THE NORTHERN EARLDOMS

THE NORTHERN EARLDOMS

Orkney and Caithness from AD 870 to 1470

Barbara E. Crawford

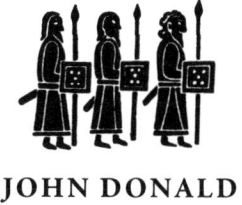

JOHN DONALD

First published in Great Britain in 2013 by
John Donald, an imprint of Birlinn Ltd

West Newington House
10 Newington Road
Edinburgh
EH9 1QS

www.birlinn.co.uk

ISBN 978 1 904607 91 5

Copyright © Barbara E. Crawford 2013

The right of Barbara E. Crawford to be identified as the author
of this work has been asserted by her Estate in accordance
with the Copyright, Designs and Patents Act, 1988

All rights reserved. No part of this publication may
be reproduced, stored, or transmitted in any form, or
by any means, electronic, mechanical or photocopying,
recording or otherwise, without the express written
permission of the publisher.

The publishers gratefully acknowledge the support of
The Carnegie Trust for the Universities of Scotland
towards the publication of this book

British Library Cataloguing-in-Publication Data
A catalogue record for this book is available on request
from the British Library

Typeset in Agmena by
Koinonia, Manchester
Printed and bound in Britain
by CPI Group (UK) Ltd, Croydon, CR0 4YY

To all friends and neighbours in the northern world of the earldoms

Contents

List of Plates	xiii
List of Figures	xv
Preface and Acknowledgements	xvii
List of Abbreviations	xxi

Introduction
1971–2012	1
Earls and Kings	4
Joint Earldoms	6
Bibliographical References for Introduction	8

1 Between Norway and Scotland: Joint Earldoms and Divided Loyalties — 10
1.1 Political and Maritime Contexts	10
1.1.1 Waterways, lordships and power centres	11
1.2 Earls of Different Kingdoms	18
1.2.1 Peripheral communities	21
1.2.2 Borders and frontiers	23
1.3 Historical Approaches	26
1.3.1 Local historians	28
1.3.2 Genealogies	32
1.4 Lordship	35

2 The Sources of Knowledge about the Joint Earldoms: Documentary Survival and Historical Reality — 39
2.1 Evaluation of *Jarls' Saga* (*Orkneyinga Saga*)	39
2.2 Runic Inscriptions	50
2.3 Latin Documents	53
2.4 Norwegian Documents	59
2.5 Scots Documents and the 'Genealogy of the Earls'	62
2.6 Liturgical Fragments	65

CONTENTS

2.7	Material Evidence	67
	2.7.1 Ecclesiastical foundations	68
	2.7.2 Secular residences: Birsay and Kirkwall	70
	2.7.3 Seals	76

3 Viking Earls: AD 870–1030 — 80

3.1	Mythical Origin	80
	3.1.1 Nordic significance of the origin myth	81
	3.1.2 Title of jarl	83
3.2	Creation of the Earldom of Orkney	85
	3.2.1 Economic interests	87
	3.2.2 King and jarl	90
3.3	Earl Sigurd I 'the Mighty' (*hinn ríki*)	92
	3.3.1 Sigurd I's death and burial c.892	96
	3.3.2 Place-name and archaeological evidence for Norse settlement on the north mainland of Scotland	100
3.4	The Tenth Century – Survival and Accommodation	103
	3.4.1 Einar: the one-eyed slave-born earl (fl.900)	105
	3.4.2 Struggle for control of Caithness	108
	3.4.3 Earldom contacts beyond Caithness and Orkney	111
3.5	Sigurd II Hlodversson 'the Stout' (*digri*)	113
	3.5.1 Expansion south and west	114
	3.5.2 Hoards, arm-rings and an earldom economy	120
	3.5.3 Earl Sigurd *digri*'s conversion and death	125
3.6	Earl Thorfinn 'the Mighty' (*hinn ríki*)	129
	3.6.1 Relationship with Olaf Haraldsson	131
	3.6.2 Caithness contested between Earl and Mormaer	134
	3.6.3 Campaigns to the Hebrides and internal rivalries	138
	3.6.4 Division of the earldoms	141

4 Medieval Earls: 1050–1150 — 145

4.1	Earl Thorfinn's Founding of the Orkney Bishopric	145
4.2	Military Organisation and Earldom Authority in the West	150
	4.2.1 Ross – the southern frontier	152
	4.2.2 Thorfinn's 'famous journey' and pilgrimage to Rome	156
	4.2.3 Ingibjorg 'Earls'-mother'(*jarlamóðir*) and problems of chronology	159
	4.2.4 Eulogy of Earl Thorfinn and developments after his death	162
4.3	Hierarchy of Power: Magnus Olafsson 'Barelegs'(*Berfættr*) and the Earls	165
	4.3.1 Royal ambitions and the role of the Orkney earldom	167

	4.3.2 Rival earls	171
4.4	Twelfth-century Earldom Society	172
	4.4.1 Events in Caithness	175
	4.4.2 Rognvald Kali Kolsson	177
	4.4.3 Frakokk and Clan Moddan, and the Celto-Norse society of Caithness and Sutherland	179
4.5	Aspiring Earls and Scottish Influence	183
4.6	Aspects of Political Geography in the Twelfth-century Earldoms	188
	4.6.1 Scapa Flow	189
	4.6.2 Castles	193
5	**Saint-Earls and Orkney's Twelfth-century Renaissance**	**198**
5.1	The Killing of Earl Magnus	198
5.2	Growth of the Magnus Cult	199
	5.2.1 Preconditions for sanctification	200
	5.2.2 Bishop William's role	202
	5.2.3 'Elevation' of the relics and 'Translation' to Kirkwall	204
	5.2.4 Kol's speech and the building of St Magnus Cathedral	208
5.3	Pilgrimages and an Age of Piety	212
	5.3.1 Earl Rognvald: pilgrim, poet and benefactor	214
	5.3.2 Earl Rognvald 'the Holy'	219
5.4	The Two Orkney Saints	221
5.5	Architectural Evidence	228
	5.5.1 Egilsay and the Brough of Birsay	228
	5.5.2 Parish churches	231
5.6	Orkney's Twelfth-century Renaissance	234
6	**Earls Constrained by the Power of Kings in the Twelfth and Early Thirteenth Centuries**	**238**
6.1	Circumstances of Divided Loyalty	238
6.2	Earl Harald Maddadson (1158–1206)	240
	6.2.1 The meeting of royal authority in the earldoms	240
	6.2.2 Harald's disloyalty and King Sverrir's anger	242
6.3	Harald, Earl of Caithness and King William	246
	6.3.1 Harald 'The Young' (*ungi*) and the Battle of Wick	248
6.4	Violence in Caithness	250
	6.4.1 Earl Harald's attack on the stewards and on Bishop John	251
	6.4.2 Punishment: papal penance and royal retribution	254
6.5	Earl Harald's Ultimate Survival	257
6.6	The Last Joint Earls: David and John Haraldsson	261
	6.6.1 Repairing relations with the kings of Norway and Scotland	262

		6.6.2 Loss of Sutherland	264
	6.7	Conspiracy in Norway and More Violence in Caithness	267
		6.7.1 The burning of Bishop Adam in 1222	268
		6.7.2 Royal vengeance	271
		6.7.3 Contextualising the evidence about the nature of Caithness society	273
	6.8	Murder of Earl John (1230)	274
		6.8.1 The end of the old line and the end of an era	276
7	**Shadow Earls: 1230s–1370s**		278
	7.1	The Angus Earls	278
		7.1.1 Royal reorganisation in the north	279
		7.1.2 Johanna and Matilda, heiresses to the earldom lands	283
		7.1.3 The new dynasty's adjustment to the north	286
	7.2	Installation as Earls of Orkney – *Hirðskrá*	288
		7.2.1 The earls' position	291
	7.3	1263 and the Problem of Divided Loyalty	294
		7.3.1 King Hakon Hakonsson's motivation and preparation	295
		7.3.2 1263 naval expedition west	297
		7.3.3 Earl Magnus Gilbertsson's circumstances	299
	7.4	The Treaty of Perth 1266	301
		7.4.1 Earl Magnus Gilbertsson's reconciliation 1267	303
	7.5	'A Northern Commonwealth' and the role of the earls	306
		7.5.1 The death of the Maid of Norway in Orkney 1290	308
		7.5.2 International and national matters: 1295 and after	310
		7.5.3 Weland de Stiklaw	312
	7.6	Earldom Minorities and Abeyance	314
		7.6.1 Trouble between Scots and Norwegians in the islands	314
		7.6.2 Malise, earl of Caithness and Orkney c.1330–c.1350	317
		7.6.3 Filling the vacuum after Earl Malise's death	320
	7.7	Developments Regarding Caithness and the Breaking of the Link with Orkney	325
		7.7.1 Alexander of Ard, eldest grandson of Earl Malise and the loser of both earldoms	325
		7.7.2 Changes in Caithness: evidence of feudalising influences	329
8	**Sinclair Earls: 1379–1470**		332
	8.1	Earl Henry I (1379–c.1400)	334
		8.1.1 Earl Henry's terms of appointment	336
	8.2	Earl Henry I's Establishment of his Authority	339
		8.2.1 The killing of Bishop William	340

	8.2.2 Malise Sperra, the dangerous cousin with a rival claim	342
	8.2.3 Shetland and the Sinclairs	343
	8.2.4 Earl Henry I's priorities	345
8.3	Earl Henry II (1400–1420) and his Grandmother Isabella Sinclair	347
8.4	Earl William Sinclair (1420–1470)	349
	8.4.1 The rule of David Menzies and the abeyance of the earldom	350
	8.4.2 Compiling the 'Genealogy of the Earls' and William's position	352
	8.4.3 Earl William's Installation 1434	355
	8.4.4 Chancellor of Scotland 1454–1456 and earl of Caithness	356
8.5	The Gathering Storm Clouds	360
	8.5.1 Earl William's position in the minority of James III (1460–1468)	361
	8.5.2 The marriage treaty and the pledging of Orkney and Shetland (1468–1469)	365
	8.5.3 Earl William's renunciation of his right to the earldom of Orkney – the excambion of 1470	368

9 The Aftermath of the Old Earldoms 371

9.1	The Revival of Sinclair Power and Influence in the North	371
	9.1.1 Lord Henry Sinclair, 'farmer' and 'leaseholder'	372
	9.1.2 Kirkwall's Burgh charter	375
	9.1.3 Earl William's family settlement	377
9.2	Sir David Sinclair of Sumburgh	378
	9.2.1 Sir David's will of 10 July 1506	381
9.3	Changing Worlds	385
	9.3.1 Turbulence in Caithness	386
	9.3.2 The Pentland Firth – a barrier at last?	387

Retrospective Summary 389

Bibliography 394
Index 417

List of Plates

COLOUR PLATES

1. Two runestones from the Brough of Birsay
2. Replica of the letter written by the lawthingmen at the Shetland Lawthing in June 1299
3. Last section of the Complaint of the People of Orkney, dating probably to 1425, against the rule of David Menzies
4. The hymn '*Nobilis humilis*' in honour of St Magnus
5. View of the ecclesiastical buildings on the Brough of Birsay
6. The remains of the church at Spittal, Caithness
7. Distant view of the Brough of Birsay
8. The surviving remains of the hearth in Room VI ('Earl Thorfinn's Hall') on the Brough of Birsay
9a, b. Two views of a cast of the seal of Earl John of Caithness c.1296
10. Broken matrix of a medieval seal found in Deerness, Orkney
11. View looking north-west across the Dornoch Firth to Sutherland
12. A prehistoric mound at Ham, Caithness
13a. View looking across Scapa Flow towards Osmundwall (Kirk Hope)
13b. Scenes of events in Earl Sigurd's life carved on a stone bench at Kirk Hope
14. Aerial view of Birsay
15. View over Houseby in the west Mainland of Orkney
16. Reconstructed scene of the twelfth-century earldom seat of Orphir
17. Cubbie Roo's castle on the island of Wyre, Orkney
18. The castle of Old Wick in Caithness
19. View of the excavated stone-built longhalls at Earl's Bu, Orphir
20a. Statue of a secular figure, probably Earl Rognvald, on Bishop Reid's Tower in Kirkwall
20b. Close-up of the 'lyre' against the leg of the statue of Earl Rognvald
21. Tingwall, Shetland, looking across the loch towards the archdeacon's church of St Magnus
22a. The unroofed ruin of St Magnus Cathedral, Kirkjubour, Faeroe Islands
22b. The fourteenth-century reliquary plaque inserted into the east gable wall of St. Magnus Cathedral, Kirkjubour, Faeroe Islands

List of Plates

23 Figure of St Magnus on an embroidered sixteenth-century altar frontal from Skaard, West Iceland
24 Statuette of St Magnus, originally from Kirkwall Cathedral
25 West front of St Magnus Cathedral, Kirkwall
26 Model of Bergenhus, Bergen, Norway
27 View of Scrabster Bay, Caithness
28 View of Ousedale (*Eysteinsdalr*) in south Caithness
29 Dornoch Cathedral in Sutherland
30 The ruins of Halkirk Church, Caithness
31 Hakon's Hall, Bergen, Norway
32 The memorial commemorating the Battle of Largs (1263)
33 A view of the Bishop's Palace, Kirkwall, taken from the roof of St Magnus Cathedral
34 Brawl Castle, near Halkirk, Caithness
35 Charter issued by Earl John between 1284 and 1293 of Nothegane (Nottingham) in south Caithness
36a A view of the north side of St Matthew's Church at Roslin
36b A close-up view of the first three initials W L S of the inscription on St Matthew's Church, Roslin
37 The Asta stone, Tingwall, Shetland
38a,b Stained-glass windows in the Town Hall, Lerwick, Shetland, depicting James III of Scotland and Margaret of Denmark
39 St Magnus Cathedral, Kirkwall
40 An aerial view of the site of Jarlshof, Sumburgh, Shetland

BLACK AND WHITE PLATES

1 The presumed skull of St Magnus, found secreted in a pillar on the south side of the choir of St Magnus Cathedral, Kirkwall
2 Part of the Skaill hoard of Viking silver found in the west Mainland of Orkney
3 Sketch of a boat-building yard near the woodlands of Easter Ross
4 The eastern extension of St Magnus Cathedral
5a The west end of the church on the Brough of Birsay
5b The plan of the church on the Brough of Birsay
6a, b Two views of the supposed head of King Magnus the 'Lawmender'
7 The supposed head of Erik Magnusson, elder son of King Magnus
8 The supposed head of Hakon Magnusson, younger son of King Magnus
9 Ravenscraig Castle, Fife

List of Figures

1.1 Map of Norway and Scotland
1.2 Map of the three parts of the earldom lordship
1.3 Map of the Pentland Firth
2.1 Textual Stemma of *Orkneyinga Saga* manuscript relationships
2.2 Section V of *Historia Norvegie* ('History of Norway') headed '*De Orcadibus Insulis*' ('On the Orkney Islands')
2.3 Plan of secular and ecclesiastical structures on the Brough of Birsay
2.4 Reconstruction of Kirkwall showing the Sinclair castle
2.5 Drawing of the 'seal of the community of Orkney' (*sigillum comunitatis Orcadie*)
3.1 Ancestors of the earls of Orkney
3.2 Map of Scandinavia
3.3 Map of the campaigns of Earl Sigurd I 'the Mighty'
3.4 Genealogical Tree of the ninth–tenth-century earls
3.5 Map of Old Norse *bólstaðr/boll/pol* names in north and west Scotland
3.6 Map of Old Norse *bólstaðr* ('farm') names and Gaelic *achadh* or *baile* ('farm') names in Caithness
3.7 Map showing the activities of the earls in the tenth century
3.8 Map of Earl Sigurd II's campaigns
3.9 Map of land routes across north Scotland
3.10 Distribution of ouncelands and pennylands in north and west Scotland
3.11 Descendants of Earl Sigurd II
3.12 Map of the extent of Earl Thorfinn's conquests
3.13 Map of certain, and possible, earldom power centres
4.1 Map of episcopal centres in the earldoms of Orkney and Caithness
4.2 Map of Easter Ross and south Sutherland
4.3 Map showing the route taken by Earl Thorfinn on his pilgrimage to Rome
4.4 Genealogical tree of Earl Thorfinn's descendants
4.5 Genealogical tree of the family of Moddan in Dale
4.6 Map of earldom bordlands
4.7 Map of Scapa Flow showing the surrounding islands and part of the Orkney Mainland
5.1 Map of medieval Kirkwall
5.2 St Magnus Cathedral, first completed church c.1150

5.3	Map of Earl Rognvald's route to and from the Holy Land 1151–3
5.4	Map of known church dedications to St Magnus in Shetland, Orkney and Caithness
5.5	St Magnus Cathedral, longitudinal section
5.6	Drawing of St Magnus Church, Egilsay
5.7	Plan of the site of St Nicholas Church, Papa Stronsay
5.8	Map of the dioceses of the archdiocese of Nidaros (Trondheim)
6.1	Map showing location of events in Earl Harald Maddadson's career
6.2	Map of events in the lives of Earls David and John
7.1	Tree of the possible means of inheritance of the earldoms by the Angus family
7.2	Map showing the reduction of the joint earldoms
7.3	The route taken by King Hakon Hakonsson's fleet in 1263
7.4	Schematic tree of the inheritance of the earldoms from Angus–Strathearn–Sinclair dynasties
7.5	The marriages and families of Earl Malise's daughters
8.1a	Roslin Castle from the north-west
8.1b	Roslin Castle from the north-east
8.2	Map of Sinclair Castles
8.3	Family relationships of Alexander Sutherland of Dunbeath
9.1.	Family tree of Earl William's marriages and descendants
9.2	Sketch of Sir David Sinclair, King Hans of Denmark–Norway and King James IV of Scotland

Preface and Acknowledgements

After a long career teaching and researching the history of the joint earldoms of Orkney and Caithness I have accumulated over the years a host of colleagues, former students and Scandinavian contacts with parallel interests in the medieval world of north Britain and the north Atlantic. We are co-workers in many fields of endeavour: primarily history and archaeology, language and place-name studies. The highlights of my retirement have been the volumes of essays written for me by many of these friends, students and colleagues: one resulting from a conference organised by Alex Woolf;[1] the other a festschrift organised and edited by Beverley Ballin Smith, Simon Taylor and Gareth Williams.[2] These four –whose own work in the fields of early medieval Scottish history, archaeology, place-names and numismatics has been an inspiration to me – deserve my special thanks.

My focus on the history of the Norse world has benefited from collaboration with William Thomson and Sarah Jane Gibbon in Orkney, Raymond Lamb (now in Caithness) and Brian Smith in Shetland. Their knowledge and understanding of the history of Orkney and Shetland in the medieval period is unmatched and our discussions and correspondence over many years have been most valuable. It is encouraging to see the new development of teaching and research programmes undertaken by the Orkney and Shetland Colleges of the University of the Highlands and Islands, and most especially the focus on the history of Orkney and Shetland at the flourishing Centre for Nordic Studies where researchers such as Donna Heddle, Alexandra Sanmark and Ragnhild Liosland are taking our understanding of Norse society and Nordic culture in new and interesting directions.

Norway has always provided an extra-special added dimension to my northern researches, and the many visits I have had to that wonderful country

---

1 *Scandinavian Scotland – Twenty Years After, the Proceedings of a Day Conference held on 19 February 2007*, ed. A. Woolf (2009, St Andrews)
2 *West over Sea. Studies in Scandinavian Sea-Borne Expansion and Settlement Before 1300. A Festschrift in Honour of Dr Barbara E. Crawford*, eds B. Ballin Smith, S. Taylor, and G. Williams (2007, Leiden)

have enlightened me and enhanced my understanding of the northern world to which the earls belonged. Among those Norwegians whose academic support and personal friendship have helped to make me feel welcome to their country and its historical traditions have been Per Sveaas Andersen (whose advice I sought all those years ago when starting out on postgraduate research), Knut Helle and Ingvild Øye, Hans-Emil Lidén, Erla Hohler, Alf Tore Hommedal, and more recently Jon Vidar Sigurdsson and Steinar Imsen. The younger generation – some of whom have been participants in the exchange programme between the School of History at St Andrews and the Centre for Medieval Studies in Oslo such as Margrete Syrstad, Torhild Øien and Regin Meyer – have developed Viking and medieval Norse studies in different and exciting ways. I would like to acknowledge in particular the recent important publications on aspects of Orkney history by Haki Antonsson (2007), Randi Wærdahl (2011) and Ian Beuermann (2012).

My own efforts in the world of Viking and Norse studies have encompassed an interdisciplinary combination of history and archaeology, with some forays into the study of place-names.[3] However, my earlier focus in the Ph.D thesis on the earls of Orkney and Caithness was entirely historical,[4] and it was only in the 1980s that I expanded my interests to include archaeology and place-names when working on the theme of Scandinavian Scotland. By reverting to the history of the earldoms in the present book I have once more confined myself primarily to written sources, with the unfortunate result that there is little archaeological information or analysis in the following pages. The fact of the matter is that there is little archaeology in the earldoms directly linked to the earls themselves. None of the pagan earls' burial places has been located or excavated; their earldom residences at both Birsay and Orphir have been only partially excavated, mostly long ago, and it is not easy to draw general conclusions from the results. Churches provide the most dominant, and to some extent the most meaningful, surviving material evidence of the earldom establishments at both Birsay and Orphir, as also of course in Kirkwall. Archaeology is far too important to be marginalised in a study of medieval earldoms and it is regrettable that there is so little archaeological information which can be directly linked to the story of the Orkney and Caithness earldoms. The present book is not the place to embark on a more general assessment of medieval culture in the north which could include archaeological evidence; that is being done by others.[5]

[3] As in *Scandinavian Scotland* (Leicester, 1987)
[4] See Crawford (1971, Introduction, p. x) for an explanation of the absence of any focus on archaeology
[5] Most recently by James Barrett, *Being an Islander: Production and Identity at Quoygrew, Orkney AD900–1600* (2012)

It may be thought that there is too great a focus in the following chapters on my own publications. The main purpose of this book is to renew, update and expand a thesis dating back forty years with the further work undertaken since then by me and by other scholars. William Thomson's *New History of Orkney* has filled the gap as a general and fully comprehensive history of the islands, and Randi Wærdahl's recent study of the 'skattlands' of Norway has put the Orkney earldom firmly into the Norwegian political and judicial context.[6] *Orkneyinga Saga* (or *Jarls' Saga* as it will be called) has received some detailed attention and different Old Norse scholars are providing further enlightenment about the significance and value of this saga evidence.[7] Little has been written about the earldom in Caithness or about the Scandinavian parts of north Scotland.[8] This book aims therefore to give a fresh assessment of the history of the joint earldoms of Orkney and Caithness based on my doctoral dissertation but taking it much further, and benefiting from the accumulation of information in the intervening forty years. The writing of this book has provided an opportunity to revisit the topic and to take a fresh look at this very remarkable long-lived northern Scottish and Norwegian political and cultural institution.

In some respects I adjust my interpretation of the role of the earls in the histories of the two kingdoms, Norway and Scotland, and in other respects I make a new bid to impress the reader with the importance of these joint earldoms as part of the Viking phenomenon, and as part of Scotland's history. The main thread in the following pages takes the story of the Viking earls beyond the Norse era and into medieval history. It will hopefully provide some enlightenment for those who have wondered 'What happened to the Vikings after the Viking Age?'[9]

Grateful acknowledgements are due to many people who helped with advice on particular aspects, and with the acquisition of illustrations. Duncan Stewart of the University of St Andrews Printing and Design Unit drew most of the maps which are such an important aid to our understanding of the earls' place in the maritime world of northern Scotland and the North Sea zone. Paul Bibire kindly contributed the stemma and notes on *Orkneyinga Saga* and provided ready help with many linguistic questions. Simon Taylor, Brian Smith, William Thomson, Robert Smart, Elisabeth Okasha and Doreen Waugh responded to requests for help and advice with particular chapters or captions. Andrew MacEwan's comments on Chapter 7 have rescued me from factual and grammatical errors.

6 Wærdahl, 2011, amplifying the earlier publications by Steinar Imsen (see Bibliography)
7 Jesch, 1993; 2005; 2006; 2010; Mundal, 1993; 2007; in press; Beuermann, 2011; and see Section 2.1 below
8 Although see Oram (1999; 2004; 2011 *passim*)
9 This was the theme of an Honours course ('The Viking Legacy') which I taught in the University of St Andrews for many years

Alison Rosie of the National Archives of Scotland gave unstinting help with the provision of the illustrations of Earl John's charter and of his seal. Dave Cowley of RCAHMS provided appropriate aerial views for the cover photographs. Other help with pictures was generously given by Geoffrey Stell, Peter Anderson, Iain Ashman, Steinar Imsen, Alf Tore Hommedal, Bjørn Bandlien, Morten Stige and Chris Lowe. Above all, my husband worked magic on many sometimes unsuitable images and turned them into publishable material. This book is a monument to his and Magnus' devoted support in so many ways over many years.

In addition I would like to acknowledge the professional care and high standards of the production team at Birlinn, headed by Mairi Sutherland, who devoted considerable time towards the publication requirements of this book and considerable patience with the author's wishes and considerations. Alicia Correa also contributed her professional expertise as an indexer, maintaining our close links from her St Andrews days. This book is published on the 600th anniversary of St Andrews University with which I have been associated throughout my academic career, as student, postgraduate researcher and teacher of Medieval History. I hope it lives up to the University's motto, which has inspired generations of those who have studied and taught within its venerable walls by the sea which unites many of the places explored and depicted in the following pages:

αἰὲν ἀριστεύειν 'Ever to Excel'

St Andrews, June 2013

Abbreviations

ON   Old Norse

These abbreviations generally follow the List of Abbreviated Titles in Watt (1963)

Abdn.Reg.	*Registrum Episcopatus Aberdonensis* (Spalding and Maitland Clubs, 1845)
APS	*The Acts of the Parliaments of Scotland*, ed. T. Thomson and C. Innes (Edinburgh, 1814–75)
ASC	*The Anglo-Saxon Chronicles*, trans. and edited M. Swanton (London, 2000)
Bann.Misc.	*Miscellany of the Bannatyne Club*, iii (Edinburgh, 1855)
Bower, *Scotichron.*	Watt, D.E.R., gen. ed., *Scotichronicon by Walter Bower in Latin and English*, 9 vols (Aberdeen/Edinburgh, 1987–1998)
CDS	*Calendar of Documents relating to Scotland*, ed. J. Bain (Edinburgh, 1881–8)
CP	*The Complete Peerage* (London, 1945)
CS	*Celtic Scotland. A History of Ancient Alba*, W.F. Skene, 3 vols (Edinburgh, 1876–1880)
CSR	*Caithness and Sutherland Records*, vol. 1, eds A.W. and A. Johnston (The Viking Society, London, 1909)
CV	Cleasby-Vigfusson. *Icelandic–English Dictionary*, Second edition with a supplement by Sir W. Craigie (Oxford, 1957)
DN	*Diplomatarium Norvegicum*, 1849–1919
DNB	*New Oxford Dictionary of National Biography* (Oxford, 2004–12) (www.oxforddnb.com/public/index.html)
DNFH	*Det Norske Folks Historie*, P.A. Munch, 5 vols (Christiania, 1852–63)
ER	*The Exchequer Rolls of Scotland*, eds J. Stuart and others (Edinburgh, 1878–1908)
ES	*Early Sources of Scottish History AD 500–1286* ed. and trans. A.O. Anderson, 2 vols (Edinburgh, 1922; Stamford, 1990)
Fordun, *Gesta Annalia*	Fordun, *Chronicle; John of Fordun's Chronicle of the Scottish nation*, ed. W.F. Skene, Historians of Scotland, vol. 4 (Edinburgh, 1872)

ABBREVIATIONS

Genealogy	*Genealogy of the Earls, Miscellany of the Bannatyne Club*, iii (Edinburgh, 1855) 63–85
Hacon's Saga	*The Saga of Hacon and a Fragment of the Saga of Magnus*, trans. Sir G.W. Dasent, Icelandic Sagas vol. 4, *Rerum Britannicarum Medii Aevi Scriptores*, Rolls series (London, 1894)
Hist.Norv.	*Historia Norvegie*, eds I. Ekrem and L.B. Mortensen (see Bibliography)
Hms. Laing	*Heimskringla* by Snorri Sturlason, part I, *The Olaf Sagas*, trans. S. Laing, revised with Introduction and notes by J. Simpson (Everyman's Library, London, 1964); part II, *Sagas of the Norse Kings*, trans. S. Laing, revised with Intro. and notes by P. Foote (Everyman's Library, London, 1961)
Hms. Finlay and Faulkes	*Heimskringla*, Snorri Sturlason, vol. 1, The Beginnings to Oláfr Tryggvason (Viking Society for Northern Research, London, 2011)
Howden, *Chronica*	*Chronica Magistri Rogeri de Houedene*, ed. W. Stubbs, Rolls series, 4 vols (London, 1868–71)
IA	*Islandske Annaler indtil 1578*, ed. Dr G. Storm (Christiania, 1888)
Inchaffray Chrs.	*Charters, Bulls and other Documents relating to the Abbey of Inchaffray* (SHS, 1908)
Kirkwall Chrs.	*Charters and Records of the City and Royal Burgh of Kirkwall*, ed. J. Mooney, Kirkwall Town Council (Third Spalding Club, 1952)
KL	*Kulturhistorisk Leksikon for nordisk middelalder: fra vikingetid til Reformationstid* (Copenhagen, 1956–78)
Magnus Saga	*Fragments of the Saga of Magnus Hacon's Son* in *Hacon's Saga* pp374–87
Moray Reg.	*Registrum Episcopatus Moraviensis* (Bannatyne Club, Edinburgh, 1837)
NRAS	National Register of the Archives of Scotland
NgL	*Norges gamle Love*, anden Række (second series), vol. 1, ed. A. Taranger (Christiana, 1912–18)
NW	*The Northern World* series, eds Barbara Crawford, David Kirby, Jon-Vidar Sigurdsson, Ingvild Øye, Richard Unger and Piotr Gorecki (Brill, Leiden)
OPS	*Origines Parochiales Scotiae: The antiquities, ecclesiastical and territorial of the parishes of Scotland*, ed. Cosmo Innes (Bannatyne Club, Edinburgh, 1851–5),
Orkney Recs.	*Records of the Earldom of Orkney 1299–1614*, ed. J. Storer Clouston, SHS, second series, vol. 7 (Edinburgh, 1914)
OS	*Orkneyinga Saga. The History of the Earls of Orkney*, trans. H. Pálsson and P. Edwards (London, 1978)
OS Dasent	*The Orkneyingers' Saga, Icelandic Saga*, vol. 3, trans. G.W. Dasent, *The Icelandic Sagas*, Rolls series (London, 1894)

ABBREVIATIONS

OS Guðmundsson	*Orkneyinga Saga Legenda de Sancto Magno, Magnúss saga Skemmri, Magnúss saga lengri, Helga þáttr og Ulfs*, ed. F. Guðmundsson, Islensk fornrit 34 (Reykjavík, 1965)
OS Hjaltalin and Goudie	*The Orkneyinga Saga*, trans. J. Hjaltalin, ed. G. Goudie, with notes and introduction by J. Anderson, 1873 (reprinted in facsimile Edinburgh, 1973)
OS Nordal	*Orkneyinga Saga*, ed. S. Nordal, Samfund til Udgivelse af gammel nordisk Litteratur, XL (Copenhagen, 1913–16)
OS Taylor	*The Orkneyinga Saga, A New Translation with Introduction and Notes*, trans. A.B. Taylor (Edinburgh, 1938)
OSR	*Orkney and Shetland Records*, vol. 1, eds A.W. and A. Johnston (Viking Society for Northern Research) (London, 1907–13)
POAS	*Proceedings of the Orkney Antiquarian Society*
RCAHMS	Royal Commission on the Ancient and Historical Monuments of Scotland
Reg.Dunf.	*Registrum de Dunfermlyn* (Bannatyne Club, Edinburgh, 1842)
Reg.Norv.	*Regesta Norvegica*, vol. 1 (1989) to vol. 10 (2012), (Riksarkivet, Oslo)
RMS	*Registrum Magni Sigilli Regum Scottorum*, eds J.M. Thomsson and others (Edinburgh, 1882–1914)
Rot. Scot.	*Rotuli Scotiae in Turri Londinensi et in Domo Capitulari Westmonasteriensi Asservati*, edd. D. MacPherson and others (1814–19)
RRS I	*Regesta Regum Scottorum*, vol. I *The Acts of Malcolm IV*, ed. G.W.S. Barrow (Edinburgh, 1960)
RRS IV (pt.i)	*Regesta Regum Scottorum*, vol. IV (part i). *The Acts of Alexander III*, eds C.J. Neville and G.G. Simpson (Edinburgh, 2012)
RRS V	*Regesta Regum Scottorum*, vol. V, *The Acts of Robert I*, ed. A.A.M. Duncan (Edinburgh, 1988)
SAEC	*Scottish Annals from English Chronicles A.D. 500–1286*, ed. A.O. Anderson (London, 1908, reprint Stamford, 1991)
Saga Book	*Saga Book of the Viking Society* (London, 1892–)
Scand.Scot.	*Scandinavian Scotland*, Barbara E. Crawford (Leicester, 1987)
Scone Liber	*Liber Ecclesie de Scon* (Bannatyne and Maitland clubs, Edinburgh, 1843)
Shetland Docs.	*Shetland Documents 1195–1579*, eds J.H. Ballantyne and Brian Smith (Lerwick, 1999)
SHR/Scot. Hist. Rev.	*The Scottish Historical Review* (1903–28, 1947–)
SHS	Scottish Historical Society (1893–)
SP	*The Scots Peerage*, ed. Sir James Balfour (Edinburgh, 1904–14)
WHNQ	*West Highland Notes and Queries*

Introduction

1971–2012

This book is a result of research carried out and written up in a doctoral thesis forty years ago.[1] It was not published at the time (few theses were in those days), although several chapters and articles were drawn from it and based on the evidence presented in it. This current book is, however, a great deal more than a rewrite. My intellectual and interdisciplinary interests have expanded in many different directions since I focused on the historical relationships of kings and earls: particularly regarding the archaeology of the Vikings and the Norse settlements in Scotland, but also concerning the place-name evidence for Norse settlement, the history of the medieval Church in the bishoprics of Orkney and Caithness, along with medieval saints' cults, most notably the cult of Magnus Erlendsson, earl and saint of Orkney.

A developing interest in archaeology led to a multi-disciplinary research project on the island of Papa Stour, Shetland, where a house site of the late Viking and medieval periods was excavated. A documentary reference to a wooden house called a 'stofa' led to the site at the Biggins and the discovery of a wooden building of the right type and date. This opened up a fascinating area of research into comparable log-timbered buildings in Norway and the north Atlantic islands. However, there are few references to this discovery and the ensuing research in the present book because it bears little relevance to the history of the earls of Orkney, having been built by the Norwegian regime for the use of royal officials when residing in Shetland.

This raises another point, regarding the absence of any real focus on Shetland's history in the present book. Shetland was detached from the earldom of Orkney in 1195 with the result that the earls lost control over Shetland and forfeited their estates there (see Section 6.2). The history of Shetland thereafter is rather different and the impact of direct rule from Norway caused it to

---

1 The Earls of Orkney–Caithness and their relationship with the kings of Norway and Scotland 1158–1470 (St Andrews PhD 1971)

develop in a distinctive way, which means that there is little to say with respect to the history of the earldom until the Sinclair earls reasserted some control over Shetland after 1379 (see Section 8.2.3).[2]

Another aspect of the history of the earldoms has come to the fore in recent studies and publications: the medieval Church in Orkney and Caithness, most particularly the role of the bishops in the two earldoms and their relationship with the earls and the kings.[3] As will be seen, that relationship was often a difficult one which resulted in some bloody and violent clashes, causing the earls great problems for their position in their two earldoms. These clashes reveal a great deal about ecclesiastical policies and the programme of increasing episcopal authority, especially the ways in which the kings of Scotland used the Church to further their own policies of increasing royal authority in the most northerly Scottish diocese. As far as Orkney is concerned, the relationship between the bishop and the king of Norway was bad for most of the fourteenth century, possibly due in part to the particular circumstances of increasing Scottish influence. There is much more to be studied and understood about the role of the Church in the history of the two earldoms.

An additional element in the present analysis of the status of the earls of Orkney and Caithness is a focus on the martyrdom of Earl Magnus Erlendsson, and the growth and spread of his cult (see Chapter 5). Saints' cults in general became of particular personal interest with the development of a research project on the cult of St Clement, which enhanced my understanding of the importance of saints' cults and what they can tell us about medieval life and culture. Again this project does not feature in the current book, for the cult of St Clement is of little relevance to earldom history, there being no evidence that the cult made any impact whatsoever in Orkney or Caithness, although it was of rich significance in Norway and Denmark (and to some extent in Iceland). Nonetheless, understanding the significance of that cult and of the royal cults of Scandinavia has enhanced my appreciation of the status which was gained by the sanctification of the Orkney saint-earls. This was a development of great importance for the earldom dynasty and one which enhanced the reputation of the Orkney earldom among the countries of northern Europe.[4]

In another respect this book is much expanded from the 1971 thesis in its coverage of the early centuries of the earldoms from the coming of Earl Rognvald of Møre and the grant of Orkney to his brother Sigurd (c.870) through to the mid-twelfth century. This period requires familiarity with and understanding of interdisciplinary studies and the importance of archaeological and place-

[2] A full history of Shetland is being written by Brian Smith, Shetland archivist
[3] See Sections 6.4, 6.7, 8.2
[4] Including also the secondary cult of Earl Rognvald (see Section 5.4)

name evidence, as well as the ability to use Old Norse sources sensitively. Using these sources of evidence for better understanding of the early centuries had already been developed by the author when writing the handbook *Scandinavian Scotland* (1987).[5] The writing of that book (and a number of further publications on the Vikings in Scotland) has provided the groundwork for the study of the Viking and medieval earldoms in Chapters 3 and 4.

Place-name, or toponymic, evidence is another area of inter-disciplinary studies with which I have been engaged since 1971, and which, as noted, was included in my study of Scandinavian Scotland in 1987. Toponymic evidence is an important basis for a better understanding of Scandinavian settlement in the Northern and Western Isles and in north Scotland, and this evidence has been used in a fairly general way to chart the spread of Scandinavian settlement in the islands and in north Scotland (see Section 3.3). Place-names have also been used in an attempt to analyse the movements of earldom forces around north Scotland,[6] while consideration of the habitative farm name Houseby in Orkney (*huseby*) has been used to provide possible evidence for policies regarding royal, or earldom, administrative structures in Orkney.[7]

The 'papar' project was another research direction which took me away from earldom history, but which has some bearing on the process of Scandinavian settlement in the Northern and Western Isles.[8] This was a multi-disciplinary project intended to compare all the islands called Papay (in the Northern Isles) or Pabbay (in the Western Isles) and locations with a Papil, Payble, or Bayble name, in an attempt to understand the reasons why these places were named after the Celtic priests whom the Norse called *papar* ('fathers' or 'priests'). It showed that the majority of the places so named were fertile (some were very fertile) and some of them very strategically located. These names possibly indicate that such places were used by the early Viking raiders as supply bases for their fleets. Were the Celtic priests' settlements left undisturbed by the Norse so that crops could be grown, and pastoral economy continue, and the products accessed for the Vikings' own needs and requirements? Were these locations given *papar* names to indicate their function as supply bases for the Viking fleets?[9] This theory relates to the earliest phase of raiding and is not therefore included as part of the earldom story.[10]

5   It was the first interdisciplinary study of the impact of the Vikings on the whole of Scotland, not just Orkney and Shetland, and Caithness
6   See Section 4.2.1
7   See Section 4.3.1
8   www.paparproject.org (Project Introduction)
9   www.paparproject.org under Hebrides ('strategic considerations')
10   The term 'Viking' will be used in this book for the period of raiding and the activities of the Norwegian seamen and warriors who flooded into western Europe from the late eighth

The foregoing explanation should make it clear that, during the intervening forty years, research projects of very different kinds have occupied my time, not many of which have been directly concerned with the history of the earldoms of Orkney and Caithness. The eclectic range of subject areas may not have been completely relevant to the earls and their history, but they have expanded my horizons beyond a narrow historical focus, and have helped to make this book of a rather different quality from the original thesis. A brief survey will now highlight some of the issues with which it is concerned, and point towards the main conclusions.

EARLS AND KINGS

The book starts off with a contextualisation of the important geographical nature underlying these two conjoint earldoms, as well as a brief survey of previous historical studies (Chapter 1). It continues with an evaluation of the different kinds of (mostly) written evidence that provides the source material (Chapter 2), and then proceeds to the origin of the earldoms and the Viking earls, based on the saga story (Chapter 3). Chapter 4 describes the period after the conversion and establishment of the Orkney bishopric by Earl Thorfinn which is the basis of the development of the medieval earldom, when the trajectory was set for the establishment of a settled society ruled by the earls. With the appearance of the kings of Norway, intent on challenging the earls' control of these fertile islands and using them for the establishment of their own far-flung imperial designs on the islands of Britain and Ireland, another feature comes into the picture which is going to be an important side of the political story, threatening the independent status of the earls.

The two earldoms have been practically established by this date, forming a joint lordship divided (or united) by the Pentland Firth. There is focus on the nature of the dual lordship which was the basis of the two earldoms, and better awareness that they remained two separate earldoms, which is a phenomenon of some interest. The questions asked relate to the family's ability to maintain control over the joint earldoms and how the rivalries and power struggles were resolved in the period when the saga sources are available. Once the saga sources cease (post-1230) we have very little evidence telling us about the individual earls, and this coincides with inheritance of the claim to the earldoms by Scottish heirs and the end of joint or divided rule by two or more members

---

century and whose activities disrupted the political structures of western Europe. 'Norse' will be used as a general term for the societies and cultures of those raiders from Norway who settled in the islands and north Scotland and who established the long-lived earldoms which are the main feature of this study (this is in accordance with my previous definition of terminology in *Scand.Scot.*, 2).

of the earldom family (see Section 7.1).

One of the main themes of the present book (as also of the 1971 thesis) is the relationship of the earls with their two overlords, the kings of Norway and Scotland. How did this relationship develop and change over time? The political interest of the phase after 1230 is concerned with the earls' role in national history and the relationship of the earls with their two kings. These are very 'medieval' themes and the Orkney and Caithness earldoms are a special addition to the corpus of 'feudal' history.[11] They continued to operate as a dual lordship subject to two quite separate national kingdoms and two different cultures. The circumstances of 'divided loyalty' become a pressing issue in the events of the twelfth and thirteenth centuries (see Chapters 6 and 7).

This period saw the rise of royal authority and the expansion of the power of kings to the furthermost limits of their national territory – or maritime dominion. In this process the earls were squeezed between the two advancing royal powers of Norway and Scotland, and one of the particular interests of this study is the process of curtailment. How and to what extent did the earls lose some of their powers and lands in the islands and on the north Scottish mainland? Again this is a very 'medieval' theme and the joint earldoms provide dramatic evidence and a very illuminating case-study of the process of the growth of royal authority at the expense of aristocratic independence. The methods used by the kings to bring their earls to heel had to be particularly effective for such peripheral parts of their kingdoms and we should not underestimate the problems faced in imposing royal officials and central systems of administration.[12] The earls nearly always survived, although their power and authority in their earldoms was curtailed, and their lands reduced by various means of appropriation. They were theoretically foremost members of the Norwegian king's 'hird' (ON *hirð*), the close circle of followers and warriors who were attached to the royal service by oaths of loyalty[13] (see Section 7.2). However, their attendance at the Norwegian royal court can only have been spasmodic.

Links with the kings of Scotland were probably less close and less formal. The peripheral place of the earls in the aristocratic community suggests that their involvement in the central events of the Scottish kingdom would have

---

11 The term 'feudal' is used rather sparingly in this book. It is not always very useful in describing the relationship of earl and king, nor as a valid description of the society in the islands. It can be used more appropriately in the context of the north Scottish mainland

12 My interpretation of the Norwegian kings' difficulty in maintaining permanent royal officials in Orkney has been questioned by Randi Wærdahl (2011, Chapters 2, 5, 6 and 7), and see below Chapters 6 and 7

13 Bagge, 1993, 284, highlighting the change from a body of warriors to a corps of local administrators

been minimal. Any contact we learn of is usually a result of the earls being on the receiving end of royal displeasure, or coming to terms after some event in which they had been less than loyal. Their traditional role as defenders of the northern Scottish maritime zone was severely tested in the situation of antagonism between the two kings, the earl's two overlords, in 1263 (see Section 7.3). There was no such institution as the Norwegian hird to keep them in close contact with the Scottish king and his court, although they would have had to do homage to the king, and swear an oath of loyalty when inheriting their earldom.

JOINT EARLDOMS

Embarking on the study of the medieval earldoms of Orkney and Caithness entailed a move into uncharted territory. These earldoms had never been looked at as a joint lordship, worthy of study as a political phenomenon in its own right. Caithness was a very peripheral part of Scottish history, and Orkney was not part of Scotland at all for most of the medieval period. The saga of the earls (*Jarls' Saga*), or *Orkneyinga Saga* as it is more usually known, had long been recognised as a remarkable example of the writing of sagas by the literate Icelanders, and appreciated for its evidence of life in the islands, and the deeds of the earls from the late ninth to the late twelfth century (see Section 2.1). But the post-saga period had been written about only briefly by Orkney historians, and also briefly (but percipiently) by Joseph Anderson in his Introduction to the Hjaltalin and Goudie translation of the *Orkneyinga saga* (Anderson 1873; facsimile 1973).

From the Norwegian side it has recently been pointed out that there has been a lack of historical writing on the 'skattlands' by Norwegian historians, and this vacuum has formed the rationale for a research project led by Steinar Imsen of the University of Trondheim (NTNU).[14] For the first time this project has brought together the history of the skattlands, peripheral Norwegian-settled communities which paid skat (tax); both the Atlantic islands (Iceland, Faeroe, Shetland and Orkney, the Hebrides) and the eastern frontier province of Jemtland, together with the northern regions of Norway beyond the Arctic circle.[15] The publications resulting from this project have already provided a substantial body of evidence for the importance of these peripheral areas in

---

14 Imsen, 2011, 13–14. See Section 1.2 below for a brief description of 'skattlands'
15 I have been privileged to participate at the regular seminar-workshops of the 'skattlands' research project, from which I have learned a great deal about medieval Norwegian government and the administration of the other 'skattlands'. This has helped our understanding of how the island groups of Orkney and Shetland fitted into the wider context of Norwegian 'skattland' administration

Norwegian history, and brought into focus the wide-ranging geographical zone of Norwegian influence which emanated from the earlier Viking era and Norse diaspora.[16]

The main research enquiry behind the skattland project is the political history of the extension of Norwegian royal authority, as well as the impact of that royal authority on the individual skattlands.[17] It is therefore focused on the High and Later medieval period, from the time of *Norgesveldet*, which is traditionally understood to mark the high point of the Norwegian medieval kingdom, before the ravages of the Black Death and ensuing political problems of the later Middle Ages. This period included the reign of Hakon Hakonsson (1217–1263), which saw the loss of the Hebrides and the corresponding gain of Iceland and Greenland under direct royal authority, and especially the reign of his son Magnus Hakonsson 'the Lawmender' (*lagabøter*) (1263–1280). King Magnus' by-name is fully justified by the evidence for a reformation of Norway's laws in his reign. First the different provincial laws were revised and then in 1274 a national law code, the *Landlaw*, was promulgated for the whole country and 'Norway became one jurisdiction'.[18] Orkney and Shetland would have been part of this legal province and the judicial standardisation must have been an important factor in incorporating the islands in the national Norwegian political community.

Caithness, however, would have continued to use traditional legal structures, although we know little of what these were. The earl may have played a role in the judicial arrangements in Caithness and the public assemblies probably continued to function. The Scottish system of sheriff courts was not extended to north Scotland until the early sixteenth century: before then Inverness was the nearest –but rather distant – centre of royal justice. The two earldoms therefore diverged markedly in judicial provision from the late thirteenth century, a situation which must have served to widen the differences between them.

The subtitle of Chapter 1: 'Joint Earldoms and Divided Loyalties' expresses the dichotomy of a situation in which two earldoms were united in the hands of one family and usually one person, but the loyalties of the family and earl were divided between two overlords. The two halves of the family's lordship were united by a waterway, the Pentland Firth, a situation stemming from the Viking Age when maritime factors created non-territorial units, usually islands, linked by the sea. In the case of Orkney, Shetland and Caithness, the islands

16 Imsen, ed. 2010, 2011; see Imsen (2011a, p.13 n.1, n.2) for further planned publications and research programme
17 As stated by Imsen (2011a, 16), the focus is an analysis of royal lordship in the skattlands, and on the individual skattland's growth into a 'provincial commune' (*provinskommune*)
18 Wærdahl, 2011, 120

were linked to the northern fringe of a land mass – very much a territorial unit – and this was going to turn into a problem. As the Middle Ages progressed, this waterway became a boundary, and eventually a frontier. We will consider this phenomenon more closely in the following chapters, and start off Chapter 1 with looking at the political and maritime contexts of our study area.

BIBLIOGRAPHICAL REFERENCES FOR INTRODUCTION

Crawford, B.E, 1978b. 'A progress report of the first season's excavation at 'Da Biggins', Papa Stour, Shetland, *Northern Studies*, 11, 25–9

Crawford, B.E., 1979a. 'A progress report on excavations at 'Da Biggins', Papa Stour, Shetland, 1978', *Northern Studies*, 13, 37–41

Crawford, B.E., 1984a. 'Papa Stour, Survival, Continuity and Change in one Shetland Island' in Fenton, A. and Pálsson, H., eds, *The Northern and Western Isles in the Viking World*, Edinburgh, 40–58

Crawford, B.E.1985a. 'The Biggins, Papa Stour – a multi-disciplinary investigation' in Smith, B., ed., *Shetland Archaeology*, Lerwick, 128–58

Crawford, B.E.1991a. 'Excavations at the Biggings, Papa Stour, Shetland, *Acta Archaeologica*, 61 (1990), 36–43

Crawford, B.E., 1992. 'Thorvald Thoresson, Duke Hakon and Shetland' in Supphellen, S., ed., *Kongsmenn and Krossmenn. Festskrift til Grethe Auten Blom*, Trondheim, 69–89

Crawford, B.E., 1993b. 'The Cult of St Clement in England and Scotland, *Medieval Europe 1992* Pre-printed papers no. 6 (Society for Medieval Archaeology), 1–3

Crawford, B.E., 1994a. 'The Norse background to the Govan hogbacks' in Ritchie, A., ed., *Govan and its Early Medieval Sculpture*, Stroud, 103–12

Crawford, B.E., 1996b. 'The excavation of a wooden building at The Biggins, Papa Stour, Shetland, in Waugh. D.J., *Shetland's Northern Links*, 136–58

Crawford, B.E., 1996c. 'Holy Places in the British Isles: some parallels to Selja' in Rindal, M., ed., *Two Studies on the Middle Ages*, Oslo, 7–29

Crawford, B.E., 1997a. 'Are the Dark Ages Still Dark?' in Hendry, D., ed., *The Worm, the Germ, and The Thorn, Pictish and related Studies presented to Isabel Henderson*. Balgavies, 1–4

Crawford, B.E., 1998a. 'Excavations at the Biggings, Papa Stour. The Rise and Fall of a Royal Norwegian Farm' in *NABO 97. Proceedings of a Summit of the Sea Conference*, St John's: Archaeology Unit, Memorial University of Newfoundland, 29

Crawford, B.E., 2000a. 'The Scandinavian Contribution to the Development of the Kingdom of Scotland' in Stummann Hansen, S., and Randsborg, K., eds, *Vikings in the West, Acta Archaeologic*, 71, 123–34

Crawford, B.E., 2001b. 'Alba. The kingdom of Scotland in the Year 1000', in Urbanczyk, P., ed., *Europe around the Year 1000*, Warsaw, 271–87

Crawford, B.E., 2001c. 'The History and Excavation of a royal Norwegian Farm at the Biggins, Papa Stour, Shetland', *Det Norske Videnskaps-Akademi Årbok 1997*, 231–44

Crawford, B.E., 2002. 'The Historical and Archaeological Background to the Papa

Stour Project', in Crawford, B.E. ed., *Papa Stour and 1299. Commemorating the 700th anniversary of Shetland's first document*. Also published as vol. 15, *Collegium Medievale. Interdisciplinary Journal of Medieval Research*, 13–36

Crawford, B.E., 2002a. 'L'Expansion Scandinave: viiieme-xiieme siecles' in Ridel, E. ed., *'L'Heritage Maritimes des Vikings en Europe de l'Ouest*, Caen, 15–31

Crawford, B.E., 2003b. 'The Vikings' in Davies, W., *From the Vikings to the Normans'*. The Short History of the British Isles, Oxford, 41–72

Crawford, B.E., 2004f. 'The Churches dedicated to St. Clement in Norway. A discussion of their Origin and Function', *Collegium Medievale*, 17, 100–131

Crawford, B.E., 2005b. 'The *papar*. Viking reality or Twelfth-century myth?' in Gammeltoft, P., Hough, C., Waugh, D., eds, *Cultural Contacts in the North Atlantic Region. The Evidence of Names*, 83–99

Crawford, B.E., 2005c. *The Govan Hogbacks and the Multi-Cultural Society of Tenth-century Scotland*, no. 3 in Old Govan Lecture Series

Crawford, B.E., 2006c. 'The Cult of St. Clement in Denmark', *Historie*, Jysk Selskab for Historie (2006, 2), 235–82

Crawford, B.E., 2008. 'The St. Clement Dedications at Clementhorpe and Pontefract Castle. Anglo-Scandinavian or Norman?' in Barrow, J., and Wareham, A., eds, *Myth, Rulership, Church and Charters. Essays in Honour of Nicholas Brooks*, Ashgate, 189–210

Crawford, B.E., 2008a. *The Churches dedicated to St. Clement in Medieval England A Hagio-geography of the Seafarer's Saint in 11th century North Europe*, Scripta Ecclesiastica Tome 1, Série Supplémentaire a Scrinium, Axioma

Crawford, B.E., 2009a. 'The 'stofa' project at the Biggins, Papa Stour, Shetland' in Falk, E. and Wallin Weihe, H-J., eds, *Living Crafts*, NHU, Chapter 23, 129–38

Crawford, B.E., 2011b. 'The Biggins *Stofa*: A Colonial Feature of North Atlantic Society' in S. Sigmundsson, ed., *Viking Settlements and Viking Society*. Papers from the Proceedings of the Sixteenth Viking Congress, Reykjavik, 2009, 31–49

Crawford, B.E. and Ballin Smith, B., 2008. 'The stofa reconstruction on the island of Papa Stour, Shetland: From historical research and archaeological investigations to cultural asset' in Paulsen, C., and Michelsen, H.D., eds, *Símunarbók. Heiðursrit til Símun V.Arge*, Tórshavn, 42–57

ONE

Between Norway and Scotland
Joint Earldoms and Divided Loyalties

1.1 POLITICAL AND MARITIME CONTEXTS[1]

The political history of the medieval earldoms of Orkney and Caithness is quite significant in the context of the wider European medieval picture. These were two earldoms which were part of two different national and political entities, but they were held by the same family, and sometimes the same individual. The question as to how the two earldoms related to each other is an important consideration, and there will be a close focus on the relationship of the two halves of this combined lordship, the offshore insular half (Orkney and Shetland) and the territorial half in the north of the Scottish mainland (Caithness). It is the very duality of this political unit which is so significant. There is the duality of medieval/feudal honour[2] and title, the duality of loyalty to two national kingdoms and territorial overlords, and the duality of relating to the histories of two very different north European societies and cultures. This duality emanated from the circumstances by which the earldoms were united in one individual's possession for most of the period under discussion but remained separate units throughout their existence.[3] They were also two independent feudal honours, two earldoms subject to two different overlords, two separate entities, and yet two halves of a whole unit of lordship, united by water. This is a distinctive political phenomenon, difficult to match elsewhere in medieval Europe, which is worthy of consideration.

---

1   This section (1.1) is drawn from Crawford (2010)
2   My use of the term 'feudal' is meant to be only a general reference to the sort of tenurial system which characterised medieval society in most European countries (although to a lesser degree in Norway).
3   Therefore, I prefer to refer to this political unit as the 'joint' earldoms of Orkney and Caithness, rather than the 'dual' earldom of Orkney–Caithness. Because they remained separate earldoms the concept of 'duality' in this respect can be misleading. Another duality, a 'cultural duality', may however be relevant. This is more usually associated with the medieval west of Scotland where the blending of Gaelic and Scots culture is becoming better recognised. In the northern earldoms the blending was primarily of Norse and Scots cultures, and with Gaelic culture becoming increasingly significant in Caithness throughout the period covered

1.1.1 *Waterways, Lordships and Power Centres*

Starting off with the all-important matter of maritime geography underlying the power bases of the earls of Orkney and Caithness, we have two groups of islands, Orkney and Shetland, located between Norway and the British Isles, and very marginal to these two territorial masses. However, the southern group, the Orkney Islands, is only a short distance from the north mainland of Scotland, where the joint earldom of Caithness was based, although separated from Orkney by the turbulent waters of the Pentland Firth, where 'the mouth of Charybdis' lay as is said in the medieval Norwegian chronicle of Theodoric the monk.[4]

This waterway and the waters separating Orkney from the more northerly Shetland Isles were no barrier to colonists from Britain who settled these islands in prehistoric times. In the Late Iron Age they were part of the kingdom of the Picts which covered the northern part of what is now called Scotland, and the name 'Orkney' dates from that period and is derived from the Celtic language which they, presumably, spoke.[5] The name Shetland is Norse,[6] and different from its pre-Scandinavian name which was *Innsi Catt* ('Isles of Cats'); this is the same totemic term as lies behind the origin of the first element of the Norse name Caithness (ON *Katanes*) for the extreme north-east portion of the Scottish mainland. The province of Cait included the whole of Caithness and Sutherland.[7] Links had therefore already been established between the north Scottish mainland and the offshore islands long before the Norse arrived.

When the Vikings dominated northern waters, the sea passage around the north of the British Isles was an important maritime feature which they needed to control. This was a crucial sea route for maintaining communication between different parts of the northern world. In order to control and police it the two provinces of the Orkney Islands (where the tribe of the Orc lived) and the north Scottish mainland (the land of the Cataibh) had to be in the hands of the same warlords and Viking pirates, and eventually their political successors. This factor made the Orkney–Caithness connection quite important; if a Norse earl had ruled the islands and a Scottish earl had ruled Caithness, control of the waterway would have been disputed. It is the importance of this waterway which led to the two earldoms becoming established and continuing to exist jointly as one lordship for 500 years. It helps to explain why the earldoms never separated and were never divided between different members of the earldom kindred.

4 A reference to the whirlpool, north-east of Stroma, known as 'Swelkie' (ON *svelgr*). Trans. MacDougall, 23 and footnote 149 (see Figure 1.3)
5 Watson, 1926, 28ff.
6 Originally 'Hjaltland', see Fenton (1973) for discussion of the 'various names' of Shetland
7 Watson, 1926, 30; the Gaelic name for Sutherland is *Cataibh*, (*i Cataibh*, 'among the Cats')

Although the Northern Isles of Orkney and Shetland had formed part of the Pictish world in the first centuries of our era, the Celtic culture they established in these islands was, if not obliterated by the Scandinavian influx in the eighth and ninth centuries AD, very much dominated by the new arrivals from the east. All traces of the Celtic language were erased, and the Vikings became the dominant component in both Orkney and Shetland.[8] So the Northern Isles were divorced from the culture of Scotland for some centuries. This was not so certainly the case in Caithness on the north Scottish mainland, where the indigenous population survived to some degree and did so increasingly further south down the north Scottish mainland through Sutherland.[9] The place-names are evidence of a very dominant Norse settlement in the north-eastern part (the 'Ness' of Caithness) (see Section 3.3.2), but this toponymic evidence becomes more evidently intermingled with Gaelic nomenclature further south-east, and westwards towards the west coast.[10] The culture of Caithness most probably became very rapidly hybridised with Gaelic as the Middle Ages progressed, in Sutherland even more so (see Section 4.4.3). Naturally, southern Scottish culture became an increasingly important element in the Norse settlements of the north Scottish mainland, particularly as the kings of Scots came to regard this territory as part of their realm, and were able, by the late twelfth century, to lead expeditions right into the heart of the Caithness earldom (see Chapter 6). The territorial part of the earls' domain was inevitably going to become integrated into the medieval Scottish kingdom. This process stopped at the Pentland Firth, however, and the islands of Orkney and Shetland remained a part of the maritime world of the North Sea and Atlantic Ocean until the islands were pledged to Scotland in 1468–9 (see Chapters 8 and 9).

In the Viking world power and expansion were based on control of the seaways, and the location of the islands in the Atlantic became obvious targets for the warriors with ships who were able to cross open seas with ease. Western Norway faces out to sea, and is divorced from the interior of the country by mountain ranges which were always a formidable barrier. However, the coastal communities have a sea route up and down the coast, sheltered by the chains of islands from the rougher waters. This is the 'north way' (the meaning of the name Norway), which leads to the northern hunting grounds and also round the southern province of Jaeren into Skaggerak and the Viken for maritime access to south-eastern Norway. It was only a stage further to cross the North

8   The extent of the obliteration of the native populations is disputed; see Smith (2001) and Bäcklund (2001) for divergent views
9   So-called because it was the 'southern land' (ON *Suðrland*) to the Norse communities in Caithness and Orkney
10   See Crawford, 1987, fig. 25

DIVIDED LOYALTIES

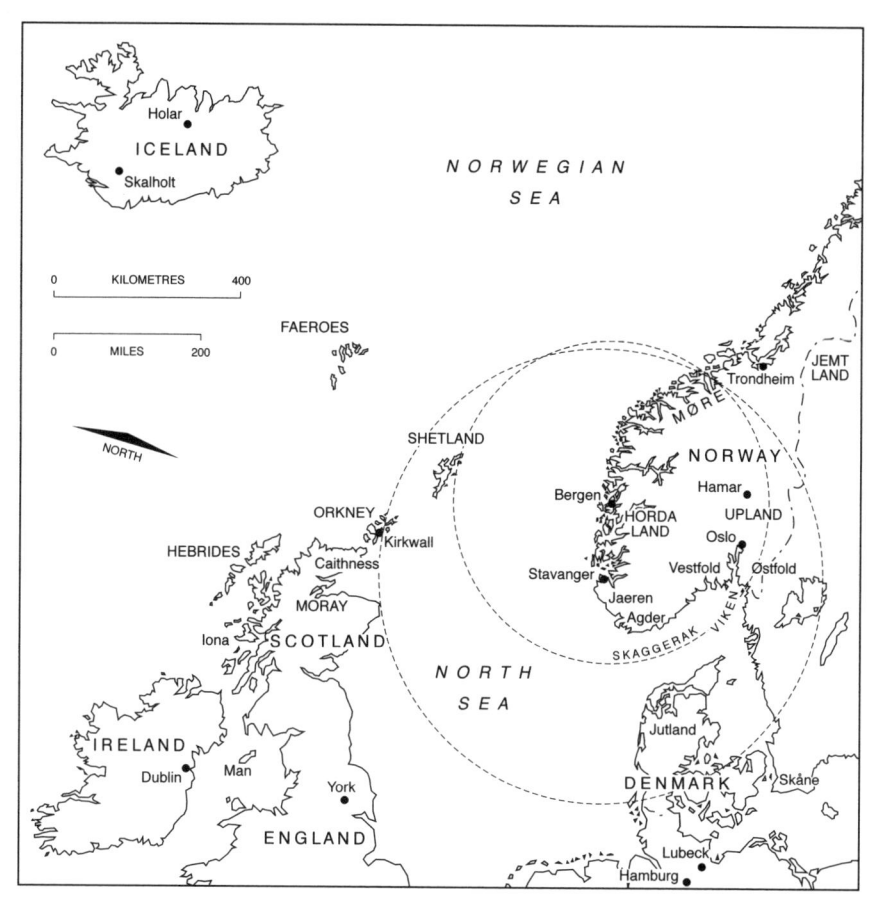

Figure 1.1 Map of Norway and Scotland, showing how the radius of maritime contact from Bergen in western Norway includes Shetland within the same diameter as the district of Møre, south of Trondheim, and the Skagerrak, the sea passage between Norway and Denmark. The radius of maritime contact from Stavanger which includes Orkney also extends to the south of Jutland.

Sea to Shetland and Orkney, and the radius of maritime contacts from Bergen in western Norway includes Shetland within the same diameter as Trondheim or the southern tip of Norway (see Figure 1.1). The radius of maritime contacts from Stavanger includes Orkney as well as Jutland in Denmark. Once the Viking ships had crossed the stretch of open water between Norway and Shetland (which can be done in twenty-four hours with a good wind), they could then sail within sight of land all the way south-west to Ireland and the Irish Sea. Shetland was a strategic base for moving further north and west to the Faeroes and Iceland, and the Orkney Isles were a nodal point in the maritime

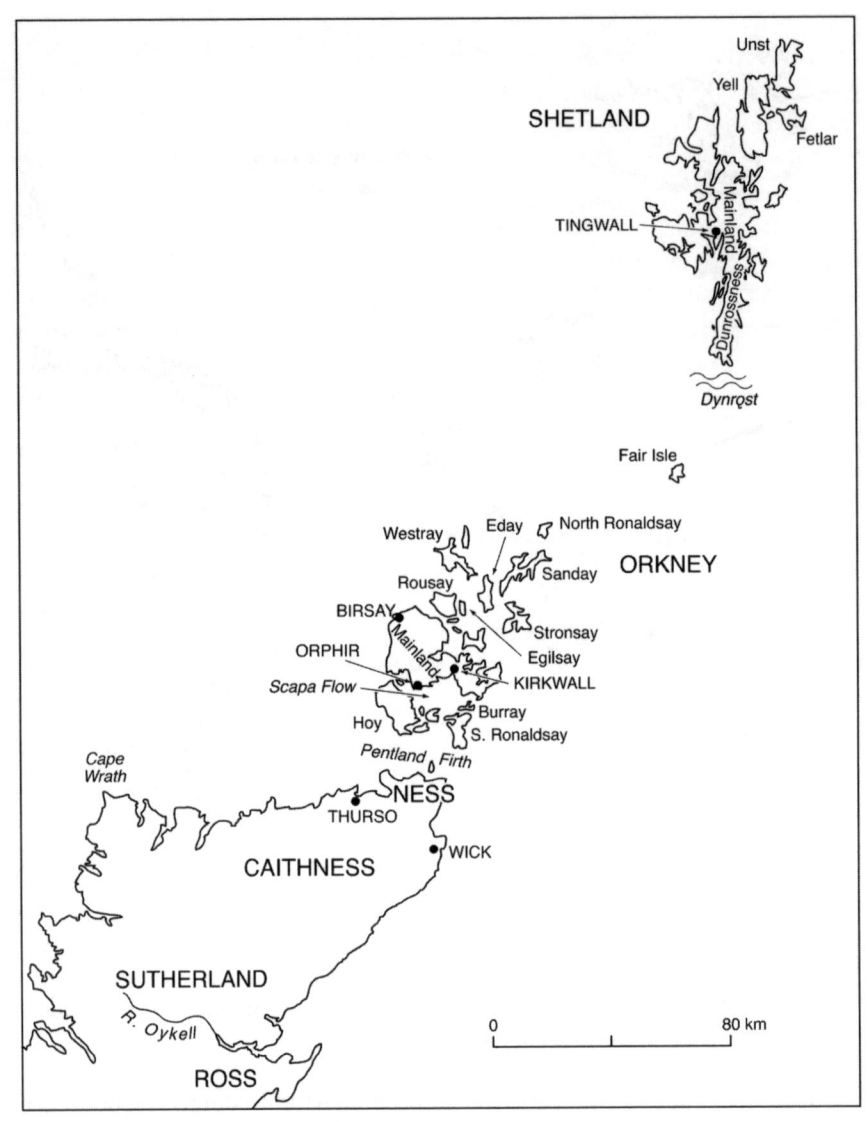

Figure 1.2 Map of the three parts of the earldom lordship – Shetland, Orkney, Caithness.

routeways around the British Isles. Situated as they are at the very north of Scotland they provide a base for access down the western and eastern coasts to the whole of England, so that control of these islands was crucial for Norwegian navies which had plans to raid or conquer Scotland and England. They provided a power base for ambitious conquerors and plentiful resources for supply of provisions.

As will be seen later, the Orkneys were a group of islands which had many favourable features for settlement and the exercise of political power. The Mainland of Orkney (the biggest central island) is surrounded by the north isles such as Rousay, Sanday and Westray, and the south isles of Burray and South Ronaldsay, all within easy sailing distance of the main power centres on Mainland.[11] One of the earliest earldom power centres was on the Brough of Birsay, on the west Mainland coast, which provided direct access to the western sea route. Orphir became an important earldom estate in the twelfth century; it lies on the north shore of Scapa Flow, the large sheltered inland sea which has provided a refuge for fleets throughout history (see Section 4.6.1 and Figure 4.7). The islands around Scapa Flow protected this inland harbour, and the island of Hoy (*Há-ey*, 'high island') provided shelter from the south-west gales. The urban centre of Kirkwall grew up at a strategic point on an isthmus connecting Scapa Flow with the route to the north isles of Orkney, and providing an accessible political, commercial and ecclesiastical power hub from the twelfth century (until the present day). Above all, Scapa Flow gave direct access to the Pentland Firth, the waterway which divided the two earldoms of Orkney and Caithness but which was the main route for sailing around the north coast of Scotland (see Figure 1.3).

Of course this waterway united the two earldoms in terms of medieval contact, rather than divided, and as already noted, made it imperative that the earls maintained control of the Firth in order to maintain control of the sailing routes. The perils of navigating the tidal streams and rips which swirl along the Firth twice a day – as well as the feared whirlpool called the Swelchie – should not be underestimated, and the sagas provide plenty of examples of disastrous shipwrecks of people whose loss caused grief and dislocation in their home country.[12] But, for the earls, with their followings and local watchmen who knew the dangers of the Firth well, it was quite possible to maintain political control over the two sides of the Firth and combine their island domain with their territorial one in a joint power base, difficult though that may seem to us today.

The joint earldoms were really a tripartite maritime lordship, consisting of Shetland, Orkney and Caithess, all three divided by rough waters. At the northern extremity, Shetland, a separate archipelago, had its own culture and distinctive geography. Composed of much harder and older rocks than Orkney (except for the southern peninsula of Dunrossness), Shetland is far less fertile with respect to arable culture, although with excellent pasture for

---

11 The main island in the Orkneys is called Mainland, spelled with a capital 'M' which distinguishes it from the Scottish mainland which is spelled in this book with a lower case 'm'
12 See Crawford, 1987, 21, for some examples

stock-raising and surrounded by rich fishing grounds. It is divided by deep voes, like miniature fjords, with large islands at the northern end of the archipelago. It was less easy to maintain political control over this extensive seascape, although the *þing* site at Tingwall[13] was well placed for access from both north and south for the Shetland farmers to attend the annual Lawthing assembly. Shetland was an integral part of the Orkney earldom until it was brought directly under the control of the Norwegian Crown in 1195 as a result of the treacherous behaviour of Earl Harald Maddadson (see Section 6.2). Once the most northerly component of the earldom had been lost, the remaining combination of Orkney and Caithness (which continued to be a joint lordship for nearly another 200 years), was pulled inevitably in a southerly direction.[14] Of the three component parts, Shetland remained the most closely connected with Norway being nearest to the western province of Hordaland and the administrative centre at Bergen. When the earls no longer posssessed Shetland, they were possibly less closely connected with west Norway, although they still had to attend the royal court for their installation and when summoned for important meetings.

The tripartite maritime lordship did not survive into the thirteenth century. But the close ties between Orkney and Caithness did survive, and Caithness was a part of the northern Scandinavian world and linked, emotionally and economically, with the Norwegian earldom throughout the twelfth and thirteenth centuries, although Scottish influences moved rapidly north in the fourteenth century and the earls' power base in Caithness was reduced during the same period. We can recognise some geographical determinism in the surviving connection between the two earldoms, for the geological situation in Orkney and north-east Caithness is remarkably similar. Both are composed of low-lying level sheets of Old Red Sandstone (Devonian) flags.[15] Farming this fertile soil would have been done by similar methods, large-scale cultivation of arable land, producing crops of barley and oats, worked by the tenants (earlier slaves) based on earldom demesne estates. These Caithness estates in the north-east part (called the 'Ness' in the sagas) and along the north coast, would eventually be farmed by the *bondi*, wealthier farmers whom we meet in *Jarls' Saga*, usually because they were being fined, or worse, by the Scottish kings (see Sections 6.4.2 and 6.7.2). There is evidence from the saga that the earls fought hard to win Caithness in the first century of the earldom (see Sections 3.4.2 and 3.6.2), and that they then frequently resided there to maintain control or

---

13 ON *þing* ('public assembly'); the assembly of either the whole population or representatives (Crawford, 1987, 206–9)
14 Crawford, 2010, 90
15 Crawford, 1987, 28 and fig. 10; Omand, 1993, 103.

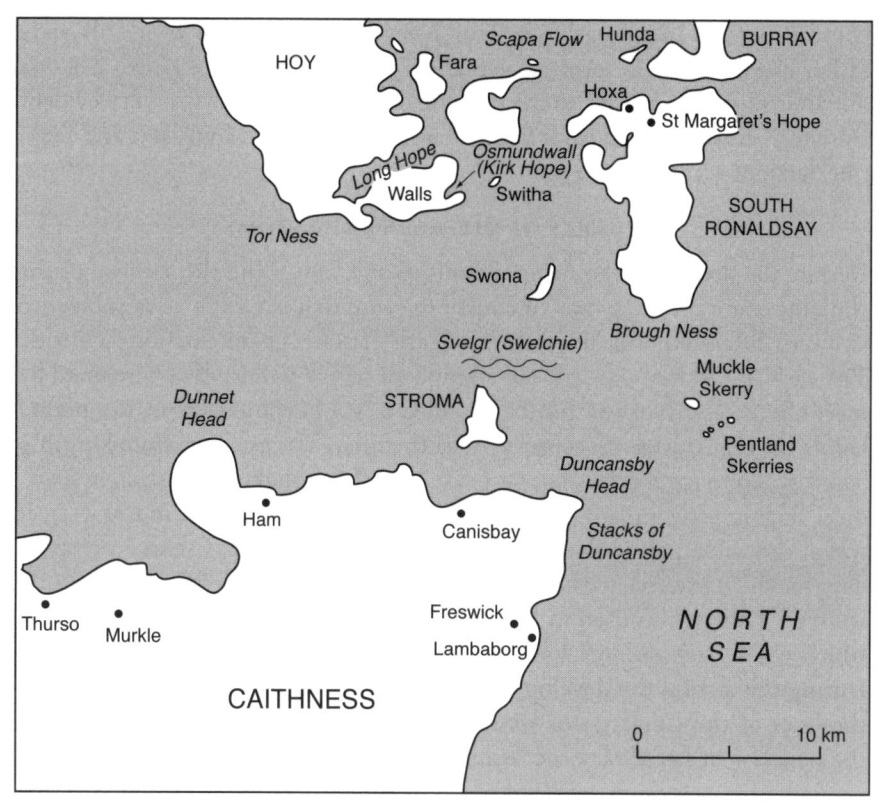

Figure 1.3 Map of the Pentland Firth, indicating the proximity of the north Caithness coast and the south isles of Orkney, although divided by the treacherous waters of the Firth. Local pilots would know how to avoid the Swelchie (ON *svelgr*, 'swirl, current, whirlpool, stream') as mentioned in the account in *OS* Chapter 74. *OS* Taylor, p. 189, n.3, gives references to saga accounts of shipwrecks in the Swelchie.

defeat their rivals. This was dictated by geography and by earldom ambition southwards, for there were campaigns to conquer and absorb Sutherland into the Caithness earldom and to conquer, but not to absorb, Easter Ross into the earldom in the eleventh century (see Section 4.2.1).

Eventually the southern frontier of earldom power retreated back to Caithness alone, as Sutherland was taken away, and north Scotland became vulnerable to royal campaigns and heavy retribution which must have reduced the wealth the earls derived from this area. To some degree it is this Scottish earldom which provides the most dramatic evidence of the attrition of lordly independence by royal authority which is a feature of medieval kingdoms everywhere, although the earls also faced crackdowns on their freedom of control in their island earldom. However, their Norwegian overlords were rather more remote in terms of actual distance, although the North Sea was not an insuperable barrier to the exercise of royal authority, as is very evident from the occasions when royal fleets arrived in Orkney (in 1098, 1151 and 1263) (see Sections 4.3.1 and 7.3.2).

1.2 EARLS OF DIFFERENT KINGDOMS

Despite the linking of the two earldoms in one family and the survival of the conjoint comital unit, it was of course the case that the earls were subject to two very different political systems and earls of quite separate national entities. The earls of Orkney were part of a kingdom where power was maintained by maritime access; Norway has been called a 'sea-borne realm' in the period before the mid-thirteenth century. After that there was a change from kingship based on sea to royal dominion based on land,[16] although administrative structures then in place maintained royal authority over the islands in the west. It was at this same period that the term 'skattland' came into use in Norway to describe those external parts of the Norwegian kingdom which paid taxes (ON *skattr*).[17] This term is used in Magnus 'Lawmender's' *Landlaw*, issued in 1274, which was a new national Lawcode introduced into the skattlands as well.[18] During this period the development of Norway into a medieval kingdom on the lines of the countries of western and northern Europe took place, and the new law of hereditary succession to the throne meant that the king was recognised as sovereign overlord of the skattland territories as well as in the Norwegian kingdom. The inhabitants of skattlands were theoretically considered to be royal subjects. This new concept developed just at the time that the Hebrides were lost, and replaced by Iceland and Greenland as skattlands, which submitted to royal overlordship in 1263–4. There was a 'state-formation process' by which the peripheral Atlantic communities were incorporated into the medieval kingdom.[19] The earls were also incorporated into this political structure nominally, although they probably retained a certain degree of independence being so far removed from the main centres of royal authority.

This is something of a contrast to the earldom of Caithness, which was part of the mainland of Scotland, and therefore always territorially part of the political structures in the kingdom, a fact which seems to have been theoretically

---

16 Imsen, 2010, 22
17 *Historia Norwegie* describes the islands in the west as 'tributary' a century earlier (*tributariis insulis*), but this definition implies the rendering of occasional tribute, rather than regular payments of 'skat' as implied by the term 'skattland' (see Section 2.3 for further discussion of *Historia Norwegie*)
18 Imsen, 2011, 16–17
19 Ibid., 2010, 30

acknowledged by the earls from almost the beginning of the earldom, at least as far as can be understood from *Jarls' Saga* (see Section 3.6). This was entirely based on territorial links, and sea power did not come into the picture. Land-based authorities have a simpler task in front of them when they develop theories of national identity and a kingdom grows towards its natural boundaries, particularly where the boundaries are defined by the sea. However, the kings of Scots were rather slow to get marching on the road to the creation of a single and undivided kingdom, for throughout the earliest period of the earldoms' history there were several political groupings in north Scotland, all of them vying with each other to dominate militarily. The ongoing struggle of the kings of Alba to defeat their rivals occupied two centuries and delayed the process of extending Scottish authority to Caithness. We will find that the earls battled with the rulers of Moray to the south (see Section 3.4), who constantly opposed the growing power of the kings of Alba (Scotland), and it was not until this Moravian dynasty was finally crushed by a series of campaigns in the twelfth and early thirteenth centuries that the Scottish kings were able to extend their authority north of the Beauly Firth.[20] They were greatly aided in their ability to lead military expeditions to the furthest north of mainland Scotland with moral justification by the mistakes made by Earl Harald and his son Earl John with regard to the episcopal authorities in Caithness (see Sections 6.4.1 and 6.7.1).

Caithness was therefore a province of the kingdom of Scotland which, despite the different ethnicity of the population and its Norse culture, was always going to be brought closer to the kingdom of which it was an integral part when the opportunity offered. It was incorporated by a punitive process of heavy fines, rather than the installation of royal officials or the confiscation of earldom lands (although the kings attempted to implement both). The bond with the king of Scots was sealed by the personal submission of the earl, symbolised by the oath of fealty and the feudal ceremony of homage, and in return the earl was granted his earldom with full freedom to run the northern province much as he liked. The nearest sheriff was based in Inverness, well to the south of Caithness, and other royal officials such as baillies and 'crowners' only appear in the documentary record for Caithness in the fourteenth century.[21]

The way in which the earl of Orkney was bound to his Norwegian overlord was somewhat different, although it involved a ceremony of submission, and each earl was supposed to renew his allegiance to each new king. These

20 Oram, 2011, 185–94
21 As noted by David Carpenter (2004, 39) in his survey of royal authority throughout Britain, there were no royal castles or sheriffdoms in Caithness in the thirteenth century and Dingwall was still the 'northernmost outpost of royal power in the 1260s'

ceremonies are mentioned in passing in the course of the saga story of the earls (and we cannot be sure that the later description was not influenced by the saga writer's experience of the earls' relationship in his own times). The record of the events of 1210 when the joint earls John and David Haraldsson went to make their peace with King Ingi and Jarl Hakon is likely to be an accurate rendering of how the two earls were reconciled, as it was recorded in an almost contemporary saga. They had to pay a large fine (for not having visited the king to give their allegiance sooner), give security and hostages and swear loyalty and obedience. Then 'in the end, King Ingi made them his earls over Orkney and Shetland, upon such terms as were adhered to until their death-day'.[22] This indicates that the grant of the earldom to the heir was not an automatic development, but conditional upon certain terms, which could be set by each king with the new earl. It was a situation which developed after their father Harald Maddadson had been tangentially involved in the Eyiarskeggjar rising against King Sverre and paid dearly for his disloyalty, losing Shetland, and having his powers over his earldom curtailed (see Section 6.2.2).

Earls in Norway were few and far between by this date, and regarded with some reservation, as can be seen from the law governing the king's hird.[23] It was a title of nobility which by that date was only granted to members of the royal family for life, and, in a situation where there was no system of primogeniture, these powerful individuals could be regarded as a threat by those already seated on the throne (and there might be more than one king sharing power until later in the twelfth century, when primogeniture was at last acknowledged as the normal method of inheritance). The earls of Orkney were always an exception, in that it was acknowledged that the sons of an Orkney earl had a right to claim the earldom, but it came to be treated as more of an official appointment with a residual inherited family right to the title. The difficulty of knowing what the terms of an earl's appointment were, and whether these differed over time will be discussed more fully below in Section 7.2.1.

The two earldoms therefore developed into somewhat different honours, both in nature and in status. We have no indication of how the earls regarded these differences but they were doubtless very well aware of them; the circumstances of their relationship with their two overlords, the king of Scots to the south and the king of Norway over the sea to the east, must have been rather important factors in their lives. They faced two ways and the dichotomy of the two cultures, Scots and Norse, was something they lived with and adjusted to, even those new earldom dynasties which moved north from southern Scotland in the thirteenth and fourteenth centuries (see Sections 7.1.3, 7.6.2).

22 *ES*, ii, 381, and see further analysis of this occasion in Section 6.6.1
23 Discussed in Section 7.2

1.2.1 *Peripheral communities*

From the point of view of the kings and royal administration the earldoms were peripheral to the political heartlands of both Scotland and Norway. The concept of 'centre and periphery' has been much used by historians in recent decades, and as the young kingdoms grew into political units the communities on the fringes of the geographical national terrain were seen to be natural objectives for domination and incorporation. As far as Norway was concerned the distances between political centre and periphery 'were immense', whether it was the Fenno-Scandinavian north, the oceanic western islands, or the forested parts of eastern Norway on the borders with Sweden. The islands off the Scottish coasts were certainly highly peripheral, if less so than Iceland and Greenland, which could only be reached by extremely long voyages of two to four weeks.[24]

It is interesting to make a comparison of the province of Jemtland on the eastern, forested frontier of Norway with the earldom of Orkney, both of them physically detached from the political centres of government, although with entirely different political structures. Jemtland was conquered by King Sverre in 1178, and was treated as a skattland like Orkney. One difference was that it was part of the archbishopric of Uppsala in Sweden, whereas Orkney and Shetland were part of the Norwegian archbishopric of Nidaros (from 1152/1153). The Jemtlanders were remarkably independent, and renowned for their self-government, and in this respect the comparison with Iceland is frequently cited by local historians.[25] Certainly their identity was regional and they considered themselves to be 'Jemtlanders' rather than Norwegian, just like Icelanders, (and also Orcadians). Steinar Imsen emphasises that these skattlands were turned into 'provincial communes', a process by which the Norwegian Crown ruled these outlying communities through a class of 'royal liegemen' (ON *hirðmenn*) but also allowing the local elites to dominate the legal and administrative operations in their locality.[26] The granting of community seals to both areas is a striking indication of how the Norwegian Crown regarded these peripheral skattland communities to be worthy of the accolade of having their own independent means of confirming their own legal judgements with sealed documents.[27] It was also probably intended that the granting of seals with the royal symbol (the lion rampant holding the Norwegian axe) included in the image would help to bind these peripheral 'provincial communes' closer to the

---

24 Imsen, 2010, 27
25 Ibid., 26
26 Ibid., 159; Imsen, 2006
27 Imsen, 2005, 156

Norwegian Crown and to give them a sense of identity with royal authority.[28] There is good evidence of the importance of possessing the seal in a difficult political situation in Orkney with the rule of David Menzies in the 1420s which is dramatically revealed in the Complaint against him (see Section 8.4.1); while a series of fourteenth-century documents from Jemtland demonstrate how the seal could be misused there in similarly dramatic circumstances.[29]

Caithness was also peripheral to the Scottish royal power centres in Edinburgh and Stirling, although more easily accessible to a land army than the Hebrides which came into Scottish possession in the 1260s. By that date Caithness had finally been penetrated by royal armies, through expeditions in the late twelfth century and in 1223 after the burning of Bishop Adam (see Sections 6.3 and 6.7.1). These were visible and memorable demonstrations that the king's peace 'should run undisturbed and the royal will be unchallenged throughout Scotland'.[30] However, the danger of having his kingdom bordering on to the realm of the Norwegian king was brought forcefully into the open when King Hakon's great naval expedition of 1263 sailed along the north coast of Scotland. Even more disturbing to the susceptibilities of the Scottish king must have been the evidence that King Hakon sent a force across to Caithness to impose a fine on the men of Caithness for ensuring their non-combatance during the time of hostilities. The letter which he wrote at the time found its way into the Scottish central archives, showing that it had been (probably) passed there by the inhabitants of Caithness caught between the two warring kings (see Section 7.3.2 for the whole story). This incident showed only too clearly how accessible northern Scotland was to a hostile Norwegian fleet – perhaps in some respects still more accessible than to a Scottish land army. Of course at the other end of the kingdom the kings of Scots had a southern land frontier which was easily crossed by hostile English armies, but the Border country was also more easily defended than the northern coastal province of Caithness. There are however some interesting parallels with the far south-western province of Galloway which King William struggled to assert his authority over at the same time as he also cracked down on Caithness in the late twelfth century.[31]

---

28 Only these two provincial communities, Orkney and Jemtland, had the privilege of including the royal Norwegian lion on their seals (Crawford, 1978a; 1979; Clouston, 1930–1; *KL sub* 'Lagtingssegl'). See Section 2.7.3 and Figure 2.5.
29 Njåstad, 2003, 163
30 Oram, 2011, 187
31 Ibid., 135–44; Gillebrigte, Lord of Galloway, was also a vassal of Henry II of England, and so owed dual allegiance, just as the earl of Caithness did

1.2.2 Borders and frontiers[32]

The waterway which divided – or united – the earldoms of Caithness and Orkney has already been mentioned several times. We can never ignore this important feature in our study of the history of the two earldoms. What role did it play, locally and nationally? The very fact that these two earldoms on the northern and southern sides of the Pentland Firth were held by the same family reflects an early medieval age of fluid frontiers and personal lordship over men and their territories.[33] That picture is exemplified by the many incidents in *Jarls' Saga* showing the earls and their relatives and followers moving to and fro across the Firth as if it was one social and political arena, without any difference of national identity. The supposed agreement between the Norwegian King Magnus *barfœttr* ('Barelegs') and the Scottish king Edgar which followed on King Magnus's war-cruise around the northern and western coasts of Scotland in 1098 may have defined the various spheres of authority in theory, but it probably made very little difference to the situation on the ground – or over the water. The constant activity of ships moving across the Firth as described in the twelfth-century section of *Jarls' Saga* certainly gives no impression that the actors in the dramatic incidents were in the least bit concerned about whether they were acting out their roles on a Norwegian or a Scottish stage (see Section 4.5). If it was then a 'boundary', it should have made the Norwegian kings wary of infiltrating the southern, Scottish, side of the Firth, and yet we hear about King Eystein Haraldsson capturing Earl Harald Maddadson in the harbour of Thurso in 1151 (*OS*, Chapter 91). The Scottish kings' authority in Caithness at this time (especially King David's) was exercised by attempting to influence the inheritance of the earls, and by promoting the Scottish Church in the area, rather than by their own royal presence (see Section 4.3.1). That authority was also expressed in a charter of King David's addressed to Earl Rognvald (as earl of Orkney) and including the local people in Orkney as well as in Caithness (see Section 4.5).[34] The Firth as a boundary did not seem politically relevant to the Scottish king either.

The next century saw a change, particularly brought about by the Treaty of Perth of 1266 (see Section 7.4). The role of kingship was changing, in that kings now considered themselves to be rulers over 'national' entities in which borders were important defining elements of that national entity.[35] The statement in the

---

32 See contributions to *Grenser og Grannelag* (Imsen, ed., 2005) on the importance of borders and frontiers in medieval Scandinavian history
33 Imsen, 2009, 12
34 *DN*, xix, no. 31; *OSR*, 17; *CSR*, 1; Barrow, 1999, 155; *omnibus probis hominibus Cateneis et Orchadie*
35 Steinar Imsen (2009, 16) gives other examples of King Magnus Hakonsson's negotiations regarding Norway's borders with Sweden to the east and north

treaty about Orkney's position being reserved specially to the king's domain, with all rights and pertinents relating to his lordship, gives a clear indication of the constitutional position of Orkney within the realm of Norway for the first time, even though the treaty is primarily concerned with the situation in the Hebrides. The Pentland Firth was a new state border and the inhabitants of Orkney and Caithness were 'subjects' of one or other of the kings,[36] which did in theory make the other side of the Firth 'foreign territory'.[37] So long as there were earls in receipt of grants of both earldoms, as they were throughout the thirteenth century, the links across the Pentland Firth would be retained. During the periods of minority or abeyance in the fourteenth century when royal officials had full authority over royal and earldom lands and rights in Orkney, and powerful feudatories in northern Scotland were exercising wardship rights over the heirs to the Caithness earldom, a tense situation must have developed across this maritime frontier.[38]

The closer incorporation of Orkney into the Norwegian kingdom is a feature of the latter part of the thirteenth century, and the introduction of the new *Landlaw* of 1274 must have been an important element in binding the island societies into the central administrative structures. The policy of developing 'provincial-communal' rule throughout the island dominions at the same time would have encouraged self-government. Was this also 'aimed at reducing the position of the earl' as argued by Steinar Imsen? It would seem unlikely that that was a prime purpose of such developments, especially if the Scottish king was regarded as a 'potential threat'.[39] The earl's main role was to defend his earldom from all external attacks, which was traditionally the function of feudal vassals, and as we know was still an important factor from the earls' installation charter which survives from the later fourteenth century (see Section 8.1.1). All earls were given fiscal privileges to carry out such functions, and arrangements for the granting of such privileges would no doubt have been included in the 'many special agreements' referred to in the reconciliation of Earl Magnus Gilbertsson with King Magnus 'the Lawmender' in 1267 (see Section 7.4.1).

---

36 Ibid., 11
37 This probably did have the eventual effect of turning the men of Caithness into 'Scots and foreigners' (ibid.) but not immediately. There is a reference in the Complaint against David Menzies of 1425 to 'foreigners from Caithness', whom he had brought in to Orkney, but it is not at all clear who exactly these 'pests' were. In 1461 raiders are said to have come from the Isles and Sudreys (Hebrides) in the following of the earl of Ross and Lord of the Isles (*Orkney Recs.*, nos xviii, xxii and xxiii). The earl of Ross had made inroads into Caithness and Orkney during the abeyance of the earldoms post-1350 (see Section 7.6).
38 As in 1357 and 1358 when the letter of Duncan Anderson and the royal writ of David II give clear evidence of incursions across the Pentland Firth into Orkney by one of the holders of the heir in wardship to the earldoms (see Section 7.6.3)
39 Imsen, 2009, 16

The clearer definition of the Pentland Firth as a 'state border' made the earl's role even more significant, and particularly when Caithness was the other half of Earl Magnus' lordship, a factor about which the Norwegian kings must have had some reservations. An important element in this border control issue was the matter of maritime relations between the two kingdoms.[40] We have a very clear statement of Earl William's fight in Caithness against the old enemy the earl of Ross in order to defend Orkney in the latter years of the Norwegian period (see Section 1.4).

Of course, as will be seen, there was increasing Scots influence creeping ever further north into the north mainland of Scotland during the late thirteenth and fourteenth centuries (see Section 7.5). This process was aided by the policy of bringing in royal feudatories such as the de Moravias, who were given grants of land and heiresses in marriage by the Scottish kings. The loss of Sutherland meant a big chunk of former Caithness earldom territory was handed over to this family who were created earls and became big players in the power games of north Scotland. Another scion of the family, Freskin de Moravia, was married to Lady Joanna, an heiress of the Caithness earldom dynasty, and through her had authority in Strathnaver, in north-west Caithness (see Section 7.1.2). The one surviving document from the second half of the thirteenth century relating to the earldom of Caithness concerns a grant by Earl John to Freskin's son-in-law, Reginald Cheyne II, of an earldom estate at Nothegane in south Caithness, with the harbour of Forse (see Sections 2.3 and 7.7.2). These landholding changes were happening in the earl's circle; we have no inkling of the extent to which society was changing among ordinary farmers, or among the tenantry of the earl's estates. In the difficult period of the abeyance of the earldom after the death of Earl Malise (c.1350) there is clear evidence that members of the Ross family and following were in control of Caithness and probably dominating matters in Orkney, and seemingly not inhibited by any definition of the Pentland Firth as a state border.[41]

The Church was also a factor in the spread of Scottish influence into the islands, just at this time, and it is considered very likely that this was a result of the impact of the Black Death and succeeding bouts of plague which decimated the ranks of the clergy in Norway.[42] Economic and social matters were rendering the frontier zone along the Pentland Firth a crossing point for mobile and ambitious members of the northern Scottish nobility and the Scottish Church.

---

40 A clause at the end of the 1266 treaty concerned shipwreck, and when the treaty was renewed in 1312 an additional Memorandum shows that there had been violent activities perpetrated by the subjects of the two kingdoms against royal officials and merchants (see Section 7.6.1)
41 Crawford, 1982, 69–70; see Section 7.6.3
42 Ibid., 70–1

The absence of an earl of Orkney and Caithness from c.1350 to 1379 probably made the situation more fluid and allowed this movement north to happen. The Pentland Firth might have been a state border, but it was not one which was easily policed, and those who were in control in Caithness were in control of the ferries and crossing-points.

1.3 HISTORICAL APPROACHES

The earldoms arose or were created in an early medieval context, which makes it of interest to those historians and linguists who look to the sagas, particularly *Jarls' Saga*, as source material for analysis (see Section 2.1). However, the actual situation of the Orkney earl and the status of his title 'jarl', or the relationship of the earls with their kings, is not necessarily of prime interest to these researchers, most of whom are immersed in the wider Norse world and the Icelandic school of saga-writing, which has much bigger social, cultural and emotional horizons than the constitutional position of the jarls.[43] Naturally enough there was great interest in *Orkneyinga Saga* among early local historians in Orkney and Shetland,[44] but the first achievement of this early manifestation of enthusiasm for medieval Nordic literature was the translation of *Heimskringla* ('Saga of the kings of Norway' by Snorri Sturlason) by Samuel Laing of Papdale, Kirkwall (as early as 1844).[45] There was already at that time the pioneering translation into Latin of *Orkneyinga Saga* by the Icelander Thormodus Torfæus (Þormóður Torfason) (1697), which was translated into English in an abridged version in 1866 by Reverend Alexander Pope of Wick. However, the first full English translation was the joint effort of the Shetlander Gilbert Goudie and the Icelander Jón Hjaltalín, which appeared a few years later in 1873 (reprinted in a facsimile edition in 1973), and which still serves a very useful purpose, not least because of the notes and Introduction contributed by the Scottish antiquary Joseph Anderson.[46] His was the first critical approach to the medieval sources to be undertaken, and includes, for the first time, a consideration of the history of the post-saga period when the earldoms of Caithness and Orkney are plunged into a darkness which is illuminated by very few written sources.[47] Since then

---

43 *Medieval Scandinavia. An Encyclopedia* (ed. Pulsiano, 1993), for instance, has only two entries in the index for 'jarl' among the many hundreds of entries, and both of these relate to the occurrence of the term as a title in literary sources, neither of which is actually concerned with the Orkney jarls
44 An exceedingly informative account of some of the early efforts to publish translations of *Orkneyinga Saga* has been recently published by Andrew Wawn (2011)
45 First published in 1844, and revised with Introduction and notes by J. Simpson and P. Foote in the 1960s, published in an Everyman edition (see *Hms* in the Abbreviations)
46 See Wawn's comparison of a passage from *OS*, Chapter 20, translated by Hjaltalin and Goudie, with that by Dasent in the Rolls Series (Wawn, 2011, 32–8)
47 Crawford, 1971, xv

there have been further translations, one by A.B.Taylor (1938), with a critical edition of the text, and a more popular translation, with only a short introduction, by Hermann Pálsson and Paul Edwards (1972). Both of these have their own particular value for the student of Norse Orkney.[48]

The earldoms of course survived into the late medieval period when the title and the position of earls as members of the medieval nobility had developed into a rather different phenomenon from that of the early earls. The rulers of feudalised medieval kingdoms regarded earls as important members of their courts and entourages whose role as fighters was still essential, but who were also meant to help maintain the rule of law, and of the kings' writ within their earldoms. The position of earls in Norway developed rather differently, and the earls of Orkney were always something of an anomaly[49] (see Section 7.2.1), although their independent position in the islands may have been tolerated because the kings were unwilling – or unable – to do away with them entirely. However, there were clear intentions of bringing the earls more tightly under royal authority, and of converting their role into something more approximate to that of appointed officials (see Section 7.4.1). Historians are interested in such developments, and the earliest generation of Norwegian historians, such as P.A. Munch and A. Bugge, were committed to understanding the role of the earls in Norway's political development. Munch in particular included the story of the Orkney earls in his monumental five-volume work *Det Norske Folks Historie* ('The History of the Norwegian People'), first published 1852–63.[50] Until recently he was alone among Norwegian historians who considered the role of the earls in the post-saga period.[51] The position of the Orkney earl in the High and Later Middle Ages has recently come under close analysis by Norwegian historians, as part of a wider study of the political administration of the skattlands[52] (already mentioned in the Introduction to this volume).

Similarly, the earls of Caithness have only in comparatively recent decades been considered of historical interest by historians.[53] The Scottish earldom was regarded as an adjunct of the Orkney earldom, and not of any great intrinsic

---

48   The standard Icelandic editions are by S. Nordal (1913–16) and F. Guðmundsson (1965)
49   Crawford, 1971, xvii
50   New editions were printed in 1941–3, at the time when notions of Germanic racial superiority were dominant in occupied Norway. See Øien, 2005, 84–5
51   When writing my 1971 doctoral thesis, Munch's History was the only secondary Norwegian source available to read on the history of the later earls, although his study finishes with the Kalmar union of 1397
52   Particularly by Woerdahl in her study of the King's Tributary Lands in the Norwegian Realm (2011)
53   Topping, 1983; Oram, 1999, 2005, 2011; MacDonald, 2003; and also Carpenter, 2003, within a British context

importance in Scottish history, as the earls of Orkney belonged to a non-Scottish world. The early Norse earldoms were of general significance because of the Viking impact on Scotland.[54] However, it is now better appreciated that the incorporation of Caithness into the medieval kingdom in the late twelfth and thirteenth centuries is one significant aspect of the growth of Scottish national identity which provides some interesting evidence about the incorporation of different ethnic elements in the composite kingdom (as with the Western Isles in the 1260s). The story of the taming of the north, and of the men of Caithness, as well as the processes by which the earls were brought to heel, provides instructive examples of the methodology of ambitious and ruthless kings in the pursuit of maintaining and extending their power over their territory. The developing consciousness of a Scottish national state led them to assert that this was their territory to dominate and assimilate.

1.3.1 *Local historians*

If we turn to the local historians of our two earldoms, the contrast between the Orkney islands and the north Scottish mainland is particularly striking. Caithness has never had a local historian of the calibre of Orcadian authors such as J. Storer Clouston, Hugh Marwick, or William Thomson, at least as far as the medieval history of the earldom is concerned. J.T. Calder's *Sketch of the Civil and Traditional History of Caithness* (1861) is indeed 'sketchy' on the medieval earls, who take up only two and a bit chapters. Reverend Angus Mackay's *History of the Province of Cat* (1914) shows a greater depth of enquiry and understanding in the three chapters devoted to the medieval period, although his interests are directed more specifically towards 'the Conflicts of the Clans' (of which there is indeed much to write about in Caithness and Strathnaver's history). Much more focused on the medieval earldom is James Gray's *Sutherland and Caithness in Saga-Time (or the Jarls and the Freskyns)* (1922), which is full of insights, somewhat romanticised at times. The very general book in the County series (*The Caithness Book*) (1973) has one chapter on 'The Vikings' and another one 'From the Vikings to the "Forty-Five"', both of them short summaries.[55] From the point of view of publication of medieval charters and other records, Caithness has been better served, thanks to the energy of the original founders of The Viking Club. The collection, editing and translation of *Caithness and Sutherland Records*, (edd. A.W. and A. Johnston, 1909) is a remarkable achievement, although the majority of the record material concerns Sutherland, and

---

54 Crawford, 1987; Woolf, 2007, *passim*
55 Earl William is erroneously said to have 'surrendered Orkney to the Crown in 1455 and was compensated with the Earldom of Caithness' (Omand, 1972, 128)

the preponderance of Caithness material concerns the medieval Church.[56] There are more articles on medieval Caithness scattered through the *Old Lore Miscellany* publications of The Viking Society. But in general the Caithness earldom has suffered from being seen as a minor component of the Orkney earls' dynastic power base and less significant in northern Highland history than the earldoms of Sutherland and Ross to the south. This may be a fair representation of the Scottish half of the joint earldom, which has to be seen in the context of the maritime world across the Pentland Firth,[57] but it fails to see the history of Caithness as that of a very interesting community in its own right.

Orkney has been fortunate in its historians, either local or non-local.[58] The history of the islands, and of the earldom, have attracted the interest of many men, and rather few women! Among those already mentioned is J.S. Clouston, whose *History of Orkney* (1932) is a monumental study of the Norse earldom, as well as a socio-economic study of Norse society in the earldom.[59] He also wrote many articles of importance for our understanding of medieval society in the islands, in *Scottish Historical Review* and *Proceedings of the Orkney Antiquarian Society*. It has been said by one of the new generation of Orkney researchers that his contribution to studies on medieval Orkney is 'second to none'.[60] There were earlier writers who immersed themselves in the history of the earldom, the first of whom, George Mackenzie, can perhaps be called the founder of modern Orkney scholarship.[61] He was an eighteenth-century Orkney lawyer who held a local position connected with earldom grain rents, and was involved in an important lawsuit which gave him access to documents concerned with traditional weights and measures, including the 1492 Rental, of which he made a copy (the only one now surviving).[62] He also wrote a book called *The General Grievances and Oppressions of the Isles of Orkney and Shetland* (1750 and 1836). The Rental was used by a local landowner, David Balfour, when he wrote his *Odal Rights and Feudal Wrongs* (1860). Historians are now fortunate to have a modern

56 The 'Introduction, Notes and Index' were prepared by Reverend D. Beaton, of Wick, who was also the author of *Ecclesiastical History of Caithness* (1909). J.B. Craven also wrote a *History of the Episcopal Church in Caithness* (1908)
57 Unless it is understood as being an integral part of the Celtic world which surrounded Caithness in the northern half of the Scottish Highlands, which is where some local historians would place the emphasis (e.g. Bramman, 1972)
58 Øien, 2005, 90–9, a historiographical study of the historians of medieval Orkney
59 The first twenty-two chapters are concerned with the medieval period, and the rest of Orkney's history is squeezed into nine chapters
60 Gibbon, 2006, 67. The many references to Clouston's writings in the following chapters are witness to their continued usefulness
61 Crawford, 1971, xi
62 Thomson, 1996, viii–ix, gives a very helpful account of Mackenzie's historical researches

edition, with a significantly important introduction explaining much about the obscurities of the rental entries and payments of skat.[63]

A number of other early Orkney rentals were published by a local Orkney sheriff, Alexander Peterkin, early in the nineteenth century, among which was the second of Lord Henry Sinclair's rental compilations, that of 1500 (actually compiled at various dates between 1497 and 1503)[64] (see Section 9.1.1).

More general accounts of the history of the islands were forthcoming in the nineteenth century, the first of them written by George Barry, minister of Shapansay, as early as 1805, although his survey is primarily of the geographical nature of the islands and the islanders,[65] with the earldom's history only occupying two chapters. Another remarkable nineteenth-century compiler who amalgamated a large amount of evidence (although unfortunately not referencing his material very adequately) was Roland Saint-Clair whose study of *The Saint-Clairs of the Isles* (1898) provides information about the earldom dynasty ('Sea Kings of Orkney') and also the earls of Caithness, more briefly. In this respect he is the only writer to have considered the two earldoms together in one book, (as this present study will attempt to do).[66] The main purpose of Saint-Clair's book was to focus on the Sinclair earls and the cadet branches of the family in Orkney, Shetland and Caithness, as well as everywhere else where the Sinclair name was established.[67] A local historian of the same generation as Storer Clouston was John Mooney, whose acceptance of the evidence of *Orkneyinga Saga* was very much in line with the nineteenth-century approach to saga sources.[68] One of his ground-breaking efforts was to collect a great deal of evidence together for his study of the martyrdom and cult of Earl Magnus (1935) which had not been done in English before, as well as editing the medieval charters relating to Kirkwall (*Kirkwall Charters*), and writing a very historically focused study of *The Cathedral and Royal Burgh of Kirkwall* (1947).

Another of J.S. Clouston's achievements was the editing and publication of *Records of the Earldom of Orkney 1299–1614* (SHS, 1914) which includes many documents relative to the administration of the islands, particularly in the time

---

63 Thomson, 1996, x–xxvi
64 Ibid., vii. The 1500 rental awaits a modern edition
65 Entitled grandiosely *The History of the Orkney Islands in which is comprehended an Account of their Present as well as their Ancient State; together with the Advantages they possess for Several Branches of Industry, and the Means by which they may be Improved*
66 Saint-Clair does however make the mistake of considering the Orcadian jarldom to have consisted of 'two principal parts – Insular and Scottish' – and he calls Caithness the 'Scottish Orcadia' (p.181), thus giving priority to the Orkney earldom
67 This approach has fostered the current Sinclairiana movement with its overblown hype about the achievements of the Sinclair earls, particularly Earl Henry I (Sinclair, 1992)
68 Torhild Øien (2005, 94–5) is rather critical of Mooney's approach to the sources

of the Sinclair earls. This was produced at just about the same time as *Orkney and Shetland Records*, another Viking Society publication edited by A.W. and A. Johnston (1907–13), which complements Clouston's collection and translation of Orkney records by including documents with a much wider scope, dating from the late eleventh century to the early sixteenth century, and also many ecclesiastical records.[69] It also is a collection of Orkney *and* Shetland records, and the forerunner of the up-to-date edition of Shetland record material by John Ballantyne and Brian Smith, who have produced two volumes in recent years to the definite advantage of researchers into Shetland history (1994; 1999).

The earls, and Orkney society in the time of the medieval earls, feature in Hugh Marwick's and William Thomson's books, alongside their many other studies and publications of a diverse nature concerning Orkney in the Norse and medieval periods. Marwick's seminal book on *Orkney Farm-Names* (1952) is an assessment of settlement evidence, as derived from toponymy, and the elucidation of the meaning of Norse farm-names in the islands relates quite often to the earls' power bases and estates. Part II ('Farm Background')is a ground-breaking discussion of 'Skatts and Rents' and the classification of land, with an important analysis of the 'earldom lands of various kinds' (p.192). Part III focuses on the chronology and meaning of habitative names, which initiated the study of Norse settlement chronology.[70] William Thomson is the most notable contemporary local historian of our time, and he has introduced a 'new era' into Orcadian historical studies,[71] and not only with regard to the medieval period. He is one of the very few with the breadth of knowledge of the wider economic and social background to be able not only to fit the Orkney evidence into the contemporary situation, but also to see Orkney's identity as a 'changing variable'. *The New History of Orkney* (1987, and updated twice, in 2001 and 2008) is a remarkable history of the islands which few localities in Scotland can match; while his edition of *Lord Henry Sinclair's 1492 Rental* has already been mentioned as a most valuable contribution to our understanding of medieval rural economies and tax structures. Many of the articles which Thomson has written on the Orkney landscape and economy over a wide historical spectrum are now collected and republished in *Orkney, Land and People* (2008).

69 As noted in my thesis (1971, xii, n.3) these two collections of documents were edited in an atmosphere of rivalry and without collaboration, although surprisingly this did not result in much overlap of material
70 Marwick also wrote a study of *The Orkney Norn* (1929), with some discussion of early Orkney documents, updated in Michael Barnes' more recent publication (1998) which includes a few annotated texts
71 Øien, 2005, 97

Few of the historians of the earldom of Orkney have considered the earldom as one half of a joint medieval lordship.[72] There is also the danger that Shetland is left out of our study because of the fact that it was taken out of the earldom in 1195 and brought under direct Norwegian rule (see Chapter 6). Shetland, especially the southern half of the long Shetland archipelago, can never be omitted from any consideration of the history of the Northern Isles because it has always been closely associated with Orkney. Moreover, we must always remember that throughout our period Shetland and Orkney were ecclesiastically tied together in the Orkney bishopric, the significance of which should not be underestimated (and probably needs more estimation).[73] From the point of view of our historiographical survey, we need to appreciate that Shetland has produced a remarkable number of local historians, such as Edmonston, Goudie and Hibbert.[74] It has also been the focus of attention by early travellers who then wrote about their experiences and impressions of this northern archipelago. One of these writers, John R. Tudor (1883), actually treated Orkney and Shetland together in his description of the islands, and he starts off with four chapters on the history of 'The Norse period'.[75] Brian Smith continues to publish in the fine tradition of local historians in Shetland; his published works range over a wide period from the Viking Age to modern social and economic history.[76]

1.3.2 *Genealogies*

Despite some reservations it is important to mention the work of genealogists, and particularly Father Richard Augustine Hay (1661–c.1736) who wrote the *Genealogie of the Sainteclaires of Rosslyn*, first published in 1835 by James Maidment.[77] Hay's mother married Sir James St Clair of Rosslyn/Roslin as her second husband, from which arose Hay's intense interest in the family, its history and its charters, to which he appears to have had access, and many of which he recorded in full.[78] This gives his *Genealogie* great worth for the histo-

---

72 The *Old Lore Miscellany* publications of the Viking Society are comprehensive in their inclusion of material from all the areas of Scandinavian settlement in the British Isles
73 Gordon Donaldson's study of the archdeaconry of Shetland (1995) has recently been expanded by Brian Smith (2003)
74 A. Edmonston, *A View of the Ancient and Present State of the Zetland Islands*, 2 vols, 1809; S. Hibbert, *Description of the Shetland Islands* (1822); G. Goudie, *The Celtic and Scandinavian Antiquities of Shetland* (1904)
75 It is the travellers who were more inclined to treat Orkney and Shetland together, whereas the local historians, being deeply involved in their own archipelago, tend to focus on its history and culture alone. See Flinn 1988
76 For example Smith, 1988; 1990; 1995; 2000; 2001; 2002; 2003a; 2009
77 Foreword to the 2002 reprint of Hay's *Genealogie*
78 These are translated in the 2002 reprint of Hay's *Genealogie*

rian of the Sinclair family and of the Sinclair earls, and although Maidment cast doubt on the accuracy of Hay's transcriptions, some of the originals of the charters which have recently been discovered (like those in the Crookston writs) show that there is no great inaccuracy on Hay's part.[79] What makes Hay's work very unhelpful for the academic historian is the amount of hyperbole in his prose sections about the Sinclair earls and their lifestyles. Much of this appears to be derived from the writings of a certain Van Bassan ('fabulous genealogist')[80] and it is very difficult to be sure what is Hay's own writing and what he has copied from Van Bassan's hyperbolic descriptions.[81] The long lists of Earl Henry's titles and powers (such as the power to stamp coins within his dominions, to make laws, and the wearing of a crown when he 'constituted laws')[82] were very likely dreamed up by Van Bassan. The passages where the list of hundreds of retainers and their sumptuous dress is described likewise appear somewhat overblown, although there can be no doubt that noblemen of the standing of the Sinclair earls, and their wives, would be surrounded with large retinues of their attendees, possibly dressed in scarlet gowns and coats of black velvet[83] which were part of the panoply of nobility in the fourteenth and fifteenth centuries. We have evidence, from his will, that similar fine clothing belonged to Sir David Sinclair (1506), illegitimate son of the last earl of Orkney; he was based mostly in Shetland, although an esteemed official of both King Hans of Norway–Denmark and King James IV of Scotland (see Section 9.2.1).

Hay's *Genealogie* has had wide circulation for a very long time, and has boosted the mystique of the Sinclair earls, emanating from their possession of an ancient and remote island earldom. They were the heirs of a long line of Orkney earls, who had held sway in the northern seas, and whose insular stronghold appeared invincible and an almost regal power base. They continued to hold their earldom of a foreign power and yet became linked by marriage with the Scottish kings, whose vassals they also were. But their possession of the islands of Orkney – and their increasing influence in Shetland – gave them an independent status which no other feudal vassal possessed. These lordly Sinclairs could sail north and reside in Orkney and be outwith the dominion of their Scottish overlord. They drew great wealth from their fertile estates, and the produce from those estates was brought into the Scottish east coast ports

---

79 Crawford, 1971, xiii; Saint-Clair (1898, 275) also comments that the recent discovery of Alexander Sutherland's testament shows that it 'agrees in every way' with Hay's transcription
80 According to Saint-Clair, 1898, 101 note, and see Clouston's comments (1932, 236)
81 He is said to have been a Dane who lived long at Roslin Castle and Saint-Clair indicates in his use of Hay's text where he thinks it has been copied from Van Bassan (1898, 101, 104, 107; also Chapter IX)
82 Hay, 2002, 17
83 Ibid., 20

and probably sold at a good profit. They appeared untouchable, and although their relationship with their Norwegian king was contractual and they could be deprived of their title in theory, that would not be widely known in Scotland (and the possibility of it happening was remote).

The era of the Sinclair earls was a successful final chapter in the history of the northern earldoms, even though for most of their rule they no longer held the joint earldoms because Caithness was acquired by the Scottish king in 1375 (see Section 7.7). The success of Earl William Sinclair in regaining the earldom of Caithness in 1455 was an apparently deliberate move to reunite the joint earldoms and recreate the cross-Pentland Firth dominance which his ancestors had had from the beginning. However, Earl William's more immediate ambition was probably to secure for himself a Scottish earldom title which his family would retain when the Norwegian title was lost, a situation which he doubtless foresaw was going to happen in the near future (see Section 8.4.4). There is one piece of evidence which suggests that the ancient link of the earldom of Caithness with the earldom of Orkney may have been considered quite important at the time that Earl William was striving to regain the title of earl of Caithness. It comes from the opening sentence of a contracted version of the 'Genealogy of the Earls' which was added to the Corpus MS of Bower's *Scotichronicon* in the late 1440s or early 1450s.[84] It says 'Note that the earl of Orkney was accustomed from ancient times to be [also] earl of Caithness'[85] and is followed by a list of the earls from Rognvald III to the Earl William who was given the earldom of Caithness by James III in 1455. This preliminary sentence has no counterpart in the full version of the 'Genealogy' (neither the version dating from 1443 nor the one dating from 1446) and is a significant pointer to the purpose of this *aide-memoire* being added to the Corpus MS. It was written there for some reason connected with Earl William's ambition to have the earldom of Caithness reunited with his earldom of Orkney.

This contracted version of the 'Genealogy of the Earls', added to a manuscript of Bower's *Scotichronicon* in the late 1440s or early 1450s, indicates that the full version of the 'Genealogy' must have been known to Bower's scribe at that time. This fact is in itself quite important for telling us that the extant Latin earldom pedigree, drawn up probably in 1443,[86] was quickly known outside Orkney (where it was drawn up).[87] It was certainly a very remarkable document, and

---

84 Bower, *Scotichron.*, Watt, ed., 9 (1998), 41; see Section 2.5 below for a full description of the 'Genealogy'
85 Ibid., 40 (*Notandum quod comes Orchadie solet antiquitus esse comes Katanesie*)
86 See Crawford (1976, 157 n.6) for discussion of the dating issues
87 Or a previous version which was originally drawn up for William at the time he was striving to be given a grant of Orkney in the early 1420s (Crawford, 1976, 158)

perhaps thought so at the time, for very few such genealogical compilations are known from Scotland (and it deserves to be better known in the history of medieval Orkney). This 'Genealogy' was an important statement of the young William's right to the earldom, and it was compiled with the purpose of proving to King Erik that William should be awarded the family title and rights which went with the title. Its importance for those of us trying to understand the complexities lying behind the inheritance of Orkney, and Caithness, in the later Middle Ages is inestimable, and it is much used in the later chapters of this book.[88]

Although the purpose of the 'Genealogy of the Earls' was specifically to prove the young William's right to be granted the earldom of Orkney by his Norwegian overlord, the way in which the list of his predecessors goes right back to the granting of the earldom to Rognvald of Møre served another purpose. This was part of the process of cultivating the past, the 'validating charter' of a dynasty's identity and power.[89] The use of saga literature for this purpose is well known in Norway with the sagas about the kings' ancestry, but the 'Genealogy of the Earls' is possibly a unique example of this being used in the post-saga period, certainly in Scotland. It gives us some indication of the value placed on the Norse sources in late medieval Orkney for a very practical purpose, as well as for reasons of 'sentiment and piety'. The cathedral canons stopped short of including the origin myth of the earls (see Section 3.1), although a legendary past was for many noble families no deterrent to the validation of its authoritative position in the present.

1.4 LORDSHIP

Lordship (Latin *dominium*) was an important aspect of the authority exercised by kings and powerful landholders throughout medieval Europe. It has been defined as 'the power of command, constraint and exploitation',[90] and such power was exercised not only through royal authority but by the aristocracy. Our national historiographies focus very much on the growth and exercise of royal power especially in 'king-centred polities' like England and Scotland, and Norway also, but non-royal power was a very important aspect of lordship in medieval society. The lordship of the earls in Orkney and Caithness should be

---

88 The reliability of the 'Genealogy' was queried by Gray (1922, 103), but my assessment as made in 1971 still stands, despite the apparently erroneous insertion of an Earl Erik who is otherwise unrecorded. See Crawford (1971, 53ff) for a full discussion of the value of the 'Genealogy' and for the difficult problems regarding the 1422 Cragy testimonial and the implications arising from the relationship of James of Cragy's wife Margaret, a daughter of one of the earls, with Earl Henry I (1971, 54–5; 1976, 162)
89 Davies, 2009, 33
90 Ibid., 2, quoting Boutruche, *Seigneurie et Feodalité* 2 vols (Paris 1959–70) at p.9

central to this study, although it is their relationship with the kings which will emerge as the main theme in their story, and the increasing exercise of lordship by the kings over the earls which will become the dominant element in that story.

In her doctoral thesis (2006) Randi Wærdahl made a marked distinction between 'indirect lordship' (*indirekte herredøme*) exercised by the kings over Orkney and Shetland, and Man and the Hebrides (see Chapter 3) and the imposition of 'direct lordship' (*direkte herredøme*) imposed on Orkney after 1195 and on Faeroe and Iceland (see Chapter 4).[91] She explains the meaning of the ON terms *ríki* (rule, realm) and *veldi* (dominion) and their use to refer to the power and authority which kings and lords exercised over a geographical area and its inhabitants. Princes (usually earls) had *ríki* 'by virtue of their personal power base or because it was given to them by the king in the form of delegated royal authority'.[92] We can note that some of the earls were called, and remembered as having been called, *hinn ríki* which was the adjectival form of the term, meaning 'the Mighty/Powerful' (CV, sub *Ríkr*). This perhaps suggests that they were famous for having ruled their earldoms as independent lordships.[93] Similarly, Cnut the Great (1016–1034) is designated *Knútr inn Ríki* (ibid.), being famous for ruling his three kingdoms in an imperial mode without any submission to an overlord.

The period AD 1000–1250 was the formative age of the shaping of aristocratic power,[94] and that is the period for which we have the Old Norse sources (see Section 2.1), providing us with a dramatic and vivid picture of the earls' exercise of power and lordship within their earldoms. Although that picture may be coloured in the early period by the saga writer's understanding of lordship in his own day (c.1200), it provides us nonetheless with many convincing instances of the earls' 'personality and direction' which was at the heart of lordship.[95] The earl's control of the men in these communities, his maintenance of their loyalty, his ability to lead them in martial enterprises, his generosity in rewarding them for their loyalty and service, are all aspects of lordship which are dramatically conjured up for us in the pages of *Orkneyinga Saga*. It is said that 'good lordship' worked through 'charisma, display and reward'[96] and we have fine examples of

---

91 This distinction is not stressed so much in the English-translated version (Wærdahl, 2011, 55–6) although direct lordship is said to be exercised by the earl on behalf of the king
92 Ibid., 55
93 Rognvald Eysteinsson is called *ins ríka* (*OS* Guthmundsson, Chapter 3), his son Sigurd *inn ríki* (ibid., Chapter 5) and Thorfinn Sigurdsson also, even though there is a full description of his submission to King Olaf Haraldsson (*OS*, Chapter 18, and see Section 3.6.1)
94 Davies, 2009, 8
95 Ibid., 40
96 Ibid., 43

generous earls, most notably Earl Thorfinn, who provided his men and others with meat and drink throughout the winter 'in the same way that kings and earls in other lands would entertain their followers around Christmas, so there was no need for anyone to search for taverns' (*OS*, Chapter 20). Once the Viking era was over there were fewer raiding campaigns by which the earl's followers in his hirð could gain wealth from booty, so the reward came in grants of earldom estates, which fulfilled the purpose of lordship and the requirement to maintain a following. The role of a good lord or earl was then to create peaceful internal conditions so that his close followers, and family, could enjoy the fruits of their estates without disturbance or raids by outside enemies.

Two examples of the earl defending his Orkney earldom from outside attack come from the very end of our period; first is the death of Earl Henry I (1400), who according to the 'Genealogy of the Earls' returned to his island earldom 'and enjoyed his lands there at the latter time of his life, and for the defence of the cuntrie was sclane their crowellie be his innimiis'.[97] The second was the occasion when his grandson, Earl William, was unable to go to meet his Danish overlord Christian I in 1460 when summoned. The reason given by both the local community and the bishop of Orkney in two separate letters is of the devastating attacks on the islands by the earl of Ross and Lord of the Isles, and telling how Earl William 'for our defence' had laid himself out 'to his no small suffering and loss, bearing the expense, labours and dangers of war' specifically (it is said) in his earldom of Caithness in putting a stop to the malicious and savage attacks 'without whose presence and defence we had been utterly lost and destroyed by the sword and the fire'.[98] This is how the local community and the local bishop saw the earl's role in the defence of his people in the final years of the Norse earldom. There must have been many similar occasions during the previous 500 years of the earldoms' existence of outside attack and destruction by the sword and by fire. Of course, maintaining good order from disruptive elements within the earldoms is another aspect of good lordship which is evident from the saga account and we can cite the example of Earl Rognvald Kali Kolsson who died while pursuing the outlaw Thorbjorn in Caithness in 1168 (see Section 5.3.2).

Once the principle of single inheritance had come into force there was the problem of minorities and the 'hiatus of power' which followed the death of an earl.[99] The central period of the history of the joint earldoms (post-1231–1379) was bedevilled by minorities and abeyance in the absence of a male heir (1330–

---

97   *Bann.Misc.* iii, 81. This was probably during a raid on the islands by an English fleet (see Section 8.2.4)
98   *Orkney Recs.*, nos xxii and xxiii; *DN*, v, pp.827 and 836 (see Section 8.5.1)
99   Davies, 2009, 113

50) (see Section 7.6). This is the period when the Old Norse saga sources have dried up, and the documentary evidence is very thin indeed. Reading between the lines it appears that these circumstances of minorities and abeyance were characterised by periods of disruption when violence broke out in the earldoms. The likelihood is that it was the absence of an adult male heir which created a vacuum of authority and unleashed tensions.[100] Such tensions were usually kept under control by the exercise of good lordship and the personal authority of the earl. However, the biggest tensions in the earldom of Orkney appear to have been those which arose over the appointment of royal officials, when royal lordship came to the fore as a rival to the earl's own exercise of lordship over his heritable dominions. These tensions between the two forms of lordship, royal and comital, are in evidence from the late eleventh century until the fifteenth century and will form one of the main themes of this study of the joint earldoms.

The good rule of an effective earl was an all-important element in the maintenance of peace in the islands and on the north mainland of Scotland. The peripheral position of the earldoms meant that the forces of royal lordship coming from Norway or Scotland were spasmodic and not exercised consistently, or sometimes not at all. In these circumstances the earl's authority was the most relevant factor, but circumstances of inheritance, of disputed control, and after the late thirteenth century of minorities meant that the protection of powerful adult earls was not always available. We will be tracking the role of the earls throughout the 600 years of the earldoms' existence and assessing, where possible, the effectiveness, or otherwise, of their exercise of lordship.

---

100 Ibid., 113. See Section 7.6

TWO

The Sources of Knowledge about the Joint Earldoms

Documentary Survival and Historical Reality

Having introduced the secondary works written by historians about Orkney and Caithness, we will now turn to the original source material which is basic to our understanding of the history of the joint earldoms. Over the 600 years of the earldoms' existence our written sources vary widely. In the beginning we have the Norse sources, sagas written in old Norse or Icelandic, the most remarkable of which is *Orkneyinga Saga*, or the saga of the 'Orkneyingers', the people of Orkney. This is a composite work derived from an earlier (now lost) version, called *Jarla sǫgur* ('Jarls' Sagas') so it is clear that it was written specifically to record the deeds of the 'jarls', or earls, and by 'jarls' was meant the earls of Orkney, the most famous earls in the northern world.[1]

In its present form *Jarls' Saga* is a hybrid text, made up of several different sagas or short prose narratives (called *þáttr*) about individual earls and including many stanzas of skaldic verse.[2] It was written to entertain and was probably read aloud to audiences in Orkney and other parts of the northern world.

2.1 EVALUATION OF JARLS' SAGA

We do not know who the author was although there have been several attempts to identify him.[3] Most probably he was an Icelander, one of the many literate, educated men who produced the stories of gods, heroes, warriors and redoubtable women which have been written down in Old Norse and form a body of literature from the Middle Ages which is unsurpassed.[4] The term 'literature' is

contd p. 42

---

1 Jesch, 1993, 230. In *Scand.Scot.* (1987, *passim*) *Orkneyinga Saga* was referred to as *Jarls' Saga*, which is a more useful description of this text, said to be 'a more precise and probably the more historically correct title' by Michael Chesnutt (1993). That term will be used in this book also
2 The complicated composition of *Orkneyinga Saga* text is summarised in the entry 'Orkneyinga Saga' in *Medieval Scandinavia. An Encyclopedia* (Chesnutt, 1993, 456–7); also more recently discussed by Beuermann (*Jarla Sǫgur Orkneyja*, 2011, 110–12). See stemma (Figure 2.1) and associated notes by Paul Bibire
3 Chesnutt (1993) provides a summary of the proposed candidates and associated references
4 See Mundal (2007) for a discussion of the saga's possible Orkney origin

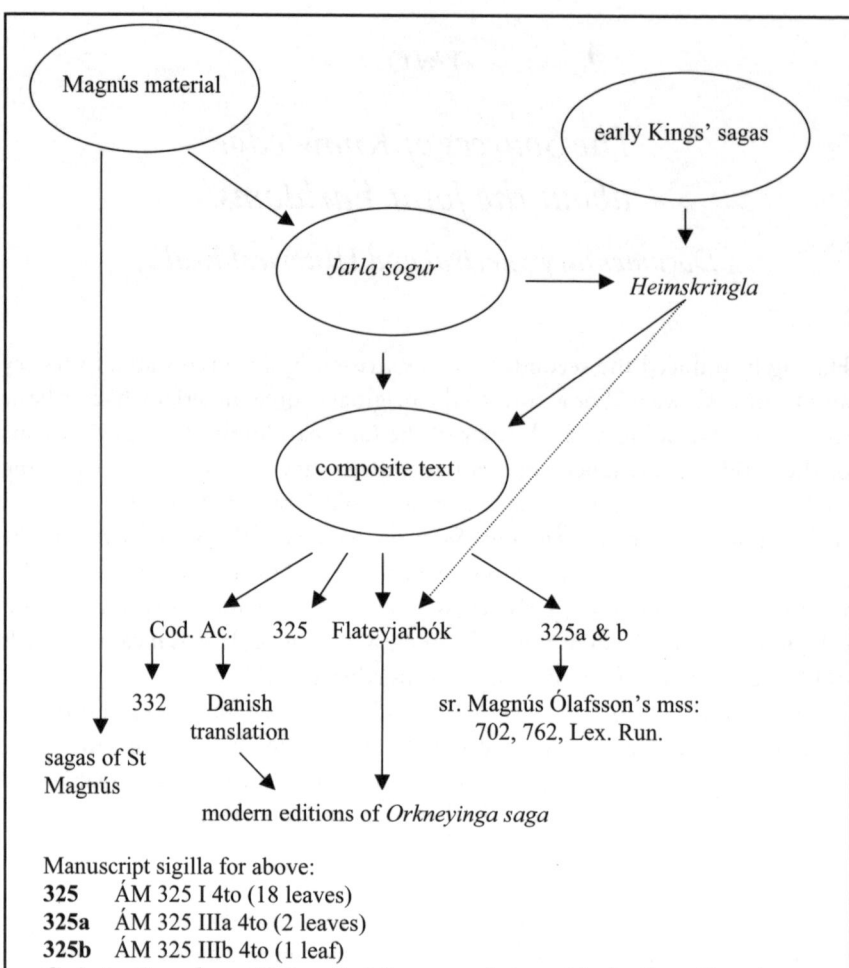

```
         ┌─────────────────┐                          ┌─────────────────┐
         │ Magnús material │                          │ early Kings' sagas │
         └─────────────────┘                          └─────────────────┘
                  │                                            │
                  │         ┌──────────────┐                   ▼
                  └────────▶│  Jarla sǫgur │──────────▶ Heimskringla
                            └──────────────┘
                                   │
                                   ▼
                            ┌──────────────┐
                            │ composite text│◀╌╌╌╌╌╌╌╌╌
                            └──────────────┘
                         ╱      │      │       ╲
                        ▼       ▼      ▼        ▼
                   Cod. Ac.   325   Flateyjarbók   325a & b
                      │                               │
                      ▼                               ▼
                     332    Danish           sr. Magnús Ólafsson's mss:
                          translation              702, 762, Lex. Run.
    ▼                           ╲
sagas of St                      ▼
 Magnús              modern editions of *Orkneyinga saga*
```

Manuscript sigilla for above:
325   ÁM 325 I 4to (18 leaves)
325a ÁM 325 IIIa 4to (2 leaves)
325b ÁM 325 IIIb 4to (1 leaf)
Cod. Ac. Copenhagen University Library ms, destroyed in the Great Fire of Copenhagen 1728
332   ÁM 332 4to (fragmentary text; copied by Ásgeir Jónsson before 1728)
Lex. Run. *Specimen Lexici Runici*, sr. Magnús Ólafsson, publ. (by Ole Worm) Copenhagen 1650
702   Uppsala Isl. R: 702, verses anthologised by sr. Magnús Ólafsson
762   ÁM 762 4to, verses anthologised by sr. Magnús Ólafsson
Flateyjarbók GkS 1005 fol.

No attempt is made here to distinguish between the textual value of **332** (representing the lost **Cod. Ac.**), **325**, **Flateyjarbók**, **325a** and **325b**, in reproducing their common direct or indirect source(s). All of these may represent distinct redactions, not direct copies of their exemplars. Prose textual variants may therefore be due to their redactors' taste, and will be evaluated by their editors' taste.

Figure 2.1 (above and opposite) Textual Stemma of likely manuscript relationships which resulted in *Orkneyinga Saga* (Paul Bibire).

Orkneyinga saga is only ever edited from Flateyjarbók, since only that manuscript gives (almost) all the Norse text. The modern text of *Orkneyinga saga* is the product of 18th- and 19th-century scholarship, and is constructed by cutting and pasting parts of Flateyjarbók, using the early modern Danish translation as a template.

Flateyjarbók is a manuscript of the Kings' Sagas, and its central text is a much enlarged version of *Heimskringla*, including narrative dealing with those other parts of northern Europe, particularly the earldom of Orkney and the Faroe Islands, which were considered as part of the wider realm of Norway. Parts of *Orkneyinga saga* deal directly with the kings of Norway, and those parts are effectively the same text as *Heimskringla*. This is unsurprising, because they are taken from *Heimskringla* in the process of excerpting from Flateyjarbók.

However, the relationship between *Orkneyinga saga* and *Heimskringla* is not this simple. The Separate Saga of St Óláfr lxxxix refers to pre-existing narrative about Orkney, there named as *Jarla sǫgur* or *Jarla saga*: mss variants give both plural and singular forms (O.A. Johnsen & Jón Helgason, 1941, I, p. 255). The Separate Saga is uncontroversially a fuller version of the saga of St Óláfr found in *Heimskringla*, and is appropriately considered to be of the same authorship. So the Separate Saga and *Heimskringla* had access to sagas or a saga about the Orcadian earls, and seem to have used it or them as source-material.

If a separate saga of St Magnús were included, the plural form 'sagas' in *Jarla sǫgur* is entirely uncontroversial. It might be less easy for a modern reader to see *Orkneyinga saga* alone as 'sagas of the Earls'. The text is cyclic, however, as were the earlier Kings' Sagas such as Fagrskinna and Morkinskinna. Although, like them, it is not broken up into separate sagas of the different earls, such division might be thought implicit by the compilers of *Heimskringla* and the texts related to it, who imposed such saga-divisions upon the earlier stories of the kings, perhaps on the model of the Separate Saga, itself not only a king's saga but a Saint's Life.

The composite text in Flateyjarbók is *Heimskringla* much enlarged with material dealing with the earldom of Orkney and with the Faroes. It may not be original to Flateyjarbók. The sections derived from *Heimskringla* in *Orkneyinga saga* were probably already present in the exemplar, **Cod. Ac.**, from which the early modern Danish translation was derived. Conflation of *Heimskringla* with a version of *Jarla sǫgur* is likely, therefore, to underlie this. Further work is needed to try to determine whether **325a** and **b**, and the mss derived from them, were also derived from this composite text, or whether they could be derived directly from the earlier *Jarla sǫgur*.

It can be argued that the selection of passages from this composite text, to form the narrative we know as *Orkneyinga saga*, may have taken place in **Cod. Ac.** or a version antecedent to it. That would produce the text as translated into early modern Danish. This guided scholars such as Jón Jónsson (1780) and Guðbrandur Vigfússon (1887) to re-select the same passages as they survive in Norse in Flateyjarbók, to create the existing text.

Alternatively, the relationship between *Orkneyinga saga* and *Heimskringla* could be even more complex. *Heimskringla* is likely to have used *Jarla sǫgur* as a source. Passages from *Heimskringla* might then have been inserted into a composite *Orkneyinga saga*. This would create the text as translated into early modern Danish. This expanded text might then have been used in the compilation of Flateyjarbók to enlarge its version of *Heimskringla* (shown in the stemma by a dotted line).

used advisedly for the sagas are not historical documents.[5] They were composed around the lives and deeds of great men, based on oral history and remembered tradition, but embellished with dramatic detail which may, or may not, be accurate. *Jarls' Saga* is thought to be more 'historical' than most, 'an early type of historical writing generally classified under the heading *konunga sögur*'.[6] It is a collection of remembered accounts, some of which are 'sketchy', while others from the period just before the first compilation was written down (c.AD 1200) are very much more detailed, and possibly first-hand.

Naturally enough, in the long period of time from the founding of the earldom to the year 1200, much had been forgotten about the earlier earls, and the possibilities for confusion about the earlier centuries were great. However, the account of the twelfth-century earldom and the events in the decades preceding the commitment of knowledge to written text c.1200 is considered to be an accurate reflection of many different aspects of life in Orkney and Caithness among the earldom elite. It has been said to be, at the very least, a 'most valuable repository of historical tradition'.[7] This is not to say that it is an easy source of evidence for historians to use, and we have to heed the warnings of those who understand the background to the writing of saga literature, and be aware, for instance, that when the information was in *Heimskringla*, or 'History of the Kings of Norway' (attributed to Snorri Sturlason), it was used in order to enhance the authority of the kings over the earls.[8] In particular, the relationship of the great Norwegian king (and saint) Olaf Haraldsson, with Earls Thorfinn and Brusi is presented as reflecting the power and authority of the king over these independent earls from the islands in the west. The issue of knowing to what extent the earls were under the kings' authority, and to what extent they lived their lives independent of that authority, will be a recurring feature in the following chapters. The example of King Olaf and Earl Thorfinn alerts us to the difficulty of using the saga text as a direct reflection of a political situation in Orkney at any given time (see Chapter 4). However, in respect of our knowledge of the earldom dynasty, its genealogy, the earls' marriages or liaisons, the names of their children, and the quarrels between rival heirs, we can be more confident that the details in the pages of *Jarls' Saga* were remembered with some reliability.

If we look at some examples of this sort of information we can perhaps develop an impression of reliability, and unreliability (in the broadest sense),

---

5 Discussion of 'Saga literature' in Crawford, 1987, 7–8; and recently Jón Vidar Sigurdsson on 'Sagas as sources', 2011, 96–101
6 Chesnutt, 1993, 456; and see Knirk (1993, 362–6) on *konunga sögur* ('kings' sagas')
7 Chesnutt, 1993, 457
8 Jesch, 1993, 230

working backwards in time from the latest chapters (using Pálsson and Edwards' translation of *Orkneyinga Saga*):

> Earl Harald was five years old when he was given the title of earl. For twenty years he was joint ruler of Orkney with Earl Rognvald the Holy. Following the death of Rognvald, Harald was Earl of Orkney for forty-eight years and died in the second year of the reign of King Ingi Bardason. After that his sons Jon and David came to power and another son, Heinrek, ruled over Ross in Scotland.
>
> (*OS*, Chapter 112)

This statement is in the very last chapter of *Orkneyinga Saga*, which is from one of the two continuations to the original *Jarls' Saga* and which has been identified as a Saga of Earl Harald Maddadson.[9] It concerns the rule of the famous Earl Harald, said – in the following paragraph – to be one of the three most powerful earls of Orkney. He was recognised as earl from 1139, although (as said in the above extract) ruling jointly with his half-cousin, Rognvald Kali Kolsson, for the first twenty years.[10] *Haralds Saga Maddaðarsonar* has been shown to be a 'coherent' account of politics (in Caithness in particular), informed by personal knowledge of the situation from descendants of participants in the events.[11]

Moving further back in time we are given information about 'Leading Families' in the mid-twelfth century:

> In Orkney at this time there were many well-born people descended from the Earls. Farming at Westness on Rousay was a man of distinguished lineage called Sigurd, married to Ingibjorg the Noble whose mother Herbjorg was Earl Paul Thorfinnsson's daughter. Their sons were Brynjolf and Hakon Pike, and both father and sons were among the chieftains of Earl Paul . . .
> Sigurd, the Earl's kinsman-in-law, married Thora the mother of Saint Magnus the Holy, and they had a son, Hakon Karl, a great leader like his father . . .
> At Knarston, Jaddvor, the daughter of Earl Erlend farmed with her son Borgar, and they weren't very popular.
>
> (*OS*, Chapter 56)

This sort of genealogical information, from a period not long before the saga was written down, is considered to be accurate knowledge about people who were known to the saga writer.[12] They were closely associated with the earls, as is said, and most of them appear in the saga narrative on other occasions. This is the saga equivalent of the charters which are historians' main source of information about families and lands in Scotland at this period, but written for

---

9 *Haralds Saga Maddaðarsonar*, Chesnutt, 1981
10 Crawford, 2004a
11 Chesnutt, 1981, 55; and see analysis in Section 6.3.1 below
12 The author appears to be deeply immersed in the social events of Orkney which is one reason why Else Mundal (2007, 17–18) thinks that he may have been Orcadian

a very different purpose. It is not a legal record nor is it given in a legal format (or in Latin), so it is a very different source of information. Its main purpose is to record the family relationships among the landowning Orcadian elite and so the human interest is foremost. This is remarkable, unique, evidence from the medieval period of Scottish history.[13]

A little earlier in time (c.1100), Chapter 42 provides some central facts relevant to what happened in the earldom:

> Later that spring in Orkney, King Magnus gave Earl Erlend's daughter Gunnhild in marriage to Kol, son of Kali Sæbjarnarson, in compensation for the death of his father. Her dowry consisted of some property in Orkney including a farm at Paplay.
> According to some people, Erling, the son of Earl Erlend, was killed in the Battle of the Menai Strait but Snorri Sturluson says he met his death with King Magnus in Ulster.
> Kol Kalason became one of the King's landholders and travelled with him east to Norway, where he and his wife Gunnhild settled down on his estate at Agder. They had two children, a son called Kali and a daughter Ingirid, both very promising youngsters and lovingly brought up.

This information about the marriage of Gunnhild and Kol links the earldom family with the foremost class of chieftains in Norway, and was a consequence of the close interest which was taken in the earldom by King Magnus Olafsson 'Barelegs' (*berfœttr*), who had brought Orkney under his authority on his 1098 expedition to the west (see Section 4.3). It shows how the earldom family was tied into the Norwegian structure of power (the two earls had been exiled from Orkney and sent to Norway). The uncertainty about the death of Erling Erlendsson is a nice example of the saga writer quoting his divergent sources over a matter of some importance – where exactly the earl's son met his death. The personal details about Kol and Gunnhild's two children is a charming piece of information which there seems no reason to doubt, but which we have no means of corroborating!

Events after the death of Earl Thorfinn in the mid-eleventh century are summarised in Chapters 33 and 34:

> After Thorfinn's death his sons took over the earldom. Paul, the elder of the two, was also very much the one in charge. They did not divide the earldom and were for the most part on friendly terms. Ingibjorg the Earls'-Mother married Malcolm, King of Scots, known as Long-Neck. Their son was Duncan, King of Scots, father of William, who was a great man, and whose son William the Noble every Scotsman wanted for his king...

---

13 Duncan, 1975, 191–2; Crawford, 1987, 7; 2003, 65

DOCUMENTARY SURVIVAL

> Some time after the brothers Paul and Erlend began ruling in Orkney King Harald Sigurdarson came west from Norway with a great army. He landed first in Shetland and sailed from there to Orkney, where his army grew considerably, and both Earls decided to join him. So he set off for England then put in at Holderness . . . on the following Sunday the stronghold which stood by Stamford Bridge surrendered to King Harald and he went ashore to occupy it, leaving behind his son Olaf, the Earls Paul and Erlend, and Eystein Heathcock, a relative of his by marriage

This passage contains some vital information which is unrecorded elsewhere, and shows just how important the saga source is for historians of eleventh-century Scotland. But how far can it be relied upon when we have no corroborating evidence that Malcolm III (*Ceann Mor*/Canmore) was married to the widow of Earl Thorfinn? In general, it is accepted by Scottish historians that the mother of Malcolm's two sons Duncan and Donald was indeed Ingibjorg,[14] although there are problems of fitting this marriage and the birth of two, maybe three, sons into the time available between Thorfinn's death (believed to be c.1065) and Malcolm's marriage to his second wife Margaret (c.1070). Ingibjorg's age has also been considered to be a problem from the fact that she had borne sons to Thorfinn who were old enough to be involved in the Battle of Stamford Bridge in 1066. It has therefore been proposed that Ingibjorg was a daughter of Thorfinn and not his widow.[15] (This chronological difficulty will be discussed more fully in Section 4.2.3.)

The earls' participation in King Harald *harðráði's* (Hardraada/'Hard-Ruler') expedition south to Yorkshire and their presence at Stamford Bridge is corroborated by an entry in the Anglo-Saxon Chronicle under the year 1066 when it reports that after the battle King Harald Godwinsson gave safe conduct to the young Norwegian prince, Olaf, and to the earl of Orkney, allowing them to return north with 24 ships.[16] This is valuable support for the accuracy of the saga account, even though the English chronicler only mentions that one earl had participated, whereas both Paul and Erlend are said in the saga to have joined Harald *harðráði's* campaign.

Chapter 12 concerns Earl Sigurd II 'the Stout' and this takes us back to the late tenth and early eleventh centuries:

> Earl Sigurd married the daughter of Malcolm, King of Scots, and their son was Earl Thorfinn. Earl Sigurd had three other sons, called Sumarlidi, Brusi and Einar Wry-Mouth.

14 Duncan, 2002, 42; and further discussion by Woolf, 2007, 265–8
15 Donaldson, 1988, 3, and references there given. This seems highly unlikely when a daughter is never named in the saga
16 *ASC*, p.199, Worcester manuscript D. The earl is named as Paul in the later Florence Chronicle, where it is also said that he had been left in charge of the ships

Five years after the Battle of Svoldur, Earl Sigurd went to Ireland in support of King Sigtryyg Silk-Beard, leaving his elder sons in charge of the earldom. Thorfinn he sent over to Scotland to be fostered by the King, the boy's maternal grandfather. Earl Sigurd arrived in Ireland, joined up with King Sigtrygg and set out to fight King Brian of Ireland. The battle took place on Good Friday. No one would carry the raven banner, so the Earl had to do it himself and he was killed.

The section of *Jarls' Saga* concerning this famous earl is thin and the saga writer seems to have had only minimal sources at his disposal. The information in *OS*, Chapter 12, summarises the 'forced conversion' of Sigurd by Olaf Tryggvesson, c.996, facts about his marriage and offspring, and his death at the famous Battle of Clontarf, 1014 (see Section 3.5.3). Yet these are some of the most important incidents in the history of the earldom, and should have been the basis for a much extended saga narrative. Indeed, the Irish accounts which mention Sigurd's role in the Battle of Clontarf are the first 'documentary' sources to confirm the name of an Orkney earl known otherwise only from the saga narrative.[17] So in this passage we have information about the battle where Sigurd met his death and know that it is giving us an accurate account, (except for the attempt to date it in relation to the Battle of Svoldur, which actually took place in 1005). However, the saga is right about it taking place on Good Friday, and gets the name of the Irish king right also. The mention of the raven banner picks up on the information about this magic banner, the making of which has been described in the previous chapter. The dramatisation of the detail about its manufacture was of more interest to the saga writer than the dry detail of political circumstances.[18]

The exceedingly important information about Sigurd's marriage to the daughter of Malcolm, king of Scots, is known only from the saga, and there has been uncertainty as to who is meant by 'king of Scots'. Was it the king of the southern kingdom, Malcolm II MacKenneth, or a 'mormaer' of Moray (who are on occasion referred to as 'kings')? In this instance it seems more likely that it is the former and that Thorfinn was therefore brought up at the court of Malcolm II, a development which would have implications for the earl's influence on the introduction of Christian culture into the earldom.[19]

The events after the death of the first Earl Thorfinn (Torf-Einarsson), known as 'Skull-Splitter' (*hausakljúfr*), who probably died in the 970s, are related in Chapter 9:

---

17 *ES*, i, 535
18 For a full discussion of the different banners, raven or otherwise, which are mentioned in the sources of this period see Jesch (1993, 232–5)
19 See further discussion of the debate on this matter in Section 3.4.3

Earl Thorfinn had five sons, one called Arnfinn, the next Havard the Fecund, the third Hlodver, the fourth Ljot, and the fifth Skuli. Ragnhild Eirik's Daughter plotted the death of her husband Arnfinn at Murkle in Caithness, then married his brother Havard the Fecund who succeeded to the earldom. Under his rule the islands enjoyed peace and prosperity

In this first century of the earldom, we are in a period long removed from the time of the saga writer, who is recording only tradition as known in twelfth-century Iceland or Orkney, much of it embroidered with myth. As regards the names of the earls' sons, we simply have to take the information on trust as there is no way of checking the accuracy of the text. The introduction of Ragnhild Eriksdaughter as a *femme fatale* and her liaisons with several of the earls is, however, another matter. With her appearance we meet the prejudiced opinions of the saga writer, weaving into his narrative the stereotypical image of the manipulative power-seeking lustful woman who prodded the menfolk into vengeful actions (her role becomes more typical and more interesting as the chapter progresses).[20]

Ragnhild was a daughter of Erik 'Blood-axe' (*blóðøx*), the son of Harald 'Finehair' (*hárfagri*) who lost out in the battle with his brother for control of Norway. What is of particular interest to us is the impact that Erik must have had on Orkney, as also his sons and his widow had after his death in 954. Erik used Orkney as a launching pad for his expeditions south to Northumbria and his sons are said in *Hakon the Good's Saga* (Chapter 5) to have used Orkney and Shetland as summer bases for piracy in Scotland and Ireland. Erik's widow, the 'wicked' Gunnhild (another saga stereotype), moved back north to Orkney from Northumbria, with a haul of taxes and booty. If only the saga writer had known more to tell us about this period than the entertainment myths of their daughter Ragnhild's perversities! There was probably some disruption in the earldom after the death of the earls Arnkell and Erlend with Erik in northern England, for although Thorfinn their brother is said to have taken control, it is also said that Erik's sons 'subdued' the islands, staying there all winter and taking skat. The marriage of their sister, Ragnhild, to Thorfinn's son, Arnfinn, may reflect a situation when the two dynasties came to some agreement over control of Orkney and its resources, and is therefore likely to be true – perhaps even including her role in her husband's demise. The association with a particular place may give the information about Arnfinn's death some credence.[21]

20 Ragnhild's depiction as the saga stereotype of a wicked woman is discussed in Crawford, 1987, 79, 218, and in Section 3.4.3
21 Crawford 1987, 9

Chapter 5 takes us back to the beginning of the earldom, and the very uncertain evidence about its founding in the late ninth century:

> (Earl) Sigurd had a son called Guthorm who ruled the earldom for a year but died childless. When Earl Rognvald of Møre heard about these deaths, he sent his son Hallad west to the islands and King Harald gave him the title of earl.

Sigurd I 'the Mighty' (*hinn ríki*) is the first recorded earl of Orkney. The story in *Jarls' Saga* and *Heimskringla* tells about the grant of the islands of Orkney and Shetland to Rognvald of Møre by King Harald *hárfagri* in compensation for the death of Rognvald's son on the king's expedition west. Rognvald transferred them to his brother Sigurd, and King Harald confirmed the grant. All the sources that we have link the conquest of Orkney with the family of Møre; the extent of King Harald's involvement may be influenced by what later saga writers thought should have been the situation, and some mention of the king's acknowledgement of the transfer of power is added on to every mention of the change of earl – as in the passage above. It was clearly important that this impression should be incorporated into the saga account of the earldom's foundation (see further discussion in Section 3.2). There is close correspondence between *Jarls' Saga* and *Heimskringla* at this point.

These extracts from different chapters taken from throughout the composite *Orkneyinga Saga* text show how the evidence about the earl's family relationships can be used with some degree of confidence, but that the more extensive narrative relating to the political circumstances is far less reliable. This is only a cursory comment on the value and usefulness of bits of the saga text as a source of historical information. Paul Bibire's analytical exposition of the different elements which make up that composite text helps the reader to be more aware of the saga writer's sources of information, and better informed as to how the different sections relate to the wider Icelandic manuscript material (Figure 2.1 'Textual Stemma'). The important manuscript compilation *Flateyarbók*, which contains the fullest text of the composite *Orkneyinga Saga*, has recently received detailed analysis,[22] and this is helping to show how that one manuscript was composed in the late fourteenth century. Different sections of *Jarls' Saga* were drawn together in it and made into a coherent – or not always so coherent – whole. In this process, elements of what it is claimed were originally from a 'serious work of history' were dramatised and the whole turned into something like a work of saga literature.[23] Attempting to unpick that seamed garment is not simple, or always possible, given the fragmentary nature of the surviving manuscripts. We have to take what there is and use the evidence it provides

22 Rowe, 2005; Jesch 2010, 159–68
23 Ibid., 2010, 173

with caution, but use it we must. It is all that survives telling us about the first centuries of the earldom and it throws beams of light onto the social structure of the ruling elements in the islands.

Skaldic poetry was closely embedded into the saga texts, and is a highly literate and sophisticated source of evidence about the earls, which is scattered throughout *Jarls' Saga*. The issue of how to use, and understand, skaldic verse, is exceedingly complex.[24] The skaldic poetry formed a core memory bank, and in some cases may have formed the main basis from which the prose text was written. A remarkable amount of this recorded poetry was composed by the earls themselves: Torf-Einar in the late tenth century is credited with five stanzas (*OS*, Chapter 8). Rognvald Kali Kolsson in the twelfth century is the most famous earl-poet, and there are twenty-eight of his stanzas in the long section devoted to his life, and above all his pilgrimage to the Holy Land in 1151–2.[25] Several other stanzas by different Icelandic poets are included in the latter section. Above all, we have the many stanzas of the Icelandic skald, Arnor Thordarson, *jarlaskáld* ('earls' skald') throughout the saga of Earl Thorfinn Sigurdsson, describing in high-flown imagery the deeds of Thorfinn and his co-earl Rognvald Brusisson and the battles they fought.[26] Arnor spent much of his career at the earls' court in Orkney, or accompanying them on their campaigns, and his poetry therefore reflects the quality of an eyewitness account. Here is rich material which is at the very heart of the 'Viking' literary achievement, and the verses are at the heart of the saga prose text, for, in some cases (especially in Thorfinn's own saga), the written prose is woven around the skaldic verse, which forms the reliable source of information which the saga writer then elaborated. Difficult though this skaldic verse is to understand and use for pure historical purposes, its survival from the tenth, eleventh, twelfth and early thirteenth centuries in Orkney tells us much about the 'high literary culture' which some of the earls were immersed in, and which revolved around them and their court.[27]

The characterisation of *Orkneyinga Saga* text as a 'national history' (*þioðarsaga*),[28] as *Heimskringla* is a national history of the kings of Norway, indicates how important this whole text is, and the varying components of it, for our study of the earldom. It is a documentary witness to the independent

24 See comments by Crawford, 1987, 8
25 Rognvald is known to have composed other poetry, especially *Hattalykill* or the 'Key of Metres', illustrating different metrical forms, which survives in a 'badly-mangled text' (Jesch, 2005, 19)
26 Bibire, 2004. Whaley's study (1998) of the poetry of Arnórr Thordarsson *jarlaskáld* greatly helps our understanding of this one poet's use of language and the meaning of his poetry
27 Crawford, 1987, 8; Jesch, 2005, 20–2
28 Jesch, 2010, 169

existence of insular and north Scottish mainland communities which developed their own distinctive culture and political structures from the tenth to the twelfth century. This wonderful source comes to an end after Earl Harald Maddadson's death (1206), when Orkney was brought under close royal control, and it has been pointed out that the Icelandic sagas about native secular chieftains came to an end also after Iceland submitted to Norwegian royal authority in 1262–3.[29] Perhaps these changes in political circumstances meant that the saga authors considered it 'unseemly' to write sagas about secular rulers once they had become the king's 'hirdmenn'.[30] Sagas thereafter were to be written only about kings and not their subjects.

2.2 RUNIC INSCRIPTIONS

Another source of historical information found in the Norse world is the corpus of inscriptions written in the runic script, in Old Norse. These show us that literacy was widespread even in the Viking Age, among a class of stone and wood carvers who produced the inscriptions, but also among the general population who, we assume, were able to read them.[31] They are mostly formal inscriptions found on memorial stones, erected in memory of individuals. But, increasingly, informal inscriptions are discovered in excavations, which indicate that the use and understanding of runic texts was more widespread and continued for longer in the Middle Ages than previously appreciated.[32] These enigmatic and often cursive inscriptions, many of them badly preserved, are not always easy to read or interpret, but in recent years there have been several publications giving expert readings and assessments of these inscriptions which are found in many different parts of the British Isles dating from the Viking Age or later.[33]

The runic material from Orkney, Shetland and Caithness is not particularly full, nor does it relate in any specific way to the earls themselves. There are more than fifty inscriptions known in Orkney, seven from Shetland and two from Caithness. Of the Orkney total, thirty-three come from the amazing series of twelfth-century inscriptions carved on the inside walls of Maeshowe,

29 Jón Viðarr Sigurðsson, 2011, 87–8
30 The hirdmen were members of the royal (or earl's) *hirð* 'a common term for the retinue of warriors accompanying kings or great men in the Nordic countries' (Bagge, on the term *hirð*, 1993, 284)
31 See discussion of the issue of 'Literacy' by Barnes and Page (2006, Chapter 7)
32 This is particularly the case with regard to the many informal runic records discovered at Bryggen, the harbour area of Bergen, west Norway, in the excavations which took place there after the fire of 1955 (Knirk, 1990). These total c.600, more than all the previous runic inscriptions known from the whole of Norway (Spurkland, 2005, 174)
33 Holman, 1996; Barnes, 1998; Barnes and Page, 2006

the prehistoric chambered tomb on the Orkney Mainland. The rest have been found in different places, many of them informal graffiti and not always of certain Viking-Age origin.[34] It is perhaps significant that the five stones from the Brough of Birsay (see Colour plate 1) is the greatest number of actual memorial stones from one place in the Northern Isles, and that is the likely location of Earl Thorfinn's Christ Church, the seat of the first bishop established by the earl in the mid-eleventh century (see Sections 2.7.2, 4.1). It does suggest that this was the place of burial of the earldom elite at that time, and signifies that those who could afford a stone memorial were buried here close to the earl's own ecclesiastical foundation.[35] We know that Earl Thorfinn was buried in Christ Kirk, Birsay, the very church he had built, but no memorial stone has been found indicating the exact location. The best-known of the Brough of Birsay stones is that with the name 'Filippus/Philippus' (the runic characters read *filibusranru*, 'Philip carved'), telling us unequivocally about an individual with a Christian name who apparently set up the stone.[36]

The Maeshowe collection of runic inscriptions is something quite different, and also different in many ways from those memorial stones just discussed. This is a totally secular record, carved by people who were associated with the earls, and specifically Earl Rognald Kali Kolsson, for they call themselves *Jorsalamenn/Jorsalafarar* ('Jerusalem farers', or pilgrims), and had probably therefore accompanied Rognvald to the Holy Land in 1150–1. Indeed, one of them signs herself 'Hlif, the earl's housekeeper'.[37] What they were doing in Maes Howe is not exactly clear, although the explicit messages in some of the inscriptions suggest that they were passing their time in vying with each other as to who was the most versatile rune-carver.[38] Some of them convey more implicit messages about the nature of women who have visited the men inside the mound, two of whom are named: 'Ingibjorg, the fair widow' and þorny, both of whom seem to have been engaged in some sort of sexual activity.[39] This survival of the most

34 The recent discovery of an informal runic inscription at the high-status site of Tuquoy in Westray merely tells us that 'Thorstein Einarsson carved these runes', but who Thorstein was is unknown and he is not mentioned in the contemporary section of *Jarls' Saga* (Owen 2005a, 204)
35 Although the stones can only be dated to 'between the ninth and twelfth centuries' (Barnes and Page, 2006, 175), the fact that they were all found around the church site on the Brough of Birsay, and one reused by being built into the twelfth-century church wall, suggests that they were closely associated with the church site; while the reused one must actually pre-date the building of the twelfth-century church
36 Barnes and Page, 2006, 170; Crawford, 1987, 187
37 *matselja*, 'the woman who divides up the food' (Spurkland, 2005, 144)
38 *þessar runar reist sa maðr er rynstr fyrir vestan haf*, 'These runes were carved by the man most skilled in runes west of the ocean' (ibid., 146)
39 Barnes, 1998, 34; Spurkland, 2005, 147–8

casual of messages left for posterity reveals something about Norse society in the twelfth century which is not so different from any other century. But they also reveal how skilled these men were in the use of runic writing and the carving of runic messages, just as they boasted. Although this can be taken as evidence for a learned and literary milieu in twelfth-century Orkney, it is thought probable that the rune-carvers were in fact visiting Norwegians or Icelanders rather than native islanders.[40] There is no evidence that such runic prowess was widespread in Scandinavian Scotland, which may suggest that the use of runes as a communication device faded earlier in the west than in Norway itself.

An additional element of Viking artistic culture is preserved among the Norse carvings in this prehistoric tomb, and that is the animal known as the Maeshowe dragon (depicted on the front cover of this book). This is one of very few surviving pieces of evidence in the earldoms of Nordic art styles which are associated with the Vikings. The style of animal is comparable with the lion on the Jellinge stone (Harald Bluetooth's memorial to his conversion of the Danes and Norwegians, dating to the late tenth century); to the St. Paul's Churchyard stone (dated to the early eleventh century); and to animals on the Scandinavian weather-vanes, such as the Heggen vane (also dated to the early eleventh century), where the animal's tail passes through the body in a similar way to the Maeshowe dragon's tail.[41] These comparable styles of animal art might therefore suggest that the Maeshowe dragon dates to an earlier period than the runic inscriptions, and the decorated terminal of the tail is very reminiscent of the eleventh-century Ringerike style of Viking art. It has, however, been said to be 'closely allied' to some monsters carved on the capitals of Urnes stave kirk in western Norway which date to the early twelfth century.[42] Some features indicate an element of Romanesque floriated style which suggests that it might be a 'last dying gesture of native northern art'.[43] In which case this engraved dragonesque animal could be dated to the beginning of the twelfth century, which would make it slightly earlier than the runic inscriptions, unless the mid-twelfth century crusaders were carving an anachronistic style of dragon.

There are other indications that Maeshowe may have had an important influence on the lives of the Norse settlers in Orkney, and certainly earlier than the rune-carvers' lasting literary additions to the great prehistoric monument. When the bank surrounding the mound was excavated in recent times, it was found that there had been some rebuilding of the bank in the mid-tenth century, dated by radiocarbon analysis.[44] For some reason the Norse community had

40 Barnes, 1991, 1998, 10; Jesch, 2006, 15
41 Mackay Mackenzie, 1936–7
42 Comments by A. Brøgger quoted in RCAHMS Orkney report, 313
43 Mackay Mackenzie, 1936–7, 173
44 Renfrew, 1979, 37

felt it necessary to adapt this bank, or to make it a more important feature. Was it because the mound was being used for open-air gatherings, such as legal assemblies?[45] Or was it because the tomb was being reused as the burial place of one of the pagan chieftains of the period? As we will see, such individuals were certainly buried in mounds or 'howes' (see Section 3.3). It is not unlikely that a Norse pagan burial of the pre-Christian period which had included rich grave-goods was later plundered. If so, the references in the runic inscriptions to the 'great treasure' which was carried away may be a twelfth-century reminiscence of such a plundering.[46] It would not be surprising if Maeshowe was considered to be a significant monument by the Scandinavian settlers who used it for their own public purposes.

2.3 LATIN DOCUMENTS

The thorough conversion of the island population in the eleventh century, along with the introduction of Christian culture and the Roman alphabet must have had some impact on the Norse cultural milieu, possibly curtailing the use of the runic script. The Latin sources complement the Norse texts and provide a 'historical' basis which we can use to give a more standard picture of the earls' relationship with kings and Church. In the twelfth and thirteenth centuries such Latin documents as have survived were drawn up somewhere else, and were referring to the earldom from an external viewpoint.

The first of these to be discussed is the Latin text *Historia Norwegie* ('History of Norway') which gives an important 'glimpse of the rise of literate culture in Norway'.[47] It includes valuable information about the islands and the earls and survives in only one copy written in Scotland.[48] The original document (not the copy, which was made c.1490–1500) is thought to have dated from the third quarter of the twelfth century and may have been compiled in connection with the creation of the archbishopric of Nidaros (Trondheim) in 1152/3, as it includes entries on the tributary islands in the North Atlantic which had been included in the new archdiocese. Its purpose was a geographical definition of those widely scattered bishoprics now under the authority of the archbishop of Nidaros. The information about Orkney and its pre-Norse inhabitants

---

45 See 'Althing and Lawthing in Orkney' by Alexandra Sanmark in *Mimir's Well – Notes from Nordic Studies* (*The Orcadian*, 1 March 2012), where it is suggested that Maeshowe may have been the site of the Orkney Althing
46 Renfrew, 1979, 37
47 Mortensen and Ekrem, 2003, 8
48 NAS Dalhousie Muniments GD45/31/1, the so-called 'Panmure Codex' which contains the 'Genealogy of the Earls' and several other copies of Norwegian and Scottish historical material. For a full analysis of this manuscript, its date and scribal identification, see Chesnutt (1986, 54–95)

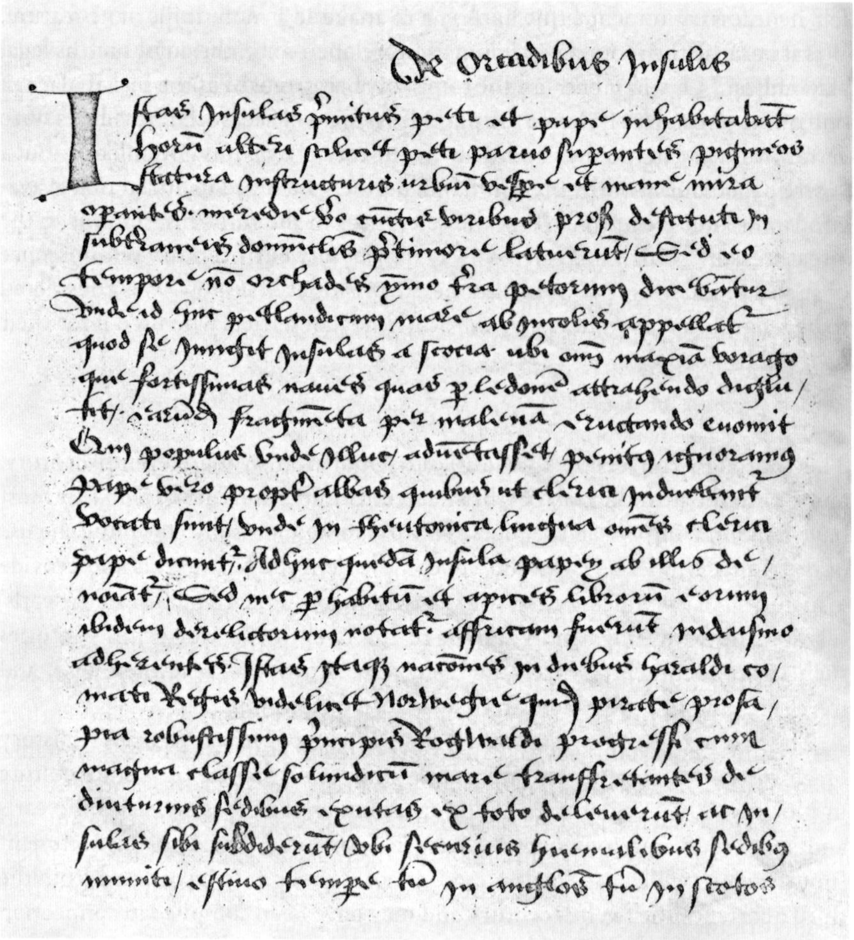

De Orcadibus Insulis

Figure 2.2 Section V of *Historia Norvegie* ('History of Norway') headed '*De Orcadibus Insulis*' ('Of the Orkney Islands') and starting off with the singular statement 'These Islands were at first inhabited by the Picts and Papae'. This is our only indication that the Norwegians knew anything about the pre-Viking inhabitants of the islands. (Photo: author; Dalhousie manus. f4r. NRS ref. GD45/35/1)

(see Figure 2.2) must have been acquired in the islands, which suggested to early commentators that it had been written in Orkney. However, the recent full edition of *Historia Norwegie* concludes that it had been compiled in Norway, perhaps eastern Norway, although the author may have spent time in Orkney, and also in Iceland.[49]

49 Mortensen and Ekrem, 2003, 23

The information which the author had acquired in Orkney is of very great interest to a historian of the earldom. This relates to the period of Earl Harald Maddadson (see Chapter 6) and the episcopal reigns of William I (d.1168) and William II (1168–1188) when a visiting Norwegian cleric would have been able to acquire what he then included in his historical account. It tells us a little of what was known (or had been handed down as lore) about the pre-Norse inhabitants and about the first earls:

Of the Orchades Islands
These islands were at first inhabited by the Picts and Papae. Of these, the one race the Picts little exceeded pigmies in stature; they did marvels, in the morning and in the evening, in building [walled] towns but at mid-day they entirely lost their strength, and lurked, through fear, in little underground houses . . .
And the Papae have been named from their white robes, which they wore like priests; whence priests are all called *papae* in the Teutonic tongue. An island is still called, after them, *Papey*. But as is observed from their habit and the writings of their books abandoned there, they were Africans, adhering to Judaism.
(*Historia Norwegie*)[50]

This passage has caused much discussion, but reflects what was remembered, in local tradition, of the pre-Norse inhabitants of Orkney. There was no living survival of Pictish culture in the north (or anywhere else in north Britain) and memory of the Picts had got embellished with folklore motifs. The author seems a little uncertain whether their priests were even Christian. The name *papae* ('fathers') had somehow got attached to them, and the islands called Papay (or one such island) was known to be associated with them. But the notion that they were 'Africans, adhering to Judaism' suggests that they may have been thought to be a particular sect which, like Irish monasticism, had distant origins in the North African monastic tradition.[51]

The author goes on to describe the coming of the Vikings (*piratae*) to Orkney in the days of Harald 'Finehair' and the conquest of the islands by 'the most vigorous prince Rognvald' who set out with a great fleet to cross the Solundic sea and 'totally destroyed those peoples after stripping them of their long-established dwellings and made the islands subject to themselves'.[52] He continues, later, to say that Orkney remained under the lordship of Rognvald's descendants 'with the proviso that they are bound to pay tribute to the Norwegian kings', and the tributary nature of the islands north and west of Britain

50 *ES*, i, 331; this translation by A.O. Anderson, is preferred to that by Fisher in Mortensen and Ekrem (65), where the term 'Picti' is translated, bizarrely, as 'Pents'
51 Crawford, 1987, 211. For a full study of the places associated with the 'papar' in the Northern and Western Isles see website www.paparproject.org
52 *ES*, i, 331. Crawford, 1987, 54–5. See Section 3.2

is stressed in a section called *On the tributary Islands* where it is said that the 'southern islands are elevated to [being ruled by] kinglets, while the northern are adorned by the protection of earls; and both [kinglets and earls] pay a large tribute to the kings of Norway'.[53] The status of the Viking settlements is unequivocally here stated to be tributary, as also in the case of the Faeroe islands, which fits with the semi-official nature of the *Historia Norwegie* as an account of the lands in the west which were recently incorporated into the Norwegian archbishopric.

There are earlier Latin documents which emanated from a different period of ecclesiastical authority in the earldoms. The first one which is known is a letter of Archbishop Thomas of York to Archbishop Lanfranc of Canterbury concerning the consecration of a bishop of Orkney (before 1073):

> There has come to us a certain cleric, sent by Earl Paul (*Comes Paulus*) with sealed letters from the regions of Orkney signifying that he has given the bishopric of his country to the same cleric. And he requests that by the accustomed order of your predecessors the bishop be consecrated by us. What he justly seeks we cannot unjustly deny.[54]

This is a most remarkable piece of evidence for the universality of the Norman Church in the British Isles, however inappropriate that term might be for the earldom of Orkney which at this date was an integral part of the Norse world (although hardly integrated into the kingdom of Norway). These two archbishops were the venerable organisers of the Norman Church in an England which, only a few years previously, had come under the domination of William the Conqueror. In theory the young Church in Orkney should have looked to the archbishop of Hamburg-Bremen, who had the whole of Scandinavia under his authority. But, for some reason, Earl Paul Thorfinsson preferred to send his chosen nominee for the Orkney bishopric to York to be consecrated, and the machinery for such a process was indeed put into action.[55] Here is the first unequivocal evidence from an ecclesiastical source for the existence of an earl of Orkney, and for his active role in the organisation of the Church in his earldom. The cleric's name was Ralph (*Rodolphus*; ON *Hrolf*).[56]

---

53 *ES*, i, 331. This appears to be distinguishing between the Hebrides, which were indeed ruled by 'kings', and Orkney (see discussion of the different titles in Crawford, forthcoming, and Section 3.2.2)

54 Author's own translation. Latin text can be found in *OSR*, no. 3; *DN*, xix (i), no. 14; Clover and Gibson, 1979, no. 13

55 Another letter was sent by Lanfranc to the bishops of Worcester and Chester requesting them to go to York to assist Archbishop Thomas in the consecration of Earl Paul's nominee; *OSR*, no. 4

56 The circumstances of Ralph's consecration and other possible double episcopal elections in the earldom are discussed in Crawford, 1996, 4, 8

In the late twelfth century a copy of a Latin document has survived in which Earl Harald Maddadson made an annual grant of one silver mark to the canons of the abbey of Scone in Perthshire:

> To his much beloved friends and men Harald, earl of Orkney, Shetland and Caithness (*Orcardensis, Hetlandensis et Catanesie comes*), greeting! Know that I have given and with this my charter have confirmed to God and Saint Michael and to the canons residing in Scone annually one mark of silver weighed to the weight of a Scots mark. Wherefore I will that every year this gift be paid to the said house by me and my son Torfinn and by my heirs for ever, for the souls of my ancestors and for my soul and my wife's, namely . . .
> Witnessed by my son Thorfinn, Laurence the Chancellor and others[57]

This is typical of many such pious grants made in medieval Scotland, but the only one to have survived telling us of the Orkney earls' generosity to the Church in Scotland. Why should Earl Harald have been so generous to the royal monastery of Scone? He had a turbulent career and was deeply implicated in rebellious actions against the Scottish king. But he was also a son of the earl of Atholl and therefore keyed into the ecclesiastical network of his paternal home territory (see Chapter 6). The naming of all three parts of his earldom making up his title of earl (Orkney, Shetland and Caithness) is an interesting – and unique – example of the usage of the three constituent parts in the earl's title. However, due to Earl Harald's involvement in the Eyiaskeggjar rebellion of 1193 he was deprived of Shetland two years later, so it seems likely that this charter, although undated, must date from prior to that event.[58] The name of his wife has been omitted – perhaps by the later copyist. It would have been Hvarflød (daughter of Malcolm MacHeth, earl of Ross), Earl Harald's second wife and the mother of his main heir, Thorfinn.

Earl Harald got into deep trouble over his problems with the Scottish bishop in his Caithness earldom, as will be discussed at length in Chapter 6. Because of these difficulties the authority of the pope of the day, Innocent III, was brought into direct contact with the earl and his northern Scottish earldom, so that two documents have survived in the Vatican register to give us a valid source of information as to the problems. Even in the formal Latin of the papal chancery they provide us with dramatic evidence of the clash between lay and ecclesiastical authority and of Earl Harald's contentious actions in defence of what he considered to be his rights over the Church in his earldom. The first one was

---

57 Author's own translation. Latin text in *OSR*, no. 13; *DN*, ii, no. 2; *Liber Ecclesie de Scon*, no. 58; Lawrie, 1910, 257
58 In *ES*, ii, 358, it is suggested that Earl Harald made this grant in connection with the peace after his rebellion against the Scottish Crown in 1196–7. If so, it would suggest that he was attempting to ignore the loss of Shetland which had been taken away from him in 1195

written in 1198 to the bishops of Orkney and Ross in response to Earl Harald's complaint about the actions of Bishop John of Caithness in blocking an annual payment which he had instituted and which was to be paid from his Scottish earldom direct to the papal see:

> The noble man, our beloved son, Harald Earl of Caithness and Orkney, has been careful to intimate to us that he had for the remission of his sins from the time of Pope Alexander, our predecessor... ordained one penny to be collected yearly from every inhabited house within the earldom of C. which from his regard for the holy apostles, Peter and Paul, he was wont to send to the apostolic see . . .
> If, after due warning, the foresaid bishop (John), shall neglect to restore the alms abstracted to this present time . . . you compel him so to do by ecclesiastical censures, refusing him by our authority the right of appeal.[59]

This did not solve the problem of the earl's quarrel with Bishop John, which escalated into a full-scale physical attack on the bishop by the earl's men in 1201, in which the bishop had his tongue cut out (and was blinded according to the saga writer's information).[60] The second papal letter ordered penance to be laid on one of the earl's followers, Lumberd, who had been responsible for the 'terrible and great outrage'.[61] Earl Harald appears to have escaped without being judged responsible for the actual attack, although his enmity with the bishop underlay the whole shocking affair, and he had to face a military expedition, led by the Scottish king, William the Lion, which came north to Caithness immediately (see Section 6.3). His son John had to face worse retribution after the second attack on a bishop of Caithness, Adam, who was killed in 1222.

Moving forward to the end of the century we have a very fine medieval charter which has survived from Caithness, giving us a ray of light about the activity of a later Earl John (1284–1303) in granting land to the powerful Reginald Cheyne 'the elder', whose wife was possibly the granddaughter of an earl:[62]

> We, John, earl of Caithness and Orkney [*comes Cattann' et Orcadie*] give and grant to Lord Reginald called 'le cheyne', the father [*patri*], lord of Inverugie, our whole ounceland of Nottingham with the harbour of Forse [*totam nostram oratam de Nothegane cum portu Forse*] . . . to be held freely and in peace with all liberties . . . but with the burden of the payment to the Lord King which is called 'Layyelde' [*servitium domini Regis quod vocatur Layyelde*] . . .
> Witnesses: Harald our uncle, Ivor MacEoth, Swain called 'of the Liverary' [*de Liverarum*], the clerk William, Walter called 'the Steward' [*Senescallus*] and others

---

59 Trans. (and original text) in *CSR*, no. 3; *DN*, vii, p.2
60 *OS*, Chapter III
61 *CSR*, no. 4; *DN*, vii, p.3
62 Kinnoull Charters (NRAS1489/Bundle 272/No 138ii). Author's own translation.

This charter is indistinguishable in most respects from other Scottish charters of the period, but it provides invaluable information about two aspects of the Norse inheritance in Caithness which were still relevant in the late thirteenth century: one is the use of the term *oratam* ('ounceland') for the land of Nottingham or Nothegane (Latheron, south Caithness), and the other is the royal due called *Layyelde* (see Section 7.7.2 for fuller discussion of these terms).[63] Additionally, the list of witnesses gives us evidence of officials belonging to the earl's household, which no other source provides in this period. The educated clerk, called William, would be able to draw up land transactions in the standard form and Latin of the noble household administrations of Scotland; perhaps, indeed, he wrote this charter, which has survived entire (except for the seal) (see Colour plate 35).

2.4 NORWEGIAN DOCUMENTS

No document similar to the above charter, showing an earl involved in land transactions, survives from his Orkney earldom in this period.[64] We do have, however, an interesting example of the widow of Earl Magnus V, Countess Katharine, making arrangements for the purchase of lands in South Ronaldsay in Orkney in a letter written at Kirkwall in 1329:

> To the honourable lord and her dear friend, Herra Erling Vidkunnson, Regent [*Drottseti*] of the king of Norway, Katharin, countess in the Orkneys and Caithness, sends God's greetings and her own. I make known to you, that I have bought of Herra Sigurd Jodgierson, your commissioner [*umbodzman*] those lands which you and *Herra* [sir] Hakon and Lady Kristin possessed in Ronaldsay. But with regard to the 45 pounds' worth which Herra Hakon and Lady Kristin owned in the lands, which were adjudged to my lord (the earl) for the debt which Herra Hoskoll owed to Earl John, and which my lord gave to me, I and Herra Sigurd have agreed, that if you send to my commissioner in Bergen your open letter, stating that you on behalf of Herra Hakon and of the heirs of the aforesaid Lady Kristin free all these lands to me, then I will, for the sake of your friendship give you 25 pounds English, and have them paid this summer in Bergen to you or your commissioner, who has the before-mentioned letter . . .[65]

This document is in Norwegian and is a rare glimpse of communication and social interaction between the earldom dynasty and powerful Norwegians at the

---

63 Crawford, 1985, 26–7
64 The laws and customs concerning the holding of land in Norway and Scotland in the medieval period were very different, and the odal law prevailing in the Northern Isles did not require written record of any land transaction as was customary in feudal practices prevailing in Scotland (Robberstad 1983; Thomson, 2001, 255; Jones, 2011)
65 *DN*, ii, no. 168; English translations in *Orkney Recs.*, no. IV, 10–11, and in Marwick, 1957, 49–50 (also ibid., 1929)

highest level. It also provides evidence of a countess acting on her own behalf as the widow of Earl Magnus V (pre-1312–pre-1321), during the minority of her son and heir to the earldoms. She refers to her father-in-law, Earl John, who made the grant of the Caithness lands discussed above. The circumstances of the land transaction are also complex and the full names of the lands concerned are listed in a second 'open' letter of Countess Katherine's, written a few days later, also in Kirkwall.[66] These lands in south Ronaldsay had evidently been the 'odal' property, that is the family property which was shared among the three mentioned Norwegians, Erling, Hakon and Kristin. One part of these lands, worth £45, had (for reason of debt) been 'adjudged' to Earl John and it looks as if there was some dispute regarding this portion, over which Countess Katherine was prepared to come to an agreement by offering to pay £25 for it.[67] The lands are named in the second letter. These two letters are the first documents written in Norwegian which have survived from Orkney.

Two slightly earlier Norwegian documents have survived from Shetland. The famous letter issued by the lawthingmen of Shetland at Tingwall in 1299 recorded the attempts by the sysselman (royal official) (see Colour plate 2), Thorvald Thoresson, to clear himself of the accusation of treachery which had been made by Ragnhild Simunsdatter on Papa Stour at Easter,[68] and a decree of the Lawthing of Shetland in 1307 concerned the case of Bjorg in Cullivoe.[69] The reason for the survival of these Norwegian documents from Shetland may be due to the fact that Shetland had been confiscated from the earls in 1195 and taken in under the Norwegian Crown and directly administered from Norway, so that these documents went into the royal archive.[70]

As the fourteenth century progressed, our documentary sources become fuller, and are particularly concerned with the governance of the Orkney earldom and the appointment of earls or administrators in the periods of abeyance of that earldom. This was a period of extreme uncertainty regarding the inheritance of both Caithness and Orkney because of the failure of the direct

---

66 DN, ii,170; Orkney Recs., no. V, 11–12; Marwick, 1957, 50.
67 Marwick, 1957, 48, 49. These arrangements are sorting out a matter of 'odal' inheritance and are not concerned with the grant of land by a superior. In Orkney most legal transactions concerning the transfer of land would have been conducted orally at the public assemblies and only gradually were replaced by written record of the transfer in the fifteenth century (Clouston, 1932, 205)
68 DN, I, no. 89;. OSR, no. 25 (transcription and translation); Orkney Recs., p.67 (translation); Reg.Norv. II, 978; Hodnebø, 1960, no. 66; Barnes, 1998, 35–7 (transcription and translation); Crawford and Ballin Smith, 1999, 49–50 (translation); Shetland Docs., 1999, no. 2 (translation); Bibire in Crawford, 2002, 9–11 (transcription and translation)
69 DN, I, no. 109; Orkney Recs., p.69–70 (translation); Shetland Docs., 1999, no. 3 (translation)
70 Now in the Danish Rigsarkiv AM 100 3, AM 100 5a

line around 1330, when Malise, earl of Strathearn, inherited both earldoms; then again on his death in 1350 there was no male heir but only five daughters to share the inheritance. The result of this was the resignation – or sale – of the earldom of Caithness to the Scottish Crown in 1374/5, which broke the dual earldom situation for the very first time (see Section 7.7.1). We have one confirmation of a grant made by Earl Malise in 1344, in which he styles himself 'earl of Strathearn, Caithness and Orkney', and by which he gives the right of marriage (*maritagium*) of his daughter Isabella, whom he also makes his heir to the earldom of Caithness, to William, earl of Ross, his brother-in-law.[71]

In 1425, a very remarkable document was drawn up in Norwegian by the lawman of Orkney and other 'good men', sealed with the seal of the community of Orkney and sent to the queen in Copenhagen. This was the Complaint against Earl Henry (II)'s brother-in-law, David Menzies of Weem, who had been given the wardship of Earl Henry's heir to the earldom, William, who was a minor on his father's death in 1420 (see Colour plate 3). David Menzies also succeeded in being appointed the royal governor in the islands in 1423, and so was in a very powerful position (see Section 8.4.1). He clearly blocked the young earl's attempts to get the necessary evidence to prove his right to be given a grant of the earldom:

> And when the Earl [William] came and asked for the aforesaid seal [to be affixed] to the evidence proving his birthright to the earldom of Orkney, and desired the goodmen [*godo mæn*] born here in the country [Orkney] to go with him to our gracious lord, the King's grace, to tell how it stood here in the country and bear true witness for the Earl, he could neither get the men nor the seal, but only Thomas Sinclair and the Archdeacon of Shetland and two servants of those who were born here in the country.
>
> (*Orkney Recs.*, 37–8)[72]

The 'seal of the community of Orkney' was an important symbol of the ruling elite's authority, and was only supposed to be held by the lawman, the most important community official (see Figure 2.5). However, Menzies had taken this seal from the lawman and used it for his own purposes, which gives a good idea of his disrespect for the customs of the islanders, different in so many ways from the feudal society he came from in Scotland.[73] The refusal of the lawman to yield up the seal to Menzies is described in graphic detail in the Complaint,

---

71 *RMS*, i, Appendix I, no. 150; *CSR*, p.138. The grant of *maritagium* gave the earl of Ross control over whom Isabella married (Crawford, 1971, 30)
72 Norwegian text in *DN*, ii, 691; Imsen, 2012, 28–33, has Norwegian text and English translation side by side
73 There are no examples of community seals having been granted in Scotland, so the practice would have been alien to Menzies

and the retribution then inflicted on him, for he was imprisoned in the tower of Kirkwall, while his house and church were attacked and looted by 'foreigners from Caithness' sent by Menzies, presumably because local men would have refused to carry out such an order. Eventually the lawman was released when his wife relinquished the seal and the Lawbook and laid them on the altar of St Magnus Cathedral. David Menzies clearly was taking the opportunity to make a great deal of money out of his control of the earldom and grant of royal rights,[74] but his regime of terror did not last long and he was removed from the Orkney scene to London as security for James I sometime in 1425.

The information contained in this Complaint gives full evidence for the maintenance of a traditional Norse society in the islands at that date. The document was written in Orkney in a form of Norwegian entirely consistent with the language of Norwegian documents of the time.[75] It is a most impressive source of information about a well-ordered society which ran its own affairs and maintained a loyalty to the earldom dynasty but whose social organisation (or the organisation of the social elite) was threatened by an incoming Scot (even though he was a member of that earldom dynasty). David Menzies of Weem seems to symbolise the looming threat to Orkney society of the inevitable process of Scotticisation which was being hastened under the rule of the Sinclair dynasty and Scottish churchmen.

2.5 SCOTS DOCUMENTS AND THE 'GENEALOGY OF THE EARLS'

There is evidence for the appearance of Scottish incomers into Orkney and Shetland from the late fourteenth century onwards (Chapter 7). Their influence was greatly increased by the numbers of Scottish churchmen who began to fill ecclesiastical positions after the devastation of the Black Death, for the language of these incomers would be influential in legal and cultural matters. The first Orkney document written in Scots dates from 1433,[76] while the last surviving Orkney document written in Norwegian is the Complaint against David Menzies of 1425. But there may have been earlier documents written in Scots in Orkney and undoubtedly there were later ones in Norwegian. None of the surviving ones has very much to do with the earls in this period of time, so an extract relating to the earldom inheritance from the sixteenth-century Scottish translation of the 'Genealogy of the Earls' has been chosen to illustrate the position of the earl, even though this translation was commissioned by a later Sinclair in southern Scotland.

74 Reference is made to Menzies' collection of rent from earldom estates, and to his unjust collection of judicial fines belonging to the earl and the king (*Orkney Recs.*, pp38–9)
75 Imsen, 2012, 13.
76 Marwick, 1929, xii

The 'Genealogy of the Earls' is a very remarkable document drawn up probably in the 1420s by Bishop Thomas Tulloch as a testimony to the just claim of the young William Sinclair, heir to the earldom, who had some difficulty persuading King Erik to grant him his earldom (see Section 8.4.2). It has survived in a Latin copy of the late fifteenth century and the Scots translation dates from the mid-sixteenth century.[77] The chosen extract (from the Scots translation) relates how the young Earl William appeared before a meeting of the bishop and chapter, in the cathedral kirk of St Magnus, and requested that they produce the evidence proving his right to inherit the earldom which his ancestors had held continuously by hereditary right:

> In our presens togidder asssemblit comperand ane magnifiit and prepotent lord Lord Wilzem of Sanct Clare Erile of Orchadie and Lord of Sinclair in the Cathedrale kirk of Sanct Mawnis martyre in Orchadie hed proponit [*proposed*] in this maner –the quhilk [*which*] Lord hes presupponit [*presupposed*] that wele and fowlie [*fully*] that thing wes knawin till ws that lang tymis afore bypast his antecessoris and progenitoris and thai Eirlis of Orchadie iustlie [*justly*] laufullie inforssable [*undisturbedly*], linialie, and gre be gre [*step by step*] be iure hereditary [*by hereditary right*] hed succedit to the forsaid Eirldome of Orchadie, and withoute ony strange geneolige enterand betuix, had be lang tyme brukit [*used*] the same quietlie.[78]

This document then sets out the history of the earldom from the very first conquest of the islands by King Harald 'Finehair' (in the ninth century) and his grant of Orkney and Shetland to Earl Rognvald of Møre down to the Sinclairs of the fourteenth and fifteenth centuries. From the information cited and the direct quotations it is clear that the author had two sources on which he relied for his information about the earldom's foundation and the descent of the earls in the saga period: one was *Historia Norwegie* and the other was some version of *Orkneyinga Saga*. The former still survives in the collection of copied documents, which also includes the Latin version of the 'Genealogy of the Earls' (see Section 2.3). This whole collection was copied down by a scribe working, it would appear, in the employ of Lord Henry Sinclair, grandson of the last earl, between 1490 and 1510.[79]

---

77 See full discussion and references to the texts of the Genealogy in Crawford, 1976, 156–8 and n.4. The Latin copy is part of the Panmure Codex, along with *Historia Norwegie* (see Section 2.3). The Scots translation, dated 1554, was done for Sir William Sinclair of Roslin, grandson of the last earl of Orkney. Both are printed in *Bann. Misc.*, iii, 65–85
78 *Bann.Misc.*, iii, 68
79 Chesnutt, 1986, 89, where it is shown that the copy of the 'Genealogy' in the Panmure Codex cannot have been commissioned by the last Orkney earl, William Sinclair (although the original 'Genealogy' was certainly drawn up at his request, as seen in the extract above)

More uncertain is the nature of the sources used by the writer of the 'Genealogy' for his information about the inheritance of the earldom in the saga period. Although it has been suggested that this information was drawn from *Heimskringla*,[80] the possibility that a version of *Orkneyinga Saga* was used should not be discounted. A manuscript of the *Jarls' Saga* would probably have existed in Kirkwall in the Middle Ages, and the genealogical information have been excerpted from it, until the end of the Norse line in 1231.[81] After that the writer probably drew his information about the Angus, Strathearn and Sinclair earls from documentary material available in the cathedral archives. At least it provides the bare bones of the inheritance, which otherwise would be very difficult to ascertain, and it is undoubted that some member of the Sinclair family ensured that it did survive by having the 'Genealogy' copied out.[82] Although it has never been the focus of scholarly attention like the saga accounts, nonetheless it is a most important piece of information about the Sinclair family's concern about their comital status at the time the 'Genealogy' was initially drawn up in the 1420s, and also when the copy was made at the end of the century.

The difficulty of knowing what manuscripts may have existed in Orkney in the Middle Ages, and the recognition that there may have been rich resources which have simply disappeared, is reflected in the attempt by the earl to gather evidence for proving his claim to the earldom in the 1420s. William Sinclair is recorded in the Genealogy as saying that 'charteris, evidentis, instrumentis, compt bukis, and otheris divers kindis of probationis was consumit by fyre, tint [*lost*] and alianat in the tyme of hostilite, and of weirs [*wars*] of unfreindfull innimiis'. He asserts that the reason was the lack of 'ane suir hows or mansioun inexpugnable' and therefore requests the bishop and canons to search in the church's 'schrinis, coperis, thekis [*protective covering*], kistis [*chests*], armoureis [*cupboards*], or chartor wardis' to find authentic documents which would prove his descent and claim to the earldom.[83] If Earl William did not possess any evidence to prove his right to his inheritance, then we can be sure that already by his time there was precious little surviving of the earldom documents. The bishop and canons were able to find the first book of *Historia Norwegie* and some

---

80 Crawford, 1976, 176, citing Storm, 1880, p.xvii
81 The information tallies closely with the saga accounts, except in one instance (Crawford, 1976, 176)
82 As Chesnutt's conclusions (1986, 89) point to the period between the years 1490 and 1510 when the Codex was copied, that suggests Lord Henry Sinclair was responsible. He was very active in reasserting the family's position of power in Orkney after the islands were pledged to Scotland (Chapter 9), and would probably have been interested in having a copy of source material relevant to Orkney, and to his family's ancestral genealogy.
83 *Bann.Misc*, iii, 69

version of *Orkneyinga Saga* along with evidence for the descent of the earldom in the post-saga period, but no sources are cited for this later evidence. It is worth noting that the majority of the sources cited in the present chapter are from manuscript material which has survived in repositories outwith Orkney.

The diverse nature of these sources is remarkable, and their very diversity makes it difficult to pull them together in a coherent assessment of the earls and their rule. As discussed, we have the Old Norse saga sources (which were preserved in Iceland), the runic inscriptions from the islands, the Latin ecclesiastical documents (preserved in English and Scottish monastic record collections, as well as the papal archives); Latin and Scots charters come from family papers, while the Norwegian land grants and administrative documents are mostly in the Danish Royal Archives (Rigsarchiv) in Copenhagen. In addition, the unique hymns of praise to Earl Magnus, the Orkney saint, have survived in Uppsala University Library in Sweden and in Copenhagen in the Arnamagnaean Collection of Icelandic manuscripts.

2.6 LITURGICAL FRAGMENTS

These are possibly the most specialised sources of all the surviving documents discussed here, requiring an understanding of medieval music notation and the beginnings of polyphony to appreciate their rarity and sophistication. The first one is the St Magnus hymn, '*Nobilis humilis*', 'a two-part syllabic piece of music . . . characterised by parallel movement in thirds'[84] with seven Latin stanzas celebrating St Magnus. The manuscript in which this remarkable hymn has survived dates from the second half of the thirteenth century, and is probably Icelandic in origin, but the hymn and its musical setting are likely to be somewhat older (see Colour plate 4). This is a very early piece of polyphonic music, and, although debate has raged about the origin of polyphony, it is now thought that this is not Nordic in origin but a feature of west-European musical development in general. For present purposes the artistic sophistication of the text of this hymn in praise of St Magnus demonstrates vividly the widespread cult of the islands' earl-saint, and the depth of devotion to him in the north Atlantic world:

> Nobilis humilis magne martir stabilis
> abilis utilis comes venerabilis
> et tutor laudabilis tuos subditos
> serua carnis fragilis mole positos
>
> [Noble, humble Magnus, steadfast martyr
> mighty and kindly one, our honourable earl

---

84 De Geer, 1988, 242

praiseworthy protector
Save us your servants
Framed in our fragile flesh
Weighed down and burdened][85]

There are six more stanzas and it is suggested that the character of the music as a *conductus* would suit it for an introductory or processional function in a liturgical context.[86] This could only have been in a cathedral or monastic setting, and the most obvious place for its use would have been in St Magnus Cathedral itself.

The second liturgical piece is the 'sequence to St Magnus' (*'Comitis generosi militis gloriosi'*) which appears to have been written in the fifteenth century, as the third line of verse eight reads *ter centeno laureatus* indicating that it was composed 300 years after the martyrdom of Earl Magnus. This is known from four manuscript fragments, all Icelandic, part of a Mass of St Magnus.[87] One of the sources has a complete musical notation, which is the Easter sequence '*Mane prima sabbati*', widely known in northern Europe.

Comitis generosi, militis gloriosi martytris certamina
Concinat Orchadi[c]a gens plaudens:nam cælica terit Magnus limina
Magnum probant opera que dei per munera agit dignus nomine
Spreto virgo sæculo annorum curriculodecem est cum virgine
(*OS* Dasent, 327–8)

[Of high-born earl, famed soldier, noble Martyr,
Now high in heav'n, let Orkney sing the praises:
Magnus in name and deed, he spurned the world,
And lived for ten long years in virgin wedlock]
(Trans. by D.P. Hunter Blair in Mooney, 1935, 285–6)

Ingrid De Geer's conclusion to her study of the music of the Orkney earldom is worth quoting in the present context: 'Strong bonds connected the Northern Isles with the further Norse area – of which it was in many respects a part. However the small crossroads realm of the Orkney Isles was also a bridgehead, a place where capacities and talents and traditions of the north and of the south met and amalgamated, and from where in turn impulses were likely to spread – to the north and to the south.'[88]

In the context of musical sophistication it was the Church which led such cultural developments, and those places where a princely family founded

85 Gilbert Márkus' trans. in Clancy, ed., 1998, 292
86 De Geer, 1988, 252
87 Ibid., 1988, 254
88 Ibid., 260

and endowed their centre of religious activity were in the forefront of such flowering. In Orkney this was the earls' cathedral built to the glory of a member of the earldom dynasty and most probably a proprietorial church of the earldom family (Chapter 9). The cultural flowering in both a secular and religious sphere was certainly a consequence of the establishment of a powerful earldom dynasty, and the Orkney earldom is a remarkable manifestation of this medieval phenomenon. The cult of St Magnus may not be greatly significant to Orcadians today – although they are very proud of the medieval architectural masterpiece dedicated to their own island saint – but in fact it was the religious fervour associated with such local cults that inspired the blossoming of medieval culture there and everywhere else in medieval Christian Europe. How and why it happened in these northern communities will be explored later (Chapter 5). For the moment we can regard the survivals of the liturgical evidence associated with the cult of St Magnus as one of the precious documentary sources which reveal, if only partially, the richness of the world which the earls inhabited, and which they helped to mould.

2.7 Material Evidence

It might be thought that the long-lived dynasty of earls would have left many material traces of their lives and burial places. But the evidence is surprisingly thin. Unfortunately, none of the burial places of the pagan earls has yet been discovered (although it is recorded where several of them are buried; see Chapter 3 for the locations of the burial places of Earl Sigurd I, Earl Hlodver and Earl Thorfinn I). Nor have any of the pagan burials excavated in Shetland, Orkney, or Caithness provided the evidence which might indicate that the dead were of the earldom kindred. Just as disappointing is the lack of any memorial tomb furniture in St Magnus Cathedral, indicating the former location of burials of the earls or their family members. The Sinclair earls may have chosen to be buried in Roslin Church, Midlothian, which was the family's collegiate foundation.[89] But the earls of the previous dynasties would certainly have regarded St Magnus Cathedral as their family burial place.[90]

---

89 It is believed that Earl William was buried in Roslin Church because of the reference in Alexander Sutherland's will (1456) that he wished to have a tombstone laid over his grave in Roslin near where his son-in-law William himself planned to be buried (Crawford, 1994, 102; see Chapter 8, n.99)

90 Craven (1901, 93–4) indicates one tomb niche on the south wall of St Magnus Cathedral which has the three 'gouttae' or tears of the Strathearn coat of arms above the arch and on a tomb slab below

The great gilded 'feretories' containing the relics of the Orkney saints Magnus and Rognvald did not survive the Reformation, although, remarkably enough, the corporeal relics themselves have survived. There could not be any more dramatic surviving material evidence of the earls than these skull and skeletal fragments, discovered hidden in two piers of St Magnus' cathedral. In the eighteenth and early twentieth centuries two lots of relics were exposed, (perhaps for the first time since the Reformation), one consisting of cranial pieces, secreted in the large north pier of the choir, the second of an almost complete skeleton, in the large south pier of the choir.[91] The latter, with the skull showing clear evidence of a blow from a sharp instrument, are the presumed relics of St Magnus (see Plate 1). The former can be identified as those of the second Orkney saint, Rognvald Kali Kolsson (see Section 5.4).

2.7.1 Ecclesiastical foundations

In addition to the mortal remains of the two Orkney saints, small stone statues of the northern saints have survived from the medieval cathedral's once richly adorned interior: one of St Magnus with his sword of martyrdom, one of St Olaf, the royal Norwegian saint with his axe, and a third possibly of St Rognvald (see further details in Chapter 5). The cathedral itself is a great monument to the earldom dynasty and the achievement of Earl Rognvald, who founded it. The huge expense of building and maintaining this great edifice must have diverted large resources of earldom income, so it is hardly surprising that there is no certain evidence of any earldom monastic foundations in the islands.[92] The development of the episcopal church on the Brough of Birsay into a monastic foundation after Bishop William's move to Kirkwall was another expensive building operation, and a necessary one in order to give the site of Magnus' burial the required liturgical status for the saint's first resting place (see Chapter 5 and Colour plate 5). This was most probably undertaken by Bishop William rather than by St Magnus' cousin and rival, Hakon Paulsson, who is unlikely to have wanted to expend his own resources on a monument to the cousin whose death he had overseen.[93] Earl Hakon was however probably responsible for building the round church dedicated to St Nicholas, at the earldom power centre of Orphir, a building that was unique in the north, and a very special re-creation of the round Church of the Sepulchre in Jerusalem (see Section 5.3).

91 Mooney, 1925, 253–4; Jesch and Molleson, 2005, 134–40
92 The surviving ecclesiastical structure on the island of Eynhallow may have been the church of a monastic community, but it is not known if this was an earldom foundation, or not (RCAHMS, 1946, no. 613)
93 Unless this had been one of the conditions imposed by the Church for expiation of the murder of Magnus, to be fulfilled after Hakon's visit to Rome

The Sinclair family mausoleum at Roslin, the church dedicated to St Matthew and founded by Earl William Sinclair in 1455, is of course a most remarkable and famed memorial to the dynasty, and especially to the last Sinclair earl of Orkney (see Colour plate 36). But its cultural connections are of a totally different order from the northern world of the earls, and it will not therefore be considered in any depth here. There is no certain evidence of any element of Nordic culture, only a possible hint of the cult of the Orkney martyr, and ancestor of the Sinclair earls.[94] There was clearly no wish to blend the cultures of the two Sinclair dynastic power bases, and no evident attempt to bring northern elements to bear on the southern Scottish world.

However, there is some evidence to suggest that Scottish-based saints' cults were imported north to the Orkney islands. Firstly the cathedral prebend of St Catherine was well endowed with many different pieces of land which appear to have been part of earldom estates,[95] and secondly, a charter (dated 1448) granted by Bishop Thomas Tulloch and the chapter of St Magnus Cathedral acknowledged that the right of patronage of the Chapel of St Duthac, at Pickaquoy, outside the burgh of Kirkwall, 'pertains and belongs not only to the Lords of Orkney, the earls, but also to their heirs and descendants, of right and custom, and will belong for ever'.[96] Nothing is known of the date when this chapel was founded, although we can assume that it is likely to have been founded not long before the date of the charter, as the cult of St Duthac of Tain was very popular in the fifteenth century.[97] Perhaps a member of the earldom family introduced this cult to the islands and endowed this chapel, which was thus considered to be in the patronage of the earl.[98] One of the cathedral prebends was also associated with St Duthac.[99] If it were not for the survival of such written charters and rentals, nothing of this would be known, for such ecclesiastical organisation disappeared at the Reformation and there is not much material evidence left, particularly not of St Duthac's chapel at Pickaquoy.

94 The corbel head on the south side of the nave which has an evident wound on the skull might represent the head of St Magnus (who was killed with a blow to his head), rather than the murdered mason's apprentice (see image in Wallace-Murphy, 1993, 22). Smout has suggested (2003, 5–6) that the ash tree Yggdrasil may be represented on the apprentice mason's pillar.
95 Thomson, 2001, 258–9. The Sinclair family fostered the cult of St Catherine on their Midlothian estates.
96 Hay, 1835/2002, 78–9. This strongly worded acknowledgement of the earldom family's eternal right of patronage suggests that this right had been threatened
97 Yeoman, 1999, 106; see now Turpie, 2013.
98 It may have been introduced into Orkney during the period of Ross power in the mid-fourteenth century. The cult was very focused in eastern Scotland (Yeoman, 1999, 106), with the cult centre being in Tain, in the earldom of Ross
99 Craven, 1901, 102–4. There is a St Duthac's Chapel at Moss of Kilimster in Caithness (Gibbon, 2006, Ref. CW11)

An ecclesiastical foundation of the earldom family in Caithness is a hospital for pilgrims in Caithness dedicated to St Magnus, of which there are still some visible surviving remains at Spittal (see Colour plate 6). It was built beside the route across the causeway mire in upland Caithness, most probably to provide a refuge for pilgrims travelling to and from the saint's resting place and shrine in Orkney (see Section 5.4).

2.7.2 Secular Residences: Birsay and Kirkwall

The significance of the Brough of Birsay in the history of the earldom of Orkney will be mentioned again in Chapter 3. It is an iconic site for historians of medieval Orkney, and a magnet for tourists; cut off as it is from the village of Birsay today, and accessible only at low tide, it has an other-worldly quality (see Colour plate 7). But it was not always cut off, and this geographical factor has not always been taken into consideration when its place in island history is discussed. The breach of the isthmus which joined the Brough to the Point of Buckquoy may have occurred during the Norse period, and, if so, this factor may lie behind the postulated change of use of the ecclesiastical buildings on the Brough from bishops' church and residence to monastic establishment founded to fill the vacuum when the bishops moved east to Kirkwall (this will be discussed more fully in Section 5.5.1).[100]

There is little doubt that both secular and ecclesiastical structures surviving on the Brough can be linked to the earls, for they are sufficiently high-status in size and sophistication to be directly connected to the upper levels of medieval society (Figure 2.3). They consist of an ecclesiastical complex and secular hallhouses which include the truncated remains of what might be a bathhouse or sauna. Lying directly on top of some of these impressive longhouses are some very different small houses with hearths stemming from a later period when the use of the site had drastically changed, as well as ancillary buildings surrounding the main site, some of which have been excavated and recorded.[101] We have here a multi-period settlement of some complexity which cannot be properly understood because much of it has not been excavated.[102] Moreover, a great deal of the site has been destroyed by coastal erosion, dramatically seen in Room VI, where only half the building has survived the erosion. Therefore our attempts to interpret the standing remains are only partial and our understanding incomplete.

---

100 Crawford, 1987, 189–90; 2005, 97
101 Hunter, 1986; Morris, 1996
102 There is also evidence that this had been an important power centre in the pre-Norse period, most notably from the magnificent Pictish standing stone with symbols and three warrior figures which was found on the Brough smashed into sixteen pieces (Ritchie, Scott and Gray, 2006, 55)

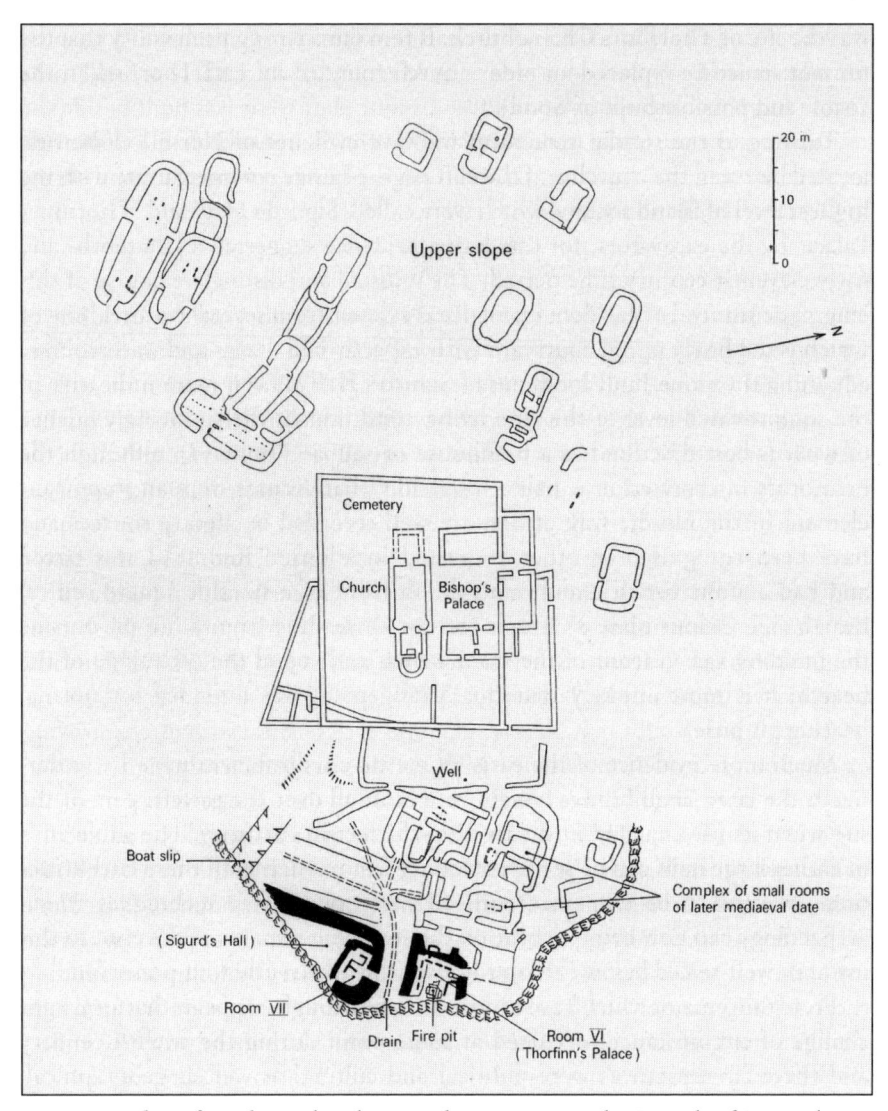

Figure 2.3 Plan of secular and ecclesiastical structures on the Brough of Birsay dating from the time of the tenth- and eleventh-century earls. (From Crawford, 1987, fig. 55)

The best-preserved part of the site is the ecclesiastical complex, with the church and conventual buildings or cloister on its north side. This is not Earl Thorfinn's Christchurch; its architectural features indicate that it is of a later date, probably mid-twelfth century. Evidence suggests that it replaced an older church, or several older churches, and the original excavators believed that this was the site of Thorfinn's Christchurch. It remains a strong probability that the present structure replaced an older church founded by Earl Thorfinn in the 1050s (and possibly built of wood).[103]

Turning to the secular structures we have evidence of Norse longhouses, located between the church and the cliff edge, of a size commensurate with the highest level of island society, which were called 'Sigurd's Hall' and 'Thorfinn's Palace' by the excavators, for the dating evidence suggested a late tenth- and early eleventh-century time period. The unusual and distinctive nature of this enigmatic survival of earldom residence is evident from several features, one of which is the finely paved courtyard with expertly laid drains and watercourses adjoining the stone-built longhouse ('Sigurd's Hall'). Even more indicative of the sophisticated level of the elite living-conditions is the surviving evidence of what is best described as a bathhouse or sauna (Room VI), although the excavators interpreted it as half a longhall.[104] Bathhouses were an important element in the Nordic way of life, are well-recorded in literary sources and have been recognised in other excavated locations.[105] Room VI was paved and had a stone bench along one side, in front of a sizeable square central hearth (see Colour plate 8). Ducts for hot air leading from a fire-pit outside the building ran in front of the stone bench and round the other side of the hearth; it is most unlikely that this arrangement was intended for normal heating purposes.

Much more evidence of the earls' domestic circumstances must lie underneath the later small houses which were built all over the eastern part of the site when its use changed in the twelfth–thirteenth centuries. The gable ends of earlier large halls can be seen protruding from underneath these later structures, waiting to be excavated with all the sophisticated techniques which archaeology can now bring to bear on the surviving remains of the past, in this instance well-sealed below the later houses and apparently well-preserved.

From the remains which have survived on the Brough it appears that an abrupt change of circumstances occurred at some point during the twelfth century and these circumstances were political and cultural as well as geographical. The politico-cultural changes were most probably connected with the events

---

103 Radford, 1959; 1962; 1983; Cruden, 1965; This older interpretation was discounted by Lamb in favour of the parish church of St Magnus, in Birsay village, being a successor to Earl Thorfinn's Christchurch (Lamb, 1972–4; 1983). See Crawford, 1987, 184–90; 2005, 97–106, for re-assertion of the arguments that the church on the Brough is the more likely location.

104 Cruden, 1965, 22. This is not to be confused with 'Room VII', a strange structure of small compartments made of upright slabs built into the north end of 'Sigurd's Hall', and described by the excavators as a 'sauna'

105 Crawford, 1987, 156. See Jarlshof in Shetland (Hamilton, 1953, 110); Reykholt in Iceland (Guðrún Sveinbjarnardóttir, 2006)

which took place after the violent death of Earl Magnus Erlendsson in 1116 and the growth of his saintly cult (see Chapter 5). The present church building is considered by architectural historians to be twelfth-century in date,[106] and it was possibly constructed as a memorial church for the saint who was buried here briefly before his remains were translated to the magnificent cathedral in Kirkwall built by his nephew and heir Rognvald Kali Kolsson. A community of monks or canons would have been brought in to care for the abandoned church site, and the cloister court and surrounding residential buildings on the north side were probably constructed for this community.[107]

The geographical factor is the evident massive scale of the erosion which has taken place, even possibly causing a breach of the isthmus connecting the Brough to the Point of Buckquoy in this period. This must have made living conditions on the Brough very difficult and may well have hastened the abandonment of the Brough as an earldom residence.[108] The Norse longhalls near the cliff edge ('Sigurd's Hall and 'Thorfinn's Palace') have been truncated by extensive erosion.[109] The bathhouse/sauna (Room VI) has been cut in half, but its survival, along with the other halls, gives us a dramatic glimpse of the living circumstances of the earldom dynasty at the height of its power and influence in the northern world.[110]

The significant impression of proximity of Church and earldom power centre in this western outpost arose from the circumstances in the period immediately after conversion. This was a time when the nascent Church needed protection and support from the secular leaders, a time when the bishops were appointed by the secular rulers, who considered them to be members of their retinue (hird). All that was going to change as the medieval Church won its freedom from state control and became financially independent with the institution of tithes and the donation of land from the faithful (most notably the earls), seeking remission of their sins. The move to Kirkwall and the building of a magnificent cathedral church for the bishop symbolised this twelfth-century change from subject priest, who was primarily the earls' chaplain, to independent prelate who eventually would become the earls' bitter opponent.

---

106 Fawcett, 1996, 212, 252

107 Useful comparison is made with a parallel situation at Selja in west Norway where a monastery was founded at the holy site associated with St Sunniva when the bishops moved to Bergen during the twelfth century (Crawford, 2005, 99–104)

108 Ibid., 94–6

109 The south gable end of 'Sigurd's Hall' was clipped by the construction of a 'boatslip' or processional way which leads up from the beach into the ecclesiastical complex (Crawford, 1987, 15 fig. 2

110 The importance of the longhall in the residences of the Norse elite of the earldoms is becoming better appreciated through more recent excavations. See Owen, 2005a, 198–206

Figure 2.4 Reconstruction of Kirkwall in the time of Earl Patrick Stewart, showing the situation of the medieval castle on the waterfront, originally built by Earl Henry I after 1379. (Courtesy Peter Anderson, 2003, p. 82)

The move to Kirkwall also symbolised the change in Orkney's political geography, as the west coast power centre was abandoned and a more central location in the Orkney islands was developed. Birsay retained an importance as an earldom and episcopal estate, but centred in the present-day village across the Bay from the Brough (see Colour plate 14). Excavations there have shown that medieval stone longhalls were built on the south side of the burn, and the medieval parish church dedicated to St Magnus on the north side of the burn was adorned with finely carved architectural elements.[111] It is likely that this area developed into the main power centre as a result of the changes on the Brough and reflects a move away from the island, so conveniently located for the western sea route, but less vital to the earls' policies once the Hebridean possessions were lost after Thorfinn's death. The whole locality around Birsay became an important episcopal estate centre probably as a result of a donation of land to the Church by one of the earls following the setting-up of the new political centre in Kirkwall.

Material evidence of the importance of Kirkwall as an earldom centre is entirely dominated by the cathedral, the proprietorial church of the earldom family and its mausoleum. The Sinclair castle built by Earl Henry I has totally disappeared. It is mentioned in Earl William's installation document of 1434, referred to as *illa turris* ('that tower') which had been built despite the promise which his grandfather (Earl Henry I) had made in his installation document of 1379 (see Section 8.4.3). It was built as a tower house 'on the Scottish pattern' and close to the inner harbour which then came much closer up to the cathedral than today (see Figure 2.4). It was actually rather close to the cathedral, and in 1614 an assault was launched from the top of the cathedral which seriously threatened the structure of the castle defences.[112] By that date, strong curtain walls had been built around the tower, with blockhouses at the corners. It was reputed to be extremely strongly built, and was a dangerous stronghold in the wrong hands, so it was demolished after Earl Robert Stewart's rebellion of 1614. Nothing whatever now remains of it and its location at the corner of Castle Street and Broad Street was built over in the nineteenth century. The alien presence of this feudal castle in Kirkwall was short-lived; its presence seemed only to encourage the powerful Scottish elements in late medieval and early modern Orkney to act as if they had no constraints (either Norwegian or Scottish) on their rule in their island empire.

111 Morris, 1996, 259; Crawford, 2005, 104–5
112 Anderson, 2003, 90–1

2.7.3 Seals

Finally, the material remains of seals are an important legacy from the medieval past which reveal much about the earl's (and the community's) status and power. It was only in the second half of the twelfth century that seals became a recognised feature of the authority of individuals in medieval society other than royal authority, and regularly used as a mark of authenticity of a document.[113] However, there is evidence that symbols had been used on banners as a mark of identity and as emblems of war long before this, and this aspect is dramatically evidenced by the story in *Jarls' Saga* and in *Njal's Saga* of the importance of Earl Sigurd *digri*'s raven banner at the Battle of Clontarf (see Sections 2.1 and 3.5.3). There is another saga story, which reveals the use of such an image on a seal, just at the date when seals were coming into use in north European history. This is the account in which Bjarni Kolbeinsson, bishop of Orkney (1188–1223), sent to the young Icelandic chieftain Rafn Sveinbjornsson a gold finger ring, which weighed an ounce, and 'on which was cut a raven (*rafn*) and his name so that he might seal with it'.[114] This appears to be the oldest evidence for the use of a private seal with emblem (a 'rebus' on the owner's name) in the northern world; this is evidence, if more evidence were needed, that the learned episcopal class in the islands was up-to-date with, or even in advance of, cultural development in northern Europe.

When the evidence for the earls' own heraldic emblem emerges in the thirteenth century it is the symbol of their sea power, the ship, which is always recorded. The early armorials show the seal of the ruler of Orkney as a gold ship with silver sails on a blue background. When the Sinclairs succeeded in being awarded the earldom in 1379, they appear to have retained the Sinclair engrailed cross, and the first surviving evidence of Earl Henry Sinclair I's seal in 1389, has the engrailed cross quartered with the Orkney ship.[115] When his grandson William succeeded in getting a grant of the earldom in 1434 he added a difference – a significant difference – to his seal; the ship is now bordered with the royal Scottish tressure.

The emblem of the earls of Caithness was also a ship, and the earliest surviving representation of it comes from Earl John's seal of 1292 or 1296, when

---

113 It should be noted that in the letter written in 1073 by Thomas, archbishop of York, regarding the consecration of a cleric sent to him by Earl Paul, there is reference to the 'sealed letters' (*literis sigillatis*) which the earl has sent (*OSR*, no. 3). This must have been a form of ecclesiastical seal at that date

114 Clouston, 1932, 196; *KL*, *sub Landskapsvåpen*; *Sturlinga Saga*, II, 884

115 This is shown as having the galley in the first and fourth quarters, and the engrailed cross in the second and third, but it is said that Earl Henry II put them the other way with the engrailed cross in the first and fourth quarters and the galley in the second and third which is the seal shown in Clouston, 1932 (plate between pp.276 and 277)

the ship is similarly shown with the royal tressure[116] (see Colour plates 9a and 9b). It would appear that the earls had different seals for Orkney and Caithness, for the Caithness ship is described as a 'lymphad [galley] with dragon heads at prow and stern, the mast terminating in a cross, and with two figures sitting therein'.[117] The Sinclair earls of Orkney did not hold Caithness until it was restored to Earl William in 1455.

When discussing seals from Orkney one has to include the remarkable seal of the community of Orkney, although this has nothing to do with the earls' own status, but with the status of the people of Orkney (Figure 2.5). This corporate seal of the community (*sigillum comunitatis Orcadie*) was granted to the Orkney people by the king of Norway probably in the late thirteenth century, and examples have survived from three fifteenth-century letters: one of 1425 sent by the community of Orkney to the queen of Norway; the Complaint against David Menzies of the same year which had the seal 'of the country and people here in the Orkneys' attached; and a letter sent to King Christian of Denmark and Norway in 1460 which was written under 'the common seal of Orkney with consent of the whole community'.[118] It had also been attached to the 'Genealogy of the Earls'. This emblem provides evidence of the early cohesion and organisation of the Orkney people.[119] The self-awareness of their public role in communicating with their royal overlord is demonstrated in these letters, and the seal of the community is a useful visible indicator of the royal link with the Orkney community.

The seal depicts the royal lion of Norway (a lion rampant, crowned and holding an axe in its paw) on a shield which is supported by two bearers. The bearers must be representative members of the Orkney community and this is a very remarkable depiction of medieval Orcadians. There is only one other Norwegian local community known to have been granted the privilege of having a communal seal with the royal arms, and that is Jemtland on the eastern border with Sweden.[120] As Storer Clouston suggested, 'it was the policy of Norway to permit – probably in fact encourage – her various dominions to display these arms as their cognisance, as a visible indication of vassalage

---

116 There is a reference to the earl's seal being affixed to the letter of agreement with the bishop of Caithness over payment of tithes (*SAEC*, 337), dating some time prior to the bishop's murder in 1222
117 See Section 8.4.1. Clouston (1930–31, 58) quoting Rae MacDonald
118 *DN*, ii, no. 691; *Orkney Recs.*, p.45; *DN*, v, no. 827; *Orkney Recs.*, p.53
119 Crawford, 1978a. Wærdahl, 2011, 121 suggests it was a combined Lawthing seal and provincial seal
120 All the Norwegian legal provinces were furnished with seals by Magnus *lagabøter* ('Lawmender') and his successors in the late thirteenth century, but these were seals used for the Lawthings' judicial decisions

Figure 2.5 Drawing of the 'seal of the community of Orkney'(*sigillum comunitatis Orcadie*) based on the remnants of the seal from letters to the Norwegian–Danish authorities in 1424, 1425 and 1460. (Copied from Clouston, 1932, facing p. 276)

and loyalty to the Crown'.[121] The representation of the two bearers gives us very interesting evidence for how the local members of the judicial elite (or 'goodmen' as they were called locally) must have appeared, probably dressed in their best garments.[122] From the surviving evidence of the seals, which are now very fragmentary, they appear to be dressed in tight-fitting jerkins with ?embroidered collars and cuffs, and breeches, again with some evidence of adornment around the thighs and knees. Most striking is the clear depiction of their boots, which gives the impression that they were made of sealskin. In fact it is possible that the whole outfit was of sealskin, and perhaps even the headgear also, which appears to be tight-fitting (although the reconstruction drawing of the seal is not clear enough to rely on such detail).[123]

121 'The Orkney Arms' (*POAS* 1930–1, 58)
122 The reason for showing these two bearers may have some thing to do with the king's desire to strengthen links with the local elite, some of whom would be closely attached to the Crown through membership of the king's hird
123 The Orkney Arms as matriculated in 1931 show the two supporters dressed in the same jerkins and breeches, with fancy boots but no head covering. By 1971, the supporters had been reduced to one and he does have a hood attached to his jerkin (Crawford, 1978)

The earl's seal and the community seal appropriately encapsulate the two powers which dominated the lives of the people of Orkney throughout our period. These were the earldom and the kingdom, both striving to exercise the authority under which the islands were governed (as already mentioned in Section 1.4). Much of the story to be be told in the following pages is about these two, earl and king, who shared the exercise of lordship over the people of Orkney.[124]

ENDNOTE

There is always the possibility that more material evidence for the earls will be discovered, or recognised. Seal matrices are something which the metal detector finds, and a recent discovery of a half of a seal matrix found in Deerness, east Mainland of Orkney, is a tantalising glimpse of just how important such finds might be (see Colour plate 10). Although we only have the lower half of the matrix, it indicates that it belonged to a woman, and one of high social standing, for only the very wealthiest in society could afford a professionally made seal matrix. The figure has a headdress which has two flowing streamers, and is kneeling as before an object of devotion. The inscription which has survived is barely legible and so far it has not been possible to identify who this aristocratic person might be. It probably dates from around 1300.

---

124 The situation between earl and king of Scots in Caithness was rather different, and there was no community seal even though the 'men of Caithness' appear on several occasions to be regarded as a cohesive body of farmers, as will be seen in Chapter 6.

THREE

Viking Earls

AD 870–1030

3.1 MYTHICAL ORIGIN

We have now looked at the range of historical and archaeological sources (Chapter 2) which give us our information about the earls, and so will turn to the completely non-historical story, or myth, of the earls' origins. This has been explained to have a 'specific meaning' as an important preliminary element in the historical account of the origins of the earldom dynasty. It is contained in the first three chapters of *Jarls' Saga*, which has recently been the subject of detailed analysis.[1] We can now better appreciate that this section introduces us to the purpose of the saga writer and the ideas about the standing of the earldom dynasty. It reveals much about the status of the earls in Norse society and history at the date when it was added in the redaction of the saga, and the mythological form is believed to carry 'ideological meaning': that is, the descent from gods and other mythical powers provided an irrefutable ideological foundation for the dynasty's power.[2]

The aim was manifold: genealogy was exceedingly significant to the status of a ruling family, and genealogical lore is an important part of Icelandic saga literature, and 'a means of historical interpretation and mythological thinking'.[3] So the stories recounted in this early section about the ancestors of the Orkney earls are intended to explain their princely status as qualities which they inherited from the prehistoric, mythical, Scandinavian north. This had a very practical significance, which was to put the earldom dynasty into a separate, independent context from the kings of Norway. This will be more

---

1 Steinsland 2011; Beuermann 2011.There is no mention of the mythical origin chapters in Clouston's *History* (1932). Discussion of the earldom family's origins in Norway in Crawford, 1987, 53, makes no reference to the first three chapters, and Thomson refers to them simply as 'daunting' (1987/2001, 24). Meulengracht Sørensen's discussion (1993) provided an enlightening analysis of what these myths tell us about the status of the earldom dynasty.

2 The redaction was written c.1230 (Chesnutt, 1993, 456), just when the Norse dynasty ended. The ideology behind this mythological introduction is discussed by Meulengracht Sørensen, 1993, 213; Steinsland, 2011, 15; Beuermann, 2011, 113–21

3 Meulengracht Sørensen, 1993, 213

fully appreciated once the history of the relationship of the earls with the kings is explored further.

3.1.1 Nordic significance of the origin myth

The context of the origin myth is set in the very far north of Scandinavia where a king called Fornjot ruled over Finland and Kvenland, 'the countries stretching to the east of what we call the Gulf of Bothnia, which lies opposite the White Sea' (*OS*, Chapter 1). The story really starts with the descendants of Fornjot, the brothers Nor and Gor and their sister Goi. They all represent the natural forces of sea, storm and burning flame, and probably have their roots in pre-Christian mythology.[4] One winter, at the time of sacrifices, Goi disappeared, so Nor and Gor made a vow to find her. They set out in search of their sister, Nor going over land and Gor searching the islands and skerries by ship. In their journies Nor conquered the Lapps and native peoples and made himself king over the coastal parts of what, of course, came to be called 'Norway'.[5] He also found his sister in Heidemark, in the Upplands district, and after fighting the local king Hrolf (who had abducted Goi) in a single combat in which neither of them was wounded, they came to terms. Nor married Hrolf's sister and Hrolf kept Goi in a reciprocal marriage arrangement. But for the purposes of the saga writer it was Gor who was more significant for he ruled over the islands 'and that's why he came to be called a sea-king'.[6] He also claimed parts of the mainland by having his ship hauled across Namdalseid to Namsen, with his hand on the tiller, thus asserting his right to all the land lying to port.[7] It was from the sea-king Gor that the earls of Møre claimed their descent, five generations down to Earl Rognvald 'the Powerful' from whom the earls of Orkney were descended (see Figure 3.1).

Seen in the context of how other genealogies were compiled the earls' genealogy is significantly different in its stress on a northern origin. *Skoldunga Saga* (which tells of the origin of the Danish kings), and Snorri Sturlason's *Heimskringla* (which uses the origin myth of the Norwegian kings in *Ynglingatal*), look to 'the immigration theory of foreign inspiration' and have Odin

---

4 Ibid., 214–15; Fornjot's three sons Aegir, Logi and Kari are clearly associated with the three elements of fire, air and water (Beuermann, 2011, 115).
5 Nor was thus the eponymous hero whose family gave names to the various districts as told in *Hversu Noregr byggðisk* ('How Norway was settled') in *Flateyar-bók* (I, 21–4) (Meulengracht Sørensen, 1993, 216)
6 *OS*, Chapter 3, and see Beuermann's discussion of the status of 'sea-king'(*sækonungr*) (2011, 121–2)
7 The significance of this episode in relation to the story of Magnus 'Barelegs' claim to Kintyre in 1098 should be noted (*Hms.* Laing, *Magnus Barefoot's saga*, Chapter. xi: *OS*, Chapter 41), see below Section 4.3.1.

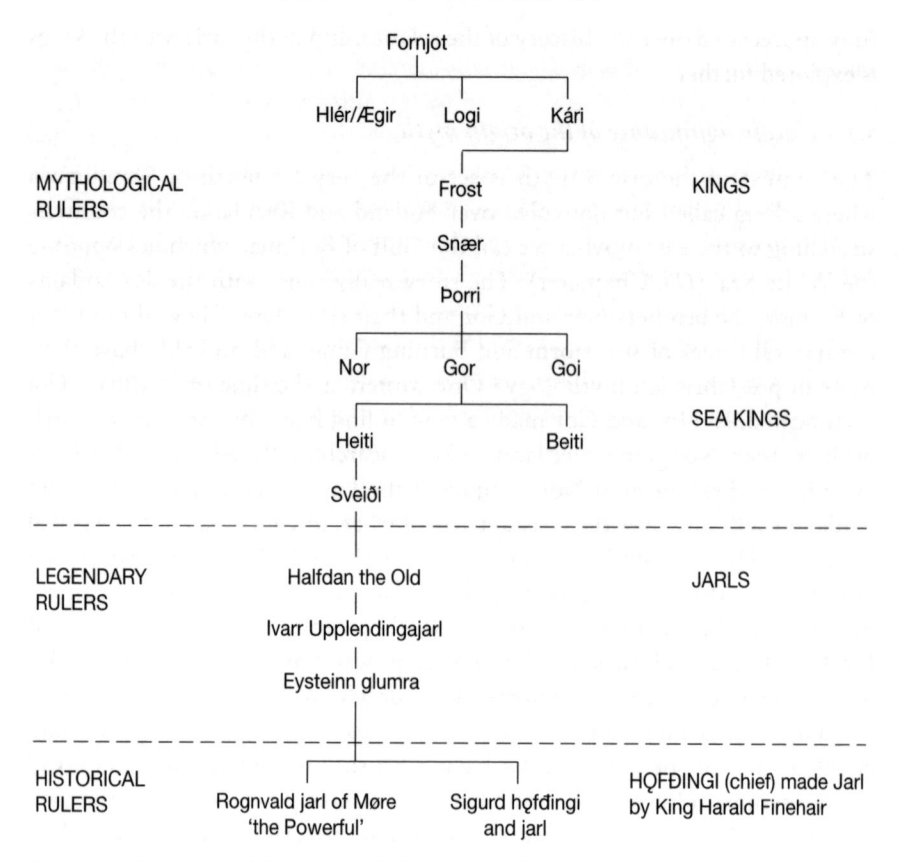

```
                        Fornjot
                           |
              ┌────────────┼────────────┐
          Hlér/Ægir       Logi         Kári
                           |
MYTHOLOGICAL              Frost                    KINGS
RULERS                     |
                          Snær
                           |
                          Þorri
                           |
              ┌────────────┼────────────┐
             Nor          Gor          Goi
                           |
                    ┌──────┴──────┐                SEA KINGS
                  Heiti          Beiti
                    |
                  Sveiði
- - - - - - - - - - -┼- - - - - - - - - - - - - - - - - - -
                     |
LEGENDARY      Halfdan the Old                     JARLS
RULERS               |
               Ivarr Upplendingajarl
                     |
               Eysteinn glumra
- - - - - - - - - - -┼- - - - - - - - - - - - - - - - - - -
               ┌─────┴─────┐
HISTORICAL                                  HǪFÐINGI (chief) made Jarl
RULERS    Rognvald jarl of Møre   Sigurd hǫfđingi   by King Harald Finehair
             'the Powerful'         and jarl
```

Figure 3.1 Ancestors of the earls of Orkney. (Based on Beuermann, 2011, fig.1)

and his three sons at the top of the genealogies.[8] The author of the *Jarls' Saga*, however, makes the Orcadian jarls go back to the original ancestor, to Fornjot himself. The reason may be that this gives the earls 'a specific Nordic self-esteem and pride', making the dynastic history of the Orkney earls senior and even more specifically Nordic than the Ynglingar.[9] The other origin myths play around with Trojan ancestry and marriage with the daughters of native families in the countries to which the ancestors of the Ynglingar and the earls of Lade emigrated. The Orkney dynasty is only linked to the extreme north and the inhospitable regions where the giants rule who were the arch-enemies of the gods but whose descendants were equal to the gods as culture heroes. This gives the Orkney jarls a special Nordic inheritance which is also linked

8 Meulengracht Sørensen, 1993, 218
9 Ibid., 219; Steinsland, 2011, 50; Beuermann, 2011, 115–17

in with Halfdan the Old, the first ancestor who bears the name of a historical character, the father of Ivarr *Upplendingajarl*, and the progenitor of the jarls of Møre (*OS*, Chapter 3). This is 'one of the great heroic dynasties', which ruled for 300 years without marrying off their women to the dynasties claiming Odin as their ancestor, and the writer of the saga was deliberately choosing the arch-enemies of the gods, the giants, as the progenitors of the earldom dynasty.[10]

So the 'specific meaning' of these three early chapters may be to set the scene for the history of the earls: indeed it is meant to do so, and we can only try to understand why this particular myth was devised at the time the saga was written – or probably even before that time. At the date the myth was promulgated the Orcadian dynasty had outlived the Møre family, and was thus the only representative of an aristocratic jarldom *ætt* ('family', 'kindred') still in existence. Genealogical origins were important to the family as such, and particularly as a powerful boost to them in relation to their overlords, the kings of Norway. This helped to give them an independence, deeply rooted in Norwegian history, or prehistory, and which in a way made them 'more Norwegian than the kings of Norway'.[11]

3.1.2 *Title of jarl*

How did a jarl, or earl, differ from a king in status and authority in medieval Norway? This is a difficult question to answer for contemporaries did not write much about such things, and we have to deduce from circumstantial evidence what an earl's position was, and how it changed over time. In English and Scottish history we know 'earl' as an exceedingly familiar and long-lived title of nobility, the 'crème de la crème of the higher aristocracy'.[12]

The ON term *jarl* is used in a double sense, and its application varied over time. The older meaning, common to Germanic societies, was that of 'nobleman', 'warrior' as opposed to the ordinary people (*karlar*, *búendr*), and this meaning is enshrined in the famous Old Norse Eddaic poem *Rígsmál* (*Rígsþula*) which distinguishes three classes of men: earls, churls and thralls.[13] The more specific meaning of 'chief', used as a dynastic title in Norse society, is what we are primarily concerned with regarding the earls of Orkney, and this was held

---

10 Meulengracht Sørensen, 1993, 219; Beuermann, 2011, 116
11 Meulengracht Sørensen, 1993, 221
12 Davies, 2009, 59. The title of earl (*comes* in Latin) became an important official title in England after the Danish conquest by Cnut the Great in 1016. Its use spread to Scotland later in the eleventh century, although the term is not fully documented until the twelfth century (Duncan, 1975, 164–5).
13 *CV sub* 'Jarl'; *KL sub* 'Jarl' col. 559. Foote and Wilson give the primary meaning of jarl as 'a distinguished man' (1970, 135). See discussion in Beuermann, 2011, 123, especially n.42

by certain powerful landed warriors and handed down to all sons in heritable transmission. This title was also conferred by kings, and historically it is very uncertain how it was appropriated by the kings in this way, although we have the story in *Heimskringla* that the unifying king of Norway Harald 'Finehair' at the end of the ninth century appointed an earl in each *fylke* ('district equivalent to a shire') with at least four *hersar* ('war-leaders') under him.[14] There was clearly tension between those dynasties which carried the *jarl* title and those calling themselves *konungr* ('king'), but, with the unifying of Norway under Harald 'Finehair', the hierarchy of kings at the top with earls below them in rank became the norm. The several chiefs who bore an earl's name as a family dignity in Norway were reduced to two thereafter: the *Háleygja-jarlar*, earls of the northern parts of Norway called Halogaland who based themselves at Trondheim in Harald 'Finehair's reign and became known as earls of 'Lade' (*Hlaðir*); and the *Mæra-jarlar* (earls of Møre) in Romsdal, from whom the Orkney earls were descended.

In the later Viking Age between the time of Harald 'Finehair' and King (and Saint) Olaf Haraldsson, the jarls of Lade were very powerful and ruled large areas of western Norway, sometimes on behalf of the Danish monarchy, which had ambitions to control southern Norway. When Hakon Ladejarl (+ 995) is said to have had sixteen jarls under him it can be understood to mean that he controlled sixteen *fylker*. Once the country was united again under Olaf Haraldsson and his son Magnus the Good in the eleventh century, only one jarl was allowed at any one time and no earl is named again until 1159.[15] The position of jarl appears in the Norwegian provincial laws (dating from the twelfth century but based on older regulations) where he stands between the *lendman* ('feudal lord') and the king, and his *wergild* ('compensation value') was half that of a king, and double that of a *lendman*, equal to a bishop.[16] After the demise of the Lade dynasty, the earldom dignity was never heritable, any new creations were few and far between, and in 1308 Hakon V's legal amendment decreed that henceforth only kings' sons and the earls of Orkney should bear the title of jarl.[17]

This decree tells us what a very special, and anomalous, dignity the earldom of Orkney had become by that date, and in some respects this was the case

---

14   *Hms.* Laing, *Saga of Harald the Fair-Haired*, Chapter 6; Foote and Wilson, 1970, 136. The youngest son of the jarl in *Rígsþula* was *konr unga* ('king') and he appears to rise above the social level of his father, which *may* symbolise the growth of Norwegian royal power under Harald Finehair (Jón Viðar Sigurðsson, 2011, 82).
15   *KL sub* 'Jarl' col. 560
16   Foote and Wilson, 1970, 136
17   *NgL*, iii, 74ff; Helle, 1964, 189

throughout its history as a Norwegian earldom. How then did it come into existence, and how did it maintain its integrity in a way that no other Norwegian earldom did?

3.2 CREATION OF THE EARLDOM OF ORKNEY

The story as told in *Jarls' Saga* is familiar and has been retold many times.[18] It concerns the exploits of members of the Møre dynasty who were believed in Icelandic tradition to be the conquerors of Orkney and Shetland; it concerns the role of King Harald 'Finehair', who as the unifier of large swathes of western Norway under his rule would later be considered to have had a hand in the establishment of the dynasty over the islands; and it concerns the actuality of the geographical situation of the islands in the lawless Viking Age. This latter point meant that those islands which lay *en route* between Norway and Scotland and Ireland were ideal raiding bases, and are likely to have been subject to control by pirate leaders who exercised fleeting hegemony in a very fluctuating manner.[19] The saga sources tell us that before Orkney was settled, it was a lair of pirates:

> It is related that in the days of Harald Haarfager ('Fine-hair') the king of Norway, the islands of Orkney, which before had been only a resort for Vikings, were settled.
>
> (*Heimskringla, Saint Olaf's Saga*, Chapter xcix)

> One summer Harald Fine-Hair sailed west over the North Sea in order to teach a lesson to certain Vikings whose plunderings he could no longer tolerate. These Vikings used to raid in Norway in summer and had Shetland and Orkney as their winter base.
>
> (*OS*, Chapter 5)

> Just about that time King Harald Fine-Hair was forcing his way to power in Norway. During the campaign many men of high standing abandoned their estates in Norway, some emigrating east, some west over the North Sea. Others used to winter in the Hebrides or in Orkney, then spend the summer raiding in Harald's kingdom, causing plenty of damage
>
> (*Eyrbyggja Saga*, trans. Pálsson and Edwards, Chapter 1)

This inchoate situation is likely to have existed from the start of Viking raiding in the west in the eighth century, but the evidence for it will have to be found in the ground, and even then it might be difficult to recognise or interpret.[20] This

---

18 Crawford, 1987, 51–6; Thomson, 2001, 25–8; Helle, 2007, 21–3; Woolf, 2007, 304–6; Beuermann, 2011, 119ff.
19 Crawford, 1987, 46–7; Woolf, 2007, 308
20 Evidence of the earliest phase of Viking raiding and settlement in the islands around Scotland

aspect of the history of the Northern Isles is prior to the establishment of the earldom and much interesting research is going on into the circumstances in Orkney in the pre-earldom phase.[21]

As far as the establishment of the earldom in Orkney is concerned we have the authority of *Jarls' Saga* that King Harald's friend Rognvald, earl of Møre, accompanied the king on his expedition west-over-sea, in which he conquered the Hebrides, Orkney and Shetland. During the campaign, Earl Rognvald's son Ivar was killed and in compensation Harald gave Orkney and Shetland to him, but Rognvald handed them to his brother Sigurd, the 'forecastleman' (*stafnbúi*) on Harald's ship. 'When the King sailed back east he gave Sigurd the title of earl and Sigurd stayed on in the islands' (*OS*, Chapter 4).[22] But how much authority does this account have? Not much, according to the opinion of those who consider that the later saga writer was interpreting the circumstances in accordance with what he knew of his own time, when the kings had full authority over earls and would never allow these earls to conquer overseas territory without any reference to the king's overlordship. This account has no doubt been coloured by later thinking and the later writers simply did not know whether the earls' ancestors had won the islands by force, or whether they owed their position to a grant from the king, but in the political circumstances of their own time 'it was necessary to stress the latter'.[23]

This sceptical approach to the sources is influenced by the belief that Harald was not in any position to be handing out lands overseas at a time when he was occupied with controlling his conquered lands in western Norway. However, Harald 'Finehair' is now getting a rather more favourable press from historians, and it is suggested that although posterity exaggerated his importance

---

is not plentiful in the archaeological record. There is doubt about the chronology of the earliest longhouses excavated by Hamilton at Jarlshof in Shetland (Graham-Campbell and Batey, 1997, 155–6). More recently excavated sites such as Scatness in Shetland provide some evidence for the early period of Scandinavian settlement (Dockrill *et al.*, 2010, 86–97), and Norwick in Unst will possibly prove to be a particularly early Viking site (Ballin Smith, 2007, 293–6). Bornais in South Uist mostly provides evidence for a well-established settlement of tenth-century date (Sharples, 2009, 107; 2012), and the longhouse recently excavated at Skaill in the west Mainland of Orkney dates from the second half of the tenth century (Griffiths and Harrison, 2011, 138)

21 Barrett, 2003, 82–8; Barrett, 2008, 415, discusses recent archaeological excavations and analyses the evidence for 'unambiguous' settlement dating to the first phase of Norse migration. The excavated headland site at Deerness in the East Mainland of Orkney is providing the material and the basis for discussion of 'chiefly' sites in an early period of Scandinavian/Viking settlement (www.mcdonald.cam.ac.uk/projects/Deerness/)

22 By handing the earldom over to his brother was Earl Rognvald attempting to 'break the initial link of dependence' on Harald? (Beuermann, 2011, 120)

23 Crawford, 1987, 53

'there are still good reasons for taking his reign as the point of departure for the political unification of Norway'.[24] Harald's relationship with such earls as Rognvald of Møre would probably entail a formal recognition of the king as their overlord although not preventing them from maintaining 'a relatively strong and independent position in their own territories'.[25] There may in fact be no valid reason to doubt Harald's leadership of an expedition (or two) west to oversee what was happening in the islands which had come under Viking influence and control during the ninth century. Whether he could control the activities of Rognvald's family in their bid to bring the islands under their dominion is, however, considered unlikely.[26]

3.2.1 *Economic interests*

What is becoming more evident, from archaeological research primarily, is the importance of economic factors in all aspects of the Viking period, including the development of political structures. Early trading centres are understood to be established and controlled by royal or chieftainly power and authority.[27] It has long been recognised that the Viking plundering of monasteries and trading centres, and the collection of ransom and tribute meant that these sea-borne pirates became the carriers of the luxury articles of western Europe. Trading centres, or towns, some of them in frontier zones, were controlled for the exchange of such goods and the manufacture of objects of war and items of everyday wear. Well-known sites where such trading and manufacture were carried out: are Kaupang in Vestfold (southern Norway), recently re-excavated;[28] Hedeby on the Schlei fjord founded by King Godred of Denmark in 808; Ribe in Jutland; and Birka in Sweden, the entrepôt centre for trading between the Baltic and the rivers of Russia.[29]

In the west we know of the importance of Dublin as a Viking town and an entrepôt between the Norwegian lands and colonial settlements around Scotland and the western world.[30] We might expect that the islands of Orkney would also be a suitable location for the exchange of goods in the Viking Age, although no evidence of a *kaupang* or beach market has yet been found.[31] Pierowall in

---

24 Krag, 2003, 185; See recent discussion of the evidence for Harald's 'unification' of west Norway by Bagge (2010, 25–6)
25 Krag, 2003, 188
26 Helle, 2007, 22; Wærdahl, 2011, 41
27 Skre, 2007, 458–61
28 Skre and Stylegar, 2004; Skre, ed., 2007; Skre, ed., 2008; Skre, ed., 2012
29 Clarke and Ambrosiani, 1991, 56–63; 73–5
30 Ibid., 102–6; Clarke, 1998; Larsen, ed., 2001; Wallace, 2008
31 Owen, 1999, 23; Distinctions should be drawn between market sites and towns (Skre, ed., 2008, 462–3), the latter founded by Scandinavian kings involving kingdoms with territorial

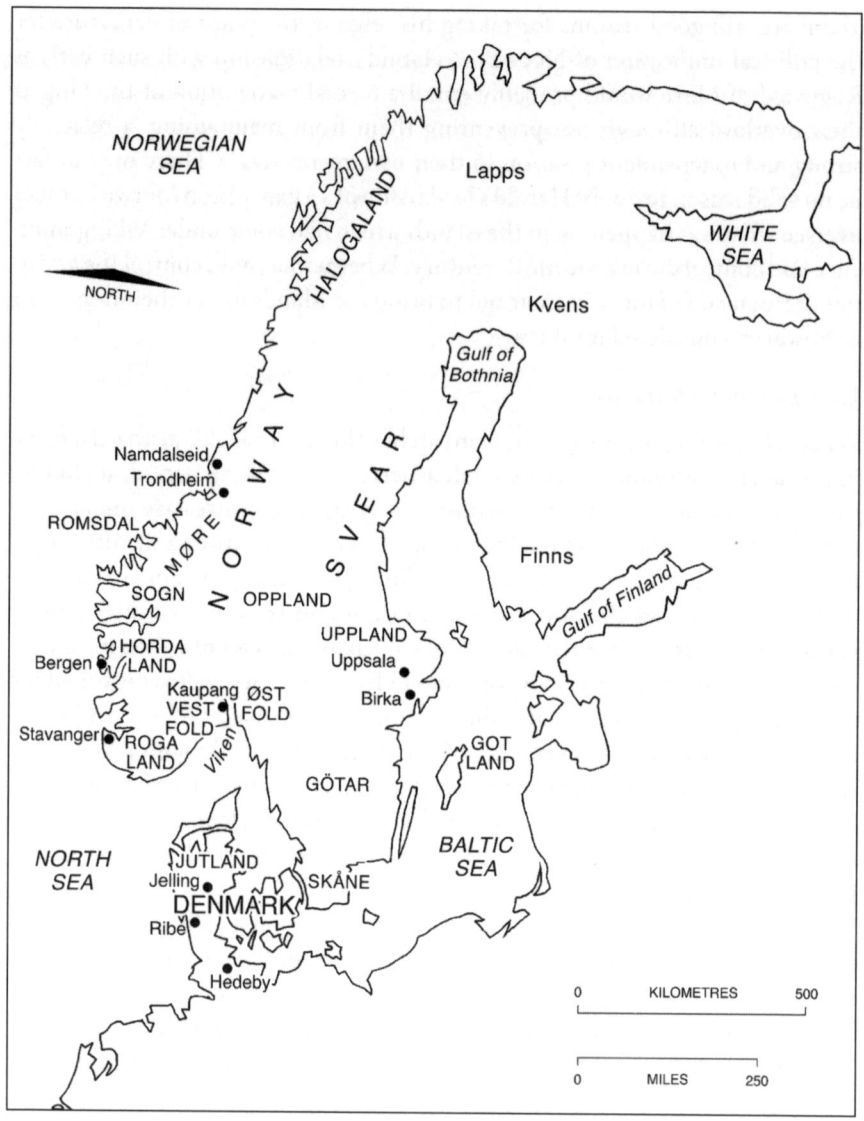

Figure 3.2 Map of Scandinavia, showing places mentioned in the text.

Westray is in a suitable geographical location for such a beach market, and the number of pagan graves found on the Links there strongly suggests that there was a Norse population of some size residing in the vicinity, which may point

---

borders, the former being tied into 'essential local and regional networks'. Neither situation is probably applicable to Orkney in the ninth century

to the existence of a community involved in some form of economic activity.[32]

When we attempt to analyse the origins of the Orkney earldom and ask how and why members of the Møre dynasty established themselves in these islands and why the kings might have been involved also, economic factors are probably very relevant. The network of trading and raiding routes which were established through the Viking ninth century necessarily included Orkney, and the islands' ideal location as a 'bridgehead' on the route westwards,[33] suitable for controlling the passage of goods between western Scotland and Ireland and the home country, would make them potentially a very profitable possession. They were also springboards for raiding and trading southwards either via the western or eastern route round the British Isles.[34] Colonial opportunities for settlement were provided by the fertile islands of Orkney, but political and economic opportunities were also on offer for a powerful dynasty with the resources and manpower to take up these opportunities and benefit from them.

The situation in Norway is obviously crucial to our interpretation of how and why the earldom of Orkney came into being. Archaeological evidence and 'Historical Speculations' have been brought into consideration. The evidence of the pagan grave material found in Norway and the many metal objects of 'Insular' origin (that is, manufactured in the British Isles and Ireland) have been analysed, and Egon Wamers' distribution map shows clearly where the raiders had come from and where they returned to with their loot.[35] Finds of Pictish, Irish and Anglo-Saxon decorated brooches and other items of adornment taken from religious objects, such as crosses, reliquaries and holy book covers, are clustered in several regions of western Norway (Trøndelag, Møre and Romsdal, Sogn and Fjordane, Rogaland) as well as Vestfold in Viken, which were political centres at the time. The very earliest finds (dated on art-historical grounds) are from Sogn and Møre and Romsdal, and it may indeed be 'significant' that it was the rulers of Møre who incorporated Orkney into their dominion in the late ninth century. Wamers' 'Historical Speculations' also suggest that Harald 'Finehair''s powerful overkingship of western Norway resulted from the benefits of Viking raiding overseas, particularly to Ireland. Harald's struggle with the Danes in southern Norway may have been first fought out in the Irish sea zone before culminating in his victory at the Battle of Hafrsfjord, in Rogaland in 868.[36] Between these two theatres of war the Orkney and Shetland islands were absolutely vital staging posts for all fleets moving between western Norway and

32 Thorsteinsson, 1968; Graham-Campbell and Batey, 1998, 129–34; Owen, 2005, 297–301
33 Wamers, 1998, 52
34 Crawford, 1987, 21
35 Wamers, 1998, 59 and fig. 2.3
36 Ibid., 71–2

the Irish Sea. They had to pass near, or through, these islands, and control of the islands was fundamental to the success of the combatants in the two battle zones. Any ambitious Norwegian chieftain, or king, who had ambitions in the western lands would therefore need to exercise power over the islands.

3.2.2 *King and jarl*

Control of Orkney and Shetland was both politically and economically important, but Harald could not maintain this single-handedly, with his main priority being the domination of the west coast chieftains and conquest of Danish-dominated southern Norway. He would have to leave the islands in the west in the hands of reliable collaborators. So the nub of the historical problem is raised – who took the initiative in gaining control of Orkney and Shetland? Was it as the saga tells us or did it happen otherwise?

Of the west Norwegian dynasties there was only one powerful enough and willing to take on this colonial challenge, and that was the Møre-jarls. The other powerful dynasty of jarls, the jarls of Hålogaland, were fully occupied at this juncture in establishing themselves in Trondheim which Jarl Hakon Sigurdsson made his main power centre, with its commercial base in nearby Lade (*laðhelle*, 'loading-place').[37] They had the whole of the north Norwegian coast to the rich hunting grounds of the Arctic under their control with its resources of furs and pelts, received as tribute from the native Lapp (Sami) population. South of Trondheim the jarls of Møre controlled the coastal lands and islands around the Romsdal fjord with fewer resources at their disposal and no evident trading centre for long-distance trade.[38] The pagan grave evidence mentioned above shows us that people from Møre were already familiar with the western Viking route and must have been traversing the seas to Shetland and Orkney for many decades through the ninth century (and probably before). It would therefore be understandable if members of the Møre dynasty were eager to take advantage of any opportunity to establish themselves in the Orkney islands, and found a new dynastic centre and commercial power base on the other side of the North Sea.

One non-saga tradition suggests that they did conquer the islands on their own account and without reference to any superior authority. This comes from the twelfth-century Latin text *Historia Norwegie* (already referred to, Section 2.3) which might be thought to be free of literary embellishments. Certainly the author, probably a learned cleric and high-ranking member of an episcopal

---

37 Andersen, 1977, 99–101; Blom, 1997, 20ff
38 Borgund near Ålesund has been excavated but does not go back to this period. Veøy in Romsdalsfjord is a possible early trading centre but on a small scale, for a more local market (Helle, 1992).

or royal retinue, discusses the conquest of the Orkney islands in a sober, realistic manner – and gives Harald 'Finehair' no role in the action at all.[39]

This text dates to the third quarter of the twelfth century and is therefore older than the surviving redactions of *Jarls' Saga* or *Heimskringla*. Because of the unique information in *Historia Norvegie* about the pre-Norse inhabitants of Orkney, the Picts and the 'papar', it can be assumed that the author must have had access to local Orkney traditions, perhaps through visiting the islands.[40] If so, there seems every reason to think that he may also have learned of the conquest of Orkney by the family of Jarl Rognvald from the same source. This information is given nowhere else.[41]

While we will never know for sure the actual facts about the creation of the earldom of Orkney, we can accept that there were two versions circulating in later centuries, one giving the initiative to Harald 'Finehair' – perhaps the official view of the Icelandic saga writers – and the other suggesting that members of the Møre family were acting in the islands on their own account.[42] What both traditions also tell us is that the sons of Jarl Rognvald made their mark in other parts of the Viking world, Rolf (Rodulfus/Rollo) in Normandy and Hrollaug in Iceland.[43] Einar eventually established the direct line of earls in Orkney (see below). Tore, the eldest son who stayed at home, was less successful and after him the Norwegian line faded into insignificance. What we can also accept is that bitter rivalry developed between the royal dynasty of Harald 'Finehair' and the Møre-jarls (despite the friendship between Harald and Rognvald extolled in *Heimskringla*). Rolf 'the Ganger', who settled in Normandy, was banished by King Harald because he had a *strandhögg* on the coast of Viken (despite his mother's pleas in elegant skaldic verse that he should be spared).[44] Jarl Rognvald himself met a violent end, killed by Halfdan Hålegg, son of King Harald, and the consequences of this murder were played out in the Orkney islands when Rognvald's son Einar wreaked vengeance on Halfdan (see Section 3.4.1). Control of the strategic islands of Orkney would appear to have been an aspect

39 See Section 2.3 for previous discussion of the conquest of the 'two races', the Picts and the Papae, by Earl Rognvald
40 Mortensen in Ekrem and Mortensen, 2003, 23
41 See Crawford (1987, 53–5) for the story in a late Irish source which also seems to be about the conquest of Orkney by the Møre family
42 A.O. Anderson thought the *Hist.Norv.* account was 'perhaps a true account of the establishment of the Norwegians' power in Orkney', and that the saga story of the gift of the islands in compensation for the death of Rognvald's son Ivar 'was probably a confirmation of the earlier seizure' (*ES*, I, 331, n.4)
43 Hms. Laing, *Saga of Harald the Fairhaired*, Chapter xxii; *Hist.Norv.*, 67–8
44 Hms. Laing, *Saga of Harald the Fairhaired*, Chapter xxiv. A *strandhögg* or 'strand-raid' was conducted by raiding Vikings who 'landed on the coasts and drove off cattle and stores for their ships'(*CV, sub strandhögg*)

of the rivalry between these two dynasties, and control of economic considerations was probably part of that rivalry.[45] Such considerations may lie at the root of the disputed origins of the Orkney earldom, although this is not mentioned in the written accounts.

The title of jarl or earl becomes indissolubly tied to Orkney for the next 600 years, and we can understand why it was used by the sons of Rognvald: because it was their family title. This must be the reason why they did not ever attempt to take on the title of king. Looking at the earldom in the context of Viking chieftaincies established around north-western Britain and Ireland, it is noteworthy that the dynasty which came to rule Man and the Isles did adopt the royal title of 'king' in contrast to Orkney.[46] The account in *Historia Norvegie* compares the two titles and describes the rulers of the southern tributary islands (the Sudreys or Hebrides) as 'kinglets' (*reguli*), saying that the southern hegemony was 'elevated' (*sublimatae*) by the rule of these kinglets, whereas the northern group (Orkney and Shetland) was 'adorned' or 'graced' (*decoratae*) by the 'protection of earls'.[47] The twelfth-century author was choosing his words carefully in distinguishing between the two dignities. By that date there was a clear hierarchy of title established throughout the north, with earls becoming definitely subordinated to kings, real kings whose powers were increasing and who distinguished themselves from 'kinglets' as well as jarls. However, in the days when Jarl Rognvald's brother and sons were installing themselves in Orkney and Shetland, the distinction between a 'jarl' and a king was not so well defined.[48] Those days were the late ninth century and according to the chronology in the Icelandic Book of Settlements (*Landnámabók*) Earl Sigurd I was ruling Orkney at the time of the settlement of Iceland (c. 870).[49]

3.3 EARL SIGURD I 'THE MIGHTY' (*HINN RÍKI*)

When we turn to consider the supposed achievements of the first Orkney earl, Sigurd, brother of Rognvald, we find his expansion onto the north Scottish mainland to be the only remembered record of his contribution to the earldom story (*OS*, Chapter 5). In fact it is the account of his death from a wound inflicted by the infected tooth of his defeated enemy, Earl Mælbrigte, and his burial in a mound on the banks of the River Oykel which takes up most of the chapter.

---

45 Andersen, 1977, 78
46 MacDonald, 1997, 31
47 *ES*, I, 330; Fisher in Ekrem and Mortensen, 2003, 65
48 Beuermann, 2011, 121ff. and especially n. 42, 126
49 Trans. Pálsson and Edwards, 16. The date of the settlement of Iceland as computed in *Landnámabók* has been confirmed by recent scientific studies of the Greenland ice core and also the tefra layer found in Iceland settlement sites and dated to 871 (Grönvold *et al.* 1995)

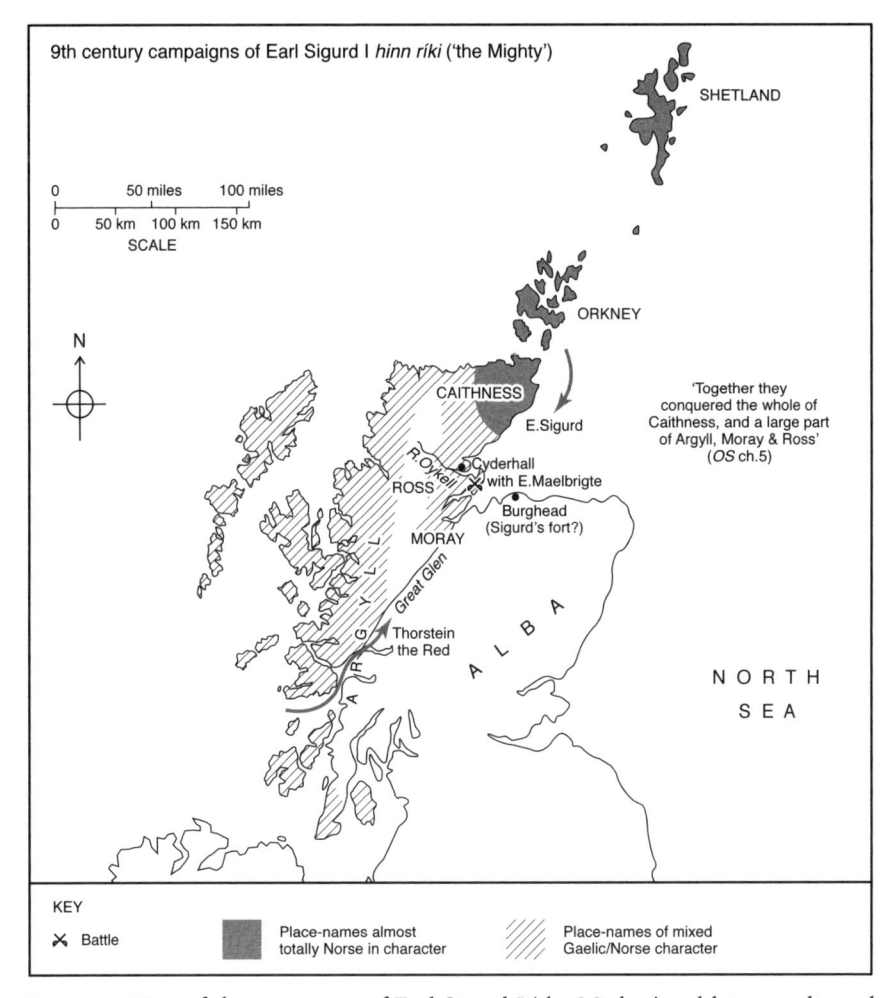

Figure 3.3 Map of the campaigns of Earl Sigurd I 'the Mighty' and his co-ordinated attack on north Scotland with Thorstein 'the Red'.

This explanation for the death of Earl Sigurd appears to reflect an Irish-Gaelic folk story motif of the 'avenging head', one of several folklore elements which it has been suggested are pointers to a mixed Gaelic–Norse culture in Orkney in the Middle Ages.[50] Was Sigurd getting his just deserts for behaving like a Celt in cutting off the heads of his defeated enemies?[51] We can also note that Sigurd is said to have strapped the severed heads to the victors' saddles 'to make

50 Almqvist, 1972–3; 1978–9, 97–9
51 Beuermann, 2011, 129. Beuermann is puzzled by the inclusion of this presentation of Earl Sigurd as dying a 'silly death' in the saga account (2011, 127–8)

a show of his triumph' (*til ágætis sér*), and that they began riding back home 'flushed with their success' (*ok hrósuðu sigri*). Perhaps his ensuing death – of a somewhat derisible nature – was told as an example of hubris for his show of unseemly pride?

The aggressive programme of conquest and settlement initiated by Earl Sigurd on the north mainland was the start of close encounters with the Celtic-speaking population of north Scotland. This was a situation which differs from the Norse conquest in the islands, where we have no saga evidence to inform us about the relationship of the incoming Norse with the native inhabitants of Orkney and Shetland. In contrast, the saga provides a picture of hard-won ascendancy by the Norse conquerors in Caithness during the tenth century.

There are many interesting aspects of this new phase of conquest which particularly concern us because it is the beginning of the link between Orkney and Caithness which leads to the circumstances of joint earldoms. First of all we should ask: why did the earls move across the Pentland Firth onto the north Scottish mainland and embark on long wars with native rulers of the area? It was a hard struggle to win control and this fact emerges clearly from the *Jarls' Saga* itself. First of all there was an opportunity to join forces with another famous Viking warrior, Thorstein 'the Red' (*hinn Rauða*), supposedly the grandson of Ketil 'Flat-neb' (*flat-nefr*) from the Hebrides, and the son of Aud 'the Deep-Minded' (*djúpauðga*) and Olaf 'the White', king of Dublin, who was also seeking to expand onto the Scottish mainland. He would have been easily able to move north-east up the Great Glen route and meet up with Sigurd in Moray and Ross. Theirs was a famous partnership, and many different Old Norse sources refer to their campaigns and their successes in conquering 'the whole of Caithness and a large part of Argyll, Moray and Ross' (*Katanes allt ok mikit annat af Skotlandi, Mærhoefi ok Ros*) (*OS*, Chapter 5).[52]

The motivation which does explain much of the aggression of war-bands in the early medieval period was the need for plunder. The leaders of war-bands on the move had to present their military followers with booty to satisfy the demand for wealth, and which sufficed for payment and reward. The Vikings plundered monasteries, towns and fertile settlements throughout north and west Europe in the ninth, tenth and eleventh centuries for this reason and to accrue wealth which they took back home. There is no evidence of any wealthy

52 *Landnamabók* says the two of them won *meirr en hálft Skotland*.What the Icelandic authors meant by 'Scotland' is always difficult to translate, but in this instance it may be that the western dominion of the Gaels is meant, i.e. Argyll. However, the statement in the *Chronicle of the Kings of Alba* (or the *Scottish Chronicle*) that 'Northmen wasted Pictland' (*ES*, 1, 395) or 'ravaged Pictavia' (Hudson, 1998, 153–4) at this time is possibly referring to the same campaigns (Crawford, 1987, 57)

monastic or ecclesiastical establishments anywhere in north Scotland north of Easter Ross.[53] But this was frontier territory which provided opportunity for expansion and settlement. If control was won as far as the Firthlands (to the Moray and Cromarty Firths), the earls and their followers would have access to the natural land route which cuts across the Highlands of Scotland, the Great Glen.[54] The Firthlands of Easter Ross were also fertile grain-growing territory, with access to good timber resources. The need for access to timber resources is likely to have been as urgent in the late ninth century as it was to the later earls in the eleventh century[55] (see Section 4.2.1).

Moray and Ross are specifically mentioned in the saga as territory conquered by Thorstein and Sigurd. Another indicative statement is that Sigurd built a fort 'southwards in Moray' (*OS*, Chapter 5), although this has caused historians some worries. It does strengthen the possibility that some control may have been exercised over the north coast of Moray.[56] The advantage of controlling both shores of the Moray Firth (*Breiðafjǫrðr* 'Broad-firth' in the sagas) would be that it enabled these sea-borne warriors to access the water routes leading to the Great Glen. However, any control which might have been established by them over the Great Glen route would have been difficult to maintain permanently and Sigurd's burial north of the Dornoch Firth certainly points to that waterway being the southern limit of effective control at the date of his death c.892 (see Section 3.3.1). The absence of any known pagan graves in Ross is an indicator that Norse settlement did not take place in Ross in the late ninth century.

These geographical factors may have been basic to the driving ambitions

---

53 There were early Christian monastic sites at Tarbat and Rosemarkie in Easter Ross. Excavations at the former (Portmahomack) have produced evidence that it was indeed attacked earlier in the ninth century from the evidence of demolition and burning which has been uncovered, as well as the destruction of Christian-Pictish sculpture (Carver, 2008, 135, 138, 144)

54 The potential of this land route, and its significance for earldom strategies as opposed to the long and dangerous sea route round Cape Wrath have been discussed in Crawford, 1986, 40–4; 1987, 22–4, 67; Crawford and Taylor, 2003, 6.

55 Crawford, 1995

56 This phrase is usually translated 'in the south of Moray' which of course points to an inland location which would be a rather unlikely place for Sigurd to build a fort; he would establish a coastal stronghold which he could access by ship. The ON *þar lét hann gera borg á sunnanverðu Mærhoefi* may be a slightly ambivalent indication from a northern perspective that he caused a fort to be built somewhere 'to the south' in Moray. The Dark Age coastal stronghold at Burghead, on the north coast of Moray, would have been an ideal location, and there is some archaeological evidence that it was attacked in the late ninth/early tenth century (Graham-Campbell and Batey, 1998, 105). A silver horn-mount of ninth-century date, apparently of Anglo-Saxon type, was also discovered there which is perhaps significant, but is no direct evidence for the fort ever having been in Norse possession.

which led Sigurd and Thorstein to come together and join forces in what appears to have been a very wide-ranging strategy of conquest (according to the saga statements). The immediate consequences would have been the settlement of Norse speakers along the coasts of Caithness and Sutherland and penetrating some distance up the straths or dales which run deep into the mountainous interior. Warfare would have been followed by consolidation of possession and the settlement of Norse speakers on the occupied land.[57] The place-names of Caithness and Sutherland are the source of evidence which give us assurance on this aspect of conquest. How long this process took is not known, for the chronology of the different names ending in the elements *-ból*, *-bólstaðr*, *-staðr* and *-setr* is not easily established[58] (see Section 3.3.2). However, we should see the process as a colonial offshoot from the lands already settled in Orkney.

How long did the partnership of Sigurd and Thorstein last? Thorstein's position may have been the more dominant of the two. He is said in *Landnámabók* to have made himself king over the territories he conquered, no doubt taking that title because his father had also been a 'king'. It is recorded in *Heimskringla* that his daughter Groa was married to a Celtic chieftain in Caithness called Dungadr.[59] If this is reliable tradition, then it suggests that he was in a position to come to terms with a native ruler who probably had retained authority in north-east Caithness, indicating that he was involved in social arrangements to the extent that his daughter was used as part of a settlement negotiation. Dynastic marriages of this kind are evidence of power politics and important indicators of political strengths and aspirations.

However, Thorstein was killed in battle, and treachery on the part of the Scots was remembered as the cause of his death. Sigurd survived, to be regarded as the conqueror of Caithness, providing the basis for future Orkney earls' claims to authority over Caithness.

3.3.1 *Sigurd I's death and burial, c.892*

Despite Sigurd's victory over Mælbrigte, 'earl of the Scots',[60] somewhere in the frontier zone between their spheres of authority, it was remembered that Mælbrigte was nonetheless the cause of Earl Sigurd's death. As mentioned, he received a fatal wound from his victim's tooth which was sticking out from

---

57 Crawford, 2004, 108
58 Crawford, 1987, 108–14
59 *Hms*. Laing, *Saga of King Olaf Haraldsson*, Chapter XCIX. In *Laxdaela Saga* Groa is said to have been married when in Orkney with Aud 'the Deep-Minded' (trans. Magnusson and Pálsson, 52)
60 A term probably equivalent to 'mormaer', 'great steward', used of members of the Moray dynasty at a later date

VIKING EARLS: AD 870–1030

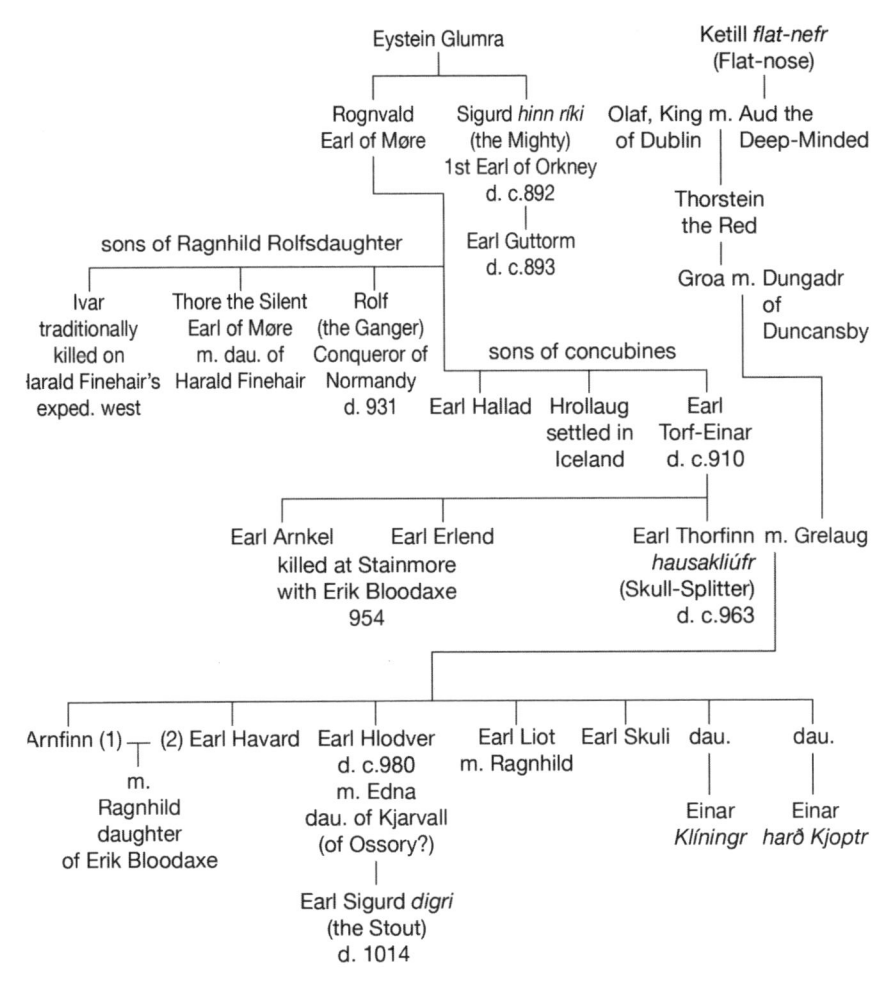

```
                    Eystein Glumra                          Ketill flat-nefr
                          |                                   (Flat-nose)
              ┌───────────┴──────────┐                             |
          Rognvald              Sigurd hinn ríki    Olaf, King m. Aud the
          Earl of Møre          (the Mighty)        of Dublin | Deep-Minded
                |               1st Earl of Orkney            |
                |                   d. c.892                Thorstein
                |                       |                    the Red
  sons of Ragnhild Rolfsdaughter   Earl Guttorm                |
  ┌─────────┬──────────────┐         d. c.893             Groa m. Dungadr
Ivar      Thore the Silent  Rolf                                of
traditionally  Earl of Møre (the Ganger)                    Duncansby
killed on  m. dau. of   Conqueror of    sons of concubines
Harald Finehair's Harald Finehair  Normandy  ┌──────┬────────┐
exped. west                d. 931      Earl Hallad Hrollaug  Earl
                                                  settled in Torf-Einar
                                                  Iceland    d. c.910
                    ┌────────────┬──────────────────┬────────┘
                Earl Arnkel   Earl Erlend       Earl Thorfinn m. Grelaug
                killed at Stainmore             hausakliúfr
                with Erik Bloodaxe              (Skull-Splitter)
                      954                       d. c.963
        ┌──────────────┬─────────┬────────┬────────┬─────┬──────┐
Arnfinn (1) ─ (2) Earl Havard  Earl Hlodver Earl Liot Earl Skuli dau. dau.
            m.                   d. c.980  m. Ragnhild            |    |
         Ragnhild                m. Edna                        Einar Einar
         daughter                dau. of Kjarvall               Klíningr harð Kjoptr
         of Erik Bloodaxe        (of Ossory?)
                                    |
                                Earl Sigurd digri
                                (the Stout)
                                d. 1014
```

Figure 3.4 Genealogical tree of the ninth–tenth-century earls from Sigurd I (+c.892) to Sigurd II (+1014).

the severed head which Sigurd was carrying back north strapped to his saddle. Sigurd's burial in a mound (indicating a pagan burial) on *Ekkjalsbakki* ('banks of the River Oykel') was also remembered, although the place of Thorstein's burial was not. This may be because of the significance of the River Oykel in the earldom conquest of the north Scottish mainland. It is mentioned on other occasions as an important boundary between Norse and Scottish territory (*OS*, Chapters 74, 78) (see Colour plate 11). The Kyle of Sutherland or Dornoch Firth, which is the estuary of the River Oykel, is the northernmost of the firths of Easter Ross, and the Pictish name Oykel was adopted by the Norse incomers as *Ekkjal*.[61] Remarkably, a place-name tells us where Sigurd's burial mound most probably was located, for the farm-name Cyder Hall or Sidera is derived from the name of an estate called *Syvardhoch*, recorded in a thirteenth-century document.[62] This is 'Sigurd's howe' (ON *Sigurðarhaugr*), and the burial mound (*haugr*) must have lain somewhere near the farm of Cyder Hall, which is on the north side of the estuary, near Dornoch, although the actual burial mound has never been located.[63]

The remarkable record of Sigurd's burial in this location, and in a pagan manner, has some significance for the reliability of the saga record of his achievements. The brief account of his conquests starts with the statement that he was 'a great ruler' (*OS*, Chapter 5). He is known as *hinn ríki* ('the Powerful' or 'the Mighty'), an epithet accorded to only one other earl. The author of the addition to *Orkneyinga Saga* known as 'Harald Maddadson's Saga' says that 'according to people who have written on the subject' the most powerful earls were Sigurd Eysteinsson, Thorfinn Sigurdsson, and Harald Maddadson (*OS*, Chapter 109). Sigurd's conquest of the north mainland of Scotland is corroborated by the spread of Norse settlement-names (see Section 3.3.2), and also attested by the pagan burials which have been found in both Caithness and Sutherland.[64] These are likely to date from the earliest spread of pagan settlers into the area from the Northern Isles in the late decades of the ninth century and early decades of the tenth century. Sigurd's own pagan burial in a prominent location on the north side of the Dornoch Firth is emblematic of his success in conquering north Scotland and therefore making it possible for his warriors and their families and followings to move into this territory and colonise it.

The study of burial mounds in Scandinavia has recently brought new understanding of the purpose of such monuments, or at least has brought new theories to bear on their potential significance. The finest examples are in eastern Sweden (Gamla Uppsala), Denmark (Jelling in Jutland) and at Borre in Vestfold, Norway. Many other mounds are known along Norway's west coast such as Storhaugen and Grønhaugen at Avaldsness on the main sailing route between Stavanger and Bergen.[65] This is the locality where Harald 'Finehair' himself is said by Snorri to have been 'buried under a mound at Haugar in

---

61 Watson, 1904, 17–18
62 *CSR*, no. 9
63 Joseph Anderson was the first to make the connection between all these name forms in 1873 (notes to Hjaltalin and Goudie's translation of *OS*, p.107, n. 2), where he says 'This place named Siward's Hoch (*Sigurd's haug*) at that early date, could be no other than the traditional site of Earl Sigurd's grave-mound'. See discussion of the possible location of the burial mound in Crawford, 1986, 38–9
64 Crawford, 1987, fig. 31; Batey, 1993; Crawford, 1996a, fig. 71
65 Opedal, 1998

Kormsund' (*Hms. Harald Fairhair's Saga*, Chapter xlv). Such mounds were evidently built and located at strategic points for symbolic purposes, and these have been explained as marking a new social and religious identity, especially in a frontier environment where two strong political powers were opposing each other. This public mode of ostentatious burial may signify times of crisis and stress, and the implantation of a new political and military elite.[66] The situation in north Scotland after the phase of Viking conquest can certainly be seen as reflecting such a new political domination. Sigurd's burial in a mound on the north side of the River Oykel, near the mouth of the Dornoch Firth, can be interpreted as a deliberate and highly visible statement made by the military retinue commemorating their dead leader's victories against the native rulers in the locality. The choice of location on a waterway which was a boundary marker made the burial mound an especially significant symbol intended to intimidate those who ruled the other bank of the waterway. It must have signified that control over the territory north of the Oykel was firmly in the hands of the new Scandinavian political and military elite.[67] However, there is no obvious surviving burial mound in evidence at Cyderhall, unlike the magnificent examples in Scandinavia.

The very mention of the earl being buried in a mound ('howe-laid' as it is sometimes quaintly translated) signifies pagan ritual,[68] and the record of scattered equipped graves throughout Caithness and Sutherland testifies to the settlement of pagan Norse men and women at this same time. The conquests of Sigurd and Thorsteinn would have enabled the settlement to take place and although we have no direct evidence from the saga of how this settlement proceeded, the distribution of Norse place-names throughout this area provides evidence for the replacement of some of the native population by Norse speakers. It could only have taken place under the protection of powerful military operators; in these coastlands the threat of attack from the surviving Celtic peoples, who probably controlled the mountainous interior, must have been real and continuous.

---

66 Opedal, 1998, 172, citing Hedeager, 1990
67 Hedeager (1990) and Myrhe (1992) interpret such mounds as evidence for new power dynasties who were in the process of building up their power (Fuglestvet og Hernaes, 1996, 142)
68 The likelihood that Thorstein was influenced by Christianity (his mother Aud 'the Deep-Minded' was indeed a Christian according to the Icelandic sources) may explain why there is no mention of his burial place in the saga sources.

3.3.2 *Place-name and archaeological evidence for Norse settlement on the north mainland of Scotland*

The study of place-names is an important part of our understanding of the extent of Norse settlement in Scotland; indeed, in many areas it is our *only* source of evidence. Wherever we recognise Scandinavian names for farms we can be sure that Norse speakers put down roots and settled in that particular locality. Opinion among philologists and historians is now tending to agree that even those Norse names which do not denote a farm but which are topographical (referring to a feature in the landscape) may also be an indication of the earliest phase of Norse settlement.[69] The lack of habitative names in a locality may merely indicate that the colony was not long-lived enough for division of farm-holdings to take place, which is what probably gave rise to the *-staðir*, *-bólstaðr* and *-setr* names. These are the habitative elements in a Norse place-name which signify a farming settlement of some kind (Figure 3.5).

The map of the linguistic regions of Scandinavian Scotland shows that Region 1, which includes the Northern Isles and north-east Caithness, consists of place-names of 'almost totally Norse character'.[70] Region 2 covers a much wider and more diverse area which is shown to include most of north Scotland, and extends down the eastern seaboard almost as far as the Great Glen. This north Scottish territory has a very mixed linguistic character, which has been studied in only a few parts, in north-east Caithness, for example, and in the southernmost frontier zone.[71] The habitative Norse place-names throughout Scotland were first plotted by W.F. Nicolaisen (1969; 1976), and we are still mostly reliant on his maps for understanding the pattern. His attempt to build a chronology based on the different names and the pattern of their distribution has been to some extent undermined by more recent assessment,[72] which casts doubt on the absolute chronological sequencing of these names. Nonetheless, Nicolaisen's maps show how the different habitative names in north-east Caithness, such as the *-bólstaðr* and *-setr* names, reflect the distribution of these farm-names, as known in Orkney. The *-staðir* names however are sparsely represented in Caithness, and there is something very specific about the distribution of these names in Orkney also.[73] South of Caithness the *-bólstaðr* names

---

69 See discussion in *Scand. Scot.* of the issues as they stood in 1987 (111), followed by further comments in Crawford, ed., 1995, 12, and more recently with reference to the topographical names of the western seaboard of Scotland, Kruse, 2005; Jennings and Kruse, 2009; Markús, 2012
70 Crawford, 1987, fig. 25; Graham-Campbell and Batey, 1998, fig. 3.1
71 Waugh, 1985; 1989; Crawford and Taylor, 2003
72 See comments and references in Crawford, ed., 1995, 9–13; 2004, 109 n.12
73 For the most recent discussion of *staðir* farms in Orkney see Crawford, 2006

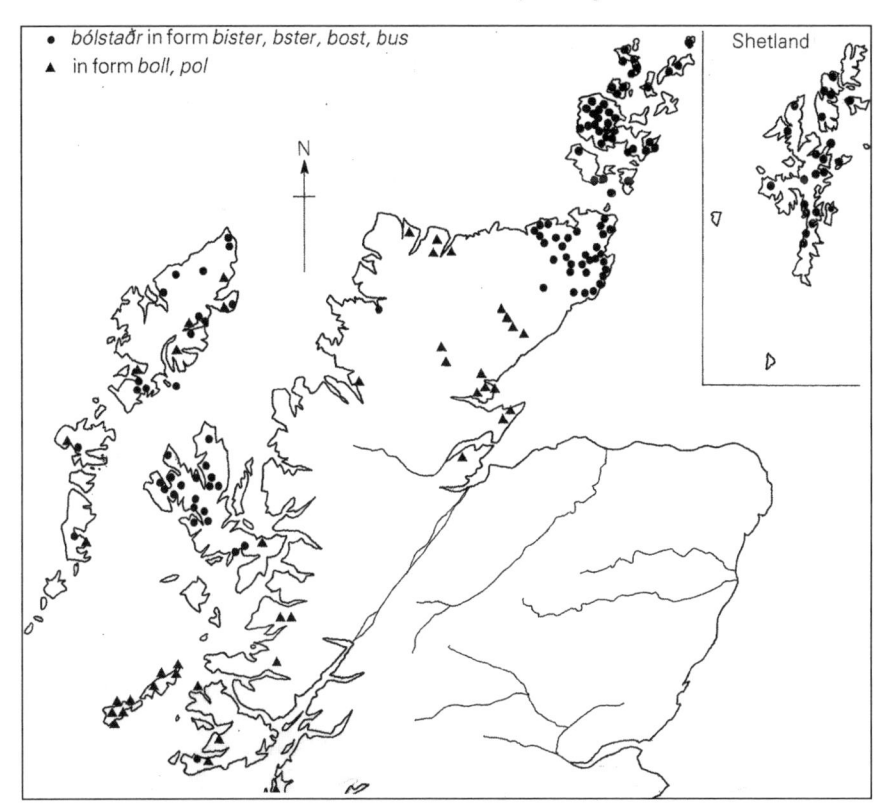

Figure 3.5 Map of Old Norse *bólstaðr/boll/pol* names in north and west Scotland, showing the extent of Viking settlements which were so well established that they had been divided. (Based on Crawford, 1987, fig. 27)

are replaced by names ending in simplex *-ból* (still a Norse element), and they are similarly found in the extreme north-west mainland, and in the Hebrides.[74]

There is no doubt that the Norse place-names of Caithness and Sutherland represent a southward movement of Norwegian-speaking settlers onto the north Scottish mainland from Orkney. As already noted, they would only have been able to move into this mainland territory in the wake of conquest and the establishment of peaceful conditions which would allow the immigrants and their families opportunities to colonise.[75] This most probably started after Sigurd's conquests in the late ninth century, but we cannot say that that is when

74 Fraser, 1995; Cox 1994; Gammeltoft, 2001, App. 2, 299ff.
75 Although the date of c.800 is generally proposed for 'the initial appearance of Scandinavians in Caithness' (Waugh, 1993, 121), large-scale permanent settlement is unlikely to have occurred until much later in the ninth century

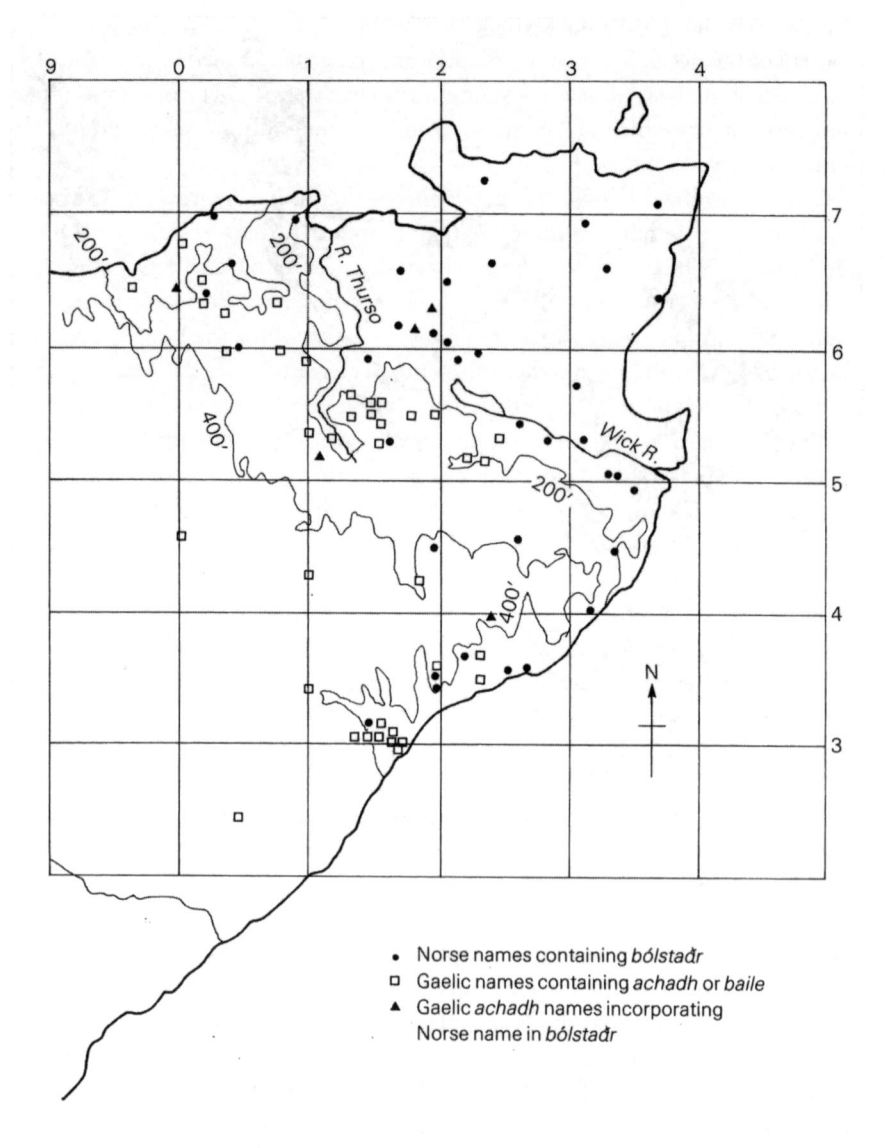

Figure 3.6 Map of Old Norse *bólstaðr* ('farm') names and Gaelic *achadh* or *baile* ('farm') names in Caithness, showing how the north-east corner north of the Thurso and Wick Rivers has no surviving Gaelic habitative names, whereas the region to the south and west of the rivers has a more mixed Old Norse and Gaelic nomenclature. (Crawford, 1987, fig. 26, based on Nicolaisen, 1982, fig. 5.1)

the different habitative names would have been given. As we will see, Norse control of the north Scottish mainland was not permanent from that time. The most recent analysis of *-bólstaðr* names estimates that these farm-names represent settlements which are likely to date very generally to 'some time in the tenth century'.[76]

Turning to the other source of evidence – that of pagan graves in the north mainland – we do not find that they help to refine the date of settlement much more closely. The burials which have been discovered in Caithness and Sutherland are rather a motley collection, and very few have been excavated with modern techniques or sophisticated analysis – except for the boy's grave from Balnakeil Bay in the far north-west of the Scottish mainland.[77] The surviving finds indicate a type of burial and quality of grave goods which compare with the Orkney corpus and suggest a similar social level of individual and of material culture. The majority have been discovered in the north-east corner of Caithness, mostly on the coast, with a cluster in south-east Sutherland. These two areas can therefore be regarded as foci of early Norse settlement, but it is not possible to date them any more closely than to the second half of the ninth and early part of the tenth century.[78] This can be regarded as fitting the period of Sigurd's conquests, and if, as stressed above, we regard those conquests as essential for settlement of Norse speakers on the land – who were also followers of the earl from Orkney – then the likely date would be nearer to the year AD 900.

3.4 THE TENTH CENTURY – SURVIVAL AND ACCOMMODATION

The whole of the tenth century appears to have been a time of violence and turmoil in the north, and Sigurd's hard-won conquests were not easily maintained. This period has been little written about and the saga story is patchy, but the indications are that the Møre dynasty struggled to establish its position in Orkney in a situation where control was fluid and rivalry with the Norwegian king's dynasty turned violent. It is quite clear from the saga sources

---

76 Gammeltoft, 2001, 162, and fig. 3, for an updated map of *bólstaðr* names
77 Batey, 1993, 157. The skeletal remains suggest that this was the burial of a young person, aged between eight and thirteen, probably male (Low *et al.*, 2000, 28). The character of the grave goods buried with him was entirely Norse, and consisted of the usual weaponry, as well as personal items. These indicate that a boy of such a young age was, surprisingly, regarded as adult, although there was no indication that he had died a violent death. The range and wealth of the grave goods certainly tell us that he had come from the upper stratum of Norse society, but whether he had died on a Viking voyage, or not, is impossible to say. The suggestion that he might be identified with the son of Rognvald of Møre, Ivarr, who was killed on Harald Finehair's expedition west (as was initially done on the discovery of the burial) is implausible, and on the present evidence impossible to prove
78 Graham-Campbell and Batey, 1998, 154

that the native aristocracy in north Scotland put up a very hard fight against the Scandinavian incomers whose struggle to control even Caithness continued for many decades. In the middle of the century Orkney was drawn into the wider sphere of Viking activity in Britain as a result of the ambitions of the son of Harald 'Finehair', Erik 'Blood-axe', for whom access to the resources of the Northern Isles was essential to success further south.

3.4.1 *Einar: the one-eyed slave-born earl (fl.900)*

The need for a powerful leader and successful warrior to maintain control over the lands won by conquest is evident from the saga record of what happened on the death of Earl Sigurd I (c.892). Hallad, son of Earl Rognvald (who succeeded his cousin Guttorm Sigurdsson, who died, childless, after a year), was sent west by his father, and was said to have been given the title of earl by King Harald. However, unable to control those Vikings who were raiding the islands and Caithness at the time, he gave up the earldom and retired back to Norway as a 'common landholder' (*hauldr*) (*OS*, Chapter 5). This opened the way for another son of Rognvald, Einar ('Torf-Einar'), to restore the family's possession of the islands, and a skaldic verse records his killing of two Danish raiders who had 'set up camp' there. This gave him full power over Orkney and he 'became a great leader' says the saga which then goes on to explain his nickname which derived from the fact that he was the first man to dig peat for fuel. As it is also said that this happened at Torfness in Scotland, usually assumed to be Tarbat Ness in Easter Ross, a part of the north mainland with which Einar has no other connection, this explanation can be understood to be a later, erroneous, linking of nickname with place-name.[79]

Einar was the real progenitor of the earldom line, but being the son of a slave-born concubine of Earl Rognvald did not give him the best start in life, and this defect of birth is developed into a literary theme by the saga writer. His father eventually agreed to let him go west to maintain the family conquests, although disparaging his chances of ruling successfully 'considering the kind of mother you have', and saying that he was glad to be rid of him. This has been shown to be a variant of a common scene in Old Norse literature, the 'provocation scene' which can be the provoking of men, usually sons by their mothers, to avenge the

---

[79] Crawford, 2004b. However, the connection with 'Torf' (ON *torf*, 'peat') may be in some way a distant echo or resonance of the situation which the colonisers met when settling in islands which provided no wood for fuel, a point made by Snorri who, commenting on Einar's nickname, adds 'as in Orkney there are no woods' (*Hms.* Laing, *Saga of Harald the Fairhaired*, Chapter xxvii). This was a situation which certainly must have meant that the Norse settlers had to change their customary way of getting fuel for cooking and warmth, although it is unlikely that the earl himself went out to the peat banks with a 'tuskar' in his hands! ('tuskar', ON *torfskeri*, 'peat-cutter' is the Orkney and Shetland word for a peat-cutting spade)

death of a kinsman, or to restore the family honour.[80] In this case, it is his lowly maternal origins which are being used as the means of provocation towards Einar, perhaps challenging him to prove himself to be the opposite of what was expected of him in the circumstances. This very fact – the slave background of the mother of a king or earl's son – is also a feature of Old Norse literature, and one which can sometimes be taken to indicate a promising future. It may indicate that the offspring was the result of alliances of socially opposite parties, and that has links with the mythic origins of royal and princely houses.[81] Einar's origin may therefore key into the mythic background of the line of the Møre jarls, set out in Chapter 1 of OS (as discussed above, Section 3.1). It suggests that this was an additional factor in the myths surrounding Einar's role in the saga as a highly significant progenitor of the line of Orkney jarls, the one from whom all the following earls were afterwards descended.

Einar of course proved himself to be a worthy warrior, remembered in the later Middle Ages as having *'be lang tyme brukit* [enjoyed the possession of] *the said Erildome, habundand* [abundant] *in mycht and riches'*('Genealogy of the Earls').[82] The writer of the saga derived most of his information from the five skaldic verses which had supposedly been composed by Einar himself about his contest with Halfdan 'Long-Leg' (*háleggr*), for this earl had another attribute, poetic skills, which has meant that his reputation lives on in the skaldic corpus of Old Norse literature. Halfdan was the son of Harald 'Finehair' whose relations with the Møre family deteriorated into a feud, and after the killing of Earl Rognvald by Halfdan and his brother, Halfdan sought refuge in Orkney from his father's retribution (*OS*, Chapter 8). At first Einar fled over to Scotland, and Halfdan set himself up as 'king' over the islands for a period.[83]

Later in the year Einar returned and fought it out in a sea battle with Halfdan who jumped overboard and sought refuge in *Rinansey* (?North Ronaldsay). His discovery was followed by his ceremonial killing, said to be a victory offering to Odin in revenge for his killing of Einar's father, Rognvald. The motivation is clearly expressed in Einar's verses, as is his scorn for his brothers' failure to carry out the vengeance themselves. The 'blood-eagling' of Halfdan, a ritual method of dispatching your enemy by slitting the backbone and cutting the ribs so that the victim's lungs could be pulled through and spread out like an eagle's wings

---

80 Mundal, 1993, 249, and see further discussion of this aspect by Beuermann, 2011, 131–3
81 This is the main thread of Gro Steinsland's thesis about the ideology of kingship which can be understood as a result of a mythic alliance between gods and giantesses (Steinsland, 1991, and see discussion of this theory as it relates to Einar in Mundal, 1993, 251)
82 *Bann.Misc.*, iii, 75
83 The difference in title from 'jarl' is exemplified here, showing again that the son of a king took the title of king

is described in the prose section, and may be a later elaboration.[84] The king's son was buried under a mound of stones, and the tax which Halfdan wanted Einar to pay was symbolically alluded to in his verses as the stones which were thrown onto the cairn:

> 'throw, good boys, since the victory is ours, stones at *Háfæta* (Longleg), I choose for him hard taxes'[85]

This skaldic reference to 'hard taxes' (*harðan skatt*) which were evidently being demanded of Einar by Halfdan – as payments in recognition of his pre-eminence over the earl – is a very important first reference to the symbol of the Orkney earls' subjection to the kings of Norway, that is, payments of tribute in bullion. Einar's rejection of the demand, followed by his killing of Halfdan, is the first violent event in what was going to be a tense relationship between the earls and their nominal overlords on the other side of the North Sea. Einar had indeed proved himself a worthy earl and risen to the challenge thrown at him by his father. It is also noteworthy that this earl's status was enhanced through association with Odin, who was the progenitor of the royal dynasty of Harald 'Finehair', and not found among the earls' mythic ancestors.[86] When was this association built into the saga account of Earl Einar? It does not appear in the skaldic verses, but it is implied in the prose passages; even the description of Einar as tall and ugly, and 'one-eyed', though still 'the most keen-sighted of men' (*OS*, Chapter 7) is an implicit reference to Odin's well-known characteristic. This is a deliberate boosting of the militaristic properties of the earldom, with pagan overtones.

Einar's final stanza was directed towards the victim's father, Harald 'Finehair', as Einar prepared for the inevitable arrival of the king seeking compensation for the killing of his son. This is even more provocative, apparently addressing the king as 'Man with the fair beard! (*Seggr með fogr skeggi*) and concluding: 'Men say that the brave King is a danger to me; I shall not be afraid of that, I have made a cut in Harald's shield' (trans. Mundal, 1993, 253).

However, when King Harald did sail west seeking compensation, Einar fled to Caithness, and a reconciliation package was negotiated by mediators. A 'fine' (*gjald*) of sixty gold marks was laid on the islands, which Einar agreed to pay on condition that the 'odal' (*óðul*) rights of all the landowners were made over

---

84 The veracity of the saga account of Halfdan's murder has been doubted, and the phrase in the skaldic verse 'torn by the eagle's talon' interpreted as something more symbolic (see discussion in Crawford, 1987, 196).
85 Trans. Mundal, 1993, 253; the epithet *háfæta* is a deliberately derisive term, being the feminine form of 'Long-leg' (*háleggr*) (Beuermann, 2011, 134).
86 Beuermann, 2011, 135–6

to him, which the *bonder* agreed to.[87] So Einar paid the whole sum, and the saga adds that the earls held 'all the estates' (*áttu óðul oll*) for a long time until Earl Sigurd Hlodversson gave them back to the farmers (see Section 3.5). The correlation was that the earl was also allowed to retain his earldom. There is nothing inherently unlikely in this record of a reconciliation between king and earl, and the payment of compensation for murder of a family member accords well with what is known about the functioning of society in the Viking period. This fine of sixty gold marks is a possible kernel of actuality in the saga story.[88] However, the matter of overlordship of land and the development of legal theory about landed possessions and acknowledgement of superiority over land was an area in which nothing had been determined as early as this (early tenth century) in Scandinavian society.

The first clash between earl and king had ended in a compromise, and the event shows that those in possession of the settled lands west-over-sea were not easily dislodged from their island possessions by those claiming overlordship from mainland Norway. However, retribution meted out by kings with superior war-fleets who appeared over the horizon in person was daunting enough for the island earls to come to terms – sensibly – for the kings went back home again and earls were left in charge of the islands. Einar appears to have enjoyed his earldom untroubled by rivals for the rest of his life, dying in his bed, unusually for a Viking earl. We are not told where Einar was buried, but it would surely be in pagan mode under a 'howe' like his uncle, Sigurd 'the Mighty', somewhere in the islands, where he was firmly based.

3.4.2. *Struggle for control of Caithness*

There is no mention of Einar being active outside the islands, only that he fled to Caithness when King Harald sailed to Orkney. He was not apparently pursued there by Harald, and it may be significant that all the negotiations over the odal rights are said to have concerned the Orkney farmers. What was happening on the north Scottish mainland? We hear nothing more until the sons of Thorfinn Torf-Einarsson 'Skull-Splitter' (*hausakliúfr*) are recorded as engaging in battles with native rulers in Caithness (*OS*, Chapter 10). The winning of land and authority in north Scotland was a hard fight, and we can

---

87 This arrangement over the farmers' odal (their family lands held with certain rights) has been much debated. If it is a retrospective interpretation of the situation in the islands regarding the earls' overlordship of all lands, it may reflect a later understanding that this was how the earls got their superiority over the farmers and not the king (see discussion in Crawford, 1987, 200–1; Krag, 2003, 188, for the traditions of King Harald's appropriation of the peasants' odal rights in Norway)

88 Crawford, 1987, 200

glean from saga evidence that there was accommodation with at least one Celtic warlord in a way which was evidently not the case in the islands (or if it was, there is no surviving evidence to give any information about it). The record of intermarriage with Dungadr, an earl in Caithness,[89] has already been referred to (Section 3.3): he was married to Groa, the daughter of Thorstein 'the Red', and their daughter, Grelaug, was married to Thorfinn 'Skull-Splitter'.[90] These are the first recorded marriages in the Orkney (and Caithness) earldom, and they indicate a settlement between a native chieftain who remained in possession of an estate in Caithness, and the Norse conquerors.[91] Such accommodation may have resulted from the threat posed to both native leaders and incoming Norse from the powerful rulers of the province of Moray.

Earl Sigurd I's battle with Earl Mælbrigte of the Moray dynasty which resulted in the death of his opponent, and Sigurd's subsequent death from a wound, has been referred to already. This first earl's burial in a pagan mound on the north side of the Oykel river shows that the Norse conquest at that time reached as far south as the Dornoch Firth, but this situation did not last. The province of Moray stretched from the River Spey to the west coast, at its greatest extent, north into Easter Ross, or even further north, and its rulers were a powerful dynasty. They are sometimes called 'kings of the Scots' by the saga writer and sometimes *rí* ('king') in the Irish annals, although they were *mormaer* ('great steward') to the kings of the southern kingdom of Alba. The significance of the province of Moray is now more fully recognised along with the powerful position of its dynasty in the whole history of the earlier Pictish period.[92] The rulers of Moray claimed to have authority over the whole of northern Scotland, so must have greatly resented the appearance of the Norse raiders and settlers on the north mainland whose leaders were bent on controlling this strategic area for their own wider ambitions. The absence of any reference to activity by the earls on the north mainland after the death of Earl Sigurd I (c.892) until the battles recorded in the late tenth century suggests that the Norse conquest had not gone unchallenged, and in fact may well have been reversed, particularly so as the later battles took place in the far north of Caithness, where Liot, son of Thorfinn 'Skull-Splitter', and his nephew, Sigurd Hlodversson, were fighting what appear to have been rearguard actions. These two are said to have fought separate battles at Skitten Moor (*Skíðamyrr*) near Wick in Caithness with an

---

89 Dungadr may be the eponymous lord of Duncansby, in the north-east corner of Caithness. See recent discussion of this place-name and its significance by Doreen Waugh, 2009, 35
90 Hms. Laing, *Olaf Haraldsson's Saga*, Chapter xcix
91 Crawford, 1987, 64
92 Woolf, 2000, 2006. The importance of Moray in the history of the earldoms will recur in later chapters.

VIKING EARLS: AD 870–1030

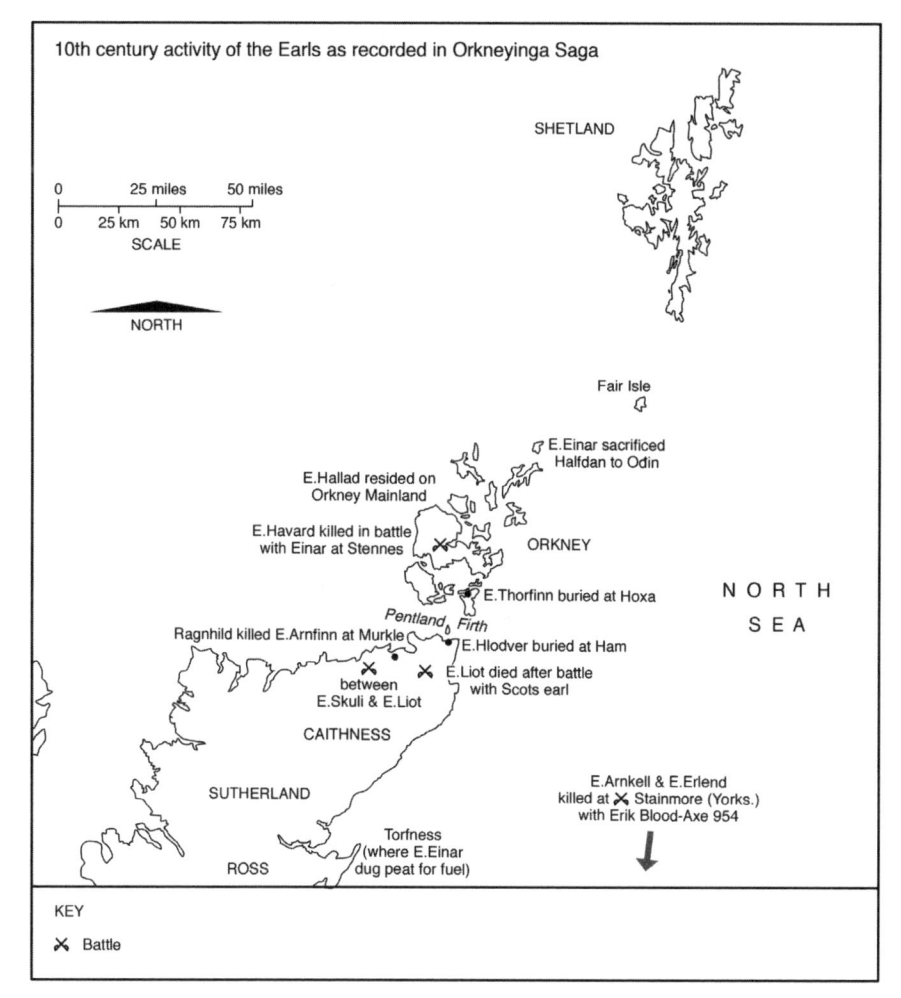

Figure 3.7 Map showing the activities of the earls in the tenth century, as recorded in *Orkneyinga Saga*.

Earl MacBeth and an Earl Finnlaech, both of whom were apparently rulers of Moray.

This was a period of contention between the five sons of Thorfinn Skull-Splitter (see Genealogical tree, Figure 3.4), and in such a situation, one of the sons (Skuli) sought help from the ruler of Moray. He is said to have travelled across Scotland and 'was given the title of earl by the king of Scots', returning north to Caithness where he gathered an army and crossed to Orkney 'to claim the earldom from his brother' (*OS*, Chapter 10). Here is the first indication that the title of earl – which would include a grant of devolved authority over the north mainland territories – was given, apparently by the ruler of Moray (if that is who is meant here by the 'king of Scots').[93] A battle was fought in Orkney, which Liot won, and Skuli fled back to Caithness, and then south to Scotland. Liot moved after him and spent some time raising troops in Caithness, but Skuli was given a 'large following' by the king of Scots and Earl Macbeth, and marched north where battle was joined in the Dales of Caithness.[94] It went badly for the Scottish army and Skuli was killed so Liot 'took over in Caithness'. He was not inclined to come to any accommodation with the rulers of Moray with the result that Earl MacBeth led another army north and battle was joined again at Skitten Moor, after which Liot died of his wounds in Orkney, having returned to the islands (*OS*, Chapter 10).[95]

Although the record of all these events in *Jarls' Saga* is brief and unsophisticated, and probably muddled as well, there is no reason to doubt the circumstances of rivalry among the sons of Earl Thorfinn I, or of the interplay between the Norse establishment on the north mainland and the claims of the rulers of Moray to overlordship. The events also reveal how the claimants to power in the earldom family were determined to dominate in the islands *and* on the mainland. Skuli tried to win power in Orkney after he had been given the title of earl over Caithness by the Scots. Liot moved into Caithness to add it to his Orkney earldom. There was no agreement to allow one brother to have the islands and another to have Caithness, and, as explained in Section 1.1.2, this suggests that they saw the mainland territory and the offshore islands as one dominion for reasons of economy and strategic control over the waterways. The fertility of Caithness must have been an additional relevant and desirable factor.[96]

---

93 The dating for this period of conflict is highly uncertain, but must have been in the 970s or 980s. Presumably it was the earldom of Orkney which Skuli was said to be 'claiming' from his brother, although the actual Norse phrase *deildi þar til ríkis* is only indicating a struggle for power. Chapters 10 and 11 are an interpolation in the earliest text of the *Jarls' Saga* (see recent discussion by Bolton, 2008, 144) and they have some interesting information about the situation in Caithness, although that information is not reliable in detail

94 A term which it has been argued (Crawford, 1987, 65; Thomson, 2001, 59) applied to the river valleys of Thursodale and Strath Halladale which run down from central Caithness to the Pentland Firth, and which can be easily used for accessing the north coast by a land army approaching from the south

95 Although according to tradition, he was buried in Caithness at Stenhouse in Watten (Gray, 1922, 26)

96 Gray asserts (1922, 35) that 'to Norway Orkney and Cat were essential. For their fertile lands yielded the supplies of grain which Norway required' and when the Norse failed to secure the grainlands of Moray, Orkney and Cat 'became still more necessary to them and their folk at home'. The first documentary evidence of cereal products being exported from Orkney to Norway and Iceland is not until the late twelfth century (Barrett, 2012, 279–30)

After Liot's death Hlodver took over the earldom 'and ruled well' (*OS*, Chapter 11). This is probably shorthand for saying that he was successful in holding Caithness as well as Orkney. The bald fact that he 'died in his bed' but also that he was buried in a mound at Hofn in Caithness indicates that he died in Caithness, but not in any battle to retain possession (see Colour plate 12). Hofn is likely to be Ham, on the north coast of Caithness, near Dunnet Head.[97] Once more we have the placing of a burial mound on the coast overlooking a waterway (as with the location of Sigurd I's burial mound on the banks of the Oykel).[98] Hlodver's mound can also be understood to be a statement of power, although this time power over the waterway which united the two halves of his dominion.

3.4.3 *Earldom contacts beyond Caithness and Orkney*

The position of the Orkney Islands was strategically important for giving access to both western and eastern sides of the British Isles and this made them essential for mobile power-seekers like Erik 'Blood-axe' eldest son of Harald 'Finehair', who appeared on the stage of the Viking world with ambitions in northern England in the mid-tenth century. In such circumstances the earls were caught up in the campaigns of agression led by their Norwegian overlords and had to follow the war-fleets of scions of the royal dynasty when naval operations were launched (this would happen again in later centuries).[99]

Erik is said to have been forced out of Norway by his half-brother, Hakon 'the Good', moving west to Orkney (c.947) which he dominated for seven years, followed by his widow and children for some years thereafter. The earls at the time were Arnkell and Erlend, sons of Torf-Einar, and they accompanied Erik on his raiding expedition to the Hebrides, Ireland and Strathclyde, according to *Jarls' Saga* (*OS*, Chapter 8). Erik was then taken as king in Northumbria and had two brief periods of power in York before falling in battle at Stainmore (on the Yorkshire–Westmorland border) in 954, along with a good number of petty Viking kings, and including the two Orkney earls.[100] Whatever the truth

---

97 According to Taylor (*OS*, 356 ; 1930–1, 43). Gray (1922, 26) suggested that it could be Huna, near John of Groats

98 There is a mound close to the cliffs near Ham (Colour plate 12).which is of prehistoric origin, but which could have been reused for a Norse burial mound (RCAHMS *Caithness Inventory*, no. 65).Taylor (1930–1, 43) mentions a mound known as the 'Earls' Cairn', at Hollandmaik, three and a half miles inland from Ham, which is perhaps rather too far away from Ham and from the coast to be a significant candidate for Hlodver's burial mound. It is a prehistoric chambered cairn (RCAHMS *Caithness Inventory*, no. 72)

99 Crawford, 1987, 61

100 The complexity of the sources and the possible confusion of two Eriks by the later medieval chroniclers are explored by Clare Downham (2004; 2007, 115–20)

of the story of the demise of the last Viking king of York, along with five (or six) Viking kings on the lonely heights of Stainmore, the participation of the Orkney earls in such adventures in northern England is quite plausible, and was to be repeated on a later occasion (1066) (see Section 4.3.1). Erik's widow Gunnhild subsequently remained in Orkney with her children, and they appear to have been in control of the islands for some years,[101] providing the saga writer with good material for some of the more fabulous 'intrigues'(as OS, Chapter 9 is headed) during the period after the death of Thorfinn 'Skull-Splitter' (c.963).

These 'intrigues' are mostly to do with the machinations of Ragnhild the daughter of Erik and Gunnhild, reputedly married to three of Earl Thorfinn's sons, and who schemed with another claimant, Einar *klíningr*. The 'hard reality' of rivalry among the sons and grandsons of Earl Thorfinn is a feature of the second half of the tenth century and tells us of the problems caused by the ability of any male descendant of an earl to claim the earldom lands and rights, in a free for all.[102] Provision for the division of the earldom among claimants may not have been made on any established pattern, as would happen in the next century. The comment about Hlodver in *Hms*. (*Olaf Haraldsson's Saga*, Chapter xcix) is that he lived the longest and 'ruled the land undivided' (*réð þa einn londin*). The violence and murders were explained by the later saga writer as being caused by Ragnhild, according to the familiar topos of the vengeful woman who prodded on the menfolk to action, seeking to build and maintain her own power.[103] All this is related as happening in Orkney, although the death of Earl Arnfinn is said to have taken place at Murkle in Caithness, where Ragnhild had her husband 'done to death', and indicating that Murkle was an earldom power centre at this time, as it certainly was later.[104]

The marriages of earls have been noted already as being a useful indicator of external contacts and alliances. Perhaps the earls' liaisons with Ragnhild are less than useful in this respect, although whatever links these liaisons created were certainly ones which keyed into the Norwegian power sphere.[105] The next earldom marriage to be recorded is that of Hlodver to Eithne, the daughter of King Kjarval of Ireland (*OS*, Chapter 11). If reliable,[106] this would suggest a

---

101 Snorri says that Erik's sons fled back to Orkney in Earl Thorfinn's latter days and 'committed great excesses in Orkney' (*Hms*. Laing, *St Olaf's Saga*, Chapter xcix)
102 Crawford, 1987, 63; Thomson, 2001, 58
103 Crawford, 1987, 218. See Section 2.1 where the depiction of Ragnhild as the stereotypical power seeker is also discussed
104 Murkle is recorded as being the place where the earl of Caithness gave his oath to Edward I in 1296 (see Section 7.5.2)
105 As Thomson comments, Ragnhild may not have been the instigator of the troubles so much as the prize for the winner (2001, 59)
106 Alex Woolf thinks that this marriage has been chronologically misplaced (2007, 283–4)

new development in this earl's diplomatic contacts which would be evidence of a more wide-ranging alliance, far to the south in the Irish Sea zone. Such a marriage would signify an interest in this area, but for what reason is not explained, as there is no other evidence recorded of Hlodver's activities.[107]

It is the marriage of Hlodver's son Sigurd which has caused historians most problems, but which is highly significant for indicating an important outside alliance. The saga simply says that he married the daughter of 'Malcolm, king of Scots', but which Malcolm is this meant to be? Opinion has been, and still is, divided as to whether this was Malcolm II MacKenneth (1005–1034) of the southern kingdom of Alba, or Malcolm MacBrigte, ruler of Moray.[108] Sigurd's success in defending Caithness against the Scots and the account of his battle with Earl Finnleik at Skitten Moor in Caithness (*OS*, Chapter 11) does not suggest that his relations with the Moray dynasty were any friendlier than previously. If the marriage alliance was forged with Malcolm II MacKenneth, this would indicate that the earl of Orkney was considered to be an ally worth having by the powerful ruler of Alba – and the reason is not hard to seek, for the combination of the two powers both north and south of Moray would keep the Moray dynasty's ambitions in check.[109]

3.5 SIGURD II HLODVERSSON 'THE STOUT' (*DIGRI*)

Sigurd *digri* had the same by-name as was later given to King Olaf Haraldsson, the Saint, and which is usually translated as 'the Stout', although it carries the connotation of 'powerful warrior'. The 'Genealogy of the Earls' describes him (in Latin) as *robustus ac corpolentus, magnus et strenuissimus bellifer* (translated into Scots as 'the wicht and corpulent, ane grete and maist stowt battellare').[110] He is said to have been 'another great chieftain, who ruled over several dominions' and he brought Caithness under his sway (*OS*, Chapter 11). This would have been an essential preliminary to expansion west, which marks the next phase of earldom history.

---

107 The name Hlodver (ON *Hloðvir*) is a highly unusual one, and appears to be the Norse rendering of Louis/Ludwig (Woolf, 2007, 303)
108 From an initial position of indecisiveness (1987, 64) I have come to be more firmly of the opinion that this was Malcolm II (2001, 75; 2004a). It has, however, recently been strongly argued that Malcolm MacBrigte, ruler of Moray, is the more likely candidate (Bolton, 2009, 145–6), as already assumed by Hudson (1994, 135–6; 2005, 75)
109 Crawford, 1987, 64. The compiler of the fifteenth-century 'Genealogy of the Earls' seems clear that it was Malcolm MacKenneth from his statement that Thorfinn was 'procreate of the dochtter of umquhill the maist excellent prince Malcolme illustrie king of Scottis' (*procreatus ex filia quondam excellentissimi Principis Malcolmi Regis Scottorum illustris*), *Bann. Misc.* iii, 75
110 Ibid; Latin *strenuus*, 'valiant' (Davies, 2009, 61)

3.5.1 *Expansion south and west*

A significant factor about the second Earl Sigurd is that he appears in the storyline of other Icelandic sagas, and also is attested in the contemporary Irish annals. This fact makes historians less nervous about accepting his historical existence. Previous earls are not attested in historical sources as such, only in the later saga literature.[111] This does not mean that they did not exist although some historians are now writing as if that is the case.[112] Certainly Sigurd *digri's* posthumous reputation is evident from his appearance in the later Icelandic Family Sagas, such as *Njal's Saga* and *Eyrbyggia Saga* as also in *The Saga of Gunnlaug Serpent-Tongue*. There the skald Gunnlaug (who was, probably, a historical figure) is said to have visited Orkney on his 'Grand Tour' and to have presented a poem to the earl, which was in the form of a *flokkr*, a shorter poem without a refrain as distinct from the more highly regarded *drápa*.[113] As a reward he was given a broad-axe 'with silver inlay all over it' and invited to stay by the grateful earl. Unfortunately, this poem was not recorded, so we do not know if this is an accurate record of a real visit to Orkney or an imagined event in the life of Gunnlaug. It does however tell us that such an event was a story worth recording in thirteenth or fourteenth-century Iceland and one which a northern audience would have thought worth hearing, so that it is an indication of Earl Sigurd's significance in Icelandic historical memory.

Although the information about Sigurd Hlodversson in *Jarls' Saga* is minimal, we do get the specific statement in *Njal's Saga* that the earl's territories in Scotland included Ross and Moray, Sutherland and the Dales, which would be not unlikely if he then expanded his authority to the Hebrides, as he is said to have done.[114] The absence of Caithness from this list may be significant, suggesting that the north-east tip of the Scottish mainland was still dominated by the native family (referred to above). This area, around Duncansby, was probably the original 'ness' of the Catt tribe (which makes good topographical and toponymical sense); the Norse term for the ness then being used for the larger territory which became the earldom.[115] We have accounts of the Battle of *Dungalsnipa* (Duncansby Head) in *Njal's Saga* (Chapter 86), in which the Scots earls Hundi, Melsnati and Melkolf were involved: and of the second Battle of Skitten in *Jarls' Saga* – in which an Earl Finnleikr challenged Earl Sigurd to

---

111 Also, of course, in contemporary skaldic verse, such as the stanzas composed by Torf-Einar
112 See Alex Woolf's arguments (2007, 307) that Sigurd *digri* may have been the first earl of Orkney – with his title received from Harald 'Blue-tooth', king of Denmark
113 *Gunnlaug's Saga*, 19. Paul Bibire provided help in understanding the significance of this passage
114 The Dales being the river valleys of the north mainland (see Section 3.4.2, n.94)
115 Crawford, 1987, 65

VIKING EARLS: AD 870–1030

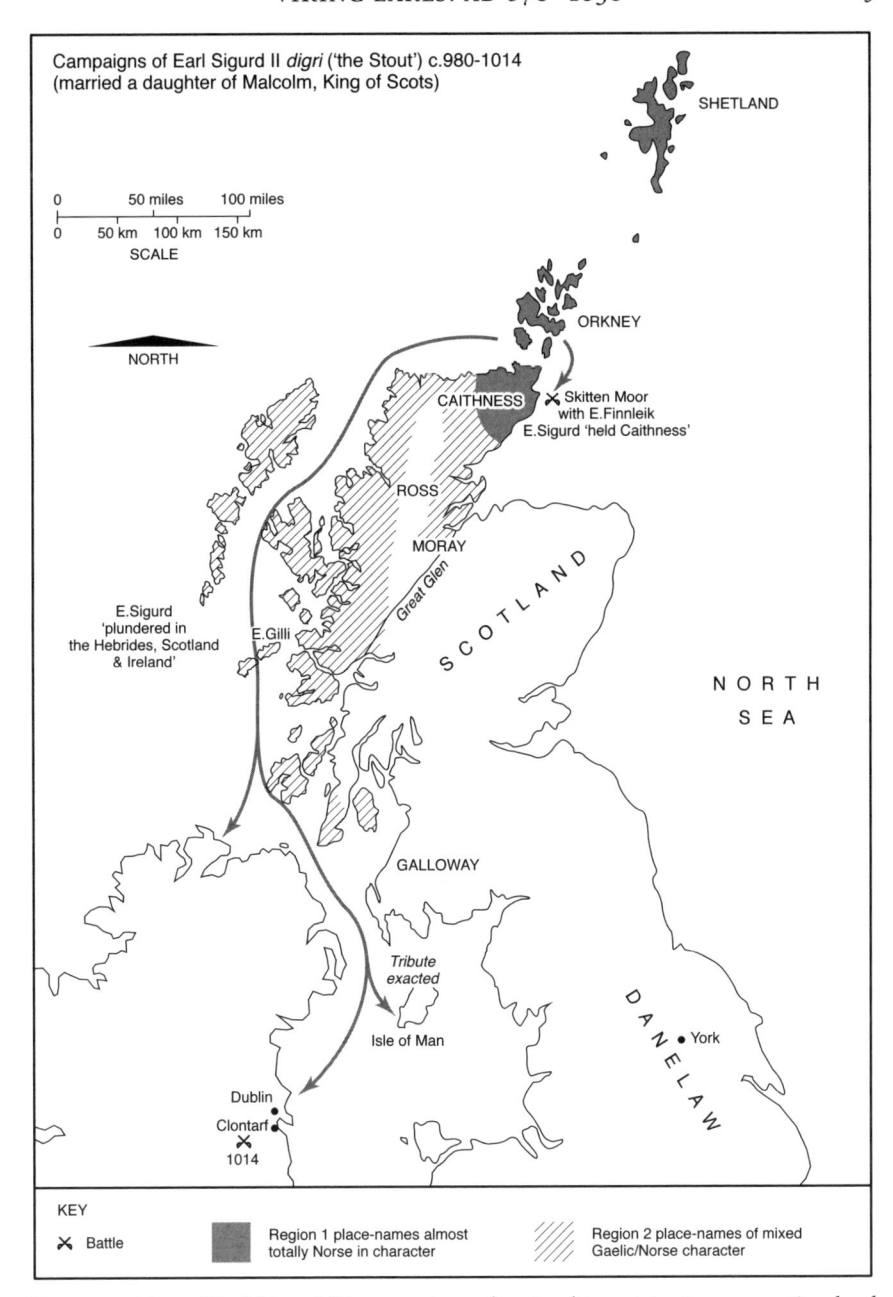

Figure 3.8 Map of Earl Sigurd II's campaigns, showing his activity in western Scotland and the Irish Sea.

combat.[116] Together these strongly suggest that there was continuing tension and hostile relations between the Norse earls and the native family, alongside the rulers of Moray, in north-east Caithness.

The story of Earl Sigurd's banner is what the author of *Jarls' Saga* was most concerned to record, and it must have been a well-known feature of this earl's battle victories and defeat, appearing as it does in both saga accounts relating to his victory against Finnleik in Caithness and his death at Clontarf. The story involves the influence of fate, the role of his mother (called a sorceress – *margkunnig* – in *Jarls' Saga*) and the magic banner, woven with the symbolic figure of a raven, the bird of Odin. As his mother predicted, it brought her son victory at Skitten but caused the death of his standard-bearer, all three of them. The importance of such banners in Viking martial endeavours is well-recorded and we need not doubt that Earl Sigurd would have had his own, whether it was woven for him by his mother or not, and whether it had the magic qualities attributed to it, or not.[117]

There is another aspect to Earl Sigurd's campaign in north Scotland which the saga writer thought worth telling. It relates to the legal status of the farmers' lands in Orkney which had earlier been restricted by Earl Torf-Einar when he paid the fine of sixty gold marks laid on the islands by Harald 'Finehair', and the farmers' odal rights were made over to him (see Section 3.4.1). There is a new development in this arrangement under Earl Sigurd II. Some sort of bargain was made by the earl with the farmers before the Battle of Skitten when he gave them their odal rights 'in return for war service' (*OS*, Chapter 11), remembered as being a reversion to a previous situation for the comment is made at the end of the chapter, 'and the farmers of Orkney got back their land-rights'. This may have been the relaxation of some sort of inheritance tax, specifically in return for getting their agreement to fight, and it may relate particularly to the requirement for them to fight in Caithness, and have been an extension of any military obligation which they had in Orkney itself.[118] This must have been a vital issue for an earl who had plans to expand his power further south, and west; future earls would need to raise troops elsewhere to fulfil their ambitious military policies. It raises the question of how committed the Orkney farmers were to supporting such policies, and whether they saw Caithness as a very separate part of their Norse world. To Sigurd it was essential that Caithness was under his control, for reasons already presented, and his main achievement,

---

116 It is possible that Finnleikr can be identified with Finlay, the father of Macbeth (Crawford, 1987, 72)
117 See Crawford, 1987, 196–7, for other examples; Jesch, 1993, 232–5
118 Crawford, 1987, 201

according to *Jarls' Saga* was that he was 'powerful enough to defend Caithness against the Scots' (*OS*, Chapter 11).

That was a basis for further expansion south of Caithness, so that the territory which had been dominated by his ancestor, the first Earl Sigurd, as far as Ekkjalsbakki (see Section 3.3.1) could be brought back under earldom control. This meant in particular Sutherland, the southern half of Caithness.[119] As noted above, we have the specific statement in *Njal's Saga* that Sigurd's territories included Sutherland, and also Ross and Moray, suggesting that his power extended south of the River Oykel, although we have no certainty as to what sort of influence Sigurd might have exercised in that area. Despite the unlikelihood of him challenging the power of the rulers of Moray in their home territory, it is not impossible that he came to a *modus vivendi* after his successes further north which would have allowed him to have free access for himself and his ships to the Firthlands of Ross and Moray (the Cromarty and the Beauly Firths – the inner reaches of the wider waterway known today as the Moray Firth, or 'Broad Firth' (ON *Breiðafjǫrðr*). It seems most likely that the Norse settlement in Ross which is evidenced by the place-names would have begun in the period of Sigurd II's successful expansion south of Caithness. The fertile coastal plains of Easter Ross have a sprinkling of Norse farm-names ending in -*ból* and -*bó*, as well as several -*dale* (-*dalr*) names, showing that Norse speakers were settled in these localities long enough for the names to become permanent features of the toponymy (see Section 4.2.1).[120]

The evident rationale behind this settlement – particularly of those names which show Norse influence in the river valleys leading west and which provided overland routes to the west coast – is likely to have been strategic and economic. Strategic needs would relate to these overland routes through the central mountainous massif to the west coast (see Figure 3.9). They could, and probably did, provide a passage for troops on horseback, and the requirement for horse transport and horse rearing is suggested by the many 'Langwell' and 'Rossall' names in this locality (see Section 4.2.1 for a fuller discussion). Economic requirements were probably of many different kinds, most obviously the produce of the coastal grain-growing lands, but undoubtedly including the

---

119 The reason why this part of Caithness should be distinguished by the term 'Sutherland' has never been explained, but seemingly relates to a particular division of territory, the 'southern portion' of Caithness. However, 'Sutherland' may originally have been a much larger territory, perhaps it was the name given by the Norse settlers in Orkney to the whole of the north Scottish mainland, just as the Hebrides were the south islands (*Suðreyjar*) from the viewpoint of those in Orkney. The significance of the ending -*land* has been discussed recently by Waugh (2009, 44–5) with particular reference to the name Sutherland

120 Crawford, 2004, 110; Crawford and Taylor, 2003, Map 2

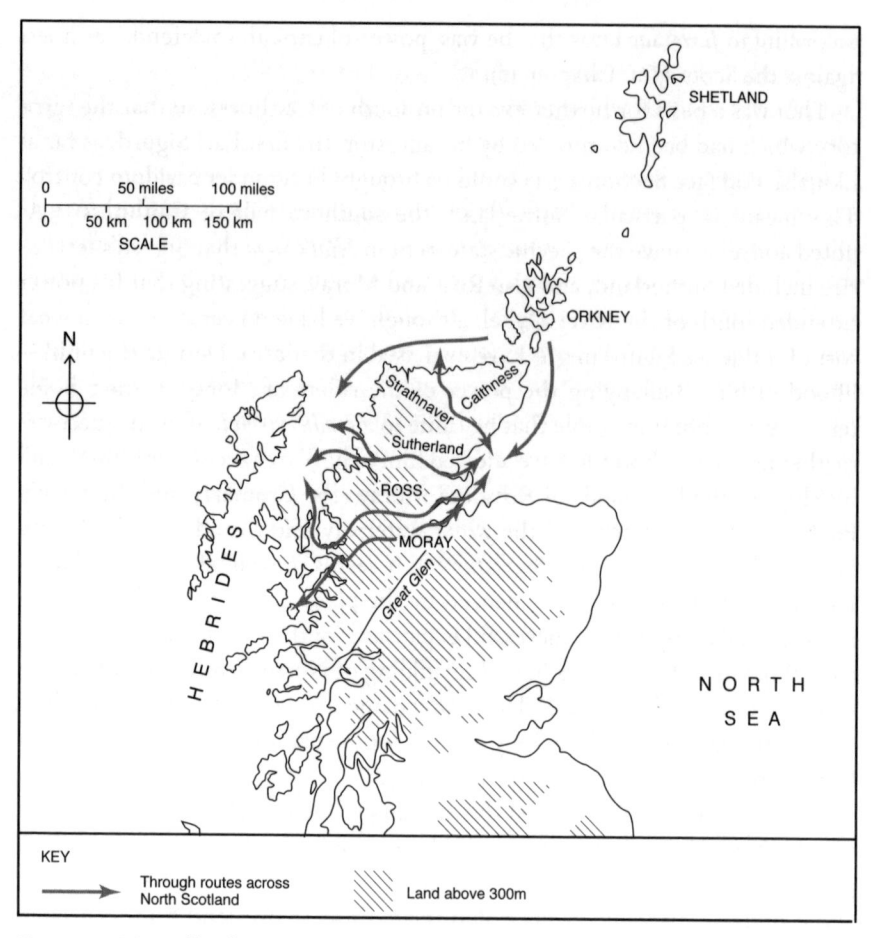

Figure 3.9 Map of land routes across Scotland showing means of accessing west Scotland from Orkney by land as well as by sea. Some of these north Highland glens have a scattering of Norse place-names even though distant from the coast. The routes are all in use today or were in the recent past.

rich timber resources of the wooded valleys of the Oykel, Carron, Conon and Beauly/Glass rivers.[121] The fine pine and ash woods of Easter Ross have been a prime resource for shipbuilding for many centuries (see Plate 3), so there is no doubting their potential for the Norse earls of Orkney who were based in totally treeless islands. The north mainland, particularly Caithness, was also lacking any source of useful timber close to hand for the repair and building of their ships, which was needed to maintain control over the maritime earldoms,

121 Crawford, 1995, 11–17; Crawford and Taylor, 2003, 6–8

and maintain contact between the two halves of the earldom lordship. Both these needs and requirements made access to the river valleys of Ross an important priority for earls whose territorial ambitions were primarily based on sea power.[122]

Another route giving access to the west coast from these sheltered firths, and an alternative means of transfer of ships and men directly to south Argyll and the southern Hebrides (in preference to sailing round Cape Wrath) was provided by the Great Glen, an artery cutting right through the centre of the Scottish Highlands.[123] Access from the north to the lochs which provide a sailing route through the Great Glen is gained from the Moray Firth (*Breiðafjǫrðr*) via the River Ness. The 'Southern Frontier' of Norse settlement in north Scotland[124] lay north of the Great Glen rift valley (from the place-names which form our evidence for Norse influence); Norse control of the Black Isle would have provided some protection for ships sailing into the inner part of the Moray Firth. Use of the Great Glen route can only have been intermittent and possible during periods when the northern earls and the rulers of Moray were not in a hostile relationship.

It is likely that Earl Sigurd II's ambitions in the west were the driving force behind initial Norse settlement and strategic policies in Easter Ross. *Jarls' Saga* is again exceedingly brief in telling us about his ambitions; Sigurd 'used to go on Viking expeditions every summer, plundering in the Hebrides, Scotland and Ireland' (*OS*, Chapter 11). For more detail (some of it considered not too reliable) we have to look to other Icelandic sagas – where Earl Sigurd plays a significant role. The historically attested fact that Sigurd became deeply embroiled in Irish politics to the extent that he participated in the Battle of Clontarf in 1014, and met his end there, makes it almost certain that he was active in Hebridean and Irish waters in the decades prior to that climactic event.

Certainly the Icelandic sources give us a picture of an earl who was very active in fighting Hebridean chieftains, such as Godfrey 'king of Man', whom he defeated (according to *Njal's Saga*); taking tribute from settlements in Man (according to *Eyrbyggja Saga*); allying with a tributary earl, Gilli of Colonsay (or Coll), whom he married to his sister Nereid, and from whom Kari (a member of Sigurd's military following) collected tribute on the earl's behalf (according to *Njal's Saga*, Chapter 85). The Irish sources give evidence of disturbance in the Irish Sea in the years 986–8 in which the Haraldsson dynasty from the Hebrides

---

122 However, it is a fact that Ross never became part of earldom territory, as discussed in Crawford, 1995, 23–4 and Crawford, 2004, 111–12 (see further Section 4.2.1)
123 Crawford, 1987, 22
124 Crawford and Taylor, 2003

was fighting for supremacy, and allying with unspecified 'Danes'.[125] There seems every reason to believe that Earl Sigurd would have been fighting in this cockpit also in order to further his ambitions to extend his maritime supremacy south-west towards Dublin.

3.5.2 *Hoards, arm-rings and an earldom economy*

Another aspect of this turbulent period is of a very different character but also gives evidence of disturbed conditions in the Irish Sea zone, and that is the peak in finds of silver hoards in western Scotland and the Isle of Man dated to 970s–980s.[126] These hoards of silver objects, some of them cut into pieces and called 'hack-silver', are closely associated with Viking raiding and trading, but when hidden by being buried in the ground can also be associated with times of uncertainty and insecurity.[127] The information about Earl Sigurd's exaction of tribute from the Isle of Man and the collection of 'skat' by Kari from Earl Gilli, which was taken back to Orkney, need not be entirely fictitious.[128] If Sigurd was a powerful and successful warrior, he would certainly have been successful in accruing wealth in the form of silver. The problem is to know to what extent these were single exactions of tribute or whether they were collected regularly enough to warrant the definition of taxes.

'Taxation' is indeed a crucial issue as regards the earls' establishment of a permanent economic basis for the collection and management of resources. This is an area where there has been debate about the nature of the earldom administrative structures and the date at which historians believe that these were established.[129] The question involves the matter of usage of bullion or coinage as a medium of exchange, the organisation of the landed wealth in the areas under the earls' authority, and whether the assessment of the income from these lands was used as a basis for annual taxation in the form of renders in kind or payments in silver. The dating of the introduction of fiscal measures has to be understood in the context of the earls' arrangements for the assessment and collection and transport of their wealth, and the organisation of officials to do this work throughout the areas under the earls' control. How sophisticated

---

125 The situation in the Hebrides, with particular focus on the Haraldsson dynasty is fully analysed by Hudson (2005), and by Downham (2007) who focuses on the 'sons of Ivarr'. Etchingham (2001, 176–9), corrects some earlier speculations in *Scand.Scot.* (1987, 66) about Earl Sigurd and his allies
126 Williams, 2004, 73
127 Crawford, 1987, 128–33, and recent discussion of the function of hoarding in Williams, 2004, 80–2
128 *Njal's Saga*, Chapter 85; Thomson, 2001, 61
129 See Andersen, 1991, for a summary of the theories and a viewpoint on the date of the earls' taxation/assessment system and Crawford, 2011, for a review and restatement

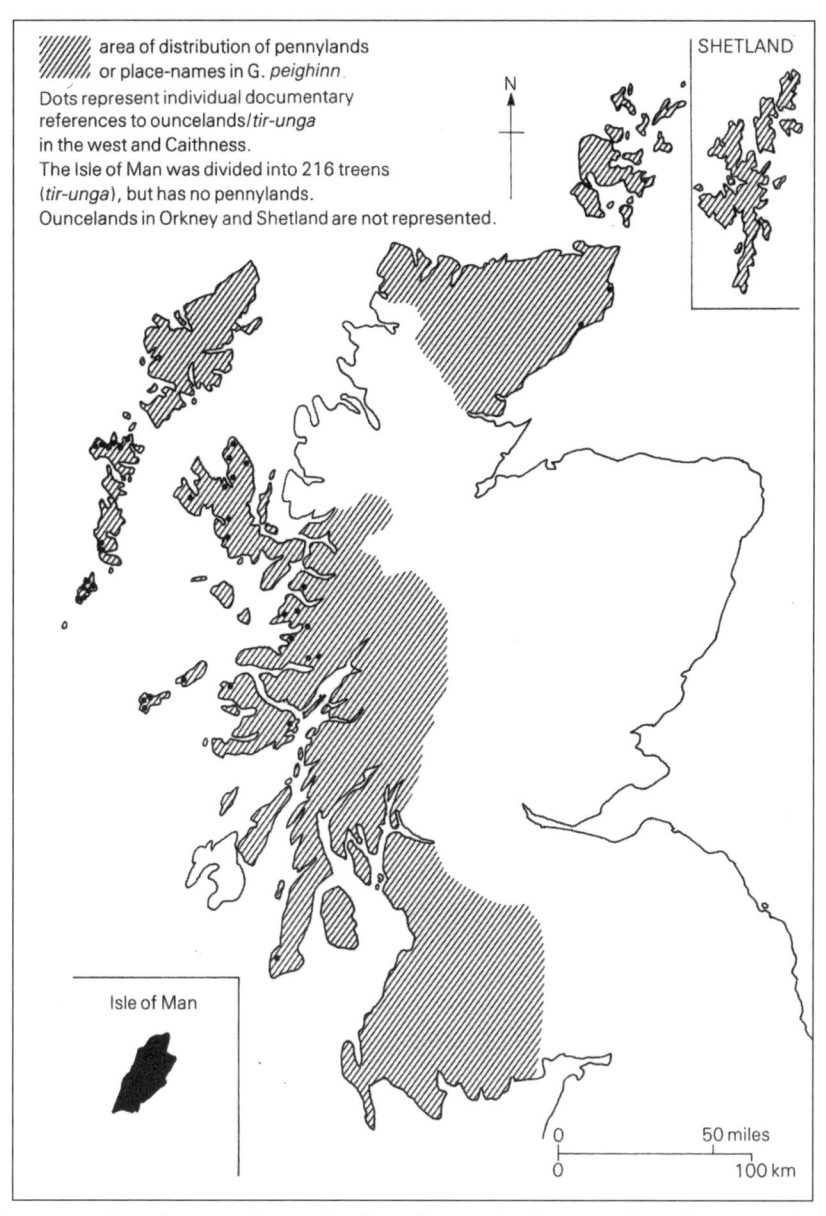

Figure 3.10 Distribution of ouncelands and pennylands in north and west Scotland (Crawford, 1987, fig. 24). This map needs refining since it was first compiled for *Scand. Scot.* because of much important work that has been done on land assessments in the west in the years since by D. Rixson (1999, 2002) and W.P.L. Thomson (2002). It still however serves a purpose in depicting the total area where these important but complex land assessments have been recorded in Scandinavian Scotland.

were early medieval warrior chieftains in their organisation of their resources? Opinions on this vary. Such organisation would have developed in fits and starts depending on the power and ability of individual earls, so that we should not expect it to appear as a readymade institution, or everywhere at the same time. The evidence that we have can be interpreted to suggest that some process of organisation of resources got underway in the period of Earl Sigurd's rule and of his son Thorfinn, and it was in the heart of their maritime empire, in the Orkney Islands, that it is likely to have happened first.

So what is the evidence? First is the physical reality of the silver hoards themselves. Viking silver hoards are composed of different elements, silver objects and ornaments, ingots and coins from countries in western Europe which already minted their own currency, and from the eastern Arabic world. Weights are also found, telling us that the silver was weighed, and the cut up pieces of silver ('hack-silver'), show that the use of silver as bullion was at quite a sophisticated level, valued in terms of weight and quality (the custom of 'pecking' which left small nicks on the silver pieces which had passed through Viking hands was a means of testing the calibre of the silver). It may even be that a particular type of arm-ring which is most commonly found in hoards of the Norse settlements of Scotland was used as a primitive form of currency, and it is sometimes known as 'ring-money'.[130] These arm-rings do approximate to a weight of 24g (plus or minus 0.8g) which suggests that they were being manufactured to some sort of standardisation, even if this was not absolute. The use of such arm-rings, some of them weighing several ounces, is debated, and they could have served various purposes, with their value as reward for military service granted by warrior chieftains to members of a retinue or hird being perhaps foremost, with use as a weight-based trade/exchange commodity being a possible secondary function.[131] This ring-money is a feature of seven hoards from Scotland (coin-dated c.950–c.1040) (see Plate 2), as well as of five coinless hoards and one single find. Examples also appear in Manx hoards during the same time period, when the earls' power was at its most extensive throughout the Viking maritime zone of Scotland and the Irish Sea which indicates an association with the northern earldom.

Secondly, we have the geographical evidence of certain territorial units known as 'ouncelands' which are a unique feature of medieval land assessment in the Northern and Western Isles, and which are recorded, for Orkney, in late

---

130 The description of ring-money as a form of 'state currency' produced in Scandinavian Scotland (Crawford, 1987, 134) was queried (Kruse, 1988; 1993), although the link with the Orkney earls is thought to be 'not unlikely' (Williams, 2004, 79) and ring-money has been described along with ingots and hack-silver as 'coinage without a king' (Barrett, 2007, 318)

131 Williams, 2004, 80

VIKING EARLS: AD 870–1030   123

medieval rentals.[132] These were valuation units which clearly were associated with the ounce, which as mentioned above was basic to the Viking monetary system, in a pre-coinage period. Such territorial units must have been originally worth an ounce of silver, for which an ounce of silver was theoretically rendered, and thus they were designated 'ounceland'.[133] By the time we have the documentary evidence of the late medieval rentals, the original assessment basis has become altered and elaborated, due to changes in landownership and changes in land value. For the present purpose we can only hazard a guess as to the date of the imposition of these ounceland units. Most recent historical analysis points to the period of the rule of the Orkney earls in the west as being the most likely time frame when one single authority was powerful enough to have the opportunity to impose a single assessment system – however crude and unrefined – in both north and west.[134] Reservations about the advisability of describing it as a 'single system' have been voiced, especially as the ounceland is divided into different numbers of pennylands in Orkney and Caithness (eighteen) and the Hebrides (twenty).[135]

Pennylands were more akin to the size of a family farm within the Orkney township unit, and clearly relate to coinage rather than silver bullion. They most probably date to a later period than the ounceland,[136] and perhaps even relate to different factors in the north and west. Their distribution is a little spasmodic in the Hebrides, for there is no evidence for pennyland units in Islay or the Isle of Man (see Figure 3.10).[137] Although we may suspect that the origin of the pennyland lies in the Orkney earldom, such an assessment unit may have been adapted to local conditions by chieftains in the west in the period after the Orkney earldom lost control of the Hebrides in the second half of the eleventh century.[138] The names 'tirunga' and 'treen' are likely to have been given to the ounceland assessment unit at a time when Gaelic was becoming the dominant administrative language in the islands.

132 Thomson, 1987; 1996; 2001, 206
133 It is known as 'tirunga' in the Western Isles and 'treen' in the Isle of Man, both Gaelic terms meaning 'land-ounce' (Crawford, 1987, 88)
134 Crawford, 1987, 80–90; Williams 2004, 94; Oram, 2011, 62–8
135 Thomson, 2002 and Oram, 2011, 66–7, express doubt on several aspects of this 'system'.
136 Williams (2004, 92) assigns both to the tenth or eleventh century, although admitting that the assessment in ounces 'may well pre-date assessment in pennies'. A possible origin in the twelfth century for the pennyland has been argued by myself (1993, 137–43), and Andersen (1991, 81) thinks both date to the late twelfth/early thirteenth century
137 See map in Crawford, 1987, 87, and Williams, 2004, 67
138 Oram, 2011a, 70–3, argues that the pennyland and quarterland units developed out of the tenth-century Gall-Ghàidheil domination in the Irish Sea and southern Hebrides and the adaptation of older systems by the Haraldsson dynasty

This aspect of fiscal organisation and earldom administration is therefore linked tentatively to the growth of Earl Sigurd's power in the late tenth and early eleventh century and the rule of his son Thorfinn 'the Mighty' (c.1020–mid-eleventh century). The discoveries of silver hoards dating to the time of these two earls tell of the accumulation of wealth in the form of bullion throughout the insular world of Scandinavian Scotland, while the recognition of ring-money as a more standardised unit of weight, assessed near enough to a standard 24g can be stipulated to be a result of earldom organisation of resources, although never to the sophistication of a minted coinage.[139] The evidence of ounceland and pennyland assessment units emanating from the earldom is another aspect of organisational abilities for the recovery of income from the lands controlled. These were presumably linked to some sort of tax or tribute system and could perhaps also have been used for the basis of other aspects of earldom organisation like the raising of troops.[140] This accumulation of evidence points to an apparently precocious development in the basis of earldom power taking place in the period when the powerful and successful earls Sigurd and Thorfinn were in control, even though they did not attempt to mint their own coins.

Geographical factors help to explain this, for the compact grouping of the Orkney islands, with the territory of Caithness accessible across the Pentland Firth, created a conjoint unit, linked by waterways, and easily controlled by the ruling earls. The similarity of the assessment pattern in both Orkney and Caithness strongly indicates that the imposition of these units was carried out by the earldom administration. There are even 'skatlands' in Caithness, as in Orkney.[141] The Caithness ounceland is however much less well documented and probably dropped out of use when the davach was introduced into the north mainland of Scotland (the davach never appears in Orkney).[142]

This remarkable assessment system which developed in the earldom territories contrasts with the situation in both Norway and Scotland, where the

139 The reason why the earls did not attempt to imitate the powerful royal dynasties of western Europe and mint their own coins, as the kings of Man and Dublin did, is a complex question which needs to be analysed in the light of a comparable disinclination on the part of the eleventh-century kings of Scots to produce their own currency
140 Crawford, 1987, 88–90. The method of organisation of the earls' fleets by means of a levy on the ouncelands and pennylands, called the 'leidang' (*leiðangr*) is currently out of favour (Williams, 1996; 2004, 69) (see below)
141 Bangor-Jones, 1987, 15. Marwick (1952, 206–7) developed a particular theory on the function of the skatland (one quarter of an ounceland) in the leidang system of naval levy, about which Thomson (2001, 214–15) is sceptical. The Orkney land assessment term is usually spelled 'skatland' (sometimes 'scatland') whereas the Norwegian 'skattlands' are spelled with a double tt (see Section 1.2)
142 Williams, 2003, 27

creation of unified kingdoms, with a single dynasty in power, only got underway in the mid-eleventh century. The extent of the Norwegian land mass, and the mountainous interior, made it a challenging task for a single dynasty to assert its authority, despite the extent of coastal territory which could be dominated with maritime control. Scotland was a mix of different chieftaincies and linguistic groupings in the late tenth century, with the kings of Alba in the southern half of the country and the rulers of Moray south of the Viking lands rivalling each other for dominance.[143] There is little evidence of any centralisation or development of state structures until the late eleventh century. Power was best exercised through command of the seas, and this was the secret of the early success of the Orkney earls. The term 'thalassocracy' for a maritime empire is not out of place in the context of a firm power base in the earldoms of Orkney and Caithness; from this power base personal authority could be extended over the north Scottish mainland and down the west coast to the distant Hebridean islands, perhaps as far south as the Irish Sea.[144]

It has already been noted that personal authority was delegated to loyal followers or members of the earldom family. Sigurd is said to have left 'agents' (*menn*) to collect the tax from Man (*Eyrbyggja Saga*, Chapter 29); Earl Gilli may have acted on the earl's behalf in the Hebrides (*Njal's Saga*, Chapter 89), and Thorfinn sent a member of his wife's family, Kalf Arneson, to the Hebrides 'to make sure of his authority there' (*OS*, Chapter 27).[145] This is the basis on which a medieval administration with hierarchical authority was established, and it was the method used by all kings to assure themselves of their authority and to access the wealth of the more distant parts of their lands. The kings of Norway might have looked to the model established in Orkney with some admiration and with a desire to emulate. Indeed, they made several attempts to bring the earldom under their own control and access some of its riches.[146]

3.5.3 *Earl Sigurd* digri's *conversion and death*[147]

Coming back to *Jarls' Saga* as our guide we still have two of the most famous incidents connected with the life of Sigurd 'the Stout' to consider: his forced conversion by King Olaf Tryggvesson of Norway within his own earldom, and his death at the Battle of Clontarf fighting to extend his authority to Ireland. Both incidents are crucial turning points in the history of the Orkney earldom,

---

143 Crawford and Clancy, 2001, 72–85
144 Crawford, 1987, 11
145 Crawford, 2004, 114; Richard Oram has reservations about the source evidence being proof of Orcadian political domination in the Hebrides (2011, 68)
146 Crawford, 1987, 91
147 See my previous discussion of these two events (ibid., 67–70)

the first for its significance in the changing of religious belief from paganism to Christianity, along with the role of the king of Norway in this development. The second for its apocalyptic quality in signifying the end of an era for the Orkney earldom, and an end of Sigurd's ambitions, in a clash which resonated throughout the Viking world. The drama of the Battle of Clontarf entered into the saga corpus of the stories of Icelanders, which means that we have other, fuller, accounts of the battle, and of Sigurd's demise, apart from the dry phrases recorded in *Jarls' Saga*.[148]

Olaf Tryggvesson (AD 995–1000) was the king who was later credited with the initial conversion of the Norwegian peoples and of the settlers in the Atlantic islands. Unlikely as this may seem, we have to remember that this was an age of extraordinary mobility when the players in the dramatic events could move around the civilised and uncivilised worlds with ease. Olaf's own career had started off bound up with the renewal of Viking raids at the end of the tenth century when he was involved in the successful raids led by Svein Forkbeard of Denmark in the sustained attack on Anglo-Saxon England. This certainly meant a close encounter with Christian societies and their religious beliefs. It is told in his saga that he was influenced by a hermit in the Scilly Isles into being baptised a Christian (*Hms.* Laing, *King Olaf Tryggvesson's Saga*, Chapter XXXII), and more reliably recorded that he underwent a confirmation ceremony at the court of the Anglo-Saxon King Æthelred, who stood as his sponsor (*ASC sub* 994).

On his return east to claim power in Norway in 996, Olaf Tryggvesson sailed round north Scotland through the Pentland Firth into the bay of Osmundwall in south Hoy where he found Earl Sigurd getting ready to set out on a Viking expedition with three ships. He requested the earl to come over to his ship and forced him to accept baptism and be Christianised along with all his people – literally at the point of a sword (see Colour plates 13a and 13b). There are varying accounts of this situation and it is added in *Jarls' Saga* that, as a result, 'all Orkney embraced the faith'. The dramatic confrontation of these two powerful Viking chieftains no doubt caught the imagination of the later saga authors, and we do not have to believe that it all took place exactly as described. But there is no reason to doubt that such an incident did take place, and that it was part of the process of the Norwegian king's assertion of his authority over the earl. Nor do we have to believe that the baptism of the Norse communities in the islands was instantaneous; this is far too complex a situation for it to be so simplistic. Much research has been done to try to assess the development of Christian belief in the islands in the preceding century, and

---

148 Above all in *Njal's Saga*, Chapter 157

even to chart a continuation of belief from the previous Pictish population.[149]

The significance of Sigurd's forced conversion is primarily that it would have enabled teaching of the new beliefs to take place, and allowed churches to have been built. One version of *Olaf's Saga* says that the king left priests behind in the islands 'to instruct the people'. This is what conversion was all about and it would take decades of such missionising work for the full adoption of the new faith and for the establishment of a Christian society.[150] That work can be understood to have been successfully prosecuted in the time of Sigurd's son Thorfinn (see Chapter 4). Of course the islands had been open to Christian influences for centuries, and so had the earls. Sigurd's mother was Irish and therefore Christian. He married the daughter of a Scottish king (which may have required some nominal acceptance of her religious beliefs). These Christian women may have had their own priests with them in the earldom household, although nothing is said in the sagas about them influencing the beliefs of their menfolk. It cannot have been a very hard decision for Sigurd to agree to baptism, especially when faced with the situation he found himself in. The agreement to let Christian priests proselytise may have been harder and a commitment to expend resources on the building of churches harder still. It is regarding these aspects of the conversion of Orkney that Olaf Tryggvesson's intervention was probably crucial.

For Sigurd the adoption of the new beliefs may have been only nominal, but Olaf's decision to keep him to his word by taking his son, called Hvelp or Hundi, as a hostage would have allowed the process of Christianisation of the islands to proceed. The son was baptised under the name of Hlodvir (his grandfather's name), but he 'didn't live long', and following his death we are told that Sigurd refused to pay homage to King Olaf (*OS*, Chapter 12). Perhaps he also reverted to old practices of worship. It is in respect of pagan or magical symbolism that the compiler of the chapters on Earl Sigurd in *Jarls' Saga* had most to say. This concerns the famous 'raven banner' woven for Sigurd by his mother Eithne (already referred to in Section 2.1), which she endowed with magical qualities so that it helped to bring victory to the warrior on whose behalf it was carried but death to the standard-bearer himself. This prophetic power had proven valid at the Battle of Skitten Moor when three of Earl Sigurd's standard-bearers were killed although he was victorious (perhaps the story of the banner's magical

149 Useful contributions pertinent to the matter of continuity of belief can be found in Crawford, ed., 2002; Thomson, 2001, 63–6. Recent excavation of church sites in the Northern Isles has helped to provide some evidence for continuity of resort to earlier Pictish sites, but with a probable break in time, as at St Nicholas Church, Papa Stronsay (Figure 5.7) (Lowe 2002; Lowe *et al.* 2000) and at St Ninian's Isle, Shetland (Barrowman, 2011, 194, 204)
150 Crawford, 1987, 70

powers developed due to this). At the Battle of Clontarf three of Sigurd's men were similarly killed when carrying the banner, according to *Njal's Saga* (Chapter 57), and as no one else would carry it, the earl tore it from its staff and wrapped it around himself, and subsequently he also was killed.

What was Earl Sigurd doing fighting a land battle outside the gates of Dublin, so far from home? The promise of the kingship of Ireland and the hand of a royal queen are mentioned in *Njal's Saga*, which used the dramatic confrontation between the Norsemen of Dublin alongside whom Earl Sigurd fought against Brian Boru, king of Munster, as the apocalyptic scenario for the end of the earl's ambitions. Horsewomen of the apocalypse – the twelve Valkyries seen riding across the heavens in Caithness in the remarkable 'Song of Dorrud' (*Darraðarlióð*) – are the most dramatic manifestation of the many portents and visions evoked in the Norse world in the wake of the battle. (*Njal's Saga*, Chapter 157). Whoever Dorrud was it is notable that the prose section recounting his experience in seeing the Valkyries weaving the web of fate for those warriors at the battle,(with the warp made of entrails and heads of the slain for the loom-weights, blood-spattered spears for the heddle rods and arrows for the weaving batten) was located in Caithness.[151] This Scottish part of the earl's dominions is a rather surprising location for the envisioning of such a powerful Nordic image as the Valkyries and their influence on the fate of warriors. However, the poem has been said by Holtsmark to have some elements of Celtic imagery mixed into the Old Norse *visionsdikt* (visionary poem), for the idea that weaving could have magical properties is probably Celtic in inspiration.[152] If so, the connection with Caithness, a milieu of mixed Norse–Celtic culture, is indicative and also unusual as there is no other evidence of Caithness having any links with Norse literary culture. Wherever the poem itself was composed, it was at some point linked with north Scotland, perhaps at a later date than the events so darkly commemorated.[153] It is indeed a fitting symbol of the interplay of Norse and Celtic worlds which Earl Sigurd straddled, and in the thick of which he met his death, mentioned in stanza 7:

> Will Seafaring men
> hold sway over lands
> who erstwhile dwelled

[151] 'On Good Friday morning it so happened that a man called Dorrud went outside his house in Caithness and he saw twelve persons (*menn*) riding up to a woman's bower (ON *dyngja*, 'the sunken weaving-house on a Norse farm')

[152] *KL sub Darraðarlióð*; and Poole, 1991, 140

[153] If the reference to the 'young king' in stanza 10 (whom the Valkyries are said to be praising) is Sigtrygg of Dublin, who was killed the year following the battle, it has been suggested that the poem was composed in 1014–15 (Holtsmark, *KL sub Darraðarlióð*), but see Poole's (1991, 122–3) discussion of the dating problems

on outer nesses:
is doomed to die
a doughty king,
lies slain an earl
by swords e'en now
(*Darraðarlióð* (Song of Dorrud) (*Njal's Saga*
trans. Bayerschmidt and Hollander, Chapter 157)

3.6 EARL THORFINN 'THE MIGHTY' (*HINN RÍKI*)

Sigurd's death, and the succeeding years of rivalry among his sons, marks an end of the Viking era in the northern earldoms, in which raiding was the predominant lifestyle of the earls, and their main means of amassing wealth. The period between 1014 and the establishment of Thorfinn Sigurdsson as the most powerful ruler in the islands and in Caithness is summarised in *Jarls' Saga* with certain dramatic incidents which delineate changes in the political and social situation.

First of all is the process of inheritance of the lands and islands of Orkney, Caithness and Shetland by the four brothers, in which the saga writer gives some suggestive details about the changes in the 'constitutional' character of the earldom power base. Because of Thorfinn's close links with the court of his grandfather, the Scottish king Malcolm, where he was brought up after his father's death in 1014, he was closely associated with Caithness from an early age. Indeed, the saga says that he was given Caithness and Sutherland by his grandfather, with the title of earl, and counsellors were appointed to govern the land with him (*OS*, Chapter 13). If his grandfather was indeed Malcolm MacKenneth (and not Malcolm, ruler of Moray), we may wonder if he had any real power to make such a grant of Caithness and Sutherland, but it could be read as telling us that by this date the kings of Scots regarded north Scotland as their territory, and under their theoretical overlordship. It also suggests that Caithness and Sutherland were regarded as a separate earldom, even though the title of earl was still a personal one and not yet firmly linked to a fixed territorial earldom. If Thorfinn had been content with that grant, the way might have been laid for the future development of a completely separate Caithness earldom.[154] However, as the saga writer says, Thorfinn grew into a tall, strong, black-haired man and 'everyone could see that he was going to turn

---

154 The fifteenth-century compiler of the 'Genealogy of the Earls' is quite specific that 'the quhilk king gaif to the said Thurfine the landis of Cathanie and of Sutherland in Scotland onder ane denomination of Erildome (*sub unica denominatione comitatus in Scocia*): and he josit tha landis togidder with the Erildome of Orchadie and Schetland and sundrie otheris dominions lyand in the kingdome of Scotland' (*Bann.Misc.*, iii, 76)

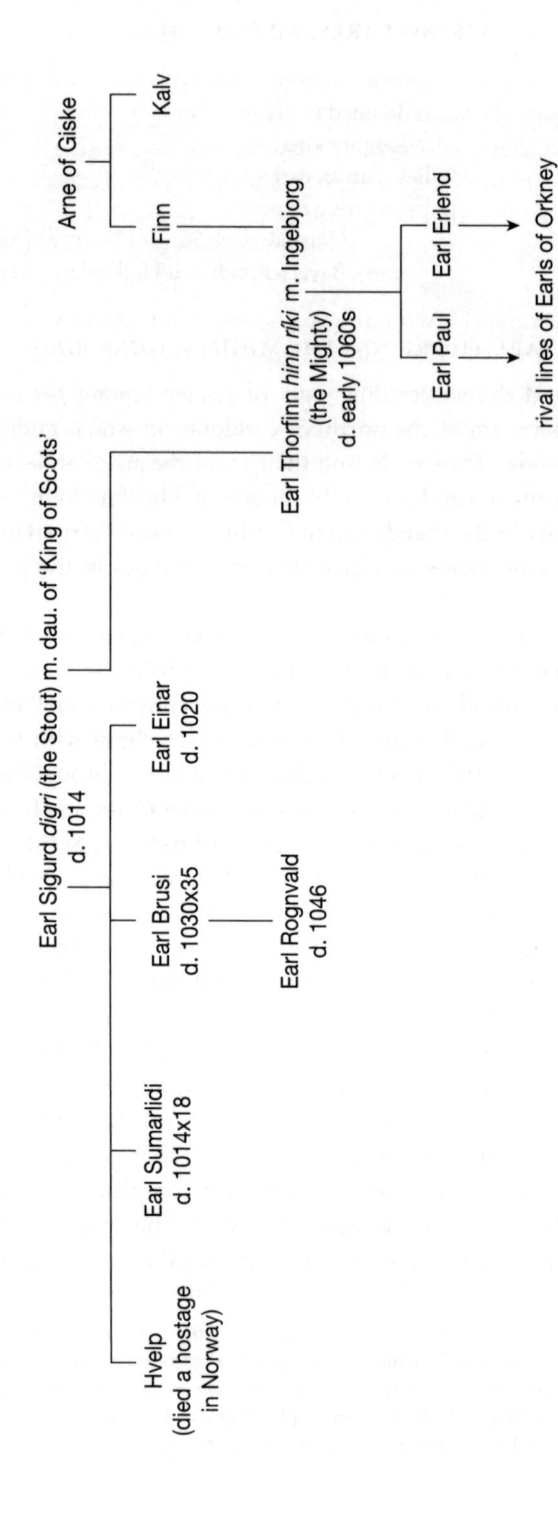

```
                                                                    Arne of Giske
                                                                   ┌──────┴──────┐
                                                                  Finn          Kalv
                                                                   │
                                                                Ingebjorg
                                                                   m.
Earl Sigurd digri (the Stout) m. dau. of 'King of Scots'
d. 1014
┌──────────────────┬──────────────────┬──────────────────┐
Hvelp          Earl Sumarlidi      Earl Brusi         Earl Einar      Earl Thorfinn hinn ríki
(died a hostage  d. 1014x18       d. 1030x35          d. 1020         (the Mighty)
in Norway)                            │                               d. early 1060s
                                 Earl Rognvald                        ┌──────┴──────┐
                                  d. 1046                          Earl Paul    Earl Erlend
                                                                      ↓             ↓
                                                                  rival lines of Earls of Orkney
```

Figure 3.11 Descendants of Earl Sigurd II.

out greedy' (*OS*, Chapter 13). On the early death of one of his half-brothers Sumarlidi, Thorfinn claimed his dead brother's third of Orkney, but another half-brother Einar, objected, saying that Caithness and Sutherland had been part of his father's realm (*ríki*), and that Thorfinn had already therefore had his share. Here it is clear that both entities were understood to be one empire or realm,[155] united by the Pentland Firth. Once he had come of age, Thorfinn made preparations to acquire the third of Orkney by force, but the peaceful brother Brusi intervened between the protagonists and brought them to agreement, as a result of which Thorfinn was given his third of Orkney, and Einar and Brusi united their shares under single rule. There was no hint yet of any claimant being earl of one or other parts of the realm; they inherited the title from their father and received some form of acknowledgement from their Norwegian overlord to whom they gave an oath of loyalty, and who agreed to allow them to hold a division of the islands, which included Shetland.

The process of inheritance of the respective earls' shares would have been followed eagerly by the farmers, or landholders, of Orkney and Caithness. They are usually referred to as *bóndi* (pl. *bændr*) in the saga, men who were descended from the original settlers in the islands, or members of distant segments of the earls' families, or those followers of the earls who had been given lands in reward for service. They had an important role to play in the inheritance rivalries, for their support or the withdrawal of support was crucial to an earl's success or failure. They also had to provide military, or naval, contingents towards the earls' expeditions and this was evidently a big bone of contention, which led eventually to the murder of Earl Einar. The story of his attempt to increase the number of ships for his raiding expeditions and the restrictions imposed on him at the farmers' assembly (*þing*) reveal limits on an earl's freedom to access resources, and it is said that because of Earl Einar's demands and harsh rule 'many people of importance left Orkney', some of them going to join Earl Thorfinn (*OS*, Chapter 14). There were checks and balances on an earl's tyranny and overweening ambitions, and in the end Einar got his just deserts, and was pole-axed in Thorkel *fóstri's* hall in Sandwick (*OS*, Chapter 16).

3.6.1 *Relationship with Olaf Haraldsson*

These same years also provide glimpses of the earls' developing relationship with the king of Norway, which is to become such an important feature of the history of the earldom. The new king in question, Olaf Haraldsson, was a

---

155 The word used in OS is *ríki*, translated as 'realm' in *OS* Taylor (more correctly than 'earldom', in *OS*, Pálsson and Edwards). Sometimes the word *eyjar* ('islands') appears to include Caithness, evidently considered to be part of the island realm and not a separate entity, even though on the mainland of Scotland.

powerful figure in life (and after death, when his role as martyr and proselytizer of the Norwegian people turned him into Norway's national saint), and he started the real process of welding the disparate parts of Norway into a single unit ruled by a single king. This process extended to the Atlantic islands also, and the story of the earls' submission to Olaf is elaborated by the saga writer into dramatic confrontations, which raise a lot of interesting aspects of the earls' relationship with the kings, even though these have been written from a thirteenth-century viewpoint.[156] The saga author knew about the process of submission and overlordship, the problem of dual allegiance and the earls' attempt to use their loyalty to another king to avoid obligations, as well as the kings' use of hostages as pledges for their earls' good behaviour. His recounting of the circumstances foreshadows the process of restriction of the earls' freedom, turning them into royal officials bound by oaths of homage and payments of tribute to their Norwegian superior rather than freebooting rulers of a thalassocracy who acknowledged no restrictions.

There is evidence from Olaf Haraldsson's reputation as a ruthless controller of his powerful *stórmenn* ('great men', 'men of rank') in Norway that he had no scruples in cracking down hard on those who were unwilling to submit to his authority, and we need not doubt that he would also have asserted his dominion over the earls. A rare entry in the Icelandic Annals about the situation in Orkney says specifically that 'Earl Thorfinn and Earl Brusi Sigurdsson gave the Orkneys into the power of King Olaf' (*þorfinnr jarl ok Brusi jarl Sigurðar synir gafu Orkneyiar i valld Olafs konungs*; IA, sub 1021, 106), which indicates that his successful inroad into the Orkney earls' independent status was well-known. Ottar the Black's poem on King Olaf says it in verse:

> Great rulers have good reason
> To regard you; trust
> You show in their strength:
> Shetlanders will serve you.
> Before your coming
> No commander so courageous
> In all the eastlands, you
> overlord of Orkney

(*OS*, Chapter 19)

The visits made by Brusi and Thorfinn to Norway and their evident submission to King Olaf indicate that there was a real growth in royal authority in this period, which meant that the king's strong reputation extended effectively to Orkney from Norway, without him having to make a personal expedition west

---

156 See Crawford, 1987, 76, and also comments by Orning (2008, 313–14) about using the sagas as records, enabling the reader to come 'relatively close to the historical reality'

to the islands.[157] Some dramatic passages in *Jarls' Saga* give a fine picture of the delicate balance of power between the earl and the king. Thorfinn plays his Scottish card:

> 'Were you ever to need my help against other rulers, my lord' he said 'it would be yours for the asking. But it's not possible for me to pay homage to you (*veita yðr handgongu*). I'm already the Earl of the King of Scots and subject to him' (*lyðskyldr*) ... The king could see how much more ambitious Thorfinn was than Brusi and trusted him less, for he realised that Earl Thorfinn could rely on the support of the King of Scots should he want to break the agreement.
>
> (*OS*, Chapter 19)

This indicates a prioritising of allegiance which is more applicable to a later 'feudal' period, but nonetheless there is reality in the process of submission of the earl to the king, the acknowledgement of superior authority, and the development of a hierarachy in the order of rule. The wise Thorkel Fosterer who looked after the young earl's interests advised him secretly not to part from the king 'without having made a settlement' and the earl 'realised that he had no choice but to let the king have his way', even though this meant that he might lose control over his ancestral lands. He was exceedingly reluctant 'to swear oaths granting those lands (*ríki*) to men with no birthright to them' (*er ekki í váru til bornir*). But he was in the king's power and realpolitik advised that it was necessary to submit and become the king's liegeman, 'just as his brother Brusi had done'. King Olaf thought that Thorfinn had agreed to everything too readily and cheerfully, so that he 'suspected that Thorfinn had no intention of keeping to the letter of the agreement'. The reader cannot know whether this reflects the actual course of events or the actual process of submission. But when we read on and learn that the agreement was about the imposition of compensation for the killing of Earl Einar we can be reasonably confident that an element of reality lies behind this dramatic literary rendering of the saga author's account of the meeting. Reality probably also lies behind the king's appointment of Earl Brusi, who was given two-thirds of the earldom, as the king's 'personal agent' (*trunaðar mann*), and who had to leave his son Rognvald behind with the king as a hostage, who 'stayed with King Olaf for a long time'. Rognvald played a foremost role in the dramatic events which saw the end of Olaf Haraldsson's career in opposition to the powerful Anglo-Danish King Cnut. He followed Olaf into exile in 1028, fought alongside him at the Battle of Stiklestad in 1030, then rescued Olaf's half-brother Harald Sigurdsson from the battlefield, and fled with him to the safety of the court of Prince Jaroslav

157 The earls may have gone to meet with King Olaf because of fear of reprisals, but also because the nature of the joint inheritance of the earldom by more than one son meant that the king's support was needed in the competition for power

in Novgorod (*Heimskringla, Saint Olaf's Saga*, Chapter ccxlv; *OS*, Chapter 21). It is said that Jaroslav thought very highly of him, 'as did everyone else'.[158] Rognvald submitted to Magnus Olafsson who had also sought safety at the court of Jaroslav, and returned with him to Norway where Magnus was hailed as king in succession to his father, Olaf. Rognvald then returned to Orkney, Brusi having died, in order to claim his father's estates, and was given the title of earl by King Magnus, along with three fully equipped warships and the third of Orkney which King Olaf 'had owned' and had granted to Brusi (*OS*, Chapter 21).[159] The story of Rognvald's relationship with Thorfinn is central to the next dramatic section of *Jarls' Saga*.

The earls of Orkney were caught up in the northern world of international politics and power struggles which make the eleventh century such an exciting period. They were players on this stage because of the importance of the islands in the maritime world of ambitious and mobile aspiring rulers determined to fill the void left by the death of the great King Cnut. It is probable that Cnut was more interested in Orkney and the Hebrides than any of the sources suggest. He certainly extended his authority northwards from England into Scotland (Alba) so that Malcolm (Mael Coluim), the Scottish king, and Mælbeath (macBeth), ruler of Moray, and Jemarc (Echmarcach) from the Rhinns and the islands submitted to him (*ASC, sub* 1031).[160] Control of the sea routes around the north of Scotland was probably a prime aim. The reference in *Jarls' Saga* to 'constant threat of war' when Danes and Norwegians who were sailing to the west and returning by way of Orkney 'often came ashore to plunder the headlands' (*OS*, Chapter 19) possibly relates to this period of the Anglo-Danish maritime hegemony. A sense of relief must have pervaded northern lands and islands when Cnut departed this life in 1035. The power brokers could revert to worrying about their own positions *vis-à-vis* their neighbours without worrying about the overlordship of the northern world by one imperial authority. For Thorfinn this meant facing up to a powerful rival from Scotland, the often-discussed 'Karl Hundison'.

3.6.2 *Caithness contested between Earl and Mormaer*

Although Thorfinn controlled two-thirds of Orkney, Caithness was still an important power base for him, for several reasons. Control of Caithness meant Orkney was secure from attack from the south; control of Caithness provided

---

158 Rognvald was a paragon of all the requirements for a successful warrior and leader: 'taller and stronger than other men, outstandingly handsome and so talented there wasn't a man to match him'(*OS*, Chapter 21)
159 Although it is said (*OS*, Pálsson and Edwards) that the king gave the earldom to Rognvald 'in fee', these words are not in the Old Norse text, and are best not used in this pre-feudal age
160 Hudson, 1992; Crawford, 2001, 77; Bolton, 2009, 147–50

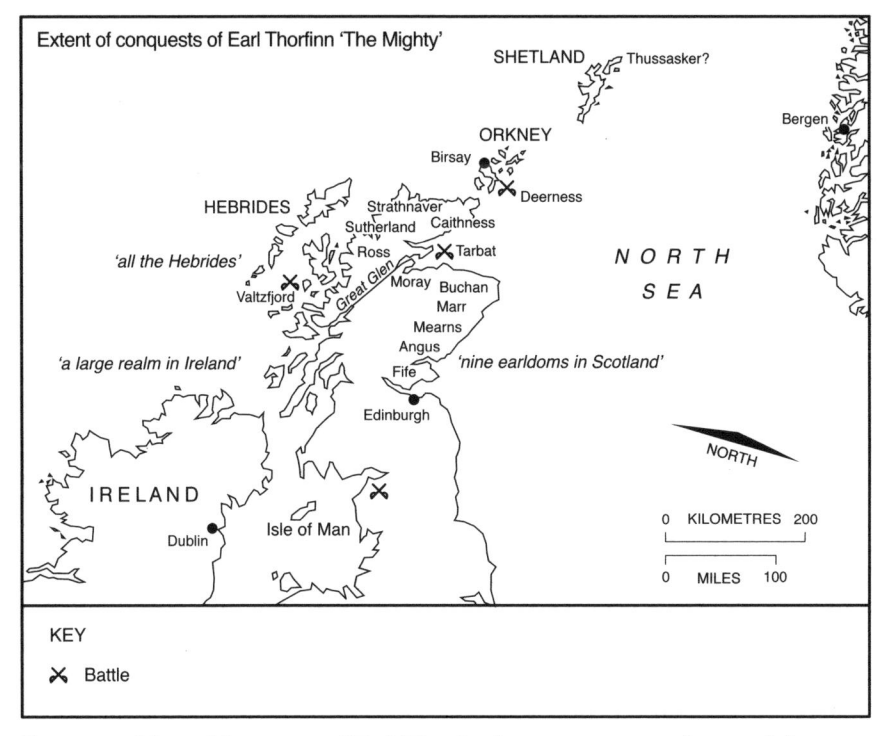

Figure 3.12 Map of the extent of Earl Thorfinn's conquests, according to *Orkneyinga Saga*, Chapter 32.

a springboard for expansion down the east coast and exploitation of rich resources in the Firthlands (see Section 3.5.1); it also provided a base for expansion down the west coast without which the earl would have had great difficulty in bringing the Hebrides under his authority. Duncansby, near the north-east point of Caithness, was evidently the important power centre for this phase of the Orkney earls' clash with native lords in north Scotland:

> Earl Thorfinn stayed on in Caithness at Duncansby, keeping five well-manned longships with him so that he had a considerable force
>
> (*OS*, Chapter 20)

In the earlier period of tension between Orkney earls and Celtic lords on the north mainland it had been in the hands of members of a native Celtic dynasty (see Section 3.3).

Chapter 20 of the saga suddenly introduces a new theme, the battle with Karl Hundison for control of Caithness.[161] Most historians seem now to agree

---

161 Bolton (2009, 143) interprets this chapter as an interpolated section, incorporated into the

that King Karl must have been a ruler of Moray, and the present consensus is that he is to be identified with MacBeth.[162] The name 'Karl Hundison' by which the saga writer knew him must have its own explanation, which we do not fully understand.[163] Whoever he was, he was a powerful warrior and determined to assert the authority of the kings of Moray over the territory north of the Oykel:

> He claimed Caithness just as earlier kings of Scots had done, and expected the same payment of tributes as from elsewhere; but Earl Thorfinn, who held Caithness, thought it no more than his proper inheritance from his grandfather and refused to pay any tribute for it.
>
> (*OS*, Chapter 20)

This led to outright hostilities, with Karl/MacBeth taking the initiative and moving his nephew Muddan north into Caithness. He was ousted by Thorfinn who pursued him south and conquered Sutherland and Ross, plundering 'throughout Scotland' (probably meaning Moray). This led to a co-ordinated campaign with Karl/MacBeth sailing north with eleven long-ships and a large number of men aboard, while Muddan was sent with a land force back to Caithness and approached from the Highland zone, from the south. This was a dangerous two-pronged attack by an enemy which apparently had effective naval forces at its disposal, and which was able to take the fight into Orkney waters, for the two warriors, Karl and Thorfinn, fought a sea battle 'east of Deerness' at the eastern end of the Orkney Mainland. Our unimpeachable source for this, and the famous victory of Earl Thorfinn, is the evidence of the verses by the poet Arnor Thordarson (*jarlaskáld*),[164] on which the prose elaboration of the battle is most probably based. The Scots were routed, and Karl retreated south to the Moray Firth (*Breiðafjǫrðr*).

> main body of the saga in a later revision. Taylor (*OS*, 58) also comments on its coherent theme, focusing on the struggle of Thorfinn and Karl Hundison, and suggests that an oral *þáttr* surviving in Caithness lies behind it
>
> 162 See arguments in Crawford, 1987, 71–2; Duncan, 1975, 100; Cowan, 1982, 33; Brunsden, 2009. Aitchison, however, supports the alternative identification with Duncan (1999, 57). Bolton (2009, 145) argues that as Thorfinn's grandfather was not Malcolm MacKenneth but Malcolm MacBrigte of the Moray dynasty, Thorfinn was therefore drawn into the family blood-feud of the two branches of the Moray dynasty, which explains why he and Macbeth/ Karl Hundison were such bitter enemies
>
> 163 See discussion in Crawford, 1987, 72, where Anderson's suggestion that Karl was an 'opprobrious' name meaning 'churl' is cited (*ES*, i, 578). However, the name Karl appears as a personal name in other contexts in this period, possibly being the Norse equivalent of Charles, a name of high status. His patronymic 'son of Hundi' ('son of a dog') might also be considered to be unflattering, but *Hundi* ('dog') or *Hvelp* ('whelp') was the name of Earl Sigurd II's son, taken hostage by Olaf Tryggvesson, and therefore unlikely to be a derogatory name
>
> 164 Whaley, 1998, 124

PLATE 1. Runestones OR8 Birsay II: OR9 Birsay III (Barnes and Page, 2006), presently on display in the custodian's office on the Brough of Birsay. These badly damaged runic inscriptions had been reused as building material in the church on the Brough. They are probably memorial stones although the inscriptions are virtually unreadable. Having been reused in the twelfth-century church, they must date to the eleventh century or earlier. (Photo: author; © Crown Copyright, Historic Scotland)

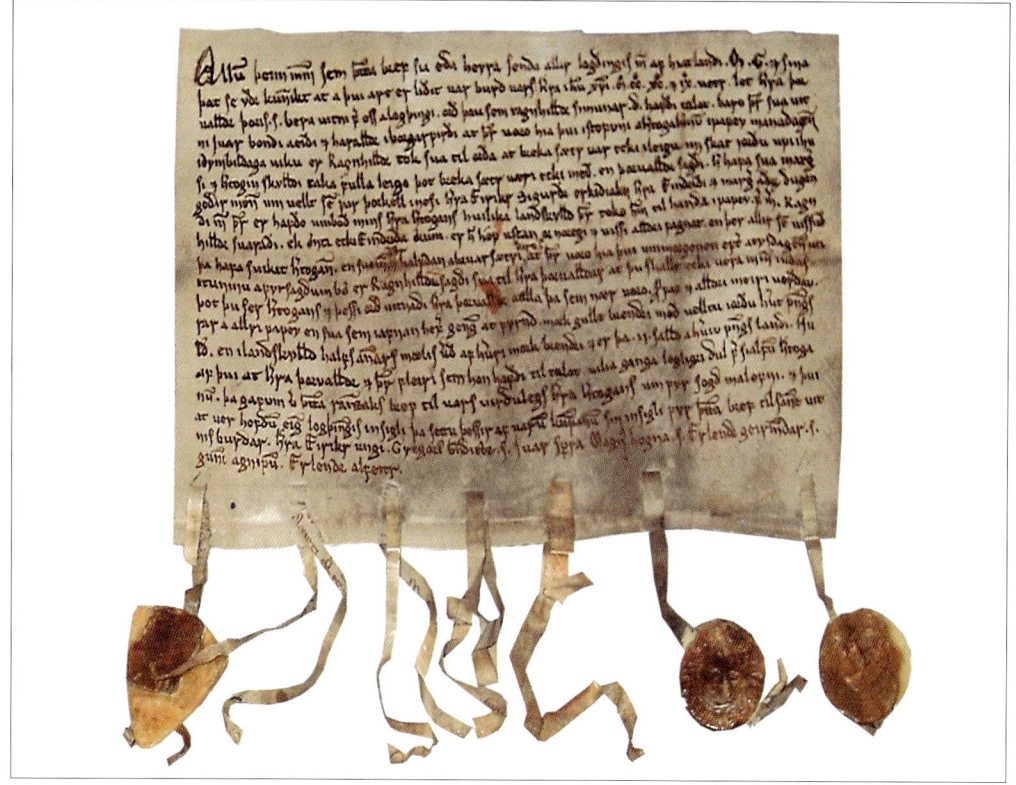

PLATE 2. Replica of the letter written by the lawthingmen at the Shetland Lawthing in June 1299 recording the events which had taken place on the island of Papa Stour at Easter time, and making an official statement about the rate of rents and taxes which should be paid by the farm of *Brekasætr* (Bragaster). This arose from the actions of the sysselman, Thorvald Thoresson, who was accused of treachery towards his lord, Duke Hakon of Norway, who held Shetland as part of his ducal 'appanage'. (Photo: author; courtesy Shetland Museum and Archives)

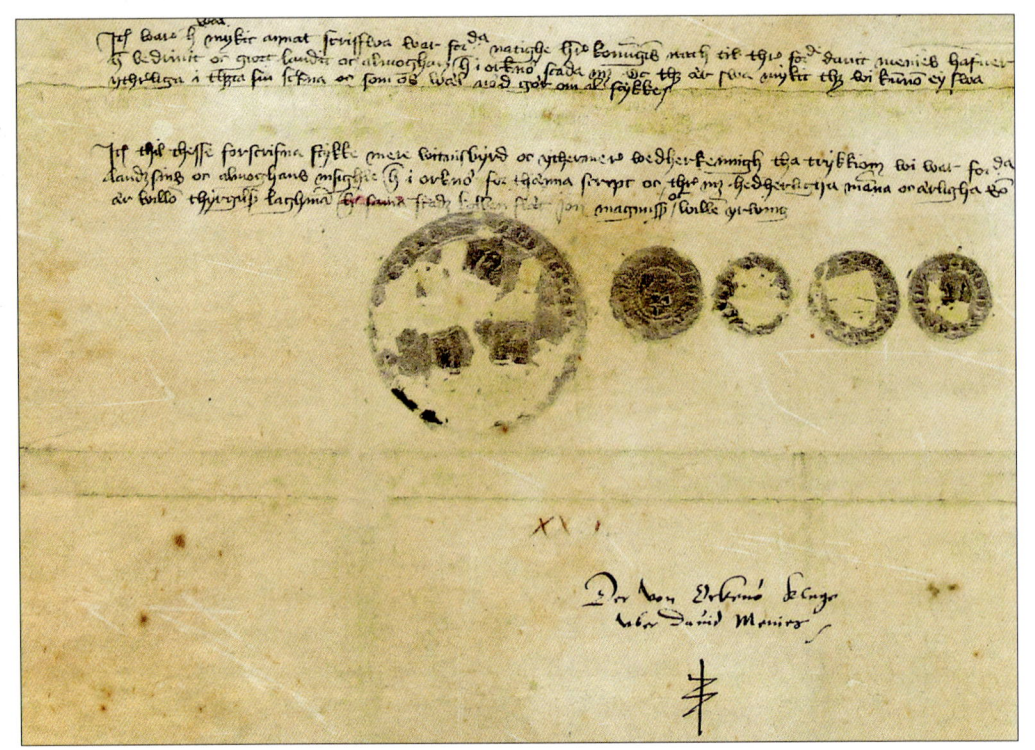

PLATE 3. Last section of the Complaint of the People of Orkney, dating probably to 1425, against the rule of David Menzies, brother-in-law of Earl Henry Sinclair II. It was sealed with the seals of the 'country and people here in Orkney' (the largest seal, of which virtually nothing survives), of the Lawman and three 'honourable and honest' men. (Courtesy Danish Rigsarkiv, journal no. D 10 Ny Kron. Række nr. 2944)

PLATE 4. The hymn *Nobilis humilis* in honour of St Magnus is a two-part syllabic tune. The MS dates to the second half of the thirteenth century. (De Geer, 1988, Fig.10) (Uppsala University Library MS c233 fol.19v–20r)

PLATE 5. View of the ecclesiastical buildings on the Brough of Birsay from the upper slope to the west. The twelfth-century church is central to the walled enclosure, with the cloister and monastic buildings on the north side. A sizeable burial-ground is on the south side of the church, where a replica of the famous Pictish stone can be seen. (Photo: author)

PLATE 6. The remains of the church at Spittal, Caithness, dedicated to St Magnus and most probably founded by the earldom family. It was a collegiate foundation providing shelter for pilgrims travelling across Caithness to visit the shrine of the murdered earl in Orkney. The hill beyond is Spittal Hill, which may have been the place of assembly of the Caithness farmers, who ran down from a hill to attack Bishop Adam in his residence at Halkirk in 1222. (Photo: author)

PLATE 7. Distant view of the Brough of Birsay from Ravie Hill, showing the good situation of this location for the earls' fleets to access the sea routes south-west and north. The probability that the Brough was connected to the Point of Buckquoy in the Viking Age would have made the bay a sheltered location for shipping at that time. (Photo: author)

PLATE 8. The surviving remains of the hearth in Room VI ('Earl Thorfinn's Hall') on the Brough of Birsay, surrounded by paving and with a flag-covered water or hot-air channel in front of the stone bench on the opposite side. This dramatic remnant of a high-status residence, now ending at the cliff edge, may be the remains of a bath-house (sauna). (Photo: author)

PLATE 9a and 9b. Two views of a cast of the seal of Earl John of Caithness c.1296
PLATE 9a. Showing the remains of the seal inscription '–IS CATANIE' (*sigillum Johannis, comitis Catanie*, 'seal of John, earl of Caithness')
PLATE 9b. Showing the galley (lymphad), the symbol of the earldom, surrounded by the royal tressure, and surmounted by a ?hare (Courtesy NRS (RH17/1/149))

PLATE 10. Broken matrix of a medieval seal found by a metal detectorist in Deerness, Orkney. It is likely that this matrix was broken on the death of the owner, but who the owner was is as yet unresolved. She is depicted kneeling, in an attitude of supplication, and must have been an aristocratic lady, or a nun. Dimensions of broken matrix: height c. 19mm, max. width c. 29mm. (Courtesy Orkney Islands Council)

PLATE 11. View looking north-west across the Dornoch Firth to Sutherland. This is the *Ekkjalsbakki* of the sagas, the estuary of the River Oykel, on the north side of which Earl Sigurd I is said to have been buried in a 'howe' or cairn (c.892). (Photo: R.M.M. Crawford)

PLATE 12. A prehistoric mound at Ham, Caithness, with the distant Orkney islands visible across the Pentland Firth. It was somewhere in this location that Earl Hlodver was buried in a 'howe' (c.980). (Photo: R.M.M. Crawford)

PLATE 13a. View looking across Scapa Flow towards Osmundwall (Kirk Hope) where Earl Sigurd II was trapped by King Olaf Tryggvesson and forced to accept Christianity. (Photo: R.M.M. Crawford)

PLATE 13b. Scenes of events in Earl Sigurd's life carved on a stone bench at Kirk Hope. (Photo: R.M.M. Crawford; Acknowledgements to Colin Watson and Anne Bignall)

PLATE 14. Aerial view of Birsay, showing the Brough in the foreground and Birsay village close by the ruin of Earl Robert Stewart's sixteenth-century palace. St Magnus' Kirk is at the head of Birsay Bay. The fertile arable lands of the Barony around the Loch of Boardhouse were always in the possession of the earls or the medieval bishops. (© RCAHMS Aerial Photography Collection Licensor www.rcahms.gov.uk)

PLATE 15. View over Houseby in the west Mainland of Orkney. The abandoned farm is in the middle of the fields with the associated chapel site at the edge of the loch. The village of Dounby lies beyond. (Photo: author)

PLATE 16. Reconstructed scene of the twelfth-century earldom seat of Orphir, on the north side of Scapa Flow. The round church of St Nicholas lies beyond the earls' timber longhall, and the stone buildings on the slope down to the stream would have been the domestic quarters of the workforce which ran the estate and managed the earl's establishment. (Copyright Iain Ashman)

PLATE 17. The small twelfth-century stone-built castle on the island of Wyre is one of the earliest surviving medieval defensive structures in Scotland, and certainly the earliest in Norway. It is recorded in *Orkneyinga Saga* as having been built by Kolbein Hruga, the father of Bishop Bjarni, from whom is derived the name by which it is known locally: Cubbie Roo's Castle. (Photo: author)

PLATE 18. The castle of Old Wick in Caithness is another early surviving defensive tower and possibly built by Earl Harald Maddadson c.1200. (Photo: author)

PLATE 19. View of the excavated stone-built longhalls at Earl's Bu, Orphir, with the surviving remaining semicircular apse of the round church of St Nicholas in the graveyard beyond. (Photo: author)

PLATE 20a. Statue of a secular figure, probably Earl Rognvald, dated to c.1300 but later placed on the sixteenth-century tower (the 'Moosie Tower') added to the Bishop's Palace, Kirkwall, by Bishop Reid. (Photo: author)

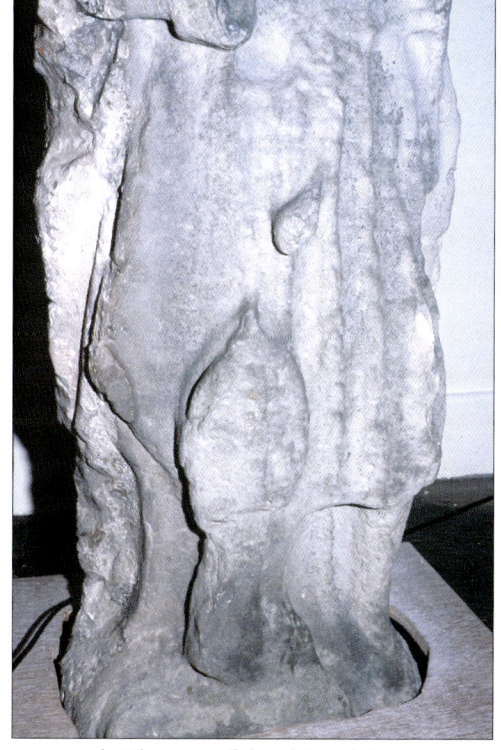

PLATE 20b. Close-up of the object sitting on a footstool against the leg of the statue. It has been suggested this may be a lyre (Crawford, 1995a), indicating the harp-playing skill which Rognvald boasted of in skaldic verse.

PLATE 21. Tingwall, Shetland, looking across the loch towards the archdeacon's church of St Magnus. There is a causeway running from the church towards the Law Ting Holm and Shetland's assembly site which projects out into the loch. (Photo: R.M.M. Crawford)

PLATE 22a. The unroofed ruin of St Magnus Cathedral, Kirkjubøur, Faeroe Islands, probably built c.1300 but never completed. (Photo: author)

PLATE 22b. The fourteenth-century reliquary plaque inserted into the east gable wall of St Magnus Cathedral, Kirkjubour, which contained relics of *magni domini be. Magni* ('the great lord, the holy Magnus' (Mooney, 1935, 276). (Photo: author)

PLATE 23. Figure of St Magnus on an embroidered sixteenth-century altar frontal from Skaard, West Iceland. He is shown wearing a circlet of nobility on his head, his sword in his right hand and a palm of martyrdom in his left. (Photo: author; courtesy The National Museum of Iceland)

PLATE 24. Statuette of St Magnus, with the garland or circlet on his head, and the symbol of his martyrdom, a sword, in his hand. It came undoubtedly from the Cathedral of St Magnus. (Photo: author; courtesy Orkney Islands Council)

PLATE 25. West front of St Magnus Cathedral, Kirkwall. (Photo: R.M.M. Crawford)

PLATE 26. Model of Bergenhus, Bryggen, Bergen, Norway, as it was before the destruction of the ecclesiastical complex in 1531. The cathedral stands on the left, Hakon's Hall in the centre behind the fortified sea wall and the sixteenth-century Rosencrantz Tower on the right. (Photo: Tore Klyve, Bergen City Museum)

PLATE 27. A view of Scrabster Bay, Caithness, looking towards the location at the head of the bay of the bishop's castle, very little of which survives. Bishop John was mutilated by Earl Harald's men who stormed the castle in 1201. (Photo: author, taken from above the present harbour, with Thurso in the distance)

PLATE 28. A view of Ousedale (*Eysteinsdalr*) in south Caithness, where the saga says that the Scots army camped on its march north in 1201/2. (Photo: author)

PLATE 29. Dornoch Cathedral in Sutherland, to where Bishop Gilbert moved his episcopal seat in the 1220s, after the murder of Bishop Adam at Halkirk in north Caithness. Some of the architecture dates from the thirteenth century. (Photo: author)

PLATE 30. The ruins of Halkirk Church, with the River Thurso in the foreground. Near here Bishop Adam was burned to death in 1222 by the Caithness farmers who revolted against the imposition of increased teinds (tithes). (Photo: author)

PLATE 31. (*Above*) Hakon's Hall on the left, Bryggen, Bergen, Norway, built in the 1260s by King Hakon Hakonsson, modelled on Henry III's Great Hall at Westminster. (Photo: courtesy Morten Stige)

PLATE 32. (*Right*) The memorial (built 1912) to commemorate the Battle of Largs (1263) is modelled on the twelfth-century Round Tower at Brechin Cathedral. It is known locally as 'The Pencil'. (Photo: author)

PLATE 33. A view of the Bishop's Palace, Kirkwall, taken from the roof of St Magnus Cathedral. The circular tower (the 'Moosie Tower') was built by Bishop Robert Reid during his episcopacy (1541–1558), and the stone figure (probably of Earl Rognvald) can just be seen high up in its niche on the south side, where it was relocated when the tower was built. The rectangular hall behind probably dates from the thirteenth century and may therefore be the building in which King Hakon Hakonsson died in December 1263 after the defeat of the Norwegian fleet at the Battle of Largs. (Photo: author)

PLATE 34. Brawl Castle, near Halkirk, the earls' 'manorial seat' (*caput*) in Caithness. It is very difficult to date this plain, square, defensive tower but (like the castle of Old Wick, Colour plate 18) it is an early example of a castle in the far north of Scotland, possibly twelfth-century. (Photo: author)

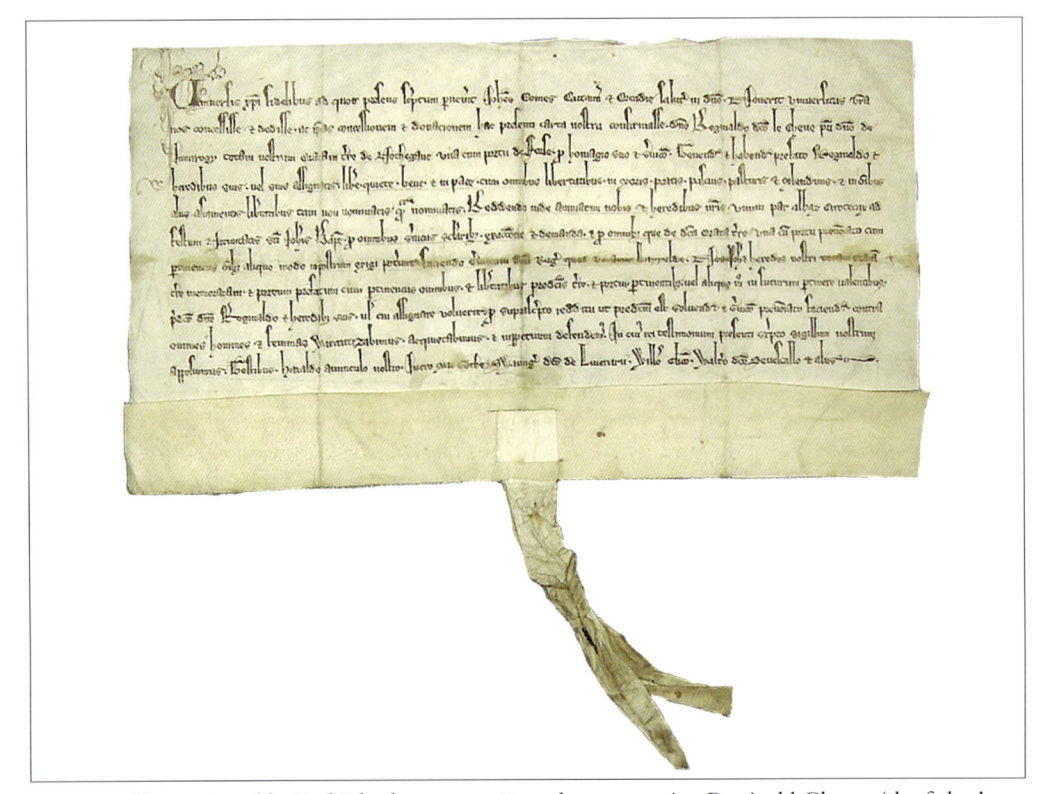

PLATE 35. Charter issued by Earl John between 1284 and 1293 granting Reginald Cheyne 'the father' the 'ounceland' of Nothegane (Nottingham) in south Caithness (see Sections 2.3 and 7.7.2). (With permission of the Hay family, earls of Kinnoull, NRAS 1489/Bundle 272, no. 138ii)

PLATE 36a. A view of the north side of St Matthew's Collegiate Church at Roslin with the famous carved inscription on the north clerestory cornice. The initials read W L S F Y C Y Z O G M iii L which is interpreted to stand for 'William Lord Sinclare Fundit Yis College Ye Zeir Of God 1450', the date probably signifying the creation of the College rather than the date of the building. (Photo: R.M.M. Crawford)

PLATE 36b. A close-up view of the first three initials W L S interspersed with the engrailed Sinclair cross (Photo: R.M.M. Crawford)

PLATE 37. The Asta stone on the road between Tingwall and Scalloway in Shetland, traditionally the location of the battle between Earl Henry Sinclair and his cousin Malise Sperra in which the latter died, probably in 1391. (Photo: author)

PLATE 38a. Nineteenth-century stained-glass window in the Town Hall, Lerwick, Shetland, depicting James III of Scotland at the time of negotiations in 1468–9 for his wedding to Margaret of Denmark, when Orkney and Shetland were pledged for the dowry which her father, Christian I, was unable to raise (see Section 8.5.2). (Photo: Brian Smith; courtesy Shetland Islands Council)

PLATE 38b. Nineteenth-century stained-glass window in the Town Hall, Lerwick, Shetland, depicting Margaret of Denmark at the time of negotiations in 1468–9 for her wedding to James III of Scotland. (Photo: Brian Smith; courtesy Shetland Islands Council)

PLATE 39. St Magnus Cathedral, Kirkwall, which was granted to the burgh of Kirkwall when it was raised to status of Royal Burgh by James III in 1486, and which has remained the property of the local authority ever since. The cathedral had probably been nominally the property of the earls since its foundation, and ownership therefore passed to King James when the islands were pledged in 1468, but he decided to hand it over to the new Royal Burgh in 1486 (See Chapter 9). (Photo: author)

PLATE 40. An aerial view of Sumburgh, Shetland, showing the famous archaeological site of Jarlshof and the ruined late-sixteenth-century 'Auld Hoose' of Sumburgh. Sir David Sinclair was designated 'of Sumburgh' and his residence would have been in the vicinity of the ruined house, where there are the remains of medieval longhouses. (Photo: author)

This did not see the end of the threat to Thorfinn's position in Caithness however, and the account of Muddan's killing by Thorkel *fóstri* is dramatic in the extreme, an incident which does not derive from any skaldic verse. Muddan made his way back to Caithness and based himself in Thurso with a 'strong force of men', suggesting that he was in a very threatening position. Thorkel was picked to go north with some troops to deal with Muddan, and managed to travel in secrecy so that Muddan was caught unawares in a house in Thurso in the middle of the night. As he tried to escape from the burning house, he was attacked by Thorkell who sliced off his head, and many of the Scots were killed, although some escaped (*OS*, Chapter 20).[165] The next showdown between the Orcadians and the Scots of Moray took place 'on the south side of the Moray Firth' on a peninsula known as Torfness, which is assumed to be Tarbat Ness (see previous discussion of the name). That the battle took place right at the frontier of Karl's territory tells us that Thorfinn had the advantage and that Karl was fighting to retain his authority in his own paternal domain. The ensuing victory of the earl over the 'mormær' made Thorfinn's reputation as the most powerful warrior in north Scotland; he had an assured power base over the whole terrain from the Pentland Firth to south of the River Oykel – as his ancestor Sigurd 'the Mighty' had had one and a half centuries earlier.

The saga writer did not know what happened to King Karl after this: 'some people say that he was killed there'. We can speculate that more probably Karl/MacBeth passed out of the saga story because he moved south and diverted his energies fighting for power in the southern Scottish kingdom of Alba, where he was king from 1040 to 1054. This may have left something of a vacuum in the north which Thorfinn was able to fill.[166] He certainly found himself in a position whereby he was able to raid deep into the kingdom of Alba, evidently laying stretches of territory under his authority as far as Fife, according to the saga account, corroborated to some extent by one of Arnor's verses:

> Shattered were the Scots' settlements . . . The true prince took payment for treachery, thrice in one short summer he struck them
>
> (*OS*, Chapter 20)

Which summer that was is a matter of guesswork. The extent of his authority in Scotland/Alba is summed up in Thorfinn's eulogy as having consisted of nine

---

165 An interesting detail from the point of view of wooden house structure, is the reference to the house as a *lopt*, which means that it was two-storeyed, with a 'balcony' (*loptsvalirnar*) which Muddan jumped over. This sounds like a sophisticated log-timbered house, similar to the *bur* ('two-storeyed storehouse'), many examples of which still survive in Norway. Whether this detail is reliable evidence for such a house in Thurso in the 1030s is uncertain, for it may be influenced by the style of houses known to the thirteenth-century saga writer
166 Crawford, 1987, 72

Scottish earldoms; this must indicate some knowledge of numbers of lordships down the east coast from Moray to Fife. Unfortunately, we have no evidence from Scottish sources that Thorfinn did indeed share in ruling this part of Scotland,[167] although we can assume that a powerful warrior with troops and ships at his disposal is likely to have played a role in the power struggles which dominate this period of Scottish history.[168]

3.6.3 *Campaigns to the Hebrides and internal rivalries*

After the death of his co-earl Brusi (1030x1035), Thorfinn had temporary possession of all the Orkneys, and with the defeat and disappearance of Karl Hundison he faced no threats to his position of strength in Caithness and north Scotland. Thus he was able to turn his attention to the west, and was clearly attempting to extend his authority over the Hebrides, and perhaps even further south, at the time when Rognvald Brusison sailed to Orkney to claim his father's share of the earldom (post-1035):

> Now, at that time Thorfinn was having a great deal of trouble with the Hebrideans and the Irish and needed reinforcements badly.
>
> (*OS*, Chapter 22)

This was in a period after the abdication of King Sihtric in Dublin, and Thorfinn and his nephew Rognvald had a successful partnership raiding in the Hebrides, in Ireland and thoughout the west of Scotland.[169] A fierce battle at *Vatnsfjǫrðr* (Waterford), attested by Arnor's verse, was a 'brilliant victory' (*bjartan sigr*).[170] It is said again that Thorfinn resided most of the time in Caithness, while Rognvald remained in the islands. At a time when his ambition was to consistently press further south-west, Caithness may have given Thorfinn an added advantage strategically.[171] However, in the years 1040–2 (when Cnut's son Hardicanute was ruling in England) he is said to have spent the winter in Orkney, and the saga writer is at pains to stress how the two earls raised their

---

167 The Scandinavian place-names in east Fife have been much discussed in the past two decades, although they are not thought to be the result of Norse settlement from the north but from England in this period (Fellows-Jensen, 1990; Taylor, 1995; Taylor, 2004)

168 The only evidence for close involvement of the Scottish kings with the northern earldom is Malcolm Canmore's marriage to Thorfinn's widow Ingibjorg, as mentioned in *OS*, Chapter 33, where it is also recorded that she was the mother of Malcolm's eldest son Duncan (Crawford, 1987, 74; 2001, 84); see Section 4.2.3

169 Crawford, 1987, 74

170 Probably Loch Vatten in north-west Skye (Whaley, 1998, 244), although Waterford in south Ireland is a possibility (Crawford, 1987, 74)

171 Particularly for gathering troops from Highland Caithness and Sutherland, who could move through the mountainous interior to the west coast for easy access to the Minch and the sea routes south (see Section 3.5.1)

troops in their different parts of Orkney. Thorfinn also raised troops in Caithness, with large numbers of Scots and Irish flocking to him, as well as many from all over the Hebrides. This great recruitment was for the reprisal campaign in north-west England, which again (according to Arnor) was a great success, with two pitched battles being fought as well as many sorties and killings.[172]

This evidence from the saga testifies to the unchallenged position which Thorfinn briefly won for himself throughout northern and western Scotland, extending even to parts of Ireland and north-west England. These were pillaging raids, after which 'they ravaged far and wide throughout England, killing, looting and burning wherever they went' (*OS*, Chapter 24). A successful warlord like he was would not have any problem recruiting warriors to follow him and help to maintain the momentum. As the poet puts it: 'No greater ring-giver ever roamed with warguard'.[173] Thorfinn was of course extremely lucky to have a famous skald like Arnor in his train, ready to laud his achievement and we are extremely lucky to have those verses to give us the flavour of his success, as well as some assurance that the extent of Thorfinn's successes was not dreamed up by a later encomiast.

However, it could not last, or at least this thalassocracy could not survive the diminution of the personal leadership of the famous warrior with full control over all parts of his inherited lands and islands. Even though, as suggested above, some administrative elements may have been laid down in parts of the domain, such as tax-raising structures and the locating of deputies, who were entrusted to maintain control on behalf of the earl and exact tribute and food renders, the weakening of the earl's power by rivals and rebels would see the whole structure unwind very rapidly. Among these variable factors, dependent on political fortunes and personal rivalries, were the earls' overlords the kings of Norway, always looking to assert their authority over the earls when their own political circumstances allowed. The trouble for Earl Thorfinn arose after the arrival in Orkney of Kalf Arneson, a relative by marriage[174] who had come to terms with King Magnus Olafsson, after repenting of his participation in the killing of Olaf at the Battle of Stiklestad.[175] Although Kalf had his uses as a powerful warrior — we are told for instance that he was sent by Thorfinn to the Hebrides 'to make sure of his authority there' (*OS*, Chapter 27) — his arrival

---

172 In revenge for the defeat suffered by Thorfinn's troops in England (*OS*, Chapters 23 and 24); see discussion of the textual problems in Chapter 24 by Jesch (1993, 230–1)
173 *hring drífr* is translated by Whaley as 'ring-strewer' (1998, 252). See Section 3.5.2 above on the function of arm-rings
174 He was the brother of Finn Arnesson, whose daughter Ingebjorg was Thorfinn's wife
175 Kalf was the one member of the powerful Arnmødling family who had fought against Olaf at the Battle of Stiklestad, in contrast to Rognvald Brusisson, who had been Olaf's foster-son and who fought alongside him at Stiklestad

evidently also caused difficulties.

The problem is plainly expressed: 'Kalf had a large following which placed a heavy burden on the earl's finances' (*OS*, Chapter 25). Therefore Thorfinn tried to get control of the third of Orkney which had been Earl Einar's and over which Rognvald had been given authority by King Magnus. But his approach to Rognvald met with resistance, who appealed to the fact that this was the king's portion, and he could not surrender it. This infuriated Thorfinn who had never fully accepted that Einar's third was confiscated by King Olaf and, warrior that he was, he determined to fight it out with his nephew. The various options open to Rognvald are expressed by the saga writer, who saw the niceties of both the earls' claims, and this probably reflects the reality of the situation. The practicalities of their respective power bases are appreciated, Rognvald having authority over two-thirds of the Isles,[176] whereas Thorfinn had his third of Orkney, but also Caithness, 'most of Scotland and all the Hebrides as well'.[177] However, Rognvald could call on support from King Magnus, and having visited Norway he returned with a 'large well-equipped army' supplied by the king (*OS*, Chapter 25). When Rognvald's and Thorfinn's fleets met in a sea battle off Roberry Head on South Ronaldsay, it was Kalf's decision to support Thorfinn which decided the outcome.[178] Arnor's verses describe the battle, and express his anguish at seeing his two patrons come to blows, with an additional verse by Bjarni *Gullbrárskáld* (another famous skald) adding to the extraordinary richness of skaldic poetry from this scene:

> I heard how you closed,
> Kalf, with Finn's kinsman,
> Sailed your ships-of-war
> Straight at his fleet;
> Keen to kill you
> Crashed upon Brusi's kin:
> Helpful, your hate,
> When you upheld Thorfinn
>
> (*OS*, Chapter 26)

The battle was not the end of the story of Thorfinn and Rognvald. Both survived and their continuing hostility, with the benign or malign influence

---

176 The term used in the ON text (*eyjar*, 'islands') is probably meant to be inclusive of the Shetland islands (Smith, 1988, 24, n.11)
177 The meaning of 'Scotland' in this context is not clear, but may be a general reference to the authority which Thorfinn was believed to have had within the province of Moray or more widely in the kingdom of Alba
178 King Magnus sent a message with Rognvald bidding for Kalf's support by promising him that he could have his estates in Norway back if he supported Rognvald in the power struggle

of the king of Norway in the background, provides wonderful material for the saga writer, which is best read in the saga itself. Rognvald's secret night attack on Thorfinn in his Orkney residence, and the belief that he had perished in the fire (*OS*, Chapter 28) was followed by Thorfinn's vengeful attack on Rognvald at the earldom estate on Papa Stronsay, when he was hunted down and killed on the beach by Thorkell *fóstri* 'because no one else would do it' (*OS*, Chapter 29). This is prime evidence for the violent nature of society in the earldom, and for the lengths to which the earls were driven by their desire for power and the need for wealth to support their ambitions. It is a continuation of the ritualised killing of Halfdan by Earl Einar (see Section 3.4.1), although in the 1040s there was no issue about the pagan nature of the maiming or 'howe-laying' of the defeated warrior. Rognvald was carried to Papa Westray for burial, possibly in St Boniface Kirk.

3.6.4 *Division of the earldoms*

During the period of hostility between the two earls it is said that Thorfinn stayed on the Orkney Mainland (*OS*, Chapter 28), but we do not know which earldom estate he stayed at, probably Birsay. When Thorfinn was in hiding, Rognvald is said specifically to have taken up residence in Kirkwall (*OS*, Chapter 29), and this is a very important first reference to Kirkwall. It was possibly in the king's third of the islands, formerly Earl Einar's. The name Kirkwall is likely to have been given with reference to a church (*Kirkjuvágr*, 'church-bay') and the pre-cathedral church in Kirkwall was St Olaf's, at the heart of the original urban settlement by the Papdale Burn (see Figure 5.1).[179] It is quite possible that this church was founded by Rognvald and that he chose to dedicate it to his foster-father, Olaf Haraldsson, whose cult as a martyr-saint developed rapidly after his death at Stiklestad in 1030 and burial in St Clement's Church in Trondheim.[180]

In the period when Thorfinn was rivalling his half-brothers for power he is said to have resided at Duncansby in Caithness, but once he was clear of all rivals to power in his realm he had his permanent residence at Birsay (*Hann sat jafnan í Byrgisheraði*) in the west Mainland of Orkney (*OS*, Chapter 31) (see Colour plate 14). This is a very significant phrase for our understanding of earldom development, and was presumably also significant for the saga author who considered it worth recording.[181] It meant that there was a certain stability in the earldom organisation, linked undoubtedly to the establishment of a

---

179 Lamb in Batey, ed., 1993, 44–5
180 See Townend, 2005, on the rapid growth of Olaf's cult; churches were founded and endowed in England (York and Exeter) already by the mid-1050s (ibid., 268–9)
181 Crawford, 1983, 100

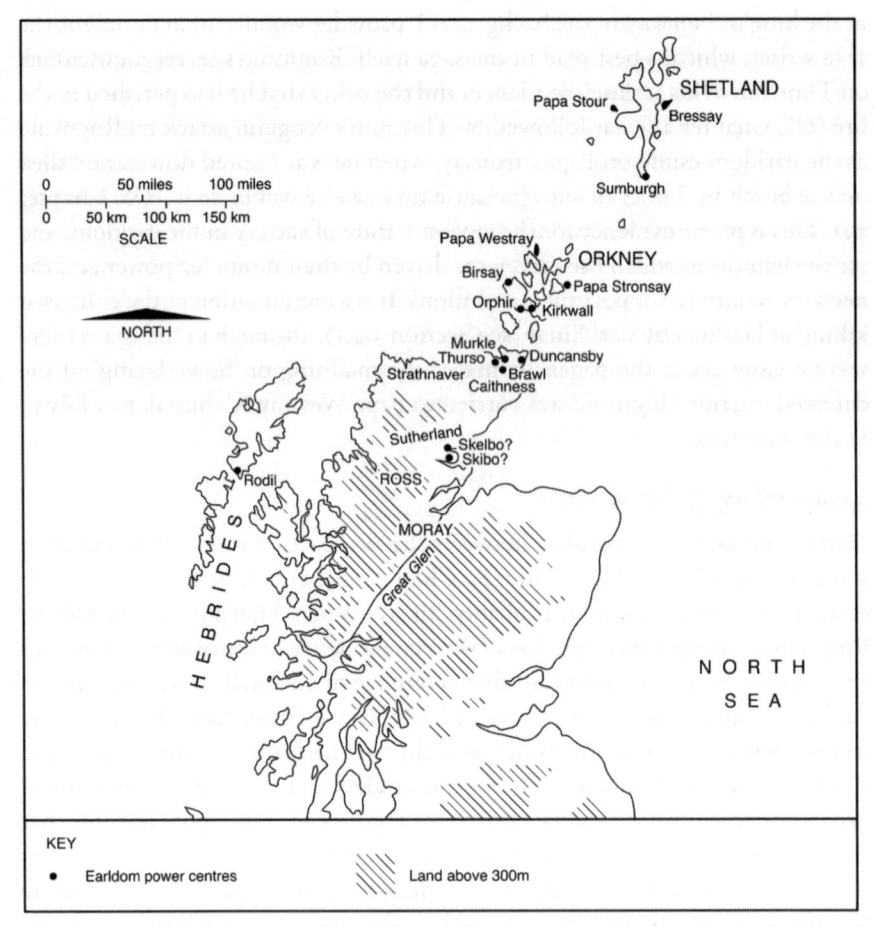

Figure 3.13 Map of certain, and possible, earldom power centres in Shetland, Orkney, Caithness and Sutherland.

bishopric at Birsay also (see Section 4.1). Normally the earls would have moved around their estates, as did every other ruler in western Europe in the tenth and eleventh centuries, maintaining control over the widely scattered territories and accessing food supplies to maintain their military following or hirð. But the fact that Thorfinn was able to reside in one place suggests that his need to maintain military control personally was no longer a priority, and that he had enough trustworthy hirdmen who would do that for him in the different parts of his realm, and extract due renders and taxes from the individual territories.

The Brough of Birsay, where the earldom residence was situated in this period, projected from Orkney's west coast, and was conveniently located for accessing the Hebridean parts of the earl's realm, as well as the Shetland Islands. It was also a good defensive point against incursions along the waterway leading via Eynhallow Sound into the heart of the Orkney islands. It was not so conveniently located for the earl's access to his Scottish earldom across the Pentland Firth which possibly indicates that by the latter part of his rule, when he is said to have resided in Birsay, Thorfinn had need to focus on the wider-flung parts of his maritime realm. The surviving remains of the secular residence, the stone-built longhalls, on the Brough, depleted though they are due to extensive erosion, are an indicator of the domestic living conditions of the highest members of the earldom elite in the islands (see Section 2.7.2). Great changes were going to occur with respect to circumstances on the Brough of Birsay in the next century, and the earl's main residence on the Mainland of Orkney moved to Orphir, on the north side of Scapa Flow, so that the Brough of Birsay ceased to be a place of residence. What we can now view is a relic of the eleventh-century earldom power centre (see Chapter 4 for further analysis).

Division of the earldoms is clearly indicated in this period. Under the rule of Thorfinn's sons, the joint earls Paul and Erlend, we are told that meetings were held to try to resolve the differences. The second one was called by 'men of goodwill' (góðgjarnir menn) on the Orkney Mainland[182] in order to try to make peace between the brothers and cousins, and it was agreed to divide the earldom in two halves, 'just as in the time of Thorfinn and Brusi' (*OS*, Chapter 35). Thorfinn we know was closely attached to Caithness, and so would have held the south isles. Brusi almost certainly held Shetland, and therefore the north isles of Orkney.[183] With Paul and Erlend the former probably had the same as Thorfinn while the latter had Brusi's half.

The saga makes quite frequent references to such divisions when there was joint rule by two or three earls. Although it is never explained how these divisions were worked out, it can sometimes be understood which earl had which portion of the islands from comments made in the text. The divisions must have been made with some equivalence of value and/or income, but it was frequently a cause of discontent and outbreaks of violence occurred. After Hakon Paulsson's death (c.1126) his sons took charge 'but they soon fell out and divided the earldom in half, which led to serious rifts between the chieftains, who formed up in two opposed camps' (*OS*, Chapter 54). It would appear that

---

182 This would have taken place at the 'assembly' (*þing*) site at Tingwall on the Orkney Mainland (Clouston, 1932, 185), the obvious place for a peace meeting between rivals, especially one called by the 'men of good will', at which a formal division of the earldom was carefully arranged and ratified
183 Smith, 1988, 27; Thomson, 2001, 70

both Shetland and Caithness were included in these divisions[184] and, as already pointed out, it seems never to have been the case that one earl took Caithness and another Orkney. Geographical logic would mean that the south isles of Orkney were linked together with Caithness, and the north isles with Shetland, while the west and east parts of the Mainland were divided near the isthmus of Scapa. Storer Clouston worked out a system of division of Orkney according to numbers of pennylands in each half or third, and he considered that the division was based on parishes, in which case the division between east and west Mainland was along the boundary of Firth and St Ola parishes, just west of Kirkwall.[185] Clouston did not bring Caithness or Shetland into his equation. A later refinement of the six divisions by the Norwegian archivist Asgaut Steinnes related these districts to the 'huseby' farms, which he saw as being the administrative centres for each district.[186] Although pennylands are unlikely to have been in existence at the time of Thorfinn and his sons, it is likely, as has been shown above, that units of territorial assessment (ouncelands) probably existed at this date (see Section 3.5.2) and had been imposed in some shape or form by Thorfinn's reign; if so, it is possible that they could have been used for the basis of an equivalence of value between the different halves or thirds.

When Thorfinn returned to Orkney from his journey to Rome, the saga writer tells us that he 'was finished with piracy and devoted all his time to the government of his people and country and to the making of new laws'. This is meant to indicate a change of lifestyle and and a new statesmanlike direction for this famous earl, which is an appropriate note on which to end the chapter devoted to 'Viking Earls'.

---

184 Crawford, 1984, 71

185 Clouston, 1919, 20; 1932, 35. Clouston's thesis is 'preposterous' according to Brian Smith (1988, 23).

186 Steinnes' theories (1959) are 'even more improbable' (Smith, 1988, 23). Thomson, 2001, 70–3; 2008, 50–1, also discards Steinnes' theoretical model of six divisions but focuses on the significance of some of the 'huseby' farms (see Section 4.3.1)

FOUR

Medieval Earls

1050–1150

The section of *Jarls' Saga* which has been central to the earldom story just discussed in Chapter 3 concerned Thorfinn's struggle for unrivalled power in his earldoms, and his campaign to extend his authority to the Hebrides. Along with the dramatic incidents in his rivalry with Rognvald Brusisson and the tense meetings with his Norwegian overlords, Olaf Haraldsson and Magnus Olafsson, these chapters have a quality and significance unsurpassed in Old Norse literature relating to the period. Fortunately for the historian of the Orkney earldom there are in addition some small crumbs of information which relate to political and religious developments in the governance of the earldom and which give us grounds for believing that the earls were leaving the Viking Age behind and becoming primarily rulers of a medieval lordship. This information is given in Chapters 31 and 32 where we first read about Thorfinn's visit to Norway to meet King Harald Sigurdsson *harðraða* ('hard-ruler') c.1050, and his subsequent journey to Rome where he had an audience with the Pope and 'received absolution from him for all his sins'. This is followed by the invaluable information that he built and dedicated to Christ 'a fine minster' (*dyrligt musteri*) at Birsay, on the west Mainland of Orkney, the first seat of a bishop, which must certainly have resulted from this papal visit.

4.1 EARL THORFINN'S FOUNDING OF THE ORKNEY BISHOPRIC

This provides some direct evidence for the deliberate Christianisation of the islands, and the creation of an ecclesiastical establishment. A formal structure of churches with priests who preached to and educated the converted communities would eventually result in the full Christianisation of the population. The forced conversion of Earl Sigurd in 995 can have had little direct effect in the islands, when it was linked to a formal, and probably nominal, submission of the earl to Olaf Tryggvesson (given up when Earl Sigurd's son Hundi died as a hostage in Norway) (see Section 3.5.3). Thorfinn Sigurdsson, however, was brought up at the court of his Scottish grandfather from the age of five, and must have been thoroughly imbued with Christian teaching even though his

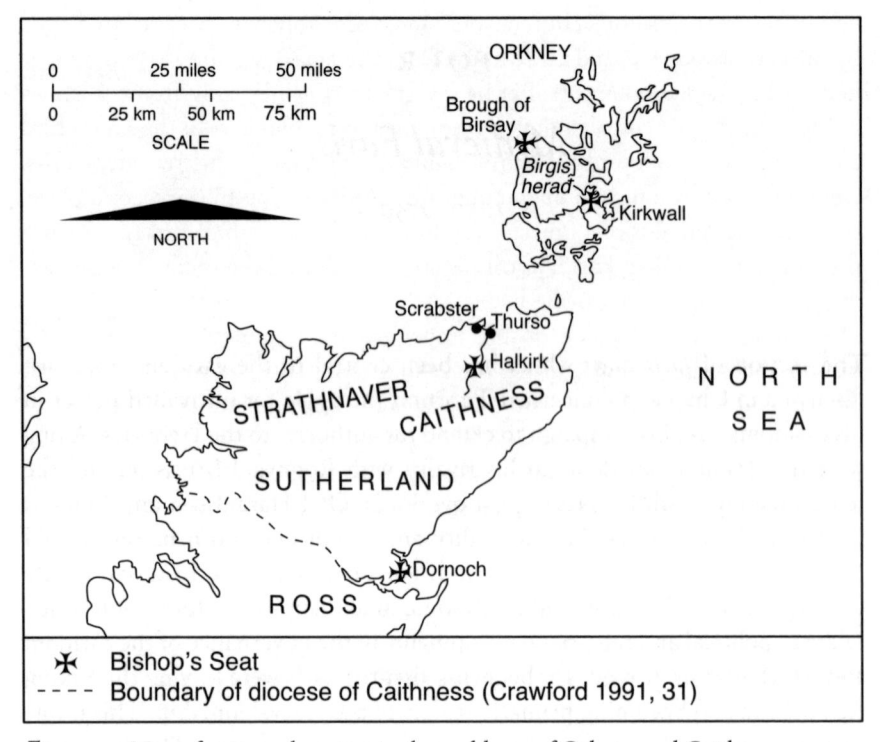

Figure 4.1 Map of episcopal centres in the earldoms of Orkney and Caithness.

famous exploits included raiding Christian peoples and ruthlessly fighting his way to power. It was no doubt the killing of so many of his enemies which was the impetus behind his pilgrimage to Rome and the need to seek remission for his sins. He was only able to undertake this once he had gained full authority, which made it safe for him to leave his earldoms for many months.

Presumably as a result of his audience with the Pope, Thorfinn embarked on a process of establishing a bishopric and supporting the maintenance of an ecclesiastical hierarchy. It is very significant that Adam of Bremen says that a bishop, Turolf, was established in Orkney 'by order of the Pope' (*iussu papae*)[1] and that he was appointed to a particular episcopal seat (*civitas*, 'city') called 'Blascona', which is thought to be a strange, Latinised version of 'Birsay'.[2] In the

---

1 Schmeidler, ed., 1917, 224; trans. F.J. Tschan, 1959, 216. Adam of Bremen wrote a history of the archdiocese and archbishops of Hamburg-Bremen c.1070. He provides the only information about the very first bishops of Orkney and the statement about Turolf's appointment may indicate that Thorfinn bypassed the authority of Archbishop Adalbert (Haki Antonsson, 2007, 89–90)
2 See discussions of this identification by Munch, 1855, 217; Crawford, 1983, 103, n.12; Crawford, 1987, 81; Crawford, 1996, 1.7; Crawford, 2005, 91; Antonsson, 2007, 87–8

first instance, the bishop's church would most probably have been located close by the earl's residence, and as we know from the saga Thorfinn resided permanently at Birsay (*Birgisherað*) after he returned to Orkney from Rome. Bishops in the early days of conversion in Scandinavia were members of the king's hird and would have followed the king around as members of his retinue, so this would be the way a bishop operated in the earldom also.[3] In the second place, there are the remains of a fine stone church on the Brough of Birsay, which is the likely successor to Earl Thorfinn's church, close to the remains of secular dwellings (see fuller discussion below).

Although the earl was probably under papal compunction to establish a bishop and support him and his household materially, he would have been determined to have a cleric who was acceptable to him, and probably a close associate. Interestingly, the name of the first bishop, Turolf (ON *Thorolfr*) is of northern origin, and this is unusual in the Scandinavian north at this period, when there were very few native clerics who had the training to be members of the higher ecclesiastical hierarchy.[4] The dedication to Christ is another indication that whoever advised Thorfinn knew the dedication of other early episcopal churches, for this was the customary dedication for first bishops' churches, especially in the western Scandinavian sphere.[5] It may suggest that Thorfinn was emulating the Norse king of Dublin, Sigtrygg 'Silkbeard', who had founded Christ Church Cathedral in Dublin c.1030, and it is noteworthy that these two episcopal churches were founded before any of the Norwegian bishops' churches (those at Nidaros and Selja were founded by King Olaf Kyrre about 1070). This indicates that Thorfinn's earldom was quite advanced in its progress towards becoming a regular Christian lordship, and this no doubt reflects the contacts which the earl had had with the Christian kingdoms of western Europe, and the head of the Roman Church.

The creation of a bishopric was essential to the establishment of a converted Christian society in the islands. It is likely that a few churches were already in existence before the bishop's church was built on the Brough. Indeed, some older pre-Norse churches may have been refounded by converted Norse settlers. As already noted, Rognvald Brusisson most probably built a church in Kirkwall where he established his power base, and other members of the earldom family

---

3   Thus, bishops prior to Turolf would have been peripatetic; see Crawford, 1996, 7, for Henry, mentioned by Adam (Schmeidler, ed., 1917, 236), as having been a bishop in the Orkneys before being appointed to Lund (?1042/7, according to Gelting, 2004)
4   Crawford, 1996, 7
5   Crawford, 1983, 104; 1987, 81, 2005, 91, as for instance in Trondheim and Dublin. This would often be accompanied by a secondary dedication and there is a tradition that the church on the Brough of Birsay was dedicated to St Peter (Radford, 1959, 11)

and retinue could have built their own private churches on their estates by the middle of the eleventh century. However, there was more to conversion than the building of baptismal churches; there was the need to establish a society ordered according to Christian principles and governed according to Christian precepts.

This is where we note the important information provided in *OS*, Chapter 31, that Thorfinn had finished with piracy and concerned himself with the 'government of his people and country and to the making of new laws' (*lagði þá hug á stjórn lyðs ok lands á lagasetning*). There seems no reason to doubt this statement, but unfortunately we do not have any evidence – contemporary or later – of what sort of new laws he might have introduced. It seems most likely that they would have concerned the establishment of Christian principles and moral code, and if we use as a model Olaf Haraldsson's laws which were proclaimed with Bishop Grimkell's advice at Moster in Hordaland in 1024, we should expect these to be concerned with the governance of the Church by the bishop, with the choice and consecration of priests who had to be supported, along with the building and maintenance of churches, and the adherence to the new Christian calendar of holy days and fast days.[6] They may also have included changes to customary pagan practices such as sacrifices, revering of ancestors, and pagan rites at burials; and changes to social customs of birth, marriage and inheritance. All these aspects of the older social organisation would certainly have to have been brought into line with Christian precepts, and the ruler had to attend to these matters with the advice and guidance of his bishop. In later centuries, Orkney and Shetland subscribed to the Gulating lawcode of west Norway,[7] but at this early period of social restructuring Earl Thorfinn himself was clearly remembered as having been responsible for the setting up of new legal frameworks, which would have superseded judicial customs already established in the islands. Presumably the Viking raiders and settlers, and the earlier earls, had already created their own communal legal structure, based on those customs that were already in place in the home country. The principle of making new laws was undoubtedly part of the ecclesiastical package which the newly established bishop had brought into the islands, and if so, it is very likely that there would have been some written record of this event, which has not survived. This was a very different principle from the oral nature of judicial affairs as practised in the local assembly (*þing*). In terms of the contemporary situation in the Scandinavian kingdoms this specific statement about Thorfinn's role as lawgiver is highly significant for our appreciation of the parallel nature of the earldom and the young Norwegian kingdom. It tells us that the earl's role

---

6 Andersen, 1977, 113, 127–8; Crawford, 1987, 83
7 Larson, 1935; Helle, 2001

mirrored that of kings in newly Christianised parts of Europe.⁸

It can be assumed that these new frameworks were imposed on Caithness and Sutherland also. The Scottish earldom was an integral part of the earl's whole domain and any changes to government and religion would have applied across the Pentland Firth as well as in Orkney and Shetland. This means that the bishop's authority would also have applied there, as he was the earl's bishop. There is very little information about what happened in Caithness in this period – all our evidence stems from the following centuries when there was violence and trouble over the imposition of Scottish bishops by the Scottish kings (see Chapter 6).⁹ This in itself tells us that an established order was being overturned, but the only evidence that can be used relative to the earlier situation are some late medieval indications that the bishops of Orkney continued to possess estates in Caithness along with the right to some financial dues from the parishes of Dunnet and Canisbay ('skat malt' and 'skat silver').¹⁰ It seems certain that these must have been a continuing relic of an earlier period when the bishops of Orkney had been endowed with lands and income in Caithness by the earls (and had never relinquished them). It is a highly unusual situation for one bishop to have any such rights in another diocese, which Caithness was from the mid-twelfth century.

Another relic of this earlier period is probably the church at Halkirk in Caithness, which seems to have been rather special, and originally non-parochial.¹¹ The name itself (ON *há-kirkja*) means 'high' church, and in the sense of being elevated in a political sense rather than topographically. It is located close to the earldom centre of Brawl, in fertile upper Thursodale.¹² (see Figure 4.1). First recorded as being the place where Bishop Adam was murdered in 1222, it was then an episcopal manor (see Chapter 6). The association with the bishops, and the Old Norse name, suggest that it had originally been founded as the Orkney bishops' main church close by an earldom estate to serve as a base for the episcopal administration of the Caithness part of the bishop's diocese.¹³ The

8 See Bagge, 2011, 182ff, for a discussion of 'what was law?' in this period. It may be that the earl had more authority to make laws in the islands where Norse society was not so long established as was the case in the Scandinavian kingdoms
9 Crawford, 1993
10 Ibid., 131–2; Crawford, 1991, 30
11 Crawford, 1993, 132–4
12 The bishops of Caithness had a castle at Scrabster, near Thurso in the twelfth century, probably a previous possession of the bishops of Orkney dating from the period when they would have needed to cross the Pentland Firth to access the Scottish mainland part of their diocese.
13 The conversion of the Norse population in the earl's Scottish earldom presumably followed the developments in Orkney. However, there may have been a stronger survival of Christian beliefs from the pre-Norse period on the north mainland of Scotland, as also of churches, and

Caithness diocese was established by King David I (c.1150), and after the violent attacks which the Scottish bishops suffered in 1198 and 1222, they moved their cathedral to Dornoch in the south of the diocese, and the former significance of Halkirk was forgotten.

4.2 MILITARY ORGANISATION AND EARLDOM AUTHORITY IN THE WEST

Uncertain though the evidence is for the effects of Thorfinn's ecclesiastical policies on his Scottish earldom of Caithness it is quite unknown if they had any effect whatsoever in the wider parts of his domain down the west of Scotland and in the Hebrides.[14] If they did, it is very unlikely that they would have survived the reduction of this part of the Orkney empire after Thorfinn's death.

There are however a few scattered pieces of evidence suggesting that some form of secular administration may have survived from this period of earldom authority in the west. The matter of the ounceland and pennyland territorial units has already been discussed (see Section 3.5.2), and the conclusion drawn that the spread of these units in the west probably relates to the period of Sigurd II's extensive campaigns in the Hebrides and Man. Thorfinn's successes in following his father's path of conquest would have strengthened any initial imposition of tax-render units, and perhaps refined them. Once imposed they would of course have proved useful to all successive chieftains who exercised control in the area, not only the earls from the north.

Did such units have a use in the important matter of raising troops? The earls looked to the islands in the west as a source of manpower, and sea power.[15] How such forces were actually raised is never described, although it has been thought likely that it was individual warriors with their personal war-bands who augmented the earldom fleets rather than the earl himself having a levy system on the model of the Norwegian *leiðangr* (*leidang*, 'naval levy'). The chieftain's military following (called his *lið*) is thought to have been the predecessor of the naval levy,[16] and the earl and his 'gödings' would all have had their own *lið*, but it appears from the phrases used in the saga as if the earls did sometimes raise levies; it is said that Thorfinn 'raised a levy throughout his realm' (*hafði hann útboð um allt ríki sitt*) for the raid on England in 1040x2, and that Rognvald did the same in his own earldom. Thorfinn certainly gathered troops in Orkney

---

it is likely that some of the dedications to Celtic saints which are recorded in Caithness may have survived from the pre-Norse period (Craven, 1908, Chapter 1; Grieve, 2005; Gibbon, 2006)

14 Crawford, 1987, 82

15 Williams, 2004, 69. These Hebridean forces had their own ships, a valuable advantage. Control of the west would have given the earl access to woodlands which he lacked in the Northern Isles (see Section 4.2.1).

16 Stylegar, 2004, 23

and Caithness, while on occasion he had a great force (*her*) from Scotland and Ireland and drew troops (*drósk honum lið*) from all the Sudreys (Hebrides) (*OS*, Chapter 24).[17] The earls' authority over the islands and Caithness would have been sufficient to organise the mustering of ships and men, either for war campaigns or for defence.[18] The earls themselves and their *lið* must have been primarily responsible for the manning of ships and supply of weaponry, but the provisioning of food supplies needed to maintain the fleet, and the organisation of such supplies was probably imposed on individual farms or districts, as it was in Norway.[19]

The mention of districts raises another possible pointer to a toponymic legacy of Norse administration and organisation of this period in Orkney, Shetland and the Hebrides, that is, the name of a district division called in Old Norse *hérað*, a term seemingly derived from *herr*, 'army'/'host'(CV, *sub hérað*). In parts of Scandinavia it may have functioned as a district associated with defensive matters, and later became associated with judicial arrangements, although in western Norway it signifies a more geographical division. In Orkney the word appears most significantly in the name *Birgisherað* where Thorfinn is said to have resided, and where he built the bishop's church – indicating a district attached to the important earldom seat on the Brough of Birsay.[20] This district eventually was divided into two parishes, Birsay and Harray, the latter name deriving from the second element of the ON name *Birgisherað*. The district called 'de Herra' in Tingwall, Shetland, has the same origin and is significantly close to Shetland's main legal assembly site, as well as the archdeacon's church.[21]

Remarkably, this same district name is found in the west, best preserved as the present name 'Harris' (Gaelic *Na Hearradh*) for the southern half of the Long Island in the Western Isles.[22] The name also survives in the island of Rum (Glen Harris) and is recorded in early rentals as a district called 'Herries' in Islay

17 Although the term leidang (ON *leiðangr*) is never used in *OS*, the use of the words *útboð* and *lið* tells us that there was a process of calling up men and ships, but on what basis is not described. It was Earl Einar's 'harsh levies' (*útboð*) in the early years of the Sigurdssons' joint earldom which caused his unpopularity (*OS*, Chapter 14).
18 The organisation of a beacon system for defence is very evident from the twelfth-century section of the saga, and place-names derived from *varð*, *viti* and *bál* throughout the islands provide toponymic evidence of places where beacons were located (Clouston, 1931–2).
19 *KL sub* 'Lide'
20 Crawford, 2005, 93, and discussion of the significance of the term *Birgisherað* (Crawford, 2006, 38–9)
21 Brian Smith (2009) shows that the 'Herra' name survived in several other parts of Shetland and these places may all have served as early legal districts with their own assembly site prior to the establishment of the central Lawthing at Tingwall
22 The significance of the strategic location of Rodil, at the south end of Harris (along with the church dedicated to St Clement) is discussed in Crawford, 1999, 117

in the Inner Hebrides. Herries is a territorial division immediately adjacent to the lordship centre of Finlaggan and facing onto the Sound of Islay.[23]

These appear to be toponymic traces of an early administrative arrangement, probably with judicial associations knowing how the Vikings carried their interest in law with them to their settlements overseas. Can we look to the earls' administration as lying behind the creation of these *hérað* districts? Any relationship between the ounceland/pennyland assessment unit divisions and the *hérað* districts has never been suggested. The appearance of this district name in such scattered locations does, however, indicate that it may have served some administrative purpose for the Norwegian settlements in the west.[24]

4.2.1 *Ross – the southern frontier*

Turning next to the Scottish province of Ross, which formed the frontier zone between the earldom of Caithness (including Sutherland) and the large and powerful province of Moray, we are dealing with a territorial unit even though it had maritime coastal links on both the east and the west. Ross was an important buffer between the earls' domain and that of the powerful 'mormaers', who, as we have seen (see Chapter 3), were the main protagonists of the earls in the tenth and early eleventh centuries because of their claim to power over Caithness and Sutherland. The province of Ross stretches across from the eastern Firthlands (Dornoch, Cromarty and Beauly Firths) to the west coast, and there are several cross-routes which provide access from coast to coast[25] (see Figure 3.9). The southernmost Firth leads into the Great Glen, the Highland Fault line with its string of lochs which enable water-borne transport to move easily across to the province of Argyll (see Chapter 3). Easter Ross therefore provided strategic opportunities for movement of armies and fleets from the east coast of north Scotland through to the west coast and the Hebrides, which in certain circumstances might have been more convenient than sailing south-west from Orkney round Cape Wrath.[26]

---

23 The Mid Ward is called 'The Herries' (Caldwell, 2008, 37, 147) and 'ye harees of Ila' in 1631 (Alan MacNiven, pers. comm.).
24 Andersson, 2006, 134–6, criticises my discussion of the name *Birgisheráð* in Crawford 2006, 38–9, as suggesting that this indicates an administrative unit around the earl's power centre in Birsay. He states that the *hérað* names in the north Atlantic settlements are only geographical divisions, or districts, without any administrative meaning. However, this does not allow for variable meanings at different dates with regard to the *hérað* names in west Norway, Orkney, Shetland, the Hebrides and Iceland (thanks to Peder Gammeltoft for discussion of Andersson's definitions)
25 See Baldwin, ed., 1986 for a collection of different studies on the history, place-names and archaeology of the Firthlands
26 Crawford in Crawford and Taylor, 2003, 6; Crawford 2004, 111–12

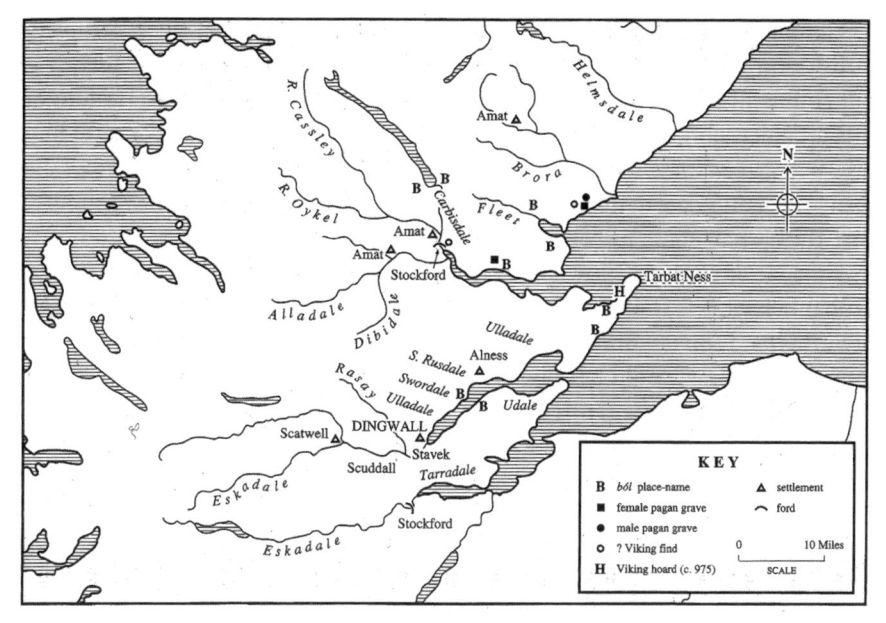

Figure 4.2 Map of Easter Ross and south Sutherland showing Norse place-names and location of pagan graves. (From Crawford, 1995, fig. 3)

For earls who ruled a maritime empire, and whose power was necessarily maintained by their fleet of ships, this area provided a vital source of wood for shipbuilding and ship repairs. Their campaigns of conquest southwards on the north Scottish mainland would give them access to the wooded shores of the Firthlands and the river valleys leading westwards, and they had regularly to battle for control of this area with the mormaers of Moray.[27] This is evident with the first earl, Sigurd I, who had a partnership with Thorstein the Red in the late ninth century, and among their conquests Ross was named (*OS*, Chapter 5) (see Chapter 3). This situation was threatened by the powerful rulers of Moray in the tenth century (as has been discussed), but towards the end of that century Sigurd II is said to have dominated Ross along with other provinces (*Njal's Saga*, Chapter 86), followed by his son Thorfinn who 'subdued Sutherland and Ross', consolidating his position by his victory against Karl Hundison at the Battle of Torfness (the peninsula of Tarbat Ness at the eastern coastal point of Ross).[28]

27 The earls are sometimes said to have been given ships by the kings of Norway, which would have been prestigious vessels for their own use. Norwegian timber resources might not have been readily available to them or their retinues unless they had close family connections with western Norway
28 Crawford in Crawford and Taylor, 2003, 4

Conquest was one thing, but how did these earls maintain their authority in Ross, and for how long was it maintained? These are questions which it is difficult to answer, for the saga tells us nothing about the earls' government of this province, and we are reliant on the Norse place-names of Ross for revealing how extensive Norse settlement was. Indicative archaeological evidence in the form of pagan grave material is so far undiscovered, which leads one to suggest that the earlier phase of conquest under Earl Sigurd I and Thorstein was not permanent enough to allow any settlement to take place, otherwise it would probably have left traces of burial evidence as has been recorded in the south of Sutherland (on the north side of the Dornoch Firth).[29] Any attempted settlement at that time would have been curtailed by the mormaers' vigorous assertion of authority in the tenth century. We have to look to the period after the Norse had been influenced by Christianity as being the more likely period of settlement, and this may have begun under Earl Sigurd II.[30] But it was probably not until the time of Thorfinn's victory over Karl Hundison and the vacuum left by Macbeth's move south (1040) (see Section 3.6.2) that Norse settlers were able to consolidate their landholdings. By that time the earl's following would have certainly abandoned overt pagan practices like equipped burials and be using Christian churchyards.

The Norse place-names of Easter Ross have benefited from close study[31] and they show that Norse speakers settled on the rich grain-growing lands of the coastal plain but that they also had authority in the river valleys running west from the firths towards the mountainous massif of the highland terrain. The '-dale' (*-dalr*) names of the valleys (like Eskadale, Dibidale, Alladale) may represent Norse control asserted from a distance and not be evidence of Norse-speaking farmers on the ground. However, the scatter of other Norse names in the valleys, ending in *-völlr* ('field', indicating a level cultivable area) strongly suggests that these were estates which were farmed by Norse speakers.[32] If the timber in these valleys was the earls' prime requirement, of necessity there would have to have been settlers in the locality who were able to manage this resource for the earls' benefit, or who could compel the native population to fell and log the timber according to requirements for shipbuilding or other domestic needs.

29 Crawford, 1995, 8, fig. 3
30 The hoard of coins and silver arm-rings discovered in the churchyard at Tarbat has been dated 990–1000 (Graham-Campbell, 1995, no. 29) and may therefore be material evidence for the activity of Earl Sigurd II's forces in the locality of the Firthlands
31 Crawford and Taylor, 2003
32 The normal habitative Norse names ending in *-byr*, *-staðr* and *-setr* may have been replaced by *-völlr* (see fuller discussion in Crawford, 2004, 116, and additional comments by Graham-Campbell, 2006, 94–119)

These river valleys also provided the routes through to the west coast, which would have been of vital use to the earls when deploying their forces on campaigns in the west. The use of such routes through Ross – and Sutherland and Caithness – would have meant that they had to be patrolled and made safe for the passage of military retinues on horseback, or for officials accessing the remoter Norse strongholds. Some of the place-names, particularly Rossall (ON *hross-völlr*, 'horse-field'), may even indicate that units were established for the specific purpose of breeding horses and for supplies of pasture or hay along the valleys.[33] We do hear in the saga of earls and other people riding inland across this area,[34] and a supply chain of riding horses, and fodder for retinues would have been a very necessary part of earldom organisation.

However, there is a question mark about the status of the province of Ross in Earl Thorfinn's empire, for it does not appear to have ever formed an integral part of the earldom administrative structure, to the extent that there is an absence of ounceland and pennyland land divisions. This suggests that Ross was administered on a different basis from the Hebrides, and the territories along the west coast of Scotland where these divisions can be traced. However, the remarkable survival of the place-name Dingwall in Ross is an important indicator of the extent of social organisation of Norse settlers in the locality. The name Dingwall, derived from *þing-völlr* (the 'field' or 'open space where the assembly met'), tells us very clearly that the Norse settlers were well enough established, and well enough organised, to have had their own public assembly, and for this to have been in existence long enough for the name to have become a permanent feature of the local nomenclature.[35] Dingwall is still today a very central place, being the county town and seat of local government, and has always been a nodal point because of its location at the head of the Cromarty Firth, accessible therefore by sea from all the coastal territories of the Firths, and also accessible from the river valleys and routeways running westwards into the hills.[36] It seems very likely therefore that it played an important role in the Norse population's social and cultural homogeneity and that the Norse-speaking settlers were dominant enough in the locality to organise their own legal, social and economic affairs.[37] How do we explain this centrally impor-

33 Another recurring name is Langwell (ON *lang-völlr*, 'long field'). See Crawford, 2004, 117–22 and fig. 2, for further details of these names and the hypothesis that they may indicate an organisation of horse transport for earldom retinues in the period when the earls were needing access to the west coast for maintaining power in the Hebrides
34 Instances are cited in Crawford, 1995, 119
35 The significance of *þing* ('assembly') sites in the Norse settlements is discussed in Crawford, 1987, 206–10; Fellows-Jensen, 1996, and will be further analysed in forthcoming publications of the Thing project (www.thingproject.eu/node/11)
36 Crawford in Crawford and Taylor, 2003, 14, 17–18
37 Crawford, 2004, 113

tant position which Dingwall had in the province when there is an absence of evidence for any earldom administration (if the lack of evidence of ouncelands and pennylands can be understood to point in that direction)?[38]

A possible conclusion to be drawn from this[39] is that the Norse-speaking settlers of Ross were independent of earldom authority to some extent, and able to set up their own framework of social organisation. We should not imagine that the settlement took place outwith the earls' control; indeed it could only have happened with their military strength helping to coerce the native population. But, once Ross was fully under Norse control, the earls may have been content to allow the settlers to run their own affairs and to be free of earldom tax demands – and in return to extract the timber for the earls' use, to patrol the routes to the west, and to maintain supplies of horses for the use of earldom retinues. All the areas brought under even nominal earldom authority would have been organised for the benefit of the earl and his close following (hird).

The above hypothesis regarding Ross's place in the earldom administrative picture is built on place-name evidence. Who may have been given the responsibility for this organisation? The suggestion has been made that it was Kalf Arneson.[40] He was certainly entrusted by Thorfinn to make sure of the earl's authority in the Hebrides after the Battle of Roberry (as the saga tells us, OS, Chapter 27). He was a close relative, with a following of men from Trøndelag (where Kalf's own estates lay), who would have had the skills to exploit the rich timber resources of Ross. Perhaps they settled in the Firthlands after leaving Trøndelag with Kalf when Magnus the Good was accepted as king in 1034, and moving west to the protection of Earl Thorfinn's domain. Such a group of settlers could have established their own assembly site at Dingwall with the sanction of the powerful earl of Orkney who had the resources and the experience to adapt his imperial ambitions and administration to local circumstances in this most vulnerable frontier locality.

4.2.2 Thorfinn's 'famous journey' and pilgrimage to Rome

Finally we come to the crowning achievement of Thorfinn's 'state-building', enhancing his reputation as a Christian prince who was on a level with other northern rulers, and an achievement which appears to have been very well-known.[41] This was his tour through Europe to Rome which took place c.1050

---

38   This discounts an earlier suggestion that Scatwell may indicate a place which rendered 'skat'. The name Scatwell more probably derives from a topographic feature (see Crawford, 1995, n.5)
39   See fuller arguments in Crawford in Crawford and Taylor, 2003, 9–10, 17–18; Crawford 2004, 113
40   Crawford, 1995, n.10; 2003, 10; 2004, 114
41   An additional reading (included in OS Taylor, 188) says 'that journey was his most famous one'

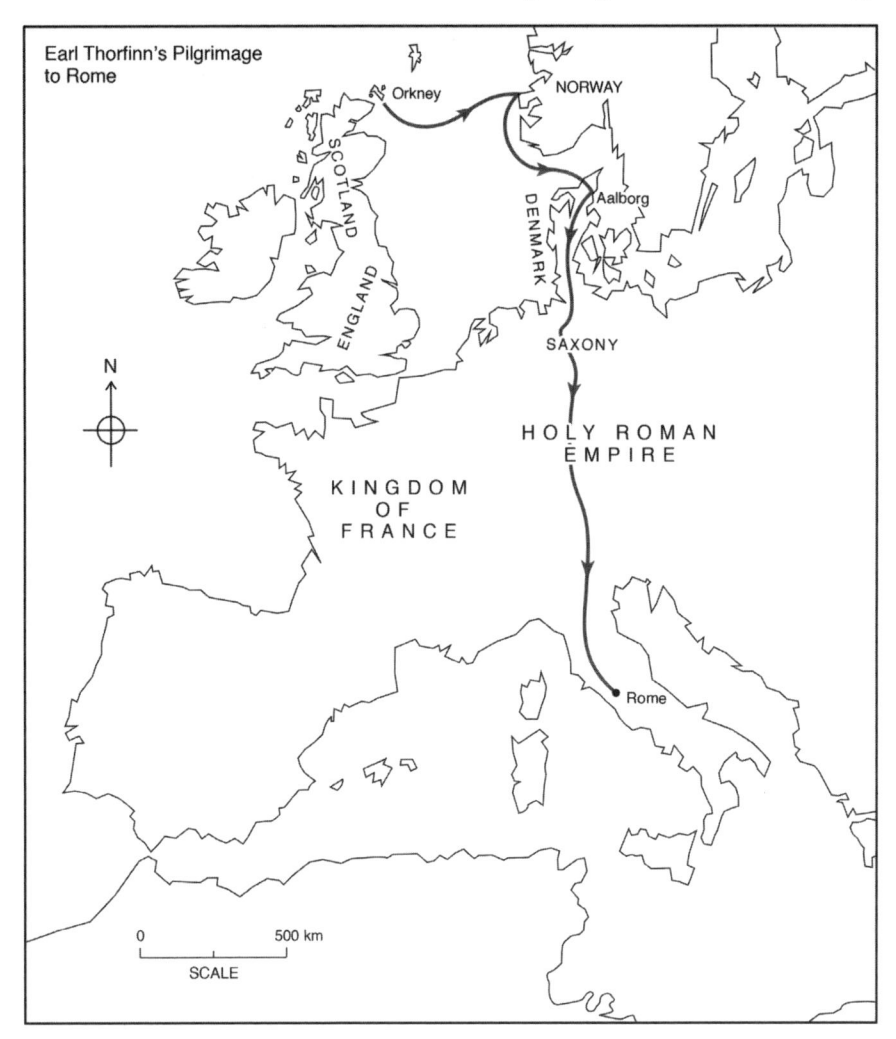

Figure 4.3 Map showing the route taken by Earl Thorfinn on his pilgrimage to Rome in the 1030s; 'and that journey was his most famous one' (*OS* Taylor, Chapter xxxi).

after he had established full authority over 'all his realm' (*öllu ríki sínu*). He went initially to visit King Harald Sigurdsson (*harðraða*) in Hordaland, with whom he was on good terms (in contrast to his relationship with the two previous kings), and then sailed to Denmark, where he stayed with King Sveinn (Estrithsson) at Aalborg. After this we are told that he announced his intention to go on pilgrimage to Rome; he travelled through Germany, meeting the Emperor Henry III (1039–56), and when he reached Rome he had an audience with the Pope (Leo IX), and 'received absolution from him for all his sins' (*OS*, Chapter 31).⁴² Such absolution, required for the murder of Rognvald Brusison and many of his following, would only have come at a price. That price would have been the financial support of a newly established church in his earldoms, maintaining a bishop and clergy with endowments. The earl then returned home and, as a consequence, ceased his war-campaigns (*Lét hann þá af herferðum*), while embarking on his new governmental arrangements and the making of new laws.

This pilgrimage to Rome followed the model of contemporary Christian rulers, such as Cnut the Great who had attended the coronation of the emperor Conrad III in 1027, Duke Robert of Normandy in 1028, MacBeth who visited Rome c.1050, and several Irish kings. It was clearly incumbent on Christian rulers of this period who had left a bloody trail in their path to power to seek absolution and make amends by promising support for the Church in their dominions. Thorfinn was 'keeping up with the Joneses' and in more ways than one. By 'hobnobbing' with the secular and ecclesiastical rulers of kingdoms and empires he would inevitably have learned a great deal about the governing methods of those more sophisticated states, and the significance of having an educated and Latin-literate clergy. Although both Norway and Denmark were only starting to develop systems of royal administration with attendant clergy, in the Holy Roman Empire a sophisticated ecclesiastical structure was well-established.

Thorfinn's route through Germany could have taken in the powerful archbishopric of Cologne on the way to Rome, although, if so, the saga author did not think this a matter of interest worth recording. It has been recently argued that such contact, in particular with the archbishop of Cologne, could have been the source of knowledge which 'provides the key to the introduction of the land-assessment system in Orkney'.⁴³ Startling as this may appear, there are good grounds for suggesting that the Cologne penny may have been the weight-standard on which the pennyland in Orkney was based. From c.1050, Cologne, like England, maintained a mark of 216g which in Cologne was divided into 144 pennies of c.1.5g each (so 1 ounce = 18 pennies). In Orkney the ounce-land was divided into eighteen pennies.⁴⁴ The Cologne penny remained very

---

42 Thorfinn *may* have passed through Hamburg and visited Archbishop Adalbert (Crawford, 1983, 103; Williams, 2004, 101), although as Haki Antonsson points out (2007, 89) this is rather unlikely considering that King Harald *Hardraða* was on bad terms with the archbishop, and also considering Adam's statement that Bishop Turolf was appointed in Orkney 'by order of the pope' (*iussu papae*)

43 Williams, 2004, 100

44 Two fragmentary Cologne pennies have been recorded in two silver hoards in Scandinavian Scotland (Williams, 2004, 77): in the Machrie (Islay) hoard dated 970–980 (Graham-

stable in this period and so would have been a good monetary basis on which the earls could model their land assessment units.[45]

If this was indeed a result of Thorfinn's experience of the sophisticated ecclesiastical economic system in the Cologne archbishopric, it may have been only one of several elements of a new governmental system which he attempted to impose in his earldoms. The key to such striking developments was the ability of educated clerical personnel in his household and retinue to keep accounts and make taxation records. Primitive though such systems may have been they would have helped to establish some standardised form of monetary or economic impositions on the diverse areas under Thorfinn's control. The extent of the ounceland and pennyland divisions over both earldoms and in the west most probably relates to imposition by one political authority, and the obvious candidates are the earls. If so, it is no wonder it was said that in those areas over which Thorfinn had imposed his authority by force 'it was thought very oppressive to live under his rule' (*þótti morgum ófrelsi mikit at búa undir ríki hans*) (*OS*, Chapter 32), and they broke away after his death.

4.2.3 *Ingibjorg 'Earls'-mother'* (jarlamóðir) *and problems of chronology*

With the date of Thorfinn's death we find ourselves right in the middle of a historical problem and one which pertains to the destiny of all the northern realms. It touches on the royal dynasties of Scotland, Norway and England, and is bound up with the apocalyptic events of 1066. Thorfinn's death has been loosely tied into the reign of King Harald Sigurdsson of Norway, who met his end at one of the battles of that year, at Stamford Bridge in Yorkshire, for Thorfinn is said in the saga to have died 'towards the end of the reign of Harald Sigurdarson' (*á ofanverðum dǫgum*) (*OS*, Chapter 32). This has been understood to mean c.1065 although it has long been recognised that there were severe problems with this date, for the saga also tells us that after Thorfinn's death, his widow Ingibjorg married Malcolm, king of Scots 'known as "Long-Neck"' (*OS*, Chapter 33), (or 'Canmore' as he is better known).[46] Their son, later King Duncan II, is known from Scottish history to have been Malcolm's eldest son (although his mother's name is never mentioned in the Scottish sources), and

---

Campbell, 1995, 21), and in the Burray (Orkney) hoard, dated 997–1010 (ibid., 51) – the only Continental coin in the hoard. It is noteworthy that these two coins should occur in hoards in Islay, a Hebridean power centre, and in Orkney, the earldom power centre. The dates of these hoards correspond with the rule of Earl Sigurd (II) Hlodversson (c.985–1014) suggesting Cologne links already in his time

45 See Section 3.5.2 for discussion of the ounceland. Williams, (2004, 102–3) proposes that the division of the ounceland into twenty pennies in the west relates to the earlier Dalriadic twenty-house unit

46 Duncan, 2002, 42–3; Woolf, 2007, 267–8; Thomson, 2012, 'Ingibjorg *jarlamóðir*'

there may indeed have been further sons of this marriage. As Ingibjorg was also the mother of the two sons of Thorfinn, Paul and Erlend, who were old enough to join King Harald's expedition to England in 1066, it does seem very likely that she must have married Malcolm some years before that event to have been young enough to bear his children.[47] Indeed it has been suggested recently that she was married to Thorfinn in the late 1040s and that Thorfinn died c.1052–4,[48] giving plenty of time for her to marry Malcolm *before* he finally won the battle for the Scottish throne against Macbeth ('Karl Hundason'), and Lulach, in 1058. The possibility has also been aired that Ingibjorg may herself have died before Malcolm became king.[49]

Her second marriage raises Ingibjorg's profile, although her significance as Malcolm's first wife was eclipsed by the famous and saintly Margaret who became Malcolm's queen, probably in 1070, and the progenitor of all succeeding medieval kings of Scotland.[50] It is interesting, and probably significant, that in the Norwegian sources Ingibjorg is consistently referred to as 'Earls'-mother' (*jarlamóðir*), a rather unusual title, perhaps the equivalent of 'Dowager'. It suggests that she had a particular and well-known role as the mother of Paul and Erlend who succeeded Thorfinn and who ruled as joint earls. Perhaps it signifies that she had responsibility for her sons in the period of their minority after the death of her husband, Thorfinn.[51] They may have been very young if Thorfinn did indeed die early in the 1050s.[52]

Another important, and significant, event is the expedition to Orkney and Wales and England which was led by Harald Sigurdsson's son Magnus in the fateful year 1058. This is well-known from Irish and English sources,[53] but is

47 Ingibjorg's marriage to Malcolm most probably occurred before 1060, if her sons by Thorfinn were old enough to accompany King Harald in 1066, and if her son by Malcolm, Duncan, was old enough to be taken as a hostage by King William the Conqueror in 1072
48 Thomson, 2012, 33
49 Ibid., 2012, 35
50 Crawford, 2006a, *sub* Ingebjorg and Margaret. It is noteworthy that Ingibjorg is referred to as *comitissa* ('countess') in the Durham *Liber Vitae*, and not as *regina* ('queen'), which William Thomson (2012, 30, and references there given) suggests indicates that she died before Malcolm won the throne. Perhaps it was her non-royal status as the mother of Duncan II which made later chroniclers cast doubt on his legitimacy
51 Thomson, 2012, 34–5
52 The date of Ingibjorg's marriage to Thorfinn is unclear, although it is suggested that it was possibly arranged by Olaf Haraldsson at the time when he and Thorfinn came to terms in 1021 (Crawford, 1987, 77). Did it take place before Kalf Arnesson came over to Orkney in the mid-1030s, which the saga says was because of his relationship with Thorfinn, Ingibjorg being his niece? William Thomson (2012, 34) thinks however it was later and that the marriage with Thorfinn came about *because* Kalf had previously come to Orkney and established a relationship with the earl
53 Woolf, 2007, 266–8. Although there is no reference at all to Magnus being in Orkney it is

not mentioned at all in the Scandinavian sources, including *Jarls' Saga* and has therefore not been discussed in relation to events in Orkney, until recently. It is now thought to signify some intention on the part of the Norwegian king and his son Magnus to ensure that they exercised authority over the young earls in Orkney, who were under age on the death of their father, Thorfinn. If their mother, Ingibjorg, was also dead by then, it would be understandable if there was concern about the situation in the earldom.[54]

Another political factor arising out of the important alliances in the area at this time is the possibility that Malcolm Canmore's final successful bid for power was launched from the north, from Orkney where he had taken refuge during his struggle with MacBeth.[55] His marriage to Ingibjorg thus linked him with Orkney at a time when the islands provided a useful base from which to launch his attack against MacBeth and Lulach (who was killed in Moray).[56] All these new ideas are helping to make sense of a complex situation which is only hinted at in the conflicting accounts about a dramatic era in the history of Orkney, Norway and Scotland. This was a time when these northern societies were interlinked through alliances and political ambitions. The alliances were made or broken according to the outcome of ambitious expeditions and fateful battles; none more so than those of 1066.

This was the apocalyptic year when Harald Sigurdsson of Norway, Harald Godwinsson of England and Duke William of Normandy fought it out for possession of the Anglo-Saxon kingdom. The young earls, Paul and Erlend Thorfinnsson, were caught up in the dramatic events of Harald Sigurdsson's invasion from Norway, and they and King Malcolm no doubt thought that they were backing a sure winner and a strong candidate in the competition for the English throne.[57] Their family links with King Harald's first queen Thora, who was a cousin of Ingibjorg, gave the earls a stake in Harald's ambitions, as also was the case with Malcolm, tied by marriage into the earldom family and, by extension, into the Norwegian royal family. Harald's invasion fleet sailed west to Shetland and Orkney 'from whence he took with him a great armed force' (*Hms.* Laing, *The Saga of Harald the Stern*, Chapter LXXXIII), and 'both earls decided to join him' (*OS*, Chapter 34). Harald's second queen Ellisiv and their daughters Maria and Ingigerd had accompanied the fleet so far, but were then

---

    assumed that he must have called there *en route* to the Hebrides and the Irish Sea because the Irish Chronicle *Tigernach* mentions that he had 'foreigners from Orkney' in his following (ibid., 266).

54 Thomson, 2012, 35–6
55 Duncan, 2002, 42
56 Woolf, 2007, 268–9
57 Crawford, 2001, 84–5

left behind in Orkney, when King Harald and the earls sailed on. However, any potential for sharing in the successes of the Norwegian candidate disappeared on the field of Stamford Bridge when Harald Sigurdsson *hardraða* earned his six feet of English soil. The earls and Olaf (King Harald's son) were permitted to return north to Orkney, and the Anglo-Saxon Chronicle says that the Norwegian party was given a safe-conduct to go first to King Harald Godwinsson, to whom they swore oaths 'that they would always keep peace and friendship in this land', after which the king allowed them to sail north with twenty-four ships (*ASC* 'D', 199).[58]

4.2.4 *Eulogy of Earl Thorfinn and developments after his death*

The death of Earl Thorfinn is marked by a section in *Jarls' Saga* (Chapter 32) summarising his achievements and including the praise stanzas composed by Arnor *jarlaskáld*, which are among the most renowned survivals of Old Norse poetry. First is the brief stanza extolling the wide extent of Thorfinn's dominions:

> Forced to heed the ring-harmer[59]
> were folk from *þursasker*
> – I tell men truly how
> Þorfinnr [Thorfinn] was regarded – as far as Dublin
>
> (Whaley, 1998, 128)

This is an important pointer to the range of Thorfinn's area of influence. The *þursa skeriom* ('Giants' Skerries') referred to are likely to be rocks off Shetland, perhaps Muckle Flugga or the Outer Skerries,[60] while the southern point of the zone under his control was Dublin on the Irish Sea. This is a succinct assessment of the extent of the earldom thalassocracy at its widest.

Then comes the eulogy of Thorfinn's lordship with its powerful imagery of the end of the world:

> The bright sun to swart* will turn,
> earth will sink in the dark ocean,
> Austri's toil will be rent,
> all the sea will roar over the mountains,
> before in the Isles a finer
> chieftain than Thorfinnr
> – God help that guardian of his
>   retinue – will be born
>   *black
>
> (Whaley, 1998, 128)

---

58 Jesch, 1993, 224
59 A poetic kenning for 'generous ruler' (Whaley, 1998, 128)
60 Crawford, 1987, 75; Whaley, 1998, 263

This is followed by a prayer for Thorfinn's soul:

> The splendid ennobler of sovereign
> Torf-Einarr's kin – and I pray
> true mercies for the precious prince –
> God keep far from harms
>
> (Whaley, 1998, 128)

These verses provide something of a contrast with the dramatic change which the saga author then tells us happened following Thorfinn's death: 'Most of the places he had conquered broke away and the people there looked for protection from those who held the lands by birthright. It was soon clear what a great loss his death was'(*OS*, Chapter 32). Firm leadership was evidently lacking, and if his sons were indeed under age at his death (as suggested may have been the case) that would not be surprising. Which locations 'broke away' is never specified so we are left in the dark as to whether it was territories on the Scottish mainland or the Hebridean islands. There is no mention that Thorfinn's sons, Paul and Erlend, ever led campaigns to reassert their father's authority in either area. The days of annual naval expeditions in the spirit of the Viking Age were coming to an end, and the maintenance of a campaigning and conquering lifestyle more difficult to sustain, especially when the resources of the earldom were divided between two earls. Moreover, from what we perceive from the saga evidence, it would appear that these earls were tied into the Norwegian cultural and political scene and did not have close contacts with Scotland.[61]

They lived in an age when it was their Norwegian overlords who had wide-ranging ambitions to conquer and dominate in the British Isles, and the earls had to fit in with their contractual obligations to follow the kings and supply them with ships manned with warriors. We have already seen that Paul and Erlend were caught up in the events of 1066 soon after they started ruling in the earldoms and followed King Harald *hardraða* south to York. After Harald's disastrous encounter with Harald Godwinsson at the Battle of Stamford Bridge, the earls are said to have come ashore and 'launched a fierce attack', in which however almost the whole Norwegian contingent perished (*OS*, Chapter 34). The earls survived and were given permission to take the young Olaf Haraldsson back to Orkney where his mother had remained. Olaf spent the winter in Orkney 'on the friendliest terms with the earls his kinsmen' (*OS*, Chapter 34) before returning to Norway to rule jointly with his brother Magnus.

The marriages of the two brothers tell us about the social milieu they moved in. Paul was married to a daughter of the famous Earl Hakon Ivarsson, while Erlend was married to Thora, daughter of Sumarlidi Ospaksson, and tied

---

61   There is no mention of them ever visiting or staying on their Caithness estates

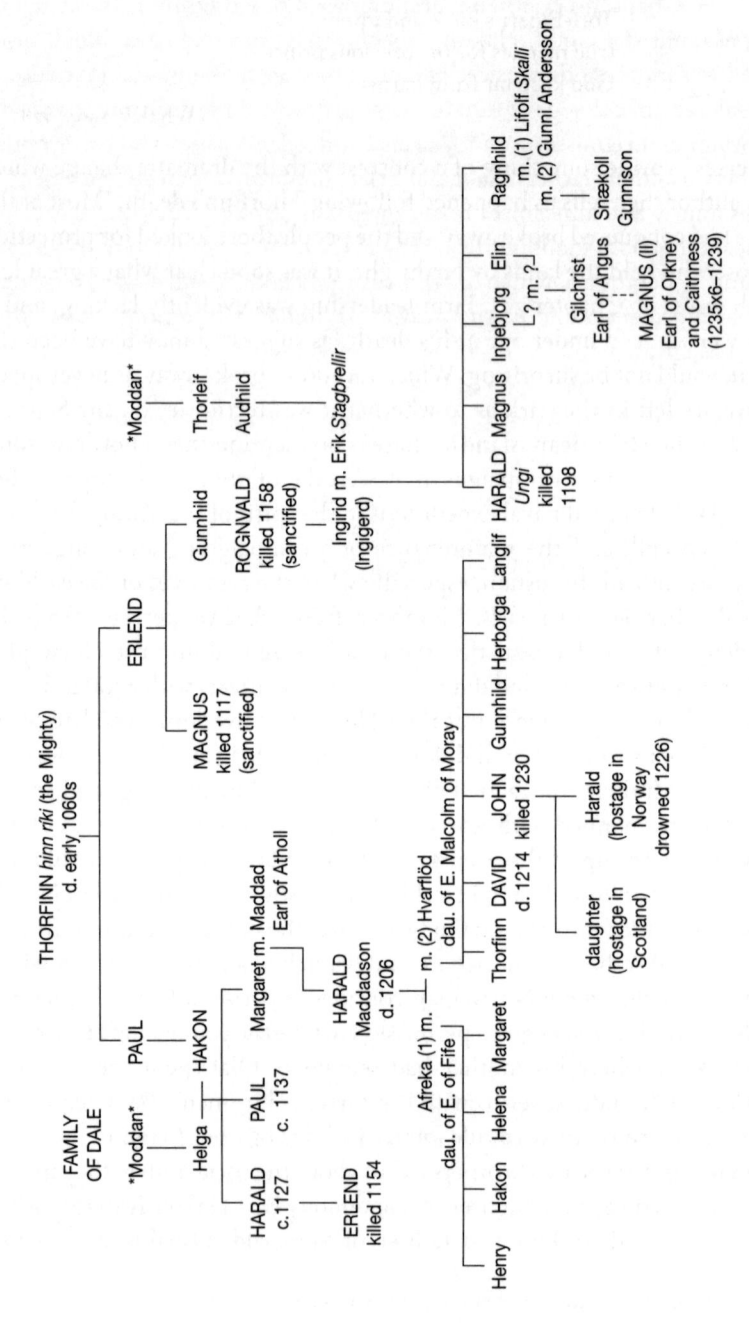

Figure 4.4 Genealogical tree of Earl Thorfinn's descendants.

into the Icelandic family network. Paul's marriage meant that his son Hakon 'considered himself more highly-born than the Erlendssons' who were his cousins (*OS*, Chapter 34), for his grandmother was Ragnhild, the daughter of King Magnus the Good. Hakon Paulsson therefore had royal blood in his veins and was indeed a direct descendant of the saintly king Olaf Haraldsson. He considered that this gave him a moral justification for lording it over his cousin Magnus Erlendsson, and the peaceful relationship which previously existed between their fathers, Paul and Erlend Thorfinsson, who had ruled the earldoms jointly and amicably, broke down. The two branches of the earldom line descending from Paul and from Erlend became rivals for power over the succeeding generations, which in the case of Hakon and Magnus resulted in judicial murder leading to the growth of a cult of saintliness around the martyred Magnus.

4.3 HIERARCHY OF POWER: KING MAGNUS OLAFSSON 'BARELEGS' (*BERFÆTTR*) AND THE EARLS

Division of the earldom was always a source of weakness. It led to one or both of the earls looking to their Norwegian overlord for support and this in itself meant submission to the Norwegian king's authority. It sometimes led to one earl looking to Norway and the other earl looking south to Scotland. Hakon Paulsson was always more closely connected to the powerful in Norway – because of his kindred link with the royal dynasty. When he was forced to leave the islands because of his troublesome nature, he sailed east to see the 'many well-to-do kinsmen' he had in Norway and Sweden (*OS*, Chapter 35; Taylor, 194). Magnus Erlendsson on the other hand spent some years in Scotland, after he had fallen out with King Magnus 'Barelegs' (*berfættr*), and also stayed at the court of King Henry I of England (according to the *Longer Magnus Saga*; *OS* Dasent, 257). The matter of the earls' relationship with their overlords, and the extent to which they were allowed to be independent operators in their island empire was becoming more crucial in a period when kings were strengthening their constitutional position as rulers above their feudal 'vassals' (although this term is not exactly appropriate for the relationship between the king and his 'hirdmen' in Norway). As was discussed in Chapter 3, the titles of 'earl' and 'king' were roughly equivalent in the Viking Age, but by the late eleventh century the hierarchical distinction was becoming more formalised, and earls were considered to be subject to their royal overlords.

There is a curious incident related in great detail in the section of the saga devoted to Hakon Paulsson's stay in Sweden which has recently been shown to be possibly significant for revealing how the relevant status of earl and king was regarded at the time the saga was written c.1200.[62] Chapter 36 is devoted to the account of how Hakon sought out a pagan soothsayer in Sweden to find out his future political destiny. This is not an unknown motif in sagas of great men; a comparable incident is recorded in the saga of Olaf Tryggvesson, where it was used to show how the great king was shaking off the world of occult practices, and carrying a message about the king's role as the great missioniser of the pagan north. The story of Hakon Paulsson's encounter with the soothsayer seems to have different messages,[63] one of which is more to do with the relationship of Orkney earls and Norwegian kings. The soothsayer suggests Hakon would be better to seek guidance from his ancestor Olaf Haraldsson the saint, who is known on different occasions to have appeared to other kings in dreams, including Olaf Tryggvesson, to advise as to the right course of action. However, the clear message is that Hakon had not been guided by his saintly ancestor and needed to seek out a pagan soothsayer to find out what lay in store for him in the future. The soothsayer's intimation that Hakon would commit a crime for which he would be barely able to atone to God is foretelling the murder of his cousin Magnus, which the medieval audience listening to the saga teller would know all about, as well as the subsequent growth of Magnus' saintly reputation. The unspoken message, which the audience would probably also be able to apprehend, was that Magnus' cousin, Hakon, was not favoured enough to be the recipient of advice from the holy martyr Olaf, even though he was directly descended from him. As a mere earl, or a would-be earl, he was not of sufficient status.

The absolute contrast between the power of a king to affect the position of the earls in their earldom, and the inability of the earls to withstand the show of power of an ambitious king with formidable naval resources at his disposal is demonstrated dramatically a few years later when King Magnus Olafsson ('Barelegs') led two expeditions west.These campaigns were instigated by Hakon Paulsson (according to the saga) during his sojourn in Scandinavia. He was a close follower of King Magnus and is said to have urged the king to conquer Orkney 'just as Harald Fine-Hair had done' (*OS*, Chapter 38), then to raid in Scotland and Ireland, leading to an invasion of England in revenge for the death of his grandfather Harald *hardraða*. In his response King Magnus warned Hakon, however, that he should not be surprised by his harsh treatment of the countries west-over-sea, which Hakon did not like the sound of at all.

The first action taken when the large army arrived in Orkney in 1098 did indeed set the tone for the drastic nature of the strategy employed for the furthering of King Magnus' ambitions; the earls who were still ruling in the

62 Haki Antonsson, 2005a
63 Discussed by Thomson 2001, 90

islands, Paul and Erlend, were seized and sent to Norway ('taken prisoner' according to Hms. *The Saga of Magnus Barefoot*, Chapter IX). Sigurd, the king's young son, was set over the islands with a body of counsellors (*OS* Taylor, Chapter xxxix).[64] This was a new and unprecedented approach to the islands' circumstances. No earl had been removed like that before, and it can only have been regarded as humiliating treatment, which may be linked to the earls' deaths, for both died in Norway in the following year, Erlend in Trondheim, and Paul in Bergen (*OS*, Chapter 42).[65] All the indications are that the royal governance of Orkney was intended to be permanent.

4.3.1 *Royal ambitions and the role of the Orkney earldom*

Control of Orkney was only the first of the ambitions of Magnus 'Barelegs', and probably not the most important of them. His sights were set on further conquests in the west and the establishing of royal authority over all the Norse settlements in the Hebrides, with quasi-imperial ideas about further extending his authority all around the Irish Sea zone, and creating a Norwegian thalassocracy. These wider horizons are not our main concern, so we will restrict our discussion to how the Northern Isles fitted into Magnus' war strategies.

In the first place, the islands were of course a vital staging post for any operations further south (as mentioned in Chapter 3), and the establishment of the young Sigurd in Orkney with counsellors shows how important they were considered to be in Magnus' overall strategy.[66] They were the forward base from which operations further west were conducted. Support and maintenance for the large war-fleet would have been provided from the islands' resources, and administrative structures probably put in place for the provision of supplies. The addition of ships and men from the earls' own levies was probably also an important requirement.

Secondly, the matter of the king's overlordship of the earls was a significant consideration. This needed to be regularised, the relationship tightened up and put on a more established basis, in accordance with the Norwegian king's relationship with his own Norwegian hirdmen. Although not mentioned, the three young members of the earldom dynasty would have been required to

---

64 The additional information that Sigurd was given the title of king and set over the Orkneys and Hebrides, and put in the charge of his relative Hakon Paulsson is given in *Hms*. Laing, Chapter XII (but not mentioned in *Jarls' Saga*)
65 The basis for this treatment may have been the failure of either Paul or Erlend to visit the kings in Norway and do homage, and receive a grant of the earldom. There is no indication in the saga that they had ever done so
66 It is recorded in the Icelandic Annals that Sigurd had power in Orkney for seven years (*hafði riki i Orkneyium vii ár*, Storm, 1888, 111)

submit to the king, and to give him an oath of loyalty during the first campaign, thus being admitted into the royal hird. Hakon Paulsson and Magnus and Erling Erlendsson were then required to follow in the king's retinue when the royal fleet moved on.[67] Magnus Erlendsson was in the king's ship, for during the Battle of the Menai Straits with the Norman knights the famous incident took place when he refused to prepare for battle and took out his psalter and chanted psalms throughout the conflict, sitting in the main cabin (of the king's ship), which aroused the anger of the king. It is said that Magnus Erlendsson had been made *skutilsvein* (cup-bearer, a rank in the king's hird), and used to serve at the king's table, but after the incident at the Menai Straits the king took an intense dislike to him (*OS*, Chapter 40).

Thirdly, there is the interesting issue as to how the earldom was organised during this period when the king was closely involved in Orkney affairs and needed to control the islands and earldom resources for his own military requirements. As said above, the indications are that royal control was intended to be permanent, and the fact that counsellors/regents were put in charge to rule on behalf of the young Sigurd gives us an indication that powerful members of the royal hird were established in Orkney, in order to oversee the administration and take over the revenues. The likelihood is that Earl Thorfinn had installed some sort of system for the collection of revenues, based on the ounceland territorial division, earlier in the century (see Section 3.5.2). If such an arrangement was already in existence, it would have been retained,[68] and there is a possibility that Houseby (*husebyer*) farms were created at this time specifically for the organisation of the collection of revenues. This hypothesis is based on the existence of certain farms called Huseby/Housebay in Orkney, which relate to farms with the equivalent name in Norway (see Colour plate 15). Although the issue of 'huseby farms' in Norway (and Sweden) is a vexed question, and the date that such farms were established is very contentious, nonetheless they are generally understood to have played an important role in royal estate administration.[69] Their role as administrative places is recognised to have been significant in the period when the kings were amassing estates, often confiscated from

---

67 As had been the case on previous occasions when the kings used Orkney as a base for campaigns further south, in 954 and in 1066 (see above Section 3.4.3 and Section 4.1.4)
68 Such an arrangement for collecting in food renders, or the obligation of providing hospitality to the lord, was known in ON as *veizla*, a term which appears in the Orkney Rentals as 'wattle' (Thomson, 1996, xv; 2001, 211)
69 References to the relevant literature are given in Crawford, 2006, 21–3. The meaning of the place-name Huseby (*husebyer*, 'farm with many houses') indicates a cluster of buildings which had specific functions, some perhaps as storehouses for royal renders. Recent studies suggest that Huseby farms were part of the *bona regalia*, the royal estates belonging to the Crown, and not the patrimonial estates of the kings (Iversen, 2011, 238–9)

defeated members of rival local dynasties.⁷⁰ Would one of the kings therefore have introduced the concept of 'huseby farms' into Orkney in the process of bringing the earldom administration under royal control? Because these farms were closely associated with royal administration in Norway, it is perhaps unlikely that the earls themselves would have adopted the royal model for their own administration.⁷¹ It may rather have been implemented by King Magnus, or those 'advisers' (*raðuneyti*) who were left in charge of administering Orkney when he set his young son Sigurd over the islands.⁷²

Finally, the position of Orkney close to the north Scottish mainland, where the earls' Scottish earldom was situated, meant that the delineation of the respective spheres of influence was becoming established and the Pentland Firth turned into a border zone (see Section 1.2.2).There does not seem to have been any intention on the Norwegian side to take over Caithness, for which the earls were subject to the kings of Scots. Once King Magnus and his son Sigurd were established in the islands, it was necessary for their relationship with the king of Scots to be regularised. The king of Scots must have felt the need to come to an agreement with Magnus about their spheres of influence, particularly after Magnus had shown his intentions with his war-cruise through the Hebrides, looting and burning, to the Irish Sea. On his return north we are told in the saga that messengers from King Malcolm (*recte* Edgar)⁷³ came to offer him a settlement: Magnus could have possession of all islands off the west coast 'which were separated by water navigable by a ship with the rudder set'(*OS*, Chapter 41). There is no information from the Scottish sources to corroborate this, but that it was well-known both in Norway and in Scotland is confirmed by the reference made to the arrangement in 1242 (*Hacon's Saga*, 249).⁷⁴ Whether or not the story of Magnus being drawn over the isthmus at

70 When Steinnes (1959, 36–46) discussed the Orkney huseby 'system', it was thought that these farms dated back to the early medieval period, which led Steinnes (ibid., 45–6) to suggest that the term had been brought into Orkney by the earls of the Møre dynasty, probably in the early tenth century
71 In Crawford 2006a, 209–11, the possibility that Earl Thorfinn might have been responsible for establishing this administrative arrangement was raised
72 Westerdahl and Stylegar (2004) have suggested that the introduction of the Huseby farms may have taken place a century later when King Sverre took the earldom into the royal administration.This was after the submission of Earl Harald Maddadson in 1195 (see Chapter 6). In Norway the creation of these farms was probably taking place earlier, during the time of the unification of Norway under Olaf Haraldsson and his successors in the first half of the eleventh century
73 Malcolm died in 1093, and was succeeded by his son Edgar
74 In 1242 Alexander III was claiming that King Magnus had won the Southern Isles 'with some unfairness' from King Malcolm. The Norwegians, however, responded that it was well known that the two kings, Magnus and Malcolm, 'had agreed it all between them what realm

Kintyre on his ship with its rudder set in order for him to claim the peninsula as an island reflects a real event, it tells us that there was a general recognition that his authority was restricted to islands.[75]

These different factors indicate what Magnus' ambitions were for the Orkney earldom and for the wider Norse–Celtic world beyond. Following his successful campaign in the Hebrides and off the coast of Wales (also in the Isle of Man), he spent the winter of 1098–9 in the west, and arranged two marriage alliances.[76] The first was the betrothal of his son Sigurd to Bjadmunja, the daughter of King Myrkjartan of Connaught (*OS*, Chapter 41), indicating his intentions of creating a permanent alliance with a powerful Irish chieftainly family. The second was the marriage of Earl Erlend's daughter Gunnhild to Kol, son of Kali Sæbjarnarson (who had died of his wounds acquired during the campaign), once Magnus had returned to Orkney and heard of the death of Earl Erlend. He was thus taking over the earl's role, in the way that a feudal overlord took responsibility for unmarried daughters of vassals who had died. This marriage had long-term consequences for the history of the earldom during the twelfth century when Gunnhild and Kol's son Kali became one of the most powerful and well-known earls of Orkney – Rognvald Kali Kolsson.

However, all these strategies for the power game which King Magnus was playing out in the west – military, strategic and political – came to naught because of the disastrous second campaign in the west led by the king in 1103 which ended with his untimely death in Ulster. 'As soon as the news of his father's death reached Sigurd in Orkney, he set out for Norway where he was accepted as joint ruler along with his brothers Eystein and Olaf' (*OS*, Chapter 43). Symbolically, Sigurd left the young daughter of the Irish king behind in Orkney. The earldom was left to its own autonomous development and, as we will see, a new power game developed between the rivals of the next generation. It is not unlikely, however, that the short period of direct royal administration would have left its mark on the islands, and the killing of the 'royal official' (*syslumann*) by Hakon Paulsson[77] was a direct result. This was only the first of such violent encounters between an earl and the royal official who had been

---

the Northmen should have in Scotland or those small isles which lay close to it', and that the Scots king had no power in the Southern Isles at that time anyway (*Hacon's Saga*, 249) (see Section 7.3)

75 The Pentland Firth is said to become 'some kind of boundary, although not a state border' with the 1098 agreement (Imsen, 2009, 11, and see n.7 for discussion of the source material)

76 Power, 1986

77 As recorded in the *Longer Magnus Saga*, Chapter XIII (*OS*, ed. Guðmundsson, 350). The term sysselman (royal official) may be anachronistic in this early twelfth-century context, as the office was not created until later in the century (Helle, 1974, 76–7, 206–8; Bagge, 2011, 235–6)

planted in the islands, with the intention of maintaining royal authority there (see Chapter 6).

4.3.2 Rival earls

The divergent political links of the cousins Hakon Paulsson and Magnus Erlendsson have already been referred to: Hakon closely tied in with his upmarket Norwegian kindred, and Magnus looking to Scotland and further south. When he abandoned his place on King Magnus' long-ship (an act of infidelity which would have had dire consequences for him if he had been found and brought back), Magnus is said to have joined the following of the king of Scots, and stayed quite a while with him, as well as in various places with friends in England and with a bishop in Wales (*OS*, Chapter 40). As long as the Norwegian king was alive, Magnus did not go back to Orkney – wisely! He did, however, go to Caithness after he had been at the Scottish court where he was 'chosen and honoured with the title "earl"',[78] presumably having been given the title by the king of Scots along with a grant of the earldom.

However, the claim to their inheritance in Orkney was what both Hakon and Magnus were more concerned about. A year or two after King Magnus' death, Hakon went to Norway and received a grant of the title of earl 'as well as all the authority pertaining to his birthright' (*OS*, Chapter 43) from the new joint kings. This was something which had not been done since the days of Thorfinn but which was by now, and perhaps as a result of the period of royal control, a necessary precondition to the enjoyment of the lands and income. Hakon then appears to have taken control of the whole of the islands, and this is when he is said to have slain the royal official who was in charge of Earl Magnus' inheritance.[79] Shortly afterwards Magnus moved across to Orkney from Caithness and 'begged to take his father's heritage' (*Longer Magnus Saga*, Dasent, 253), and Hakon agreed reluctantly – if Magnus were to receive a grant from the kings. Magnus therefore went to see King Eystein in Norway who 'gave him a friendly welcome and handed over to him his patrimony, half of Orkney and the title of earl' (*OS*, Chapter 44). We do not know what other conditions were imposed, or whether the kings retained any rights to land or income which had been taken into the royal administration by King Magnus.

The need for the aspiring heirs to receive a grant is very clearly set out in these passages in the saga, and was apparently a prerequisite for any settlement between the two. Indeed it seems to have established an acceptable division of

---

78 *Longer Magnus Saga*, Chapter 11, trans. Dasent, p.251
79 This was probably the east Mainland, north isles of Orkney, and Shetland, which had been in Erlend's possession. So Magnus' grant of Caithness does not appear to have been connected to the nearest part of Orkney across the Pentland Firth, the south isles

power and wealth, for the two cousins are said to have got on well together for a period. They had joint charge of the defences, and a poem was composed in their honour (which has not survived) relating how they fought and killed a chieftain called Dufniall (Donald) who was their second cousin,[80] while they also put to death a Shetlander called Thorbjorn, at Burra Firth (*OS*, Chapter 46). This situation did not last however, and the saga relates how their relationship became tense due to the stirring of troublemakers, particularly those attached to Hakon's following.

The martyrdom of Earl Magnus will be discussed in a later chapter (Chapter 5) when we look at the story of the 'saint-earls'. As regards the situation in the earldom and the political circumstances we are now moving into the final section of *Jarls' Saga* (*OS*, Chapters 58–108) when the saga writer was writing about events which had taken place within living memory of those people from whom he acquired his information. So the story is vividly retold with a great deal of well-informed detail, and with the apparent benefit of personal knowledge of the localities. Events in both Orkney and Caithness are central to this period of the earldom story.

4.4 TWELFTH-CENTURY EARLDOM SOCIETY

The storyline in this section of *Jarls' Saga* revolves around the rivalries of the earls descending from Paul and Erlend and many of their relatives and close associates. What sort of society do we perceive in the pages of the saga and through the many details which are given about the most powerful players in the eventful world of the earldoms of Orkney and Caithness? There is plenty of evidence about the wealthier sections of society and the most ambitious individuals, but very little indeed about the ordinary workers on the land. It was, of course, the deeds of the powerful which medieval Icelanders or Orcadians wanted to hear about (and this section was certainly written by one who had close connections with Orkney and Orcadians from whom he probably drew his information).[81]

Society may have moved on from the previous centuries when Viking earls went raiding every summer, and met with the farmers at the Spring assembly in order to raise a naval levy. Violence, however, was still endemic, and personified by the maverick Swein Asleifsson, whose 'violent and unpredictable behaviour' dominates some forty chapters of the saga,[82] and whose way of life retained a

---

80   This 'chieftain' may well have been Donald (Dufniall) Ban, son of King Duncan I who held the Scottish throne for two brief periods (before being captured and maimed in 1097–8) as recently suggested by Thomson (2012, 2–8)
81   See above Section 2.1 for discussion of the saga's authorship
82   Thomson, 2001, 109

great deal of the older style. The authority of the earls should have helped to control individuals of this type. They had a call on the loyalty of those who submitted to them, and on all the farmers in their earldom division, which should have given them the authority to maintain peaceful conditions. But Swein Asleiffson switched loyalty very easily, and as a buccaneer who led his own individual raids in the west and who thus had his own sources of wealth he was not too dependent on the patronage of the earls.[83] His lifestyle was an echo (and more than an echo) of the older Viking world; he raided far and wide in the west with his own fleet of warships, and in north Scotland; he had his own following of eighty men whom he entertained in his large drinking-hall in Gairsay and whom he managed to maintain at his own expense (*OS*, Chapter 105); he had estates in Caithness as well as in Orkney, and was deeply involved in the Celto-Norse society of north Scotland, pursuing a vendetta and blood-feud with Clan Moddan, another non-earldom family which was a dominant force in this unregulated society (see below).

Swein's high profile in the pages of the twelfth-century section of *Jarls' Saga* may be due to his rumbustious and old-fashioned lifestyle, which made for good saga material. It was, nonetheless, the doings of the earls which were usually central to the story, for they were at the head of the Norse societies in both Orkney and Caithness, and their abilities (or disabilities) were crucial to the well-being of the farming communities. They had the wealth and status to lead the farmers and to win their loyalty and they had the power to maintain peace and justice. There was also the all-important duty and requirement to see to the defence of their earldoms. However, they did not rule alone, and we can see from the evidence of the saga that they had their retinues (hird) or military followings, and their close advisers. The ON term used for these men was *raðgjafi* ('counsellor'), a term which was applied to three named close advisers to three twelfth-century earls. A similar, and relatively unusual term, *raðuneyti*, is used for the body of earls' counsellors.[84]

An even more unusual ON term, *gæðingr*, (Anglicised as 'göding' by Clouston) is specifically associated with the Orkney earldom in this period, and is used of the upper strata of the landed aristocracy. Its definition is not entirely certain, being translated either as 'man of property'[85] or in general usage as 'good-man' or 'man of good family'.[86] These men would certainly have been

---

83 Barrett, 2004; Beuermann, 2009
84 'especially one of the council of a king or princely person' (CV *sub raðgjafi* and *sub raðuneyti*) (Clouston, 1932, 160–1, 190, 191)
85 The term has been seen to be the equivalent of *lendirmenn* in Norway (CV) who were powerful members of the aristocracy endowed with royal estates by the kings
86 Thomson, 2001, 106; Clouston, 1932, 158

the recipients of grants of earldom estate by the earls, and they would have owed obligations in return. A very relevant factor in the enclosed society of the earldoms was the interrelationship of these men with the earls, most of whom would have been bound by marriage and kindred ties with the earldom family.[87] They are named and shown to be linked through marriage with the grand-daughters of Earl Paul I, where it is said 'these were all the earls descendants and gödings in Orkney'(*OS* Taylor, Chapter xxxiii). A list of the whole of the Orkney aristocracy in the time of Paul II uses a different term – *göfgra manna* – meaning 'noble or worshipful/well-born man' (CV, *sub göfugr*), who, it is added 'were come of the earls' kin' (*OS*, Chapter 56).

Land was the basis of the power of these families, most of whom would have had their own family 'odal' estates as well as grants of earldom land. Clouston considered that the term 'göding' (*gæðingr*) became restricted to the earls' 'vassal chieftains', although it may originally have been a general designation for a chief in Orkney.[88] Certainly it was grants of earldom land which would have been of particular value to these families for the earls possessed the best land in the islands (and undoubtedly also in Caithness). Thomson cites several instances recorded in the saga of earl's 'gödings' established on earldom estates, such as Olaf Rolfsson occupying Duncansby in Caithness, Kugi entrusted with Rapness on Westray, Valthiof on earls' bordland on Stronsay.[89] Clouston believed that it was under Earl Thorfinn that this 'göding' class was created, for he put valuable fiefs into their hands and gave them 'greater responsibilities and authority' than they had previously possessed. He points to the comment that Thorfinn 'set up men to keep watch and ward over the islands', and we have already seen in Chapter 3 that the earl put Kalf Arneson in charge of the Hebrides. Undoubtedly it was necessary to delegate authority over the different parts of the earl's domain, to maintain control at home when the earl was campaigning far away, and it may well be that this period saw the creation of a 'feudal' class of men bound to the earl by bonds of homage and loyalty who were given parts of the earldom estate to hold in return for service.[90]

Whether this policy created a typical 'feudal' society according to the meaning of the term as known in other parts of medieval Europe is a matter for debate.[91] One can look to Norwegian society for a model, where feudal tenure

87 Jon Vidar Sigurdsson (2008, 105) mentions the importance of *vennskapsbånd* between the earls and the 'gödings', meaning a bond of friendship (or clientage)
88 Clouston, 1932,158–160; in *Orkney Recs.*, 393–4, Clouston cites all the references to the 'gödings' in *OS*, where he refers to them as 'the semi-feudal nobility'
89 Thomson, 2008, 43–5
90 Imsen, 2003, 74–5
91 Imsen (ibid.) defines it as a 'feudal political system'; Duncan (1975, 192) describes twelfth-century Orkney society as 'heroic' rather than 'feudal'.

was not the norm, even though the 'landed men' (*lendirmenn*) had a relationship with the king approximating to what is known in medieval European societies.[92] But the island world of Orkney, Shetland and Caithness may have had its own indigenous social development which was modelled on neither Scotland nor Norway.[93] The 'republican' method of self-government in Iceland was another result of the phenomenon of Viking exploration and settlement where a society developed which was quite different from that of the home country, and indeed quite unlike anywhere else in Europe. In Orkney and Caithness the geographical circumstances were particularly conducive to the development of a feudal hierarchy and landowning elite with a moderately wealthy class of tenantry who appear in the pages of *Jarls' Saga* under the general name of *bondi*.[94] A lower class of labourers provided the manpower to work the land and fulfil the labour requirements which an arable-based economy demanded, but whose status is not clear, whether free or unfree.[95] The agricultural wealth of these communities provided a surplus which enabled a military oligarchy (the earl and his 'gödings') to spend its gains on a lifestyle of leisure and warfare and indulge in some conspicuous consumption.

4.4.1 *Events in Caithness*

The parallel nature of social development in both earldoms is evident from the saga, although we know less about Caithness than Orkney in this respect, and we might suspect that the saga writer presents the social make-up of Caithness as being more purely Norse than it may have been in reality. Both sides of the Pentland Firth had to be in the earls' hands for requirements of defence and security, as already stressed. Many of the events of this section of *Jarls' Saga* took place across the Firth in Caithness, and the establishment of a semi-feudal class of earldom 'gödings' can be seen operating there too. When we read in the saga about the arrangements for defence of the islands under Earl Paul II we are also told that Olaf Rolfsson crossed over to Duncansby in Caithness and had *yfirsókn* there (this was a grant of authority with lands) (*OS*, Chapter 66).[96] Duncansby was an earldom centre where Thorfinn had resided and its position was evidently very important for defence of the north coast and control of sea

---

92 Imsen (2003, 74) defines the political structures at 'state level' in Norway as 'absolutely feudal'. See Bagge's recent discussion about the situation in Norway (2011, 243)
93 As Clouston (1932, 142) says, 'Orkney was a self-governing state whose lines of development can never be elucidated merely from analogy'
94 Clouston, 1932, 180–1
95 There is one reference in *Jarls' Saga* to unfree members of Earl Thorfinn's household when the women and slaves (*ófriálsum karlmǫnnum*) were allowed to leave the burning house (*OS* Guðmundsson, 72; Crawford, 1987, 211)
96 Clouston, 1932, 163

traffic through the Pentland Firth. Both Olaf Rolfsson and his son Swein Asleifsson possessed authority in Duncansby as devolved to them from the earls, and the dramatic burning of Olaf and five of his men in their house by Olvir Brawl (*OS*, Chapter 66) is recounted as taking place there. Swein later held the stewardship of Duncansby under Earl Rognvald (*OS*, Chapter 82), and also had an estate at Freswick. Olaf and Swein's main family (odal) estate was the island of Gairsay, centrally located in the Bay of Firth in Orkney. This was where Swein is said to have overseen the sowing of his crops before embarking on his summer raiding expeditions south to the Irish Sea (*OS*, Chapter 105).

Olaf Rolfsson had a 'large following' in Caithness, among whom are named Asbjorn and Margad, the sons of Grim of Swona, who had gone fishing with Swein during the time that his father was burned to death at Duncansby. These two, along with their father Grim, then ferried Swein over the Firth to Knarston at Scapa, for which Swein gave Grim a gold ring. It is obvious that the islands of Swona and Stroma were strategically important, perhaps as outlook posts, and the farmers who lived on them possibly played a useful role as ferry men, certainly in this instance. Both islands play a role in movements across the Firth at different times (see Figure 1.3).

Some dramatic events took place in Caithness, linked to Freswick and 'Lambaborg'[97]. When Swein held the stewardship of Duncansby and was raiding in the Hebrides, he put Margad Grimsson in charge of the stewardship, but that caused trouble as Margad was a bully and killed Hroald, causing rival gangs to line up (*OS*, Chapter 82). There was a stand-off at Lambaborg, where Swein joined them and these troublemakers then embarked on a robbery spree and gathered all the loot into the fortress. Earl Rognvald went over to Caithness to try to sort out this situation and besieged Swein in Lambaborg, who escaped and sailed south to Scotland, plundering the monastery on the Isle of May, in the Firth of Forth. The impression from these stories of illegal happenings and killings in Caithness is that different localities there could be used as pirate bases for the stronger and most violent of the 'gödings', and that the earl had to go in person to sort the situation out.

There is evidence that some of the earls had grants of Caithness or were holding authority there. For instance Earl Harald Hakonsson 'held Caithness from the king of Scots' and lived there for a long time (*OS* Taylor, Chapter liv). This was after the death of Earl Hakon Paulsson (c.1123) when his sons fell out and divided their inheritance. Harald's mother was Helga, daughter of Moddan, and Earl Hakon's mistress, and she and her sister Frakokk 'had a lot to say in the government of Earl Harald' (*OS*, Chapter 54). They also had

---

97 This may have been the site now known as Buchollie Castle although Taylor suggests it was the Broch of Ness, in the southern part of the Bay of Freswick (*OS* Taylor, 390)

a lot to do with the unintended death of Earl Harald (?1128) who was killed by the poisoned shirt which Helga and Frakokk had been making for Earl Paul (*OS*, Chapter 55). As a result they were banished to Sutherland by Paul where they brought up Erlend, Earl Harald's son, with the intention of claiming the earldom of Orkney for him.

4.4.2 *Rognvald Kali Kolsson*

First of all however, Rognvald Kali Kolsson[98] came to claim the earldom of Orkney which had been granted to him by King Harald Gilli in 1135 and the people he looked to for support against Earl Paul (who would not agree to giving up any of the earldom) were the earl's deadly enemies in Caithness. Rognvald first sent envoys over to Caithness and Sutherland to Frakokk Moddan's daughter and Olvir *rósti* ('Brawl') promising to share the land with them if they would support his claim to getting hold of half the earldom from Earl Paul (*OS*, Chapter 63). Clearly these were powerful allies to have in his planned attack on the earl. Earl Paul was uncertain how to respond to this rival but he was advised to go to Caithness 'to see his friends and kinsmen and find out how much support he could raise' (*OS*, Chapter 65).[99] The sea battle of Tankarness off the east Mainland which ensued between Earl Paul's forces and the twelve long-ships of Frakokk's fleet ended in the capture of five of Olvir *rósti*'s ships and the dispersal of the rest. When Rognvald led his second campaign the following year to win his half of the earldom, he succeeded in winning support in Orkney without any assistance from Frakokk and her family, and he and Earl Paul divided the islands (which probably included Caithness).

Rognvald very successfully created a network of alliances in a situation where he embarked on his campaign without any base of support in the islands or in Caithness.[100] He was an outsider coming in to claim authority in a society where a single earl was already well entrenched, and interestingly he looked to the Scottish connection to help him win power. This Scottish connection led through Frakokk and her family to the Atholl family and beyond, as far as the royal dynasty, and King David in particular. This was a result of Frakokk's creation of a marriage alliance between her niece Margaret and Maddad, earl of Atholl, cousin of King David. She is reported to have boasted: 'Now that I've

---

98 Rognvald was a nephew of Earl Magnus Erlendsson and inherited a claim to the earldom through his mother Gunnhild, Earl Magnus' sister (see Thomson, 2001, 102–3, for useful analysis of Rognvald's claim)
99 It is not clear if Paul had a grant of the earldom of Caithness and whether he had any powers to raise troops south of the Firth; it does not sound from this suggestion that he should attempt to raise support there as if he had any right to demand it as earl
100 Thomson, 2001, 103–4

married off Margaret Hakon's daughter to Earl Maddad of Atholl, we've many a good claim to Orkney, for he's the best-born of all the chieftains of Scotland' (*OS*, Chapter 63). They had an even better claim once a son was born, and the son of this union, Harald Maddadson, was to become one of the greatest Orkney earls. The acceptance of Harald as Rognvald's co-earl also opened the way to greater Scottish influence because of King David's ambitions to extend his authority north of Moray into Caithness and Sutherland.

The complexities of this period, and the cross-currents of Norse and Scottish influences which came together in the dramatic events in north Scotland in the first half of the twelfth century are revealed in the pages of the saga for all to read. This remarkable narrative is the fullest source of evidence that has survived for any part of Scotland in this period. But it is in its way as difficult to interpret as the driest documentary source, although for different reasons. We have for a start to take into account the one-sided nature of the narrative, and recognise that the narrator's interpretation of the motivations of the main actors is only his personal viewpoint. Although very well-informed about events in Orkney and in Caithness at this period, he can hardly be expected to have any depth of knowledge of the situation in Scotland, or the difficult political situation in the provinces to the south of Sutherland where the Scottish kings faced big challenges to their authority from the descendants of MacBeth and Lulach, rulers of Moray, who had been defeated by Malcom III in the 1070s and 1080s.[101] Malcolm's son David was faced with continued rebellions in the area which he was successful in containing during the 1130s. Once Moray was under royal control, this ambitious ruler could look north of Inverness to extend his authority over the north mainland of Scotland in a more effective way than the nominal overlordship which had hitherto been exercised. This entailed controlling who was to be given a grant of the earldom of Caithness and manipulating which of the individuals who had a claim would be the easiest to dominate. Although King David's manipulating hand is not clearly mentioned in the saga, we can nonetheless assume that the marriage between Maddad of Atholl, the most powerful chieftain in the southern Highlands (and possibly David's cousin), and Margaret, daughter of Earl Paul, provided a means of some royal influence being exercised over the circumstances in the northern earldom.[102]

---

101 Oram, 2004, 90ff.
102 This may have been a result of the king's need to complete his tight control of Moray as much as his wish to dominate affairs in the Norse areas of north Scotland (Oram, 1999, 9; 2004, 98)

4.4.3 *Frakokk and Clan Moddan, and the Celto-Norse society of Caithness and Sutherland*

The most obvious manipulator of events regarding marriage alliances and claims to earldom authority was the powerful woman Frakokk Moddan's daughter whose malign influence runs like a thread through the dramatic events of the early-twelfth-century section of the saga. It is difficult to know whether her role in these events has been highly coloured by the saga writer or whether she was as dominant as the story tells. Although unrecorded in any other source, we can accept that she existed because the author was writing about people and events which had occurred probably within living memory of older people at the time of his writing, and certainly within the time-span of recent history. We can therefore be certain that the events are real and that Frakokk's role was as significant as it is portrayed. But perhaps her role has taken on something of the supernatural already by the time of the saga being written down. The most obvious example of this is the incident in which she and her sister Helga embroidered the poisoned shirt for Earl Paul, but which Earl Harald put on by mistake, with deadly consequences (*OS*, Chapter 55). Frakokk and Helga are portrayed as warning him that if he put on the garment his life would be 'at risk' and they are described as pulling off their bonnets, and tearing their hair in their efforts to stop him. This incident is built up into a dramatic precursor to Earl Harald's sudden death, in which these two were remembered as being implicated. Even more mysterious is the death of Earl Paul which was apparently engineered by Helga's daughter Margaret, through the agency of Swein Asleifsson (*OS*, Chapter 75). The role of women in these inexplicable deadly events is one which was good for the dramatic recounting of the story. It may be, of course, that it reflects reality.

Who then was Frakokk Moddan's daughter and how did she come to be so implicated in earldom politics, and able to manipulate the way things developed? She was a daughter of Moddan of Dale, simply described as a 'rich and honoured man' but whose origins are obscure.[103] The Dale in question is most likely Thurso Dale, 'the only great valley of Caithness',[104] and the fact that Moddan's son Ottar is said to have been jarl in Thurso strengthens the family's link with this particular part of Caithness.[105] Frakokk herself was however based further south in Helmsdale (Strathdonan), which runs inland from the southeast coast of Sutherland and located south of the Ord, which divides Caithness

---

103 Williams, 2007, 132
104 Gray, 1922, 53
105 See Williams (2007, 133–5) for full discussion of whether Moddan may have been of the same family as a previous jarl Muddan or Mutadan (Karl Hundason's nephew killed in Thurso by Thorkel Fostri c.1041)

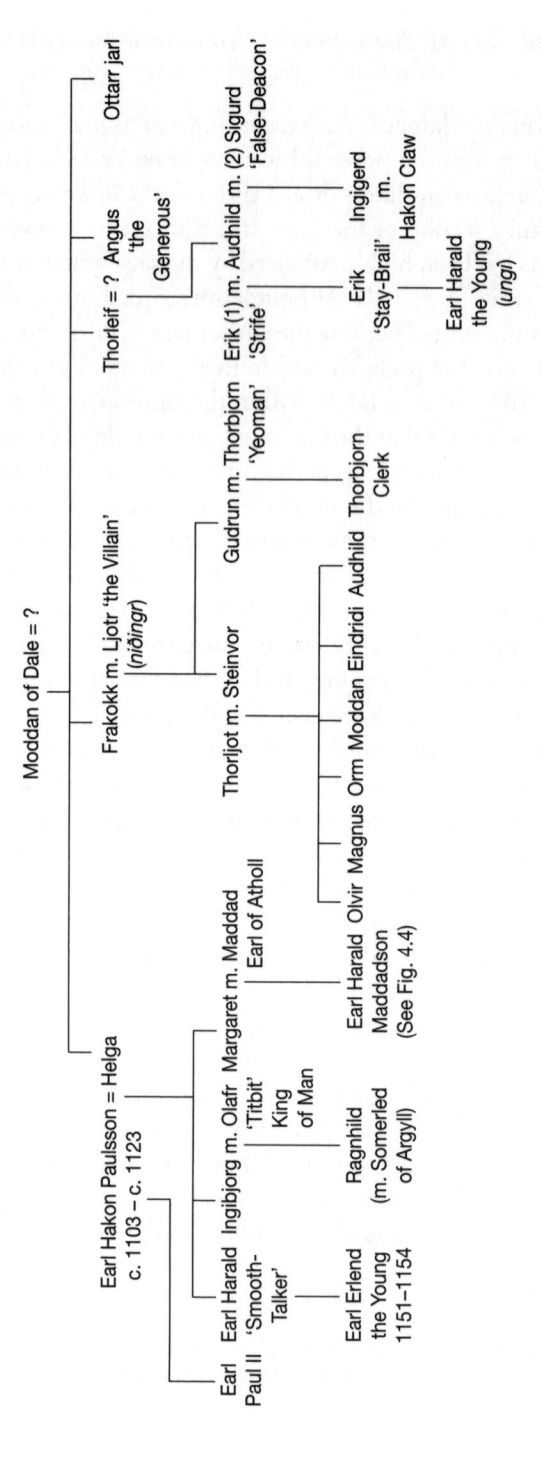

Figure 4.5 Genealogical tree of the family of Moddan in Dale. (Based on Williams, 2007, fig. 11)

from Sutherland. It may be that this was her husband's estate as she was married to Liot *nithing* ('renegade/villain') evidently a powerful Sutherland landowner, whose Helmsdale estate she would have continued to hold after her husband's death. The saga is explicit that Frakokk and her sister Helga resided here after they were banished from Orkney, and Rognvald Kali's envoys went there to discuss allying with Frakokk against Earl Paul. Finally, it was in Helmsdale that Frakokk was killed when burned in her house by Swein Asleifsson who approached the house site from the north-west arriving unexpectedly from Atholl (*OS*, Chapter 78).[106] It has been suggested that the Moddan family probably held the hill land of the upper parts of the valleys of Strathnaver, Sutherland, and Caithness with control of the important land routes across to Sutherland and the estates held by Frakokk.[107] Their territorial power base was central to the highlands of north Scotland and less dependent on maritime connections than the power bases of the Orkney earls.

Reading between the lines of the saga story concerning these characterful individuals (as we are always tempted to do) we can glean a little insight into the nature of the mixed Celto-Norse society which had developed in north Scotland in the couple of hundred years since the ninth and tenth-century conquests by the earls. We have already seen that Caithness was bitterly fought over by Norse earls and Celtic chieftains (see Section 3.4.2). A native dynasty survived into the tenth century at Duncansby, which was however firmly in the hands of Earl Thorfinn in the early eleventh century. The Clan Moddan kindred was established at Thurso further west along the north coast of Caithness in the twelfth century. The names of the sons and daughters of this family point to a mixed linguistic culture. Of Moddan's children two daughters had Norse names – Helga and Thorleif – while Frakokk's own strange name is likely to have had a Celtic origin. One of his sons had a Celtic name – Angus – and the other's name –Ottarr – is possibly Norse. Frakokk's own daughters had Norse names as did most of her grandchildren, with the exception of her father's name – Moddan – which is given to one of the grandsons.[108] The preponderance of these names is Norse, and it is likely that it was Norse culture which was dominant and Norse speech which was the norm among this upper level of Caithness–Sutherland society. This was especially the case when connections with the earldom family were close with Helga being Earl Hakon's mistress and the main ambitions of the two sisters being to insert their off-spring and protégés into positions of

---

106 Gray (1922, 59) mentions that tradition records her residence to have been at Carn Shuin, on the east side of the River Helmsdale near Kinbrace
107 Gray, 1932, 53; Williams, 2007, 137
108 Another of the grandsons was called Magnus, which in the 1130s doubtless reflected a wish to commemorate and perpetuate the name of the saint-earl

power within the Orkney earldom. Undoubtedly however this Celto-Norse kindred would have been bilingual.

Other information which can be gleaned from the saga about the mixed cultural or linguistic nature of society in Caithness is very sparse, but one interesting comment in *OS*, Chapter 92, has been interpreted as indicating the use of a Gaelic term for a hospitality rent. When Earl Harald boarded out his men in various places in Caithness during Easter 'Then the men of Caithness said that the Earl was on *commaid* (ON *á kunnmiðum*) (*OS* Taylor, 307 n. 4, 397). This may have been an intended pun on an ON phrase 'to be on familiar fishing-grounds' (*at vera á kunnmiðum*), and as it is attributed to 'the men of Caithness' it sounds like a local phrase which was unfamiliar to the saga writer. It is very likely derived from the Gaelic word 'conveth' (Gaelic *commaid*) which was the term for a well-established hospitality rent throughout Scotland north of the Forth.[109] If so, it must have come from the Gaelic-speaking world to the south and might at this date have been introduced by earls who were familiar with this term in Gaelic Scotland.[110]

Mention of the place-name in Caithness called *Asgrimserg* ('Asgrim's erg' or 'shieling') in *OS*, Chapter 103, indicates transmission of the Gaelic word for 'shieling' (*airigh*) into Old Norse.[111] In actual fact this name was adopted by several different Scandinavian communities around the British Isles, and even as far north as the Faroe Islands.[112] Why this particular place-name element should have passed into Old Norse toponymy is not clear, but it could indicate that the shieling system was worked by Gaelic speakers who inhabited the upland settlements during the summer months, herding cattle, sheep and goats. The term for the transhumance huts and pasturelands certainly passed into common usage among the Norse communities.

These two terms gleaned from *Jarls' Saga* are merely two recorded elements of linguistic influence from Gaelic to Old Norse, which on their own do not suggest that the Gaelic-speaking population had great influence on Norse society in north Scotland. However, there must have been much more transmission of cultural influence which has escaped being recorded, and we have to remember that the saga author was writing from a fixed viewpoint of the earldom elite of Norse society. The work that has been done on Gaelic and Norse folklore stories and elements has brought out the likelihood of a mingling of stories, myths and motifs in the Scandinavian societies of northern

---

109 Almqvist, 2005, 30
110 This suggestion differs from those made previously in *Scand. Scot.* (1987, 213)
111 The sixteenth-century translator of the saga has a gloss on the word 'erg' in Chapter 103 when he says 'or setr as we call them' (*OS* Taylor, 333)
112 Crawford, 1987, 213, and references there cited

and western Scotland, and it is thought to be highly probable that 'much of the transmission took place within the borders of the Orkney earldom'.[113] We can perhaps be more specific and say that it was the Caithness earldom which was most probably the melting pot, and that it was among the Celto-Norse society of north Scotland that this mingling of ideas and beliefs took place. Naturally, such influence might then have spread across the Pentland Firth to Orkney, and possibly even further north.[114] Frakokk's court in Helmsdale and her wide kindred links are very likely to have provided fertile ground for the transmission of mixed cultural ideas among the elite of the locality, which included aspiring claimants to the Orkney earldom who then moved across the Firth and established themselves in the islands.

4.5 ASPIRING EARLS AND SCOTTISH INFLUENCE

We have already seen that after the death of Earl Hakon, his son by Helga, Harald, lived in Caithness ' for a long time' (*OS*, Chapter 54) and was given a grant of the earldom by the Scottish king. Following his death, his young son Erlend was brought up by Frakokk who doubtless intended that he would succeed to his father's position. King David would support those earls whom he could influence and who might be used as a counter-balance to the aspiring Norwegian earl, Rognvald Kali Kolsson, who was successful in winning support in Orkney at his second attempt in 1135 (*OS*, Chapter 71). Earl Paul then agreed to divide the islands with Rognvald, although probably reluctantly, as an earlier attempt to persuade him had been unsuccessful.

Because we have so much evidence from the saga about the ploys of the different power groups in the game of power-seeking and power-sharing it is difficult to be certain from the saga narrative as to the course of events and the cause of the twist and turn of how the events turned out. The most mysterious happening was the disappearance of Earl Paul (*OS*, Chapters 74, 75) who was captured by Swein Asleifsson in Rousay and taken into captivity in Atholl where he was put into the care of Earl Maddad and Margaret, Earl Paul's sister. His continued presence was a barrier to the ambitions of these two for the promotion of their son Harald to power in Orkney (who was only three at this point), and so Paul was blinded and maimed, as a result of which he died, or was killed, and was certainly 'out of the saga'. Only two years later (in 1139) Earl Rognvald was persuaded to accept the five-year-old Harald Maddadson as his co-earl, which was a quite unprecedented situation, and certainly suggests that very strong pressure from the highest quarters was brought to bear on

---

113 Almqvist, 1978–9, 89; 2005, 27
114 Chesnutt, 1968; De Geer, 1985, 243

Rognvald. It would appear that David I was pushing for the acceptance of the young half-Scottish Harald as earl, who would need to have guardians and counsellors in charge of his half of Orkney for many years to come (and also in Caithness, although it is nowhere said that Harald was given a grant of Caithness by David I).[115]

The possible role of the Church in these events is indicated by a reference to the visit of a Scottish bishop to Orkney two years after Earl Rognvald came to rule in Orkney (1138). He is described as arriving at Earl Rognvald's farm at Knarston, where the earl was celebrating Christmas (*OS*, Chapter 77) and was recognised by Hrolf, the earl's 'hird-priest' as 'Bishop Jon of Atholl' who had come on a mission.[116] He went to Egilsay to meet up with Bishop William of Orkney and stayed a few days; then the two of them set out to meet up with Earl Rognvald and told him about the 'private arrangement' between Swein Asleifsson and Earl Maddad that Harald Maddadson should have half of Orkney and the title of earl but that Rognvald would be the senior of the two, even after Harald had come of age. Swein was probably acting on behalf of King David in this negotiation. The impact of the bishop's visit –with Swein alongside him – and the authority of King David behind them no doubt impressed on Rognvald the advisability of accepting the suggested arrangement. However, this would have to be proposed to and agreed by the farmers, which apparently it was, for it is said that after the Earl had held a meeting in Caithness during Lent, an agreement was concluded 'by sealing it with sworn oaths of all the best men of Orkney and Scotland'. This indicates that Caithness was included in this agreement and that the men of both earldoms ('Orkney and Scotland') were party to the unprecedented arrangement of having a minor acknowledged as earl.

From this development it can be recognised that the Scottish king was involved in the internal affairs of the earldoms, albeit through his cousin Earl Maddad, and the power broker Swein Asleifsson. It is very difficult to know how much reliance one can put on the abundant information provided by the saga writer about Swein's close connections with King David especially the events recorded in OS, Chapter 83. These include the reported conversations of Swein and the king, who is said to have offered compensation to all those who had been robbed by Swein on his travels south to Edinburgh, and who offered to bring Swein's wife south from Orkney and give Swein a position in his kingdom. He is then said to have sent messages north to Orkney with gifts, asking Earl Rognvald to make peace with Swein. None of this is confirmable, but there does exist one charter of David's addressed to Rognvald, and possibly

---

115 Forte, Oram and Pederson, 2005, 286
116 Probably this was John, bishop of Glasgow (1114x1118–1147), but designated 'of Atholl' because of the connection with Earl Maddad in Atholl (*OS* Taylor, 388)

Harald, showing that there were official contacts with the earl, although on a quite different subject. It is worth quoting it in full – this is the first known Scottish charter addressed to an earl of Orkney, along with another earl and the *probis hominibus* ('good men') of Caithness and Orkney:

> David, king of Scots to Reinwald, earl of Orkney, and to the earl and all goodmen of Caithness and Orkney, greeting. I command you and ordain that as you love me you shall love the monks living at Dornoch in Caithness and respect their men and property whenever they come among you, not permitting anyone to do them harm or insult them.[117]

This is a fairly simple and typical royal mandate of the period which reveals much, however, about royal and ecclesiastical policy in the north. First of all it shows that King David was ordering Earl Rognvald, as earl of Orkney, to do his bidding, suggesting that Rognvald must have acknowledged King David's authority in the negotiations mentioned above. The second, unnamed earl who is also addressed must be Harald, who was still under age.[118] But in addition the king addressed his mandate to the good men of Caithness *and Orkney*, a rather surprising extension of royal command to the people of another kingdom.[119] The monks who are to be protected were possibly a monastic community of Céli Dé based at Dornoch, where there was a cult of St Barr,[120] and it is likely that this community was linked into plans which King David and Andrew, the Scottish bishop of Caithness, had for the diocese.[121] This mandate is however concerned to protect the monks and their officials when they were moving around the north of Scotland and the islands,[122] an indication of royal policy regarding the establishment of Scottish ecclesiastical structures in Caithness (see Chapter 6).

The complex story of rival earls continues, when Erlend, the son of Earl Harald Hakonsson 'Smooth-Tongue' (*slettmali*) succeeded in winning power in both Caithness and Orkney. He had been brought up by Frakokk in Sutherland so had a mixed Celto-Norse cultural background, and his campaign to gain authority was based in Scotland, and relied on Scottish support. He is said to have spent much time in Thurso after the death of his uncle Earl Ottar, and

---

117 *Reg.Dunf.* no. 23; *DN*, xix, 31; Lawrie, *Charters* no. 32; *OSR*, no. 11; *CSR*, no. 1; Barrow, 1985, 155; *Reg.Norv.*, I, 82. This mandate is undated, but probably dates to 1140–45

118 There is no name or initial included, and the title 'earl of Caithness' is omitted

119 As Barrow (1999, 9) comments, this is a rather remarkable instance of King David addressing the earl of Orkney and men who were the lieges of the king of Norway

120 Barrow, 1997, 83–4

121 Ibid.; Oram, 1997, 15. Bishop Andrew was a Benedictine monk from Dunfermline (Crawford, 1991, 31)

122 It has been suggested that they may have had a trading station at Dornoch (*RRS* I, 44)

he was fostered by Anakol, described as 'a viking, a ruthless man of Hebridean origins' (*OS*, Chapter 92), who acted as Erlend's *raðgjafi* (see Section 4.4). After Rognvald's departure on crusade (1151), Erlend went to receive a grant of half Caithness from King Malcolm (grandson of David I), sharing the lands with Harald Maddadson. But the desire to gain possession of the Orkney earldom was a driving ambition, as always (no earl was ever content with possession of Caithness alone), and Erlend gathered a force from his friends in Caithness and crossed to Orkney 'to seek recognition'. He sought half of the earldom from Harald who was assembling a force to oppose this new claimant, and it was decided that Erlend should go to Norway to get a grant of Earl Rognvald's half from King Eystein, Rognvald being far distant on a pilgrimage to the Holy Land, from which he might very well never return.

This information from the saga about Erlend's claims to earldom power and possessions gives us a very good description of how the process of claiming your inheritance and of getting official recognition worked, even when there was a relative already in possession of both lands and authority. The claimant had to have a good blood link and be of the earldom *ætt* ('kindred'), as of course Erlend was, being a son and a grandson of earls; he had to have powerful backers and win the acknowledgement of the farmers in the earldoms, and he had to have a grant of official recognition from the king of Scots for Caithness and from the king of Norway for Orkney. Even if another earl was already in possession, such strong claims had to be acknowledged, and the authority and lands divided, so long as the claimant had enough powerful backers to put the legitimate claim into practice. In twelfth-century feudal Scotland this was an outmoded and irregular system, and the king of Scots could only attempt to manipulate the traditional arrangements from afar through the agency of powerful operators like Swein Asleifsson, and eventually the Church.

The unpredictable element was the willingness or unwillingness of the earl already in possession to agree to share or not. This was a very tricky business and depended on a number of factors, chief among them being the military preparedness and support which an earl might have for when the inevitable fighting occurred. In Erlend's case it turned out that he was given not Rognvald's half by King Eystein but Harald's, which led immediately to a fight between them, around the fortress at Cairston, near Stromness (*OS*, Chapter 92). Harald must have been worsted in the adventure for he agreed to hand over to Erlend his half of the earldom and had to swear oaths never to claim it back. The need to have such arrangements ratified is evident from the statement that these oaths were 'witnessed by a number of important men in the islands', and Harald departed across the Firth to Caithness and on further south to join his kinsmen, no doubt to plan his comeback and revenge. An assembly was then summoned by Swein and Erlend at Kirkwall to which men came from all over the islands, and Erlend presented his case for taking over Harald's share, proving his official grant from King Eystein. He is even said to have produced letters from Eystein which must have been the official notification of the grant. This official endorsement by the king of Norway of a new earl's claim had by this date evidently become fully recognised as being an important requirement. However, the involvement of the men of Orkney in these changes of earl and the need of the new claimant to have their agreement points also to an elective element in the process.

When Rognvald did arrive home safe and sound late in the year 1153, the outlook for peace in the islands was not good. Two earls in Orkney and one in Caithness – but aspiring to return to his estates in Orkney – meant that two would ally against the other; the die was cast when Rognvald renewed his friendship and alliance with Harald and broke off relations with Erlend and his protector Swein.[123] The so-called War of the Three Earls ensued (*OS*, Chapters 94–9) which resulted in the death of Erlend after much manoevring and jockeying for advantage, all recounted by the saga author with detailed descriptions of the geography and sea routes around the islands which he evidently knew well. Swein and Harald were finally reconciled and the saga story moves on towards the death of Earl Rognvald (which will be discussed in Chapter 5).

From the point of view of the place of Caithness in the earls' social and administrative control of their realm two mini-sagas from this latter period of Earl Rognvald's life are quite revealing of the problems they had in controlling the activities of lawless men in this society. One concerns Thorbjorn Clerk, Earl Harald's counsellor, who fell out with Earl Rognvald due to a dispute over their retainers Thorarin 'Bag-nose' and Thorkel. He was 'driven away by force' and went across to Caithness 'and stayed there for some time committing various crimes, raping and killing' (*OS*, Chapter 100). After Thorbjorn killed Thorarin, Earl Rognvald 'declared him an outlaw throughout the land' which meant he should have left the territory under the earls' control, but Thorbjorn simply went into hiding in Caithness, and it was in tracking him down that Earl Rognvald met his end. Then we hear about a well-connected but 'terrible bully' Gilla Odran who fled from Scotland due to 'much trouble and killing in the kingdom' and was received in Orkney by the earls[124] who made him their steward in Caithness, which suggests that such bullies were needed to keep control of earldom rights and incomes from that area. However, due to a dispute over the stewardship, a local farmer Helgi was killed by Gilla, who then moved west and became the captain of one of Somerled's ships. Swein

---

123 Clouston, 1932, 109
124 This is an early example of Orkney being a haven for Scottish outlaws; later treaties between the kings of Norway and Scotland included clauses to prevent this (see Chapter 7).

Asleifsson pursued him and having got involved in the battle in which Somerled was killed he then tracked Gilla Odran down in *Myrkvafjǫrðr* (probably Loch Glen Dubh in Kylestrome, *OS* Taylor, 402) and killed him with fifty of his men (*OS*, Chapter 101). These stories suggest that the earls may have had some difficulty in controlling wilder elements who established themselves in Caithness where they were able to lead a life of lawlessness without the earls being always able to exercise their authority to maintain peace, as they were mostly able to do in Orkney.

In contrast to this aspect of violence Caithness provided the earls with the opportunity to hunt deer in the uplands there, which they were wont to do every summer (*OS*, Chapter 102). This was a sport which was not available in the islands, and it also provided a valuable source of food and other useful items like antlers. These were both important assets for the earldom elite who liked to indulge in the high-status sport of hunting and also needed large reserves of food supplies.

4.6 ASPECTS OF POLITICAL GEOGRAPHY IN THE TWELFTH-CENTURY EARLDOMS

Both Orkney and Caithness were the centre of the earls' world, with the Pentland Firth as the binding waterway running between the two halves. From that central world their influence and their authority reached further out into every island from the Outer Skerries north-east of Shetland to Stroma in the Pentland Firth and along the north Scottish coast, down the east side of Caithness and Sutherland to the Dornoch Firth. Naval expertise was essential for the maintenance of their influence and authority over this widespread maritime empire, but it was their landed possessions, the earldom estates, which were the key to their wealth and power. As far as Orkney is concerned we have a very good idea of which estates belonged to the earls from the saga account and the late medieval Rentals. William Thomson's map of the earls' bordlands[125] gives an impressive indication of the widespread pattern of these manor farms throughout the islands, both those recorded in the Rentals as 'bordlands', and those localities which had previously been earldom estates but which had passed into the hands of the Church in later centuries (see Figure 4.6). This map tells us of the manorial pattern of lordship in Orkney where 'large farms and formidable chiefs'[126] dominated the local communities. It brings us nearer to a 'feudal' pattern of landownership than anywhere else in north Scotland, or in western Norway.

---

[125] Thompson, 2008, fig. 45
[126] Ibid., 33

Strategic considerations underlay the earldom estate pattern and their development into power centres. The number of large manorial farms in the north isles of Orkney – in Westray, Sanday and Stronsay – indicates that there were originally single large earldom properties on these islands which have been identified as strategically significant, enabling the earls or their 'gödings' to command vital sea routes from the north and east.[127] The farm of Housebay in Stronsay has been the subject of particularly interesting in-depth studies.[128] These identify the great fertility of this earldom estate and the significance of its 'central place' as an earldom power centre, with also some very suggestive place-names round about indicating (a rarity in Orkney) that it was also a place of heathen worship, with particular reference to Odin. Housebay's position at the south-east extremity of Stronsay was strategically located to control the main navigation route leading east from Orkney across the North Sea to Norway.[129] The Stronsay Housebay proves the importance of the farms with the 'huseby' name and this recent assessment demonstrates links with the earls and political operators like Swein Asleifsson.

4.6.1 *Scapa Flow*

Within the Orkney earldom Scapa Flow became an important part of the earls' political landscape in the twelfth century, and can perhaps be called the 'nerve centre' of the joint Orkney–Caithness lordship. Scapa Flow is a vast natural harbour providing safe refuge from the tides and cross-currents of the Pentland Firth, as well as providing secure vantage points from which the Firth could be policed, passing traffic controlled, and passage to and from Caithness secured.[130] The accounts of the activities in these waters recorded in the twelfth-century section of the saga give us boundless information as to how the earls and their followers, and opportunists like Swein Asleiffson used this maritime landscape in their games of strategy to gain advantage over their opponents, and triumph over their deadly enemies.

An important factor in earldom political geography of the period after the 1130s is the change of the earls' centre of operations from Birsay to Orphir, on the north side of Scapa Flow. The settlement on the Brough of Birsay was probably handed over to the Church after the reburial of Magnus Erlendsson, thereby declining in importance as an earldom residence.[131] Both the earl and

127 Ibid., 39
128 Stylegar, 2004, 8–13; Thomson, 2008, 37–51
129 Ibid., 45
130 Omand (1993, 103) refers to this 'superb natural anchorage' whose sheltered waters have a 'low energy wave environment'
131 The only reference to earls in Birsay after the translation of Earl Magnus' relics occurs c.1155 when

THE NORTHERN EARLDOMS

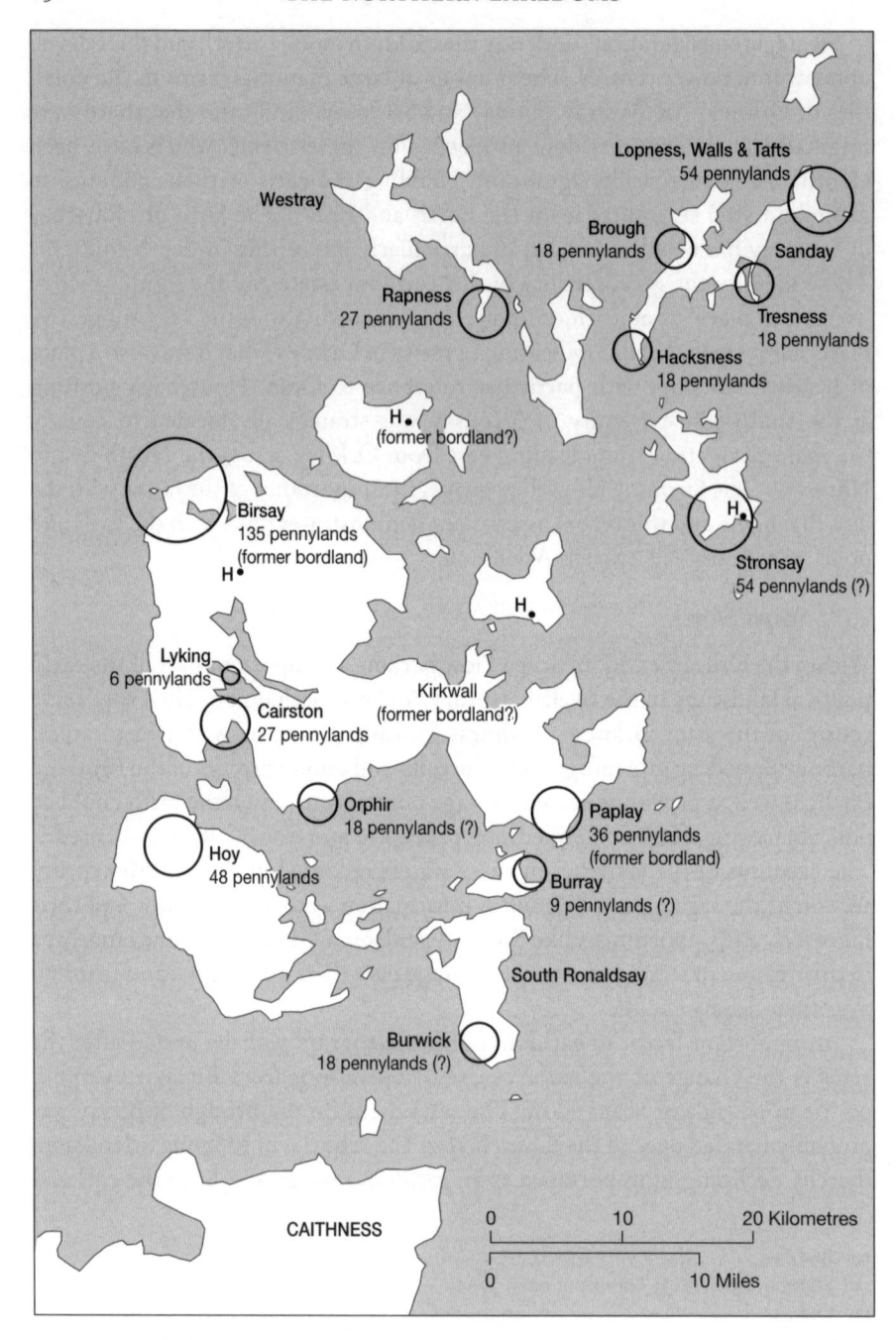

Westray

Lopness, Walls & Tafts
54 pennylands

Brough
18 pennylands

Sanday

Rapness
27 pennylands

Tresness
18 pennylands

Hacksness
18 pennylands

H.
(former bordland?)

H.

Birsay
135 pennylands
(former bordland)

H.

H.

Stronsay
54 pennylands (?)

Lyking
6 pennylands

Kirkwall
(former bordland?)

Cairston
27 pennylands

Orphir
18 pennylands (?)

Paplay
36 pennylands
(former bordland)

Hoy
48 pennylands

Burray
9 pennylands (?)

South Ronaldsay

Burwick
18 pennylands (?)

CAITHNESS

0   10   20 Kilometres

0   10 Miles

Figure 4.6 Map of earldom bordlands based on Thomson (2005, fig. 45) with the addition of 'huseby' farms (H) from Crawford (2006). The Scottish term 'bordland' was used of those lands held directly by Scottish feudal landowners and not rented out ('Land providing supplies for the lord's table'). As the map shows such mensal estates were distributed throughout the Orkney islands, and, if not described as 'bordland', they can be recognised in the Rentals by the absence of any skat payment from such lands (ibid., 1996, xix). They consisted of the very best arable land, and were strategically located. Division of the earldom among claimants would mean that these bordland estates would be divided also according to their value. That such earldom estates also existed in Caithness is suggested by the names Murkle Boardland near Murkle and Borlum near Sandside.

---

the bishop moved their main seats to the central Mainland, the earls to Orphir and the bishops to Kirkwall where the body of the murdered Earl Magnus was enshrined in the new St Magnus Cathedral. This led to the development of Kirkwall as the ecclesiastical, political and commercial heart of the earldom. Kirkwall was well placed to become the nexus of the earldom, being at the most strategic crossing-point between the south-facing waters of Scapa Flow and the south isles of Orkney and the north-facing waters of Wide Firth, leading to the north isles. It linked east–west land routes with north–south sea routes. The crossing-point was called Scapa (ON *skalp-eið*,' the dividing isthmus') and this important 'aith' or portage was where men and goods (and maybe ships) could be transported between the inland waters of Scapa Flow and the Peerie Sea and Wide Firth Bay. The many instances of shipping being funnelled up to Scapa from the south show us how important this passage was.[132]

Another recurring reference is to the mooring of ships at Knarston where for instance Swein was dropped for him to proceed to Earl Paul's estate at Orphir (*OS*, Chapter 66), and where Earl Rognvald is twice said to have disembarked for his farm at Knarston, on the first occasion in order to hold his Christmas feast there (*OS*, Chapters 77, 94).[133] This name, and the farm, has now disappeared but its location is still remembered and it was situated on the west side of Scapa Bay, near Lingro. The farm name itself (ON *Knarrarstaðir*), tells us that it was located near good mooring for 'knarrs', a general term for a transport ship, latterly of freight and cargo, but probably originally of men.[134] The location of such a name close by the 'aith' at Scapa reveals that this was a very important

---

Swein is said to have 'found Earl Rognvald in Birsay'. Perhaps the earl was there to administer the establishment of a community of monks at the former bishop's seat (see Section 5.5.1)

132 The name Scapa Flow was derived from this portage at the northern end of the sheltered harbour basin

133 See Crawford, 2006, 34–7, for a fuller discussion of the three Knarston names in Orkney

134 Jesch, 2001, 130ff.

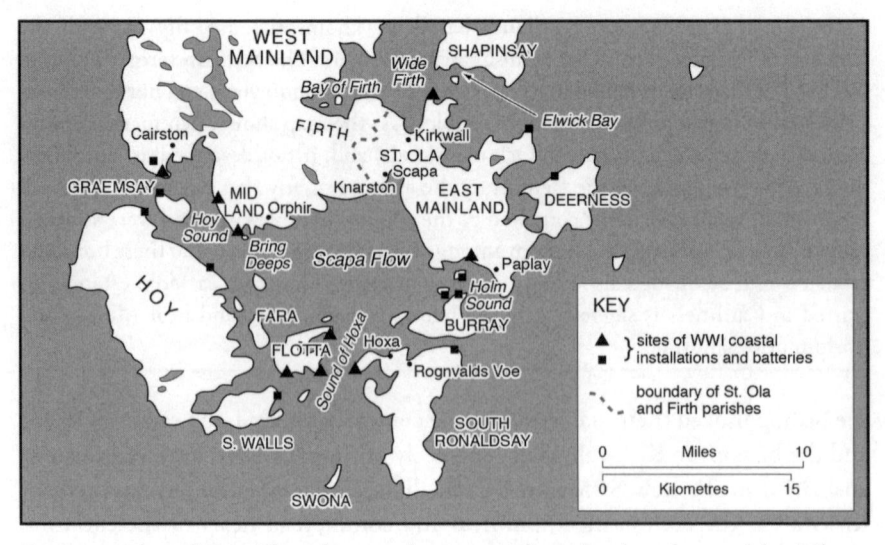

Figure 4.7 Map of Scapa Flow showing the surrounding islands and part of the Orkney Mainland. The strategic location of the earldom residence at Orphir can be assessed in relation to the maritime access points and the transit route across the isthmus at Scapa to Kirkwall. Also shown are sites of WWI coastal installations as an indication of the location of strategic defence points (as relevant in the twelfth century as in the twentieth). (Information drawn from maps kindly provided by Geoffrey Stell)

place for those who spent their lives moving around the islands by ship and who needed to moor their 'knarr' while visiting Kirkwall or Orphir (Figure 4.7).

As the entries about Swein and Rognvald disembarking at Knarston in order to go to Orphir show, it evidently served as a mooring place for visitors to the earldom estate of Orphir, which became the most important earldom residence at this time. Orphir is first mentioned at the time of Earls Paul and Harald Hakonsson in the 1120s/1130s, when many incidents took place there including the murder of Swein 'Breast-Rope', and the embroidering of the 'poisoned shirt' by Helga and Frakokk c.1128. It clearly became these earls' favoured residence, and the location gives us an understanding of why that should be. Orphir is situated in a south-facing position with a very good outlook across Scapa Flow, giving the earls an excellent view of shipping sailing into the Flow from the south and west [135] (see Colour plate 16). Orphir's position meant that the earls were within easy reach of Kirkwall where much of the political activity was

135 Knarston similarly had an excellent view across the Flow to the south as the description of Bishop John's arrival at Knarston shows, when 'a ship was seen sailing north across the Pentland Firth' and the earl and his hirdmen watched it sail up to Knarston and the bishop disembark (*OS*, Chapter 77)

focused after it was developed into a power centre with ecclesiastical importance as the location of the island saint's relics. Orphir was however sufficiently detached from the growing cult centre of the martyred Magnus, who had been killed by Paul and Harald's father Hakon, and whose saintly status was therefore not particularly appreciated by the kindred of Earl Hakon (see Chapter 5). The dividing line between the two halves of the earldom ran just west of Kirkwall (along the boundary of St Ola and Firth parishes), and Orphir was well within that part of Orkney belonging to the Paul line of earls (see Figure 4.7).

The Earl's Bu at Orphir was an earldom bordland, but a smaller estate than Birsay, being only 18 pennylands compared with Birsay's 135.[136] The site of the earldom farm has great archaeological potential and has been excavated at different times over a long period, but the surviving structural remains are 'difficult to interpret'.[137] The early excavations uncovered impressive stone walls and footings of medieval ('late Norse') buildings to the north of the round Church, but these have not been satisfactorily interpreted, nor dated. It does seem clear that none of these structures represent the drinking-hall of the earls mentioned in the twelfth-century section of the saga. Nonetheless the situation of a prestige settlement site and the remains of a prestige church located close by does conjure up the material situation of the twelfth-century earls' living circumstances, visualised in the reconstruction drawing by Iain Ashman (see Colour plate 16). There is much more which could be done to elucidate this site, and recent excavations and survey work have brought to light some different, and intriguing, features of the late Norse domestic comital economy.[138]

4.6.2 *Castles*

A significant feature of 'feudal' society appeared in the earldoms at this date – the 'castles' mentioned in the saga text, which were defensive stone structures built for protection in a violent age. There are in fact some surviving stone towers which are generally thought to originate in this period, remarkably early examples from the age of castle building. This is a big contrast to Norway where it was highly unusual for members of the aristocracy to have their own castle, and royal castles were few and far between, the earliest dating from the time of King Sverre (1177–1202).[139]

---

136 Thomson, 2001, 224
137 Graham-Campbell and Batey, 1998, 192
138 Such as the small horizontal water-mill (Graham-Campbell and Batey, 1998, 193–4) (shown on the reconstruction drawing, Colour plate 16) which was apparently part of the domestic functioning of a large household with plenty of grain to consume, grown on the fields around the Earl's Bu
139 Lidén, 1974, 11; Bagge, 2011, 132

The most famous, and best-preserved surviving castle is Cubbie Roo's Castle on Wyre, a small stone defensive tower, surrounded by ditches (see Colour plate 17), which is actually referred to in the saga:

> At that time there was a very able man called Kolbein Heap farming on Wyre in Orkney. He had a fine stone fort (*steinkastala*) built there, a really solid stronghold.
>
> (*OS*, Chapter 84)

We are not actually told why Kolbein felt the need to build himself a stone castle at that time (during the joint reigns of King Harald Gilli's sons, 1136–mid-1150s), whether for defensive purposes, or for a display of his wealth and power.[140] It is certainly doubtful that it could have been used as a permanent residence, and is much more likely to have been built for occasional need of defence.[141] The nearby farm on the island, the Bu, is where the main residence would probably have been situated. On another, later, occasion Hanef the royal steward fled to Wyre after the killing of Earl John Haraldsson in 1230, and took refuge in the castle that Kolbein Heap had built (*Hacon's Saga*, 171).

The small stone tower at the centre of the complex still stands to a maximum height of almost 8 feet (2.5m), and the tower itself measures nearly 8m square with walls over 5 and a half feet thick (nearly 2m) at the base.[142] It was probably at least two floors high with an entrance at the first floor accessed by retractable ladder. Excavation of the enclosing defences showed different phases of construction, with two ditches, one of them rock-cut. The stone masonry is very fine and the external plaster coat of lime mortar is characteristic of early building elsewhere.[143] The link with Kolbein Hruga is expressed in the traditional name of 'Cubbie Roo's' Castle, and there seems no reason to doubt that he was the builder. If so, where did the model of a stone-built keep come from and the expertise in building it? The same issue arises with the Romanesque achievement of St Magnus Cathedral, where the work of masons from England and Scotland is fully evident (see Chapter 5). Members of the wealthy earldom circle were very familiar with the world of the Anglo-Normans who had stone-building perfected to a high art, and we can be certain that this is where the inspiration came from.[144] There is no parallel to this form of stone tower (as seen in Cubbie Roo's Castle) in contemporary Norway, where the first stone

---

140 The purpose and function of castle building in medieval England has been much discussed in recent years (see for instance Platt, 2007, 51)
141 Ritchie, 1985, 87
142 RCAHMS, 1946 *Inventory of Orkney*, 237
143 Ibid., although this does not prevent the RCAHMS *Inventory* from expressing doubts as to the twelfth-century date of the structure
144 Ritchie, 1993, 121

fortifications developed during the reign of Sverre in the later twelfth century. They are much more massive in structure, and without the square towers already known in France and England. This stone keep on Wyre is among the earliest survivals of stone-built fortifications in Scotland.[145] It was probably not alone, for there are references to other castles in the saga story of this period, such as Cairston near Stromness which was attacked by Earl Erlend and Swein 'all day with iron and fire' (*OS*, Chapter 92).[146] A *kastali* is also referred to on the island of Damsay in the early 1150s (*OS*, Chapter 66). Not documented are a keep at Westness on Rousay and the possible fortified structure at Castlehowe in Paplay in the East Mainland (*OS* Taylor, 384), but these are likely to be later in date.[147] An important point relating to the earls' position in the islands is that none of these castles appear to be earldom castles, which might indicate the inability of the earls to maintain full authority over the powerful 'göding' class during this period.[148]

Across the Firth in Caithness we find more survivals of what appear to be early fortifications. The castle in Thurso was a very important earldom stronghold and is mentioned several times. A settlement between Earls Rognvald and Harald was discussed at the castle (*kastal*) in Thurso in 1154 (*OS*, Chapter 94), and it was attacked by Scottish forces in 1198 (see Chapter 6). Unfortunately nothing of this earliest castle survives, but it was believed to lie on the south side of the town.[149] Second to Thurso as an earldom base was Wick, where Earl Harald spent the winter 'in residence' (*OS*, Chapter 92). Perhaps the well-preserved stone tower at Old Wick can be identified with Earl Harald's castle (see Colour plate 18). It has no diagnostic features but is now recognised to be twelfth or early-thirteenth-century in date.[150]

One of the best-recorded castles is Swein Asleifsson's 'Lambaborg', where he and Margad Grimsson gathered forces 'ready to make a stand' (*OS*, Chapter 82). The saga writer makes the comment that it was a 'safe stronghold' (*vígi*) and stood on a sea cliff 'with a stoutly built stone wall to landward'. As mentioned above, Swein and his following of sixty men robbed and looted around Caithness, taking the loot into the stronghold. Eventually they made a daring escape down the cliffs when Earl Rognvald arrived. The Broch of Ness near Freswick suits the location of these stirring events,[151] and it is worth noting that the name

145 Ritchie, 1985, 87
146 Clouston excavated this castle in 1927 (1928–9, 59–66; 1932, 105)
147 There is a full discussion of the source material relating to these Norse castles in Orkney in S. Grieve's unpublished MA thesis Norse Castles in Orkney (University of Glasgow, 1999)
148 Grieve, 1999, 116
149 Myatt, 1993, 7
150 Close-Brooks, 1986, 103; Ritchie, 1993, 121; Gourlay, 1993, 14–15
151 www.caithness.org/caithness/castles/lambaborg

Lambaborg indicates that there was a pre-Norse broch at the site, for the term used by the Norse settlers for these stone towers was 'borg' (the origin of the word 'broch'). Perhaps it was the broch which was used by Swein for his stronghold, for there does not appear to be a structure contemporary with his time on the site.

There are many more medieval castles in Caithness, which gives an indication of the warlike nature of society on the south side of the Pentland Firth.[152] The violence portrayed so realistically in the full and detailed saga account of the earldoms of Orkney and Caithness in the twelfth century gives us no doubt that this was a warlike and violent society, among the elite of the earldom kin, the 'gödings' and their followers.

We know that this is what the saga-teller's audience was prepared to hear about, and probably wanted to hear about. But was it overplayed for the purpose of making a good story more horrific? Maybe, and perhaps the numbers given as being killed on the occasions when the rivals clashed and when the feuds were being played out were exaggerated. But we cannot doubt that this society was violent, just as the earlier Viking age had been violent. Indeed, it is said, in contrast to the other parts of the Norse world, that the Orkneys were 'the last Viking-Age frontier', and that the personal warrior abilities of the Orkney earls are stressed in the Old Norse literature.[153] However, by the twelfth century the violence was internalised in the settled communities of Orkney and Caithness and Sutherland, so for that reason seems more shocking. Whether it was any more violent than the contemporary societies of Norway or Scotland is a difficult question to answer, although it is thought to have been more violent than contemporary Iceland, where life appears from the sagas to be comparatively more peaceful.[154] We have in these saga accounts a full, frank, realistic and convincing presentation of the way of life in these Nordic and Celto-Norse societies of north Scotland and the islands. So we have the evidence, but, remarkable as it is, we cannot know whether it is telling us about a society which was normal in European terms, or abnormal. Certainly that society was developing tendencies similar to those of other societies, but perhaps the norms of these other medieval societies were not quite so normal in Orkney and Caithness. One of the big differences is that the societies in both areas were barely under royal control, which was a force for taming the wilder

---

152 The contrast between the numbers of castles in Caithness and Orkney is commented on in Crawford, 2005, 202, and the reason is suggested that the earls exercised more control over their Orkney earldom than their Scottish one. This contrast needs closer examination as do the earldom power bases in Caithness
153 Jon Vidar Sigurdsson, 2008, 97
154 Ibid.

elements of warlike societies in the medieval age. We will see in Chapter 6 how royal lordship was imposed on the earls and how they were brought within the governmental systems of the medieval kingdoms of Scotland and Norway. Perhaps the societies in the earldoms became more peaceful as a result.

FIVE

Saint-Earls and Orkney's Twelfth-century Renaissance

Before looking at the impact of the royal fist in the mailed glove we turn first to developments within the earldoms which resulted in the sanctification of two of the earls, Magnus Erlendsson and his nephew, Rognvald Kali Kolsson. This result meant the adornment of an earldom dynasty with two saints, which is a notable political and religious feature of secular lordship in northern Europe. Several royal dynasties managed to achieve such a creditable enhancement of their status, but for the Orkney earldom to do so is exceedingly impressive. If historians of the twenty-first century are impressed, how much more so must twelfth-century contemporaries have been? This religious and cultural development gave the earldoms – most especially Orkney – a status and fame beyond what would ever have been gained under usual circumstances, considering the islands' peripheral place in the medieval world.

5.1 THE KILLING OF EARL MAGNUS

The breakdown in the relationship of the cousins Hakon Paulsson and Magnus Erlendsson has already been briefly referred to (see Section 4.4.2). Their quarrel escalated into a violent encounter on the island of Egilsay at Easter-time 1117.[1] Our evidence for this development rests primarily on the chapters which are central to the rule of Hakon and Magnus in *Jarls' Saga* (Chapters 44–53) which were written at least fifty years after the event, and the two saga accounts (the Shorter and Longer Magnus Sagas) written even later.[2] Inevitably the story will have become influenced by the growing cult of the murdered Magnus in the intervening period. However, the saga gives sober details of the peace meetings held, first at the place of assembly on Mainland (probably Tingwall) at Lent, where both sides formed up in battle order, but where attempts at reconciliation by most of the 'noblemen of the isles' (*stórmenn*) resulted in an agreement

---

1 Reasons for preferring 1117 above the other postulated dates of 1115 and 1116 are presented by Haki Antonsson (2007, 77–8).
2 See recent discussions of all the sources for the martyrdom and development of the saintly cult in Jesch and Mollesen, 2005, 129–34; Haki Antonsson, 2007, 5–23

being reached with oaths and handshakes of friendship. A further meeting was then fixed for Easter on Egilsay, 'to confirm the peace and goodwill'. However the account of the journey to Egilsay is tinged with the supernatural, suitably heightening the tension surrounding the doomed earl's progress towards his martyrdom.[3]

The themes of foreboding and treachery are skilfully interwoven in this account, with Hakon arriving prepared for a military encounter and with a greater number of ships than had been agreed. Magnus is described as the innocent victim who spent some time in the church on the island before being seized and led to his execution, after negotiations broke down. According to the account of the Hebridean Holdbodi, who was one of Magnus' companions, Hakon would have agreed to Magnus being imprisoned, but he was forced (or persuaded) by his followers to agree to his rival's execution, as it was insisted that one of the two earls should be killed. 'Better kill him then,' said Hakon, 'I don't want an early death: I much prefer ruling over people and places' (*OS*, Chapter 49).

The method of killing Magnus by the blow of an axe to his head delivered by Lifolf, Earl Hakon's cook, has been dramatically confirmed by the discovery of male skeletal material in St Magnus Cathedral in Kirkwall (see Section 2.7 and Plate 1). The remains of two individuals were found hidden separately inside two of the nave piers (one skeleton was contained within a small wooden 'kist' which might have been the interior of the saint's shrine). The skull of one of them bears the marks of a severe head wound across the top which was most likely caused by a blow from an axe, identifying it as the head of Magnus.[4]

5.2 GROWTH OF THE MAGNUS CULT

The killing of an earl in the course of bitter disputes between rival claimants over power and possessions was not an unusual event in the history of the two earldoms. The results of the killing of Earl Magnus, however, were nothing less than momentous, for the growth of a saintly cult which developed in the following decades was to bring fame and glory to the earldom family and be the reason for the building of perhaps the finest surviving example of Romanesque architecture in Scotland, the cathedral dedicated to St Magnus in Kirkwall. Exactly how and when and why this development took place is not easy to analyse, even though we have both *Jarls' Saga* and the other accounts to give us a broad outline of events. Clearly there were several groups and actors involved: the earldom family, and especially the next generation of members of the

---

3   Crawford, 1998, 28; 2004d (Magnus Erlendsson)
4   Jesch and Molleson, 2005, 135

Erlend line; the church in the islands, and particularly the bishop, William; and the islanders themselves, whose piety and belief in the sanctity of the murdered earl, and his power to work miracles on their behalf, was an important component in the growth of the cult, as it was in all other saintly cults.

5.2.1 *Preconditions for sanctification*

In the first instance there was the important matter of where Magnus' body would be laid to rest, and details about this come from one of the most moving passages in the whole of *Jarls' Saga*, where his mother Thora, weeping, pleads with Earl Hakon to be allowed to bury her son. Rarely do medieval historians have intimate and personal details of this kind illuminating the brutal events of the period. Earl Hakon is said to have shown some remorse and to have wept himself, before giving his permission for Magnus' body to be taken to Birsay and buried in Christ Kirk, in the church built by their common grandfather. It cannot have been a welcome development for Earl Hakon to have the body of his cousin – in whose death he was deeply implicated – interred in the church so closely associated with the earls' main residence. Even more unwelcome must have been the belief in the sanctity of the buried earl which grew up during the reign of Hakon's son Paul. Another striking passage describes how Earl Paul sat silent 'and flushed deep red' when it was urged by the farmer from Westray, Gunni, that the relics of Earl Magnus should be moved to Kirkwall (*OS*, Chapter 57).

The rapid developments of a spiritual and emotional nature which lay behind the growth of a saint's cult like that of Earl Magnus Erlendsson can be best understood by looking at how this happened in the context of contemporary cults of royal saints, particularly with respect to the rulers of the Scandinavian countries.[5] The growth of a successful cult around a national secular leader is nothing unusual, in fact it is almost the norm, as we know from the cult of King Olaf in Norway (after his death at the Battle of Stiklestad in 1030), of King Knud in Denmark (after his murder in the church of Odense in 1086), and of Duke Knud Lavard who was murdered by his brother at Ringsted in Denmark in 1131.[6] This was a feature of the recently converted societies in the Scandinavian kingdoms, among which Orkney was numbered. It also happened in a formative stage of development of secular and ecclesiastical rulership.[7] It can be said that elements of national identity and religious fervour, alongside ecclesiastical

---

5   Crawford, 1984, 65
6   King Erik Jedvardson of Sweden was also killed in battle in 1160 against a Danish pretender to his throne and a cult appears to have been developing towards the end of the century (Haki Antonsson, 2005, 159; 2007, 127–39, 139–44)
7   Haki Antonsson, 2007, 145

pretensions as well as political rivalry, all played a part in the growth of cults associated with these saintly rulers, including that of Magnus of Orkney.[8] The rivalry of the two earldom lines was the basic political situation lying behind the changing circumstances and Magnus' relatives and supporters came to be a very important element in the promotion of the cult. It was in the interest of the Erlend line of earls to 'cash in' on the growing belief in the sanctification of the dead earl. They had been politically disadvantaged by the loss of power following on from Magnus' execution and Earl Hakon's sole rule over both Caithness and Orkney; he is said to have 'made heavy exactions from the friends of Earl Magnus who he thought had taken most part against him'(*OS* Taylor, Chapter lii). However, Magnus' nephew, Rognvald, the only male heir to the Erlend line, through his mother Gunnhild, Magnus' sister, had a direct claim to the lands of his murdered uncle, and he used the developing cult of sanctity as a platform on which to base his own just and incontrovertible right to inherit the titles and possessions in both earldoms.

However, saints were not made by political activism alone. There were certain requirements which had to be fulfilled for the process to happen, among them the wishes of the local people who venerated the dead person, the support of the local bishop, the proof of miracles taking place in the vicinity of the dead person's tomb, and some evidence of the incorruptibility of the surviving relics when 'elevated', or taken up out of the grave. All these elements feature in the saga account, although the chronology of how they all happened is not very clear. The authors of the three Icelandic texts had a collection of miracles upon which they could draw; it was exceedingly important that these be recorded, and the task of compiling such collections was entrusted to learned clerics who were well-established in the ecclesiastical hierarchy.[9] The resulting record was called *Jarteinabók* ('Book of Miracles') and it is included in *OS* Chapter 57. Some of the miracles occurred at the grave in Birsay, followed by a 'good many' in Kirkwall after the saint's relics had been transferred there (and probably placed in St Olaf's Church). Another notable aspect of the miracles, which have recently been analysed, is the nature of the cures. Eight of them are cures for madness, or 'devil possession', which is a rather high proportion compared with the cures which are recorded as having been effected by other northern saints.[10] Otherwise the cures are said to be for leprosy,[11] paralysis, blindness, lameness,

---

8 Crawford, 1998, 25
9 Haki Antonsson, 2005, 150
10 Ibid., 153
11 Those afflicted with leprosy are said to have come from Shetland, which is an interesting precedent for the known prevalence of leprosy in Shetland in the later historical period (Crawford in Crawford and Ballin Smith, 1999, 42)

and for healing cripples.

One factor which emerges rather clearly from the record of miracles in the *Jarteinabók* is the prominent role played by Shetlanders who sought cures at the shrine of St Magnus, and who were to the fore in promoting his cult. This is welcome evidence of Shetlanders' participation in such momentous events in the history of the earldom, for in general Shetlanders feature rarely in the saga account. The main reason for this enthusiasm must stem from Shetland's association with the Erlend line of earls, for Shetland and the north isles of Orkney were part of its possessions.[12] The main proponent was a blind Shetland farmer called Bergfinn Skatason who is said to have made one journey south to Orkney to keep vigil at the grave in Birsay, taking two cripples with him; all three were cured. Later on he made a second trip south, after the relics had been translated to Kirkwall, and, with his son Halfdan, who was leprous, kept vigil at the church where they lay. Halfdan was completely healed. Bergfinn is also cited as being involved in the miraculous cure of a tenant of his called Thord, and again in making a vow to give money to the shrine to aid the healing of his nephew Ogmund who had fractured his skull badly. Many other miraculous cures to Shetland men and woman are recorded (*OS*, Chapter 57). As we will see, while he was delayed in Shetland, Bishop William had pressure put on him to recognise Magnus' sanctity and elevate his relics.

The small number of cures recorded as having affected Orkney men and women is notable; moreover the Orcadian Gunni, who did take an active part in pressing to have the earl's relics translated to Kirkwall, was from Westray which lay in the Erlend half of the Orkney earldom. He thought it best not to say that Magnus had appeared to him in a dream and ordered him to go to Birsay and tell of his wishes 'because he was afraid Earl Paul would hate him for it' (*OS*, Chapter 57). The Shetlanders were however far enough removed from the centre of earldom power and authority to have no fear of repercussions. The number of parish churches known to have been dedicated to Magnus in Shetland is a certain indication that enthusiasm for this saintly member of the Erlend line continued to run deep in this northern half of the earldom (see below and Figure 5.4).[13]

5.2.2 *Bishop William's role*

The role of the local bishop in the establishment of a cult was exceedingly important; indeed it could not happen without his concurrence and direction. Bishop William 'the Old' (1102 or 1112–1168) was closely connected with Earl

---

12 Crawford, 1984, 71; Haki Antonsson, 2007, 73
13 Crawford, 1984, 75

Hakon and his son Paul, and his seat was based in the cathedral established at Birsay by Earl Thorfinn, under the close supervision of the presiding earl. It is not surprising therefore that William is said in the saga to have shown some reluctance to believe in the stories of miracles occurring 'by calling it sheer heresy to spread them around' (*OS*, Chapter 56); his response to the idea of translating the holy relics 'was cool' (*OS*, Chapter 57), and it is also said that 'for a long time he doubted the saintliness of Earl Magnus' (*OS*, Chapter 52). Another complicating factor was the apparent presence of rival bishops in the north at this time. Evidence from the York archiepiscopal records shows that bishops were being appointed to Orkney by these northern English archbishops in opposition to those appointed by the archbishops of Hamburg-Bremen who claimed authority over all the bishoprics in Scandinavia.[14] The sporadic evidence for such dual appointments continues from the late eleventh century to the 1130s when the papacy was actually brought into this struggle to ensure that the king in Norway supported the York-appointed bishop.[15] It is most likely that the alternative York appointment referred to in the period 1109 x 1114 was the candidate of Earl Magnus, whose links with England during the early part of the century have already been mentioned (see Section 4.3.2). Of course after 1117 and the death of his patron, this alternative bishop, called Ralph Novell, would have had some difficulty keeping a foothold in the islands, and he may have been forced out of his see.[16] Certainly he is only on record thereafter in an English context. Any claim which the archbishop of York had made to authority over the Orkney bishopric became void in 1152/3 when the archbishopric of Nidaros was established which included all the bishoprics in the islands of the north Atlantic.[17]

In what way can this complicated situation help our understanding of the growth of the cult of St Magnus and Bishop William's support in furthering it? Despite his close attachment to the Paul line of earls (Hakon Paulsson and his son, Paul Hakonsson), Bishop William was eventually convinced of the sanctity of Magnus by two miracles, although sceptical historians might suggest that there were other factors which persuaded him of the wisdom of assisting the cult to become a recognised phenomenon. The change of heart is presented in the saga as taking place after he had visited Norway, and the possibility exists that his contacts in Norway convinced him of the need to support the popular

---

14 Crawford, 1983, 107–8; 1984, 68; 1996; Haki Antonsson, 2007, 93–5
15 Crawford, 1996, 5, 10–11
16 It is possible that Ralph Novell might have been able to establish himself in Caithness, with which earldom Magnus had been particularly associated. The Scottish kings were not active in creating a Scottish diocese in Caithness until the 1150s (Chapter 6)
17 Crawford, 1983, 111; B. and P. Sawyer, 1993, 115

enthusiasm for the sanctity of Magnus and to take the lead in developing the cult – whether these were political contacts, ecclesiastical ones, or both. The first miracle happened when the bishop was delayed by bad weather in Shetland. After the ship's captain made the suggestion that if they got favourable weather the bishop should cease to oppose the translation of Magnus' relics, William agreed to honour the vow if the weather improved sufficiently for him to sing Mass back home at his episcopal seat on the Sunday of the following week (*OS*, Chapter 57). Although this change of weather happened to the extent that he was able to sing Mass at home 'the very next Sunday', it took a second miracle to succeed in finally converting him to the cause. A sudden attack of blindness (appropriate for the blind refusal to recognise the evidence for the sanctity of the relics) was cured after the bishop prayed at Earl Magnus' grave and vowed that he would translate the holy relics 'whether Earl Paul liked it or not' (*OS*, Chapter 57). This whole scenario has to be contextualised in the changing political situation in the earldom, for Bishop William's reliance on the protection of the Paul line of earls was becoming less essential. His position as sole bishop was unchallenged by the 1130s, whereas Earl Paul's sole possession was threatened by the new challenge arising in Norway from the powerful combination of the heir to the Erlend line, Kali Kolsson (soon to be renamed Rognvald), and his father Kol, prepared to advance their claim to the earldom on the 'Magnus ticket'.[18]

5.2.3 *'Elevation' of the relics and 'translation' to Kirkwall*

Although the chronology of events regarding the development of the cult is 'far from clear' and Bishop William's involvement is presented 'more or less in a historical vacuum',[19] we can glean from the saga account that a conjunction of very significant events all came together in the years 1135–7. Bishop William's visit to Norway was evidently crucial in several respects, for he must have become aware that the young Rognvald and his father Kol were planning to launch an expedition to claim power in the earldom and that King Harald Gilli confirmed Rognvald's claim (in the spring of 1135).[20] At some point after his return to Orkney – and his miraculous conversion to recognising Earl Magnus' sanctity – Bishop William arranged for the bones to be raised from their burial place in Birsay and to be tested for purity. This 'elevation' was part of the process of establishing the incorruptibility of the relics, and in the case of Magnus the bones were washed and 'shone brightly'; a knuckle bone tested three times in consecrated fire would not burn 'but took on the colour of gold' (*OS*, Chapter

18 Crawford, 1998, 30
19 Haki Antonsson, 2007, 76–7
20 Ibid., 78

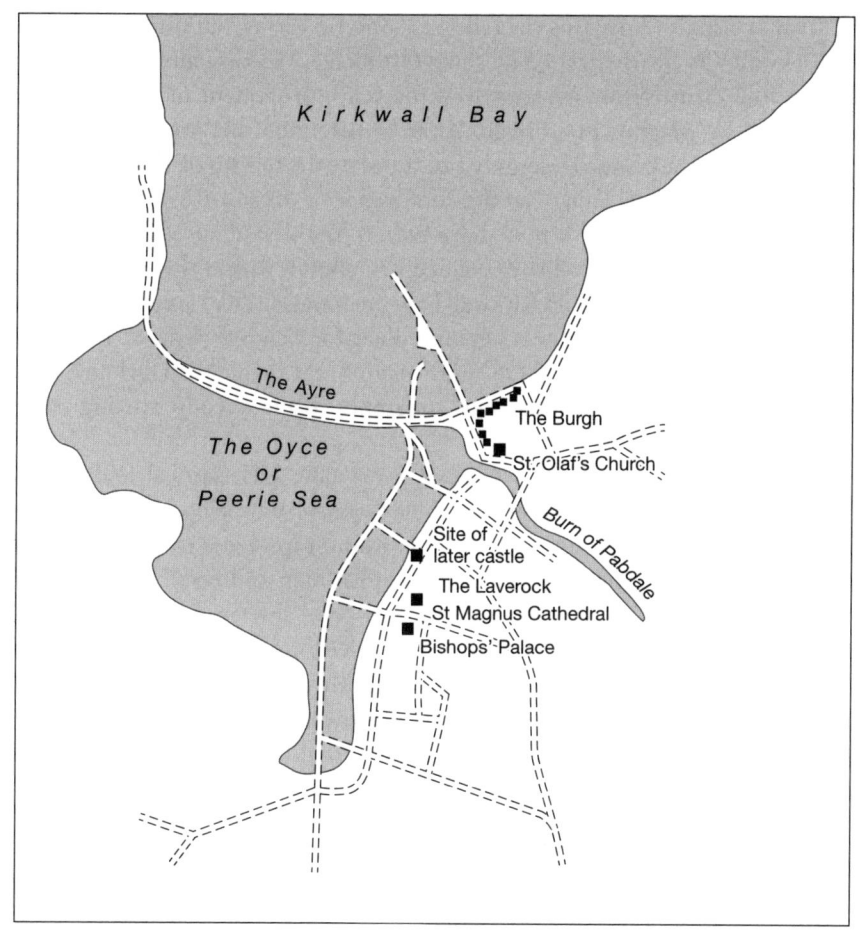

Figure 5.1 Map of medieval Kirkwall. (paparproject.org.uk, based on Hossack, 1900, map facing p.5)

57). This was sufficient for the requirements of 'canonisation' at the time, so the relics were enshrined and placed above the altar in Christ Kirk in Birsay. The saga writer estimated that this happened twenty-one years after the murder, which gives a date of 1137–8.[21] The day was St Lucy's Day (13 December), an important day in the development of a saintly cult, and a law is said to have been passed decreeing that both that day as well as the anniversary of the death of Magnus (16 April) should be celebrated, as indeed they continued to be in communities commemorating Magnus' martyrdom.

21 It is suggested by Haki Antonsson that this date cannot be correct and that 13 December 1135 is the most probable date for the *elevatio* (2007, 78)

It is not clear for how long the relics remained in Birsay, but their translation to Kirkwall was clearly desired by some Orcadians. We have already seen that Gunni, the farmer from Westray, was the brave proponent of such a move, as ordered by Magnus in a dream. After he recounted his dream, there was pressure to get the bishop to comply and translate the relics to Kirkwall, despite the opposition of Earl Paul. Can the connivance of the pro-Rognvald party in this strategy be detected? It must have been to the advantage of the opposing earldom line to have the relics enshrined in a church within their own half of the islands.[22] Why else should Kirkwall have been chosen? Kol's reported speech clearly urges his son to create a new cult place for Magnus' relics at Kirkwall, and to build a stone minster there 'more magnificent than any in Orkney' (*OS*, Chapter 68), which is a barely veiled reference to the already existing stone church at Birsay (see Section 5.2.4).

The situation of Kirkwall was ideal for a new ecclesiastical and proto-urban centre. It is at the heart of the whole Orkney archipelago, located at the northern end of the isthmus which leads from Scapa Flow to the Oyce and Wide Firth, which provides a crossing-point for men and possibly ships from the south to the north Orkney isles.[23] It had good sheltered harbourage and excellent cultivable land at Papdale nearby.[24] Kirkwall was an earldom estate and first mentioned in the saga as the place where Earl Rognvald Brusisson took up residence in 1046 and 'gathered in all the provisions he needed for the winter there'(*OS*, Chapter 46). It is very likely that he was the founder of the church dedicated to St Olaf, which became the parish church, because he had fought alongside the king at the Battle of Stiklestad, and was a close associate; it was presumably this church which underlies the name Kirkwall (*Kirkjuvágr*). If so, it must have been founded less than sixteen years after the death of Olaf (as Rognvald was killed in 1046), which is evidence for the very rapid growth of the cult of the saint-king.[25] Kirkwall was already therefore an earldom estate centre and traders would probably have been based there in the second half of the eleventh century. It is said to have been a 'market town' (*kaupstaðr*) when

---

22 The boundary between the two earldom halves lay to the west of Kirkwall (Clouston, 1919, 20, 25) at the western boundary of St Ola's parish
23 Crawford, 1983, 112–13. See Section 4.6.1
24 For further information about Papdale see the 'papar' website (www.paparproject.org.uk under 'Orkney')
25 It is not impossible that the name Kirkwall (*kirkju-vágr*, 'church-bay') was given with respect to the cathedral – and that the use of this name in the saga for Rognvald Brusisson's estate was retrospective. A parallel situation exists with regard to the name Kirkjubour ('church-farm') in the Faeroe Islands where a church dedicated to St Olaf existed before the cathedral of St Magnus was founded there in the 13th century. Was the name Kirkjubour originally given with reference to the church of St Olaf or the cathedral?

Magnus' relics were translated there in 1136/7, although the saga writer adds that there were only a few houses there at that time (in contrast to the time at which he was writing). This proto-urban centre must have been one of Erlend's and Magnus' estates, being in the East Mainland half of the earldom, and therefore part of Rognvald Kali Kolsson's due inheritance. The groundswell of opinion to have Magnus' relics transferred there, with which Bishop William concurred, can only therefore have been driven by the foresight and ambition of the pro-Rognvald party in the islands, which wished to remove the relics away from Christ Kirk, Birsay (where they were under the sceptical and hostile watch of Earl Paul), and transfer them to a location under its own control.

This move was of course going to be to the advantage of the bishop, who no longer needed to be under the protection of Earl Paul and who doubtless wished to have his own episcopal base free of secular control.[26] By the mid-twelfth century the Church in Scandinavia was beginning to break free of lay control and the move to Kirkwall fits in with this general process. In fact the building of St Magnus Cathedral at Kirkwall was in the van of this movement, for it was already in course of construction by the time that Trondheim Cathedral was erected over the burial place of St Olaf in the second half of the twelfth century. Trondheim (or Nidaros) was already a trading centre (called Kaupang), by this date. The proto-urban nature of Kirkwall's situation may similarly have been a relevant factor as an episcopal residence, for bishops were supposed to be based in towns which were centres of population.[27] The building of his own cathedral which would be his prime seat and usual place of residence, with sufficient revenues to be independent of the secular power, was every bishop's ambition in the period of exceptional growth of ecclesiastical power in the twelfth century. That ambition would be fulfilled with the inspiration and generous support of the new earl Rognvald, and his father Kol, who developed a strategy based on the growing cult of Magnus to help them win over the men of Orkney to their cause.

We therefore have a situation in which Bishop William probably acceded to the earl's demand for the translation of the relics to Kirkwall, and he led a grand procession from Birsay which took the holy relics to Kirkwall and placed them 'above the high altar of the church that stood there at that time' (*OS*, Chapter

---

26   Saga evidence shows that Bishop William also resided on the island of Egilsay where Magnus had been murdered. It was already episcopal estate at this time and the church on the island was therefore a 'bishops' church' (*residenskirker*) which made the island a refuge for the bishops away from the Brough of Birsay which was the earls' residence. However, the new cathedral was not built on Egilsay, even though this island was the actual location of Magnus' martyrdom
27   Crawford, 1983, 112

57). This must have been the church dedicated to St Olaf located near Papdale Burn in the lower town.[28] The bishop was most probably assured of the support of Rognvald Kali Kolsson and his father in the development of the cult centre and building of a cathedral at Kirkwall before he embarked on this physical and political breach with the existing earldom establishment, but the saga gives no hint of how the process developed.

5.2.4 Kol's speech and the building of St Magnus Cathedral

The political changes which took place during the years 1136–7 appear to have happened with different unseen political forces at work in both Scotland and Norway. As has been discussed, it is probable that the spiritual forces associated with the dramatic development leading to the sanctification and canonisation of the martyred earl also contributed to these changes. They had certainly driven the bishop to lead the translation of the relics to Kirkwall, and Kirkwall was the place chosen because of its detachment from the old earldom centre in Birsay and because it was in the Erlend and Magnus half of the Mainland earldom estates.

We can only puzzle out the thread of development from what the saga tells us, and the saga writer probably had his own agenda in recounting the events as they were remembered and had been told to him. Top of his agenda was the story of the aspirations of Rognvald and his supporters, their reverses and successes, and the eventual defeat and mysterious removal of Earl Paul from power (which has already been discussed in Section 4.5). The reputation of Rognvald Kali was greatly enhanced however by the linking of his campaign to the saintly reputation of his kinsman.[29] This aspect of the significance of the growing cult and the role of the saint as the patron and protector is expounded in a speech which is put into the mouth of Rognvald's father Kol at a meeting held in the Henn Isles in western Norway before embarking on the second expedition against Earl Paul in 1137. He is the inspirational figure who gives the advice to Rognvald to look to his uncle the holy Earl Magnus, 'the true owner of the realm'. He urges him to make a vow that if he is given his inheritance and legacy by Magnus and succeeds in winning power, then he will 'build a stone minster at Kirkwall more magnificent than any in Orkney',[30] and have it dedicated to his uncle. He is to provide it with all the funds that are needed, and in addition to see that the holy relics and the episcopal seat are moved

---

28 The approximate site of this church is known, and one late medieval doorway survives in the vicinity of St Olaf's Wynd, off Bridge Street (Lamb, 1993, 46)
29 Haki Antonsson, 2007, 80
30 The implication being that it was to be finer than the existing church on the Brough of Birsay, which was Earl Paul's place of worship

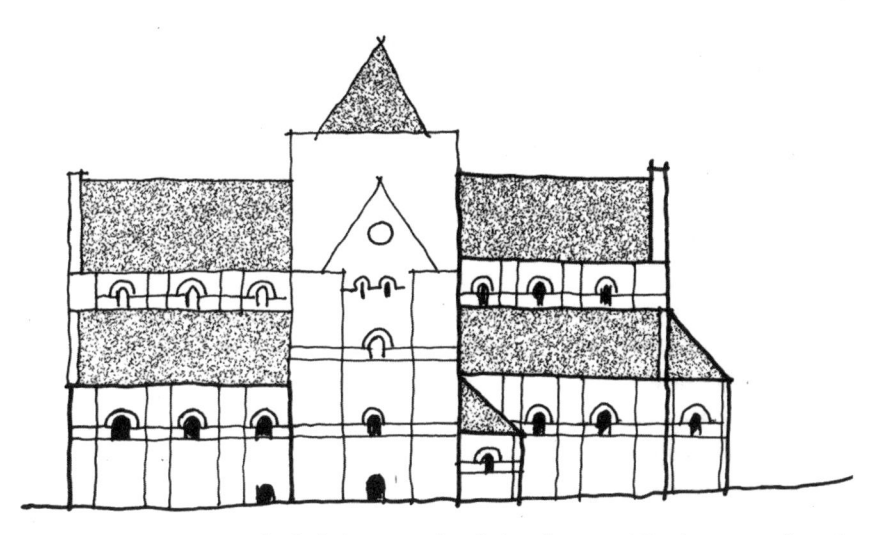

Figure 5.2 St Magnus Cathedral, first completed church c.1150 (Cruden, 1988, fig. 10), showing the original east end with an apse, before its replacement with a square chancel in the early thirteenth century.

there (*OS*, Chapter 68). Once again, the emphasis is that this development is to happen in Kirkwall, which suggests that the relics were already in Kirkwall when he made this speech (or is believed later to have made a speech like it). Kol is capitalising on a developing situation which could provide Rognvald and his supporters with invaluable moral strength in their forthcoming campaign. Everyone 'thought it a great idea and the vow was solemnly sworn' so the fleet of six large ships, five cutters and three cargo ships set sail for Shetland, with the impression given that a crusade was being embarked upon.

The ideology built into these preparations for Rognvald's expedition against Earl Paul resonates with contemporary ideas which associated princely saints with specific dominions, especially concerning St Olaf and the kingdom of Norway. The idea that these saints were protectors of the lands they had ruled when living, and were the patrons of their successors in power – who ruled with their specific permission – was well-established in Scandinavia.[31] It is most evident from the Letter of Privileges issued after the coronation of King Magnus Erlingsson in 1163/4, in which he acknowledged St Olaf as his ultimate overlord. But already in 1134 King Harald Gilli is said to have vowed that if St Olaf would aid him in his struggle against King Magnus 'the Blind' (*blindi*), he would build a church in honour of the saint in Bergen at his own expense (*Hms. Magnus the Blind and Harald Gille's Saga*, Chapter VII). The closeness in

---

31   Haki Antonsson, 2007, 208–10

time with Kol's speech and the similarity of situation and vow strongly suggest that the Norwegian pattern was followed (or seen later to have been followed) by those seeking power in Orkney in a struggle between two rulers. The saga stresses that Rognvald was a close friend of King Harald, and had been since the two met in England; he and Kol had been Harald's principal sponsors when the latter had to undergo the ordeal before King Sigurd, and Rognvald was Harald's staunchest supporter in his dealings with Magnus *blindi* (*OS*, Chapter 62). Such close personal relationships would inevitably mean that ideas about the roles of the saintly protectors of their lands would be shared, so we can be reasonably sure that Rognvald embarked on his crusade believing that the strong support of his saintly uncle would be a boost to his personal struggle for power. He is reported to have said during his second campaign that both God and his uncle the holy Earl Magnus would strengthen his position and keep him in power in Orkney (*OS*, Chapter 73).

Earl Rognvald's second expedition resulted in many men coming over to him in Orkney, and he asked Bishop William to arrange a settlement between him and Earl Paul. However, the truce and power-sharing arrangement did not last for long as Earl Paul was kidnapped and taken south to Atholl and kept in confinement at the court of his sister Margaret and Maddad of Atholl until his mysterious disappearance (see Section 4.5). In the short space of a few months the political situation in the earldoms completely changed, for once it was realised that Earl Paul was not going to return, 'all the people of Orkney submitted themselves to Earl Rognvald' (*OS*, Chapter 76) who became the sole ruler of the land (until the power-sharing arrangement with Harald Maddadson was set up two years later). It was in this time-period that the building of the cathedral is said to have commenced in accordance with the vow that Rognvald had taken at his father's bidding.

The building of the fine Romanesque cathedral church in Kirkwall shows beyond all doubt that the patrons were familiar with the best examples of such buildings in Scotland and northern England. Although we know that Earl Rognvald, and particularly his father Kol, were the main patrons and funders of the building, it is highly likely that Bishop William was also involved, as he had been instrumental in the elevation of St Magnus' relics and their translation to Kirkwall. It could well have been the bishop[32] who had the contacts with ecclesiastical centres further south which had already built, or were in the process

---

32 Bishop William was a 'clerk of Paris' and had therefore had his theological training in northern France, which was the main area of contemporary Romanesque building developments. John Mooney (1947, 29) also believed that Bishop William may have been more involved than the saga allows and suggested that Stavanger Cathedral was used by Bishop William as a model for St Magnus'(pp.30–1). See n.35

of building, fine examples of Romanesque architecture. It is generally agreed that the inspiration for the cathedral in Kirkwall was the magnificent cathedral in Durham, which was completed in 1133. Masons from Durham came north to build the abbey in Dunfermline (c.1128) and they may have moved on to Orkney when work started on Kirkwall cathedral soon after Rognvald's access to sole power in 1137, although some of the architectural features do suggest direct links with Durham itself.[33] All we are told is that the ground plan 'was drawn up' and 'builders were hired for the work' (*OS*, Chapter 76); this in itself must mean that master craftsmen came from those places in the Anglo-Norman world where stone churches were in the process of being constructed.

The chosen location for the building was along the shore of the Oyce well south of the earldom estate and St Olaf's Church near Papdale Burn. This was quite detached from the secular settlement, and was doubtless deliberately set apart as a separate ecclesiastical centre, which grew into the bishop's part of the town, later called the Laverock.[34] The site was on a steep slope above the shore and fronting onto its own harbour area where the bishop's ships could moor, alongside other merchant vessels which would have been attracted by ecclesiastical trading business.[35] In the first instance – and continuing for many decades – the shore here would have been used by the ships bringing stone from the quarries (at Head of Holland in the East Mainland) for the building construction.

Progress was apparently rapid in the first years, and focused on the choir, the first phase of which was perhaps completed c.1142.[36] This was designed to house the relics and as a completed structure it would have been consecrated when the relics were transferred here from St Olaf's Church, although the saga gives no information about that (Figure 5.2). The east end at this time ended in an apse, of which nothing has survived as it was totally rebuilt in the early thirteenth century when there was greater need for space for pilgrims (see below). The first building stage included the crossing and the transepts with three bays of the nave. At some point in the early phase of construction there were difficulties with funds, as the saga explains, and Earl Rognvald raised money, after calling the farmers to an assembly and offering them the chance to buy their odal estates and forego any need to pay an inheritance fee in the future. This was

---

33 Cambridge, 1988, 111–21; Fawcett, 2011, 30–1
34 Hossack, 1900, 7; Lamb, 1993, 46
35 This situation is very similar to the position of the cathedral in Stavanger, which is located above the harbour area, at the head of a sheltered fjord. The first bishop of Stavanger is recorded c.1130, and the building of the cathedral probably started soon after (Lidén, 1988, 74)
36 Cruden, 1988, 82

agreed to at the rate of one mark for every 'ploughland' (*plógsland*). So a land tax or levy was imposed on all cultivable land in the islands which in some way was understood to be, or presented as, a redemption sum for odal possessions.[37] It must have helped to keep the building campaign moving, which allowed Earl Rognvald and Bishop William to embark on their two-year pilgrimage to the Holy Land in 1151.

5.3 PILGRIMAGES AND AN AGE OF PIETY

Earl Rognvald was not the first earl to go on a pilgrimage to the Holy Land. Hakon Paulsson is also recorded as having 'set out on a long journey overseas' and having travelled south to Rome, then continuing on to Jerusalem (*OS*, Chapter 52). He embarked on this journey c.1120 and the purpose must have been to expiate the sin of involvement in his cousin's murder.[38] Doubtless Hakon had to undertake further commitments, such as grants of land or money to the Church, and it is thought very likely that the Round Church at Orphir was built by him on the model of the Church of the Holy Sepulchre at Jerusalem which he would have visited when in the Holy Land. This earldom estate church was an unusual architectural adornment at Orphir which became the usual earldom residence at this time rather than Birsay (as already mentioned above, Section 4.6.1; see Colour plate 19).

The church was probably in existence when Svein Breastrope was murdered (during the time of Earls Harald and Paul) when there is a reference to a 'fine (*dyrlig*) church' near the great drinking-hall at Orphir (*OS*, Chapter 66).[39] Although of modest size (only 5.8m/20ft internal diameter), it was a remarkable building in the context of early-twelfth-century Orkney and certainly one of the first stone churches to be built in the islands. It is the only medieval church of circular plan known to have existed in the whole of Scotland and is an example of a European-wide resurgence of interest in circular church plans inspired by the Church of the Holy Sepulchre in Jerusalem. The direct model for this building was probably Scandinavian, where examples from this period are known to have existed in Schleswig and Roskilde, associated with Danish royal residences, and at the royal centre of Tønsberg in Norway.[40]

Another interesting feature of this church is the dedication to St Nicholas, telling us that this saint was popular with Hakon, and possibly telling us that he

37 This imposition and the name of the land unit (*plógsland*) has caused discussion and there are different interpretations of what it signified (Crawford, 1987, 201–2; Andersen, 1991, 80)
38 The sixteenth-century Danish translation of *Jarls' Saga* adds that Hakon 'got absolution for his deed from the Pope' (*OS* Taylor, 213)
39 Summary of the excavations at the Earl's Bu, Orphir, in Graham-Campbell and Batey, (1998, 191–4)
40 Fisher, 1993, 375, 377; RCAHMS, *Orkney*, no. 483; Ekroll, 2012, 60–1

had brought back some relics with him from Rome to be used for the dedication to this saint, whose cult was spreading widely in western and northern Europe at the time.[41] In Scandinavia the cult was patronised by royalty. King Sigurd *Jórsalafari* ('Jerusalem-farer') and his co-ruler Eystein founded churches in Trondheim and Bergen dedicated to Nicholas, and Sigurd was probably inspired by the cult of this saint when he travelled through Europe and Byzantium on his pilgrimage to Jerusalem in 1108–11.[42] Earl Hakon was closely connected with the Norwegian aristocracy as already noted (see Section 4.3.2), and during his visits to Norway would inevitably have become aware of the high status of the new cult of Nicholas. Doubtless he would have wished to emulate the patronage of this saint in his own territory, and the evidence of dedications suggests that the cult was taken up by the earldom elite, for other churches apart from Orphir were dedicated to Nicholas – at Paplay (Holm) and on Papa Stronsay which were also earldom estates.[43] Because of the known growth in popularity of the cult of Nicholas in the twelfth century we can be sure that the churches dedicated to him date from this period, unlike dedications to the apostolic saints which could have been given at any date. Indeed, it might be possible to regard the earldom family's enthusiasm for the cult of Nicholas as a deliberate attempt to counter the growing cult of Magnus. The dedications to Magnus are rather few in Orkney, although, as noted above, more numerous in Shetland, while conversely there are no full church dedications to Nicholas in Shetland, only a chapel in Out Skerries.[44] Certainly the Round Church at Orphir and the dedication to St Nicholas are indications of the cultural interests of Earl Hakon and his sons who represented the Paul line of earls.

This European link and the adoption of a high-status international saintly patron did not, however, succeed in becoming the dominant hagiographic manifestation in the islands. The winning team was to be the supporters of the native saint, and this is in line with the general Scandinavian pattern, where a dozen 'official' cults of native saints flourished in the eleventh and twelfth centuries. They were adopted by bishops as patrons of the diocese, and helped to

---

41 The cult of Nicholas spread after the transfer of his relics to Bari in Italy from Asia Minor in the late eleventh century (Farmer, 1978, *sub* Nicholas)

42 Sigurd was also married to a daughter of a Novgorod prince who had herself founded a church dedicated to Nicholas in Novgorod (Garipzanov, 2010)

43 William Thomson (pers. comm.) points out that the parish church of Evie in the West Mainland was also dedicated to Nicholas. Later on it was a large block of bishopric territory 'managed as a single unit and let out on a long lease', which may suggest that it had been earldom land originally at the date when the dedication was chosen for the church

44 Cant, 1975, 33.There do not appear to be any dedications to Nicholas in Caithness (Gibbon, 2006), which may be explained by the links which Magnus had with Caithness and Hakon's lack of interest in Caithness.

enhance the identity of the bishoprics during a formative period in the growth of episcopal power.[45] The secular rulers who were blood relations of the saint also benefited greatly from their links with the holy man, as with the brother of Knud Lavard in Denmark, and Magnus Olafssson, son of the royal saint of Norway. Similarly, in Orkney, Rognvald succeeded in winning sole power with the inestimable advantage of being the nephew of Saint Magnus.

5.3.1 Earl Rognvald – pilgrim, poet and benefactor

Although Rognvald himself won fame as a holy man after his death, he never quite made it into the front rank of native saints. This was not due to any lack of effort on the part of the bishop of the time, Bjarni Kolbeinsson. However, the surviving earl, Harald Maddadson, did not need the growth of another family cult, particularly not another member of the alternative earldom line, to ensure him of his possession of the earldom, for he was already in possession and had been for decades when his co-earl Rognvald was killed in 1158.

Before we come to Rognvald's death, however, we should look at this earl's achievements in life, some of which were manifestations of his piety, while others were manifestations of his skills in more worldly activities. As noted

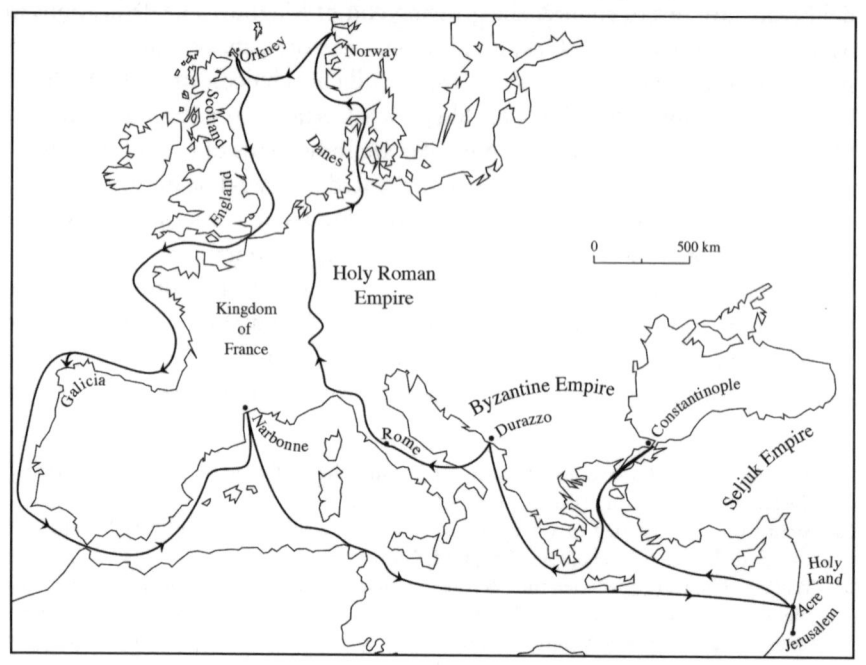

Figure 5.3 Map of Earl Rognvald's route to and from the Holy Land 1151–3. (Copyright the author)

45   Haki Antonsson, 2005, 147–9

above (see Section 4.4.2), Rognvald came from an outside position and with no personal knowledge of Orkney to win power in the earldom, with the aid of his holy uncle. The name he had been given at birth – Kali – was his grandfather's name on his father's side and not a name which had any connection with the earldom dynasty. When putting forward a claim to the earldom, he therefore changed his name to Rognvald, chosen by his mother after the former earl, Rognvald Brusisson, said to have been 'the most able of all the earls of Orkney'; and this was seen as an auspicious sign (*OS*, Chapter 61). Rognvald was a model ruler. He was good-looking, well-liked by all people and 'of more than average ability' (*OS*, Chapter 58).[46] He was an accomplished and innovative composer of skaldic poetry, which is preserved in the section of the saga devoted to him, thirty-two verses of which can be directly attributed to him, and proving that his boastful first stanza is not exaggerating where his poetic skills are concerned.[47]

The famous first stanza lists the nine skills which he claims to have mastered:

> At nine skills I challenge –
> A champion at chess:
> Runes I rarely spoil,
> I read books and write:
> I'm skilled at skiing
> And shooting and sculling
> And more! – I've mastered
> Music and verse[48]
>
> (*OS*, Chapter 58)

This indicates a remarkable set of accomplishments, and ones which are particularly appropriate to the contemporary twelfth-century age, when the upbringing of a young man included activities appropriate to a more leisured lifestyle. It presents Rognvald as very different from his Viking ancestors who would have boasted of the battles they had won, or of how many warriors they had killed.[49] Indeed, it has recently been suggested that Rognvald is deliberately presented by the writer of his section of the saga (which could almost be called 'Earl Rognvald's saga') as a model ruler who did not indulge in warlike behaviour.[50] In the many events which are related it shows that he was willing to forgive people who had acted against his will, to give quarter (Chapter 72), to

---

46 Mundal, in press
47 Bibire, 1988; Jesch, 2006
48 The word used in the last line (*harpslótt*) indicates that his musical skills were in harp-playing, an important detail (as will be seen later)
49 Jesch, 2006, 10
50 Mundal, in press

settle conflicts peacefully, on one occasion asking the bishop to act as mediator, and even paying other men's penalties in order to achieve peace (*OS*, Chapters 82 and 85). Is this all part of his presentation as a saint-like figure, leading up to his violent death and canonisation? In the complex circumstances in which Rognvald had to fight and trick his way to power it seems highly unlikely that he was entirely blameless of any involvement in the reprehensible deeds which did occur; the possibility that he used Swein Asleiffson to do the necessary dirty work – like the kidnapping of Earl Paul and his subsequent disappearance – has to be entertained, even though this aspect may have been glossed over in the saga.[51]

Another unusual circumstance of Rognvald's early reign was brought about by his agreement over the division of Orkney with Harald Maddadson in 1139, when Harald was only five years old, a quite unprecedented age for a claimant to be given recognition. However, there were apparently weighty political considerations, and it may be that he came to this arrangement in return for recognition of his own rights in Caithness (see Section 4.5). There was also a commitment that Rognvald would be the senior of the two even after Harald came of age, and that his decision would have priority in any disagreement (*OS*, Chapter 77). The dual rule was amicable and once Harald had reached manhood (aged seventeen) in 1151, Rognvald must have considered the political situation in the earldoms to be in good hands, allowing him to depart on his famous pilgrimage to the Holy Land.

This celebrated enterprise takes up five complete chapters and is a unique account of such a journey by a northern magnate from this period. That it was considered a remarkable achievement can be seen from the record (*sub* anno 1151) in the Icelandic Annals:

> The journey to Jerusalem of Earl Rognvald Kali of the Orkneys: and of Erling Skakki.[52]

The impetus was personal piety rather than the call to join a crusade, and the presence on the journey of Bishop William added an extra religious dimension to the venture. However, after the fleet had sailed through the Straits of Gibraltar, Rognvald tarried a while in Narbonne, although some of the rest of the company went straight on to Jerusalem. The mix of religious and secular

---

51 Else Mundal points out that some of Rognvald's own poetry includes references to violent activities, which are not included in the prose narrative, further increasing the suspicion that the saga writer gives us a very sanitised picture of his hero
52 Erling Skakke was a powerful Norwegian *lendirmann*, a jarl, and later regent of Norway, who married King Sigurd's legitimate daughter Kristin, and whose son Magnus Erlingsson succeeded to the throne in 1161

experience is very evident from the events recorded in verse – included in the saga – describing Rognvald's relationship with the lovely lady Ermingerd at the court of her father, the count of Narbonne (*OS*, Chapter 86). These verses show strong influence of courtly love poetry, possibly the first such examples in skaldic verse. [53] Further verses, many of them Rognvald's own composition, record events which occurred during the rest of the journey, such as his swim across the River Jordan and his approach to Jerusalem with a cross on his back and a palm branch in his hand (*OS*, Chapter 88). Having visited Jerusalem, the party made its way back north via Constantinople, where they were received by the Byzantine emperor and the Varangian Guard, then travelled by horseback across Bulgaria to Apulia and to Rome, eventually arriving back in Orkney at Christmas 1153. This example of medieval piety is famous because we know so much about it from the preservation of the skaldic verse, but Rognvald's saintliness was not based on this pilgrimage alone. There are two other factors in Rognvald's life which were more important: one is his building and endowment of the cathedral, the other his death in pursuit of an outlaw.

Kol's vision to build a cathedral to house the relics of St Magnus and Rognvald's drive to achieve this by funding it resulted in the flourishing of a saintly cult which made Orkney one of the pilgrimage centres of northern Europe, and gave Rognvald a certain aura through his close association with his martyred uncle. These factors alone provided a very favourable basis for his future saintly reputation. As far as the bishop and cathedral clergy were concerned this would have put Earl Rognvald on a pedestal. Unfortunately we know very little of the Church's side of the story, for ecclesiastical matters are only referred to in *Jarls' Saga* through a filter – the story of the earls. The funding of this ambitious architectural concept is only glancingly referred to in the saga account. Once, in relation to the project as outlined, Kol urges Rognvald to provide funds and 'let it be endowed so that the foundation might increase' (*at sá staðr mætti eflask*) (*OS* Taylor, Chapter lxviii). Following that we hear about the lack of funds which led to the agreement with the farmers who paid a land tax to enable it to be moved forward. Rognvald was certainly long remembered as its generous benefactor by the cathedral community for it is stated in the 'Genealogy of the Earls', written in the early fifteenth century:

> efter the obite of Erile Halcon, succeddit Erile Rolland, quhilk first fundit the kirk of Sanct Mawnis martyre, and dotat ('endowed')the same with gret possessions riches and rentis. [54]

53 Bibire, 1988, 219–20; Jesch, 2006, 11
54 *Bann.Misc.*, iii, 77; *post obitum Comitis Hacon successit Comes Rollandus qui primo fundavit ecclesiam Sancti Magni martyris, illamque magnis possessionibus diviciis et redditibus dotavit.* As Mooney (1947, 18) notes, this statement was made in a document drawn up by Bishop

We cannot be certain as to what sort of 'possessions, riches and rents' these were, but this statement suggests that they were not inconsiderable, and they would have consisted primarily of estates, the income from which would have been used to endow clerical positions in the cathedral and maintain the fabric. It is clear from episcopal resources mentioned in the later rentals which estates (with their skats) had been given to the bishops by the earls; these were extensive estates in Birsay, a great part of St Ola parish around Kirkwall, the island of Egilsay with the adjacent east side of Rousay, and four 'eyrislands' ('ouncelands') in Westray.[55] It has been suggested that Evie in the West Mainland was also an original earldom endowment of the bishopric.[56] The date at which these tracts of land were granted to the bishops is difficult to ascertain (except that Bishop William's residence in Egilsay, mentioned several times in the saga, indicates that the island was episcopal property before the murder of Magnus). There is information from the later Middle Ages about the prebends that were attached to the different offices in the cathedral, and which funded the canons' positions, as well as the head of the Grammar School and the master of the 'sang school'; some of these were probably original endowments by the earldom family.[57] One very notable feature of the earldom family's position with regard to the cathedral foundation is that it appears to have remained a private possession of the earls. The evidence for this peculiar situation comes from the period after the acquisition of Orkney by James III of Scotland when he transferred his rights in the ownership of the cathedral to the burgh of Kirkwall in the royal charter of 1486 (see Chapter 9).[58]

There is a very different piece of evidence which may also be testimony to the continuing high regard in which Rognvald was held by the cathedral community: for many years a medieval statue has been located in a niche high up on the Round Tower (an addition made by Bishop Reid to the Bishop's Palace in Kirkwall in the 1550s). The statue is considered to date from the fourteenth century and may represent the holy earl, Rognvald.[59] Originally located in the cathedral, it must have been removed and placed high up on Bishop Reid's Tower in the Reformation period, and that fact alone signifies that the figure had some particular importance for the cathedral community at that time. It certainly represents a layman, from the dress, and possibly a nobleman as the

---

Thomas Tulloch and the canons of the cathedral who knew all about the revenues resulting from the endowment
55 Clouston, 1932, 150
56 Thomson, 2001, 225; and above n.43
57 Clouston, 1925–6, 31–6; De Geer, 108, 96–100
58 Mooney, 1947, *passim*; Andersen, 1988, 63; Cant, 1995, 105; Anderson, 2003, 81, 83; Crawford, 2012a
59 As suggested by Crawford 1995

trace of a rose coronet can be distinguished on his forehead[60] (see Colour plates 20a and 20b).

A most significant feature is the object resting on a stool in front of the figure, which is very difficult to determine. If it is a lyre, as has been suggested,[61] then the identification with Rognvald Kali would be virtually certain because of his skill at playing the harp, and composing poetry, of which he boasted in the verse just quoted above.[62] Perhaps this stringed instrument was such a well-known attribute of Rognvald's reputation that it was decided to put it in a prominent position on his memorial statue. The instrument of his martyrdom (a spear) may also have been depicted in his left hand, or indeed a model of the church which he founded, but this part of the carving has entirely disappeared.[63] If this is a statue of Orkney's second saint, a figure revered among the cathedral clergy for his role in the founding of the cathedral and remembered for his generosity in endowing it, it would be a remarkable piece of evidence of Earl Rognvald's standing among the ecclesiastical community.

5.3.2 *Earl Rognvald 'the Holy'*

It was undoubtedly the cathedral clergy and the next bishop, Bjarni Kolbeinsson (1188–1223), who were the promoters of the cult of Rognvald, called 'the Holy'. That he was a popular earl, and also a good ruler, appears to have been the case from the positive statement made about him in the saga:

> Earl Rognvald was deeply mourned, for he had been much loved in the isles and in many other places too. He had been a good friend to a great many people, lavish with money, moderate, loyal to his friends, a many-sided man and a fine poet.
>
> (*OS*, Chapter 104)

In addition to this fine reputation and his pious benefactions, there was a certain requirement for him to meet a violent death as an innocent victim in order to attain saintly status.[64] On this occasion it was not over a quarrel with a rival

---

60 An earl's coronet or ribbon very clearly adorns the forehead of the St Magnus' statue in The Orkney Museum (Blindheim, 1988, 168) (see Colour plate 24)
61 Crawford, 1995, 35–7
62 De Geer, 1985, 220–27. Linking harp-playing and poetry composition in the final line of Rognvald's first stanza may suggest that the two skills were associated. The saga writer himself notes that Rognvald was a 'fine poet' (Chapter 104), and the addition of a harp to his statue would be the best way of expressing this well-known attribute
63 The statue was removed to the Orkney Museum in 1995 and a replica put on the Round Tower in its place
64 The 'sanctity of secular leaders was intimately linked with violent death' in the twelfth century (Haki Antonsson, 2007, 182–3)

in the earldom family, but in a fracas with a lawless and powerful member of the Celto-Scandinavian kindred, Thorbjorn Clerk. Thorbjorn was a grandson of Frakokk, and became closely involved with Harald Maddadson's entourage when the latter was accepted as co-earl, acting as Harald's foster father and chief counsellor (*OS*, Chapter 77).[65] However, he also became embroiled in a feud with Swein Asleifsson after the burning of Frakokk, and took part in the killing of two of the men who had been involved in the burning. He married Swein's sister but then rejected her, and displayed another side of his violent nature when he wrecked a peace meeting between Rognvald and Harald in Thurso by turning up with a strong force and immediately attacking Rognvald's men. Thirteen of Rognvald's men were killed there and Rognvald was wounded in the face (*OS*, Chapter 94). This is how the antagonistic relationship between Rognvald and Thorbjorn developed which led to the killing of Thorarin 'Bag-Nose' and the outlawing of Thorbjorn as discussed above (Section 4.5).

Thorbjorn spent his exile in Scotland ('with the King of Scots') but sometimes returned secretly to Caithness to his friends there (being exiled meant that he was banished from both Orkney and Caithness). So when Earls Rognvald and Harald went to Caithness for hunting deer in the late summer of 1158 they heard that Thorbjorn Clerk was hiding up in Thursodale waiting for the opportunity to attack them. Such a situation could not be tolerated and Rognvald and Harald collected a large force together and set out up the dale. The next day they reached Forsie, where Thorbjorn was in hiding at the farm of his close friend Hallvard Dufuson. The outcome was inevitably going to be violent, and specific details are given of how Rognvald was caught at a disadvantage when his foot got trapped in the stirrup of his horse, and one of Thorbjorn's men thrust a spear at him causing a fatal wound. The account was written or told to the saga writer by someone who was present and knew all the details of how the skirmish developed around the dying earl. The personal note is also evident from the mention of the stain 'we can still see' of Earl Rognvald's blood on the boulder 'as if it had been newly spilt' (*OS*, Chapter 104). This is a hint of the supernatural element which a saintly death required, and which was no doubt part of the build-up to his sanctification. Rognvald was taken back to Kirkwall and buried in the cathedral, but it was not until thirty-four years after his death that the elevation of the relics took place when Bishop Bjarni Kolbeinsson led the move to have his saintly status recognised. Miracles are mentioned, as also the Pope's permission, although there is no official record of either.[66] However, the event was known outside Orkney as is seen from the entry in the Icelandic

---

65 Thomson, 2001, 115
66 It is unlikely that the question of papal sanction would have been invented by the saga writer (Haki Antonsson, 2009, 194). This information must have come from Bishop Bjarni

Annals under the year 1192 'Earl Rognvald sanctified'.⁶⁷

Bishop Bjarni was a powerful bishop who was also a supporter of Earl Harald in his submission to King Sverrir (see Chapter 6). He would have been fully aware of the benefits to the cathedral community of the promotion of the cult of Magnus by Rognvald and his generous endowments. Apart from making Orkney a centre for pilgrimage – and all the wealth which that brought the cathedral – it also gave the bishopric great status within the newly erected archdiocese of Nidaros (Trondheim). When this was created in 1152/3, Orkney was one of the five North Atlantic dioceses brought within it and the only one with its own established native saint's cult. This put Orkney on a par with the Norwegian dioceses of Nidaros, Bergen, and Oslo which also had local saints' cults in the making.⁶⁸ The bishops had every reason to be grateful to Rognvald for giving their diocese this enhanced status.⁶⁹ Bjarni's promotion of Rognvald had therefore everything to do with gratitude to the great benefactor,⁷⁰ and this promotion was an additional boost to the reputation of Orkney, and Kirkwall especially, as the resting place of not one, but two earldom saints.

5.4 THE TWO ORKNEY SAINTS

Although the two cults were very different, one becoming almost a universal saint's cult in north Europe, the other remaining very much a local cult within the ecclesiastical milieu of the Orkney earldom, the elevation of two members of the earldom dynasty to sainthood was an impressive achievement and must have brought great prestige to the comital family. At a time when the cult of St Olaf was boosting the fame of the Norwegian royal dynasty and the cults of St Knud and Knud Lavard doing the same for the Danish kings, we cannot doubt that the cult of Magnus, and the aura of sanctity around his nephew, Rognvald, also brought fame to the earls and recognition that their island earldom had a special place in the world of northern sainthood.

The spread of churches and altars dedicated to Magnus, along with the surviving statues, are our main source of evidence for the depth and extent of belief in the saint's miraculous powers. In addition the written record of a *Vita*, the surviving liturgical material, as well as the precious evidence from musical manuscripts which have preserved the Magnus hymn, demonstrate the importance of the cult in ecclesiastical circles (see Section 2.6). It has

---

67 Storm, 1888, 120; it has been suggested that the original *Jarls' Saga* may have been written in the time of preparation for the translation of Earl Rognvald's relics (Foote, 1988, 197)
68 Haki Antonsson, 2007, 97–8
69 Crawford, 1998, 35
70 There was an attempt by Archbishop Eskil and the canons of Lund Cathedral to make King Erik *emune*'s murder in 1137 appear as a martyrdom. He had been a benefactor and generous patron of the Danish Church (Haki Antonsson, 2007, 155–6)

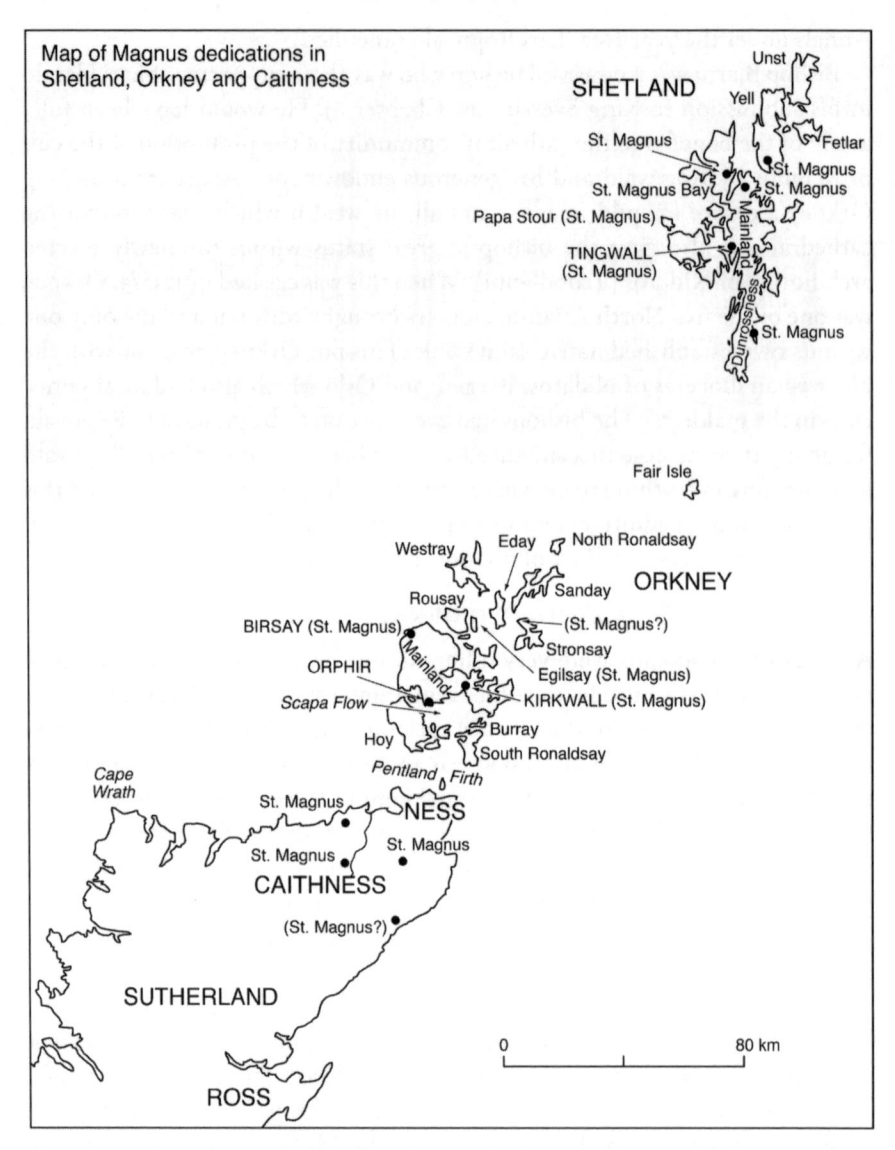

Figure 5.4 Map of known church dedications to St Magnus in Shetland, Orkney and Caithness (assumed in the case of Papa Stour, Shetland). The preponderance of these dedications is in Shetland, which supports the theory that the cult was fostered especially among the Shetlanders (Crawford, 1984).

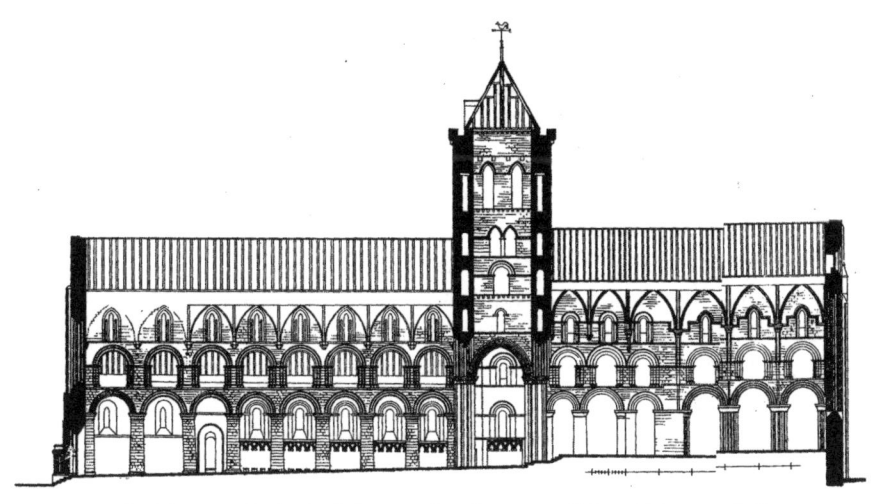

Figure 5.5 St Magnus Cathedral, longitudinal section (MacGibbon and Ross, 1896, fig. 226). Many features of this fine Romanesque cathedral link its building with both Durham Cathedral and Dunfermline Abbey, so that it has been assumed that the professional masons and workforce of builders moved north to Kirkwall. If so, the cost would have been immense, and the difficulties of finding sufficient funds is revealed in *Orkneyinga Saga*'s account of Earl Rognvald's attempt to raise money by imposing a tax on every 'ploughland' in the islands. St Magnus Cathedral is only a half-scale version of Durham and should more appropriately be compared with Dunfermline, which was probably slightly larger. However, the functional parallels of St Magnus Cathedral with Durham Cathedral, in that both were bishops' churches and also reliquary churches, is an important consideration (Cambridge, 1988, 121–2). No doubt the need for important liturgical arrangements and the requirements of pilgrimage probably helped to dictate the general architectural status of this great Orcadian building achievement. These requirements would be the concern of the clergy and Bishop William in particular.

already been noted above (see Section 5.2 and Figure 5.4) that popular fervour for Magnus was particularly strong in Shetland, and the number of dedications to him in Shetland, compared with Orkney, bears this out. Five parish churches are known to have been dedicated to him in Shetland, among them the premier archdeacon's church at Tingwall[71] (see Colour plate 21), whereas only three certain ones are recorded from Orkney, where the total number of parish churches was appreciably more than in Shetland.[72] The Orkney churches

71 Cant, 1975, 15–19; Crawford, 1984, 75
72 Moreover there are other toponymic indications that St Magnus was associated with areas around St Magnus Bay in Shetland, including the island of Papa Stour, where the church dedication may also have been another Magnus example (Crawford, 1984, 77)

dedicated to Magnus are the three places associated with his martyrdom and burial, on Egilsay, at Birsay, and the cathedral in Kirkwall, all of which reflect the saint's passage from life to death, to burial and to sainthood.[73] The absence of any others may be surprising but perhaps reflects the antipathy of the alternative earldom line, that of Hakon Paulsson and his sons, to the cult of the man with whose murder they were associated. As mentioned above (see Section 5.3), these earls appear to have looked to St Nicholas as their alternative saint-protector, perhaps adopting him as their dynastic saint.

How about the earldom of Caithness, with which Magnus was originally associated? Three Magnus dedications are recorded, but it is possible that there may have been several more, as the dedications of a large number of churches in Caithness are unknown. The three are Spittal near Halkirk, Bannaskirk near Watten, and Shebster south-west of Thurso.[74] Spittal (Hospital) was an earldom foundation providing accommodation for pilgrims travelling across Caithness to and from Orkney[75] (see Colour plate 6). There is a possibility that there may have been another Magnus dedication at Dunbeath, on the south-east coast of Caithness, where post-Reformation evidence records that there were plans to create a trading burgh at Inver, to be called 'Magnusburgh'.[76] There do not appear to be any dedications to Magnus in Sutherland, where Bishop Gilbert was accorded saintly status, and whose family would be unlikely to encourage the cult of the earl of Caithness. [77] There is no evidence of any other church dedications to Magnus in Scotland and only a few in England, of which the most significant is the church at the north end of Southwark Bridge in the City of London.[78]

There is no doubt that Magnus' fame was widely acknowledged in Scotland as can be understood from his inclusion among the Scottish saints of the *Aberdeen*

---

73 Eric Fernie comments on the appropriateness of these three sites, conforming to standard hagiographical practice (1988, 146). It should be noted that St Magnus Church in Birsay is in the village and not on the Brough. The three churches were also in places closely associated with the bishops: Birsay as the original episcopal seat; Egilsay as an episcopal residence, and St Magnus Cathedral in Kirkwall as the newly founded episcopal seat
74 Beaton, 1909, 316; McKinlay, 1914, 302
75 Crawford, 1982, 62–3; Grants of provision to the Hospital of St Magnus at Spittal appear in fifteenth century Scottish Supplications to Rome (Dunlop and MacLauchlan, eds, 1983, nos 697, 716)
76 Crawford, 1990, 15. There was a fair on the feast of Magnus, and an 'image' of St Magnus is listed in a 1501 inventory of the furnishings of Dunbeath Castle (Crawford, 1990, 15, 19)
77 Gilbert's relics at Dornoch Cathedral were venerated after his death c.1245, although no formal canonisation proceedings are known to have taken place (Watt, 1977, 41). His feast day (1 April) is included in the *Aberdeen Breviary* where the readings include some interesting references to his role as guardian of royal power and builder of castles in north Scotland (Macquarrie, ed., 2012, 98–100)
78 Bull, 1912–13, 138–40; De Geer, 1985, 112–3

Breviary.[79] The office for commemorating his martyrdom and translation most probably originated in Kirkwall Cathedral, indicating that the sources for his life, and evidence of his miracles were known there and would have been included in the cathedral Library. There are also references to his appearance at moments of national significance, such as at the Battle of Bannockburn:

> Quhilk sene was efter singand with greit mirth,
> Upon the se rydand ouir Panetland firth
> Ontill Orkna, againe hame til his awin:
> The common voce said it was Sanct Mawin.
> Quhairfor King Robert out of Abirdene
> Fyve pund stirling, as my author did mene.
> Onto the tempill of Sanct Mawnis gaif.
> I heritage, the quhilk zit that tha haif
> For the uphald,as I can richt weill ges,
> Of braid and wyne and walx (on) to the mes.[80]

The grant made by King Robert to the cathedral of St Magnus in Kirkwall out of the burgh of Aberdeen's revenues is well-recorded, and consisted of flour and a cask of wine, for the Eucharistic bread and wine, as well as one hundred shillings (£5).[81] It continued to be made throughout the fourteenth century.[82]

The fame of Orkney's saint also spread north of the joint earldoms, and his cult was widely adopted in the Atlantic islands of Faeroe and Iceland, notably at the episcopal level. In Faeroe the cathedral church at Kirkjubour was dedicated to him: there is a reliquary shrine surviving at the east end on the exterior wall of the roofless stone church which contained the 'great lord, the holy Magnus' sainted relics' according to the fourteenth-century inscription on the stone plaque[83] (see Colour plates 22a and 22b). In Iceland the southern episcopal seat at Skalholt also had a Magnus relic as is reported in the annals under the year 1298.[84] These two cathedral churches must therefore have had good relations with the bishops of Orkney at the time for them to be honoured with relics of the Orkney saint; this is important evidence for continued connections between these Norse communities into the high Middle Ages. The cult spread out from Skalholt more widely throughout the southern Iceland diocese where four of the five Magnus dedications are located, including a hospital (at

79 Macquarrie, ed., 2012, 100–14
80 Stewart, 'Buik of the croniclis of Scotland', III, 239
81 *RMS*, I, App.1, no.10. As pointed out by Barrow (2005, 215), this appears to be a continuation of earlier grants made by King Robert's predecessors
82 *RN*, vols 4, 5, 6, 7 *passim*
83 Mooney, 1935, 276
84 Haki Antonsson, 2007, 19–20

Gaulverjabær) which was also dedicated to him.[85] It appears that the bishops of Skalholt promoted the cult in the first decades of the fourteenth century, culminating in its formal adoption at the Althing in 1326.[86] The promotion of the cult in Iceland at this time probably led to the compilation of *Magnús saga lengri* (the 'Longer Saga of Magnus'), a hagiographic work based on two older texts, *Orkneyinga Saga* and the now lost Latin 'Life of St Magnus' which was composed in the 1170s by Magister Robert (probably an English cleric who was prior of St Frideswide's in Oxford).[87] This Longer Saga of Magnus was probably written by an abbot of Munkaþverá, a monastery in north Iceland. He was a member of a circle of learned writers who were interested in the papacy and papal matters, which may explain the dubious reference to a miracle of a bone of St Magnus being seen by the papacy in Rome, as recounted in the *Longer Magnus Saga*. Some late medieval embroidered altar frontals from Iceland include St Magnus among other northern saints (as the example from Skaard in western Iceland shows (see Colour plate 23).[88]

In Norway, evidence for the popularity of Magnus is not found in church dedications but known from several statues of the saint which have been preserved.[89] These mostly date from the very late Middle Ages, as do representations of Magnus in wall paintings in Denmark. There was one altar dedication to Magnus in the cathedral church of Nidaros (Trondheim), another in Lund Cathedral in Skåne, and another in Viborg cathedral in Jutland, as well as two other altar dedications in Danish churches.[90] The feast days of St Magnus (16 April and 13 December) are listed in the Church Laws and are in the calendars of both Norway and Iceland, being used also for dates in documents and chronicles.[91] The continued high regard in which St Magnus was held among the powerful in Scandinavia is seen from a 'Gavebrev' of Queen Margaret of Denmark and Norway, dated 1411, in which she gave donations for pilgrims to all the holy places of Europe and the Holy Land, among which is payment for one pilgrim to 'St Magnus in Orkney', listed between St Thomas of Canterbury and the Three Kings in Cologne.[92] All these different sources of evidence give a superficial impression of the depth and extent of Magnus' popularity which must once have existed throughout Scandinavia (except evidently in Sweden).[93]

85 Cormack, 1994, 121
86 Magnus' feast day had been observed already at the time of the earliest manuscripts of the lawcode *Grágás* in the mid-thirteenth century (Haki Antonsson, 2007, 20)
87 Haki Antonsson, 2009, 195–6, 197–9
88 Blindheim, 1988, 177–9
89 Ibid., plates 30A, 30B, 31
90 Ibid., 165
91 Mooney, 1935, 279
92 Erslev, 1881–2, 377
93 The evidence for a relic of St Magnus which was apparently once in the church of St Vitus in

Conversely, we are very hard put to it to find any evidence for the spread of Rognvald's cult. The scene of Swein Asleifsson's death in the pits outside the gates of Dublin in 1171 is made poignant by the 'last words' of Swein in which he puts his trust in the 'holy Earl Rognvald' whose retainer he was (*OS*, Chapter 108). This gives an indication of the very local nature of the cult when Orcadians call him 'holy'. The 'Genealogy of the Earls', as well as mentioning Rognvald's generous endowment of St Magnus Cathedral, gives him a special eulogy, calling him 'wys and of gret vertue' adding that through many deeds of piety he was 'diwlgat and wirschippit and honorat for ane halie man'.[94] There are no known churches or altars dedicated to him although surely there must have been one in St Magnus Cathedral, where he would have been culted, especially among the cathedral clerical community. No liturgy has been recorded nor has a *Vita* survived. However, his feast day is listed in a calendar in a fourteenth-century Icelandic manuscript under 21 August where his name – *Reginvalldi comitis* – is entered.[95]

There is some remarkable surviving sculptural evidence from Kirkwall itself which demonstrates the well-established nature of these 'native' cults alongside that of the great Scandinavian king and martyr Olaf Haraldsson. Three small but sophisticated stone-carved medieval figures have survived: Earl Magnus with his ducal coronet and the sword, emblem of his martyrdom, in his right hand (see Colour plate 24); Earl Rognvald (as has been discussed in Section 5.3.1) with traces of a ducal coronet also and maybe his harp or lyre by his side (Colour plates 20a and b); and King Olaf, dignified and authoritative, wearing a royal crown and with a halberd in his right hand. These three figures were originally in the cathedral, adorning some piece of church architecture, and encapsulating the character of their age.[96] The most remarkable surviving evidence of the two cults of Magnus and Rognvald, uncle and nephew, is the skeletal remains which have remained immured in the cathedral pillars since, probably, the Reformation period (see Section 2.7 and Plate 1). Nowhere else in Scotland has both sculptural evidence and corporeal evidence of local saints survived like this, and these survivals link us back with the people who revered these earls, with the churchmen who fostered their cults, and with the medieval age of saints in a way that is deeply moving and impressive.

Prague is discussed by Mooney (1935, 255–60)

94 *Bann.Misc.*, iii, 77: *predictus virque fuit sapientia et virtute pollebat per plura bona pietatis opera famabantur venerabaturque et reputabatur pro sancto viro*

95 De Geer, 1985, 100

96 The dating of these figures does not appear to be contemporary. Blindheim (1988, 168–9) thinks that the Magnus figure dates to c.1300 while St Olaf dates to 1400 or later, and he suggests that the sculptor could possibly have been following an earlier model of St Magnus

5.5 ARCHITECTURAL EVIDENCE

Architectural developments are another aspect of the surviving inheritance which resulted from the death of the two earls when their relics were elevated to saintly status. In Kirkwall the cathedral building proceeded apace, once funds had been raised, and changes in architectural style give some indication of the date of the changes. It is thought that Bishop Bjarni was responsible for some of these developments, and for the introduction of the Transitional and Gothic design in the reconstruction of the pillars and the transepts of the central tower.[97] He also added the two transeptal chapels in place of the original eastern apses, and these may have been modelled on those in Trondheim cathedral, as the pinnacles on the angle buttresses certainly appear to be. The sandstone ashlar utilised here is a professional advance on the 'rumble' masonry hitherto employed,[98] which points to the work of masons brought in from the south. It is conjectured that Bjarni may also have been responsible for the three doorways in the west front,[99] although the west front was not completed until many years later (see Colour plate 25). The eastern extension of the choir, or presbytery, which gives the cathedral such an individual character, is also probably from Bishop Bjarni's time (see Plate 4). He was acting in response to the needs of pilgrims who from c.1200 must have flocked into the cathedral to visit the shrines of the two saints. This choir extension virtually doubled the length of this eastern part of the cathedral with the addition of three bays and the rectangular east gable, and the great east window of c.1230.[100]

5.5.1 *Egilsay and the Brough of Birsay*

Another relic of the faith and fervour which marked the Church's life during the growth of the cult is the Church of St Magnus on Egilsay, built to mark the spot where the earl was martyred, and with a dominant west round tower which acted as a visible guide to the faithful approaching by sea, and from which the sound of bells would have added an audible invitation to the pilgrim. St Magnus, Egilsay, is something of a mystery in Orkney's architectural heritage as it is a difficult building to date, so we do not know whether it was built by Bishop William, or by one of his successors (William II or Bjarni). It is almost certainly not the church in which Magnus is said to have prayed the night before his death, but a successor built by one of the bishops on an island which was their regular place of residence during the twelfth century.

---

97 Cant, 1988, 129
98 Ibid., 132
99 Fawcett, 2011, 112, stresses the quality of the carving of the capitals of the pillars in the door recesses.
100 Ibid., 116.

Figure 5.6 Drawing of St Magnus Church, Egilsay (MacGibbon and Ross, 1887). This church marks the location of Earl Magnus' killing, although not the exact spot (according to tradition). It must therefore have been a very important pilgrimage site, along with the church in Birsay where Magnus was buried, and the cathedral in Kirkwall where his relics were enshrined. This explains the quality of the building and the special feature of the round tower which would have served as a very visible monument for pilgrims approaching Egilsay by sea from north or south.

The masonry is of a timeless quality, with similarities to Irish church building, although the round tower is unlikely to indicate close affinities with Irish round towers, being more closely related to round towers attached to churches in East Anglia and southern Scandinavia.[101] The complete absence of any red ashlar stone similar to the cathedral masonry suggests that it was not built at a time when those masons were active in Kirkwall, or surely their influence would have been apparent.

If we return to Birsay to find out what happened there after the cathedral seat was moved to Kirkwall, there is an even greater puzzle to try to sort out, for big political as well as big environmental changes occurred. We have seen (see Section 4.6.1) that the earls moved out of Birsay, and the estate at Orphir became

---

101 Fernie, 1988, 158–9

their accustomed residence. The reason for this may have been two-fold: first, the burial place of Earl Magnus at Birsay, and the enthusiasm for the growing belief in his sanctity meant that the location was not considered appropriate for the earls of the alternate line (i.e. Hakon and his sons), to whom the saintly cult must have been unwelcome, and so they abandoned it as a residence. Bishop William removed himself with the relics of Magnus to Kirkwall, and built up a new episcopal base there, well beyond the control of Earl Hakon (see Section 5.2.3). Second, the location became more difficult of access because of geomorphological coastal changes and this may have been an additional factor in the earls' move away from the Brough.[102]

The surviving ruined church on the Brough of Birsay is a fine building which was evidently one of high status. It was modified at some point with extra altars being inserted in the eastern angles of the nave, intended to increase the number of clerics for maintaining worship.[103] The apse may also have been added at the same time, housing the altar in more appropriate circumstances. In front of the altar a grave was excavated, probably that of the founder. The foundation stones of a small western tower indicate that such a tower was certainly intended,[104] although never completed, or perhaps dismantled half-built. On the north side there is a cloister surrounded by three ranges of rooms appropriate for a small monastic community (see Plates 5a and 5b).[105]

The analogy of parallel circumstances at Selja in western Norway can be usefully applied to help provide a possible explanation for the changes which occurred at the Brough.[106] Selja is an island which was the seat of the early bishops of west Norway before they moved into Bergen c.1070. It was the sacred site associated with the burial of St Sunniva and the holy 'men of Selja'. Her relics were transferred to Bergen c. 1170 and the empty religious site on the island filled by Benedictine monks from St Albans in England who established a monastic community and church dedicated to St Alban. Such a scenario fits the architectural collection of buildings on the Brough of Birsay. On the analogy of the buildings at Selja it would seem most appropriate to explain the ecclesiastical circumstances at the Brough as a monastic foundation established to fulfil the religious requirements for a sacred site associated with the first burial place of St Magnus.[107] Once his relics had been moved to Kirkwall, a commu-

---

102 Crawford, 1987, 189–90 ; 2005, 94–6, 106
103 Radford, 1959, 9; Fawcett, 2011, 50
104 The evidence of tusking stones in the outer west wall of the nave shows that the tower was planned before the west gable was built
105 See description in Crawford, 2005, 99, 101
106 Crawford, 2005, 99–104
107 Rather than an episcopal 'palace' as interpreted by Radford (1959, 9, 15–16)

nity (perhaps of Benedictine monks) was brought in to care for the empty tomb, and provide the round of commemorative prayers and requisite liturgical services. The cloister and surrounding offices would have been adapted to house this community. This may have taken place soon after the transfer of the relics c.1130.[108] It is very difficult indeed to be certain of the exact date of the building of the church on the Brough,[109] or to hazard a guess as to why the tower was never built – or was dismantled. Selja has a fine western tower which was an integral part of the abbey church there, serving a useful purpose as a visible symbol of the holy place for those pilgrims arriving by sea. Undoubtedly this was also the intended purpose of the unbuilt tower on the Brough of Birsay as with the surviving round tower on St Magnus Church, Egilsay. The imperative of the cult of the murdered Earl Magnus has meant that these two churches were planned, founded and erected, and remarkably have survived, along with the Romanesque cathedral in Kirkwall, built to house the relics of the island saint.

These three important pilgrimage churches are the best surviving examples of medieval ecclesiastical architecture in the earldoms. But in the same period Orkney Shetland and Caithness were thickly covered with churches and chapels, which sprang up as a result of a century or more of Christian teaching. This inspired the converted populations to found and build their own family places of worship and install their own priests.

5.5.2 *Parish churches*

After the founding of a bishopric at Birsay c.1050, the earls would have led the way in building churches on their estates followed by other members of the earldom family, the earls' hirdmen and their 'gödings'. Church and chapel sites are associated with the high-status settlement names and known estates of powerful members of society.[110] Because it is very difficult to date the church and chapel sites we can rarely be certain about the date of their foundation. In a few cases where excavation is possible and has taken place it can be ascertained that the church is of twelfth-century type in its architectural features, such as

---

108 Who would have been responsible for the establishment of this monastic community? It is unlikely that Earl Hakon would have been willing to be involved in such a memorial to his sanctified cousin, although he may have been under papal compulsion to endow it with the earldom estates in Birsay to expiate his sin. Earl Rognvald was tied up with his grandiose plans for the memorial cathedral in Kirkwall. Although Bishop William or his successor was instrumental in founding and building the memorial church on Egilsay, it seems likely that one of them would also have been the active agent in the transformation of their church on the Brough into a monastic foundation

109 See comparative plans of early bishops' churches in Scandinavia in Crawford, 2005, fig. 7

110 Gibbon, 2006, 215, 222, App. 5

the site of St Nicholas Church on Papa Stronsay. This was a parish church on an earldom estate, with two altars at the east end of the nave in addition to the altar in the choir (like the church on the Brough of Birsay) and significantly dedicated to St Nicholas (see Section 5.3 and Figure 5.7). Certain features suggest that it may have been deliberately located on a pre-existing Pictish religious site.[111]

The formation of ecclesiastical organisation in the earldoms involved the establishment of parishes. As in most parts of northern Europe this was a twelfth-century development and it would seem likely that it was initiated under the supervision of the long-lived Bishop William *Senex* ('the Old') (1103–1168). Organisation would have been required because all the separate parts of the two earldoms were divided into parishes, either based on pre-existing territorial units or newly established ones. Within these new ecclesiastical groupings one church was designated the main parish centre where renders had to be made. These were the tithes of all income, one-tenth of the annual increase in arable harvest or pastoral produce. The collection, storage and transport of this wealth, as well as the coercion of the population, must have required a great degree of organisation by the church officials, doubtless assisted by the earldom authorities. This process of parochial organisation extended over Caithness but perhaps not until the establishment of a separate bishopric of Caithness by the Scottish king in the mid-twelfth century. The dispute over tithes which occurred in Caithness and came to a head with the murder of Bishop Adam in 1222 may have resulted from the changed arrangements for tithe imposition which probably came about under the new Scottish regime, as will be discussed in Chapter 6. The earl's tacit encouragement of the attack on the bishop may suggest that the earls were also reluctant participants in the imposition of tithes.

The establishment of parishes, and payment of tithes created a new sense of community throughout Europe,[112] especially when the parish church was designated as the only church to be used for baptism and burial. The surviving parish churches throughout Orkney, Shetland and Caithness are still important centres of community involvement, and most of them would have been established in mid- to late-twelfth century, although the institution of parishes may have taken some time to be finally structured.[113]

This new network created by the parish structure was all-inclusive and of a different order from the family and political networks. It had its own hierarchy of priests linked to the bishop whose authority extended over the whole earldom

---

111 Lowe, 2002, 91
112 Sawyer, 1988, 42
113 Gray (1922–3) looks to Bishop Gilbert's episcopacy (1222–44) as the time when the parish structure of Caithness and Sutherland was refined with the organisation of his new cathedral's funding arrangements

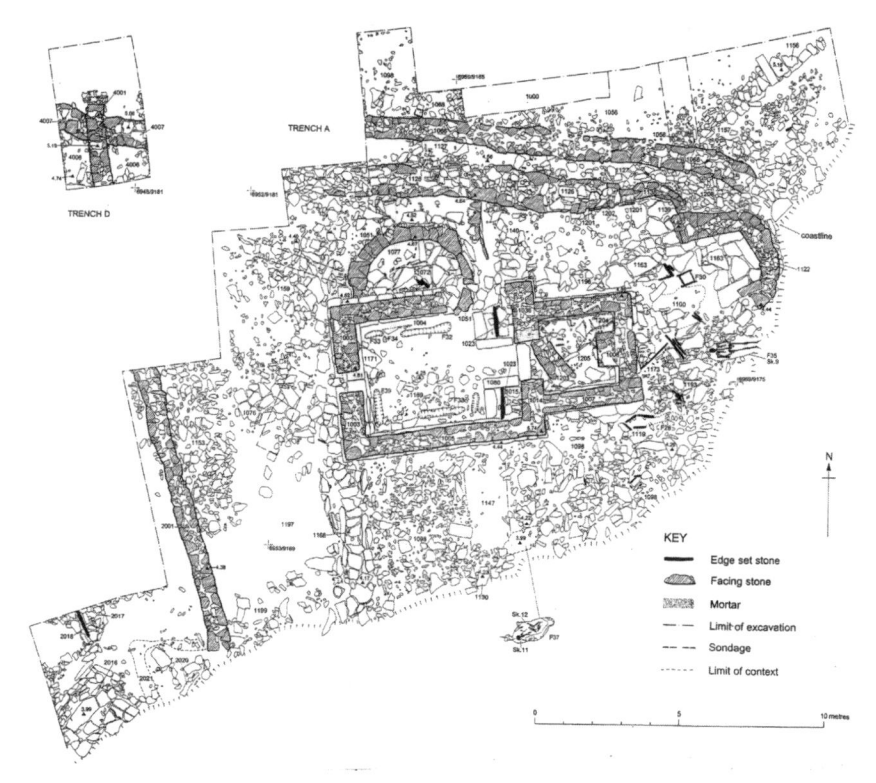

Figure 5.7 Plan of the site of St. Nicholas Church, Papa Stronsay, after excavations in 1998–2000 (Courtesy Headland Archaeology). This excavated church site is of great significance for several reasons, not least being the evidence for its location in direct association with a site of some importance in the early Christian period. However, there is a connection with the earls which is most relevant for the concerns of this book. The murder of Earl Rognvald Brusison c.1046 took place on this island, where the earl had gone to collect malt for his Yuletide ale. Clearly the island was an earldom estate, which is to be expected considering its arable fertility. The dedication to St Nicholas is also an indication of earldom ownership as it is now recognised that Earl Hakon Paulsson's side of the dynasty appears to have fostered the cult of St Nicholas, perhaps in opposition to the growing cult of his cousin, the murdered Magnus (see Section 5.3). The excavated church is a building 'of some sophistication' (Lowe, 2002, 87), with a square chancel added onto the unicameral church, and with three altars, two in the corners of the nave as in the church on the Brough of Birsay (see Plate 5a) which implies a liturgical arrangement of some complexity. These features were probably added on to an earlier church in the twelfth century when the dedication to Nicholas may also have been given.

territory and was co-terminous with the earldom boundaries. The building of churches also provided new community gathering places without respect to hierarchy or rank, at least once they had become parish churches which all the population of the parish were bound to attend and with whose priest they had a personal bond. This new structure was established alongside the secular hierarchy of the earldom family and followers. The elevation of one member of the earldom family to sainthood and another to the rank of holy man was itself a community matter, for the people of Orkney were deeply involved in this process as we have seen. The fervour of the Shetlander Bergfinn and the Westray farmer Gunnie, as revealed in the saga, shows us how the ordinary islanders were able to participate in – and indeed to influence – the development of the cult and its direction in the face of Earl Hakon's antagonism, and Bishop William's initial scepticism.

Once Bishop William had been convinced of the reality of the sainthood of the murdered Magnus and the power of his relics to achieve miracles, he became an important component of the cult's development. He was deeply involved in the transfer of the relics to Kirkwall and the building of his new cathedral there. As a powerful and energetic organiser of the growing Church he would also have been involved in the formation of an ecclesiastical network of parishes throughout his diocese.[114] It is perhaps not surprising that the memorial lead plaque discovered in his tomb described him as *primus episcopus* ('first bishop')[115] for in many ways his episcopal reign saw a new start in Orkney's church history, which at the time must have been regarded by his own clerical community as a new beginning for the episcopacy.

5.6 ORKNEY'S TWELFTH-CENTURY RENAISSANCE

The cathedral of St Magnus is a symbol of Orkney's place in the Renaissance of culture and learning which flourished in twelfth-century Europe.[116] That century was a remarkable period with the expansion of education, and the revival of Classical learning, primarily in a Christian, ecclesiastical guise. This became possible because of the more peaceful conditions in Europe, advocated by the Church and helped by the increasing power of kings. The extension of royal power was accompanied by a growth in the Church's authority, helped by the protection afforded by the kings, to whom the Church in return gave

---

114 Gibbon, 2006, 282, 290–3; 2007, 246
115 Crawford, 1996, 9 n.51; Mooney, 1924–5, 243ff., where it is described how the bones of Bishop William were moved to the east end of the extended choir many decades after his death. This was probably the occasion when the lead plaque was put in with the bones, which helps to explain the retrospective definition of William as 'first bishop'
116 Crawford, ed., 1988, 11

religious sanction and the benefits of spiritual ceremonies such as crowning and anointment.

The organisation of the Church was developed accordingly, and the hierarchy of bishoprics and archbishoprics, under the direct headship of the Popes was established. Norway was granted the privilege of having its own archbishopric of Nidaros (Trondheim) in the middle of the century and all the Atlantic sees were gathered in under its control and subject to its authority.[117] This was a very important means of binding the island communities, including Orkney, into the Norwegian ecclesiastical sphere. The cathedrals became centres of learning and promulgated the teaching of Christian beliefs throughout their dioceses. The cathedral buildings were powerhouses of prayer and liturgy, where music must have played a large part in the cultural life of the cathedral community. This would have been as true of St Magnus Cathedral as of any other cathedral for 'No functioning cathedral of that size and importance ever in music history existed without music.'[118] This was enhanced by the cult of St Magnus which inspired songs and hymns of praise and worship, of which some liturgical fragments have survived (and which have already been discussed in Section 2.6).

The flourishing of new monastic orders is a very significant feature of the twelfth-century Renaissance. These orders flourished because the nobility desired to found monasteries, and expended large amounts of their worldly wealth in so doing, while numberless men and women were prepared to take the vows of poverty, chastity and obedience in order to follow the monastic calling and enter these enclosed communities. Noble families wished to found and endow houses of monks or nuns on their estates, and to earn religious fame and eternal reward for so doing. The Orkney earls, however, appear to have preferred to spend their wealth, and earn their everlasting salvation, in founding the episcopal seats of Christ Kirk at Birsay, and St Magnus Cathedral in Kirkwall, as *Jarls' Saga* tells us. Evidence for the founding of monastic communities in the earldoms is more circumstantial, although it would appear that the burial church of St Magnus on the Brough of Birsay was taken over by a community of some order of monks or lay canons who must have been installed there after the saint's relics were transferred to Kirkwall (as discussed above). The surviving ecclesiastical ruins on Eynhallow, an island in the sound between Rousay and Mainland, are most probably of monastic origin, but whether this community was founded by the earls or one of the 'göding' families is completely unrecorded.[119]

---

117 Imsen, ed., 2003; Crawford, 2009
118 De Geer, 1988, 242
119 See RCAHMS (1946) 12th Report, ii, *Inventory of Orkney*, no. 613, for a full discussion of the controversial evidence which has been adduced to identify this ruin as a former Cistercian abbey

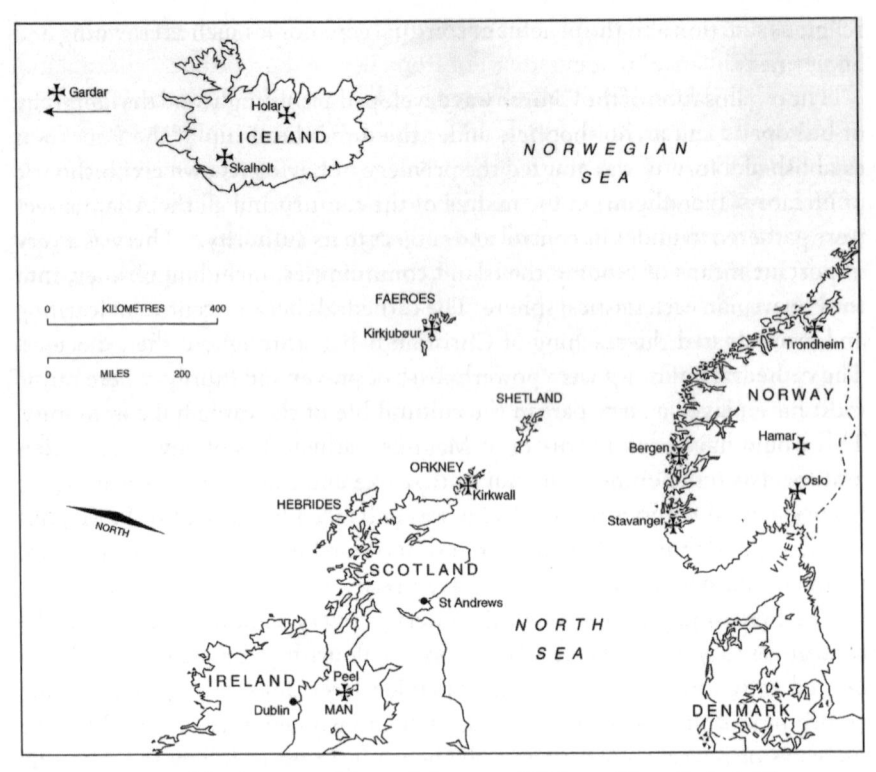

Figure 5.8 Map of the dioceses of the archdiocese of Nidaros (Trondheim). The crosses mark the sites of the episcopal sees which came under Trondheim once Cardinal Nicholas Breakspear had established a separate Norwegian Church province in 1152 or 1153. The islands in the north Atlantic and around the British Isles, which had been settled by Scandinavian speakers in the Viking Age, were brought under the authority of the new metropolitan church province. This gave the Norwegian Church an independent status and detached it from the authority of the archbishopric of Lund, which had been the metropolitan Church since 1102, and from the archbishopric of Hamburg-Bremen which had exercised authority over the Scandinavian churches before then. As far as Orkney was concerned it also removed the islands from both the metropolitan Church of York which had sought to exercise authority in Orkney, and also from the aspiring Scottish Church (which still did not have its own archbishop, and was going to be put directly under the authority of the papacy). This development had two important results: it tied the Orkney islands firmly into the Norwegian ecclesiastical sphere, and it caused the churches in Orkney and Caithness to be separated, so that Caithness was theoretically part of the Scottish Church province thereafter. This led to problems, as discussed in Chapter 6.

So for most of the twelfth century Orkney was 'a northern reflection of southern brilliance', making it part of Romanesque Europe and a cultural unit which rivalled kingdoms: 'the Orkney earldom produced its poetry and saga, its saints and its cathedral, its pilgrims, crusaders, monks and bishops.'[120] These all revolved around the court of the earls, which must have been a cultural centre of some magnificence, with the cathedral forming the most impressive status symbol of all, founded by the earls and funded by them. Perhaps this achievement aroused the envy of their overlords, the kings of Norway and Scotland, who increasingly would have been unwilling to tolerate semi-independent earls sitting in splendid isolation on the periphery of the kingdom. This situation could not last, for the twelfth century was not only the century of cultural renaissance but also the century of expanding royal power and might. In the next chapter we will see how the earls' independent position was directly challenged by the kings of Norway and Scotland.

120 De Geer, 1988, 260

SIX

Earls Constrained by the Power of Kings in the Twelfth and Early Thirteenth Centuries

We have already seen how a powerful and ambitious king of Norway was determined to implement a ruthless policy towards the earldom of Orkney when King Magnus 'Barelegs' pursued campaigns of conquest in the west in 1098 and 1103 (see Section 4.3.1). The demoting and removal from Orkney of Earls Paul and Erlend was an unprecedented occurrence which must have been a humiliating experience for the sons of Thorfinn, who did not long survive their exile to Norway. Their sons, heirs to the earldom, were compelled to join King Magnus on his war-cruise in the Hebrides, and the king's son was put in authority over Orkney, with advisers. However, the ephemeral nature of such a policy of control was only too evident on the untimely death of King Magnus, when the young Sigurd returned to Norway to claim his right to inherit his father's kingdom. Even the contumacious Magnus Erlendsson, who had flouted all the conventions of loyalty by refusing to fight, and abandoning the king's warship, survived to claim his share of the earldom, and be given a grant by King Eystein (*OS*, Chapter 44).

The exercise of authority by the kings over the earls needed that authority to be established by personal visits on a regular basis, for at that time the kings of Norway had no administrative structures which could help to implement that authority on their behalf on a permanent basis. This would change as the twelfth century progressed.

6.1 CIRCUMSTANCES OF DIVIDED LOYALTY[1]

The twelfth century saw the kings of Norway and Scotland begin the process of establishing their power and authority over the distant parts of their realm, or territory over which they claimed lordship, and over reluctant earls or rebellious ones in these localities. Whatever the circumstance of King Magnus' supposed agreement with the Scottish king over the boundary of their spheres of influence (see discussion in Section 4.3.1), a frontier situation was going to develop along the north and west Scottish coasts as the kings of Scots began

---

1 This section is based on Crawford, 2010, 84–6

the slow process of establishing direct lordship in the further reaches of their kingdom. The circumstances of joint earldoms, for which homage was owed to two different kings was, by AD 1100, foreshadowing a very problematical situation for the earls.

Indeed, the situation would eventually develop whereby the overlords came to resent their earl being subject to another sovereign. Even worse, it might happen – and did – that the two overlords would fall out and come to blows. What did the earls do then? How did they prioritise their loyalties (because prioritise they had to according to feudal custom)? It was not an unknown situation elsewhere in feudal Europe that vassals held lands from different overlords, who might fall out. When that happened the vassal had to prioritise his fealty, and the concept of liege loyalty when the liege lord had first call on a vassal's loyalty was supposed to sort that out.

However, earls were members of the nobility who held titles granted by their overlord, and whose title represented some sort of official character; accordingly, to hold two such positions in different kingdoms was *not* very common. The closest comparison to the joint Orkney and Caithness earldoms appears to be the complex case of the Norman Beaumont family who owed allegiance to the duke of Normandy (and king of England) as counts of Meulan and earls of Worcester, but who were also vassals of the kings of France. If war broke out between Normandy and France, the count/earl was in trouble from one or other of his masters. He was, as has been said, 'perched uncomfortably on the horns of a dilemma'.[2] The Beaumont twin Waleran was the one who was 'caught out by the contradictions of his dual allegiance' and lost both his French lands and the Honour of Worcester in England, being left with only the viscountcy of Evreux in Normandy.

The 'contradictions' of the Orkney–Caithness earls' dual allegiance must have become very clear during the twelfth century, although the problem is already acknowledged in the saga account of Earl Thorfinn's meeting with Olaf Haraldsson in the 1020s. His speech, as invented by the saga writer, was possibly reflecting the attitudes of c.1200:

> Were you ever to need my help against other rulers my lord, it would be yours for the asking. But it's not possible for me to pay homage to you. I'm already the earl of the king of Scots and subject to him' (*því at ek em áðr jarl Skota konungs ok honum lýðskyldr*).
>
> (*OS*, Chapter 18)

One doubts whether Thorfinn would have given priority to his Scottish lands and his relationship with the Scottish king in this way, but the saga writer knew

---

2   Crouch, 1986, 77

that the situation was anomalous and that there was a conflict of loyalty which raised potential difficulties for the earls.

If the earls themselves foresaw any such difficulties they never appear to have entertained doing the obvious thing and dividing the two halves of their lordship among heirs, creating two lines and two separate dynasties of earls. Despite the rivalry and violence among different members of the earldom family, which the saga author is keen to recount, there is no indication of a movement towards a division of the earldoms between different heirs. There were plenty of divisions of the lands among sons and heirs in the eleventh and twelfth centuries, because all scions of the earldom family had a right to claim the earldoms. These divisions seem usually to have included lands in both Orkney and Caithness, but there was never an agreement to give one earldom to one claimant and the other to a second. Powerful earls fought hard to retain both, as we will see Earl Harald did in the second half of the twelfth century.

The change towards single inheritance by one individual happened during the thirteenth century. The last case of joint inheritance was when John and David Haraldsson shared power in the period after their father's death; but that only lasted from 1206 until 1214 and then Earl John ruled alone after his brother David's death, until 1230.

6.2 EARL HARALD MADDADSON (1158–1206)

Earl Harald was a powerful and dominating figure in the north during his long life, but it was his fate to be earl at a time when more powerful and very ambitious kings were ruling in both Scotland and Norway. They regarded it as their duty to establish direct overlordship over the peripheral parts of their kingdoms, and they wished to establish proper authority over the nobles who ruled these territories, be they earls in Scotland or 'hirdmen' in Norway. Harald's half-century of rule over Orkney and Caithness saw a remarkable growth of royal authority when both kings implemented direct action to bring the two earldoms under central control.

6.2.1 *The meeting of royal authority in the earldoms*

In Caithness the enforcing of the Scottish kings' authority over the north mainland was first undertaken with the Church in the vanguard. This area – Caithness and Sutherland – would have come within the episcopal sphere of the bishops of Orkney after Earl Thorfinn founded a bishop's seat at Birsay in the 1050s and established Bishop Turolf there (see Section 4.1). Turolf and his successors were members of the earls' hird and would have had authority in the area which the earl himself dominated, and that would have included the whole territory of the two earldoms, both Orkney and Caithness.

A century later this was a situation which was not to be tolerated. In 1151, King David is said to have sought papal approval for the inclusion of the see of Orkney in a Scottish Church province under an archbishop of St Andrews.[3] Caithness was already considered by then to be a part of the Scottish ecclesiastical sphere, and at approximately this date Andrew, bishop of Caithness, had been elected, who is recorded witnessing Scottish royal charters and being given grants of land by the king.[4] At the same time, David I issued a mandate to Earl Rognvald (Kali Kolsson) and another unnamed earl (perhaps Harald Maddadson) and 'all the good men of Caithness and Orkney' requiring them to protect certain monks wherever they were travelling in the area.[5] As already discussed above (see Section 4.5) this is indicative of the Scottish Crown's attitude towards the northern territories and islands and their populations, which were being addressed as if they were the Scottish king's subjects (or subject to the Scottish king's writ).

The Church was therefore used as a powerful tool of the Scottish Crown when royal authority was being extended throughout northern Scotland, and most especially in Caithness.[6] Earl Harald's reaction to the Scottish clerical advance was hostile and there were several clashes over ecclesiastical policies, providing the Scottish kings with a moral imperative to invade the earl's territories late in the twelfth century and early in the thirteenth century.[7] Once they had demonstrated their ability to physically confront the earl with military force in the far northern reaches of their kingdom, the inviolability of his position was breached, and submission followed.[8]

The kings of Norway could also breach the earls' inviolable position in the islands, and had done for centuries. Their ability to sail unannounced over the North Sea made their arrival even more dangerous and inescapable, as on the occasion when King Eystein Haraldsson landed in Orkney in 1151 and then moved across to Caithness where he trapped Earl Harald in Thurso harbour and forced him to hand over his realm into the king's hands, and ransom himself with three marks of gold.[9] It did not seem to matter to King Eystein that Harald was in his Scottish earldom at that point. To some extent it looks as if the kings of Norway regarded the earl's Scottish domain as subject to their

---

3 In John of Salisbury's *Historia Pontificalis* (Chibnall, ed., 1956, 72); Crawford, 1991, 29
4 Barrow, 1999, 156, 255, and *passim*; Crawford, 1991, 31–2
5 Lawrie, 1905, 100, no. 132; Barrow, 1999, no. 155
6 See summary of events by R. Andrew McDonald, 2003, 107–10
7 Crawford, 1993, 136
8 The earls could, of course, have fled across the Firth to Orkney, as Earl Harald tried to do in 1196 (*SAEC*, 316), and Earl John in 1222 (see below). However this provided no defence against the implementation of reprisals against them in their Scottish earldom
9 *OS*, Chapters 91, 92. As the encounter with Harald took place on board the king's boat it was perhaps not a technical breach of the Scottish king's authority over the territory of Caithness

own authority (as the Scottish King David did with regard to Orkney). During his great war expedition of 1263 King Hakon Hakonsson sent a detachment across the Pentland Firth and imposed fines on the men of Caithness in order to ensure their neutrality during the course of his expedition west to establish his authority over the Hebrides. He, or another king, even communicated with them by letter, referred to as *littera regis Norwagie missa Cataniensibus* ('Letter of the king of Norway sent to the men of Caithness') which was at one time in the Scottish treasury.[10] (see Section 7.3.2).

The final ten years of Earl Harald's life (1196–1206) were full of dramatic and violent encounters between the earl and his two royal overlords. Indeed, there can be few examples in medieval Europe of such a sustained attempt by a vassal to defy his two different overlords as we know Earl Harald did so recklessly in these years. Because of the very public way in which he defied his kings, and their dramatic action in curbing this overmighty vassal we have several different sources which we can draw on. From Norway the saga of King Sverrir gives an eyewitness account of the earl's submission to Sverrir. For our understanding of what happened in Caithness we have first of all the final four chapters of *Orkneyinga Saga*, which are quite separate from the *Jarls' Saga* texts, and have been regarded as an independent 'Earl Harald's Saga'.[11] The information here is also derived from someone who was very close to the events described, and it seems likely that the person was Rafn, lawman of Caithness, who figures several times in the later sections, and whose son Andreas had Icelandic connections.[12] Because of the importance of Harald's story for the Scottish Crown's authority there is also information in Fordun's *Gesta Annalia*, which is related to the account in the Melrose Chronicle;[13] while the English chronicler Roger of Howden acquired a great deal of information about Earl Harald (probably from Reinald, bishop of Ross) during his visits to Scotland.[14]

6.2.2 *Harald's disloyalty and Sverrir's anger*

However, before we investigate the circumstances of Harald's encounters with the Scottish king, we must attempt to analyse why he fell into deep disfavour with his Norwegian overlord, as a result of which he lost the northern third of his maritime empire, the Shetland Islands. This catastrophe was the first impact of his overweening ambition which the Norwegian king countered with harsh reprisals. It resulted from Harald's tacit support for a rising against King Sverrir undertaken by the so-called *Eyiarskeggjar* or 'Island-Beardies'.

10 *APS*, I, 109; Crawford, 1976–7, 98; 1985, 37
11 Discussed by Chesnutt, 1981, 36–7, with reference to Taylor's analysis (*OS* Taylor, 91–4)
12 Chesnutt, 1981, 46–7, drawing on Nordal's introduction to his edition of *OS* (1913–16)
13 Bower, *Scotichron*. Book ix, Watt, ed., 5 (1990), 113, and notes on 243
14 Duncan, 1999, 135, 144; Howden, *Chronica*, iv, 10–12

EARLS CONSTRAINED BY KINGS 243

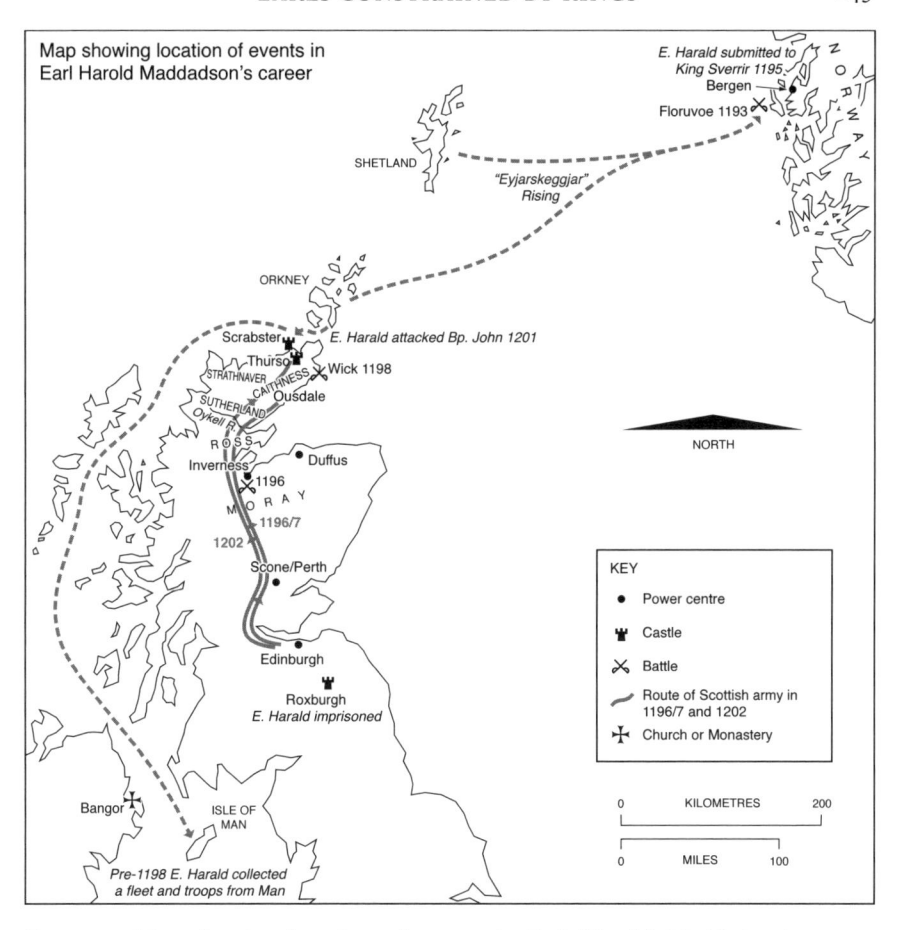

Figure 6.1 Map showing location of events in Earl Harold Maddadson's career, and depicting the range of his involvement in Norway and Scotland as far south as Roxburgh (where he was imprisoned) and the Isle of Man, where he is supposed to have collected troops.

The information in the addition to the text of *Jarls' Saga* says very little about this event, being more interested in what was happening in Caithness, but the concluding chapter does record that the earl's relative Olaf *jarlsmágr* and Jon Hallkelsson raised an army in Orkney to lead the rising, and that their candidate for king was Sigurd, the illegitimate son of King Magnus Erlingsson (*OS*, Chapter 112).[15] Although the Island-Beardies were thoroughly defeated at the Battle of Floruvoe (near Bergen) in 1193, with all the main leaders being killed,

15   This is only recorded following the much more detailed account of the Caithness events, which actually occurred *after* the rising against Sverrir

the saga writer said that King Sverrir 'grew to hate Earl Harald very bitterly, blaming him for the mustering of the army'.

The reasons for Harald becoming embroiled in this attempt to remove Sverrir, who was regarded as an imposter by the supporters of the previous king Magnus Erlingsson, are probably due to his determination to remove a rival to his own position who had appeared on the scene in the 1180s. This was Harald 'the Younger' (*ungi*), grandson of Earl Rognvald Kali by his daughter Ingirid, who had an unimpeachable claim to a share of both earldoms. He had already been given the title of earl by King Magnus before the latter's death in 1184. If a rising against Sverrir was successful and Sigurd Magnusson replaced him on the throne – due to the support of the earl and men of Orkney – then Harald *ungi* would have lost any royal support for his claim.[16] However, the rising was unsuccessful and Harald *ungi* survived to be a real threat to the older Harald which was to become all too evident a few years later.

The plan to restore Sigurd Magnusson failed, although at the time it may have seemed quite possible that it would have succeeded, for, as the saga says, the force raised in Orkney 'was very powerful'. King Sverrir blamed the earl for the organisation of the rebellious force, and the threat of reprisals must have faced Earl Harald.[17] He recognised that submission was the only possible way for him to emerge from the debacle with any hope of survival. So, in 1195, he went to Bergen with Bishop Bjarni and 'all the best men from the Orkneys' – no doubt to help plead his case – and submitted unconditionally, throwing himself on the king's mercy. The meeting was held at an assembly of bishops which was taking place in Bergen. The account in Earl Harald's saga is very brief, simply telling that the king took the whole of Shetland 'with all its taxes and revenues' and since that time the earls of Orkney 'have not ruled in Shetland'.[18] The account in Sverrir's saga has much more detail of the occasion, and of the speeches of king and earl, which we have confidence in believing to be mostly accurate because it was written so close to the time of happening. The earl was accused of disloyalty, and a charge was brought against him of *hervígi* ('slaughter') in Norway because of his support for the rebels.[19] The earl recognised that he had incurred the king's wrath, but tried to excuse himself due to his old age and his inability to control all of his men in the Orkney islands. He did not plan the uprising he said, although admitting that he did not prevent

16 Topping, 1983, 115–16
17 It is said in Sverrir's saga that the king planned to send an army to the Orkneys to punish them for their 'treachery' (*svicræði*) (Orning, 2008, 164)
18 *OS*, Chapter 112. This statement does not take into account Earl Harald's reassertion of control over Shetland on King Sverrir's death in 1202
19 Orning, 2008, 164

it because he could not oppose everyone. Then he makes the remarkable statement, which was unlikely to be believed, that the Orkney men did not entirely obey him, that many of them went out and plundered in Ireland and Scotland or robbed merchant ships, contrary to his will[20] (perhaps he was referring to the likes of Swein Asleiffson). However, he recognised that it was no use making a long speech, and he laid his case in God's power and the king's. Then he went forward and fell at Sverrir's feet.

The drama of the occasion is evident from the description of the meeting of liegemen (the hird), in the yard outside Christchurch, the cathedral which formerly stood on the headland above the harbour at Bergen (see Colour plate 26). The hirdmen stood around the king's seat and some sat in front. Sverrir was slow to respond, but said that he would show mercy, bidding Earl Harald rise and be at peace with God and with him. The terms of the agreement to be made he would declare 'at leisure'. When it was made, and written down, it was surprisingly harsh in comparison with agreements made on other occasions when men had behaved treacherously towards King Sverrir.[21] The earl was put in charge of the Orkneys again,[22] but with restricted rights over some income (half the legal fines had to go to the king), as well as losing the northern half of the earldom, the Shetland Islands, which were taken directly under royal authority. In addition, the lands of those who had joined the rising in Orkney and Shetland were confiscated. There was a three-year term during which relatives could ransom the lands back, but, if they were not ransomed, they came into the king's hands perpetually.[23] Bailiffs (sysselmen) were appointed to oversee the new royal estates, and also to collect in the legal fines from Orkney.

This was the start of a new administrative relationship between the islands and Norway. They were from then on to be more directly controlled by the Norwegian kings' officials, and the intention was obviously to make them better integrated within the Norwegian kingdom. The office of sysselman was established by King Sverrir throughout Norway in the 1170s, as a result of the need for economic resources and military requirements during the civil wars.[24] The sysselmen implemented the king's authority in the areas of the country brought under his control, and they were usually appointed to have authority

20 *ES*, ii, 345; *Sverres Saga*, 179–80
21 Orning, 2008, 216, 226–7. This was a 'strict coercive lordship' and uniquely different from Sverre's treatment of other earls (Wærdahl, 2011, 74–5)
22 There was no apparent attempt to divide the earldom with Harald *ungi*
23 *ES*, ii, 346; *Sverres Saga*, 180. It is assumed that the earldom estates in Shetland became royal estate, although not those in Orkney
24 Helle, 1974, 206; Bagge, 2011, 287–8

in districts with which they had no previous links. The situation in Orkney could be regarded as another part of the kingdom which required to be brought more directly under royal control. The dangers of having semi-independent earls in an island environment far outside Norwegian political control, where rebels could plan to unseat the incumbent on the throne with impunity, may have been the reason why Sverrir determined to clip Earl Harald's wings more severely than was usually the case with disaffected and disloyal hirdmen. He no doubt realised the difficulties of maintaining personal authority over the island earls in circumstances where he faced threats to his own security of tenure from internal opponents. However, it was not going to be a simple matter for the officials to maintain royal authority in the islands, as we will see.

6.3 HARALD, EARL OF CAITHNESS, AND KING WILLIAM

Not very long after his foolish involvement in the attempt to replace Sverrir on the throne of Norway with a rival claimant, Earl Harald also became embroiled in disturbances in northern Scotland which threatened the Scottish king's position in Moray. In this respect it can be deduced that it was his second marriage which took Harald into the maelstrom of events in this area. He was first married to Afreka, daughter of Earl Duncan of Fife (d.1154) and sister of Earl Duncan II (d.1204), which bound him to one of the most powerful families of southern Scotland. The saga says that there were four children from this marriage, Henry, Hakon, Helena and Margaret (*OS*, Chapter 105). However, for some unknown reason Harald repudiated Afreka and took as his second wife, Gormflaith (Hvarflöd), daughter of Malcolm MacHeth, earl of Ross, and they had six children, Thorfinn, David, John, Gunnhild, Herborga and Langlif.[25] This alliance with the daughter of the 'arch-rebel' of King William's reign (*OS* Taylor, 408) seems likely to have been the direct cause of Harald's involvement in the risings which took place in Moray in the 1190s. Fordun's Chronicle says very clearly that before this Harald had been a good and loyal vassal, but that he was incited by his wife to rebel.[26]

However, it is thought that Harald is likely to have been involved in the earlier troubles in the north in the 1180s in support of Donald MacWilliam, who was a descendant of Ingibjorg's marriage to Malcolm, just as Harald was a

---

25 Despite the non-Norse origins of both wives, the preponderance of the names of Harald's children were Norse, while some of the non-Norse ones reflect the names in the Scottish royal family (David, Henry and Margaret, although not Helena). It has been suggested (Gray, 1922, 113) that the son of his second marriage, called John, was named after the English king John Lackland, who ruled from 1199 to 1216

26 Bower, *Scotichron*. Book viii, Watt, ed., 4 (1994), 419

descendant of her marriage to Thorfinn.[27] If so, Harald was unusually circumspect in the events surrounding the MacWilliam rising for he is not mentioned specifically as having been involved. Looking at the broader issues of the earls' interests in the parts of Scotland bordering on their own lands of Sutherland and Caithness we should remember that their predecessors had conquered Ross in the tenth and early eleventh centuries, and that a layer of Norse settlement can be perceived there, which had provided the earls with access to the economic resources of Easter Ross (see Section 4.2.1). Perhaps Earl Harald saw a way of reviving earldom interests in the area through his marriage to Gormflaith. He certainly identified himself with the MacHeth cause at this point, although he had not apparently done so before.

In addition, the earl probably saw a threat to his ancestral lands from the encroachments of the Moray (de Moravia) family, members of which were the right-hand loyal vassals of the Scottish king and who were to be very successful in establishing themselves as the most powerful feudal nobles in the area.[28] Since being given the lands of Duffus in Moray c.1130, this family had been in the van of activity to establish royal authority in Moray, and after Earl Harald's death were going to establish themselves further north when they were given Sutherland in grant by the Scottish king (see Section 6.6.2). It would seem that it was the likely threat they posed to his position within Caithness, as well as to his wife's family's position in Ross, which impelled Harald in 1196 to lead a force into Moray, when his son Thorfinn fought a battle with 'the king's men' near the castle of Inverness.[29] This gives a clear indication as to the cause of the earl's discontent, even though the chronicler Roger of Howden states that Harald did not wish to start battle against King William when the king entered Caithness later that year or in 1197.[30] Whatever the cause, the king saw this as an opportunity to enter the earl's own domains with justification, and Fordun says that he crossed the Oykel and subdued 'both the provinces belonging to the men of Caithness', while Howden gives specific details about part of the royal army reaching Thurso and destroying Earl Harald's castle there.[31] This was the first time that a Scottish army had reached the north coast of the kingdom and it was a triumphant signal of the king's determination to establish direct control over all the territory which was nominally under his authority.

27 Oram (2011, 142–3) points to the saga tradition which tells of the descendants of Ingibjorg and Malcolm being claimants to the Scottish throne. The failure of the offspring of Ingibjorg to maintain their hold on the Scottish throne lay behind the MacWilliam risings
28 Crawford, 1985, 31
29 Uncertainty over what happened in Ross after the suppression of the MacHeth earldom in 1168 is discussed by A. Grant (2000, 110ff.).
30 *Chronica*, iv, 10; see Oram, 2011, 157–62 for full discussion of these events
31 Bower, *Scotichron.*, Book viii, Watt, ed., 4 (1994), 419; *SAEC*, 316

6.3.1 *Harald 'the Young'* (ungi) *and the Battle of Wick*

The ensuing attempt to cut back Harald Maddadson's authority in his Scottish earldom was done in the time-honoured way of using an alternative claimant to the earldom; and the candidate who had already been lurking in the wings for some time was Harald *ungi*, grandson of Earl Rognvald. The latter section of *Orkneyinga Saga* is primarily concerned with the struggle of the younger Harald to assert his claim to both earldoms (*OS*, Chapter 109 is headed 'Harald the Young').[32] The children of Erik 'Stay-Brails' (*stagbrellir*) and Ingirid, daughter of Earl Rognvald, all come into this chapter, which is very well informed about the individuals concerned and about what happened in the ensuing showdown between the two Haralds. It was probably written with some inner knowledge of the Caithness situation[33] and it has been argued that it was written with sympathy for Harald *ungi's* cause and is partial in its use of evidence.[34]

Harald *ungi* is said to have sailed from Norway to Shetland, which was then directly under Norwegian authority since Earl Harald's submission to Sverre in 1195; he 'travelled from there to Caithness' (probably avoiding Orkney deliberately) and then on to Scotland to request a grant of the half of Caithness which his grandfather Rognvald had held, 'and the king agreed' (*OS*, Chapter 109). He travelled back to Caithness 'to gather forces' and was joined there by his brother-in-law Lifolf 'Bald-pate' (*skalli*), who had a good many well-born kinsmen around, and so was well integrated into Caithness society. Lifolf was the young Harald's 'principal adviser and in charge of his troops', and these must have been local troops raised in Caithness. Harald *ungi's* father, Eric 'Stay-Brails', had been brought up in Sutherland by Frakokk, and was probably heir to estates there which had been held by the Moddan family.[35] This rival to Harald Maddadson was thus deeply embedded in north Scottish society, and he carried the torch of the rival earldom line, which stretched back through Rognvald the Holy and St Magnus to Erlend Thorfinnsson. The threat to the old Earl Harald's authority was real and well entrenched in Caithness.

It was not, however, ultimately successful, and the final showdown came in a battle which is the last battle between earldom claimants that is recorded. This was the traditional way of resolving a power struggle, but it was not to be ultimately decisive any longer, with the new direct action policy of the Scottish kings to be physically involved in determining what happened in this northern

---

32 The saga writer says nothing about the older Earl Harald's involvement in the events in Moray

33 Chesnutt, 1981, 46, suggested that the saga writer's informant was Rafn, the lawman of Caithness, who is referred to several times in this latter part of the saga narrative

34 Chesnutt, 1981, 49; although Duncan says that this part of the saga is 'strongly on Earl Harald's side' (1999, 144)

35 Gray, 1922, 59

earldom. The saga account leading up to the showdown includes direct speech, telling us that this battle was of sufficient importance in the history of the earldoms for it to generate such dramatic literary embellishment. The rivalries and tensions among some individuals in Harald *ungi's* forces are skillfully played up, with Lifolf's leadership being challenged by the 'great dandy' Sigurd *murtr* ('Mite' or 'Minnow') who questioned his strategy(*OS* Taylor, 343). The differing size of the two forces is explicitly detailed, with the older Harald assembling 'quite an army' while the younger Harald's force was 'modest'. The older earl clearly thought he had the advantage, and he took the initiative, sailing his 'very much larger forces'[36] over to Caithness and landing on the east coast near Wick, where the battle took place.[37] The quality of the 'tough and well-equipped' fighting men in Earl Harald's army is noted, the 'bishop's kinsmen' being specifically mentioned.[38] The younger Harald's force was no match for this experienced, and probably well-led, army, and once Lifolf *skalli* and Sigurd *murtr* had been killed then the remainder scattered, and the killing of Harald *ungi* 'near some peat-diggings' may indicate that he was in flight. The result was that the older Harald laid the whole of Caithness under his rule and then went straight back to Orkney, 'boasting of his great victory'. The death of *Haraldz jarls unga* (*IA*, 121) was notable enough to be recorded in the Icelandic Annals under the year 1198.

It has been claimed that this section of the saga is biased in favour of Harald *ungi* and that this is reflected in the reporting of events, and the omission of some facts which were unwelcome to the pro-Scottish faction in Caithness.[39] It is certainly the case that the saga writer included a passage which brings out the proto-martyrdom aspect of Harald *ungi's* death, commenting that people in Caithness thought that he was a 'true saint', apparently building a church where he was killed, and noting that his burial place was there 'on the headland' (*OS*, Chapter 112). Features of a supernatural nature are recorded, a light being seen that same night over the place where his blood was spilt, which was part of the build-up of a sanctification process (see Section 5.3.2 on

---

36 Earl Harald's ability to raise such a large force is rather surprising, seeing that he no longer could call on support from Shetland, or indeed from Caithness at this time. However, the evidence which Howden gives, that Harald had previously been to Man and collected ships and troops there may provide the explanation. There seems no real reason to doubt the veracity of Howden's information in this respect, as has been done by Chesnutt (1981, 38)
37 Howden and the independent Old Norse source *Fagrskinna* (trans. Finlay, 2004, 302) give the location of the battle and Harald *ungi's* death as being at or near Wick, which has more validity than local tradition linking it with Thurso (Chesnutt, 1981, 41)
38 Bishop Bjarne Kolbeinsson who has previously been mentioned as having 'plenty of kinsmen in the islands' (*OS*, Chapter 109; Crawford, 1996, 12–13)
39 Chesnutt, 1981, 49

Earl Rognvald's cult). It is also said that miracles were performed which were an indicator of the dead Harald's wish to go to Orkney and join his kinsmen, Magnus and Rognvald, the two saints of the Erlend line. This is an interesting example of how in the twelfth century the sanctity of secular leaders was linked to their violent death (as was seen above in the case of Harald's grandfather Earl Rognvald), and is also an example of the cultivation of defeated leaders by their followers.[40] It would have been extraordinary if this attempt to promote the sanctity of Harald *ungi*, the third member of the Erlend line to be a recognised family martyr, had been successful. But in this case there was no ecclesiastic to take up the cause of sanctification, and Bishop Bjarni was firmly committed to the older Harald's cause. The Scottish bishop of Caithness at this time, John, was more occupied with other matters in connection with the old Earl Harald (see below). A popular movement on its own without powerful ecclesiastical or political promoters was unlikely to succeed. What is particularly interesting is this evidence of the local population in Caithness supporting their own candidate for earl and for saint, and rejecting the authority of the older Orkney earl. Caithness was an independent community and developing its own social identity which perhaps involved having its own earl and not being attached to the Orkney earldom. This independent tendency manifested itself also in the events which followed.

6.4 VIOLENCE IN CAITHNESS

6.4.1 *Earl Harald's attack on the stewards and on Bishop John*

The next rival opponent to Earl Harald to be put in charge of Caithness, was the king of Man, Rognvald Gudrodsson,[41] a grandson of Earl Hakon Palsson through his daughter (as was Harald Maddadson similarly). According to the saga, King William sent a message to Rognvald who gathered troops from the Hebrides, Kintyre and Ireland and moved north to take over the whole of Caithness. According to Howden, Rognvald bought the earldom 'saving the king's yearly revenue' (possibly some payment made by the earl rather than income from estates).[42] King Rognvald was said to be 'the greatest fighting warrior in all the western lands' by the saga writer (*OS*, Chapter 110), and was no doubt thought to be a good match for the recalcitrant Earl Harald. As always, the Orkney earl had the safe refuge of his islands to retreat to, and he

---

40 Haki Antonsson, 2005, 158–60, 176, 182–3
41 The confusion over which Rognvald this was has been satisfactorily settled by Duncan, 1999, 155, n.51; see discussion in McDonald, 2007, 110
42 *SAEC*, 318. There is no indication that Rognvald was ever given the title of earl (as a king himself he would have considered it a lesser dignity). The contract with King William must have been financially advantageous to him (see discussion by McDonald, 2007, 111)

simply waited there until King Rognvald had departed back to the Hebrides, leaving behind three stewards in charge of Caithness,[43] Mani Olafsson, Rafn 'the Lawman' (*lögmaðr*) and Hlifolf 'the Old', who were clearly of local stock, and just as clearly prepared to collaborate with the Scottish regime and King William's appointee. This was dangerous policy, however, for Harald then engineered the murder of Hlifolf by dispatching an assassin across the Firth to do the deed.[44] Such ruthless elimination of royal officials was to be repeated later on in Orkney after King Sverrir's death.

The killing of stewards was one thing, but the attack on a bishop was something else, and it was on account of the maiming of Bishop John in 1201 that Harald was forced to make his submission to King William. What led the old earl to make such a rash move with potentially dire consequences for his independent position in his Scottish earldom? It was undoubtedly the result of a build-up of tension and suspicion between the earl and the bishop which had its roots in the anomalous situation in which the earldom of Caithness had originally been within the bishopric of Orkney (see above), but which had changed when Scottish bishops were appointed. King David had used the Church as a vehicle for the advancement of his political influence in the north, and the development of the bishoprics of Moray, Ross and Caithess is evidence of this policy.[45] The appointment of the Scottish Bishop Andrew in Caithness (1145x47) coincided with the end of the threat posed by William FitzDuncan and can be regarded as part of the policy for withdrawing Caithness from the Norse sphere and extending royal control over north Scotland.[46] There is little evidence, however, for Bishop Andrew's activity in Caithness, and he was primarily occupied with central affairs at the royal court until his death in 1184. Only in one respect do we hear of any connection with Earl Harald; from the later papal letter we know that he confirmed a grant by the earl of a payment of an annual due of one penny from every inhabited house in Caithness which because of Harald's regard for the blessed Peter and Paul was collected specifically as alms for the needs of the Roman Church.[47]

This payment is very reminiscent of the due called 'Peter's Pence' which was paid in England from as early as King Alfred's reign (it was believed), and which was later adopted in Denmark and introduced into Norway by the papal legate Nicholas Breakspear when he established the archbishopric of

---

43 Probably in 1200 (McDonald, 2007, 110)
44 The name of the murderer is never given although he is said to have met and spoken with Rafn 'the Lawman', who was his kinsman.
45 Oram, 2004, 103
46 Crawford, 1991, 29
47 *CSR*, no. 3; *DN*, vii, 3

Nidaros in 1152–3.[48] It was thereafter collected from Orkney, as a diocese of the archdiocese of Nidaros, and Earl Harald's grant of such a due from his Caithness earldom must have followed that imposition for by the 1150s Caithness no longer came under the jurisdiction of the bishop of Orkney. As noted, the first Scottish bishop of Caithness, Andrew, had confirmed this grant, but his successor, John, obstructed the payment.[49] The papal letter of 1198 instructed the bishops of Orkney and of Rosemarkie (the diocese of Ross) to restrain John from preventing the payment[50] (see Section 2.3). The reason for the new bishop to go directly against his predecessor's action, and to bring papal censure on himself as a result is quite extraordinary, and not easy to understand. However, it provides evidence of friction between the earl and the bishop which would appear to have arisen out of contention between what the Scottish bishop saw as his role in the diocese, which went counter to the earl's traditional position in the area. Underlying this tension we can guess was a determination to root out all Orcadian influence and perhaps some residual episcopal powers which the Orkney bishop may still have attempted to exercise in Caithness and Sutherland. 'Peter's Pence' was not paid in Scotland,[51] and perhaps Bishop John saw its imposition in Caithness as undesirable evidence for the perpetuation of Norwegian/Orcadian custom. But as far as the papacy was concerned that was not a problem; the only problem was its blocking by the Scottish bishop, so Pope Innocent III instructed the Norwegian bishop of Orkney (Bjarni, the earl's kinsman), along with Reginald the bishop of Ross to ensure that the 'abstracted alms' (*elemosinis subtractis*) should be restored, without any appeal being allowed.

This must have been a cause of some satisfaction for Harald 'the noble man our beloved son' (*dilectus filius nobilis vir*) as he is called in the papal document.[52] But only three years later Earl Harald risked censure himself by launching an attack on Bishop John at the episcopal castle of Scrabster, on the north coast of Caithness. This incident suggests that the antagonism between the two had continued to simmer and deteriorated into personal violence against the bishop, the specific reason being, according to Fordun, because the earl blamed the bishop for 'encouraging discord and opening up a breach between himself

48 Crawford, 1974, 17
49 He is specifically said to have forbidden the payment by those who were appointed by his authority in the diocese; perhaps meaning that the collected dues should not be paid by the church officials (but retained within the diocese?)
50 *CSR*, no. 3
51 Crawford, 1974, 15–17
52 Earl Harald had intimated to the papacy that this payment was made for the 'remission of his sins', an easy form of contrition when the due was collected from every house in his earldom

and the lord king by making accusations against him'.[53] This takes us back to the relationship of Earl Harald and King William, which we saw above had been rendered unstable due to the earl's involvement in the troubles in the province of Moray to the south of his earldom. In 1196 or 1197 (Fordun says in both years), King William had sent an army into the heart of Harald's earldom when he eventually captured Harald and lodged him in Roxburgh Castle until he had 'placated' the king. After they were reconciled, Harald left his son Thorfinn as a hostage for himself, but Fordun tells us that when he then broke his word, Thorfinn was blinded and mutilated and ended his life in prison (as mentioned earlier, Thorfinn had been involved in the battle against the king's vassals near Inverness). The saga also records that Thorfinn was blinded (*OS*, Chapter 112). Howden gives further details that point to some lack of reliability, or untrustworthiness on the part of Harald, who was supposed to bring hostages to the king at a pre-arranged meeting at Nairn, but failed to do so. He allowed the hostages to escape and attempted to offer two of his grandsons instead. He is said to have explained his failure to bring Thorfinn 'because in that land there is no other heir'.[54] Certainly there were occasions when Harald did not live up to his promises and could doubtless have been regarded as a faithless vassal, which was a dangerous game to play with kings like William the Lion and Sverre.

There are other pieces of evidence pointing to Harald's tendency to enter into independent negotiations which might have been regarded as verging on the treasonable. He was, for instance, in contact with King John of England, for in 1201 Adam 'chaplain of Orkney' and his associates were recorded as going north to Orkney on the king's affairs, while in the next year a safe-conduct was issued for Harald, earl of Orkney, and Adam, the earl's chaplain, to come to England to confer with the king.[55] There is plenty of evidence to show that King John had ambitions with regard to the rulers of the Celtic kingdoms and brought them into a feudal relationship with him.[56] This is particularly evident where the Celto-Norse rulers of Man were concerned, notably King Rognvald Gudrodsson, who got sucked into the English orbit after the resurgence of

---

53 Bower, *Scotichron.* Book viii, Watt, ed., 4 (1994), 427
54 *SAEC*, 317, a rather strange excuse when Harald had two other sons of his second marriage, John and David, who did succeed their father to the northern earldoms. Was Thorfinn controlling some other family lands, perhaps inherited from his mother?
55 *Pipe Roll Soc. ns.*xiv, 1936, 244; *CDS*, i, 324; Crawford, 1971, 81; Duncan, 1999a, 253–4. It is very unlikely that Harald did go south considering the trouble he was in in the north; perhaps it was King John who was attempting to embarrass King William (his vassal) by being in contact with the Scottish king's vassal
56 Carpenter, 2004, 278–84

Norwegian interest in the Hebridean situation in 1210.[57] He became John's liegeman and received grants of land and corn in Northern Ireland. By this date Earl Harald was dead, but the evidence of the safe-conducts already cited shows that for some reason there had been moves to establish contact with the earl of Orkney by King John at an earlier date. Such contact could of course of itself indicate disloyalty as far as the earl's Scottish overlord was concerned.

It may be that it was due to the bishop informing King William of these contacts (which he had perhaps heard about in ecclesiastical circles in the north) which led to Earl Harald's fury, and his accusation that the bishop was fomenting discord between himself and the king. Certainly the attack on the bishop was a very physical one and deliberately appropriate in its retributory nature. The earl sailed across to Thurso and led his troops up to the bishop's castle at Scrabster (see Colour plate 27); it is said in the saga that the bishop went out to greet the earl with some kind words of welcome, but he was taken captive and the earl 'had his tongue cut out and a knife driven into his eyes, blinding him' (*OS*, Chapter 111). However, the papal document prescribing punishment for the perpetrator only refers to the cutting out of the bishop's tongue.[58] Fordun's account mentions both blinding and mutilation of the tongue, but also adds that the bishop retained the use of his tongue and of one of his eyes.[59] The implication is that this punishment was inflicted because the bishop had been a spy and an informer. An evident interpolation comes next in the saga which supplies a miraculous explanation for the healing of the bishop's tongue and eyesight: this resulted from a meeting between the wounded bishop and a woman who said she would help him and who was evidently the holy virgin St Tredwell.[60] After the bishop was taken to where the saint rested, his sight and speech were restored.[61]

6.4.2 *Punishment: papal penance and royal retribution*

Harald's anger was also directed against 'those he thought most guilty of treason against him' and after they had surrendered the bishop's castle to him without

---

57   This was the same Rognvald who had been given authority in Caithness in 1198 by King William (McDonald, 2007, 131–2, 138)
58   *CSR*, no. 4
59   Bower, *Scotichron.* Book viii, Watt, ed., 4 (1994), 427
60   Tredwell, or Triduana (called Trollhæna in the ON source), was a Pictish princess who offered her eyes on a twig to the suitor from whose attentions she wished to escape. She was considered therefore to have powers to help those with eye afflictions
61   The cult of St Triduana was centred at Restalrig near Edinburgh, the place of her burial, but the place-name Kintradwell in Sutherland (south of Helmsdale) bears witness to her cult in north Scotland, as well as in Orkney from the existence of St Tredwell's chapel on Papa Westray (MacIvor, 1962–3, 251)

a fight, he 'imposed severe punishments and heavy fines' and had all the men of Caithness swear oaths of allegiance to him 'whether they liked it or not' (*OS*, Chapter 111).[62] Then he took the property belonging to the stewards who had been appointed by King Rognvald (and perhaps King William) – who had fled back south – and he settled in Caithness with a large army.

The old earl appeared invincible: he had killed his rival the Scots-supported earl in a great victory at Wick; he had murdered one of the stewards who had been put in authority in Caithness by his cousin, Rognvald Gudrodson, the king of Scots' appointee; he had maimed and rendered the Scottish bishop harmless; he had reduced the episcopal stronghold and killed the bishop's guard; he had inflicted severe punishments and heavy fines on the men of Caithness and forced them to submit to his authority. Moreover, he escaped papal censure for the attack on the bishop, for the blame fell squarely on the shoulders of one 'Lumberd' who is named in the papal order as the culprit, and to whom penance was to be administered. The order was made by Pope Innocent III, the same pope who had supported his *dilectus filius nobilis vir* Earl Harald against Bishop John in 1198, so one might wonder if Harald avoided retribution because Innocent knew of the previous situation in which the earl's grant of 'Peter's Pence' from his Caithness earldom had been thwarted by the bishop. The papal order only says that Lumberd was compelled to cut out the bishop's tongue 'by certain of the earl's army' (*a quibusdam, ut dicit, de exercitu Comitis est cohactus*),[63] with no specific mention of the earl's personal involvement.

Remarkable insight is gained from this papal order about Rome's concern with matters which had taken place on the fringes of the European world.[64] The attack on Bishop John had infringed the protected status of a member of the highest rank of the Church hierarchy so it was necessary for someone to carry the can for the misdeed, and the order for seeing that penance was carried out was made to the Bishop of Orkney, Bjarni Kolbeinsson, the earl's kinsman.[65] Lumberd had already been to the papal curia, and he carried the letter back to Orkney with its instructions for his punishment. This gives full details about how he had to walk naked – except for breeches and a short and sleeveless woollen vest – throughout the countryside where the bishop had been mutilated and in the surrounding region (in the locality of Thurso and Scrabster), for fifteen days 'with his tongue tied with a thin cord and pulled out

---

62 The papal letter of early September 1202 says that when the castle was being reduced 'nearly all who were in it were killed' (*CSR*, p.6)
63 *CSR*, p. 5
64 Crawford, 1993, 135
65 This suggests that Bishop Bjarni would have to follow the penitent Lumberd around the northern part of Caithness while he fulfilled the requirements of the papal order

beyond his lips and the cord tied round his neck'.[66] He had to carry rods in his hands and when he came to a church he was to be disciplined with the rods and then had to lie on the ground, remain in silence and fast until the evening, when he could partake of bread and water. In addition, Lumberd had to leave for Jerusalem within a month of this ordeal and spend three years there 'sweating in the service of the Cross'; for eleven years he had to fast every sixth day on bread and water unless a priest gave him indulgence because of bodily infirmity or summer heat.

Although Harald escaped papal censure, this incident, which the Church took so seriously, must have weakened his position *vis-à-vis* the Scottish king. Certainly Harald's submission to William appears to have followed on from it. Indeed, William's reaction was immediate and swift, and according to Fordun, 'he did not delay' but sent an army north before Christmas 'to attack the earl'. The saga focuses more on the earl's requisition of the stewards' property, and the reaction of the king when the stewards told him of what had happened; he 'flew into a rage' and promised to pay double compensation to anyone who had lost their property (*OS*, Chapter 112). It is also noted that the 'truly massive army' was raised by William immediately after Christmas. Clearly the decision to march north in mid-winter made an impression on contemporaries. But despite the size of the force it achieved nothing, for Harald – as usual – was able to retreat to his island earldom, and 'came back immediately once the army had returned home'.[67] The saga writer believed that King William himself marched north with his army, and is specifically said to have camped at *Eysteinsdalr*, near the boundary between Caithness and Sutherland.[68] His camp 'extended from one end of the valley to the other, quite a distance'. Fordun reports that despite – or rather because of – the failure of his expedition to bring Harald to his knees, William was planning a naval expedition to Orkney in the following spring, 1202.[69]

Perhaps it was this threat which forced Harald to submit voluntarily. He came to Perth under the safe-conduct of Roger, bishop of St Andrews,[70] and through the intercession of the bishop and other men of standing reached an agreement with the king, swearing that in all things he would abide by the judgement of the Church. On payment of compensation (or fine) amounting to the large

---

66 *CSR*, p. 6; Crawford, 1993, 135
67 Bower, *Scotichron*. Book viii, Watt, ed., 4 (1994), 427
68 The name has survived as Ousdale, a farm which lies in the steep valley near the Ord, the line of hills which divides Caithness from Sutherland (Colour plate 28)
69 Bower, *Scotichron*. Book viii, Watt, ed., 4 (1994), 427
70 Bishop Roger had been at the English court with King John at the time when Earl Harald received a safe conduct to confer with the English king, which suggests to Duncan (1999a, 253) that he must have been connected with the issuing of the invitation to Harald

sum of £2,000 of silver, he was restored to his earldom. The saga account has some discrepancies but gives specific details about King William's demand that he be granted a quarter of all the revenues from Caithness.[71] Harald then called together the farmers and leading men who accepted these conditions that they were to pay the king of Scots a quarter of all they possessed.[72]

6.5 EARL HARALD'S ULTIMATE SURVIVAL

It is hard to see what permanent advantage King William had gained from all this expenditure of effort directed at curbing the independence of Earl Harald, apart from a useful contribution to the royal treasury.[73] The earl does not seem to have suffered any permanent loss of land or rights in his earldom, and was restored to his former position in Caithness without any restriction of his powers or permanent reduction of income. There is no further mention of royal stewards being appointed alongside him. The imposition of heavy fines appears to have been considered the most effective way of bringing the earl to heel rather than any confiscation of earldom land, which then had to be administered, in dangerous circumstances. As will be seen, the same policy was followed after the burning of Bishop Adam in 1222 (see Section 6.7.1).

The earl had however, lost his eldest son (by his second wife) and chief heir Thorfinn in the struggle with King William, which was probably the most grievous result of the conflict with his Scottish overlord. Strangely, the saga writer says nothing about Thorfinn's death after blinding in captivity as his father's hostage, although Fordun adds that he was mutilated and ended his life in prison. For Harald to take the eldest son of his second marriage to Hvarflöð as his chief heir gives an indication of the importance of that marriage. Its importance is also very evident from Harald's refusal to take back his first wife Afreka, when this was demanded by King William as one of the conditions of coming to terms in 1198, on the occasion when Harald offered payment to have a grant of Caithness after his defeat of Harald *ungi*.[74] Thorfinn's appearance as witness to his father's grant to the abbey of Scone (see text quoted in Section 2.3) also tells of his participation in his father's display of public piety by this grant of alms to one of the most important abbeys in Scotland.[75]

---

71 Possibly it was the total of the farmers' payments which amounted to the £2,000 paid by Harald to the king at Perth
72 It would appear as if this information in the saga has become misplaced and is more relevant to an earlier situation, perhaps 1196/7 (Crawford, 1971, 82–5). The saga account of the Eyjarskeggjar rising and Harald's submission to Sverrir which follows the submission to William is certainly in the wrong place (see n.15)
73 Crawford, 1985, 32
74 *SAEC*, 318
75 Obviously this grant must have been made before Thorfinn's death in captivity, and most

Harald's piety as seen from the grant of 'Peter's Pence' from throughout his Caithness earldom has already been discussed, although this benefaction to the Holy See may have been made primarily to demonstrate his independence of the Scottish Church's establishment in Caithness. Another tantalising piece of evidence which points to Harald's public role in religious life comes from a lost charter, recorded as having been in the royal treasury, concerning the granting of peace and protection to the monastery of 'Benkoren' by Harald earl of Orkney.[76] Although undated, this almost certainly refers to Harald Maddadson, and the monastery in question is thought to be Bangor in County Down, Northern Ireland. The likelihood that it was Earl Harald who was in a position of power in Northern Ireland can be seen from the fact that in 1170 a fleet from Orkney is recorded as being in action against the king of the Ui-Meath on the border between County Antrim and County Down.[77] Presumably Earl Harald issued the charter when he returned to Scotland, and for some reason it ended up in the royal archives. It shows that the earl was offering protection to an ancient Irish monastic establishment and is further evidence of his good relationship with the Church, although, as with all the other pieces of evidence, it would not be difficult to show that the earl's public acts of piety could be interpreted as serving his political interests.

The promise made by Earl Harald when he paid King William the fine of £2,000 after the attack on Bishop John that 'in all matters he would abide by the judgement of the Church'[78] reveals that he was considered to be a wayward son, and had gone against the Church's teachings in certain respects, in particular in taking a second wife. It might be expected that he would have had to make donations to churches in his earldoms in expiation of the violent deeds he committed, but we have no evidence for any such. However, there is evidence that he had churchmen in his household, active clerics with whom he must have been in close contact over matters of policy and his relationship with senior churchmen. First of all was his kinsman, Bjarni Kolbeinsson, bishop of Orkney, described as his 'dear friend' (*kjær venn*), on whom he could call for help when faced with the wrath of his Norwegian overlord. Bjarni accompanied him to Bergen when he submitted to Sverrir in 1195 and probably interceded on his behalf; he also had to oversee the penance laid on Lumberd after the 1201 attack. The earl had his own household priest Laurence, named as a

---

likely before the onset of trouble between Harald and King William, in which Thorfinn was deeply implicated (see above). The name of Harald's wife is omitted, perhaps because Hvarflöð was Harald's second, bigamous wife, and was thus unacceptable to the Church

76 *APS*, 1, 116; Topping, 1983, 109–110
77 Topping, 1983, 111–12
78 Bower, *Scotichron*. Book viii, Watt, ed., 4 (1994), 429

witness to the grant to the abbey of Scone, and also mentioned by Howden in 1196 when Laurence, the earl's priest, was demanded as a hostage by King William.[79] He was clearly a figure of some importance in Harald's household, and Harald refused to hand him over.[80] The earl's chaplain Adam was named on two occasions in 1201–2 as being involved with the earl in diplomatic contact with King John, as already mentioned above.

Earl Harald was 'altogether a dangerous man'[81] and guilty of many murders and killings, which would count against him in the eyes of the Church. Apart from his violent reactions against any rival to him in his earldoms, he ruthlessly dispatched one of the stewards put in charge of Caithness (as already seen), and then after King Sverrir's death dealt similarly with the Norwegian sysselman in Orkney, Arni Lorja. Details are given in *Böglunga sögur* (Sagas of the Bagler) that the sysselman whom Sverrir set beside the earl in Orkney survived for as long as Sverrir lived 'and earl Harald dared say nothing against him'; but on Sverrir's death in 1202 he caused him 'to be treacherously murdered' and 'laid Orkney and Shetland under himself again, with all its taxes and dues, as he had had it before'.[82] This is apparently reliable evidence that the old earl bided his time and then dispatched the hated symbol of royal control. After Sverrir's death, the inheritance of the kingdom of Norway was in doubt and there was no royal successor capable of taking any direct action against the earl in the islands.

Harald is said to have died two years after King Inge became king in 1204, so for the last four years of his life the redoubtable warrior was able to rule his two earldoms as he had in previous decades, without any rival and without any royal official intervening. The saga author adds that 'according to people who have written on the subject' Harald was one of the three most powerful earls of Orkney, along with Sigurd Eysteinsson ('the Mighty') and Thorfinn Sigurdsson ('the Mighty') (*OS*, Chapter 112). It must indeed have seemed like that in the last few years of his reign, and more particularly because he survived the onslaughts of royal power in both his earldoms, in situations which none of his predecessors had had to face. Even despite the loss of his chief heir, he must have been satisfied that the two other adult sons from his second marriage, David and Jon, were able to inherit both earldoms, and to share power, while a son from his first marriage, Henry, is said to have ruled Ross, although no other evidence

---

79   *SAEC*, 318
80   This was when he also refused to take back his first wife, in contradiction of another of King William's demands.
81   Carpenter, 2004, 256
82   *ES*, ii, 380. In the final pages of *Orkneyinga Saga* it is said that after Sverrir took Shetland from Harald in 1195 'the earls of Orkney have not ruled in Shetland' (*OS*, Chapter 112).

survives to corroborate this statement in the saga.[83] If reliable, this information suggests that Harald had been able to maintain some authority over Ross, and this no doubt resulted from his marriage into the MacHeth dynasty, and helps to explain his involvement in the troubled events in Ross in the 1190s. As far as Earl Harald's achievement goes it demonstrates that the power of Scottish kings was not yet sufficiently well-established or well-supported to be able to remove this powerful northern earl, nor yet to permanently reduce the earl's control of his ancestral territories.

It is tempting to regard Harald Maddadson as more deeply integrated within Scottish society and the first earl who was more Scottish than Norwegian. His grants to the canons of Scone must reflect a continuing commitment to the Atholl family's benefactions to the abbey (see Section 2.3).[84] Further evidence of an important link between Caithness and Scone is the grant of the church of Kildonan, in Helmsdale, to the canons of Scone. It is suggested that this must have been granted originally by Earl Harald because of his known generosity to the canons.[85] There is a lack of evidence for any benefaction to the Orkney Church or the earldom saints, but then these saints were members of the alternative earldom line. Both his marriage links were with women of noble Scottish families, who were rather unlikely to have settled in Orkney or integrated into Norse society. The determination to retain full control over Caithness, brooking no rival, either to earldom status and rights, or in respect of ecclesiastical control, says much about where his priorities lay. This was his Scottish earldom and the base for his operations against the Scottish Crown which occupied so much of his time; it was not simply the further side of the Pentland Firth which had to be controlled for the sake of the islands' security. The loss of Shetland in 1195 meant that the earldom properties were thereafter focused around the Pentland Firth, which from then on was very central to earldom operations. This may have had unintended consequences. Shetland was a nodal point between western Norway and the North Atlantic islands of Faeroe and Iceland, so when it no longer formed part of the earldom then the Orkney islands were less of an integral part of that northern maritime world. The earldom lost its most Norwegian sector and probably became less Norwegian as a result.

83 It appears odd that a son of Harald's first marriage (to Affreka) should have ruled in Ross and not a son of his second wife, the daughter of Malcolm MacHeth
84 Earl Malcolm of Atholl granted the most important church in his earldom, Logie Rait, to Scone abbey (*RRS*, ii, 340).
85 *OPS*, ii, pt.ii, 735; Cowan, 1982, 39. In Bishop Gilbert's constitution for the cathedral at Dornoch the church of Kildonan with all its revenues and pertinents was reserved for the prebend held by the abbot of Scone (*CSR*, nos 9, 45)

Harald was, however, fully conversant with both Norse and Scottish cultures and would have been bilingual, brought up for the first five years of his life in Atholl but then moving north to Caithness and Orkney. His island earldom was of vital importance to him, particularly as a secure refuge in his confrontation with King William. But maintenance of his position in Caithness would seem to have been a prior commitment on which he focused his policies.

The overall legacy of Earl Harald's reign suggests that priorities had changed. Because of the attacks on him in Caithness and the need for him to have a secure foothold in the difficult and tumultuous world of north Scotland, he needed to have a network of family alliances which would give him support in his struggles to maintain independent status. His wives' family networks must have appeared more useful for him (particularly the MacHeth network of his second wife) than any marriage within the Norwegian world. Unfortunately, we know very little about the marriages of Harald's children, which would give us some indication of close social links with either Scottish or Norse society. The one piece of information that has survived about marriage negotiations is indicative; *Sturlinga Saga* reports that Saemund Jonsson, a powerful Icelandic chieftain, communicated with Earl Harald about marrying the earl's daughter Langlif, but negotiations broke down, for Saemund would not go to Orkney for the wedding and the earl would not send Langlif to Iceland.[86] This gives us a message about the reduced social links between the earldom dynasty and Norse communities further north, although there were still close contacts between Iceland and other sections of Orkney, and Caithness, society.

6.6 THE LAST JOINT EARLS: DAVID AND JOHN HARALDSSON

The last chapters of *Orkneyinga Saga* end with the statement that the brothers John and David ruled the earldom jointly after their father until David died (1214) when Earl John became sole ruler in Orkney. It is interesting to see that the earls, and John in particular, faced some of the very same problems as their father had with regard to the kings of both Norway and Scotland. John also got embroiled in another bad situation regarding the Church. Although he was a far less controversial figure than his father, he nonetheless had to come to terms with both overlords, and also with the Church. In contrast to his father, John ended his days with a humiliating death, killed by the combined opposition of Norwegian royal official and rival claimant.

---

86 *ES*, ii, 238n; *OS* Pálsson and Edwards, 14

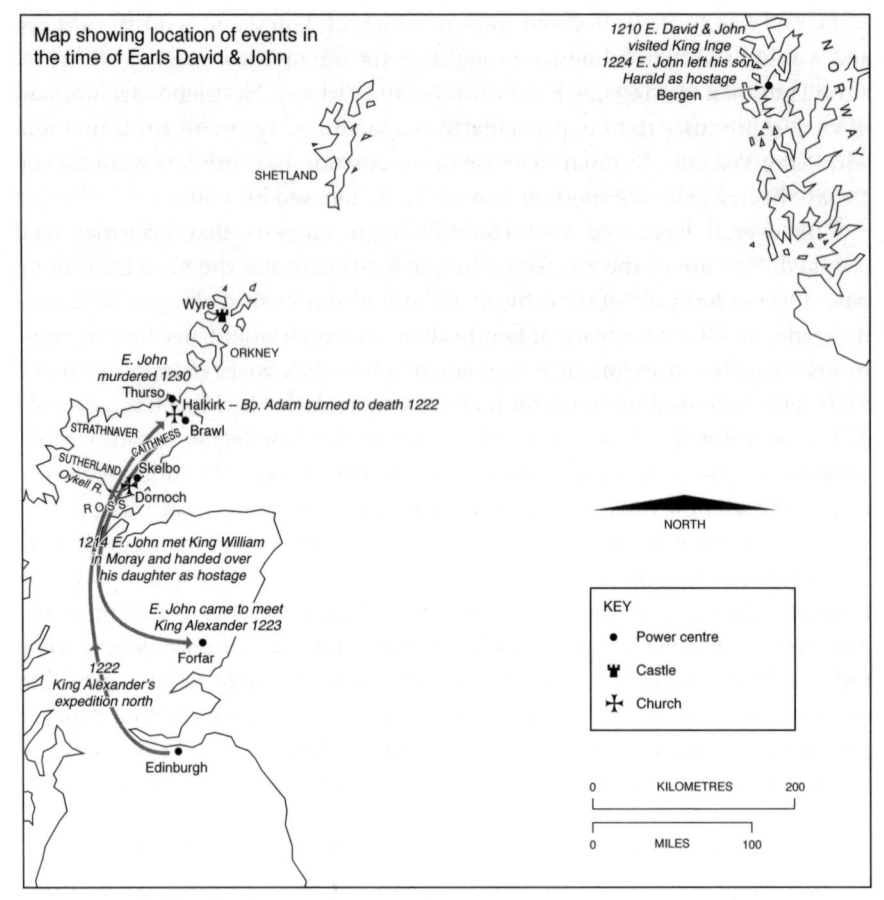

Figure 6.2 Earl Harald's sons David and John were also deeply involved in events in Norway and Scotland, but they are the last earls whose activities we can map. After the murder of Earl John, the saga evidence comes to a halt and there are very few documentary sources providing any facts about the new earldom dynasty from Angus in Scotland.

6.6.1 *Repairing relations with the kings of Norway and Scotland*

The need to repair relations with their Norwegian overlord was obvious. The new earls' father, Harald, had reasserted his rights in Orkney, brought Shetland under his authority again and murdered the royal sysselman on Sverrir's death in 1202. Nothing displayed better the arrogance of the old earl and his disregard for the authority of his Norwegian overlord. The new earls were under obligation to go to Sverrir's successor in Norway, seek a grant of the earldom of Orkney and do homage and come to terms. However, the political situation in Norway after Sverrir's death was very uncertain, and so the earls 'held the lands as their father had done, so long as there was civil war in Norway'.[87] Not until the peace of Kvitingsøy in 1208 were the rivals in Norway reconciled and after that the earls sent Bishop Bjarni to Norway. He found King Ingi and Jarl Hakon in Bergen and transmitted the message that the earls wished to be reconciled, so safe-conducts were issued for the earls to come the following summer (1210) and have the terms of their appointment agreed. There is also a reference to an expedition west by a naval force, which was accompanied by the king's officers to Orkney and Shetland, which must have given the earls a flavour of the new regime's determination to re-establish the former royal authority. The naval force (of Vikings, as they are called) went as far as the Hebrides where it plundered and burned which caused the two kings of Man, Rognvald Gudrodsson and his son Godred, also to go to Norway and be reconciled. There are some interesting differences in the saga account between the reconciliation of the earls and of the kings of Man.

The earls were accompanied by Bishop Bjarni for their meeting with King Ingi and Jarl Hakon, but it does not seem as if his presence helped the earls, who had to pay a large fine and give security and hostages as well as swearing loyalty and obedience. But, 'in the end, King Ingi made them his earls over Orkney and Shetland, upon such terms as were adhered to until their death-day'.[88] We do not know exactly what these terms or conditions (ON *vilkør*) were, nor whether they differed from those imposed on Earl Harald in 1195, but the clear implication is that the earls were tied down with very specific terms of appointment which must have reduced their freedom of control over their earldom and changed the character of their authority.[89]

Nothing of this sort is said about the kings of Man. They were frightened into becoming reconciled with Inge as a result of the plundering raid in 1209, and when they went to Norway the following year it is said that they paid the 'outstanding taxes' (*skatta*) which were due,[90] swore an 'oath of allegiance' (*trúnaðareiða*), 'received their lands in fief' (*tóku síðan löndin í lèn*), and went home again. There is no mention of them being 'made kings'. The 'skat' was clearly the tribute which had never been paid to Sverre or his son Hakon, as

---

87 *ES*, ii, 380 from *Böglunga Sögur* II (called 'Ingi Bardsson's saga' or 'Hakon Sverri's son's saga' in *ES*, i, lxii)
88 *ES*, ii, 381; *Böglunga Sögur* II, 121. This is the only evidence that Shetland was ever returned to the earls after it was detached from the earldom in 1195, and has to be interpreted alongside the *Orkneyinga Saga* statement that the earls never held Shetland again after 1195. It is possible that David and John were given a temporary grant of Shetland for their lifetime
89 Crawford, forthcoming
90 The kings of Man do not appear to have acknowledged the Norwegian kings' authority for a very long time (since 1164)

well as that due to Inge, in return for which they were granted their lands in 'len'.[91]

So by this date it can be seen that the basis of the earls' relationship with their Norwegian overlord was under firmer constraints of vassalage and obligation than those exercised over the kings of Man.[92] It must be presumed that the conditions of Earl Harald's settlement in 1195 were restated, and that a royal sysselman was appointed to oversee the administration of the Crown estates and the division of judicial fines between king and earl. We certainly know that at the end of Earl John's life, such an official, called Hanef *ungi*, 'then had the stewardship on behalf of the king'.[93] We will return to Hanef later.

The first information that we have about the earls in Scotland comes from Fordun who records that in 1214 King William travelled to Moray and 'made peace with the earl of Caithness', then took the earl's daughter south with him as a 'hostage' (*obsidem*).[94] Whether the earl had been involved in troubles in Moray is not stated, but clearly relations were in a fragile state. It is likely that this was the first time that the earl had attended his Scottish overlord since his father's death in 1206, and this may have been a cause of some tension between them. The taking of the earl's daughter was doubtless in order to arrange for her marriage to a suitable member of the Scottish nobility and thus strengthen ties with Caithness (Chapter 7).[95] It is likely that William attended to strategic matters on the Ross–Caithness frontier at this time.

6.6.2 *Loss of Sutherland*

The old King William died soon after his meeting with Earl John, but if the earl thought that his position in north Scotland might be less threatened by William's successor, Alexander II, he found out that this was not to be so. Alexander was involved in the political process of detaching Sutherland from Caithness, which had already begun under his father, and which would result in the creation of a new earldom for the de Moravia family. How this could happen is not at all

---

91 A 'len' was a grant of royal estate or emolument made to a close follower (*håndgangnemann*) of the Norwegian king, who had swon an oath of loyalty, and it is generally translated as 'fief'; but the arrangement was not as prevalent or as structured as is usual in the feudalised countries of medieval Europe. Such 'len' could be given as personal favours or as more official grants

92 Wærdahl, 2011, 79–80, where the 'indirect lordship' over the kings of Man is contrasted with the conditional re-instatement of the earls

93 *Hacon's Saga*, 155

94 Bower, *Scotichron*. Book viii, Watt, ed., 4 (1994), 473. This must be Earl John, probably indicating that Earl David was dead by this date

95 Similarly two of King William's daughters had been handed over to King John in 1209 (when the two kings made a treaty of peace at Norham), as 'hostages' for the maintenance of good relations, and to be married to royal princes

clear. Sutherland had always formed part of the earldom and diocese of Caithness but had something of a separate identity, which can be perceived from the reference to 'both provinces of the men of Caithness' referred to by Fordun in 1196 (see Section 6.3). The separate nature of Sutherland meant that it could be easily developed into a unitary lordship and earldom created especially for the de Moravia family who had been in the van of the royal advance into the province of Moray in the twelfth century.

The first member of the family known to have possession of lands in Sutherland was Hugh, son of William, who granted Skelbo and 'Ferenbeuthlin' and all the land of Sutherland 'lying between these places and the marches of Ross'(most of Creich parish) to his putative relative Gilbert of Moravia when Gilbert was archdeacon of Moray (c.1211).[96] Hugh, grandson of Freskyn de Moravia, was therefore handing out some of his Sutherland property to a powerful ecclesiastic who eventually became bishop of Caithness and had an important role to play in the reorganisation of the Church in his diocese. This remarkable personal grant would appear to have been made with strategic considerations in mind, as it comprised the southern frontier of Sutherland as far west as the march with Ross. This was the territory running along the northern side of the Dornoch Firth to the River Oykel, which as we have seen was the important southern frontier of the earls' conquests many centuries before (see Section 3.3.1). It is fairly certain that King William was closely involved in these developments on the northern frontier of Ross for he confirmed the grant of these lands to Gilbert de Moravia (c.1214) who was a royal servant and known to have been particularly concerned with the keeping and building of castles in the north.[97] This may have been planned as part of King William's 'peace-making' with Earl John in 1214.

Hugh son of William de Moravia must have held large swathes of Sutherland for him to make the grant to Gilbert c.1211; and his son William was called 'lord of Sutherland' (*dominus de Sutherlandiae*) before 1222, being created earl of Sutherland later. The 'Genealogy of the Earls' states that King Alexander 'took the earldom of Sutherland' away from Earl Magnus II (in the 1230s).[98] This formed part of the new strategy of the Scottish Crown to encroach on the southern frontier of the Caithness earls by using the de Moravia family as its loyal vassals and frontiersmen, a more successful policy than bringing in a king of Man with a distant connection to the earldom, or royal stewards who were

---

96   *CSR*, no. 5, dated c.1211; *RRS*, ii, 520, is a confirmation of the grant by King William dated c.1214. See Watt, 1977, *sub* 'Gilbert de Moravia' for analysis of his relationship to Hugh, son of William de Moravia, and for a full discussion of Gilbert de Moravia's role in the north
97   Watt, 1977, 415
98   *Bann. Misc*, iii, 77; Crawford, 1985, 33

vulnerable to attack. The dangers that still plagued the Scottish kings' rule in Moray and Ross are very evident in the rising which occurred the year after King William's death when the MacHeths and the MacWilliams united and entered Moray in insurrection. This time they were defeated not by the royal army but by a native dignitary in the north, Ferchar Maccintsacairt, who was co-operating with the Crown, no doubt with his own interests in mind.[99]

Another aspect of this royal policy of establishing loyal royal and administrative elements in the south of the Caithness province is the ecclesiastical one. Just as the first two Scottish bishops were instruments of royal policy in the earldom, even more so was Bishop Gilbert de Moravia, who was elected after the death of Bishop Adam 'in the presence of the king and the chief men of his army' according to Fordun.[100] This suggests that it happened during Alexander's expedition to impose penalties on the north in 1222, and one can be fairly sure that royal pressure was applied in making sure that this favoured royal servant was put in charge of the unruly diocese. Gilbert was in possession by 10 April 1224 and held the diocese for over twenty years, during which time he implemented big changes to the ecclesiastical organisation of the Church. The most drastic change was the demoting of the chief church of the diocese at Halkirk in Thursodale, where Bishop Adam had been killed (see Section 6.7.1), and its replacement with a new cathedral at Dornoch in Sutherland, in the heart of that strategic lordship which had been granted to Gilbert some years earlier. It is not known at what date the cathedral was established at Dornoch (see Colour plate 29),[101] although the translation of the bones of the murdered Bishop Adam – presumably to the new cathedral – in 1239 suggests that the building may then have been in a state to receive them.[102] This change of location indicates a retrenchment policy and an acknowledgement that the only firm base for the establishing of Scottish episcopal authority was in the most southerly part of the diocese (see Figure 4.1).

Impressive evidence of Bishop Gilbert's administrative powers and organisational ability is supplied by the Foundation Charter for his new cathedral's constitution. This is an ambitious and costly blueprint for the establishment of a cathedral chapter and the assigning of revenues from the different parishes to maintain prebends in the cathedral. Ten canons were created, five of them

99 McDonald, 2003, 43–4
100 Bower, *Scotichron*. Book ix, Watt, ed., 5 (1990), 115
101 In the Foundation Charter of the new cathedral constitution (1222–1245; *CSR*, no. 9) there is a reference to the cathedral church prior to this time as having been served by only one priest, and the decision to build a new cathedral is explained as being due to the poverty of the location and the frequent hostilities, which must be a reference to the circumstances at the previous chief church of Halkirk (Crawford, 1993, 133)
102 Watt, 1977, 417

being diocesan dignitaries such as dean, precentor, chancellor, treasurer and archdeacon. Six parishes were reserved by the bishop for his own use, and he also had the patronage of all the parish churches in the diocese (which is very unusual).[103] Clearly the bishop had ambitions plans for the control of all parishes throughout his diocese.[104] It is unlikely that this reorganisation would have been welcome to either of the two earls, of Caithness or of Sutherland.[105] Bishop Gilbert did earn saintly status locally however, and his tomb in Dornoch Cathedral came to be venerated, although no formal move to canonise him appears to have taken place.[106]

6.7 CONSPIRACY IN NORWAY AND MORE VIOLENCE IN CAITHNESS

Earl John was not only finding his freedom in his Scottish earldom increasingly constricted, he also had problems in his relationship with the new king of Norway, the young and ambitious Hakon Hakonsson. In 1223, Hakon was confirmed in his claim to the throne, and his rival to power Earl Skuli Bårdsson was given the northern third of Norway to rule. Previously, in 1217, Skuli's third of the kingdom had included one third of the skattlands, and at that time it is said in Hakon Hakonsson's saga that Skuli had sent letters west to Earl John in the Orkneys, and they had the king's seal on them, but the king was unaware of this (*Hacon's Saga*, 27).[107] The content of the letters is unknown, but the fact that Skuli had sealed them with the king's seal suggests that he wanted their content to carry more weight. Maybe he was attempting to win Earl John's support for some proposal for his position in the skattlands (probably including Shetland), which he preferred to keep secret from King Hakon. Earl John is named the very next year as being present on the occasion when Hakon's mother, Inga of Varteig, underwent the ordeal of the hot iron to prove the veracity of her claim as to who was the father of her son.[108]

In 1223, the Council meeting in Bergen included Earl John and Bishop Bjarni from Orkney, Archdeacon Nicholas and Gregory Kikr from Shetland (the royal sysselman), and it was arranged that Skuli's third of the skattlands would be returned to King Hakon.[109] The following year, Earl John also came

---

103 *CSR*, no. 9; Crawford, 1993, 144 n.3
104 As Watt comments (1977, 417), it is possible that this was only a blueprint at the time of Bishop Gilbert's death and its implementation must have taken a long time
105 Decades of dispute between the bishops and the earls of Sutherland over landholdings in the diocese resulted from this reorganisation, until a settlement was reached in 1275 (Watt, 1977, 416)
106 Watt, 1977, 417
107 *ES*, ii, 428; Crawford, 1971, 156; Wærdahl, 2011, 80–1
108 Helle, 1972, 134–5
109 Ibid., 136–7

to Hakon in Bergen 'and made atonement to the king in those quarrels which were between them', and left his son Harold there as hostage (*Hacon's Saga*, 90). This is an indication of the deep distrust which King Hakon harboured for Earl John, and one would like to know if the division between them was connected with the terms of the settlement of 1210 and spheres of authority in Orkney, or maybe Shetland. It was not the end of undefined trouble in the west. Two years later Earl John was again in Bergen with Earl Skuli, Simon, bishop of the Hebrides and the abbot of Iona, for a meeting with the king. They had come for the resolution of some issues and the king decided their cases 'all with the advice of Earl Skuli' (*Hacon's Saga*, 134).[110] In that same year, the earl's son Harald, who had been held as a hostage for his father's good behaviour, was drowned, as recorded in the Icelandic Annals, but it is not said where or how.[111] The attempts of both Norwegian and Scottish kings to exercise some power of control by the same means – of taking the earl's children as hostages – is an indication of the earl's overlords' determination to enforce his loyalty and obedience. In 1228, however, relations with King Hakon appear to have improved as the earl sent him 'many good offerings' and the king sent a good long-ship and many other gifts in return (*Hacon's Saga*, 149–50).

6.7.1 The burning of Bishop Adam in 1222

The time when Earl John was so busy attending meetings in Bergen was the same time that he was affected from being implicated in the shocking murder of Bishop Adam. Once again an attack on the bishop of Caithness caused reverberations around ecclesiastical circles.[112] Once again the earl acquired some blame for the deed, which was used by the king of Scots as a justification for intervention and harsh reprisals. However, the underlying cause this time was the extension of ecclesiastical authority in the form of increased teinds (tithes) which enraged the Caithness farmers. It would appear as if Bishop Adam was attempting to force Caithness into line with the rest of the Scottish Church in this respect, and perhaps other matters.[113] According to different accounts it appears that two kinds of teind were involved. The farmers were objecting to the raising of the butter teind from a customary rate of one *spann* of butter for every twenty cows to one for every fifteen, then

110 *ES*, ii, 461; Helle, 1972, 139
111 Storm, 1888, 127
112 As Adam was of the Cistercian order and had been abbot of Melrose, his death was widely reported among Cistercian houses, as from the Irish Cistercian house of Duisk (Nicholls, 1983, 96)
113 The papal letter issued in recognition of King Alexander's actions says that the dispute was over teinds 'and other rights of the church of Caithness' (*super decimis et aliis Katanensis ecclesiae juribus questione*) (*CSR*, no. 10)

twelve, and then ten cows (so making it a full tenth of the increase).[114] (*OS* Anderson, 200). However the Annals of Dunstable say specifically that the earl had objected to increased demands for a hay teind about which both he and the bishop 'had made promise to the king of Scotland'.[115] There were many problems over the payment of teinds throughout Europe and particularly it appears, the hay teind, which in a northern locality like Caithness with a good pastoral economy must have been an important item of production.[116] In the very next year, 1223, a letter was written by Pope Honorius III to the people of the Hebrides, in the diocese of Sodor, which was also under the jurisdiction of Nidaros, ordering them to pay all their teinds of butter and cheese.[117]

The trouble in Caithness therefore arose out of a general resentment at the Church's demand for tithes. In that diocese the situation was particularly inflamed because of the changes in the Church's episcopal leadership which entailed changes to traditional obligations. The bitter relationship of Earl John's father and Bishop Adam's predecessor would be well-remembered. The flames of resentment were fanned into a raging attack on Bishop Adam and the events leading up to the attack are dramatically recounted in the separate account headed 'The Burning of Bishop Adam' (only found in the Icelandic manuscript *Flateyarbók*).[118] This took place at Halkirk, which was the chief church of the diocese at the time[119] and where the bishop was staying, while Earl John was 'a short distance off', no doubt at his estate at Brawl, across the river (later known to be the 'caput' or chief place of the earldom) (see Colour plate 30). The Caithness men were holding a meeting on a hill nearby, and as Rafn 'the Lawman' is mentioned as playing a part in the negotiations with the earl it would appear that this was a meeting of the local *þing* (assembly). The saga account says that the Caithnessmen attempted to get the earl to intervene, but he would have nothing to do with it. Rafn 'the Lawman' tried to persuade the bishop to 'spare the inhabitants', or there would be consequences, and a man was sent again to the earl to ask him to make peace, but the earl would not interfere. The result was an attack on the bishop's house and the murder of the bishop's chaplain, a monk called Serlo, after which the bishop himself was

---

114 The *spann* was a Norwegian measure of weight and no doubt a long-established render which had been used when Caithness was under the authority of the bishop of Orkney

115 This is verified by the papal letter which refers to the agreement reached by the mediation of certain ecclesiastics in the presence of the king, and the decree which the bishop issued as a result had both the royal seal and the earl's seal appended to it (*SAEC*, 337)

116 Crawford 1985, 28–9

117 *DN*, vii, no. 10

118 *OS* Dasent, 232–3; *OS* Hjaltalin and Goudie, 200–1

119 Crawford, 1993, 132–4

taken into a small house (his kitchen,[120] according to the papal letter) which was set on fire and the bishop burned inside it.

Andrew of Wyntoun's verse chronicle says they:

> tuk hym out, qwhar þat he lay,
> Off his chawmyr befor daye
> Modyr nakyt his body bar
> Þai bande, dange and wondit sare . . .
>
> Himself bundyn and wondit syne,
> Þai put hym in his awyn kechyn
> In þar felony and þar ire
> Þar þai brynt hym in a fyre[121]

The two main accounts apportion the blame for this event differently. The saga's account most likely derived from the lawman, Rafn, who is cited as playing a crucial role in the events leading up to the attack, and who may possibly have provided a first-hand account to the saga author.[122] If so, he presents the earl as playing no part in the actual attack but as refusing to play any mediating role, although begged to do so. The earl's response was that there were two alternatives, one of which was that the situation was not to be endured. But he would not say what the other was (suggesting that he did not actually incite the farmers to attack the bishop). This addition to the account has a ring of reality, giving the impression that the reporter had actually witnessed and heard what he told the saga writer. Earl John's inactivity meant that he could therefore be considered culpable, and 'it was because of this that many believed him to be party to the crime' as Fordun comments, but adding that 'he proved on the testimony of good men that he was innocent and had offered no support or advice to those ruffians'.[123]

> Howevir þat it hapnyt was
> Þe erl was purgit of þat casse[124]

The Annals of Dunstable, however, depict Earl John as playing a much more aggressive role in the events. He is said to have murdered the bishop's chaplain in fury at not getting back the charter which he had earlier sealed (agreeing to pay the teinds), as well as wounding a nephew of the bishop. He gave the

---

120 This is likely to have been the *eldhus* ('fire-house') of a medieval Norse farm, which was usually quite a separate building from the dwelling-house
121 Andrew of Wyntoun, *Original Chronicle*, Book 7, Chapter 9 (Amours, ed., v, 85)
122 Chesnutt, 1981, 46
123 Bower, *Scotichron.* Book ix, Watt, ed., 5 (1990), 115
124 Andrew of Wyntoun, *Original Chronicle*, Book 7, Chapter 9 (Amours, ed., v, 85)

orders for the bishop to be bound to the doorpost of the kitchen and for the house to be set on fire. On top of that, when the bishop appeared to be escaping the flames unscathed, he caused him to be thrown into the fire and the bodies of the other two thrown in with him.[125] This belief in the major role played by the earl in the crime is reflected in the Chronicle of Melrose, and may be an inflamed rendering of the events by monastic chroniclers who liked to find a single scapegoat for such deeds, rather than a general culpability among the wider farming community.

6.7.2 *Royal vengeance*

Whoever the main culprit was in this attack on the bishop and his chaplains the violence could not be allowed to go unpunished, and King Alexander seized the opportunity to crack down hard on the earl with righteous vengeance, and even harder on the Caithness farmers. He is said to have stopped on a journey south when he heard the news, even though at the borders of his kingdom as the papal letter says (at Jedburgh according to Fordun), and gathered together an army for an expedition north to avenge the murder.[126] Both Fordun and the Annals of Dunstable say that the king went with the army to Caithness, the Annals telling how the earl fled 'and in exile roamed about among the isles of the sea',[127] suggesting that he retreated to his Orkney earldom, in time-honoured way.

However, as his father, Earl Harald, in 1202, Earl John deemed the wisest course to be to agree to the terms imposed by the king, although no details are given as to when he did so. They were wide-ranging and punitive; the full teinds of hay had to be rendered by the earl and his heirs and his men; within six months he would bring to the king's feet the heads of those who had taken part in the crime; he resigned half his earldom into the king's hands; he bestowed lands on the Church; he promised to go on foot to Rome and obey the mandate of the Pope concerning these things.[128] According to Fordun, the earl handed over the perpetrators to the king for punishment, and they had their limbs cut off and were subjected to 'various tortures'.[129] The horrific nature of the retribution was widely known, and the Icelandic Annals give specific details of eighty men having their hands and feet chopped off, from which many of them died.[130]

---

125 *SAEC*, 336
126 *CSR*, 26; Bower, *Scotichron*. Book ix, Watt, ed., 5 (1990), 115
127 *SAEC*, 337
128 Ibid.
129 Bower, *Scotichron*. Book ix, Watt, ed., 5 (1990), 115
130 *IA*, 126. More details, perhaps exaggerated, are added in the Annals of the Irish Cistercian house of Duisk that the king caused them to be killed, castrated their sons and flung out their wives (Nicholls, 1983, 96)

There are few incidents in the history of Scotland so revealing of the brutality of a king's vengeance and for which Alexander was praised in the papal letter of encouragement.

The consequences of this royal vengeance were long-lasting. The poor unfortunates who had suffered maiming – those who survived – also appear to have forfeited their lands. The papal letter approved the excommunication which had been publicly pronounced by the four Scottish bishops on the perpetrators, and ordered them to place these lands under interdict 'until suitable satisfaction has been given'.[131] A document which was at one time in the Scottish royal treasury refers to the 'quitclaiming of the lands of the bondi of Caithness for the slaughter of the bishop', proving that they had to pay either the Church or the king to redeem their lands.[132] The earl also had to pay a large fine which he handed over to the king the following year at Forfar where the court spent Christmas, and he was then able to recover the half of his earldom resigned the year before.[133] This occasion is recorded also in Wyntoun's *Original Chronicle*:

> Þar borowit þe erll þan his land
> Þat lay unto þe Kingis hand
> Fra þat þe byschope of Catenas,
> As yhe before herd, perist was [134]

The 'borowit' land (Scots for 'ransomed' or 'redeemed') is unlikely to have included Sutherland which, as we have seen, was by this date mostly in the hands of the de Moravia family. Otherwise the earl survived this dreadful incident with most of his Caithness earldom intact, except of course for the lands which he had to give in compensation to the Church. As already seen (see Section 6.5), the king did not apparently wish to have royal estates in Caithness which had to be administered, he preferred to crack down on the earls with harsh fines. Earl Harald had paid £2,000 in 1202 and Earl John probably had to pay a similar amount to redeem half of his earldom. As with the fine of the men of Caithness mentioned above, some of this money may have been converted into an annual tax raised from the earldom, for there is evidence later in the century that the earl of Caithness was liable for an annual fine.[135] Whatever the initial reason for such fines it suggests that the kings preferred to impose

---

131 *CSR*, 26
132 *APS*, 1, 110; it is likely that this redemption took the form of an annual fine of a number of cattle which the men of Caithness appear to have been still paying later in the century (Crawford, 1985, 32)
133 Bower, *Scotichron*. Book ix, Watt, ed., 5 (1990), 117
134 Andrew of Wyntoun, *Original Chronicle*, Book 7, Chapter 9 (Amours, ed., v, 87)
135 Crawford, 1985, 32

fines for misdemeanour rather than to confiscate land. Royal officials in the far north of Scotland are far less in evidence than in Moray where an administrative system had been in existence for some time.[136]

6.7.3 *Contextualising the evidence about the nature of Caithness society*

This is probably the clearest evidence of the power of the king to punish perpetrators of violence against the Church in medieval Scotland. Are there any other known incidents of such dramatic proportion, and with such horrific consequences for the population of a district? Why should it happen in Caithness? There are perhaps some deductions one might draw from the way this resistance of the local *bondi* turned into such a disastrous incident in the history of the earldoms.

First is the situation already mentioned of the imposition of new custom which derived from a different culture onto a society which already had its own established ecclesiastical arrangements. There is evidence that the imposition of tithes caused problems in many different parts of north Europe, but were church officers attacked or bishops murdered because of the community's fury at such impositions?[137] It would appear that circumstances in Caithness aggravated the situation into becoming much more of an extreme reaction.

Second, one may perceive a community which organised its own judicial affairs in a way which differed from the parts of Scotland where feudalised methods of royal administration imposed a different style of communal governance. The role of the lawman Rafn as recounted in the saga gives us a glimpse of another social arrangement and tradition, derived of course from the Norse establishment in north Caithness. This is the only evidence that we have of a lawman in operation in the Norse communities of Scotland at this date (including Orkney), and it is highly significant that it comes from Caithness, telling us of established judicial arrangements developed since the Norse conquest of north Scotland. What we do not know is whether this judicial arrangement was imposed by the earls of Orkney after they had conquered Caithness, or whether it was instituted by the *bondi* themselves. The impression given by the account is of a community which was meeting according to its own organisational structures, and relating to the earl only through the agency of

---

136 Crawford, 1971, 98. Gilmakali, a royal judge in Caithness (*iudex Catanie*) is named soon after 1222 (*Moray Reg.*, 333) but may have operated in the south of the province, while the Norse Lawman functioned in the north. A mandate of Alexander II's protecting the ship, men and goods of the abbot of Scone names all the king's 'sheriffs, bailiffs and his other good men of Moray and Caithness', indicating that some royal officials may have been appointed in Caithness during this reign (*CSR*, 12; *Scone Liber*, 73)

137 Crawford, 1985, 28–9

the lawman. If this was the norm, then it appears to correspond with the judicial arrangements in Norway where legal assemblies strove to keep themselves free of control by the king or powerful *lendmenn*. It is not how one expects that these matters were arranged in these earldoms where the earls were leaders of the community and participated in the meetings of *þing* assemblies. At least in Orkney clashes between the earls and the Orkney farmers are recounted in the saga as happening at the *þing* (see Section 3.6). Perhaps the nature of Caithness society had developed differently and the farmers were more independent of the earls.

Whatever implications there might be from the evidence of the burning of Bishop Adam about the nature of Caithness society, it is difficult to avoid the conclusion that in this frontier zone between Scottish and Norse societies tensions were endemic and could produce flash points, as the events of 1202 and 1222 show. Violence against some Irish bishops in this period has been compared with the attacks on Bishops John and Adam and understood as being features of frontier areas.[138] These might be frontiers between different secular powers or between secular and religious authorities, situations which prevailed in Caithness compounded by differences of race, language and custom. The toxicity of this mix helps to explain the violence of events as recorded in the sagas and other chronicles which give us such vivid accounts of the tragic outcomes of these situations. Being enmeshed in such a complex web of conflicting loyalties and political systems meant that the 'men of Caithness' suffered harsh reprisals and heavy financial penalties were imposed on them. In 1201, Earl Harald is said to have laid 'severe punishments and heavy fines' (*stórar refsingar ok...gjöld stór*) on those men of Caithness who were thought guilty of treason against him, while they also had to pay the king of Scots a quarter of all they possessed because of the treatment of the royal stewards (*OS*, Chapters 111–12). After the murder of Bishop Adam, those responsible had to pay dearly for the redemption of their lands. One wonders what the total impact of these economic reprisals was on the nature of society in the earldom of Caithness during this process of painful adjustment from being part of the northern cultural sphere to becoming integrated into the Scottish kingdom.

6.8 MURDER OF EARL JOHN (1230)

Both Fordun and the chronicler of Melrose gloat over Earl John's violent end, which they see as the vengeance of God for the sufferings of the venerable Bishop Adam.[139] How did this come about? It happened because of the same

---

138 Brendan Smith, 2002, 244
139 Bower, *Scotichron*. Book ix, Watt, ed., 5 (1990), 117

threat which had haunted John's father, the claim of a kinsman to land and authority. This kinsman came of course from the rival line, a great-grandson of Earl Rognvald called Snaekoll Gunnison, a son of Harald *ungi's* sister, who appeared once it became clear that Earl John had no male heir after the drowning of his son Harald in 1226. *Hacon's Saga* tells us that Snaekoll laid claim to some estates of his relatives in the islands, but the earl held them 'and would not let them go', and because of this 'enmity arose between them'.[140] Earl John asked Snaekoll if he was going to follow the example of his uncle and lay claim to the Orkneys from him, adding that he intended to keep them from him, as his father kept them from Harald *ungi*. The situation looked dangerous so Snaekoll went to the sysselman Hanef *ungi*[141] who had the stewardship in the islands from the king, and 'they had great company there, all together'.

Once again a royal sysselman in Orkney was implicated in a violent death, only this time it was the earl who was killed. The details in *Hacon's Saga* provide a fluent and vivid account of how the two rival parties clashed, and also tells of a 'ruffianly' member of Hanef's party called Olvir *illteit* ('Ill-Will'), a ship's commander of the recent Norwegian expedition to the Hebrides, who had stayed behind in Orkney when it returned to Norway. In the autumn of 1230, these two parties both went over to Caithness (perhaps for the hunting?) and stayed at different lodgings in Thurso. The saga gives a realistic account of how Hanef's party were drinking when someone burst in and warned them to prepare themselves as the earl intended to make an attack on them in the night. Hanef and his brother Kolbein, along with Snaekoll, armed themselves and set out to attack the lodging in which the earl slept. He leapt into an underground closet or cellar,[142] but the attackers found out where he was and jumped in after him. It was Snaekoll who found the earl beside a barrel and slew him, along with other members of the earl's following. The earl was said to have nine (stab) wounds.

Such a miserable and violent end of the last earl of the old Norse line is a sad reflection of the nature of the earldom inheritance traditions by means of which claimants could appear with justifiable claims on the family lands and the family title.The two earldom lines from Paul and Erlend continued to rival each other right to the end of the period of Norse inheritance. It also reflects

---

140 *ES*, ii, 480; *Hacon's Saga*, Chapter 169
141 Wærdahl, 2011, 81. Hanef was an Orcadian and a great grandson of Kolbein Hruga, of the Wyre family. He had two brothers Kolbein and Andrew who are also present in Orkney at this time. They were cousins to Snaekoll (Clouston, 1932, 219)
142 ON *undirklefi*, which indicates that it was some sort of subterranean storeroom, or cellar, where barrels were kept. Stone cellars appear to be incorporated as basements under wooden houses in thirteenth-century Norway

the evident tensions which existed between the earls and the royal officials, who ill-advisedly sided with new claimants in the power struggles. In this instance it perhaps also reflects the stubborn and aggressive attitude of Earl John, who was not prepared to compromise, just as he failed to advance any compromise between the bishop's demands and the resistance of the *bondi* in 1222. His death saw the end of a man who failed to live up to the expectations of how an earl should conduct himself, with justice and temperance, and with regard for the rights of his friends, relatives and those under his rule.

The report in *Hacon's Saga* even gives details of the aftermath of this unprecedented situation. Hanef and his brothers went out to Orkney and took refuge in Cubbie Roo's Castle on Wyre (see Section 4.6.2), which must have been their family possession. They brought in stores, evidently preparing for a siege against the expected attack by the earl's relatives and friends, who (the saga says) went out to Wyre to besiege the castle.[143] However, relatives and friends of Hanef and his companions assembled there and tried to make peace, so a truce was declared. This was to last over the winter and then in spring both parties were to go to Norway and lay their case before King Hakon.

6.8.1 *The end of the old line and the end of an era*

Although the murder of the earl had taken place in Thurso in the earl's Scottish earldom, and within the jurisdiction of the Scottish king, yet the parties concerned agreed to go to King Hakon in Norway for judgement, and not to King Alexander.[144] Of course, the party guilty of murder consisted of a claimant to earldom lands in Orkney and the royal official with their supporters, so it was more appropriate that they should seek justice in Norway. Because Hanef was a member of the king's hird he was brought before a court meeting of all the king's liegemen in Bergen, and was immediately taken up to the royal fortress along with his brothers Kolbein and Andrew, and Sumarlidi Hrolfsson, perhaps to avoid any retribution. Olvir *illteit* and others who had been involved in the murder were taken out to Toluholmr for execution, and it would appear from one version of the saga that a kinsman-in-law of the earl called Sigvaldi Skjalgson was the chief prosecutor on behalf of the earl's family members. Five men were beheaded, but Snaekollr was not considered to be guilty enough to be executed, perhaps because he was thought to have had a just claim on earldom land and rights, but a claim which was rejected by Earl John. Rather strangely he is said to have 'remained long with Earl Skuli and King Hakon'.[145]

---

143 *Hacon's Saga*, 156
144 Crawford, 1971, 159
145 *ES*, ii, 485. Snaekollr never appears to have laid any claim to the earldom thereafter, probably disqualified because he had been closely involved in the murder of Earl John

Presumably the arrangements for the inheritance of the earldom lands and appointment of a new sysselman for Orkney were attended to in the aftermath of the judicial settlement. The next dramatic and tragic event took place in the autumn of 1232 when all the 'best men of the islands' returned to Orkney in one ship which was lost and everyone went down with it.[146] We do not know exactly who was included in this tragedy[147] but it left no immediate male member of the earldom kindred who could lay any serious claim to the lands and title of the earldom of Orkney and the inheritance therefore passed to a member of the Scottish house of the earls of Angus. This break in the direct line of inheritance meant that the new dynasty claimed the earldom of Caithness; once that claim to the Scottish earldom had been acknowledged, the new earl must have proceeded to get a grant of his Orkney earldom. This differed radically from the previous situation when inheritance of the Orkney earldom had taken precedence. Unfortunately, the lack of sources means that there is virtually no information as to what this changed balance of priorities meant for the joint earldoms.[148]

The new earl can have had few close family links in either of the two earldoms, so how did he adjust to the circumstance of being earl in the north of Scotland with a claim to lands and rights in the islands of Orkney? All we can deduce is that priorities must have been somewhat changed, and in the power vacuum the Norwegian royal position in the islands was probably strengthened. *Hacon's Saga* concludes its comment on the loss of the Orkney ship by saying 'and many men have waited long for redress for it' (*ok hafa margir menn þess seint bætr beðit*).[149] This suggests that the impact on island society caused by the wiping out of so many members of the earldom kindred and following was very disruptive, but we have no other information of any kind to amplify this statement.

---

146 This event was recorded in *Hacon's Saga*, Chapter 173, and in the Icelandic Annals (Storm, 1888, 129), where it is referred to as *göðingaskip af Orknéyium*, 'the Orkney gödings ship' (see Section 4.5.1)
147 Wærdahl (2011, 120) makes the interesting comment that all these individuals were members of the royal hird in the earldom who had been summoned to Bergen for the judgement process
148 The 'Genealogy' provides no insight whatsoever into the inheritance of the Scottish family of Angus, merely saying that Earl Magnus II succeeded to Earl John, without mentioning any relationship between them (*Bann.Misc.*, iii, 77)
149 Own translation, with help from Paul Bibire as to possible meaning. Dasent's translation 'many men have had to atone for this later' (*Hacon's Saga*, Chapter 173) suggests that legal reparations were in train for some time, but without any clear reason for such a situation

SEVEN

Shadow Earls

1230s–1370s

Having left the troubles outlined in Chapter 6 behind us, we move forward into a new era, which is like 'the plunge of a train into a tunnel'[1] because of the paucity of the sources from Orkney and Caithness and the resulting darkness of this period of the earldoms' history. No longer do we have the saga author's personal account of events in the earldoms with descriptions of the geographical locations; nor do we have evidence telling us about the tensions and disputes between bishop and earl. The personalities are missing and the personal circumstances. There was no imperative to write about earls who were increasingly subjugated to the royal will (a point made in Section 2.1) and to a centralising bureaucracy. Moreover, the new earldom dynasty was far removed from the literary world of the Icelandic saga writers. In the place of the sagas we have a few charters, but the practice of drawing up land charters was adopted only slowly in the northern earldoms. The internal history of the earldoms is therefore limited primarily to the complex inheritance developments throughout the period covered by this chapter; but we will also be assessing the crucial position of the earls in the wider political relationship of Norway and Scotland.

7.1 THE ANGUS EARLS

There is enough evidence to show that the right to inherit the earldom of Caithness resided in a member of the family of the earls of Angus, and that right must have been strong and unchallengeable, as already on 2 October 1232, about the same time as the loss of 'the göding ship' (*gæðingaskip*), the title of earl of Caithness had been taken by a member of the house of Angus.[2] This was so close to the time when the ship was lost (in the autumn of 1232) that it is more probable that the Angus claim had been put forward already after the murder of Earl John.[3] This would indicate that the right of the Angus family to claim the earldom was closer than any of the earl's kin who went to Bergen

---

1 Clouston 1932, 215
2 Anderson, 1873, xlvi, n.1; Crawford, 1976–7, 109; 1985, 34
3 Crawford, 1971, 8

for the trial of Earl John's murderers. It must have passed to the Angus family through marriage with a female descendant of the earls, but was this Earl John's daughter, taken as hostage by King William in 1214, or was she a sister of Earl Harald *ungi*?[4]

The continuous use of the forename Magnus by the line of Angus earls suggests a kindred link with the Erlend line of earls. This name would of course have been particularly favoured in the Erlend line because Magnus Erlendsson's saintly reputation gave such a prestigious stamp to his kindred. It was noted above (see Section 6.3.1) how the miracles which were said to have been performed after the Battle of Wick – fought between the two Haralds of the Paul and Erlend lines – were believed to demonstrate the dead Harald *ungi*'s wish to go to Orkney and join his kinsmen, the saints Magnus and Rognvald. The marriage of one of Harald *ungi*'s sisters into the house of Angus is the most likely means by which the name Magnus became a marked feature of the Angus family dynasty.[5] There were three sisters (daughters of Ingirid and Erik 'Stay-Brails'), Ingibjorg, Elin and Ragnhild (*OS*, Chapter 104). Ragnhild is said to have been married to Lifolf *skalli* ('pate'), Harald *ungi*'s supporter in Caithness, and it is possible, although unproven, that either Ingibjorg or Elin was married to Earl Gilchrist of Angus. Earl Magnus II (the first Orkney earl of the Angus line) is likely to have been their son. The sisters had a brother who was called Magnus *mangi* but he was killed at the Battle of Sogn with King Magnus Erlingsson (*OS*, Chapter 109) (see Figure 7.1).

7.1.1 *Royal reorganisation in the north*

The route though which the claim to the earldom of Caithness was transmitted to the Angus family is unproven because of the few sources available. When the male line died out, as was the case on the death of Earl John without an heir (his son Harald having drowned in 1226), the title and associated earldom lands were evidently passed via a female member of the alternative earldom line to her male offspring who would have been thoroughly assimilated into the mainstream Scottish nobility.

The Crown would seize the opportunity to reorganise the conditions of the earls' position in the north according to its requirements and overall strategy. This was the means by which the Scottish Crown finally emasculated the independent troublesome northern earldom. We know that Earl John's

---

4 See Crawford, 1971, 9–12, for the alternative theories put forward by older historians.
5 Gray, 1922, 107–8, where he quotes Skene *in extenso* and agrees with the strength of the argument that the consistent use of the name Magnus for the Angus earls must reflect inheritance from the Erlend line of earls; Gray further argues that the son of one of Harald *ungi*'s sisters was also married to the nameless hostage daughter of Earl John

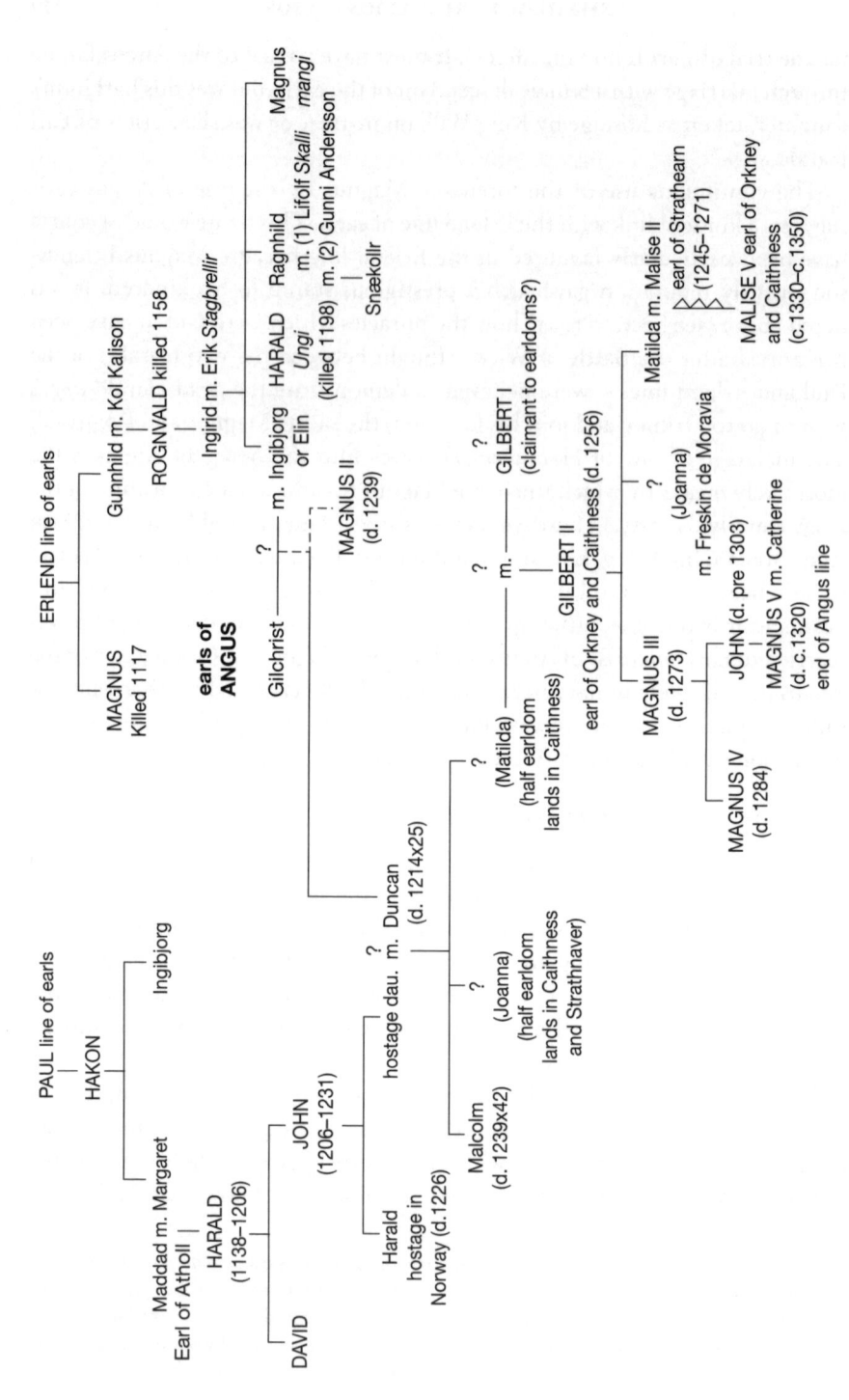

Figure 7.1 Tree of the possible means of inheritance of the earldoms by the Angus family.

daughter was taken as a hostage in 1214 (see Section 6.6.1); this was standard procedure by which an earldom family would be tied into the Scottish nobility through an arranged marriage, and the opportunity to marry her to someone suitable would not be missed, although we have no more evidence about this daughter or whom she married.

Some form of reorganisation process can be dimly glimpsed through surviving documentary sources. As we have already seen (see Section 6.6.2), the southern province of Sutherland was detached in stages from the Caithness earldom, a process which was finally completed in the 1230s when Hugh de Moravia had his position and lands elevated into a separate earldom of Sutherland. At roughly the same time we have evidence that an Earl Magnus (II) was given grants of the Caithness earldom in two halves, called the earldom of north Caithness and the earldom of south Caithness, although only after the earldom appears to have been held temporarily by others.[6] What exactly constituted the two halves of Caithness is unclear, but they presumably reflected earlier land divisions among earldom family members.[7] These charters were no doubt granted by King Alexander with the usual feudal conditions and promises, and we can guess that this process was completed during a visit by the king to Inverness in 1236. It is significant that this Earl Magnus (II) was present in the royal retinue during the king's stay in the north, evidenced from his witnessing a royal charter at this time, the first known occasion when an earl of Caithness witnessed a Scottish king's charter. It can be assumed that the king had by this time granted Magnus his two halves of Caithness. It may well have been the occasion also when the Sutherland earldom was created, and 'taken' (*cepit*) from Earl Magnus, as the 'Genealogy of the Earls' says.[8] The reason for depriving the new earl of the territory of Sutherland, which had formerly been part of the earldom of Caithness, is not known, but the circumstances of the failure of the direct line and the installation of a new dynasty in Caithness provided Alexander II with the opportunity to take such high-handed action.[9]

As regards the new earl's position in Orkney it can be assumed that he received a grant of the earldom because the death of Earl Magnus II is recorded in the Icelandic Annals in 1239, which designated him 'earl in the Orkneys' (*IA*,

---

6 Gray, 1922, 104–5; Crawford, 1976–7, 110; 1985, 34. This suggests that there was a hiatus while the circumstances of the inheritance were established and the rightful heir was acknowledged. *CP*, x, App. A, examines the parentage of Earl Magnus (II)
7 Despite assumptions to the contrary by some older historians (for example, Clouston, 1932, 221), it does not appear that south Caithness equalled Sutherland (Crawford, 1976–7, 110, n.7; 1985, 34, n.85)
8 *Bann. Misc.*, iii, 77; Crawford, 1971, 105
9 There was also Alexander's wish and need to reward William, son of Hugo Freskin, for his long and loyal service during the rebellions in the north (Gray, 1922, 80)

130). This is the only information which can be used to show that Magnus in all probability must have been given a grant of the earldom of Orkney by King Hakon Hakonsson, which otherwise goes unrecorded in the Norwegian sources. Following his death it appears that there was another break in the direct inheritance of the earldom, and earls called Gilbert are noted in the 'Genealogy of the Earls', in the Icelandic Annals and also in Scottish sources. The 'Genealogy' mentions two earls called Gilbert, the first said to have succeeded Earl Magnus, with no relationship specified, the second said to have been the son of the first one. The existence of the first Earl Gilbert has been doubted, but the 'Genealogy's' sparse information can be read as indicating that the first Gilbert may not have been successful in getting possession of both earldoms. It simply says that he succeeded Earl Magnus II, but then that his son Gilbert II succeeded him and '*josit* [enjoyed] *the Eirldomis of Orchadie and Cathanie in Scotland*'. The compiler was stressing the second Gilbert's established position in both earldoms.[10] We can assume that this second Gilbert did indeed visit Norway and receive a grant of the title and of his earldom rights, for his death in the year 1256 is noted in the Icelandic Annals where he is called 'Gilbert, earl in the Orkneys' (*Gibbon, jarl in Orkneyjum*) (*IA*, 133). In the following year his daughter Matilda, married to Malise (II) earl of Strathearn, is called 'daughter of sir Gilbert, former earl of Orkney and Caithness'.[11]

The earl, or earls, called Gilbert must therefore have had a recognised heritable claim to the title which they were granted after the death of Earl Magnus II in 1239, and they continued to give the name Magnus to the eldest son through the second half of the thirteenth and into the early fourteenth century. It is not at all clear what relationship the first Earl Gilbert had with Earl Magnus II, and the fact that no relationship between the two is mentioned in the 'Genealogy of the Earls' indicates that they were not father and son, although certainly related in some degree.[12]

A complicating factor is the evidence that there were heiresses around whose claim on the Caithness earldom lands was strong and who are known to have inherited the earldom, or to have passed that claim on to their descendants.

10   *Bann.Misc.*, iii, 77. A shortened form of the 'Genealogy' was added to Bower's *Scotichron.* in the Corpus MS (see Section 1.3.2) where it is said that Gilbert II was a son of Magnus II. However, this differs from the full version of the 'Genealogy' and it is suspected that Bower's scribe had simply elided the information in the fuller version which he was copying and missed out Gilbert I, thus making Gilbert II appear to be the son of Magnus II instead of the son of Gilbert I
11   *Inchaffray Chrs.*, 76
12   Gray (193, 116) thought he was either a son or brother of Earl Magnus. See Crawford (1971, 13–14), for discussion of the problem

7.1.2 *Joanna and Matilda, heiresses to the earldom lands*

An enigmatic reference, which has survived only in the Panmure Codex,[13] indicates that two sisters inherited the earldom of Caithness, or at least that the claim to the earldom reverted to them after it had been held by another individual for a brief period of time.[14] The Latin sentence suggests that they may have been claiming their inherited rights for some while, but exactly how that right had come to them is not explained (although it may have been in the missing section of the document).[15] The sisters were called Joanna and Matilda, and the former is quite well-documented as the wife of Freskin de Moravia, a nephew of William de Moravia, earl of Sutherland; the fragmentary account simply mentions that she was the elder sister and was married to *domino Freskino* ('sir Freskin'). The identification of the other sister, Matilda, has proved something of a problem, but she was clearly an heiress of importance.[16] Joanna's marriage to a member of the de Moravia family certainly tells us of *her* importance as a northern heiress, so important that she was married into the family which had been promoted by the king as the counterpoise to the native earldom dynasty. There is further evidence which points to her high status.

Joanna is well-known to historians of north Scotland because of her landholding position in Strathnaver. She gave a bloc of lands in upper Strathnaver to the cathedral church of the diocese of Moray sometime prior to 1269, for the perpetual service of two chaplains. The lands are named and were only a portion of her total landholding in Strathnaver.[17] She is called in that charter *nobilis mulier, Domina Johanna* ('the noble woman Lady Joanna'). This was not

13 See discussion of this Codex and its contents in Section 2.5 above
14 '... for a year and a half, and died a virgin without progeny, and thus the earldom reverted to the first sisters Joanna and Matilda, of whom Joanna, the eldest sister, was married to Sir Freskin as noted above. Scarmclath 7 August 1373'. This was written at Scarmclath in Caithness evidently at a time in the fourteenth century when there was uncertainty about the inheritance of the Caithness earldom lands; and referring either to the situation after 1239 in the previous century, or referring to the period after the demise of the Angus earldom in the 1320s (as argued by A. MacEwen, 2011, 16)
15 The existence of this fragment from the Panmure Codex detailing the right of the two sisters to the earldom is printed in *Banntyne Misc.*, iii, 43: . . . *per annum et dimedium, et obit virgo sine prole, et sic dictus comitatus revertebatur ad primas sorores Johannam et Matildam, quequidem Johanna soror senior nupta fuit domino Freskino ut supra notatum est*. It is fully discussed in Crawford, 1971, 15–16; also 1976–7, 111–12; 1985, 36
16 Crawford, 1971, 16–17; 1985, 35–7; and 2011a, for recent analysis which was rebutted by A. MacEwen (2011, 18) who has proposed that Matilda should be identified as the Matilda who was the wife of Earl Malise (II) of Strathearn
17 *Moray Reg.*, no. 126; *CSR*, no. 13; Gray, 1922, 110. These lands were granted back to Reginald Cheyne, and his wife, Mary, one of Joanna's daughters by the bishop of Moray in an arrangement by which a rent of 12 marks would be paid twice yearly at the canonry in Elgin (see discussion of this charter in Crawford, 2000, 8–9).

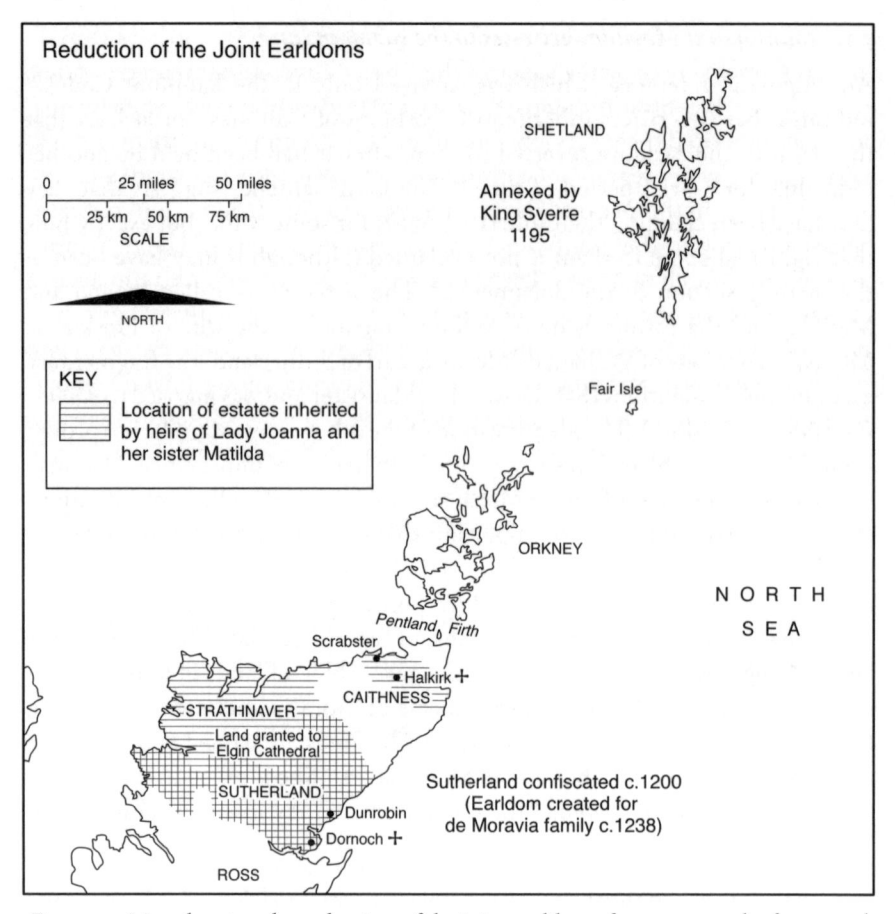

Figure 7.2 Map showing the reduction of the joint earldoms from 1200 to the fourteenth century.

the only land she held, as it is known from her daughters' inheritance that she had also had some of the lands of the earldom of Caithness – in accordance with the statement in the Latin fragment that the earldom of Caithness 'reverted' to her and her sister. How had these two sisters come to inherit that position? Her sister Matilda's name suggests that they were members of the Angus family.[18]

It has been suggested that Joanna had a right to these lands through a connection with the family of Moddan in Dale, whom we have already met (see

---

18   The name Matilda was used in the Angus family at this time, as also in the Orkney dynasty later in the century. The information from the Latin sentence that Joanna had a sister called Matilda was unknown to any of the older Scottish historians who have in the past attempted to explain Joanna's position, such as Skene (*CS*, iii, 448–53).

Section 4.4.3). That family were established in Dale (*i Dali*) in north Caithness, which is more likely to be the valley of the Thurso River rather than the valley of the Naver.[19] Was Strathnaver part of earldom territory? If it was, then Joanna must have inherited these earldom lands during her lifetime. Strathnaver was a division of the wider region of Caithness, which developed a separate identity from Caithness in this period. The first recorded use of the name is in the 1269 charter referring to the grant which Joanna made of lands in Upper Strathnaver to the Church of Moray. Later, in 1286, her possession of Strathnaver is designated as a separate feudal holding or *tenementum*.[20] In neither charter is it said to be in Caithness, only in the diocese of Caithness.[21] The *carta originalis* ('original charter') of Strathnaver is also referred to and this would have set out the terms on which the lands were held by Joanna, but which unfortunately has not survived. So the circumstances as to how, and why, these lands had come into Joanna's possession are quite unclear.

One thing we can be fairly certain about is that the feudal tenure which is evidently in place in 1269 would have been newly created by the Crown for the 'noble woman Lady Joanna' and her husband Freskin; if so, it would have been a part of the feudal reorganisation of the whole of Caithness which we have seen was already underway with the two grants of north and south Caithness to Earl Magnus instituted in the mid-1230s. It seems most likely that it was the feudal reorganisation of this *tenementum* which helped to create Strathnaver's separate identity.

Joanna's naming in the Strathnaver charter as *nobilis mulier* ('noble woman') with the distinguished title of *Domina* (Lady) may be taken as indicating that her claim came directly from one of the earls. Was that Earl John (1206–1231)? As the elder of two sisters, Joanna could have been named after her father – or grandfather.[22] The likely connection between Earl John's name and the heiress's name Joanna has been frequently made, always with the suggestion that she was the daughter of Earl John. The naming pattern might indeed indicate that her name was chosen by the hostage daughter *for her own daughter* in memory of her father, whose heiress she was.[23] As, however, there is no evidence whom

19 Gray, 1932, 110; Williams, 2007, 136–7
20 *Moray Reg.*, no. 263; *CSR*, no. 1
21 Crawford, 2000, 2–3; Strathnaver later became part of Sutherland, after the creation of the regality of Sutherland in the seventeenth century
22 Gray also suggested that Earl John himself was named after King John of England, with whom John's father, Earl Harald, was in close communication (Gray, 1922, 113; see above Section 6.3)
23 The name of her younger sister, Matilda, also had high-status associations, perhaps with particular reference to Countess Matilda, wife of Earl David of Huntingdon, brother of King William

the hostage daughter married, if she married at all, it is best to leave this as only a theoretical possibility. Perhaps more likely is the proposal that the two sisters could have been daughters of Earl Gilbert II, who died in 1256.[24] The 'Genealogy of the Earls' tells us that Earl Gilbert had a daughter called Matilda, although saying nothing about an elder sister called Joanna.[25] This Matilda married Malise II, earl of Strathearn, and she carried the claim to the earldom of Caithness along with some of the earldom lands which were eventually inherited by her great-grandson, Malise V in 1330 (see Section 7.6.2).

The discovery of the fragment in the Panmure Codex has shown that there were two important sisters who shared the inheritance of the lands of the earldom of Caithness, either on the death of Earl Magnus II in 1239 (during their lifetimes) or on the failure of the Angus line after the death of Earl Magnus V in c.1320 (long after their deaths).[26] The actual processes of apportioning the earldom lands, and the details of the marriages which were arranged for the final settlement are still open to conjecture.[27]

7.1.3 *The new dynasty's adjustment to the north*

All this evidence about Joanna and the other heirs to the earldom indicates that by the mid-thirteenth century the landholders in Caithness were of a different cultural elite from the previous earldom family members. With their familial and territorial connections now firmly linked to the south, it is perhaps unlikely that they would have spent very much time in northern Scotland. Lady Joanna and her husband Freskin would have dwelt primarily in his castle of Duffus on the rich laigh lands of Moray, or further south in Strabrock in West Lothian. The grant of her lands in upper Strathnaver to the cathedral church in Moray shows clearly where their prime loyalties and spiritual interests lay; and that was not in Caithness, or with the cathedral church of Dornoch, but in the province of Moray from which the de Moravia family took its name.

24 As suggested by Andrew MacEwen (2011, 18) who argues that the two heiresses were daughters of Earl Gilbert (II) and sisters of Earl Magnus (III) (2011, 17, 15) which possibility was also recognised in Crawford (1971, 16)
25 The absence of any reference to Joanna in the 'Genealogy' would be due to the fact that none of her descendants got possession of either earldom, whereas Matilda successfully passed the claim on to Earl Malise (V) of the Strathearn dynasty
26 This latter suggestion would mean that Earl Magnus (V) left an under-age heir (the one mentioned in the Panmure fragment, who died unmarried without any children). It is indeed likely that Magnus V's widow Katherine was active on behalf of an under-age son between the death of her husband and the inheritance of Earl Malise of Strathearn in c.1330 (see Section 7.6)
27 Another claimant to the earldom is documented in 1330 when Simon Fraser presented a complaint relating to the earldom of Caithness on behalf of his wife Margaret, *unius heredis comitis de Caithnes* (*APS*, i, 551; *RMS*, i, App.ii, 716; Skene, 1880, iii, 450; Crawford, 1971, 25, 41)

The new political scenario created by the de Moravia family's rise to political and territorial dominance in north Scotland resulted from the successful reorganising policies of the two kings William and Alexander. It was achieved by determined pressure on the native earldom dynasty, and the insertion of members of the de Moravia family who were loyal to the Crown. The creation of the new comital lordship of Sutherland (1230), the contrived election of a bishop of the same family (1222/3) and the arranged marriage of an earldom heiress to another member of the same family (c.1245–50) are fine examples of the powers of feudal kingship to manipulate political, ecclesiastical and social circumstances in a remote part of the kingdom to its own advantage. In this process the kings were much aided by natural disaster such as the loss of the Orkney earldom elite in the *gæðingaskip* and the recurrent breaks in the male line of heirs, allowing the kings to arrange marriage contracts of the surviving heiresses with suitable members of the Scottish feudal nobility.

What impact did the introduction of a new line of earls have on the situation in the north? First and foremost it must have been the case that the inheritance of the Caithness earldom by members of the Angus dynasty through the female line strengthened the Scottish element in the earldom's history. This was of course what the kings had intended, and the different parts of Caithness were now firmly held by feudal charter on terms and conditions which were most probably in accordance with usual Scottish comital arrangements. The earls themselves would have dealt with their lands in Caithness in accordance with established feudal convention, with which they were familiar (as we know they were doing later in the century), although the tenurial arrangements of the farmers (*bondi*) may have continued according to the traditional Norse custom.

The establishment of the earls in Caithness now came first, and only once the recognised heir had inherited his Scottish earldom would he claim his rights in Orkney and go to receive a grant from the king in Norway. This is certainly different from the previous situation when Orkney was the prime component of the dual earldoms, and in this respect, as in others, 1231 saw the end of an era. How the Angus earls coped with the very different social and cultural circumstances in their joint earldoms is a complete unknown. To whom did they turn for advice as to their conduct in the very different world of Norwegian power politics? Possibly the churchmen in office in Orkney at the time.

The Orkney earldom by this date (and since 1195) was a changed dignity, which had to be claimed by a descendant of the previous earl, and in the post-1231 circumstances that would be the heir who inherited the earldom of Caithness. The Orkney earldom was then granted on certain rigorous conditions, dictated by the king of Norway, and the earl had to accept that he ran his island earldom in conjunction with the royal official, the sysselman.

The assumption by the Orkney historian J.S. Clouston was that the Angus earls 'had only a nominal and titular connection with the isles'[28] and that it was doubtful whether Orkney was ever more than an occasional residence, or whether they in any 'real sense' identified with its affairs.[29] This is a very difficult area to make any judgement about as we have so little evidence of the earls' activities. Where did these earls reside? We have no evidence that they retained any landed possessions in their former home territory in Angus, and the separation of their earldom title from that of the earldom of Angus is certain.[30] As with any feudal lords, they would move around their estates, and if they had no others, then they would have to reside on their northern estates. The impression that their association with Orkney did become firmly established, certainly later in the century, is discussed below.

7.2 INSTALLATION AS EARLS OF ORKNEY – HIRÐSKRÁ

First we will consider the changed position of the Orkney earl in Norway, during a period when the kings were developing their authority and administration along the lines of western European feudal kingdoms. As royal appointees to the earldom of Orkney the earls had an official position with certain known responsibilities, which they promised to adhere to when installed as earls. They were members of the royal hird (*hirð*), the king's following of warriors with particular obligations to serve the king; and in the code of conduct for members of the hird called *Hirðskrá*, the earls of Orkney have their own particular place.[31] Along with earls appointed over Iceland, they are distinguished from earls appointed over Norwegian inland territory as those 'whom the king sets over his skattlands'.[32] In the case of Orkney they are said to be given their title on the conditions which were arranged in the agreement between King Sverrir and Earl Harald (see Section 6.2.2), as also according to the 'special arrangements' made in the settlement between King Magnus Hakonsson and Earl Magnus Gilbertsson in 1267 (see Section 7.4.1).

The clause following[33] gives details of the process of investiture of an earl

---

28 Clouston 1932, 228
29 Imsen (2000, 174–5, 2003, 76–7) also states that these earls spent 'most of their time on the Scottish mainland' and 'for longer and longer periods of time preferred to stay in their mainland fiefs'
30 One piece of evidence shows that the titles were held jointly for a brief period, when Malcolm who was earl of Angus at the time appears as a witness as 'earl of Angus and Katanie' (Caithness) in 1232, before Earl Magnus' right to Caithness was recognised
31 The surviving texts of *Hirðskraa* date from later in the thirteenth century, but some of the provisions date back to earlier in the century (Imsen, ed., 2000a, 27; 2000b, 166) and these would have applied at the time of the Angus earls.
32 Imsen, ed., 2000a, 81 (Chapter 15); Wærdahl, 2011, 83–4
33 Imsen, ed., 2000a, 82–3 (Chapter 16)

and regulations concerning his conduct. At a 'public meeting' (*þing*) he was given the title of 'jarl' and led forward by the king to the high seat, where he was seated, 'a good distance out from himself (the king)'. The new earl was then presented with a sword and standard after which he had to swear an oath on holy relics, the same oath as for a duke.[34] He promised to be obedient and faithful to the lord king, both secretly and publicly, and to hold his 'grant of lands' (*luta landz*) in accordance with the conditions imposed. He would render all obedience and observe all the oaths the king had sworn to the people of the land.

The honour and privileges accorded to an earl are specified along with the restrictions.[35] He could have his standard borne before him when he rode or rowed into town, but not if the king preceded him. He could have his military following when not in the king's presence, but it was never to number more than six. An earl had full governmental powers over his earldom, which included all judicial fines but these were to be taken according to the law and with the provision of mercy.[36] An earl must never alienate any of the lands he ruled over.[37] He was not to have a bigger retinue than the king unless with permission (and the matter of the size of his hird features prominently). Nor could he associate with any men who were opponents of the king or against whom the king harboured anger.

In times of war military support had of course to be rendered by the earl and all his men, while reciprocal help was to be given to the earl in his need by the king as good men thought advisable. The duty of provision of assistance in peaceful or unpeaceful conditions and the requirement for the earl to accompany any royal expedition is stressed. Watch duty and reconnoitring were to be carried out together if the king and earl had their followings on joint military activities, while the drawing of lots and division of booty were to be performed according to allocation of numbers (this could be one of the earliest clauses). There is focus on the necessity for the earl's loyalty, while the circumstances of any accusations of treachery or unreliability are given detailed consideration as to how such cases were to be dealt with.[38] If the earl failed to attend the

---

34   Imsen, ed., 2000a, 71 (Chapter 17); see summary in Thomson, 2001, 180
35   Imsen, ed., 2000a, 84–6 (Chapter 17)
36   As already seen (see Section 6.2.2), Earl Harald was only allowed to keep half of the *sakøre*, the judicial fines from Orkney.
37   These were the estates which the earl was granted to hold for the duration of his lifetime consisting of the ancient manor farms ('bordlands') and 'auld erledome' estates which the earldom family had acquired over the centuries, plus the 'kingslands' or royal estates probably originating in the lands confiscated after the Eyiaskeggjar rising of 1193 (see Section 6.2.2). See Marwick (1952, 192), Thomson (2001, 222–6) and Wærdahl (2011, 76) on the different categories of earldom land
38   The details of how the case of an earl accused of treachery was to be dealt with might be usefully considered to apply to the situation in which Earl Harald found himself when at

king, and his treason was notorious, then he would be considered guilty, and his followers and those who were loyal to him would all be considered to be *ubota menn* ('non-compensationable').

These terms were applicable to all those who had the dignity of earl (not that there were very many in thirteenth-century Norway), and not all earls were of like standing with the earls of Orkney. Usually earls were given their titles for life, as a mark of honour or of privilege for foremost members of the royal family. Indeed, *Hirðskrá*[39] says that there were three ways in which the king bestowed the title of jarl in Norway:

> to his legitimate sons, sometimes his legitimate brothers or anyone closely related. To whom he granted those parts of the kingdom where he thought best, and on those conditions which he ordained. But this was never hereditary even if such a claim was made. The strict restriction is repeated; 'it is first of all made known that such earldoms never have been heritable and never have been inherited, as it appears' (*Er det da aller først gjørt vitterlig at slike jarledømmer aldri har vært til arvs og aldri har gått i arv, slik det er nok av døme på*)
>
> Secondly, there was no part of the country which was customarily designated as an earldom, but the kings offered earls such pieces of territory as they judged best (sometimes in Frostathingslaw, sometimes in Gulathingslaw, sometimes in Viken and most often in Oppland), and sometimes spread all over different parts of the country in small components. Very often the kings have taken back that which they gave to an earl in one part of the country and granted him lands in another part. There are no farms, landed property or odal land in any place in Norway which can be called earls' lands, but each had so much and on those conditions which the kings have thought best.
>
> A third point (which judicious men have most preference for) relates to situations when wise kings have frequently had to deal with complaints by earls, sometimes about themselves, sometimes about their predecessors; it is therefore particularly appropriate that the king has the power to respect his patrimony and promote him whom he finds most loyal and who applies himself to fulfilling his command, both inside the country and abroad. Because the whole land is his (the king's) odal and inheritance, and it is not certain if that had gone better even if any other were tried.[40]

It is interesting to compare these regulations with the circumstances of the earls of Orkney, whose position was quite distinctive, for they had an acknowledged

---

King Sverrir's mercy in 1195 (see Chapter 6)

39 Imsen, ed., 2000a (Chapter 14)
40 Author's translation of Norwegian translation (Imsen, ed., 2000a, 79) of Old Norse text. A fourth clause is added saying that for long periods there have not been earls in Norway and that situation has pleased the people best, as 'the lesser folk's rights were seldom served best when lordship was divided among many' (Imsen, ed., 2000a, 81)

hereditary right to claim their title, which made them a very different species.[41] There is no mention of this hereditary right in Chapter 15 (about earls in the skattlands) where the earls of Orkney are lumped together with the earl whom the king set over Iceland.[42] The kings do not ever appear to have attempted to ignore this hereditary claim, which is rather surprising when the matter of heredity of an earldom within the country was so strictly legislated against. When the break in the inheritance after the death of Earl John exposed the weakness of the earldom dynastic situation this might have been taken as an opportunity by King Hakon to attempt to bring the earldom permanently into the royal administration system, in the same way as Shetland had been absorbed for the previous forty years. But he did not do so, which suggests that the Orkney earldom's heritable status was considered too established to be changed (as also in 1308, nearly eighty years later).[43]

7.2.1 *The earls' position*

We know nothing of the circumstances as to when and how Earl Magnus II visited Norway to present his claim, but, as already noted, the inheritance of the Caithness earldom probably took priority on that occasion. That inheritance, and the evidence that Earl Magnus' grant of the earldoms of north and south Caithness had been made by the Scottish king in the mid-1230s must have been presented as a strong and convincing argument for the validity of his claim to be granted the Orkney earldom as well. Even though it should have been simple for King Hakon to refuse to acknowledge that claim and to govern the islands entirely through his sysselmen he does not appear to have considered that possibility. Indeed, such a royal official would have been appointed already in 1232 to succeed the captured Hanef *ungi* and to attend to royal interests in Orkney. The fact that the king accepted Earl Magnus' claim and acknowledged the strength of his right to inherit the title must be taken as evidence that the king and his advisers felt this was the best course to take for the safe governance of this skattland territory.

We can only wonder whether Earl Magnus II was granted his title as Earl John and David had been in 1210 (see Section 6.6.1), although that is unlikely as he had not committed any breach of trust, as they had by not attending the

---

41 Imsen, 2000, 168; 2003, 69; Wærdahl, 2011, 162
42 There was only ever one earl in Iceland, Gissur Thorvaldsson, who was named as earl by Hakon Hakonsson in 1241 as the promoter of the king's policy to bring Iceland under Norwegian royal authority (Wærdahl, 2011, 91–99).
43 Even when Hakon V abolished the title of earl in *den store skipan* of 1308 an exception was made for the earldom of Orkney, as also for royal princes (Helle, 1974, 264; Imsen, 2000, 168). Wærdahl (2011, 162) comments that 'Tradition and history combine to explain why the earldom of Orkney survived'

king in Norway for the renewal of their father's grant (who had died four years previously). Was Magnus granted it on similar terms to those arranged with Earl Harald *ungi*, who was the member of the Erlend line who had been killed while fighting for the perpetuation of that line's claim against the overbearing Harald Maddadson? The likely kindred link of the Angus earl with the Erlend line (as suggested above) may have given Earl Magnus II good standing in King Hakon's eyes, and may have been presented as a favourable factor by contemporary churchmen.[44]

Another useful comparison which can be made concerns the conditions of appointment of jarls within Norway. The king's freedom to make such conditions as he thought best for the earl's office is stressed repeatedly, as well as his stated freedom regarding which parts of the kingdom and which royal lands an earl was allowed to hold. The king had complete freedom to dictate the terms of the earl's appointment and these would have been adjusted according to the political circumstances and the character of the individual being honoured. We might expect therefore that the conditions of the earls of Orkney's appointment would vary according to circumstances. It should also be noted that Chapter 15 was drawn up after the events of the disastrous expedition of 1263 and the Treaty of Perth of 1266, when Earl Magnus III had visited King Hakon in order to come to terms after his failure to participate in the naval campaign to the Hebrides (see Section 7.3.3). The settlement of 1267 was of course made in the aftermath of those dramatic events, and would probably affect the terms upon which the earl was reappointed. But for his father (Earl Gilbert II) and the Angus relative who preceded him (Earl Magnus II) the terms of appointment might have been quite different and less restrictive.

The matter of royal lands and the issue of land taxes (skats) brings up a very difficult question. Within Norway the earls had almost full royal authority in their 'len' and all royal income.[45] The details of how income from the islands was collected in from Orkney and how it was distributed are never mentioned in *Hirðskrá*, and there is no evidence about this until the late medieval Rentals.[46] The rents from the royal estates would have gone into the royal treasury after 1195, as also half of the judicial fines (see Section 6.2.2). But what happened to the skats, which were collected in from all 'odal' lands in Orkney? From the later Rentals it is known exactly how much was collected and what a rich

---

44 Current circumstances in the Orkney Church are very poorly recorded. However, the bishop in office at the time, Jofreyr (Godfrey), would appear to have been a royal Norwegian appointment (he had been provost of Tønsberg). He appears to have suffered from some paralytic illness (Watt, *Fasti*, 250; Thomson, 2001, 137)
45 Helle, 1974, 210
46 Thomson, 1996

source of income it was. We cannot believe that these would all have been left in the hands of the earl after the imposition of terms in 1195 and 1210. So did they all become part of royal income from the islands? It is most likely that there would have been some division of the skats, and that this division would vary according to the circumstances of each earl's appointment.[47] If the family's right to claim the earldom was recognised after the break in the direct line in 1231–2, we can assume that possession of the earls' own odal family lands would have been acknowledged. Would Earl Magnus II also have been granted the rights to *some* of the land taxes paid from farms throughout the earldom when he came to claim the earldom from King Hakon? We cannot expect that the earls of Orkney would have been appointed on exactly the same terms as earls within Norway. The way in which the submissions of 1195 and 1267 are referred to gives a clear indication that the earls of Orkney were treated differently – and particularly so because of their disloyal, or even treacherous, behaviour at these times. The events of 1263 provide a dramatic demonstration of how Earl Magnus III could be caught on the 'horns of a dilemma' regarding his loyalty to two kings, as we will now see.

7.3 1263 AND THE PROBLEM OF DIVIDED LOYALTY

On Earl Gilbert's death in 1256 his son Magnus (III) succeeded him, as we know from the 'Genealogy of the Earls' (which, unusually, also provides the information that Magnus' sister was called Matilda).[48] He was the unfortunate earl who had to face the situation of hostility between his two overlords, the kings of Norway and Scotland. The inherent problem facing the holder of the dual earldoms has already been mentioned in Section 6.1, arising out of a situation whereby a single individual was both an earl of the king of Scots and an earl of the king of Norway. If and when his overlords fell out, and the relationship between them deteriorated into outright hostilities, the choice facing the earl was intolerable, for he was inevitably going to offend one of his overlords by supporting the other one. By the mid-thirteenth century the kings of Scotland and Norway ruled over kingdoms with defined geographical limits, although in the case of Norway these were maritime borders which stretched across the

---

47 The late medieval Rentals refer to the king's skats and the earl's skats, showing that by the end of the medieval earldom the skats were certainly divided between them. Steinar Imsen (2000a, 177; 2008; 2009, 18) expresses different opinions about this matter; Wærdahl (2011, 166–8) inclines towards the view that the kings always had royal sysselmen in the earldom to collect in their skats, fines and rents; see Crawford (2011, 48–52) 'Recipients of Skatts after 1195' for my recent consideration of the problem

48 The reason for the inclusion of Matilda, Gilbert's daughter in the 'Genealogy' was because the Strathearn line inherited their right to the earldoms in 1330 from her, as noted above, n.25)

North Sea and included the Northern Isles of Orkney and Shetland, as well as the Hebrides (*Suðreyar*, 'Southern Isles'). The earls of the Angus line accepted this situation when they were granted the earldom of Caithness and sought the acknowledgement of the kings of Norway of their claim to the earldom of Orkney. Presumably they never envisaged the possibility of their two overlords coming to war.

However, the aspirations of ambitious kings did lead to a situation in which they clashed on the western maritime frontier. As far as the Norwegian king was concerned it was a matter of protecting his overlordship of skattlands which had been part of the Norwegian king's dominion since 1098. King Hakon certainly did not appear to contemplate invading Scotland or extending the bounds of his authority beyond what had earlier belonged to his predecessors (although that was mostly only nominal).[49] The Scottish kings were, however, proactive in pressing their advantage on the west coast, according to the situation in the rest of their kingdom. This could only be pursued effectively if the rulers in the area recognised that their primary allegiance was to the king of Scots; from the 1220s onwards, feudal lords who were answerable to the king and linked in with Scottish affairs were placed in positions of authority in the west.[50] In 1244, King Alexander made a diplomatic approach to King Hakon in an attempt to acquire possession of the Hebrides (which the Scots believed had been won unfairly by King Magnus 'Barelegs'), and even offered to pay silver to acquire possession. That offer was rebuffed and so Alexander prepared for an expedition, primarily directed against Ewen of Argyll. The dilemma of dual allegiance also faced Ewen, and the charge of treason is said by the chronicler Matthew Paris to have been laid against him by the Scottish king[51] which demonstrates the extremely dangerous conditions such vassals found themselves in, in a situation of enmity between their two overlords. However, that danger was averted temporarily by the death of King Alexander in Kerrera on his expedition to the west in 1249.[52]

After Alexander III assumed personal control of government in 1260 or 1261 the issue of the ownership of the Hebrides was raised again. Further approaches to King Hakon met a stone wall, as a result of which attacks on some of the

49   Helle, 1973, 8, although see below for the demands which King Hakon made on the men of Caithness
50   McDonald, 1997, 98
51   *SAEC*, 360–1; McDonald, 1997, 100–101
52   King Alexander's dream on the eve of his death in 1249 is recorded in *Hacon's Saga* (Chapter 265) when he is said to have been visited by the three men who were interpreted as Sts Olaf, Magnus and Columba, and who were warning him to turn back from his intended hostile action in the Hebrides. This is an interesting indication of the importance of the saints of the Norwegian dominions around the coasts of Scotland who it was thought might influence the actions of the Scottish king

islands in the west were orchestrated. The 1262 campaign against the inhabitants of the Isle of Skye seems to have been directed deliberately against the authority of the king of Man, who had Skye under his direct lordship, and it was thereby a challenge to the authority of King Hakon.[53] Raids by an individual like the earl of Ross on one island are one thing, but a full naval expedition by a king of Norway across open seas in order to reassert his authority over those distant islands is something else. We need to understand the motivation and ability of King Hakon to achieve this, and to assess the impact such a naval expedition had on the earldoms of Orkney and Caithness and the earl of the time, Magnus (III) Gilbertsson. It would appear that an important consideration for going to war in 1263 was the king's concern for Norwegian dominion over the Shetland islands and Orkney earldom.[54] This factor contributed to King Hakon's decision to gather together his great naval force and commit his kingdom to the expense, and himself to the dangers, of an expedition in far waters.

7.3.1 King Hakon Hakonsson's motivation and preparation

In 1263, Hakon had been reigning for forty-six years. But his undisputed position of authority was only secured in the 1240s after he had succeeded in dominating his political rival Jarl Skuli, and had gained papal dispensation for his coronation, which took place in the summer of 1247. In the 1250s, his heir Magnus was appointed king and crowned in 1257, along with his queen, followed by a law in 1260 which made the Crown automatically hereditary in Hakon's family.[55] This strong position of legal authority vested in the king and his successor was the basis for the establishment of agencies of central government such as a chancery, a permanent council, and national assemblies of prelates, magnates and representatives from the free population. In effect Norway was thus in the process of becoming a medieval state on the model of other national monarchies, and in line with the rest of Europe.[56] The king's authority was enhanced by the building of castles, churches and palaces, exemplified by the fine stone building on the quay in Bergen ('Hakon's Hall'), modelled on Henry III's Westminster Hall[57] (see Colour plate 31).

This new position of internal strength was reflected in the ambitious foreign policy which was advanced in the 1250s, when the 'leidang' (*leiðangr*, national naval levy) was summoned from the whole country for negotiations with the

53 McDonald, 1997, 106
54 Helle, 1973, 9–10
55 Helle, 1973, 11
56 Bagge, 2011, *passim*, 290–2
57 Ekroll, 1997, 46; Paulsen, 2011, 64–81

rulers of Sweden and Denmark. Over 300 ships were reportedly called out for a raid against Denmark and for the following peace negotiations, which constituted 'fore-runners' for the 1263 expedition, and which were intended to 'force negotiations and concessions by a show of naval strength'.[58] This expansion south and east is a new change of direction which was going to dominate Norwegian foreign policy in the future, but Hakon also maintained the traditional connections with the isles in the west and with Iceland and Greenland to the north-west. These last two both submitted and became integral parts of the Norwegian kingdom in the last years of Hakon's reign. So the 1263 expedition should be regarded and understood in the light of his remarkable success in pursuing power and authority along the frontiers of the kingdom in the previous decades. It was in the same way part of the old king's policy of asserting claims and receiving recognition in the surrounding maritime regions. Material and economic advantage were not the driving factors but rather prestige for a king whose authority had been unchallenged for over two decades.[59]

Of course it was mistaken confidence, and the rationale for setting out on such an expedition was misconceived. The world in the west had changed, and was changing fast. The days of the early medieval thalassocracy were over, when the Vikings ruled the waves and when the earls of Orkney had authority stretching from the northern tip of Shetland to the southern Hebrides (or even eastern Ireland: see Section 4.2). By the thirteenth century the sea road from Norway to Dublin via Orkney and the Hebrides was increasingly unimportant commercially. The north–south maritime axis decayed and new territorial links were beginning to cross from Scotland's political heartland to the Hebrides, and from Galloway to Ulster. Colonial ventures from England to Ireland and links from the Isle of Man to England were becoming the new state fault lines of national territorial ambition.[60] It is not to be expected that the Norwegians were aware of these changing geopolitical circumstances. However, they should have been aware of the ambition of the Scottish king and his growing ability to organise the resources of his kingdom on the northern and western maritime fringes.

We have seen in Chapter 6 how the previous two Scottish kings had cowed the men and earl of Caithness into submission by harsh fines and reprisals, in order to make this northern territory an integral part of their Scottish kingdom. King Alexander III benefited from that 'achievement' which enabled him to counter successfully the threat of any residual loyalty which the resident population of Caithness might have had for the Norwegian king, which might have inclined

58 Helle, 1973, 12
59 Ibid., 13; Andersen (1973, 27–32) examines the varying opinions of Norwegian historians about King Hakon's motivation and achievements
60 Thomson, 2001, 138

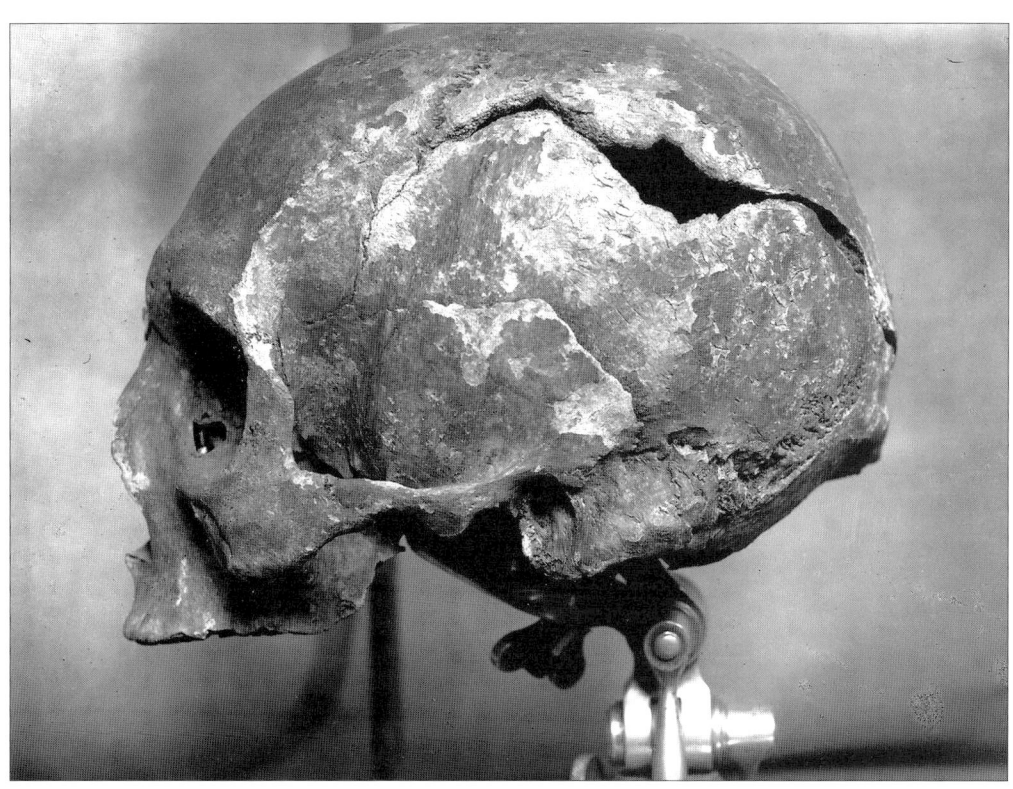

PLATE 1. The presumed skull of St Magnus, found secreted in a pillar on the south side of the choir of St Magnus Cathedral, Kirkwall, in 1919. The two splits back and front of the fissure are the result of blows from a sharp weapon, which is in accordance with some of the written sources' description that Magnus was killed by blows on his head from an axe. (Jesch and Molleson, 2005; Orkney Library and Archive)

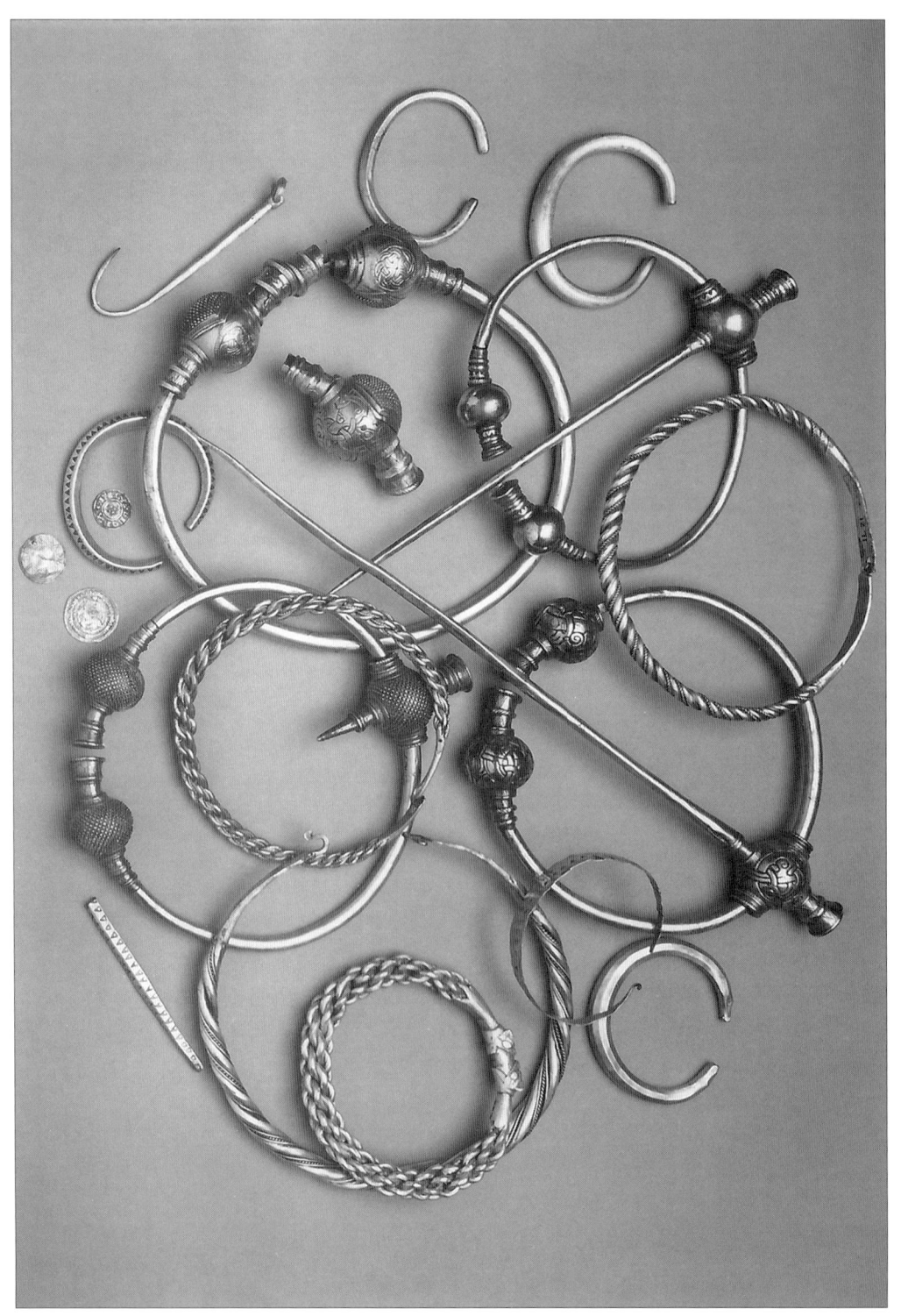

PLATE 2. Part of the Skaill hoard of Viking silver found in the west Mainland of Orkney in the middle of the nineteenth century which consisted of silver arm-rings, 'thistle-brooches', twisted silver necklets and bracelets and coins, as well as cut-up pieces of 'hack-silver'. The small wrist or arm-rings seen at the upper left, upper right and bottom are examples of the 'ring-money', discussed in Section 3.5.2. In total the Skaill hoard probably weighed 8kg. (© National Museums Scotland)

PLATE 3. Sketch of a boat-building yard near the woodlands of Easter Ross, with the woods of Guisachan behind (Crawford, 1995; drawing by Mike Taylor, Tain)

PLATE 4. The eastern extension of St Magnus Cathedral, probably built by Bishop Bjarni Kolbeinsson (1188–1223) to provide more space for pilgrims to the shrines of St Magnus and St Rognvald (© Crown Copyright, Historic Scotland)

PLATE 5a. (*Above*) Looking towards the west end of the church on the Brough of Birsay, showing the intended location of the tower. (Photo: author)

PLATE 5b. (*Right*) The plan of the church which shows the inserted niche altars at the north end of the nave and the semicircular apse probably added on to the square chancel. (After Radford, 1959; © Crown Copyright, Historic Scotland)

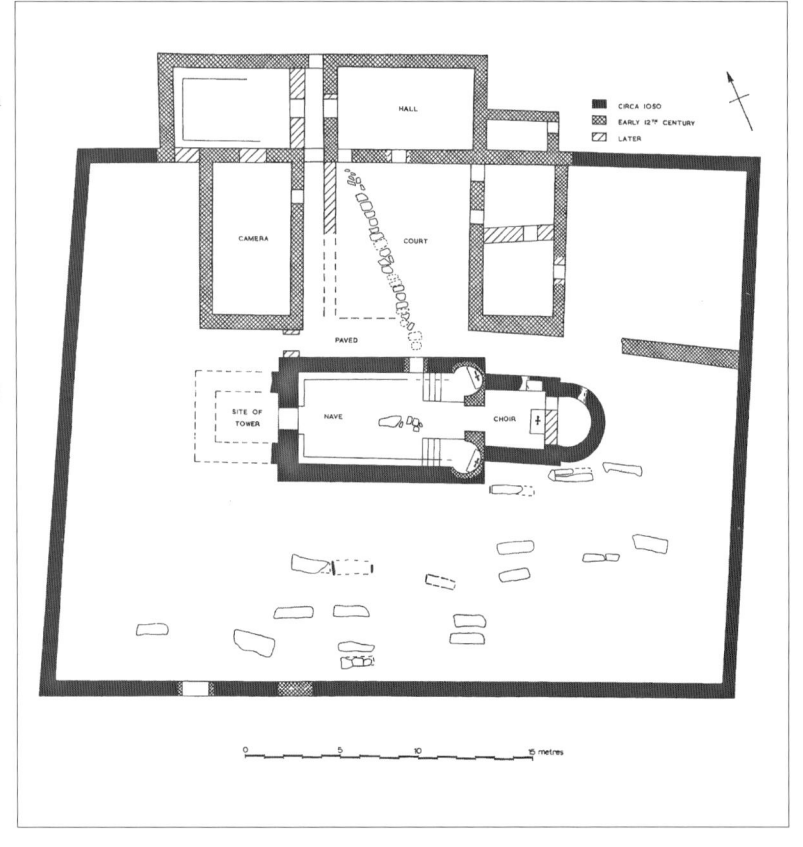

PLATE 6a and 6b. (*Above and overleaf*) Two views of the supposed head of King Magnus the 'Lawmender' in Stavanger Cathedral. (Photo: Morten Stige)

PLATE 6b.

PLATE 7. The supposed head of Erik Magnusson, elder son of King Magnus 'the Lawmender', in Stavanger Cathedral. After inheriting the throne in 1281, he married Margaret of Scotland, daughter of Alexander III, and their daughter Margaret, (the 'Maid of Norway') inherited the Scottish throne, but died in Orkney, at the age of nine, *en route* to Scotland in 1291 (see Chapter 7). (Photo: Morten Stige)

PLATE 8. The supposed head of Hakon Magnusson, younger son of King Magnus 'the Lawmender', also in Stavanger Cathedral. He was given the title of 'Duke' and granted a third of the kingdom as his ducal 'appanage', which included the skattlands of Shetland and Faeroe. Shetland's earliest document of 1299 was a letter addressed to Duke Hakon by the lawthingmen of Shetland (Colour plate 2). The indicator that he was a duke can be seen from the garland of flowers (*kranz*) worn around his head. Hakon succeeded his brother as king in 1299. (Photo: Morten Stige)

PLATE 9. Ravenscraig Castle, Fife. Old print dated 1839.

them to support Hakon's ambitions to reassert his authority in the islands to the west. We have none of the information which the saga has provided previously about the events and people of Caithness, but their dangerous and vulnerable frontier situation is very clearly demonstrated by the treatment they received in 1263 and the years following. The particular interest of the 1263 campaign for this present study is once more to see how this northern Scottish earldom suffered from being caught in the middle of the clash of loyalties engendered by the political situation. Their dilemma reflects the earl's, and that was because they were the residents of one half of his double earldom.

7.3.2 1263 naval expedition west

The campaign and King Hakon's preparations are fully recorded in the king's saga (*Hacon's Saga*, Chapters 316–26). The naval levy gathered at Bergen in May, and two men were sent to Shetland to procure pilots for navigating the sounds and sea passages; these were Jon Langlifsson[61] and Henry Scott, whose surname shows that he was of Scottish origin. They sailed to Shetland and then to Orkney where they found King Dougal of the Isles, then back to Bergen, perhaps taking Earl Magnus with them. Certainly Earl Magnus joined the levy and is said specifically to have sailed with the naval force west, having been given a 'good' long-ship by the king (*Hacon's Saga* Chapter 319). Of course, his presence was very important for the arrangements for the fleet's stay in the islands. Another notable figure accompanying the expedition was Gilbert bishop of Hamar, formerly archdeacon of Shetland, whose role as a high-ranking cleric and one who was able to negotiate with the Scots was exceedingly useful (and may indicate why the king was determined to get him appointed as bishop of Hamar in 1260; *Hacon's Saga*, Chapter 302).[62]

The king's fleet sailed out from Bergen in late June in fair weather and made the crossing to Shetland in two or three days (two nights at sea). The ships stayed there in *Breiðeyarsund* ('Broad-islands Sound') for nearly two weeks and then moved south to Orkney where they anchored in Elwick Bay in Shapinsay, conveniently close to Kirkwall. They were there for the feast of St Olaf (29 July) when the king heard mass in his 'land-tent', and feasted the ships' crews on board his own long-ship which he had had specially built for the expedition. Moving on to Rognvald's voe (St Margaret's Hope) the fleet lay at anchor for a

---

61 Probably a grandson of Earl Harald Maddadson whose daughter had the unusual name of *Langlif* ('long life')
62 It seems very likely (from his name – Gilbert – and from the fact that he had been archdeacon in Shetland; Watt and Murray, 2003, 339) that he was a member of the earldom family. If so, this suggests that a relative of Earl Gilbert was well-established in an ecclesiastical position in the Northern Isles before 1260

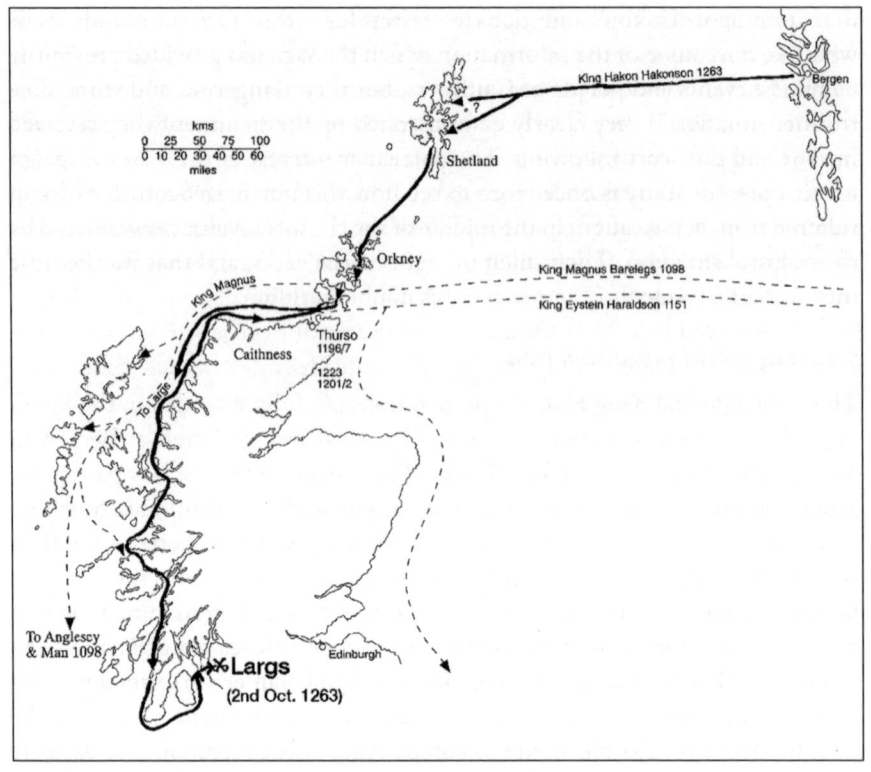

Figure 7.3 The route taken by King Hakon Hakonsson's fleet in 1263. (Based on author's map in MacNeill, P. and MacQueen, A., *Atlas of Scottish History to 1707* (1996), 448)

while, perhaps to collect in stores for the journey ahead. While there the saga reports that men were sent over to Caithness and 'laid a fine' on the people, in order to secure their submission. If they did not agree, they would have to 'undergo hard terms' (*Hacon's Saga*, Chapter 319). This is the first indication of the difficult circumstances lying ahead for the people of Caithness and the earl also, whose conflicting loyalties were going to be stretched impossibly at this testing time. So significant was this situation that the event is recorded in skaldic verse:

> First for life-ransom
> Took from Ness dwellers [*the people of Caithness*]
> That wise king of Northland
> A tribute for peace
>
> (*Hacon's Saga*, p.346)

The term used for 'fine' and 'tribute' (ON *gjald*) gives us no indication as to whether this was exacted in silver or in kind.[63] Whatever the nature of the demand it would not have enamoured the men of Caithness, who 'agreed to the fine'; nor would they have been pleased with Earl Magnus, whom they may have felt had failed to secure them any peaceful terms, or who had failed to assure the king of the peaceful intentions of his Caithness earldom. This harsh treatment may indeed have influenced the earl's subsequent behaviour. It is added that 'King Hakon sent men there to receive it', but this would not have included Earl Magnus. The next – and last – thing we hear of Earl Magnus is that he stayed behind in Orkney when the royal fleet sailed out across the Pentland Firth and on round Cape Wrath to the Hebrides, because more ships were arriving from the east.

7.3.3 *Earl Magnus Gilbertsson's circumstances*

The effect on Earl Magnus of this last great Norwegian expedition to Scotland is our main concern, so we will attempt to study the situation from the angle of the northern earldoms rather than the results of the campaign in the west and its effects on the kingdom of Scotland.[64] We have to put ourselves into the earl's shoes in order to try to understand his response in this difficult and dangerous situation.[65] He was an earl of two kingdoms and his loyalties were therefore split between two kings. The problem of divided loyalties has been raised already and the crisis brought on by King Hakon's aggressive campaign to restore his authority in the Hebrides in the face of Scottish opposition meant that Earl Magnus had a stark choice to make. Either he followed his Norwegian overlord to engage in a situation of conflict with his Scottish king, or he stayed out of the conflict and attempted to remain neutral. In some respects it might have been acceptable to his Norwegian king if he had remained behind in his Orkney earldom to attend to King Hakon's business there and make preparations for the returning fleet. But we know that he cannot have done that because when the Norwegian fleet sailed back north after the disastrous encounter at Largs in the Firth of Clyde (see Colour plate 32), there is no mention in *Hacon's Saga*

---

63 The record of a letter from the king of Norway to the men of Caithness is listed in the Scottish Treasury (*littera Regis Norwagie missa Cataniensibus*) (*APS*, I, 109) and possibly relates to this situation. Munch suggested that it could have been written by King Magnus after the conclusion of peace in 1266 (*DNFH* trans. Tennent, 1862, 94). In conjunction with King Hakon's attitude and treatment of the men of Caithness this letter does open up the possibility that he believed he had some residual rights of authority over the 'men of Caithness'

64 McDonald (1997, 106–15) gives an account of the campaign

65 Ibid., 117–19, for a full discussion of the problems of divided allegiance which similarly faced the various rulers in Man and the Isles and their responses

that Earl Magnus was waiting to welcome his king and entertain the royal party with the resources of his Norwegian earldom. What compounded this bad situation was that the return to Norway was delayed and the king decided to stay the winter in Orkney; and what made that situation even more disastrous was that Hakon took ill and died in Kirkwall, and received temporary burial in St Magnus Cathedral (see Colour plate 33). We have the full and remarkable account of all this in *Hacon's Saga* (Chapters 328–30), but there is not one mention of the earl or what had happened to him during these events. He had vanished out of the story.

If we turn to the situation in the earl's Scottish earldom, there is enough evidence to show that King Alexander was active in preparing for the Norwegian expedition, which indicates that Earl Magnus may have been under some robust pressure from his Scottish overlord. The fact that Alexander had taken the initiative in 1261 and 1262 in sending envoys to Norway, and then probably initiating the attack on Skye by the earl of Ross, leads us to assume that he would be well ahead in his preparations for the Norwegian expedition in the following year. The fortunate survival of the early exchequer records for the year 1263 shows that Alexander employed the tactics of hostage-taking in the north and west. From Caithness in particular a large number of hostages were taken whose expenses were charged to the account of the sheriff of Inverness at a penny per day.[66] They were no doubt taken as a form of surety for the loyalty of the province, and it may well be that this tactic ensured the loyalty of the earl. Or the earl's loyalty may have been ensured by the imposition of fines of which there is evidence also from the Exchequer Rolls. In both 1263 and 1266 he paid fifty marks to the king as part of the fines he owed for those years, and there can be little doubt that these fines had something to do with the tense situation in the north at that time.[67]

This evidence points directly to the earl's loyalty being constrained by such measures. He clearly did not actively participate in the defence of the north, for his authority in his earldom was superseded by a special royal commission to the earl of Buchan and Alan Dorward in the area.[68] He was most likely cowed into submission, and probably hoped to ride out the events of the summer of 1263 without forfeiting his lands or Scottish earldom. If he had stayed in Orkney and been there to receive his Norwegian overlord returning from Largs, he would certainly have lost both. Moreover, the nightmare situation was not over with the retreat of the Norwegian fleet back to Orkney and the decline and death of the old warrior Hakon in the Bishop's Palace in Kirkwall

---

66 *ER*, i, 13, 19
67 Crawford, 1976–7, 114; 1985, 38
68 *ER*, i, 20

in December. Relations between the two countries remained tense until the final peace treaty of 1266, and throughout this period Caithness was a frontier line and a war zone.[69] In the autumn of 1264, a Scottish army 'took much goods from the men of Caithness because King Hakon had laid a fine on the men of Caithness' (*Magnus Saga*, Chapter 2). There is possibly some corroboration of this in the Scottish records, for an entry from 1265 in the Exchequer Rolls refers to 200 cows of the fine of the men of Caithness.[70] Although there was fear that the Scots were going to attack Orkney at this time, it is manifestly clear that it was Earl Magnus' Scottish earldom which bore the brunt of the aftermath of the war campaign, as it had during the campaign itself. The unfortunate 'men of Caithness' whom we hear about so often in the records, were non-combatants who had the misfortune to live in this strategic war zone; they also lived in a fertile agrarian territory and could afford to pay the fines demanded from both kings to ensure their non-participation. The hardship which resulted from these impositions can only be guessed at.

7.4 THE TREATY OF PERTH 1266

Negotiations for peace eventually took place, although hostages from Caithness (and Skye) were recorded as still being in custody in 1264 or 1265, which shows that continuing measures were felt to be necessary to secure the compliance of these regions.[71] The successor to King Hakon was his son Magnus, whose inclinations were more towards peace than war (see Plates 6a and 6b), and Norwegian embassies approached King Alexander with attempts to come to a formal ratification of the events of the year 1263, and the changed political situation which had resulted. Three years and four embassies after the encounter at Largs, peace was finally concluded when Norwegian legates met with King Alexander at Perth, and peace terms were drawn up in what was a far-reaching and ground-breaking settlement between the two countries.[72] The diplomatic form of the transfer of land mirrored the document known as 'final concord' which was used in both England and Scotland as legal acknowledgement of the release of rights in property in exchange for payment of money, either a token amount or a substantial sum.[73] This is what the 'treaty' was in effect, and seen in

---

69 Crawford, 1976–7, 115; 1985, 38. See McDonald (1997, 115–16) for details of the situation in the west at this time
70 *ER*, i, 19–20. However, an entry in *Magnus' Saga* (Chapter 4) tells that the fine which the men of Caithness had paid in 1265 was seized by Lord Dougal as the 'great sum' was being carried south, which suggests that some of it had been paid in silver
71 *ER*, i, 20
72 McDonald (1997, 119–24) has a full consideration of the terms of the treaty. These are known from the later reissue in 1312 (*APS*, I, 420–1; *DN*, viii, no. 9, no. 482)
73 Lustig, 1979, 48–9

that light helps to clarify what the negotiations must have been about. Neither party was victor or vanquished, but concerned with an amicable exchange of rights, which resulted, however, in an irrevocable change of political direction for the Hebrides.

There were two particular ways in which the treaty impinged on the Northern Isles. After the clause transferring the Isle of Man and the rest of the Sudreys (Hebrides) to King Alexander, there is the express statement concerning the islands of Orkney and Shetland 'which the said king of Norway has reserved specially to his domain, with their demesne-lands, homages and rents, services and all their rights and pertinents within their borders'.[74] There had been no doubt about this before, since the 1098 agreement between King Magnus 'Barelegs' and King Edgar which had decided the boundary between the two kingdoms, when it appears that the position of Orkney and Shetland was never in question.[75] However, for the first time the constitutional position regarding the Northern Isles was now laid down in the formal document between the two countries drawn up in 1266. The same phrase is used with regard to the rights in the Western Isles which were being ceded to Scotland, although the situation in the two archipelagoes was very different, and it is likely that the same generalised terms have their origin in the Anglo-Scottish social and feudal background which lay behind the treaty's diplomatic origins.[76]

The second clause which impinged on Orkney was the stipulated arrangement for the payment of the 'annual'. This was the sum of 100 marks which it was agreed should be paid annually by the king of Scots to the king of Norway, as 'indemnification' and 'recompense for labour and pains', providing a perpetual recognition of the former overlordship of the Hebrides. It helped to sweeten the bitter pill of abandonment of Norwegian rights over their former skattlands in the west, and was a face-saving element, but it only stored up problems for the future. This was because the payment was to be given and rendered to the king of Norway and his heirs and assignees 'for ever'. It was specified that it was to be paid on 1 July each year in Orkney in St Magnus church (Kirkwall cathedral), into the hands of the bishop of Orkney or the Norwegian king's baillie 'specially deputed by him', or to be left in the custody of the canons of the cathedral for the use of the king of Norway, and they would give 'letters of discharge and receipt'. Furthermore for the next four years 1,000 marks were

---

74 Donaldson, 1999, 35; *cum dominiis, homagiis, et redditibus, serviciis et omnibus juribus et pertinentiis suis infra easdem contiguis dominio suo* (*DN*, viii, 9; *APS*, i, 78)
75 The 1098 arrangement was referred to when the Scottish envoys came to visit King Hakon in 1242 in an attempt to persuade him to relinquish the Sudreys (*Hacon's Saga*, Chapter 245; see Section 4.3.1)
76 Lustig, 1979, 48–9

to be paid in addition to the 100 marks, in the same place and at the same time. It should be noted that the earl is not mentioned as having any involvement in this transaction, although in most circumstances such a responsibility would have been laid on the earl as the king's special deputy. However, Earl Magnus was not available to play any role in these peace negotiations,[77] although it is likely that the earl would become involved in the matter of these payments in the future (see Section 8.1.1).[78]

The Treaty of Perth is an impressive piece of evidence for medieval statecraft and the use of medieval diplomatic.[79] It may in theory have clarified the political situation and regularised the 'state border' between Scotland and Norway.[80] But as far as Earl Magnus was concerned, nothing had changed, and he was still subject to two kings, with his loyalties divided between them. The two earldoms were still conjoined by the maritime frontier of the Pentland Firth, and that waterway linked them even though it was henceforth a frontier between the two kingdoms. He had been placed in an intolerable situation by the hostilities between his two overlords, kings of Norway and Scotland. He had to make reparations for his inability to act as a loyal vassal in those circumstances. We have no evidence of how he came to terms with King Alexander except for the evidence of fines paid, but we do have the statement in *Hirðskrá* about his meeting with King Magnus Hakonsson 'the Lawmender' (*lagabætir*) the year following the peace negotiations at Perth (see Section 7.2.1).

7.4.1 *Earl Magnus Gilbertsson's reconciliation 1267*

The occasion was the second time that an earl had had to attend his Norwegian sovereign in the aftermath of a failure of loyalty. The first occasion in 1195 was dramatically recorded with plenty of detail as to how the earl submitted to Sverre, and the terms that were imposed on him (see Section 6.2.2). In 1267, we are provided with only the dry statement in *Hirðskrá* about the 'many special agreements'(*þeim flæirum æinka malom*) 'about which terms were made' (*sem komo isættar giærd þæira*) between King Magnus and Earl Magnus 'which were settled at Bergen' (*þa er þæir sættozt i biorg'vin*) 'in the year from the birth of

---

77 In contrast to the arrangements for the 1312 treaty between King Robert I and King Hakon V of Norway (which repeats the terms of the 1266 treaty), when Earl Magnus IV witnessed on behalf of both his kings (*RRS*, v, no.25; *Orkney Recs.*, no. I). See below
78 See Crawford (1971, 229–31) for an attempt to trace the payments of the annual 100 marks or 200 nobles during the thirteenth and fourteenth centuries. In addition there is mention of a sum of xl lib. being paid by the sheriff of Inverness into English accounts in 1295, which it is said should have gone to the king of Norway as the payment for certain islands (Stevenson, 1870, ii, cccxlv)
79 Fully examined by Richard Lustig (1979, 49ff.)
80 Imsen, 2009, II, 16

our lord Jesus Christ one thousand two hundred and sixty seven winters and the fourth year of the rule of King Magnus son of King Hakon'.[81] However, this provides the information that some serious agreements must have been implemented about the role and powers of the earl in the administration of Orkney, and his relationship with the royal officials appointed over the islands. A document must have been drawn up recording these 'many special agreements' (*þeim flæirum æinka malom*) which sadly has not survived. The repetition of the full dating clause gives the impression that it may have been copied from a formal document.

It is not possible to make a certain assessment of the nature of the agreement. Was it punitive (as in 1195) or was it a more even-handed arrangement for the governing of the islands?[82] The trouble is that we have no idea how serious a failure of loyalty the earl's absence from the 1263 campaign was considered to be. If he had been constrained to remain neutral by threats or hostage-taking or actual imprisonment by his Scottish overlord, then King Magnus might have regarded Earl Magnus' defection with some leniency. As argued above, the disappearance of the earl in the years of tension in north Scotland might very well be an indication that he was under such compulsion. Certainly the promptness with which he attended his Norwegian overlord after the restoration of peaceful conditions indicates a willingness to come to terms with King Magnus, but whether he went on his own initiative, or whether he was summoned is not said. Perhaps the terms were more on the lines of the 1210 reconciliation with Earls David and John (which are not referred to in *Hirðskrá*). They had had to pay a large fine, give security and hostages and swear oaths of loyalty, but were made earls again on such conditions (*vilkør*) as they kept until their death-day (see Section 6.6.1). Like them, Earl Magnus was bound to attend his new overlord (King Magnus VI Hakonsson) to do homage anyway[83] and that always provided the occasion for adjustment of terms of appointment.

The Norwegian king of the time, Magnus *lagabætir*, was a very different sovereign from either his father (Hakon Hakonsson) or great-grandfather (Sverre), both of whom were warlike and harsh on rivals. King Magnus was more interested in the good governance of his kingdom and the institution of the legal framework of governance. His famous law revision (*Landlaw*) was

81 Author's translation. Original Old Norse text in Imsen, 2000, 80
82 The use of the term *skilorð* ('conditions') which were set down for Harald's reconciliation contrasts with the phrase quoted above for Earl Magnus' reconciliation (*æinka malom*, 'special agreements'). This phrase does not particularly imply that legal reprisals were imposed
83 Earls David and John had not of course attended their Norwegian king to receive their grant of earldom title, lands and right since the death of their father Earl Harald. Earl Magnus Gilbertsson must have done homage already and received his earldom grant from King Hakon before he sailed with the fleet back to Orkney in 1263

completed by 1274 and the Hirdloven (*Hirðskrá*) also drawn up about the same time.[84] It is therefore very likely that the king's predisposition to codifying and regularising legal arrangements and organisation of his hird's standing and conduct would be very relevant in the rectifying of his relationship with the earl of Orkney after the events of 1263–6. The 'many special agreements' may therefore have specifically concerned the relationship of the earl and his lord along the lines of the *Hirðskrá* chapters relating to the earl's conduct (see Section 7.2). Perhaps they included restrictions on the earl's activities relating to his Scottish earldom or to his Scottish overlord, and to specifying what his military role was to be in the aftermath of the preceding years of warfare. Probably they would lay down how royal rights were to be preserved and how the royal officials were to operate in the earldom. The details are unknown to us, but some reference to the division of lands and skats would inevitably have been included (which and how many of the skats were to be returned to the royal treasury and what proportion the earl would be allowed to keep); [85]what was to be preserved as royal estate and what granted to the earl as his demesne land, with certain restrictions on alienating any of the lands to others. Above all, a king who understood and cared about the exercise of the law would take care to regularise the legal procedures and perhaps to adapt any local customs to the legal norms which were being established in Norway, with reference to the rights of the indwellers in the islands. The matter of judicial fines may have featured, although it is likely that the division of fines between king and earl as specified in the 1195 arrangement would stand. Finally, the role of the Church or the relationship with the bishop was a possible item; the latter was going to feature largely in later appointments (see Section 7.6.1).There is no mention of any cleric accompanying the earl in 1267, as we know that Bishop Bjarni had done in 1210 and 1195.

If the reconciliation between king and earl was as suggested above, then it does not seem certain that there would have been any punitive measures. Maybe Earl Magnus had to pay a fine; certainly he would have sworn an oath of homage and commitment to keeping the terms of the 'many special agreements'. It is likely that he would have returned to Orkney a chastened 'vassal', and with more binding regulations covering his behaviour as an earl than had previously been in force.[86] The position of the earl was now more as royal officer than independent chieftain, and his authority was delegated to him by the king; 'in principle his duty was to manage the country on behalf of the sovereign'.[87]

84 Imsen, ed., 2000, 24
85 Wærdahl (2011, 85) considers that all taxes would go to the king
86 Ibid., where the opinion is expressed that it is 'difficult to believe that he subsequently enjoyed full rights to govern his earldom'
87 Imsen, 2000, 18

This brought the position of earl in Orkney nearer to that of the earl in Iceland, an appointment which was made just at this time.[88] Nonetheless, the earls of Orkney still had a hereditary right to claim the earldom, although there is no reference to this in *Hirðskrá*, whereas there *are* strict statements about the non-hereditary nature of the earls of the 'internal' sort (those appointed to the honour with estates within Norway).[89] The Orkney earldom was inherited from father to son – and once by a brother – under the Angus earls. However much the kings wished to restrict the power of the earls of Orkney they do not appear to have attempted to prevent the inheritance of the right to claim (prior to 1350), and a claimant was always granted the earldom. That claim would be presented by the individual who had already inherited the Scottish earldom,[90] and that in itself may have been a cogent reason for the kings of Norway awarding the claimant the Orkney earldom also.

7.5 'A NORTHERN COMMONWEALTH'[91] AND THE ROLE OF THE EARLS

The Treaty of Perth laid the foundations for furthering the development of social and diplomatic relationships between Scotland and Norway. The period from 1266 to the early fourteenth century was one in which close contacts were established between these two kingdoms, as also with England, creating a royal and aristocratic circle of diplomatic, commercial and social networks across the North Sea. It was a time when the earls were sometimes called upon to act on behalf of their kings in the developments which took place. Their role as earls of the two kingdoms gave them a significance which probably enhanced their status, in contrast to the preceding period when this role was potentially dangerous and sometimes humiliating. Most of the information we have about them comes from those occasions when they were evidently involved in affairs of state from their witnessing the documents which were being issued. Their role was probably more important than these attestations signify, and especially with events like the death of the Maid of Norway in Orkney (see Section 7.5.1), but any information about their position on these occasions is exceedingly sparse.

What evidence there is suggests that the earls of the Angus kindred were required, as earls of Caithness, to participate in important events involving their Scottish sovereign's international position. For instance, Earl Magnus II,

---

88 Crawford, 1971, 181–2
89 Imsen, ed., 2000a, 79
90 This interpretation differs from that previously propounded when the inheritance of the Orkney earldom was thought to take precedence (Crawford, 1976–7, 112; 1982, 68)
91 The title of a book by Gordon Donaldson (1990) which is concerned with the relationship of Scotland and Norway from the Viking Age to the early modern period

who was only earl for a few years from 1236 to 1239, witnessed, along with numerous other Scottish earls, a statement issued to the Pope concerning the Treaty of York (1237).[92] This is the first evidence that we have of an earl being involved in a central act of the Scottish kingdom concerning a national matter. The next earl of the Angus dynasty, Magnus (III) Gilbertsson, was caught up in the crisis of 1263 as we have seen, and he was most likely forced to, or decided to, remain out of the war expedition being undertaken by his Norwegian overlord. Whatever the circumstances it was impossible for this earl to participate in any of the negotiations undertaken in the years following and the final arrangements for the treaty of peace drawn up at Perth. The next Earl Magnus IV, son of Earl Magnus Gilbertsson, was earl at a time when relations between his two countries were as close as they were going to be for centuries to come, and his Norwegian king, Erik Magnusson, was betrothed to Margaret, the daughter of his Scottish king, Alexander III, in 1281.[93] After their marriage and the birth of a daughter to Erik and Margaret and Queen Margaret's subsequent death, and after the loss of King Alexander's two sons, the Norwegian princess (herself called Margaret) was declared to be the nearest heir to the Scottish throne. The name of Earl Magnus IV was one of many Scottish earls and barons listed on the declaration of 5 February 1284.[94] This is the only evidence surviving of this earl's participation in a public occasion, and he died later the same year and was succeeded by his brother John.

The tragic next phase unfolded after the accidental death of Alexander III in 1286 and the accession of his granddaughter the young princess Margaret, the 'Maid of Norway', as his heiress to the throne of Scotland. The plans for her transfer to Scotland and the negotiations for her planned marriage to the young prince Edward, son of King Edward I of England, occupied the attention of the rulers of the three kingdoms of Scotland, Norway and England for some time.[95] Many parliaments and assemblies convened in the latter decades of the century, and one might imagine that the new earl of Caithness and Orkney would have been an important figure in the negotiations of these years. The first and only occasion when Earl John participated was at the parliament at

---

92 The earl witnessed as earl of Caithness only (*CDS*, i, no.1655 where the erroneous date of 1244 is copied from Matthew Paris' *Chronica Maiora*, iv, 383–4; *CDS*, v, 25–6)

93 In the marriage contract the islands of Orkney were used as security for the completion of the contract, so that the 'whole land of Orkney with all the rights which the king of Norway had or might come to have in the same' would pass to Scotland if Norway failed to complete the contract (*APS*, I, p.79; *DN*, xix, no. 305)

94 *APS*, I, p.82; *DN*, xix, no. 309, where it appears to be uncertain whether he was designated earl of Orkney or Caithness (see Crawford, 1971, 112)

95 Articles by Barrow, Helle, and Prestwich, in *Studies Commemorating the Anniversary of the Death of the Maid of Norway* (*Scot. Hist. Rev.*, lxix, 1990)

Birgham in March 1290 when he was the last of the earls listed as witnesses to letters issued by the parliament ratifying the Treaty of Salisbury.[96] These letters were concerned with the proposed marriage of Margaret of Norway to Prince Edward, which was information the earl could usefully have transmitted back to King Erik.

7.5.1 The death of the Maid of Norway in Orkney 1290

We can assume that Earl John hastened back to Orkney to make preparations to welcome formally the young Margaret (aged only nine) when she arrived from Bergen *en route* to Scotland.[97] A payment was made in August to William Playfair, the messenger of the earl of Orkney, bringing letters from Sir John Comyn to King Edward concerning the reported arrival of the Maid of Norway in Orkney.[98] The date of departure of her entourage is very uncertain, but it appears to have been late September when the royal party arrived in Orkney.[99] The rigours of the sea voyage may have been too much for the young girl, and she died either on the voyage or shortly after arriving in Orkney.[100]

There is no evidence coming out of Orkney about these dramatic events, but we do have the remarkable record of expenses sent in to the English Exchequer by Edward's envoys who travelled north across Scotland to welcome the Maid and her entourage, intending to meet her in Orkney.[101] They left Newcastle on 15 September and reached Duffus in Moray ten days later. They sailed north via Invernairn, Cromarty and Dornoch to Skelbo where they 'spoke with the Scottish messengers' on 30 September/1 October, and probably received the sad news of the Maid's death. However, they continued north to Wick where they stayed on 4/5 October, and then returned south. They may have continued to Wick in order to view the dead girl's corpse before it was conveyed back to Norway.[102] For the second time in this century the death of a member of the Norwegian royal family had occurred in Orkney, and it is most likely that this second death also took place in the bishop's palace in Kirkwall. The

---

96 *APS*, I, 441; *DN*, xix, nos 340, 341
97 It appears to have been due to King Erik's wishes that his daughter be sent to Orkney for transferring to Scotland, so that final marriage negotiations with English and Scottish envoys could be conducted in Norwegian territory (Helle, 1990, 151)
98 *CDS*, ii, 463; *DN*, xix, p.267
99 Duncan, 2002, 194, n.75
100 The only details that are recorded come from the later enquiry into the imposter ('False Margaret') who in 1300 claimed that she was the young queen who had survived (Helle, 1990, 155–6)
101 *DN*, xix, no. 349; Crawford, 1982, 62–3, with full discussion of this journey and references
102 *ES*, ii, 695. Certain proof of her demise was only ascertained by viewing her corpse, and thus being able to assure the Scottish and English authorities of the fact of her death

later enquiry recorded that she died in the arms (*imellom hænder*, 'between the hands') of Bishop Narve of Bergen.[103] Earl John was surely present in Orkney on this occasion, unlike his father in 1263 (although he is not mentioned in the later account).

The consequences of this untimely death were many, and the course of Scottish history was changed as a result. The lack of a direct heir to the throne led to the 'Great Cause' and the internal rivalries between the Competitors to the Scottish throne, which themselves led to Edward I's domination of Scottish affairs and thus the Wars of Independence. The present concern is to see if we can understand how these events impacted on Earl John and the situation in his earldoms.

When the hearings into the claims of the different Competitors opened at Berwick under the presidency of Edward I in June 1292, King Erik Magnusson's name was among them (see Plate 7). His procurators asserted that he had a valid claim to the kingdom of Scotland as the father of the dead queen, Margaret. They also used the occasion to raise financial demands concerning the revenues of Scotland between the death of Alexander III and that of his granddaughter.[104] This may have put Earl John in something of a quandary, as he was obliged to support such claims being put forward by his Norwegian sovereign. The probable usefulness of his role in the proceedings concerning Erik's claim is evidenced by the letters of safe-conduct for him and his valet dating to the previous 13 May 1291. The first was for Earl John to go to King Edward with his household, before 24 June, and the second for his valet, William de Crumbacy, recently sent to the king, to return to the earl's lordship before 31 May.[105] These were probably visits to Edward in connection with the convention at Norham (which Earl John was not present at).

Erik was never a serious contender for the Scottish throne, and the battle between John Balliol and Robert Bruce 'the Competitor' dominated the events at Berwick.[106] Bruce's claim may have appeared to be the more persuasive to the Norwegian delegation, and before the final hearings started, negotiations were underway for a marriage between Erik and Bruce's grand-daughter Isabella. Clearly a Scottish queen from the Bruce party was perceived to be a good way to maintain friendly – and profitable – relations with Scotland, and its next

---

103 *DN* vi, no. 100
104 Helle, 1990, 152
105 *CDS*, ii, 129; *DN*, xix, 371; *CSR*, no. 20; *RN*, ii, 630, 631, where the name of the valet Wm. de Crumbacy (Cromarty?) is corrected from 'Grumbaig'. The very fact that the earl required a letter of safe-conduct for travel within the kingdom of which he was an earl suggests that his business was concerned with the affairs of his Norwegian king
106 Stones and Simpson, 1997–8

king. That was not how it worked out. It is noticeable that Earl John was never named as a supporter of either Bruce or Balliol, and the reason is doubtless because of his commitment to King Erik's claim. This fact alone would mean that he had little reason to become involved in the developing political situation in Scotland at this stage, and indeed the impression from the absence of Earl John's name is that he kept aloof from these developments.[107] Even after Balliol had won the competition and been declared king, Earl John failed to attend Balliol's first parliament of February 1293, and was named as a defaulter along with the earl of Carrick and two others.[108]

7.5.2 *International and national matters: 1295 and after*

With the year 1295 a new phase started which was to lead to the Wars of Independence in which every Scottish magnate was inextricably involved, none of them able to stay neutral; we will attempt to establish what role Earl John played in this period.[109] First of all there were was a build-up of international alliances involving Scotland and Norway. These concerned reconciliation between the two kingdoms over the arrears of the 100 marks 'annual' which should have been paid to Norway, and the late queen's dowry, which the Scots had made no effort to pay despite attempts by Edward to make them do so.[110] Unsurprisingly, Earl John was a member of neither the Norwegian nor the Scottish embassies to Philip IV of France in 1295. However, on 28 August 1296, at the parliament at Berwick King Edward issued letters of protection to Earl John of Caithness to last until Michaelmas and the year following.[111] Clearly a long absence was planned, but where was the earl going? It is unlikely that he was going to Flanders to be one of the Norwegian hostages required in the 1295 treaty, but possible that he was going to be in Norway, and was ensuring the safety of his Scottish estates while away.[112]

Another indication of the detached role played by Earl John in the series

---

107 Crawford, 1971, 118. He is never named as a member of the many embassies from Norway which negotiated with Scotland and England over the different aspects leading up to the official treaties
108 *APS*, I, p.447. The main reason for Earl John's absence (along with the earl of Carrick and two Bruce supporters) may have been due to his involvement in preparations for the marriage of Isabella Bruce to King Erik, which took place in 1293 (Crawford, 1971, 120)
109 Crawford, 1971, 120ff.
110 Nicholson, 1959, 123
111 *CDS*, ii, 839; *CSR*, no. 24
112 Diplomatic activity with Norway was renewed in 1297 and safe-conducts issued for several Norwegians moving between Scotland and Norway. Among these were the brothers Henry and Weland Stiklawe who had been in the service of Alexander III but who entered into the service of King Erik at the time of his marriage to Isabella Bruce (Crawford, 1973; 1990; and see below 7.5.3)

of events which the English government/King Edward initiated in Scotland at this time is seen from the record of the earl's oath of homage to the English king. He was one of very few not to do homage in person or by proxy during the king's tour of Scotland in July, or at Berwick in August 1296. The document containing his oath of fealty is the very last of all the hundreds in the Ragman Rolls. Edward's tour took him to Elgin, the furthest point north, on 26 July, and Earl John did homage at Murkle in Caithness on 5 August.[113] Some royal official must have been sent north from Elgin to receive the earl's oath and he had to go to an earldom estate, Murkle, at the most northerly point of Earl John's Scottish earldom, near Thurso.[114] This suggests that the earl, or his proxy, had come over from Orkney especially to fulfil his obligation as a Scottish earl to do homage to King Edward.[115]

The earl's detachment from the unfolding events in Scotland is understandable, given the peripheral position of the Scottish earldom of Caithness.[116] Even if his sympathies lay with the younger Robert Bruce, which seems likely, he was unable to do much in his Scottish earldom to help the Bruce cause, for he was surrounded by feudal magnates whose sympathies increasingly were with the English, like the Cheynes,[117] and both the earls of Sutherland and Ross.[118] It has been suggested that Orkney, rather than Rathlin, may have provided a refuge for Robert Bruce after his defeat at the Battle of Methven in 1306.[119] If so, this occurred after Earl John's death and in the minority of his heir, Magnus, when we know, again from the English records, that a certain individual called Weland de Stiklaw had a grant of the wardship of the young heir to the earldom of Caithness in 1302/3 (see Section 7.5.3).

The wardship of the young Magnus V was granted by the English authorities, but the basis of Weland de Stiklaw's northern situation stemmed from

---

113 *CDS*, ii, 803
114 In the sixteenth century it was designated Murkle Boardland, which indicates that it was earldom demesne land
115 The first known representation of an earl's seal is affixed to his writ, bearing a ship with a double tressure of fleurs-de-lys around (see Colour plates 9a and 9b)
116 Crawford, 1982, 64. Of all the Scottish earls it is said that only the attitudes of Caithness and Fife towards Bruce remain uncertain (either for or against), after Bruce raised the standard of revolt in 1306 (Barrow, 1965, 219). This was in the period of minority of Earl Magnus V, after the death of Earl John
117 Reginald Cheyne 'le fils' had married Mary de Moravia sometime prior to 1269 and thus entered into the first rank of Caithness landholders, for Mary had inherited one quarter of the Caithness earldom lands from her mother Lady Johanna
118 Crawford, 1971, 123–4
119 Barron, 1909, 90–94; Mackay, 1914, 88–9. Geoffrey Barrow (2005, 215–20) is however not convinced by the arguments put forward to support the case of Bruce having retreated north and regards a Hebridean location as being the most probable

his established position in the kingdom of Norway. Before discussing Weland de Stiklawe we will turn to the situation in Norway to find out what we can about the circumstances of the kings' influence in Orkney and the extent to which they were in charge of the administration of the islands. In contrast to the preceding centuries there are now no saga accounts to give us any detail or a general outline of the kings' policies towards Orkney and the earls. Unfortunately, there is, as yet, no documentary evidence of an administrative, judicial, or commercial kind to provide supplementary information (as there is for Shetland around the turn of the fourteenth century).[120] So we are reliant on hints of how the earls related to their Norwegian kings. Apart from the information in the Icelandic Annals which record the occasions when the earls of the Angus line died or went to Norway to receive the grant of their earldom, there is very little else.[121] However, the Icelandic Annals also record that in 1300 Earl John was betrothed to the infant daughter of King Erik and Queen Isabella Bruce.[122] This was the year after the death of Erik, when his brother Hakon had succeeded him on the throne, a king with rather a different outlook on matters of state and with different policies regarding the feudal baronage (see Plate 8). This nominal betrothal may therefore have been a result of the widowed queen's desire to ensure the protection of her fatherless daughter in a changed political situation, especially as this princess had a potential significance as the only living offspring of the previous king. Queen Isabella may also have looked to Earl John as a good link with Scotland for her daughter's future[123]. However, this arrangement did not last long as Earl John was dead before 1303. This one brief piece of information from the Icelandic Annals provides us with a glimpse of Earl John's close personal contact with the Norwegian dynasty at this point in time, and would appear to confirm that he was also closely connected with the Bruce element in Scotland at the time of the contest over the throne.

7.5.3 *Weland de Stiklaw*

The Bruce connection is very relevant when we turn to a figure whose career was closely interwoven with both Norway and the earldoms at this time. He is

---

120 There are two documents, dated 1299 and 1307, which have been fully analysed for what they reveal about the Norwegian administration in Shetland at that time. See contributions by Helle and Imsen, to the publication of the 1299 Conference (Crawford, ed. 2002) (see Colour plate 2)
121 Magnus Gilbertsson died in 1273 and his son Magnus IV received the title of earl from King Magnus in 1276 (*IA*, 69) .Some versions say in Tønsberg (*ES*, ii, 669)
122 *IA*, 52, 72, 387 (*fest dottir Eireks konungs Joni jarli Magnussyni i Orkneyium*, 'the daughter of King Erik betrothed to Earl John Magnusson of Orkney')
123 See recent discussion of Isabella's significance as the long-lived queen dowager of Norway by Randi Wærdahl (2012)

the 'Master Weland' who crops up on many different occasions in the North Sea arena, and whose career is very relevant as an adjunct to both earldoms. Weland was a career churchman and royal administrator, who must have had useful qualities in a period when those with connections on both sides of the North Sea could play an important role in the stirring international events which unfolded. We know far more about Weland than we do about Earl John due to the former's frequent appearance in both Scottish and Norwegian royal administrative documentary sources.

Weland started off his career, along with his brother Henry, in the diocese of Dunkeld (although they were probably from north-east England)[124] and he entered royal service as clerk of the chamber, and briefly chamberlain, at the end of Alexander III's reign.[125] The link with the Bruce family (which is seen already in the 1270s) is certainly interwoven with Weland's move to Norway, which happens in the early 1290s at the same time as Isabella Bruce married King Erik. Weland was with Isabella in Bergen when envoys, including his brother Henry, arrived from her father, the new earl of Carrick, bringing clothes and furnishings.[126] His connection with the Bruce family must explain Weland's banishment from Edward I's dominions c.1296, although he is recorded acting as a Norwegian envoy to the English court at Westminster several times thereafter.

Weland is said to have 'come into Edward's peace' by the year 1302–3 (when he presumably did homage), and was granted the wardship of the young Magnus, earl of Caithness, by the English king.[127] This is a remarkable piece of evidence for the standing of a cleric who had been in the employ of the king of Norway; he must have been well-known to the administration of the king of England from the many times he had served on embassies in the period of frequent negotiations between Scotland, England and Norway. He also had a high position in the Norwegian administration for he was a member of Hakon V's close circle of advisers in 1305, when he was included among the sixteen members of a royal council which witnessed the king's receipt of Queen Eufemia's dowry.[128] His placing in the list before the chancellor is said to indicate that he had acquired

---

124 The name Stiklaw is thought to be derived from the place now called Stickley near Blyth in Northumberland

125 See Crawford (1971, Appendix; ibid., 1973 and 1990a) for full discussions of Weland's career and references; also Watt, 1977, 516–17

126 *DN*, xix(i), no.390;*CDS*, ii, no.675; see Crawford (1990a, Appendix 183–4) for discussion of the items named in the inventory

127 Crawford, 1973, 334. If Robert Bruce had taken refuge in Orkney after the Battle of Methven in 1306 (see above), Weland of Stiklaw's presence in the locality, as a Bruce supporter, would have been helpful

128 *DN*, iii, 61

the rank of baron.[129] It is not unlikely that during the period of minority of the heir to the two earldoms he would have exercised some authority in Orkney, more especially when he had been awarded powers of guardianship over the young heir Magnus V in his Scottish earldom of Caithness.[130]

7.6 EARLDOM MINORITIES AND ABEYANCE

Magnus V's minority is the first of which we have any evidence. Such occasions were going to beset the inheritance of the earldoms in the following period, and they provided opportunities for Norwegian royal authority to be firmly established in Orkney without the presence, or intervention, of an adult earl. In Caithness the situation also enabled powerful individuals to get their hands on earldom property and income and control economic direction. It also provided opportunities for trouble over the collection of royal and earldom rents. The young earl came of age c.1310 and was closely connected with the negotiations between his two kings, Hakon V and Robert I, resulting in a renewal of the Treaty of Perth in 1312.[131]

7.6.1 *Trouble between Scots and Norwegians in the islands*

An interesting Memorandum which was agreed in Inverness at the same time shows that there had been violence in Orkney and Shetland between Scots and Norwegians. The Norwegian royal official, called 'seneschal' (steward) in this instance (*domini regis Norwagie senescalli in illis partibus deputati*) had been collecting royal farms in Orkney and Shetland and had to redeem himself with them when attacked by Scots.[132] King Robert promised to pay 600 marks in St Magnus Cathedral for damages done in Orkney, while compensation for injuries committed in Shetland was to be made after investigation. On the other side, amends were sought by Scots for the imprisonment of merchants of St Andrews in Norway and for the imprisonment of Sir Patrick Mowat and the

---

129 Helle, 1977, 404. As suggested by Watt (1977, 517), this high status may reflect his close association with the dowager queen Isabella

130 Crawford, 1971, 209; Randi Wærdahl (2011, 165–6) does not agree with the suggestion that because of Weland's known status in the Norwegian kingdom and his powers of guardianship of the young earl he is likely to have been the royal representative or sysselman in Orkney in this period

131 *APS*, I, p.461; *RRS*, v, 24 which is the indenture kept by the king of Scots and which Earl Magnus sealed as earl of Orkney on behalf of his Norwegian king

132 *APS*, I, p.102; *DN*, ii, 114; *Orkney Recs.*, p.3; *RRS*, v, 25. The seneschal/steward called 'Sir Bernard Peff' is identified as Bjarne Audunsson (*RN*, iii, no.407 n.3). Bjarne had the title of 'herra' and was a member of King Hakon's inner circle of advisers (Helle, 1972, 599). He was the king's chancellor from 1311 so his position in Orkney and Shetland is likely to have pre-dated his appointment as Chancellor

spoiling of his goods in Orkney by the Norwegian king's baillie (*ballivus*). The Norwegians promised to liberate and restore their goods to them. Earl Magnus was considered by both kings to be important enough to attest the Agreement on behalf of both of them; as 'earl of Caithness' (along with Bishop Ferchard of Caithness) he gave an oath on behalf of King Robert, and as 'earl of Caithness and Orkney' his seal was attached to the indenture on behalf of King Hakon, along with Bishop William of Orkney.[133]

The evidence for violence against the steward who was collecting royal rents in Orkney is most probably an indication of trouble which had been manifested in the earldom during Magnus V's minority or on his accession to his inheritance. There must have been some underlying tension that accounted for the perpetration of an apparently unprovoked attack on the royal official, which King Robert seems to have recognised was unwarranted from his agreement to pay compensation. What lay behind the complementary attack by the Norwegian king's baillie on Sir Patrick Mowat and the spoiling of his goods in Orkney is unknown, but is certainly further indication of tension between incoming Scots in the islands and a Norwegian official.[134]

Earl Magnus V's period as earl did not last long. Although there is no record of his death in the Icelandic Annals or elsewhere, it has been suggested that he was dead by August 1321 when a letter of King Robert's was addressed to the baillies of the king of Norway in Orkney.[135] This is a rather remarkable and unusual document, described as 'well-composed' and with no known model.[136] It refers to the previous treaty renewed between Hakon 'last reigning, of good memory' and himself, King Robert, and specifically the clause that no enemy of either of the foresaid kings would be received within their kingdoms, and especially if the accused was guilty of treason.[137] It then continues by naming Alexander Brown, 'our enemy, convicted of the crime of treason' who had been received recently by the baillies within their bailliary of Orkney, but who had refused to deliver him to Sir Henry Sinclair, King Robert's baillie in Caithness.[138] The letter demanded to know if this action had been taken by

---

133 Unfortunately the seal has not survived, so it is not known which earldom it represented. Can any deductions be drawn from the use of his Caithness title when acting on behalf of King Hakon, and the absence of his Orkney title when giving an oath on behalf of King Robert?
134 Members of the Mowat family were powerful royal officials in north Scotland (heritable sheriffs and lords of Cromarty) in the thirteenth century. They appear as landowners in Caithness sometime after this evidence of Sir Patrick Mowat's activity in Orkney
135 This probably indicates that the earl was no longer alive, otherwise the king's letter would have been addressed to him (Anderson; *OS* Hjaltalin and Goudie, p.lv; Crawford, 1971, 23)
136 Barrow, *RRS*, v, 164
137 *DN*, v, 68; *Orkney Recs.*, p.8 (trans.); *RRS*, v, no. 195
138 A group of conspirators, including a Richard Brown, had been sentenced to be drawn, hanged

them on the instruction of the king of Norway, or on their own authority. It continues with another complaint about the treatment of Scots ('men of our country') in Orkney who were oppressed with 'continuous injuries and annoyance', and wished to know if that also was perpetrated on the authority of the baillies or by royal command.

It is difficult to know if this evidence of further trouble in Orkney was a symptom of deteriorating relations in the wider sphere of the North Sea trading zone (of which there is further evidence),[139] or whether particular circumstances in Orkney exacerbated the situation. The vacuum which probably resulted on the death of an earl with no adult heir may well have meant outbreaks of violence, which were more likely to have occurred when an earl's combined overlordship of Orkney and Caithness was missing. This was particularly the case regarding relations between the two earldoms, for the earl himself was the one figure whose overarching authority should have kept the two earldoms peacefully together. Otherwise the different political systems on the north and south shores of the Pentland Firth could lead to strife, especially if there were individuals in Caithness who had been given authority over an underage heir and who saw it as their right to attempt to access his rents and incomes from the Norwegian earldom. Such problems may explain some of the tensions which we can glimpse in the 1312 Agreement and the 1321 letter. The 'malefactors of the kingdom of Scotland' attacking Sir Bernard Peff/Bjarne Audunsson in 1312 and seizing the royal rents which he had been collecting may well have been relatives and guardians of the young Magnus V, while the imprisonment of Sir Patrick Mowat and spoiling of his goods in Orkney by the baillie could indicate that there had been a similar intrusion by an earldom cohort into the administrative sphere of the royal baillies. In 1321 King Robert refers in the most general terms to the injuries and annoyance which 'men of his country' were suffering in Orkney, and which give us no clue as to who these people were and what their business was in Orkney. Nor is there any evident reason why the royal baillies in Orkney should have received the traitor Alexander Brown and refused to hand him over to Sir Henry Sinclair. However, the minority of an earl could perhaps explain how such free-for-all situations developed, and especially if the baillies, or sysselmen, in Orkney at these times had an enhanced power base and were given authority over earldom rights and incomes (and

---

and beheaded at a parliament at Scone on 4 August 1320 (Barrow, 2005, 429) exactly a year previously. Perhaps Alexander Brown was a relative, also associated with this conspiracy of men who mostly belonged to the old Balliol party. An Alexander Brown and other Scots were pardoned by King Edward II in April 1321 (*RN*, iv, 126). The appearance of Henry Sinclair is the first evidence of any Sinclair connection with north Scotland (Crawford, 1971, 217)

139 Crawford, 1971, 170

full powers over royal rents and rights) in the circumstances where an under-age earl and his guardian had not been given any rights or authority over his Norwegian earldom, but who considered themselves entitled to claim such rights. This is certainly known to be the case some decades later, after the death of Earl Malise, when a powerful Scot wrote a threatening letter to the Orcadian people ordering them to stop paying rents and dues to the royal officials in Orkney (see Section 7.6.3).

The total absence of any reference to Earl Magnus V after 1320 strongly suggests that he was no longer alive. In that year he was one of many earls and noblemen who sealed the Declaration of Arbroath.[140] In the preceding year he is mentioned, along with his wife, the countess, as having been present at an assembly in St Magnus Cathedral, concerned with Bishop William's conduct regarding matters in his diocese, and financial irregularities in particular.[141] But after that there is no indication of what the state of the earldom was (except for King Robert's Letter of 1321) until 1329 when the Dowager Countess Katherine negotiated two land transactions in Orkney, evidently as a widow (discussed in Section 2.4). It seems most likely that she was responsible for the upbringing of her son, the heir to the earldoms, during his minority, but, if so, he never reached maturity. The 'Genealogy of the Earls' does not say that Magnus V left any heirs, but on the other hand it does not say the he left no children (as was said of Earl Magnus IV.[142] The assumption is that for some years, between 1320 and 1330, another minority intervened in the succession of the two earldoms. In 1330, they both passed to Malise, earl of Strathearn, indicating that there was no surviving male heir of the Angus line.[143]

7.6.2 *Malise, earl of Caithness and Orkney c.1330–c.1350*

This time there was a real break in the earldom inheritance. The Angus kindred had been in possession of the earldoms from c.1232 to 1320, and had adapted to the difficult challenge of holding earldoms of the two kingdoms jointly, surviving the situation of warfare between the two kings in the 1260s. Changing to a different Scottish noble family, with a distant claim, was another test of the continuing connection between the two earldoms, and the 'Genealogy of

---

140 *APS*, i, 474–5
141 *DN*, ix, 85; Crawford, 2003, 148–9
142 *Bann. Misc.*, iii, 78. As Earl Magnus (V) only came of age after 1310 any heir that he left in 1320/1 must have been a minor
143 This may have been the occasion when the earldom 'reverted' to the two sisters, Joanna and Matilda as said in the Panmure fragment (see Section 7.1.1). If so, it was necessary to go back two generations in the Angus family tree – and the male descendant of Matilda was identified as the nearest heir. Malise would thus have derived his right to inherit the earldoms from his great-grandmother

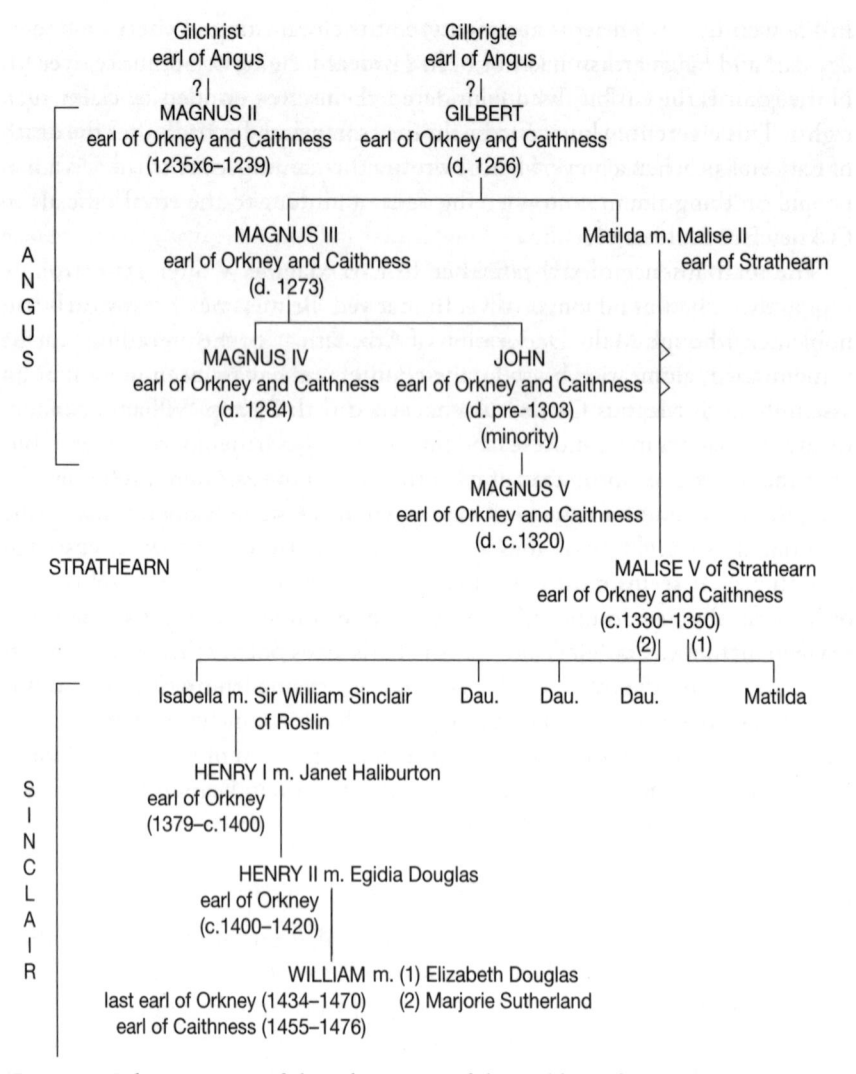

Figure 7.4 Schematic tree of the inheritance of the earldoms from Angus-Strathearn-Sinclair dynasties. (Based on Crawford, 2003, fig. 17)

the Earls' suggests that Earl Malise of Strathearn had to go to some lengths to prosecute the strength of his claim to the two earldoms successfully. There is an unusually long statement that Malise succeeded 'be just succession linialie ... as lawfull aire [heir] be law of heritage till bayth the Eirldoms of Orchadie and of Cathanie, lyk as the strenchthis, evidencis, and charteris of the confirmationis thairupon maid of bayth the kingdomis of Scotland and Norwege cleirlie makis manifest'.[144] There is also mention at the beginning of the 'Genealogy' that King Magnus Eriksson (in 1330) had ordered the bishop to make a search in the records for Earl Malise looking for 'all charters, evidents, and letters of previledge pertinent to him concerent the Erildom of Orchadie'.[145] There may have been a protracted period before the heir's claim was established, for it was possibly at this point in time when the right of inheritance reverted back to the two sisters, Matilda and Joanna – long dead – and Matilda's descendant, Malise of Strathearn was awarded the earldom.[146]

For the first time, the earl of Caithness and Orkney was a major Scottish magnate, although Malise was soon to forfeit his earldom of Strathearn. This was due to his connections with Edward Balliol in the difficult times of the late 1330s. It was fortuitous for the disinherited earl that he had other lands and titles to provide him with the status and income that he required. He was thus more active in the north than might otherwise have been the case, and the indications are that he visited his Norwegian overlord to be invested with the earldom of Orkney.[147] It can therefore be assumed that during the latter period of his time as earl (from c.1340–50) Malise would have been mostly resident on his estates in Orkney and Caithness. After his death, when he left no male heir but only a troupe of daughters, the door was opened to the exercise of power in Caithness by those who were dominant in the neighbouring area to the south.

This was particularly the case with the different branches of the powerful family of Ross, and especially the earl of Ross, whose daughter Marjory Malise married as his second wife. This marriage symbolises Malise's identification with the most powerful family in north Scotland, and enabled the Ross clan to exercise control over the earldom of Caithness and also to extend their tentacles of power into the islands of Orkney.[148] The most significant piece of evidence for this development is the 1344 grant which Earl Malise made to his brother-in-law, William, earl of Ross, giving him authority over the marriage of Malise's eldest daughter Isabella. In the same charter he makes Isabella his

144 *Bann. Misc.*, iii, 78 (*Cui Magno quinto jure successionis linealiter successit dominus Maliseus comes de Stratherne in Scotia, tanquam heres legittimus jure hereditario, ad utroque Comitatus Orchadie et Cathnes, sicut clarissime manifestant munimenta evidencie et carte utrorumque regnorum Scocie et Norwegie confirmacionis desuper confecte*)
145 Barry, 1805, 406. This passage appears only in the Scots translation, but was omitted in the *Bannatyne Miscellany* edition
146 Another claimant to the earldom of Caithness (Simon Fraser, on behalf of his wife Margaret), was trying to get a share of the lands of Caithness in 1330 (as noted in n.27)
147 Due to the union of the Norwegian and Swedish Crowns at this time King Magnus Eriksson resided primarily in Sweden. It seems likely that Malise must have gone to Sweden for his investiture as two of his daughters were married to Swedish noblemen (Erngisl Suneson and Guttorm Sperra) as recorded in the 'Genealogy of the Earls' (*Bann. Misc.*, iii, 80–1)
148 Crawford, 1982, 68–9

heir to the earldom of Caithness, failing a male heir of himself and his wife Marjory, and Earl William promises to defend the earldom of Caithness.[149] This signifies Earl Malise's weakness because of his parlous political situation in Scotland which probably made his position very insecure.[150] He needed to make a bond with another, more powerful landholder, perhaps against other powerful landholders in the region, most probably the earl of Sutherland. It is an indication of the changing circumstances in the north of Scotland which threatened the integrity of the joint earldoms.

7.6.3 *Filling the vacuum after Earl Malise's death*

We do not know the circumstances of Earl Malise's death c.1350, but it is tempting to speculate that he may have died as a result of the plague which was sweeping over northern Europe at that very time. That situation certainly caused deep economic problems within the Scandinavian kingdoms, and probably dislocated governmental institutions.[151] It is known to have hit the Atlantic islands only from an entry in the Icelandic Annals under the years 1349–50 saying that the sickness came to Shetland, Orkney, the Sudreys (Hebrides) and Faeroe (*IA*, 404). Otherwise there is no indication of how badly the communities in Orkney and Caithness were affected. However he died, Malise left a very difficult situation behind him with no male heir and five daughters (see Figure 7.5). This provided the opportunity for the Ross clan to fill the vacuum in Caithness and we get hints of what this meant from a few surviving documentary sources.

Thanks to the 'Genealogy' we have full details of the marriages of four of Malise's daughters. Matilda, his eldest daughter by his first wife, married Weland de Ard, from a family based in the district of Aird, just south of Ross. Isabella, the eldest daughter of the second marriage, heiress to the earldom of Caithness, married Sir William Sinclair, while the next two were married to Scandinavian noblemen, as already mentioned.[152] The Norwegian administration thus had the opportunity of being able to establish its officials in Orkney without any competition from an adult earl, although opposition was evidently forthcoming. First of all, King Magnus may have attempted to rule the islands through one of the Swedish sons-in-law of Earl Malise. For the first time the husband of an earl's daughter was himself given the title of earl. This was Erngisl who had the title in 1353, and according to the 'Genealogy' came to Orkney and held a part of the lands of Orkney 'by law and reason of his wyfe' (*jure ac ratione*

---

149 *RMS*, I, Appendix i, no. 150; *CSR*, no. 91
150 Penman, 2004, 108
151 Vahtola, 2003, 562–5
152 The fourth daughter of this marriage does not seem to have married (*Bann. Misc.*, iii, 78).

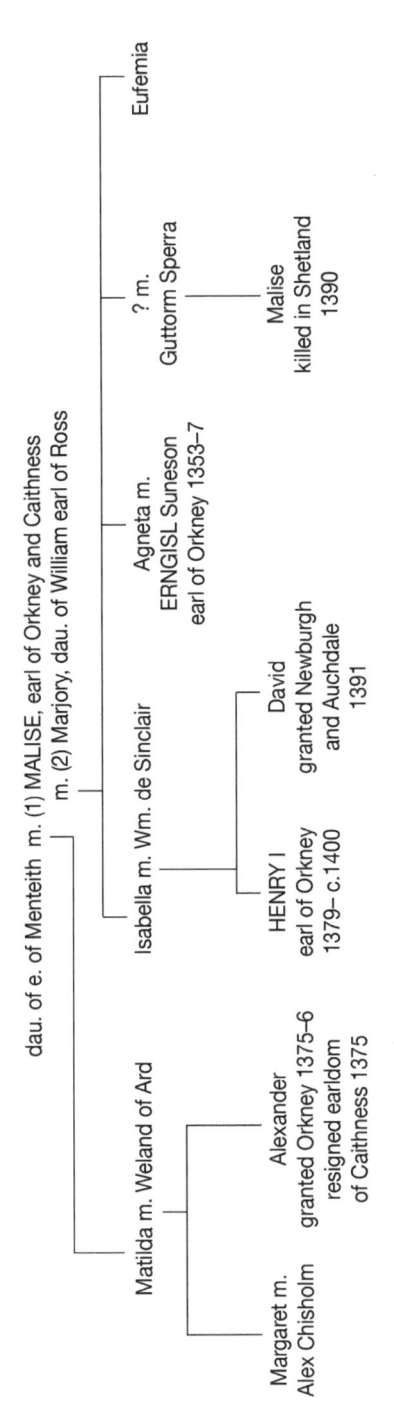

dau. of e. of Menteith m. (1) MALISE, earl of Orkney and Caithness
m. (2) Marjory, dau. of William earl of Ross

```
┌──────────────┬─────────────┬──────────────────────┬──────────────┬──────────┐
Margaret m.   Matilda m.    Isabella m. Wm. de Sinclair   Agneta m.        ? m.           Eufemia
Alex Chisholm Weland of Ard                               ERNGISL Suneson  Guttorm Sperra
                            ┌──────────┬──────────┐       earl of Orkney 1353–7
              Alexander     HENRY I    David                               Malise
              granted Orkney 1375–6  earl of Orkney   granted Newburgh                killed in Shetland
              resigned earldom  1379– c.1400  and Auchdale                            1390
              of Caithness 1375              1391
```

Figure 7.5 The marriages and families of Earl Malise's daughters.

sue uxoris gavisus est).[153] But, not surprisingly, this does not seem to have been a satisfactory arrangement, and as his wife had died by 1360, without leaving any children, his right to these lands would have lapsed, although he went on using the title of earl for some decades.[154]

More specifically we know that those who controlled Malise's eldest grandson and presumed heir were trying to get their hands on the income from the Orkney earldom. A letter written by the people of Orkney ('your community of Orkney', *communitas vestra orkadensis*) to King Magnus Eriksson and his son Hakon Magnusson[155] in 1357 informs them that they had received a letter from Duncan Anderson a 'Scottish potentate' (*potens de Scocie*) in which he warned the whole community, and specially the deputies of the king of Norway, that he held the true and legitimate heir of Malise, once earl of Orkney.[156] He had heard that the said king of Norway had 'sequestrated the fruits and farms of the earldom into his own hands' and ordered them not to allow the dues of the said earldom 'belonging to those parts' to be collected until the heir was presented to them, threatening them with the prospect of the dues being collected twice.

Probably as a result of the attempt by Duncan Anderson to get his hands on the earldom income from Orkney, a letter of King David II was issued in 1358 to his sheriff and baillies of Inverness and the holders of those places as well to the 'crowner' of Caithness (*coronatori Katanie*)[157] forbidding anyone to enter the lands or harbours of Orkney unless for purposes of pilgrimage, trade or other peaceful business.[158] This is known only from a later Norwegian copy, suggesting that it had been sent to Orkney or Norway, and had probably been issued in response to a request from the Norwegian authorities.

The same year, an entry in the Exchequer Rolls records that the income from the land of former Malise of Strathearn within the earldom of Caithness (belonging to Isabella, wife of William Sinclair) had been collected by the earl

---

153 *DN*, ii, 319; *Bann. Misc.*, iii, 80. His name is expressed differently in the Latin and Scots versions ('Hergisill, born in the parts of Swecie' or 'Here Ginsill de Swethrik')
154 Crawford, 1971, 171–2
155 Hakon (VI) Magnusson came of age in 1355 and was given Norway to rule, while his father continued to hold the skattlands, as well as part of Norway and Sweden
156 *DN*, ii, 337; *RN*, vi, 458, 459. Duncan Anderson was chief of the Clan Donnachie, a powerful clan in Atholl.The heir in question was probably Alexander of Ard, the son of Malise's eldest daughter by his first wife
157 This is the first reference to the office of 'crowner' in Caithness, a provincial judicial office which was held hereditarily, and in Caithness by the Gunn family. It is evidence of the Scottish Crown's extension of judicial powers into north Scotland, an area where it lacked a 'direct, property-based presence' (Oram, 2011, 208)
158 *DN*, iii, 358; *RRS*, vi, 203

of Ross 'without a reason' (*sine causa*).[159] This extension of Ross power north also moved across the Pentland Firth, for in 1364 documents were drawn up in Kirkwall concerning a grant of Ross lands in Scotland – the first evidence of such a grant concerning Scottish lands being issued in the islands.[160] Moreover, the witness list of these documents is very indicative (two canons of the church of Caithness; Eufemia of Strathearn, one of the heirs of the former lord Malise earl of Caithness; Thomas Sinclair, bailiff of the king of Norway; and Alexander Sinclair). The Caithness imprint is very clear (and it can be noted that Malise is entitled 'earl of Caithness' only) with members of the Sinclair family who were in this Ross circle, one of whom was apparently an official of the king of Norway, in Orkney.[161]

A few years later, a very remarkable document has survived from this period of change in Orkney, providing further evidence of trouble in the islands in the abeyance of the earldom. Such periods were evidently occasions for the development of different factions which then competed in the struggle to get hold of power and revenues.[162] On 25 May 1369, an agreement was drawn up between Bishop William (IV) of Orkney and the 'honourable and well-born man' Hakon Jonsson.[163] Although his position is never stated, the assumption has been that Hakon Jonsson was the royal official in Orkney, the sysselman (or perhaps more like a governor because of his aristocratic status).[164] He was certainly a powerful individual in both Norway and the Northern Isles, and in that position had clashed with the bishop over sums of money and amounts of butter which were royal dues (indicating that the butter skats had been misappropriated, and had been impounded by the bishop).[165] The quarrel went further than merely the matter of disputed payments, for the supporters of Bishop William and of Hakon Jonsson had been involved in something like outright war, each following having seized the lands and property of the other faction.

A group of twenty-four arbitrators (twelve probably chosen by each side) were to settle the disputes, and in addition they recommended that the bishop

159 *ER*, I, 570. In 1368 salt was sent to Caithness in vain, from interference by the earl of Ross (*ER*, ii, 308)
160 *Abdn.Reg.*, i, 106; Anderson's Introduction to *OS* Hjaltalin and Goudie, p.lxi; Crawford, 1982, 69
161 See Crawford (1971, 219–21, and below) for analysis of Thomas Sinclair's position in the Ross entourage, and his establishment in the north. He was the father of Alexander Sinclair, who witnessed the 1364 charter alongside him
162 In 1367 Sir William Keith is recorded as having the wardship of the heir of William Sinclair *per excambium* ('through exchange') (*APS*, I, 528–9)
163 *DN*, I, 404; *Orkney Recs.*, p.15; *RN*, vi, 1366
164 See Clouston 1932, 231; Wærdahl (2011, 165) gives details of Hakon Jonsson's relationship with the royal family
165 Thomson, 2001, 156

and the 'most powerful men' (*rikest*) of the country should be first and foremost in all councils with respect to the bishop, the king and the people, 'according to the laws and customs of the country'. This is an indication of resentment at a situation which had been developing; the intimation is that the royal official and his men had been dominating affairs to a greater degree than was acceptable, and exercising power on behalf of the Norwegian government to an extent that was resented.[166] Similarly, the bishop was to have 'good native men of the Orkneys and Shetland' in his service as other bishops have in the realm of Norway, a clear indication that Scotsmen had arrived in the islands in the episcopal followings and clerical administration.[167]

For the first time since the saga period the circumstances besetting the main body of wealthier farmers in the islands are revealed, as well as their attempt to solve the violence and faction which had developed to a dangerous degree in a period when there was no adult earl, and no obvious heir to the earldom. The matter of competing jurisdictions, those exercised by the Church and by the public courts, is given a prominent place in the agreement, and there are references to the procedures to be employed against those who had committed violent acts. They are to atone for their crimes according to 'the law and custom of the country', and the final sentence of this clause proclaims that each side is to be safe from the other 'except by the law'.[168]

There are many underlying currents of social unrest in the islands in this period of the abeyance of the earldom, as revealed in this document. The clash between Church, represented by the bishop, and secular authority, represented by the Norwegian royal official, is most in evidence. The resentment of the local population at being ousted by incomers in the councils (those of the king, Church and people) was probably directed as much against Norwegians as against Scots.[169] Economic difficulties may have been a very important factor, for by this date the impact of plague on the island communities was probably severe – or perhaps the impact was less severe than it was in Norway? If so, it could have been the case that the Norwegian Crown was making the most of the situation in which it had full authority to ensure export of all food renders

---

166 Ibid., 157
167 This is known from the names of Scottish clerics which appear in the sources about this time. Those named in the 1369 document included William of Buchan, archdeacon of Orkney, and Walter of Buchan, canon of Orkney, among others with Scottish names
168 This may concern the matter of revenue from fines as suggested by Wærdahl (2011, 165), and it strongly indicates that the bishop's court and the public courts were both competing for jurisdiction over certain crimes. Perhaps Bishop William was exercising what he considered to be the Church's rights according to Scottish ecclesiastical practice
169 This aspect was discussed by both Munch (*DNFH*, v, 916) and Clouston (1932, 232) (see Crawford, 1971, 174)

from the royal and earldom estates to Norway (and this situation may explain the appointment of the powerful Hakon Jonsson as sysselman/governor whose remit was to extract as much as possible). The seizing of 'property' or 'goods' (*godz*) by the bishop and his men and the reciprocal seizing of 'property' by Hakon Jonsson and his men which had been going on is likely to have been food renders and rents. What other 'goods' would have been seized by both sides in this way? Whatever it included, the general picture of lawlessness and competition for control of Orkney's produce is indicative of some severe social stress or dislocation. Once more this evidence of lawlessness occurs in the absence of an earl, and indicates that direct rule from Norway was causing problems. In the twenty years from 1350 to 1369 royal control had become well-established and was evidently particularly resented.

7.7 DEVELOPMENTS REGARDING CAITHNESS AND THE BREAKING OF THE LINK WITH ORKNEY

In the mid-1370s there were significant new developments which give indications of the pressure which the two kings applied to the problem of the joint earldoms. It was twenty-five years since a single individual had had both earldoms in his possession, and it was rather unlikely that either of the two kings, Robert II or Hakon VI Magnusson, would have been happy to see this situation revived. Nonetheless the right which the male heirs of the previous earl had to inherit or claim the earldoms was a powerful fact which neither king seems to have been able to ignore.

7.7.1 *Alexander of Ard, eldest grandson of Earl Malise and the loser of both earldoms*

Of course, the inheritance circumstances in the two earldoms were different and the grandsons of Earl Malise would have been well aware that the eldest grandson had a prior claim to Caithness, whereas any grandson had the right to present his claim to the earldom of Orkney. The eldest grandson's right to Caithness certainly prevailed (that of Alexander of Ard, the son of Malise's daughter by his first wife Matilda),[170] even although Earl Malise had attempted in 1344 to ensure that the daughter of his second wife Marjory, was his heir to Caithness (see above). We know that Alexander was considered the rightful heir to Caithness because in March 1375 he resigned to the king the castle of Brawl (Brathwell), and the land of the same with all other lands and rights in the earldom

---

170 The 'Genealogy' says that he succeeded to his grandfather 'in the principal manuring or mans of the Erildome of Cathanie be resson of his mothir' (*in principali manerio sive manso ratione sue matris Comitatus de Cathania*) (*Bann. Misc.*, iii, p.79)

of Caithness (and elsewhere) which were his by reason of inheritance from his mother Matilda of Strathearn[171] (see Colour plate 34). The 'Genealogy' says that Alexander 'sald and alienat' the earldom to King Robert,[172] so he possibly received some monetary compensation. This is followed by a long digression on Alexander's inheritance of Caithness (as well as a portion of the Orkney earldom lands) which suggests that this inheritance arrangement must have had some bearing on the reason for which the 'Genealogy' was compiled.

Alexander was also considered to have priority in the claim to be granted authority in Orkney, for he was created 'Lieutenant, Captain and Keeper' (*procuratorem, capitaneum et custodem*) of Orkney by King Hakon (VI) for a year on 30 June 1375.[173] As such he was allowed to keep half of the 'rents and income, pensions and revenues' (*redditum, proventuum pensionum et obvencionum*) which belonged to the earldom of Orkney or had of old belonged to it, but the other half he had to return to the royal treasury at Bergen. Over and above that, however, all that was due to the king 'by royal right' (*iure regio*) had to go entirely to him. As regards judicial dues Alexander was allowed to appropriate these for his own use except for those due from manslaughter and 'inemendable causes' (*orbotamal* as they were called in Norwegian) which were specially reserved to the king by royal right.

A second document was issued on the same day addressed to the people of Orkney informing them that King Hakon had handed over to Alexander *land wart her med yder* ('our land here with you', i.e. Orkney which was in their care), with all those things which belonged to the kingdom and to the earldom. This was on condition that next midsummer Alexander was to report on his 'right and reason' to the 'lordship or the earldom' (*herradømit æder jærlsdømit*), to give a full account of the revenues he had collected, and to show how the contest between the bishop of Orkney and himself was turning out.[174] There are many important things that can be gleaned from these documents concerning Alexander's appointment. Although the specific details of royal and earldom rights are lacking, it is clear that the two spheres of authority and income

---

171 *RMS*, I, no. 614; *CSR*, p.161. The castle of Brawl was therefore considered to be the 'caput' of the earldom, or principal manor, as stated in the 'Genealogy' (see n.170). Alexander also resigned other lands at the same time, and it has been suggested that this voluntary surrender of all his Scottish possessions was done as part of a deal with King Robert II perhaps in return for support in his claim to the earldom of Orkney (Boardman, 1996, 75; Thomson, 2001, 158)

172 *Bann. Misc.*, iii, 79

173 *DN*, ii, 437; *Orkney Recs.*, p.18;

174 *DN*, ii, 438; *Orkney Recs.*, p.19. This document addressed to the people of Orkney is in Norwegian and the titles Alexander is accorded are *Höfudzmanne, gøimara ok rettom syslomanne* ('headman' or 'governor', 'keeper' and 'right sysselman'), but in no other way (i.e. as earl). See Wærdahl's discussion (2011, 166–7) of the significance of the term *Höfudzmanne*

were separate, or meant to be kept separate. Does this reflect the conditions of appointment of a sysselman in times of minority and would this have been the range of Hakon Jonsson's powers? Or were these special arrangements for a claimant to the earldom – who might in fact be given the title of earl, if he fulfilled all the demands laid down in these documents? We do not know, but there is no doubt that the king, with the advice of his councillors, was able to vary the terms of appointment according to the individual being appointed. If Alexander had acquitted himself well in his role as headman, captain and keeper and was given the title of earl in the following year, then we can be fairly sure that he would not have been granted any lesser powers than he was being granted in 1375. His appointment as earl then would have included both the 'lordship and the earldom', and he would have kept all the earldom income, and retained authority over the collection of royal dues, of which he may have been allowed to keep a proportion, returning the remainder to Bergen, as stipulated in 1375. However, he was never given the opportunity, for he failed to be awarded the title of earl, as we will see.

Another strong impression given by the letter addressed to the people of Orkney is that the king was striving to ensure that the troubles which had clearly been dominating affairs in the islands would be allayed by this appointment. The 'contest' with the bishop is referred to; the people, both 'lay and learned' were enjoined to obey Alexander and his officers, and not to return any dues to any other man, under pain of treason (which harks back to the attempt of Duncan Anderson to collect income on behalf of the heir in 1357, and suggests that there were others around who were determined to do the same at this time); there is a reference to 'troubles' befalling the country, in which circumstances the people are to be obedient to Alexander in all matters 'affecting the security of the country'; the bishop and royal liegemen are specially enjoined to assist and help Alexander 'with respect to justice and to law', which was particularly necessary 'if any foreigners or natives attempt to force him or his officers from their right and ours', and especially 'if anybody will prejudice our country of Orkney'. Then both the bishop and the royal liegemen and the people were enjoined to be loyal and keep their oaths to the king and the Crown of Norway.[175] One does not have to read between the lines to get the message that a very difficult situation had existed and a great deal of underlying violence had permeated the islands during the previous decades when there had been no adult earl in control. The royal authority was ensuring

175 Imsen (2000, 171) comments on a 'peculiar' clause which informs the people of Orkney that Alexander and his officers were to dispense law and justice to everybody, the intention of which seems, however, to be to inform the people of the terms of Alexander's appointment: it does not require the people of Orkney themselves to ensure that the law was not violated

that someone was put in charge who was acceptable to the community, while at the same time ensuring that he did not get the full powers of an earl. When, and if, such an appointment was made, it would of course change the circumstance of a minority situation – when the royal authorities were in the advantageous position of being able to benefit from the opportunity to draw in all income to the royal treasury.

This eldest grandson of Earl Malise, Alexander de Ard, therefore has an important place in the history of the two earldoms. In the same year (1375) as he was granted royal and earldom rights in Orkney for a trial period he resigned Caithness to King Robert II – and the family lost their Scottish earldom. Due to his resignation of Caithness, the joint earldom situation, which had existed for 500 years, ended.[176] It is possible that this change was in some way responsible for the grant of the governorship of Orkney only a few months later. Because Alexander did not have the Scottish earldom title, he was not immediately created earl of Orkney, and as it turned out did not receive a grant of it a year later either. Why he failed to have the grant confirmed is not known, but it may be suspected that he did not succeed in establishing his authority over the troublesome opposition, whether the bishop or the rival claimants, his own cousins. Instead, his cousin Henry Sinclair, son of Isabella of Sinclair/Strathearn, was awarded the title of earl at a grand investiture in Marstrand (on the coast of Scania) on 2 August 1379, and the era of the Sinclair earls had arrived.

There is evidence from the year 1373 of contact between King Robert II and Orkney, and also of enquiries being made into the circumstances of the inheritance of the earldom lands in Caithness.[177] Perhaps the two were connected; this was the year after the death of Earl William of Ross, when the power of the Ross family collapsed, and it seems likely that the Scottish authorities decided to make moves to extend their authority north in order to prevent any repetition of the lawlessness which had previously prevailed in north Scotland. Therefore the initiative for the resignation of his earldom by Alexander to the Crown which took place two years later seems likely to have come from King Robert, and his sons.[178] The lands which Alexander resigned with the castle of Brawl must have been quite meagre. Earl Malise had held a reduced portion of the original Caithness earldom lands and these lands were themselves divided

---

176 Although only for eighty-five years, as his half-cousin twice removed (Earl William Sinclair) had it regranted to him in 1455 (see Section 8.4.4)

177 A Scottish nuncio is recorded as having gone to Orkney in 1373 on the king's business (*pro negociis Regis*) (*ER*, ii, 390; Crawford, 1982, 71). It was in August of the same year that the Latin document recording the inheritance of the earldom of Caithness by Joanna and Matilda (see Section 7.1), was drawn up at Scarmclath in Caithness

178 Alexander's right to the earldom of Strathearn was also resigned at the same time (*RMS*, i, no. 615), and granted to David Stewart, who had been created earl of Strathearn in 1371

among his five daughters. Thus Matilda held one-fifth of what the earldom lands had been in Malise's time; the other four-fifths were held by Alexander's cousins who all had their own portion of Caithness earldom lands.[179] So the earldom which the Crown acquired in 1375 can have been worth rather little. However, the gaining of the title to the earldom may have provided some rights which helped the Crown to extend its authority over the area. The earldom of Caithness thereafter was in the hands of the king's son, David Stewart, and other members of the royal family, until passing to Sir George Crichton in 1450. Five years later it was acquired again by the current earl of Orkney, Earl William Sinclair, and the two earldoms were very briefly reunited in the possession of the same individual.

7.7.2 *Changes in Caithness: evidence of feudalising influences*

This chapter has been resolutely focused on firstly, the problems of understanding the inheritance of the earldoms in the period of the Angus and Strathearn earls, and secondly, the position of the earls at a time of dramatic international happenings in the north. These included some of the most significant events in Norwegian and Scottish history: the last naval expedition of King Hakon west-over-sea, and the international Treaty of Perth which resulted in the transfer of the Hebrides to the Scottish kingdom: the voyage of the heiress to the Scottish throne to Orkney *en route* from her Norwegian home to her new kingdom, and her tragic death in Orkney. As already stressed, the deaths of the old king Hakon Hakonsson in the winter of 1263 in Kirkwall, and the death of his great-granddaughter, the Maid of Norway, in Orkney in 1290 brought the islands into sharp focus as a centre of the northern maritime world in the thirteenth century. These events reflected an era of contacts by sea in the Scandinavian north when warfare, peace-making and marital negotiations were conducted within the centuries-old network established in the era of Viking mobility and Norse settlement. It has been a theme of the chapter to try to establish what the role of the earls was in these events, whose own maritime empire straddled the Norwegian and Scottish worlds. The very problems which they faced in a world where their two overlords were in a state of enmity have been seen to be acute, and their political survival was a rather remarkable achievement. Unfortunately, details of how they managed to survive are not known, as we lack the evidence of how they planned their survival policies in the dangerous world of international contests over maritime and territorial boundaries.

Nor do we have very much in the way of evidence to know how these earls

---

179 Crawford, 1971, 33–4; 1982, 72

governed their earldoms and ran their households, or how they strategised over marriage alliances and other important personal matters. There is only one document which throws any light on the earls' domestic arrangements for running their estates, and that is a charter which Earl John Magnusson granted to Reginald Cheyne *patri* ('le pere'), lord of Inverugy, of land at Nothegane (Nottingham) in Caithness, with the harbour of Forse (dated between 1284 and 1293 and already discussed in Section 2.3)[180] (see Colour plate 35). This is a grant of an *oratam* of land at Nothegane made in an entirely feudal fashion, with the grantee being obliged to render a pair of white gloves at the feast of St John the Baptist each year. It shows that Scottish norms of landholding were certainly in existence at this date in the landowning circles of Caithness, whatever older norms of 'odal' custom may have persisted among the farming (*bondi*) class.[181]

There are however two elements in the document which hark back to an older Norse period; the territorial unit which is transferred is called an *oratam*, that is the Latin word for the 'ounceland', which (as discussed in Section 3.5.2) was the largest territorial unit in Orkney, and of which a few examples survive in Caithness. Whenever this territorial unit was imposed on Orkney– by the earls– it was also extended to Caithness, although how widely we do not know. By the later medieval period it had been replaced in Caithness by the usual Scottish term for a territorial unit, the 'davach', and so is very rarely recorded. Then the grant of this ounceland carried with it an obligation to pay a royal due which, as it says, is called 'Layyeld' (*servitium domini regis quod vocatur Layyeld*), and which is undoubtedly the same as the assize of 'Lawyeld' paid by the earldom of Caithness earlier in the century.[182] Although it is not certain for what reason this due had been exacted, it clearly had a Norse name,[183] and probably stemmed from the punishments inflicted on the earl or the people of Caithness after the violent events of the 1190s and 1230s (see Sections 6.4 and 6.7).

The witness list provides some informative – and unique –evidence about the household and entourage of the earl in the late thirteenth century. First named is the earl's 'uncle Harald', and as there is no evidence of a Harald in the earldom family during the previous generation, it seems most likely that this was Earl John's maternal uncle. If so, the name hints at a northern origin for Earl John's mother.[184] Uncle Harald is followed by 'Ivor MacEoth' who is likely

---

180 Crawford, 1971, Frontispiece. Rannald Cheyne 'le pere' married his son Rannald Cheyne II to Mary, daughter of Lady Joanna and Freskin de Moravia
181 Transferring land orally would still have been the norm, probably according to customary odal tenure
182 Crawford, 1971, 101–2
183 Derived from ON *lögr* ('law') and ON *gjald* ('fine/payment)' (Crawford, 1971)
184 Crawford, 1971, 22

to be a member of the MacKay clan, and if so, this offers some evidence for the MacKay family in the north, and evidently in the earl's train.[185] The remainder of the names are of members of the earl's household, giving us a glimpse of the feudal status of this noble earl: Swain, 'called of the Liverance',[186] William 'the Clerk', and Walter 'the Steward'. So this list of witnesses provides an eclectic mix of names of different ethnic origin, Norse, Gaelic and Scottish, (the latter including Rannald Cheyne, the beneficiary of the grant). We can extrapolate from this witness list to suggest that the wider social mix in Caithness probably consisted of the same ethnic and linguistic elements.

Naturally Caithness would have been the first of the joint earldoms to be influenced by Scottish language and feudal customs which this charter exemplifies. Perhaps it was the first occasion on which earldom estates were granted out by feudal charter, for it is likely that a magnate like Rannald Cheyne 'le pere' would only accept a grant of such land with a feudal charter of this kind. We have seen above (see Section 7.1.2) that the *tenementum* of Strathnaver was also held by a charter dating to a few decades earlier. In that respect we can perceive the influence of Freskin de Moravia, a member of the family brought in by the Scottish kings to tame the north. Earl John's charter was granted to another Scottish family which was already linked by marriage with the de Moravias. This is the way the Scotticising process advanced in Caithness, probably pushed forward by those families moving in to the area who wanted to hold land on the same terms as they had in the south.

Orkney would still be primarily, perhaps almost without exception, Norse-speaking at the date of this charter. That situation would change, however, during the course of the fourteenth century, as has been indicated in several ways in this chapter. It would, nonetheless, be a long time before any feudal charters were granted in Orkney. The biggest agents for change were the Sinclair earls to whose era we will now turn.

---

185 Crawford, 2000, 9–10. He can perhaps be identified with Ymar Mackay or 'Iye Mor' who is said to have been the chamberlain of the bishop of Caithness and the holder of twelve davachs of land at Durness (MacKay, 1906, 37)
186 Swain's name suggests he was of Norse extraction, but his office is that of a feudal household Comptroller, in charge of equipment and clothing

EIGHT

Sinclair Earls

1379–1470

The period of the three Sinclair earls forms a memorable epilogue to the ancient Norse earldom of Orkney. The Sinclair earldom was rather different from the previous Strathearn, Angus and earlier Norse earldoms. For one thing Earl Henry I, Earl Henry II and Earl William were also lairds of Roslin in southern Scotland. Cousland, Roslin and Pentland in Midlothian were all baronies of the Sinclairs, but Roslin became their most important seat where the family built their main fortified residence, on a dramatic rock site above the River Esk.[1] (See Figure 8.1.) William, last earl of Orkney, founded the flamboyant collegiate church of St Matthew nearby, on the slope above the castle in the 1440s (see Colour plate 36). So although the problem of the joint earldom situation was no longer relevant, since the earldom of Caithness had been 'sald and alienat' by Alexander of Ard to King Robert II in 1375 (see Section 7.7.1), the situation of dual allegiance was still a very real problem under the rule of the Sinclair earls, who owed allegiance to the king of Scots for their Midlothian lands and to the king of Norway for their Orkney earldom. The problem was even more acute, for the Norwegian earldom was now held by one of the most powerful nobles in the Scottish kingdom, which had certainly not been the case when the earls of Caithness were the holders of the Orkney earldom. This situation of double allegiance to two different kings was completely anomalous in the world of late medieval nation states when the ambitious Scottish kings regarded it as a matter of national pride that they should control the rich islands off their northern coasts. It is quite remarkable that the Sinclair earldom managed to survive for 95 years in such a perilous situation, particularly when two of the earls were very powerful figures in the government of the Scottish kingdom. To understand how they survived and how the situation finally ended with the events of 1468–70 will be the main purpose of this chapter.[2]

---

1 Earl Henry Sinclair was the first of the family to call himself 'lord of Roslin', and does so in his Installation document of 1379 (*Orkney Recs.*, 21; *DN*, ii, no. 459; Crawford, 1971, 224)
2 Crawford, 2003, 76; 2004e

Figure 8.1a Roslin Castle from the north-west.

Figure 8.1b Roslin Castle from the north-east (MacGibbon and Ross, 1887). This was the Sinclair seat in Midlothian and it remained the most important residence of the family even after Henry Sinclair was awarded the earldom of Orkney in 1379 by King Hakon VI Magnusson.

8.1 EARL HENRY I (1379–C.1400)

We have seen how Alexander of Ard was appointed 'governor, keeper and right sysselman' over Orkney in June 1375 for a year, after which he was to go to King Hakon (VI) Magnusson to 'give evidence of what right and reason he asserts he has to the lordship or the earldom' (see Section 7.7.1). We do not know whether he ever did attempt to assert his right, and for the next four years there is total silence as to the state of government in the islands. The 'Genealogy of the Earls' is more concerned with the inheritance of the daughters of Earl Malise, as will be seen. It does not even mention Alexander's grant of authority over Orkney, but focuses on the appointment of Henry Sinclair, telling us that he and his mother (Isabella Sinclair or Strathearn), along with his cousins Alexander of Ard and Sir Malise Sperra went to visit King Hakon, when Henry was created earl.[3] This was in August 1379 when the party, along with other members of the Sinclair retinue, went to Marstrand (on the west coast of Sweden, formerly Denmark), as we know from the Installation document in which Earl Henry acknowledges his grant of the earldom and the promises he has given regarding his role as newly appointed earl.[4]

Interestingly, there are two clauses in the Installation document concerning both cousins, Alexander of Ard and Malise Sperra, and they are very different. The first is a promise that Malise should 'cease from his claim and altogether demit his right' to the lands and islands of Orkney, so that the king and his heirs will have no 'vexation or trouble' from Malise and his heirs. The second refers to any 'compact or understanding' or any treaty which Henry may have made with Alexander of Ard, and which must not lead to trouble, as in the case of the 'precautions taken with regard to Malise Sperra'.[5] We do not know how Henry Sinclair won the confidence of King Hakon, or how he managed to outwit his cousins in what had probably been a period of tension in the islands since Alexander's appointment in 1375. From the reference to a compact with Alexander it seems likely that Henry bought his cousin out of the competition. But the position of Malise Sperra was clearly problematical. He was one of the 'friends and kinsmen' who promised to adhere to the clauses of the document along with the new earl; and he was also one of four hostages who were left behind in Marstrand until all the requirements regarding letters of surety had been fulfilled. Once released and returned to Scotland he continued to be a problem and the situation was only relieved with his death in 1389 or 1390.

---

3   *Bann.Misc.*, iii, 81, where there is a reference to *certas... pactiones conditiones et appunctuamenta* (' certain agreements, conditions and settlements') which Earl Henry made with King Hakon (VI) Magnusson
4   *DN*, ii, no. 459: trans. in *Orkney Recs.*, no. XI
5   *Orkney Recs.*, 24

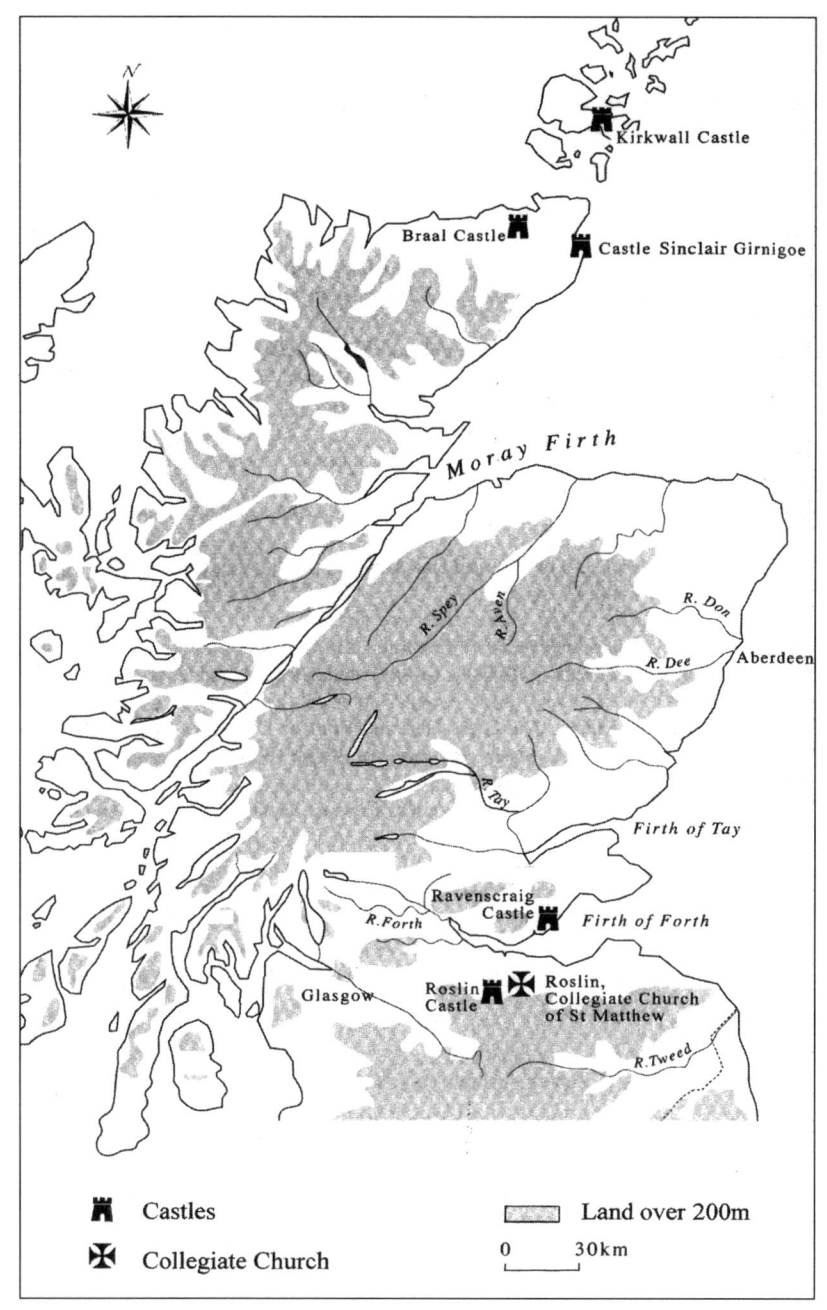

Figure 8.2 Map of Sinclair Castles (Oram and Stell, eds, 2005, fig. 9.1) showing the distance separating the family's two lordships – Roslin and Orkney (including Caithness after 1455).

The appointment of Henry as earl brought a new status to the Sinclair family, which had never had its lands elevated to an earldom in Scotland. This dramatic development in the fortunes of the family must have entailed a certain amount of adaptation to the completely different national, political and cultural circumstances in the islands of Orkney.[6] They certainly seem to have adapted to the northern conditions, and imprinted the stamp of the Sinclair clan on the islands (and Caithness), where the name of Sinclair is one of the most common family names today. Although they were deeply involved in central Scottish affairs (Earl Henry II and Earl William in particular), these earls appear to have taken good care to see that their family and followings represented them in the administration of the earldom and were given grants of land to establish their own power bases. Indeed, the role of Henry's mother, Isabella Sinclair, appears to have been particularly significant in this respect (see below). Managing their Midlothian estates, as well as their northern earldom, seems to have caused them no problems, as far as can be ascertained. Maritime communications between the Firth of Forth and the Pentland Firth were not so difficult, and these earls were evidently able to adapt to a lifestyle where the sea was vital to their success (see Figure 8.2).[7]

8.1.1 *Earl Henry's terms of appointment*

The Installation document incorporated Earl Henry's promises to his overlord King Hakon VI who 'has appointed us of his grace to rule over his lands and islands of Orkney, and raised us to the state of earl over his foresaid lands and islands, with that dignity which is required therefor'.[8] The first clauses are concerned with military service outwith the islands of Orkney, when the earl had to attend upon royal summons with a hundred good men or more 'fully equipped in arms'. Defence of Orkney 'or even the land of Shetland'[9] was also a

---

6 As noted above (Chapter 7), members of the Sinclair family were previously acquainted with Caithness and Orkney; Sir Henry Sinclair being the Scottish king's Baillie in Caithness in 1321 and Thomas Sinclair being the Norwegian king's Baillie in Orkney in 1364. Sir Henry's grandson, William, had been betrothed to Isabella de Strathearn in the 1350s, eldest daughter of the second marriage of Malise, earl of Caithness and Orkney. Connection with the earl of Ross was evidently the means by which Thomas and William Sinclair gained their positions in the north at that time (Crawford, 1971, 219–23).
7 The Sinclair earls' maritime links may have resulted in them holding the position of Admiral of Scotland. Earl Henry II is alleged to have been the first known holder of the office (*CP*, x, 196; McMillan, 1923, 12; Crawford, 1971, 277 n.1; Wade, ed., 1937, p.xiii). Earl William is called 'admiral of the fleet' in Bower's *Scotichron.* when accompanying the royal fleet to France in 1436, but perhaps so-called only for that occasion (Bower, *Scotichron.* Book xvi, Watt, ed., 8 (1987), 249, note 2).
8 *Orkney Recs.*, 21
9 This does not mean that Shetland had become part of the earldom again, as it has been interpreted. See Crawford, 1967–8, 157

requirement, with men gathered from the islands, and with the 'whole strength of our kin, friends and servants' (implying those might come from Scotland). If his lord the king should invade other lands or kingdoms, the earl was obliged to provide help and service, and he promised to assist the king or his officials if they came to the Orkney islands for any reason. This was the normal duty of provisioning which was incumbent on all feudal vassals, as were several of the clauses regarding attendance when summoned, and not raising war or litigation against any persons which might cause harm to the king or his kingdom. In the midst of these clauses there is a promise not to build castles or other fortifications within the islands without the king's consent – which was blatantly disregarded in the following decades by Earl Henry Sinclair (or his son) who built a castle in Kirkwall, as is stated in the Installation document of Earl William in 1434 (see Section 8.4.3).

It was not the purpose of this list of promises to state what the new earl had actually received with the grant of the dignity of earl, and the general term of 'earldom and lordship' is all that is used in the document. This term probably covered both earldom lands and rights and royal lands and rights,[10] and it cannot be imagined that the new earl would have been granted any less than his cousin Alexander had received when put in charge of 'all those things and appurtenances which belong to the kingdom and to the earldom with smaller things and greater, nothing excepted' for a year in 1375.[11] There is one clause only in the 1379 document which concerns royal lands and rights. It comes at the very end, after the list of signatories, and contains a promise by the new earl not to assume to himself the royal lands and rights, or to intromit with these lands and rights within the earldom which the king and his predecessors have reserved. If in the future Earl Henry was to receive 'special letters' about the royal lands and rights, then he would be bound by a particular obligation to the king.[12] This postscript suggests that King Hakon was at the last minute adding something to a traditional installation list of promises, and the reason would be in order to maintain control over the royal lands and rights which experience had probably shown could only too easily become absorbed into the earl's own landed possessions and become part of his power base.[13]

There were other stringent requirements to ensure that the new earl would fulfil the promises he had made. Letters had to be returned to King Hakon sealed by eight Scottish magnates and two Scottish bishops confirming that

10 See discussion in Crawford, 1967–8, 159, n.13; 1971, 186, n.2; 1983a, 37
11 *Orkney Recs.*, 19; Crawford, 1971, 184
12 *Orkney Recs.*, 26
13 In Earl William's charter of 1434 this promise had been moved from its position in the 1379 document and added to the main clauses (Crawford, 1971, 185, and see below)

Earl Henry had fulfilled certain conditions before the four hostages who were left behind in Norway would be released. Only one such letter has survived, concerning the alienation of any lands or rights in the earldom (which Earl Henry had promised in his grant not to sell or make over to anyone in wadset or pledge), which was issued by the new earl at St Andrews on 1 September 1379 and sealed by the named sureties, the first one of whom was the bishop of St Andrews.[14] But it appears that the remaining requirements were not fulfilled for in the following June King Hakon released the hostages in order for them to go to Scotland and ensure that the required letters were returned.[15] They also had to return 180 of the 1,000 nobles which the new earl had promised to pay as a 'just debt' (*iustum debitum*) to the king or his official at Tunsberg at Martinmas, and which had evidently not been fully paid. Whether this payment represents something like a feudal 'relief'[16] which vassals customarily had to pay their overlord when doing homage (and which Earl Henry certainly did by the kiss of fealty referred to in the document), or some other debt payment, is unclear. It has been proposed that this was the debt for the 'annual' payment due for the preceding five years.[17] We can also note that the new earl was indebted to Hakon Jonsson for certain sums of money, which may be connected with the 'just debt'. He issued a charter on the same day as his installation promising to pay 200 nobles in Kirkwall at two terms (next Pentecost and Martinmas).[18]

Although the earl's position is clearly seen from the terms of his Installation document to be similar to that of a life fief, and Henry promises that on his death the 'earldom and lordship with the lands and islands and with all right' will return to the king and his heirs, nonetheless it is acknowledged that a male heir of the earl can claim the earldom and lordship and seek the consent of the king.[19] The hereditary principle was still recognised and incorporated into the regulations and restrictions which had been imposed on the earl, and this made the earldom of Orkney a continuing anomaly in the political establishment of the Norwegian kingdom. Despite the fact that there had been no earl

---

14 *DN*, ii, no. 460
15 *DN*, ii, no. 465
16 Randi Wærdahl (2011, 243) interprets the 'just debt' as probably a 'fee for the fief', but as Earl William did not have to pay any such sum in 1434 (no such sum is referred to in his Installation document), this seems unlikely (see Section 8.4.3)
17 Crawford, 1971, 227–32
18 *DN*, I, 158. This document was transcribed in 1380 and 1384, suggesting that this was a regular obligation or permanent debt. Then in 1389 another obligation was issued by the earl to pay £140 Scots sterling over the next four years and giving permission to Hakon Jonsson to uplift the earl's farms, rents and escheats from the islands of Sanday and Ronaldsay if he failed to return the sum (*DN*, ii, 515; *Shetland Docs.*, 14; Crawford, 1971, 232)
19 *Orkney Recs.*, 24

for thirty years (excluding the tenure of the son-in-law of Earl Malise, Erngisl Suneson) during which period royal officials had dominated island affairs, it is clear that the hereditary principle was strong enough to reassert itself and allow the establishment of a new dynasty. The practicalities of maintaining peaceful conditions within the distant insular skattland may have been imperative. As has been deduced from the documents of Alexander of Ard's appointment, this period had been disturbed by rivalries among Earl Malise's heirs and their Scottish protectors (see Chapter 7). King Hakon must have been persuaded of the ability of Henry Sinclair to establish peaceful conditions within the earldom, despite the incipient problems which are referred to in the Installation clauses, as regards the cousins Malise Sperra and Alexander of Ard, and also the current bishop of Orkney.

As far as Bishop William (IV) is concerned the clause gives startling evidence of the tensions that continued to exist between the secular authorities and the Church. This was evident from the 1369 agreement as also from Alexander of Ard's appointment in 1375 (see Section 7.7). In 1379, the new earl has to promise to make no 'league' with the bishop or establish any friendship with him except with the express permission of the king. In fact he was to assist the king against the said bishop until the latter had done all those things which the king desired or 'may reasonably demand of the said bishop'.[20] We can assume from this that the bishop had been encroaching on royal rights and powers in some way, and doubtless these had included financial resources as seen in 1369.[21] It seems likely that this occurred because of the power vacuum when there was no earl for thirty years after Earl Malise's death, and Bishop William became in some respects the earl's replacement, challenging the authority of the royal sysselmen. The difficulties which the king clearly faced from this powerful cleric are likely to have been another reason why the earldom was restored, and why Henry Sinclair was chosen to be the heir who was finally successful in being awarded the honour and the authority of earl. It was recognised by King Hakon that the only hope of restoring peaceful conditions and of re-establishing the customary relationship with the islands lay in the restoration of the earldom, and the awarding of the rights, powers and dignity of earl to the family member with the best credentials for establishing authority over the islands, over the rival heirs and over the bishop.

8.2 EARL HENRY I'S ESTABLISHMENT OF HIS AUTHORITY

This detailed document in which the new earl agrees to stringent conditions of appointment is a remarkable source of evidence about governmental authority

20 *Orkney Recs.*, 24
21 Crawford, 2003, 150

in Norway in the late fourteenth century, and for the administrative reorganisation which was taking place at that time.[22] The determination to exercise control over the earl's freedom of action is clearly expressed in the very last Reversal clause, which has been added after the list of sureties (as was the clause discussed above concerning the royal lands and rights), suggesting that it also was an afterthought added after the main document had been drawn up. If the new earl did not act in accordance with the list of promises he had made, then 'the promotion and favour' which he had gained would be entirely cancelled in all aspects, and he and his heirs would have no right of claiming the earldom or 'the lands and islands aforesaid'.[23] This is a bold expression of royal intent and purpose, telling us how King Hakon VI intended to retain the exercise of royal authority over this skattland, and of the value which he placed on it. However, in practice it would have been very difficult indeed to maintain such strict royal control over the activities of a powerful feudatory with an extensive power base in another country. The political situation in Norway soon changed, for King Hakon died the following year (1380), and was succeeded by his eleven-year-old son Olav as king of Denmark and Norway. The joint Danish–Norwegian monarchy continued for the rest of the Middle Ages. The earls of Orkney were therefore obliged to attend their Scandinavian overlord in Denmark, and contact between earl and king may have become more distant as a result. On the death of her son Olav in 1387, Queen Margrete was elected Danish regent and was successful in being elected regent of Norway in the following year.[24]

8.2.1 *The killing of Bishop William*

The very difficult situation which clearly had existed in the earldom would not be quickly or easily addressed. Too many entrenched positions had been established in the preceding years of minority of Malise's grandsons and heirs. Perhaps the first powerful position was that occupied by Bishop William (IV), whose dominance and antagonism to the royal representatives has already been discussed. Earl Henry's promise in his installation charter to make no 'league' with the bishop or establish any friendly relations with him, except with the king's consent, may suggest on the face of it that he had no quarrel with Bishop William, and that the king feared he might support the bishop's regime. It may be that the bishop had helped to push forward the Sinclair claim, especially as Alexander of Ard had certainly been in opposition to him. Who then was responsible for the violent death of Bishop William as reported in the Icelandic Annals in 1382 or 1383, where the 'mournful tidings' (*hormulig tidendi*) from

22 Wærdahl, 2011, 172, 243
23 *Orkney Recs.*, p.26
24 Oleson, 2003, 723

Orkney of his 'killing' (*drepinn*)is briefly noted? (*IA*, 282, 414). It is not certain which faction decided that things would be better with Bishop William out of the way.[25] Perhaps this combative prelate would not willingly adapt to the new political scenario established by the re-creation of the earldom and the appointment of Henry Sinclair with power of control over royal and earldom finances. Such a development may have been detrimental to the position which Bishop William had won for himself and the Church in Orkney during the abeyance of the earldom.

It may also be that the divisions in the wider Church at this very time had something to do with Bishop William's demise. We know that the Church in Orkney was plunged into a difficult situation from the effects of the papal Schism which had broken out in 1378. It was particularly problematical in the islands because both Roman and Avignon popes attempted to make appointments. The former should have been the accepted papal authority because Norway followed the Roman popes, and as bishops of the Norwegian province of Nidaros the Orkney candidates should have adhered to them. However, Scotland supported the schismatic Avignon popes who also attempted to make episcopal appointments in Orkney, doubtless supported by the newly appointed Sinclair earl.[26] Had Earl Henry fallen out with Bishop William over their alignment with different popes? Very soon after the bishop's death, in 1383, a member of the Sinclair family, Robert, was described as 'elect of Orkney', provided by the Avignon pope. This was in opposition to John, elected by the cathedral chapter and then provided to his office by the Roman Pope Urban VI, but not until 10 February 1384.[27] Had Earl Henry been trying to insert his candidate and relative into the position? If so, he was not successful for Robert Sinclair does not appear to have ever been in possession of his diocese or in receipt of income (except for the traditional allowance from the Scottish Crown revenue of Aberdeen), and finally in 1391 he was translated to the see of Dunkeld by Clement VII. This suggests that both ecclesiastical and other ruling groups in Orkney were committed to the maintenance of the Norwegian links and the *status quo* regarding Church loyalties. At this time of heightened tension in Church affairs a clash may have occurred over the bishop's position which resulted in his death. We do not know whether Earl Henry was involved, but perhaps mindful of the promises he had made in his Installation document

---

25 If Earl Henry did establish friendly relations with the bishop, then possibly the attack was carried out by leaders of the community who were liegemen of the Crown and loyal to the interests of their Norwegian overlord (contra suggestions made previously, Crawford, 2003, 150 and n.75)
26 Crawford, 2003, 151
27 Watt and Murray, eds, 2003, 326

he may have refrained from protecting the bishop. The situation of double appointments and rival bishops continued until the end of the Schism in 1418 and caused difficulties for some of the Roman bishops of Orkney, John Pak (1396–1397 x 1418) in particular.[28]

8.2.2 *Malise Sperra, the dangerous cousin with a rival claim*

In order to establish his authority in his earldom Earl Henry's first challenge was to satisfactorily neutralise his main opponent and cousin, Malise Sperra. After Malise was released from being held in Norway as hostage in 1380 he appears to have spent his time attempting to establish his position in the north. From a judgement of the king's steward in Bergen in 1386 it is clear that he had appropriated the Shetland estates of two powerful Norwegians, Jon and Sigurd Hafthorsson, and put his men in charge of them, apparently illegally, for the steward's letter was ratified by the lawman of Bergen, saying that Malise had seized the aforesaid property without a legal judgment.[29] In the following year there is evidence that trouble had flared up between him and his cousin, Earl Henry, and Malise had come off worst. A submission was drawn up in Edinburgh in which Malise condoned and remitted all actions of injuries and offences done by the earl, his men, or whomsoever in his name, to Malise, his men, and possessions. Moreover, he promised to restore, pay and make satisfaction for all injuries, offences, and things usurped from the earl up to the present day by him or his men.[30] There is no hint of where this violence had taken place.

Malise's activities were certainly focused in the north.[31] Rather surprisingly we next learn that he had gained a position of authority in Norway, when in 1389, along with Earl Henry, he witnessed and sealed the document acknowledging Erik of Pomerania's claim to the Norwegian throne.[32] This shows that Malise was a member of the governing council and also that he had been knighted,

---

28 Ibid., 327
29 *Shetland Docs.*, no. 13; *DN*, I, no. 501.These estates had belonged to Fru Herdis Thorvaldsdatter, a wealthy heiress in Shetland who died post 1360. There was some uncertainty over the ownership of these lands, and Malise may have considered himself to have some rights of claiming them. His father's family (Sperra) is recorded in 1299 in Shetland (*Shetland Docs.*, no. 2), so Malise probably held family lands in Shetland
30 Hay, 1835, 57; Saint-Clair, 1898, trans. p.511
31 In 1387 Malise is called 'lord of Skuldale', probably Skouthal in the parish of Watten, Caithness
32 There are two versions of this document, one in Latin (*DN*, iii, 484)the other Norwegian (*DN*, xviii, no. 34). In the latter Henry Sinclair comes second after the archbishop and before the other bishops. Immediately following is 'herra Malise Sperra riddere' (Sir Malise Sperra knight). However, Malise's name is missing from the Latin document (Crawford, 1971, 235 n.2)

probably by Queen Margrete.³³ He had therefore gained a position of honour in the Norwegian kingdom, and his appearance following this in Shetland may suggest that he had been given a grant of royal authority as sysselman or governor in Shetland.³⁴ This may have been to compensate for the judgement against him three years earlier over his possession of the lands of Fru Herdis in Shetland. Whatever authority he had acquired in Shetland was apparently enough to antagonise Earl Henry and the final showdown between the two took place soon afterwards in Shetland. This is a very significant indicator that whatever powers Malise had been given posed a threat to the earl's interests, and this is the first time since 1195 that we know an earl of Orkney was physically present in Shetland. The clash between the two was well enough known to be recorded in the Icelandic Annals (and nowhere else):

> Sir Malise Sperra killed in Shetland and he had previously captured the earl in Orkney.
>
> (*Lögmanns-ánnall (E)*, IA, 284)

> Malise Sperra killed in Shetland, and 7 men with him by the earl of Orkney, and from that same field of action a 'swain' fled and came to Norway in a 6-oared boat and 6 men with him.
>
> (*Gottskalks Analer*, IA, 367)³⁵

Malise Sperra made his mark in life in the north and was remembered in Orkney and Scotland long after his death.³⁶

8.2.3 *Shetland and the Sinclairs*³⁷

This was evidently a fight to the death between rival members of the earldom

---

33 It has been suggested by Eldbjørg Haug (1996, 219) that Henry and Malise had been summoned to fight in the war which led to the Battle of Falköping, and that Malise had been knighted after the battle
34 Crawford, 2004e; Crawford, 1971, 235–6, 239
35 The phrase *a þui sama vettfangi flydi einn sveinn* may be taken to indicate that the 'field of action' was the 'thing' site at Tingwall. This is specifically a law term for the 'place of summons' (CV *sub vettfangr*), implying that it is the scene of a crime (*KL, sub Pileskud*). The standing stone on the road between Tingwall and Scalloway is traditionally supposed to mark the site of the killing (see Colour plate 37)
36 Crawford, 1983a, 38
37 It would have been about this time that Earl Henry was in contact with the Venetian Zeno brothers, and exploring the North Atlantic, if the Zeno 'narrative' could be believed, and if he could be identified with the local ruler called 'Zichmni' in that 'narrative'. It is not impossible that Earl Henry would have been willing and able to explore northern waters beyond Shetland (Crawford, 2004e), yet there is no evidence to show that he did, apart from the Zeno 'narrative' which is now generally considered to be a fabrication by a later member of the Zeno family in the sixteenth century. (Cuthbertson, 1996, 128–34; Smith, 2002; Cooper 2004; Wikipedia, 2010, 'Zeno Brothers')

family along traditional lines. But in 1389[38] it was also a fight between the earl whose authority was theoretically confined to Orkney and his cousin who probably represented royal Norwegian interests in Shetland. It was part of the process by which the earl recovered some influence in Shetland and from this period the Sinclair earls increasingly brought Shetland within their sphere of authority. Malise Sperra was a threat to the earl because of his claim to the earldom, and his good standing with Queen Margrete. He was an heir-in-waiting, and if he defeated (and killed) Henry, he stood a good chance of being accepted as the best choice of the surviving heirs of Earl Malise, who could then lay claim to the earldom.

Moreover, it would appear that Henry Sinclair's mother was at that date the ultimate heir to his cousin's landed possessions, through a process of inheritance reversion (see below). Malise Sperra was childless and in the event of his death, all his lands would revert to his only surviving aunt, Isabella Sinclair (who was Earl Henry's mother), as indeed they did.[39] This important factor about Isabella Sinclair is stated quite clearly in the 'Genealogy of the Earls':

> Swa that sche, modir of the forsaid Eirle Henrie the first, succedit til all hir sisteris, and till all the sonnis and dowchteris of tham, as anerlie ane and lawfull aire of the Eirledome of Orchadie and of the landis of Cathanie belangand till hire as till ane anerlie sister.[40]

Although Shetland is not mentioned here, Isabella's right to inherit all her nieces' and nephews' lands would have included Malise's Shetland property, which reverted to his aunt, in addition to the Orkney and Caithness estates inherited from his mother. This circumstance most probably explains the arrangement made in a charter of April 1391 drawn up in Kirkwall not long after Malise's death, in which Earl Henry granted lands in Aberdeenshire to his brother David, for his 'good service' and specifically for his 'right and any claim in the localities of Orkney and Shetland concerning him by reason of his mother Isabella Sinclair in any way (*aliquo modo contingente*).[41] That is, David was renouncing any claim to these lands in Earl Henry's favour, and the specific mention of Shetland most probably indicates the inclusion of Malise Sperra's paternal estates there – which had reverted to Isabella on Malise's death. This is the first indication since 1195 of any possessions by the earls in Shetland,

---

38   See Crawford 1971, 236 n.3, for discussion of the alternative dates of 1389 or 1391, but the former is probably the more likely year
39   Crawford, 1983, 40
40   *Bann. Misc.*, iii, 82: *sic quod ipsius antedicti quondam Comitis Henrici primi mater successit omnibus sororibus ejus, eorundemque filiis et filiabus, tanquam unica et legittima heres Comitatus Orcadie, et terrarum de Cathnes, sibi tanquam uni sorori debitarum*
41   *DN*, ii, 530.525; *Orkney Recs.*, p.27

and it appears to be the beginning of the Sinclair connection with Shetland.[42] Although Shetland remained separate from the earldom, it certainly came within the sphere of influence of the earls and members of the Sinclair family from this time.[43]

Two surviving charters provide evidence of Sinclair influence and presence in Shetland in the period following the death of Earl Henry I (1400). First is a grant in 1412 of royal lands and income from North Mavine (the extreme north-west part of the Mainland of Shetland) to Alexander von Klapam.[44] He can with fair certainty be identified with the Alexander of Claphame who witnessed the charter of 1391 in which Earl Henry granted lands to his brother David in return for the resignation of all his inheritance rights from his mother, discussed above. Alexander was therefore a member of Earl Henry's following and his name points to an origin in Fife, but he appears from the 1412 charter to have acquired some credit with the current ruler of Denmark and Norway, King Erik, who calls him his 'true servant and man'. The second charter is more official in nature and shows that in 1418 King Erik entrusted Shetland with all royal rights in a life grant to John Sinclair, the son of Earl Henry I 'by reason of the services done by his father and others of his kin'.[45] This indicates the family's dominance in Shetland, so that nearly forty years after the grant of the earldom to the first Sinclair earl, Shetland was granted to the present earl's brother.

8.2.4 *Earl Henry I's priorities*

The reference just cited in John Sinclair's charter suggests that Earl Henry had remained on good terms with his Norwegian king, and the surviving indications are that he not only fought for his dominant position in the islands but that he devoted some thought and planning to ensuring that his inheritance was not dissipated among family members. As well as the 1391 charter in which he bought out his brother David's claim on their mother's estates in Orkney and Shetland with a grant of estates in Aberdeenshire, there is record of a charter dated 1396 in which his daughter Elizabeth Sinclair and her husband John Drummond de Cargill renounced all claims to the earl's lands *Infra regnum*

---

42 The list of witnesses (including the archdeacon of Shetland, but *not* the bishop of Orkney) from both Orkney and Shetland, indicates the importance of this document. Four of them were entitled *dominus*, which has been interpreted as showing that these men had been knighted by the king of Norway (Wærdahl, 2011, 170), but see Clouston's doubts on that score and his discussion of what the title might indicate in terms of the lands held by these men (*POAS*, iii, 1924–5, 14–16)

43 See Crawford, 1971a, 358–60; 1983, 37–8

44 *DN*, ii, no. 623; *Shetland Docs.*, no. 18

45 *DN*, ii, no. 647; *Shetland Docs.*, no. 20

Norwagie, 'within the kingdom of Norway', in favour of the earl's male issue.[46] This shows awareness of the daughter's rights to a share of her father's estates which was part of odal custom in Norway and Orkney, quite different from Scottish custom, and which the Scottish earl was not going to allow to weaken his son and heir's inheritance.

From a letter written by Richard II of England to Queen Margrete of Denmark–Norway we catch a glimpse of Earl Henry's activities in a North Sea maritime arena in the period after he had sealed Erik of Pomerania's acceptance to be Queen Margrete's heir. This letter refers to complaints which the earl has made to Queen Margrete about the 'intolerable and extreme hurt' which had been committed against him by Richard's subjects, but adding that the same earl and his *subditi* ('subjects'), together with French and Scots, had made war against King Richard notoriously, in light of which the king does not feel inclined to make a favourable response to the request for safe-conducts (which presumably had included Earl Henry).[47] We do not know where these attacks had taken place, whether by Englishmen on the earl's Orkney lands or by the earl's men on English subjects in the Borders, but it is likely that this evidence of unfriendly relations was part of the fishing disputes which were building up in this period. A few months later, however, in March 1392, Earl Henry was given a safe-conduct by Richard to last until Michaelmas, with permission to travel with twenty-four persons.[48] In some way Earl Henry was closely involved in negotiations taking place at this time between Richard II and Queen Margrete and these sources give us a glimpse of some wide-ranging contacts which suggest that he was prominent in the Anglo-Scottish hostilities, just as his son was going to be. He had certainly participated in the Otterburn campaign in 1388.[49]

Evidence from a few charters issued by Earl Henry at Roslin shows that he divided his time between his southern estates and Orkney. His wife, Janet Haliburton, daughter of the lord of Dirleton, would most probably have resided at Roslin, administering the estate there, along with her son, the younger Henry, while the earl was north. Her husband increasingly must have resided in the north during the 1390s, as the 'Genealogy' says that he 'reterit to the parties of Orchadie, and josit thame to the latter tyme of his lyfe'.[50] Although

---

46 Anderson's introduction to *OS* Hjaltalin and Goudie, lxvii; Crawford, 1971, 241–2
47 Perroy, no. 130; *RN*, viii, 29. Discussed by Tuck, 1972, 76–9
48 *Rot. Scot.*, ii, 115b; Saint-Clair, 1898, 99. Other safe-conducts were granted – one in April, for six persons to come to England from Norway for treating on the alliance between Richard and Queen Margrete and another in July for the Archbishop of Trondheim and the Bishop of Oslo and Bergen (Tuck, 1972, 80)
49 Boardman, 1996, 280
50 *Bann. Misc.*, iii, 81

the compiler of the 'Genealogy' was at pains to stress the earl's northern connections, he could hardly make up the following statement that Henry died in the Orkneys defending his country, and 'was sclane [slain] thair crowellie be his innimiis'. It seems likely that Earl Henry was a victim of the continuing disturbed conditions in northern waters which dominated this period.[51]

8.3 EARL HENRY II (1400–1420) AND HIS GRANDMOTHER ISABELLA SINCLAIR

It has already been noticed (see Section 8.2.3.) that the 'Genealogy' provides the very specific information that Isabella de Strathearn (Sinclair), mother of Earl Henry I, survived all her sisters and her sisters' children, and succeeded them as the only surviving heiress of Earl Malise and as the 'ane and lawfull aire of the Eirledome of Orchadie and of the landis of Cathanie'; with the exception of the portion of these lands which had been inherited by her elder half-sister, Matilda, and which had been alienated and sold by Alexander of Ard to the king of Scotland.[52]

The 'Genealogy' continues by giving the very interesting information that after the death of her son Earl Henry I, Isabella came north to Orkney 'and baid continuallie thar', and that many good witnesses who were still living (this was in 1424) saw her 'and spak with hir at lenth'(*labiisque sunt locuti cum ea communicantes ad plenum*).[53] Although nothing more is said about the state of the earldom after the death of her son the first Sinclair earl, this significant statement is made about his mother's presence in the earldom which leads one to suggest that this venerable lady may have taken over the administration of the earldom for the rest of her lifetime.[54] As the sole survivor of Earl Malise's daughters, and surviving her son's demise, it would appear that she was considered to have inherited the earldom lands and rights of Orkney from him in a reversionary inheritance procedure which is recognised as operating in Scandinavian inheritance law.[55] At the very least it implies that her grandson did not

---

51 The English chronicler Walsingham records that a fishing fleet landed in Orkney in the year 1400 and spoiled some of the islands, which may have been the occasion of the earl's violent death (*Annales*, 1865)
52 The 'Genealogy' has previously mentioned – presumably not by chance – that Henry's mother (*eius matre*) was a member of the party which went to Marstrand in 1379 for his installation as earl (*Bann. Misc.*, iii, 81)
53 *Bann. Misc.*, iii, 82
54 Crawford, 2004e
55 This custom recognised a parent's right to inherit from a dead child (Sawyer, B., 1991, 214; Sawyer, B. and P., 1993, 182)), and the example of Queen Isabella Bruce who inherited her daughter Ingebjorg's estates (who pre-deceased her mother) shows the same principle in practice at the level of the royal family in Norway (Wærdahl, 2012, 106)

immediately succeed his father, because of the priority of his grandmother's claim – to whom, says the 'Genealogy' 'succedit her nevo [grandson] Henri the secund'.

If we turn to Earl Henry II, we find that he was primarily a Scottish nobleman, and that his northern earldom does not appear to figure in his career. He was very closely bound up with central events in the history of Scotland, and soon after succeeding his father he participated in the Humbleton campaign of 1402, where he was one of five Scottish earls captured by the English. By the middle of 1405 he had become the principal military commander of the Scottish forces in southern Scotland. During the next few years he was one of a small group of guardians of Robert III's son and heir to the throne,[56] and in 1406 was captured with the young Prince James at sea and taken into captivity. After Henry returned to Scotland, his brother John was regularly in England with the exiled king.[57]

In these circumstances it seems very probable that the matriarch Isabella was in Orkney (as the 'Genealogy' says) and attending to the earldom affairs in the absence of her grandson, and in her own right as the survivor of her generation with hereditary rights to the family lands in both Orkney and Caithness. Was the second Henry ever actually installed as earl? There is no evidence to suggest that he ever went to Norway or Denmark to visit King Erik. It is significant that the Installation documents of both his father and his son have survived, but nothing of the kind exists to show that Henry II had received a grant of any lands or title or that his right to the earldom was acknowledged.[58] He is however recorded as using the title 'earl of Orkney' in Scottish sources. The 'Genealogy', as well as suggesting that he succeeded his grandmother (as noted above), also says that 'at the last he decessit ondoutit erile of Orchadie and Schetland', which may be implying that he only did have the 'ondoutit' title towards the end of his life (he died in 1420).[59]

Some uncertainty about the nature of Henry II's title can be gleaned from these phrases in the 'Genealogy' suggesting that his grandmother exercised some prior right to the earldom lands and rights (although not of course the title) during most of his life as successor to his father. As the eldest daughter of

56 Boardman, 1996, 280–1
57 Brown, 1994, 18
58 The circumstances in which his grandmother inherited the family lands in the earldom from her son, the first Earl Henry, may have meant that it was not considered appropriate or necessary for Henry II to receive a grant
59 The use of the phrase 'at the last' (*ultimo*) does hint at Henry II having the earldom rights only towards the end of his life and perhaps after the death of his grandmother. It should be noted that the Latin version does *not* include Shetland, which may have been added only when the Scots translation was drawn up in 1554

Earl Malise's second marriage (the grant of whose marriage –*maritagium* – was made to the earl of Ross in 1344), Isabella is likely to have been in her sixties when her son, the first Earl Henry, died c.1400. How long she lived thereafter is unknown, but John Sinclair, brother of Henry II, was given the grant of Shetland by King Erik in 1418 (see Section 8.2.3).[60] In 1416, David Menzies, Henry's brother-in-law, was (in the event of Henry's death) made 'Tutor testamentary' for Henry's son and heir William, plus all other male and female children as heirs of Orkney until they came of age, and this gave Menzies rights over men, lands, rents, possessions and movable goods in Orkney 'baith in ye law and by ye law'.[61] In the Complaint of 1425 it was said that Menzies had been collecting earldom rents the year before William's father's death.[62] Whatever rights Isabella Sinclair had been exercising in the earldom would certainly have ceased by then, and we can assume that she was dead. This was only shortly before Henry II himself died (in 1420), which chimes with the 'Genealogy's' statements that 'at the last' he died undoubted earl having succeeded his grandmother. This does not however mean that he had then received a grant of the earldom from King Erik, and he may simply have used the title to give him commensurate status while employed in affairs of state during the reign of James I.

8.4 EARL WILLIAM SINCLAIR (1420–1470)

The difficulty which the son and heir of Henry II had in getting a formal grant of his earldom rights suggests that King Erik deliberately delayed granting them because of Henry II's failure to go to the royal court for a formal installation. If he had failed to visit King Erik and never received a grant of earldom rights, then the king might well have felt justified in withholding a renewed grant of authority from his son in accordance with the clause in Earl Henry I's installation document (see Section 8.1.1). The delay of fourteen years (until 1434) may suggest, indeed, that he intended not to make any grant at all to William Sinclair. This would have been, however, difficult to maintain, and

---

60 It can be noted that John Sinclair's grant mentions the services which had been done by his father 'and others of his kin' (*pretextu per pii recordii genitorem meum et ceteros de cognacione mea*) (*DN*, ii, no. 647)), but with no specific mention of his brother Henry II (see discussion in Crawford, 1971, 361)

61 Original charter of disposition in the Monzie papers (Ref. XS1 MS A005. Archival and Special Collections, Maclaughlin Library, University of Guelph). Thanks to Professor Elizabeth Ewen for providing me with a photocopy

62 *Orkney Recs.*, p.39; Crawford, 1971, 250. These rights should not have been operative until the death of Henry II (i.e.1420), as they were part of his testament for the regulation of his affairs after his death (information from Hector MacQueen)

once more there is evidence of attempts to put in place alternative arrangements for the governance of the earldom. This situation provides abundant surviving documentary material as it had in the 1370s, and these sources give us a remarkably full picture of island society in the period when Norse culture was probably still dominant, but Scottish influences were moving in.

8.4.1 *The rule of David Menzies and the abeyance of the earldom*

We have already seen what a powerful position David Menzies had as 'Tutor testamentary' to the young William, with full rights over lands and men in the islands according to the letter of 1416. When he was given a grant of authority by King Erik in 1423, Menzies demanded safeguards for the 'claim and settlement' which he had had with the father of the young lord William.[63] Before this grant however, his position had been challenged by a grant which King Erik had first made to the Orkney bishop, Thomas Tulloch, on 17 June 1420,[64] consequent to the death of Henry II, a new departure in royal policy. The close co-operation between kings and bishops is to be an important feature of the period of William Sinclair's earldom. The 1420 document is a sweeping grant of 'all the Orkneys with all royal rights' which was probably intended to include earldom rights as well, which at that time would be considered to have reverted to the Crown. Undoubtedly this would therefore have clashed with the authority which had been entrusted to David Menzies by Earl Henry II. So two years later, on 10 July 1422, Bishop Thomas issued another letter announcing that he had been given the castle and fortress of Kirkwall 'with the country of Orkney and the countship in the same place'.[65] The castle referred to was the one which had been built directly against the prohibition in Henry I's Installation document (see below). It must have been a symbol of authority for anyone exercising power in the islands and the bishop's first grant would have meant little without it. The purpose of this second grant was to affirm that the bishop should indeed be exercising the rights of an earl, symbolised by the Sinclair castle in Kirkwall.

The trouble that this caused can be assumed from the fact that in the following year another document gives us clear evidence that the previous grants to Bishop Thomas had probably never been implemented. This time it was David Menzies himself who was given, on behalf of King Erik and Queen

---

63 *DN*, ii, no. 676; *Orkney Recs.*, pp.35–6. It should be noted that this reference to Henry II does not refer to him as earl or indeed by name, probably because he had never been installed as earl

64 *DN*, ii, no. 657; *Orkney Recs.*, p.31. For the previous relationship between bishops of Orkney and the royal authorities see Chapter 7

65 *DN*, ii, no. 670; *Orkney Recs.*, p.33. This document differs in several ways from the previous grant (Crawford, 1976, 163)

Philippa, 'the earldom and country of Orkney', but with the apparent qualification 'as much as there rightly belongs to the Crown and kingdom of Norway'.[66] This must have replaced the previous grant to the bishop, but allowed Menzies to maintain the rights he had been given over the earldom by William's father which are expressly referred to. There is no mention of the castle in this grant and it is possible that the young William Sinclair had managed to make good the family assertion of its rights over the castle.[67] There were other members of the Sinclair family who were also playing a role in the events of these years: Thomas Sinclair was closely connected with the young William, accompanying him to Denmark when he attempted to get a grant of the earldom at about this same date. The two protagonists, David Menzies and Thomas Sinclair, and their followings had a bitter power struggle.[68]

The evidence for this struggle is fully evident in the remarkable 'Complaint of the People of Orkney about the misrule of David Menzies' (Figure 2.5),[69] which tells us so much about the disturbances which had taken place and about the ruling elite in Orkney, which objected to the heavy-handed governance of Scottish incomers and in particular, the uncle of the young heir to the earldom (referred to in Section 2.4).[70] This was sent to Queen Philippa along with a letter of appeal that the young earl be appointed their governor.[71] These documents reveal a great deal about the position of the young heir, William, at that time, and the attitude of the people of Orkney towards what they considered should be his rightful powers within the earldom. The authors refer to the 'discords and controversies' which had arisen between their governors, that is the bishop and the earl, reports of which had reached the queen's ears, but which had now been reconciled. They refer to the enquiry which the queen's chaplain had made as to why the 'aforesaid earl interfered with our government of the lands of our lord the King' and responded that it was with the 'unanimous desire and with the counsel and assent of all of us that our aforesaid earl undertook the said rule'. They continued with the request that she should 'appoint our earl and no other as our governor, and that he may maintain and govern the royal lands' until he shall come to the royal presence. They then make a strong

---

66 DN, ii, no. 676; *Orkney Recs.*, pp.35–6. See assessment of the relationship between Menzies and the bishop at the time of this document in Crawford, 1976, 165 n.47
67 Crawford, 1976, 165
68 Ibid., 161; Imsen, 2012,16
69 The heading given in *Orkney Recs.*, 36 (English trans.) to the unheaded document; Norwegian text in *DN*, ii, no. 691. It is undated but probably that document referred to as the 'written instructions' in the letter written by the community of Orkney to Queen Philippa in March 1425 (*DN*, vi, no. 423; Crawford 1976, 169)
70 Imsen (2012, 11, 20–1) analyses the social self-awareness of the Orkney community
71 *DN*, vi, no. 423; *Orkney Recs.* pp.45–8 (English trans.)

statement that as he comes from an 'illustrious, ancient and noble stock and family' so he is bound to be most acceptable and 'plenary' for all those things which 'seem' (*videntur*) to pertain to our said lord the king in Orkney. They also make reference to 'strangers who have been appointed governors in our affairs' from whom they have suffered 'innumerable losses, indignities, and shame'. The use of the phrase 'very often' with respect to these governors indicates that they are referring to others apart from David Menzies, perhaps harking back to the problems which arose in the 1360s, in the previous period when the earldom had been in abeyance (see Section 7.6.1).

The Complaint covers a myriad matters –thirty-six items, some with full details pertaining to the administration of the islands and economic and judicial practices.[72] The earl's incomes are named, such as the judicial fines which belonged to the king and to the earl but which David Menzies had collected harshly and unreasonably. These documents give clear evidence of the problems which arose when royal officials were appointed to administer royal rights at the time when an adult earl considered that he should be the 'governor' and have a grant of those rights. The overlapping nature of these rights and incomes continued to lead to great difficulty in the administration of them when two authorities claimed rights of appointment, and by inheritance in the case of the heir to the earldom.[73] The disparity between Scottish feudal practice and the automatic inheritance of his title by the son and heir of an earl, and the Norwegian customary appointment of the earl as a royal official – whose claim had to be recognised by the Crown – is brought sharply into focus in the illuminating information contained in these documents, which the misrule of David Menzies had instigated.

8.4.2 *Compiling the 'Genealogy of the Earls' and William's position*

Yet, despite the evident wishes of the community of Orkney as demonstrated in these documents,[74] the young earl was not installed for another nine years (on 9 August 1434). This was despite the fact that he drew up an early form

---

72 The main issues are familiar from social unrest in southern Norway at this time, concerning indignation with foreign bailiffs, and their lack of respect for old laws and good custom (Imsen, 2012, 9)

73 The young heir, William, is referred to as 'the earl' throughout the Complaint and Letter to the queen, although these documents date some ten years before he received a formal grant of the title. As noted, his father always used the title 'earl of Orkney', even though he never apparently went to receive a grant or was installed by King Erik (Crawford, 1976, 169, and n.61).

74 The 1425 Letter was sealed with the seal of the community of Orkney (*communitas Orcadensis*), as was the 'Genealogy' (*Bann. Misc.*, iii, 84). See Crawford, 1976, n.50; 1978 on the Orkney seal; and Section 2.7.3 above

of the 'Genealogy' (as is mentioned in the Complaint of 1425), when he tried to get the seal of the community of Orkney to be affixed to this document proving his birthright, and some local 'good men' in the islands to accompany him to King Erik, but was prevented by David Menzies.[75] That early form of the 'Genealogy' has not survived, the existing version, dating from 1443/6, was compiled for Erik's successor, King Christopher, but it is likely that the existing version was based closely on the earlier one, at least from the requirement that the compilers were aiming to prove William's descent from all previous earls 'linealie, gre be gre'('degree by degree'), and to show how his predecessors had a long-established right to the earldom and all its pertinents.[76] It was not only William Sinclair who had to go through this process, the 'Genealogy' relates how he reminded the bishop and chapter that his great-great-grandfather, Malise of Strathearn, had had similar letters from King Magnus Eriksson (1332–1355) requiring that the bishop of the time deliver to him relevant documents proving his own claim after the failure of the direct line of inheritance.[77]

However, Earl William's efforts were not successful in convincing King Erik of the justifiable nature of his claim to be given a grant of the earldom along with authority over royal lands and rights in the 1420s. It is therefore uncertain who was given this authority after the end of David Menzies' rule.[78] In April 1426, the Norwegian chancellor caused several transcripts to be made of Orcadian documents from the previous century and these may have borne some relevance to the situation in the islands at that time. On the other hand their copying could have been part of the search for information regarding the renewal of the Treaty of Perth which was made at Bergen in July 1426.[79] This was needed because of the long time during which the 'Annual' (the payment of 100 merks, or 200 nobles, in recognition of the surrender of the Hebrides) had not been paid (see Section 7.4.1). In October 1426, Bishop Thomas and two other clerics wrote to King Erik acknowledging that they would receive all

75 Crawford, 1976, 166
76 See Crawford (1971, Appendix A, pp.51–3) for detailed examination of the purpose and dating of the original text
77 Barry, 1805, 406; Crawford, 1976, 167. This section is only in the Scots version of the 'Genealogy', and has been omitted from the *Bann. Misc.* publication
78 David Menzies spent some time in England as a surety for the payment of James I's ransom in 1424, but was granted permission to return to Scotland in July 1425. He appears not to have returned to Orkney and it must be presumed that he came to an agreement with the young William to allow him to take over control of the earldom lands and rights (Marwick, 1927–8, 14–15)
79 *DN*, ii, nos 687, 688; vi, no. 426. The treaty between James I and King Erik is mentioned by Bower and the reason for its renewal (Bower, *Scotichron.* Book xvi, Watt, ed. (1987), 319); *DN*, viii, nos 276, 277, 278. Bishop Thomas of Orkney had a special mandate from King Erik to give an oath on his behalf

future payments on his behalf.[80] There is a possible indication in the wording of this document which hints that the royal appointee was someone else, and that someone else was most probably Thomas Sinclair, who was in good favour with King Erik as can be seen from the Complaint of 1425 in which he is said to have been granted royal letters of protection for himself, his men and all his possessions and property.[81] The fact that there is no evidence of infighting in the islands during the period 1426–34 strongly suggests that the situation must have been acceptable to Earl William, and the likelihood is that he and his relative Thomas Sinclair co-operated in administering Orkney during these years.

These were also years in which William was building up his power base and political relationships in Scotland. He married Elizabeth Douglas sometime before 1432 as in that year they had a papal dispensation allowing them to remain in marriage.[82] She had been married twice before and it may be that this was not Earl William's first marriage either.[83] As with his father's marriage to Egidia Douglas (granddaughter of King Robert II) this brought William into the heart of the most powerful kindred in Scotland, and one with royal connections (his wife was a granddaughter of King Robert III). He was thereafter closely connected with the royal court and it would appear that King James I even interceded with King Erik to make a grant of the earldom of Orkney to William (as mentioned in his Installation document), which he finally secured in 1434. This delay of many years before King Erik granted William rights in the earldom is quite remarkable, and may reflect dissatisfaction with the situation before William's succession, when his father had made no attempt to visit his Norwegian king to gain an acknowledgement of his claim. However, it could be noted that as Earl Henry II had given no oath of loyalty nor made any promises to abide by any installation requirements, then King Erik had no grounds for accusing him of disloyalty or of failure to abide by his promises. It may be that the king was simply wishing to break the heritability of the earldom, disband the dignity and rule the islands in the same way as Shetland. As Shetland had been granted to the late earl's brother as a life fief in 1418 and as William Sinclair and his relative Thomas Sinclair appear to have been in control in Orkney between 1425 and 1434, it seems that the Sinclair grasp of

---

80 *DN*, ii, no. 689
81 *Orkney Recs.*, 40. He was a knight in 1434, and was entitled 'Warden' (*custos*) of Orkney in 1435 (Crawford, 1976, 161, 170–1). Imsen (2012, 16) thinks that he had letters of protection simply as a royal liegeman rather than having been given a grant of royal authority
82 *DN*, xvii, 495. In that document they are both said to be resident in the diocese of Orkney
83 He was thereafter deeply involved in the legal dispute over Elizabeth's claim to the earldom of Mar and Garioch (Crawford, 1971, 275)

power and authority in the Northern Isles was complete. What was lacking was the formal bestowing of the ancient honour and dignity on the incumbent and there is no doubt that William Sinclair wanted that rather badly; despite not having been installed as earl he called himself earl of Orkney throughout this difficult period.

8.4.3 *Earl William's Installation 1434*

The earl's installation finally took place in Copenhagen on 9 August 1434, and the Installation document reflects that of his grandfather of 1379, although with various clauses amended to make them relevant to the changed circumstances.[84] The clause concerning the payment of 1,000 nobles is omitted, which indicates that that payment in 1379 had been for some reason other than a 'feudal relief', otherwise one would expect a similar payment to have been demanded in 1434 (see Section 8.1.1). Clause 3 in which Earl Henry promised not to build any castles or other defences within the islands now includes a promise that on Earl William's death 'that tower' (*illa turris*) which had been built in the town of Kirkwall without the king's consent and against the tenor of his grandfather's appointment would be yielded up along with the whole of Orkney. This indicates that the tower was in Earl William's possession already – indeed, as suggested above (Section 8.4.1), he had probably been allowed to keep control of it in the 1420s.

The two significant final clauses which in 1379 were added at the very end of the document have now been moved to the end of the main clauses and *before* the list of signatories. Moreover, the second of these two clauses, concerning forfeiture, was altered, the earl now promising that in the event of him failing to fulfil any of the promises he would go to the king and before him and the Council would agree to make satisfaction for whatever he had omitted to do. If after due and repeated summons he still failed to appear, he acknowledged that he would forfeit the earldom. The following sentence on the loss of the earl's heirs to claim the earldom in the event of forfeiture was dropped.

Earl William says that he was unable to leave noble men as hostages, as Lord Henry earl of Orkney 'our grandfather and predecessor' had done (in 1379 four friends and kinsmen had been left as hostages for the fulfilling of the conditions of appointment) (see Section 8.1.1). On this occasion one relative and five supporters are named who provided their seals on Earl William's behalf, and they all appear to be prominent members of the Orkney community (some of them recorded elsewhere as burgesses and baillies of Kirkwall) who had

---

84 *NGL*, anden række, I, no. 74; there is no translation into English. See Crawford (1971, 278–81) for full consideration of the differences between the two Installation documents and *Orkney Recs.*, p.48, for a brief summary of those differences

accompanied William to Copenhagen.[85] As they are given the title *domini* and listed as *armigeri* ('arms-bearers'), they had been knighted, perhaps on this very occasion, by King Erik. The ultimate demand in the Installation document, that Earl William had to prevail upon his Scottish overlord, King James, to add his seal to the open letter which the earl had to return – and thus become in effect a surety for the earl's allegiance to his other feudal overlord – was a condition which it was impossible for the new earl to fulfil. This was recognised by the admission that if the earl was unable to to arrange this (after having made several diligent attempts), then he would be excused. We do not know if any of the letters of surety were returned, as none have survived (as one of Earl Henry's did survive). In the event it did not much matter for shortly after this King Erik abdicated, and the uncertainty over the succession to the throne meant that there was no one in power who would be interested in ensuring that any letters of surety were returned.

King Christopher the Bavarian was finally accepted as king of Norway in 1442 and evidence shows that Earl William did make attempts to contact him, and it may have been for such an occasion that one of the copies of the 'Genealogy' (the Latin version) was compiled, for it is dated May 1446.[86] However, there is no evidence that the earl was ever in contact with his new Scandinavian overlord, or that he did homage to any of them after King Erik; the reason must be that the political situation in Scotland was beginning to make it very difficult indeed for such contact to be maintained.

8.4.4 *Chancellor of Scotland 1454–1456 and earl of Caithness*

Earl William proceeded to play a very important role in the events of the reign of James II (1437–1460). He was of course the son of Egidia Douglas and married to Elizabeth Douglas, so that he was closely connected with the family that controlled the country during James' minority. However, his wife Elizabeth died in 1451 which cut off his close link and he did not support the Douglases in their contest for power, being firmly on the side of the young king during the final clash in 1455.[87] He was chancellor from 1454 to 1456 and would not have been able during this period to attend to his earldom in the north, having to be active alongside the king during the final struggle with the Douglases.[88] In 1455, he accompanied the 'great gun' to Threave Castle in Galloway, which resulted in the fall of the castle to the royal forces, and he was high in King James' favour thereafter, for a brief period. He built up his power base at Roslin, which in 1456 was erected

---

85 Crawford, 1971, 281, n.1
86 *Bann. Misc.*, iii, 85; Crawford, 1971, 283
87 McGladdery, 1990, 88–9
88 Crawford, 1971, 284–5

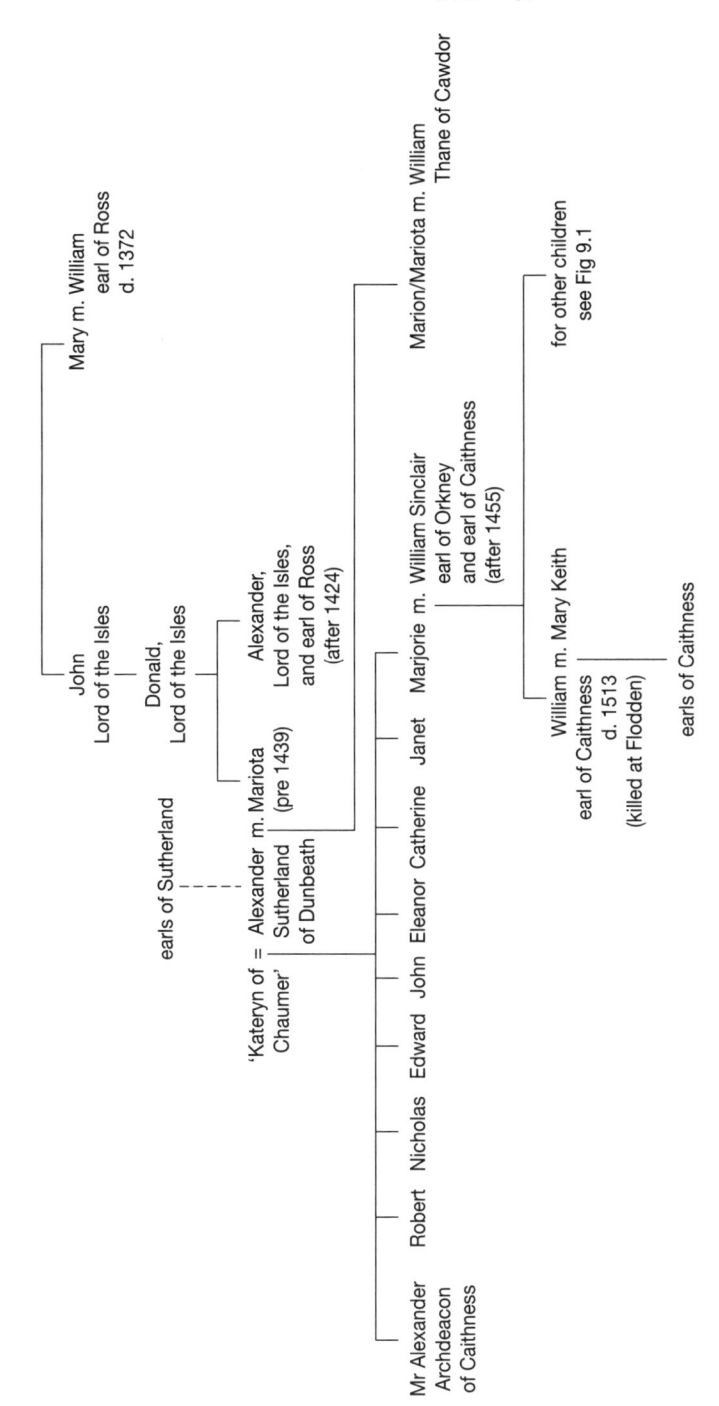

Figure 8.3 Family relationships of Alexander Sutherland of Dunbeath.

into a Burgh of Barony 'for the zele, singulare lufe and affection that we have till our weill belovitt cousin and chancelar William' as the royal charter says.[89] Prior to this, in 1446, William had founded the Collegiate Church of St Matthew at Roslin, a monument testifying, even though unfinished, to the wealth, status and ambitious aspirations of the earl[90] (see Colour plates 36a and 36b).

Above all, in 1455, he had succeeded in regaining the earldom of Caithness for his family. Since that earldom had been resigned to the Crown in 1375 it had passed through the hands of members of the royal family, as already noted (see Section 7.7). It was then in abeyance from 1434 to 1452 until being re-created for Sir George Crichtoun who was in high favour at the time. But just two years later he resigned all his 'conqueist' lands into the king's hands, evidently because of illness, and died shortly afterwards.[91] A year later, on 28 August 1455, the earldom of Caithness was granted to William Sinclair, the chancellor, in the same month as the fall of Threave Castle, in which William had been so closely involved. We can assume that he had requested this restoration of his family's ancient dignity and that it was readily granted by the grateful king, although it was said to have been given in compensation for William's claim and right to the Lordship of Nithsdale along with other rights which had been granted to the earl's forebears Egidia and William Douglas.[92] Moreover, the earldom, along with all William's other lands in Caithness which he had resigned into the king's hands, was erected into a Barony. These other lands must have been the earldom estates which had passed to his great-grandmother, Isabella Sinclair, and which she had inherited from her sisters, as the surviving daughter of Earl Malise's second marriage. They were now reunited with the portion which Alexander of Ard had inherited (called in the 'Genealogy' 'the principal manuring or mans of the Eirldome of Cathanie' *principali manerio sive manso*)[93] and which he had alienated to the Crown in 1375 (see Section 7.7.1). This 'caput' was the estate of Brawl (near Halkirk), with the castle, which is likely to have been built in the previous century (see Colour plate 34). Although the dramatic development of 1455 did not re-create the former extensive earldom possessions in Caithness, nonetheless the combination of the two earldoms reverted back to the circumstances before the death of Earl Malise. The restoration of the Caithness earldom title to the family must have been a matter of some satisfaction to Earl William. The double earldom had been re-created: so had the problems which this situation engendered.

89   Hay, 1835/2002, 76
90   Hay, 1835/2002, 27; Crawford, 1994, 101; Maggi, 2008, 2
91   Crawford, 1971, 286
92   Hay, 1835/2002, 73
93   *Bann. Misc.*, iii, 79

At about the time that he recovered the earldom of Caithness, there is evidence that Earl William had a relationship with a woman of northern origin, Marjorie Sutherland, daughter of Alexander Sutherland of Dunbeath,[94] whom he eventually married as his second wife. We know quite a lot about the earl's involvement with this family because Alexander Sutherland's will, dated 1456, has survived and provides a great deal of information about social and economic circumstances in this northern context.[95] Earl William's first wife Elizabeth Douglas, died in 1451, but it is not certain when the second marriage took place, although the 1456 will refers to children already born of Earl William and Alexander's daughter Marjorie.[96] The fact that Alexander Sutherland only refers to her as 'Marjory my douchtir' in his will and never as wife of the earl or 'Countess of Orkney and Caithness' clearly intimates that she was not the earl's wife at that point, although some of their children had already been born. This indicates that their relationship had been ongoing for some years before 1456, although for how long is unknown. It is likely that Marjorie was an illegitimate daughter of Alexander Sutherland, and was thus unsuitable for marriage to the powerful earl of Orkney and chancellor of Scotland. Evidence suggests that Alexander's legitimate daughter Marion, by his wife Mariota of the Isles, and the only child to be left his lands in his will, including Dunbeath, was his only legitimate child.[97] His other nine children, including Marjorie, were probably born to the woman whom he refers to in his will as 'Kateryn of Chaumer'. Although her illegitimate status would make Marjorie an unsuitable spouse for Earl William, an irregular union with her would not cause any problems. It is therefore very remarkable that he eventually married her,[98] and the successful nature of their union is evidenced by their offspring, numbering at least fourteen (see Figure 9.1).

Alexander Sutherland's will was drawn up at Roslin on 15 November 1456 and gives a wealth of information about his connections and economic circumstances in the north of Scotland.[99] He had acquired a number of lands, which

---

94 A. MacEwen (1982) sorts out the family connections of Alexander Sutherland with the earldom family of Sutherland
95 *Bann. Misc.*, iii, 99; a photograph of the will is in Crawford, 1990, centrepiece
96 Alexander left one thousand pounds, 'to the barnys gottyn and to be gottyn betuix thame' (*Bann. Misc.*, iii, 98), and also leaves them all the lands of the earl's in Caithness which had been wadset to him (see below)
97 Crawford, 1990, 12; 2004e
98 The first reference to 'Countess Marjory', wife of Earl William, appears to be the grant of the lands of the earldom of Caithness to their son William Sinclair in 1476 (*RMS*, ii, 1267)
99 He may have died shortly after, and money was left in his will for purchase of a 'throuch' stone to be lain over his grave, which was to be prepared near where the earl's burial place was intended to be in the Church of St Matthew, Roslin

were mostly pledged ('wadset') to him in return for loans of money. Those in Caithness had been wadset by Earl William, who was evidently in need of money, possibly because of a policy of land purchases in Orkney (see below). These purchases were connected with the fears which the earl had for his landed position in Orkney. It was just at this time that the king's policy for the Northern Isles was becoming evident. Earl William was probably preparing to establish personal landholdings for his successors which could not be subverted by royal ambitions for possession of his rich island earldom.

8.5 THE GATHERING STORM CLOUDS

The standing of Earl William at the court of King James changed dramatically in the winter of 1456–7. From being the all-powerful chancellor, and the firm supporter of the young king in his struggle to overcome the Douglas threat to his authority, Earl William appears to suddenly lose all political influence. His last known act as chancellor was on 20 October 1456, and after that both he and Bishop James Kennedy, who had also been a prominent figure in the government, are no longer of any significance. The reason is not far to seek. With internal security established, and having reached the age of twenty-five (his full majority) in November 1455, James was governing his own affairs, and turned his attention to foreign policy, showing an aggressive expansionism in several directions. In particular, trouble over the 'Annual' payment for the Isles was forcing Scottish policy in response to renewed Danish demands.[100] Legates from Scotland and Denmark were meant to discuss the problem at a meeting in Paris at Whitsun 1457.[101] But an international incident caused by the capture in Orkney of the governor of Iceland during the winter of 1456–7 meant that King Christian of Denmark–Norway asked for the meeting to be postponed.

Was this the intended purpose of the offence against the governor of Iceland? It appears from a letter dated April 1457 which King Christian wrote to James II that the governor had sought shelter in Orkney during a storm, but that he and his wife and household following had been captured and imprisoned, while the governor's goods had been seized along with the royal tribute and ecclesiastical rents which were being transported to Denmark.[102] This was a serious breach of international propriety, and could not have happened without the earl of Orkney's knowledge or indeed his connivance. Had the earl in fact deliberately engineered this incident in order to delay the negotiations, knowing of

---

100 Crawford, 1971, 299
101 In May 1456 Christian had made a treaty with Charles VII of France in which Charles had promised to bring his good offices to bear to enforce payment of the annual sum of 100 marks (Wegener, 1856, no. 55)
102 Crawford, 1985, 235

the plans which the young king was preparing for the Northern Isles? It cannot be determined whether the earl was removed from the chancellorship before or after the attack on the governor of Iceland, but the coincidence of the two events might suggest some connection between them.

As far as the king's policies were concerned James might have wished to avoid negotiations over the 'Annual' which could only be resolved by some reparations for the years of non-payment. But he could not avoid responding to the pressure which was being applied by both Christian and King Charles of France, who was acting as mediator in the affair. King Christian kept up the pressure, even threatening reprisals in 1458 if James did not agree to meet to negotiate over the issue – and intimating that he would take the matter to the Pope.[103] Embassies visited King Charles in France in July 1459, and a meeting of both parties took place at Bourges in October 1460, when a marriage alliance proposal was brought forward by Charles as the way to resolve the hostility. The Scottish delegates responded aggressively, demanding that all claims to the arrears of the 'Annual' should be remitted in a marriage alliance agreement, and further that all the Danish king's rights in Orkney and Shetland were to be given to Scotland, with an additional marriage payment of 100,000 crowns for the bride's adornment.[104]

8.5.1 *Earl William's position in the minority of James III (1460–1468)*

These demands were audacious and most probably emanated from King James himself, although he had been killed a few months previously. This fact alone would explain why the marriage negotiations got no further at this point.[105] Our problem is to know what the earl's position was, and how he intended to engineer the circumstances to his own advantage in this political stalemate. Although on the face of it a development along the lines of the Scottish embassy's demands at Bourges might help his own difficult position as a vassal with divided loyalties, it does not appear as if that was his preferred solution.[106] He was doubtless fully aware of the ultimate ambitions of King James to acquire not only possession of the royal rights in the islands of Orkney and Shetland but also his own earldom rights and powers. The Danish marriage was the means by which the Scottish king had hoped to gain a foothold in Orkney and

---

103 Crawford, 1971, 304
104 Crawford, 1969, 39;1971, 305
105 The Danish ambassadors said that their instructions did not allow them to proceed with a marriage alliance (Crawford, 1969, 39)
106 The comment that William 'evidently continued to favour Scottish plans concerning Orkney and Shetland' (Crawford, 1969, 43, n.4) does not seem to be likely on reconsideration of his position

Shetland in his ambitious policy for the acquisition of the islands, and establishing royal authority there. If the earl could prevent the furthering of this marriage policy, he could stave off the inevitable results. The sudden death of James II at Roxburgh in August 1460 might therefore have been regarded as an opportunity to delay the marriage plans and the subsequent effects on his own position in the islands.

But how was he going to manage his relationship with his Danish overlord, who was a king with widespread ambitions in his territorial possessions and desperately in need of all sources of income, because of his difficult financial circumstances? There is no evidence that Earl William had been in contact with King Christian between his accession in 1450 and the events of 1460. But there is good evidence to show that Christian made vigorous attempts to contact the earl immediately after the collapse of the negotiations at Bourges. Two letters dating to February 1461 and June 1461 were sent to Christian in response to his own communication in which he had evidently demanded the earl's attendance. The first was from the baillies of Kirkwall, and the second from the bishop of Orkney, presenting the earl's excuses.[107] The demand for the earl's attendance at this point suggests that Christian had been stirred into action by the report of the Scottish demands at the Bourges meeting. A second request was sent on 8 December 1461 for the earl to come next St John's Day and do homage as he had not yet sworn his oath of fealty.[108] Earl William never did visit Christian to do fealty, and clearly wished to sever all contacts. He must have realistically come to appreciate that his circumstances would not permit him to be a vassal of two kings. The minority of the young James III meant that Earl William was once more at the helm of state in the kingdom, and as a prominent figure in the Scottish political sphere he would be very ill-advised indeed to do homage to another king.

Who then was managing the royal estates and revenues in the earldom at this particular time? From a few years later there is record of letters passing between King Christian, the lawman of Orkney and the new bishop, William Tulloch, which give clear indication that the royal rents and taxes (skats) from Orkney were not being received, and the implication was that these had been diverted to the earl by his officials in the islands.[109] The king was attempting

---

107 *DN*, v, no. 827; *DN*, v, no. 836; English translations in *Orkney Recs.*, nos xxii and xxiii. The first letter excused the earl 'for his long absence from your majesty'; the second said that a recent raid by the earl of Ross would prevent him from visiting Christian so soon as he intended; see Thomson (2001, 196–8) for details of this attack on Orkney.
108 Huitfeldt, 1599, 123; Crawford, 1969, 41–2
109 *Kirkwall Chrs.*, 110, a translation of the version of the letter in Taranger, 1912, iii, 139–40, deriving from Huitfeldt, 1599, 158

to use the lawman and the bishop as royal administrators, and Bishop William certainly proved himself to be a loyal servant of the Danish king throughout this difficult period.[110]

This situation explains an attack on the bishop which was reported by the Danish chronicler Arild Huitfeldt, who says that it was a result of the bishop's loyal conduct and close relationship with the king of Denmark. Christian wrote two letters, one to the Scottish Council and the other to James III on 31 May 1467, complaining about the imprisonment of the bishop – presumably in Orkney – and the enforcement of oaths while he was bound in chains. The kidnapping was said to have been carried out by the son of the earl. This was presumably the eldest son, William, who was the only son of the earl's first marriage with Elizabeth Douglas.[111] The bishop was soon released, and we are left wondering if this incident was a random attack by the young son of the earl or if his father had any part in the affair. If he did, then it mirrors the attack on the governor of Iceland which had occurred a decade earlier, and which has been interpreted as having been instigated by the earl who was attempting to upset the negotiations which were underway with Denmark (see above).

Certainly, the matter of the marriage with the Danish princess had been raised again just before this second incident, which coincided with the rise of the Boyds in the Scottish political scene. Earl William had been a regent during the first years of the minority of James III, and was therefore able to divert the matter of James' marriage in another direction, and he led an embassy to England in 1461. But, with the death of the Queen Mother and Bishop Kennedy in 1463 and 1465, power in government passed to the Boyd family and there is no evidence that Earl William had any connection with them, and in fact was probably opposed to them.[112] So, when the matter of the 'annuale of Norway', as well as the question of the young king's marriage, was raised in the parliament of 1466, Earl William was no longer in any position to influence the direction of such matters, and the attack on the bishop would appear to have been the result of a reaction to developments of which the earl and his family disapproved. From then on the advance towards the Danish marriage and the concomitant change in the political circumstances in Orkney appears inexorable.

That Earl William was well aware of this future development is apparent from a land-purchasing policy which he was evidently pursuing within his island earldom. The evidence for this comes from the surviving Rentals of Orkney

---

110 Crawford, 1969, 43
111 This was the so-called William 'the Waster' who is usually said to have been disinherited by his father, because the inheritance of the earldom of Caithness passed to the eldest son of the earl's second marriage, also called William (Crawford, 1971, 318; 1985, 245) (see below)
112 Crawford, 1985, 237

which were compiled by his grandson Lord Henry Sinclair in 1492 and 1500,[113] after the loss of the family earldom and when Henry was striving to recoup some of the family's landed wealth in Orkney (see Chapter 9). As part of this process he was concerned to list all those lands, called 'conqueist' (conquest),[114] many of which are said to have been acquired by his grandfather, the last earl. This acquisition process was on such a large scale that it has been estimated that one third of all the privately owned lands in the islands were acquired by Earl William.[115] It is not said when these transactions took place, but it must have been over a number of years before the loss of the earldom in 1470 because of the scale of the enterprise.[116] It seems not unlikely that the purchasing policy was started in the 1450s when James II's ambitions for the acquisition of Orkney and Shetland became clear. If so, it is possible that the evidence for William Sinclair's debts to Alexander Sutherland as revealed in the will of 1456 (see Section 8.4.4) may have been caused primarily by his need for money to pay for these land purchases in Orkney – and also in Shetland.[117] It has been suggested that the sale of land by the odallers in Orkney may also have been a result of the economic depression which as is evident from the 1492 Rental had existed for some period of time in the north.[118] This may partly explain why so many odal families were willing to part with outlying portions of their family lands. But the amassing of such a sizeable estate of purchased lands would appear to have been driven more by the earl's own requirements and foresight, rather than as a response to the needs of odal farmers in the islands.[119]

The accumulation of evidence gives us some understanding of the awkward position in which Earl William found himself in the reigns of James II and III. We see once more the earl perched on the horns of a dilemma, although this time prioritising his liege lord was not a difficult choice to make (as it had probably been in 1263; see Section 7.3). The situation for an earl who was a powerful figure in the Scottish kingdom was nonetheless an uncomfortable one. However, the anomalous position of being the vassal of two kings was

---

113 Peterkin, 1820; Thomson, 1996
114 'Conquest' lands were personal, acquired lands (not inherited) which the family retained when the earldom estates passed to the Scottish Crown.
115 Clouston, 1923/4, 61; 1932, 256; 1927, *passim*; Thomson, 1996, xix
116 One transaction certainly took place before 1460 as it was with Bishop Thomas Tulloch who resigned in that year (Crawford, 1971, 294)
117 The earl also had other huge expenses at this time, like the building of Roslin Collegiate Church, started probably in 1446 (Crawford, 1994, 101)
118 Thomson, 1984, 139–41
119 Crawford, 1971, 294–5; 1985, 241.This policy paid off as can be seen from a document issued by James III in 1471 recognising that he had no right to the conquest lands of Earl William in Orkney and Shetland (Crawford, 1985, Appendix, and Chapter 9 below)

finally going to be resolved, although not in a way which can have been satisfactory to that vassal.

8.5.2 *The marriage treaty and the pledging of Orkney and Shetland (1468–1469)*

In the early months of 1468 there were moves to revive the marriage negotiations, and also to solve the problem of the 'annuale of Norway', as is known from the Scottish parliamentary record, and from a letter King Christian wrote to James asking him to fulfil all previous treaties made between their two countries.[120] Huitfeldt gives a précis of James' reply to this letter; the young king excuses his ignorance of the matter which he says is due to lack of experience, although adding that the pension had not been paid in his grandfather's or great-grandfather's time, but he would send legates to Copenhagen to deal with this and other matters concerning peace.

At the same time as he raised the matter of the 'Annual', Christian must also have made one final demand for the earl of Orkney to visit him, for Huitfeldt says that James III sent a knight called David Cranstoun to excuse the earl, who could not go because he was prevented by business. Christian had to be satisfied with this excuse because of the marriage negotiations which were then beginning and he replied on 1 May. Earl William's relationship, or non-relationship, with his Danish overlord finally ended with this letter. Unsurprisingly he played no part in the ambassadorial arrangements which followed for the marriage negotiations.[121] More surprising is the inclusion of Bishop William as a general member of the Scottish embassy, for as bishop of Orkney he had no formal position in the Scottish Church. However, as a Danish speaker he would have been a useful participant.[122] His relationship with King Christian continued to be close.

King James' two charters of commission to his embassy are dated 28 July, and the second one entrusted the actual marriage negotiations with Denmark to Lord Avondale and the earl of Arran, giving them complete powers to contract a marriage with Christian's daughter Margaret. At the beginning of August the embassy sailed for Copenhagen and the alliance between the two kingdoms and the marriage treaty were completed on 8 September. There is no record of the negotiations which took place, as there is of those in 1460, but it can be assumed that the Scots would not have reduced their demands for the transfer

---

120 Crawford, 1969, 37; 1971, 325
121 Crawford, 1971, 326–9, and discussion of the theories pertaining to the absence of the earl from the embassy (also ibid., 1969, 48–9)
122 King Christian later requested that the bishop might be with the young Princess Margaret until she had learned the language of her new country

of Orkney and Shetland from those previous negotiations. Christian must have been prepared for the end of his hopes for repayments of the arrears of the 'Annual'; even in 1460 Charles VII had recommended that its remission should be part of the dowry agreement. But it was over his failure to come up with the remainder of the dowry payment in ready cash that the islands were brought into the equation. How the bargaining proceeded is unknown, but it was Christian's notorious penury which must have forced him to allow the Scots to get some way towards achieving their aim.[123] Of the 60,000 florins of the Rhine which he promised to pay only 10,000 could be provided immediately. Presumably the Scots demanded the transfer of Orkney and Shetland as payment of the remainder. However, Christian only *pledged* 'all and sundry our lands of the islands of the Orkneys, with all and sundry rights, services and their rightful pertinents, pertaining or that in whatsoever manner may pertain to us and our predecessors, kings of Norway, by royal right'[124] until the 50,000 florins had been paid. The Scots conceded one-third of the royal revenues with Linlithgow Palace and Doune Castle as the future queen's dower.[125]

Many questions have been raised about the nature of the transaction, the intentions of the participants and what was actually pledged.[126] For the purposes of this study it is important to investigate how the circumstances of the mortgage situation affected the earl's position. It must have been the case that superiority over the earldom was included in the transfer of royal rights.

As has been seen, the king raised a member of the earldom family to the dignity of earl when he gave him a grant of his earldom and installed him (see Sections 7.2.1 and 8.1). He could also grant the land and earldom of Orkney to people other than the earl. Naturally the earl was supposed to do homage to each new king. This, however, Earl William had failed to do, when requested by Christian to attend him. The earl may therefore have been in breach of his duty to his Danish overlord, and possibly in danger of forfeiting his grant of the earldom (which was threatened in the earl's Installation document in a situation where he was considered to have failed to abide by the promises he made: see above).[127] If this was the case, then the pledging of royal rights in the islands in the marriage treaty would have included the earldom lands as well as royal

---

123 See arguments against the theory that Christian 'colluded' with the Scots over their demands in Crawford (1969, 49 ff.) and Crawford (1971, 330–1)
124 *Kirkwall Chrs.*, 107
125 MacDougall, 1982, 78
126 Crawford, 1971, 329–35, for discussion of the main issues
127 In King Christian's letter of 8 December 1460 demanding Earl William's attendance the next St John's Day this was said to be *sub poenis in legibus Norvegiae contentis* ('under threat of penalties contained in the laws of Norway') (Huitfeldt, 1599, 123) which may be a reference to the terms of the earl's Installation charter, or to the Hirdlaw (see Chapter 7)

estates in Orkney. So, if Earl William had not submitted to King Christian or done an oath of homage to him, this would have meant that King James did not have to directly deprive Earl William of his earldom estates, when he acquired the earl's right of his earldom in 1470.

Shetland had not been included in the original marriage treaty, which transferred only Orkney.[128] Thus far, King Christian may have felt that he had emerged from an embarrassing situation with no great loss of prestige. He had resisted the Scots demands for the transfer of Shetland as well as Orkney, and had made a prestigious marriage alliance while promising a very handsome dowry of 60,000 florins of the Rhine. Orkney was pledged for 50,000 of that sum and the ambassadors stayed in Denmark over the winter of 1468–9 while the 10,000 florins were supposed to be collected and handed over. However, Christian's penury was such that this did not prove possible and in May 1469 he was compelled to issue an additional document pledging 'all his lands of the islands of Shetland' for 8,000 florins.[129] The document explains that he was unable to pay this sum 'hindered by the insults of our enemies and rebels' and by other 'unlooked-for events'. It can be assumed that the remaining sum of 2,000 florins was raised and paid over as there is some evidence of a tax being levied for the dowry payment.[130]

The embassy then returned to Scotland almost immediately with the young princess, and the royal marriage was celebrated on 10 July 1469 (see Colour plate 38). The news that came with her that Shetland had followed Orkney in coming into Scotland's possession would have been an additional welcome wedding present. As far as the earl was concerned, the addition of Shetland did not impact on his position as earl, as the lands which he held in Shetland were family estates which would not have been much affected by the change of sovereign.

8.5.3 *Earl William's renunciation of his right to the earldom of Orkney – the excambion of 1470*

We do not know what Earl William's reaction was to the news from the returning ambassadors that Orkney and Shetland had been pledged in partpayment for the dowry of the new queen. But we might guess that he would have been somewhat dismayed. The pledging of the islands meant that the Scottish Crown's possession of the islands was in theory only temporary, and

---

128 For the background to the pledging of Shetland see Crawford, 1983a
129 The Latin text of the Shetland transfer is printed in *NgL*, second series, II, i, no. 116; also as Appendix in Crawford, 1969, 52–3. English translation as Appendix in Crawford 1967–8, 175–6; *Shetland Docs.*, no. 25
130 Crawford, 1967–8, 166; 1971, 332

no one was to know that it would result in permanent cession. In the event of the islands being redeemed, the earl would once more have been in a very difficult situation as regards both his sovereigns, and King James would not have gained what he clearly desired to have. Perhaps this situation worsened the earl's fortunes; the most direct way for the king to ensure himself of permanent possessions in Orkney, in the event of the islands passing back under Danish sovereignty, would be to acquire the earldom and retain it in his own hands, although that in itself would result in a very difficult situation.

The problem of what exactly was passed over to King James in the impignoration has been the subject of some discussion.[131] The two documents concerning the pledging of Orkney and Shetland are quite non-specific in their terminology; very similar terminology is used in both documents, although the landed situation differed greatly between them, there being no earldom lands or powers in Shetland.[132] The general term of 'lands and islands of Orkney' which were pledged 'with all and sundry rights' can be understood to be wide-ranging and to cover all royal and earldom estates, as well as the right to skat from the lands of the odal farmers.[133] It also gave King James superiority over the earldom and its lands and rights, but in order for him to have permanent, actual legal possession he had to persuade, or command, Earl William to resign his right to the earldom to the Crown.[134] And this is just what Earl William did one year later. On 17 September 1470 he resigned the castle of Kirkwall and 'all his right in the earldom of Orkney' (*toto iure comitatus Orcadie*) to the king, receiving in exchange the castle of Ravenscraig and surrounding estates in Fife and a raft of other concessions.[135]

This transaction is known as the 'excambion' and it has been a matter of some concern among historians to understand whether Earl William received adequate compensation for the resignation of all his right to the ancient earldom, its lands and incomes. However, it should be appreciated that what he was resigning in 1470 was 'all right of his earldom', that is the grant which he had received in 1434 and the right which his successors had to continue to claim the earldom. The lands which went with that grant, the rich earldom estates,

---

131 Crawford (1967–8; 1971, 333–8) contra Mooney's arguments (1947, 14, 187, 190, 204) that it was only the royal estates which were pledged by Christian
132 A comparison of the phraseology of the two documents is in Crawford, 1967–8, 166
133 Crawford, 1967–8, 168
134 The conclusion has been that 'sovereignty' was not transferred from Denmark to Scotland by this transaction, but only acquired thereafter by 'prescription and administrative integration' when Scotland refused to go along with Denmark's attempts to redeem the Northern Isles: see Goodare's (1999, 238–9) comments on Donaldson's (1984) theories about the gradual process of this development
135 *RMS*, ii, nos 996–1002

had already passed to King James by the pledging of Orkney in the marriage treaty. The earl was not resigning those in 1470, but his 'whole right' (*toto iure*) to be given a grant of the earldom and its pertinents.[136] In addition, the castle of Kirkwall was included in his resignation. It has already been seen that this castle was built illegally against the provision of the 1379 Installation document (see Section 8.4.3), and Earl William had promised in his Installation document that it would be returned to the Crown on his own death.[137] It was, therefore, held only so long as he was earl, and by the resignation of his right to the earldom the castle therefore reverted to the new superior. In these circumstances it could not remain in the possession of the former earl, even though he continued to retain his own family (conquest) lands in the islands.

Instead of the *turris* ('tower') in Kirkwall, William received a more than adequate replacement with the grant of Ravenscraig Castle in Fife (see Plate 9). This was an impressive modern fortification which had been built by James II's queen, Mary of Gueldres, and which, along with the lands of Wilston, Carberry and Dubbo, comprised half the modern Burgh of Dysart on the south coast of Fife. The Sinclair family had had connections with Dysart since the mid-fourteenth century, as well as commercial interests there, so the acquisition of Ravenscraig made a fine *caput* ('head', 'chief place of a barony') to the new family honour, which was erected into a barony sometime later in the century.[138] An additional number of charters gave the earl a series of privileges, including a handsome annual pension of 400 marks,[139] which does not give the impression that he was being forced into a disadvantageous position in this 'excambion'. Even though he may have come under pressure to resign his earldom rights to the Scottish Crown, he no doubt realised that with the circumstances of the pledging of the Northern Isles he was placed in a very difficult position and one which had an uncertain outcome. The Scottish Crown's acquisition of the earldom rights in Orkney would certainly have posed problems if the islands had been redeemed, but it can be assumed that even at this early date there was an intention never to let this happen.[140]

One of the charters granted to Earl William as part of the 'excambion' has particular interest for what it reveals about the earl's long-term planning and his understanding of the nature of the changes wrought by the transaction.

136 Crawford, 1967–8, 169
137 Ibid., 170 n.65; 1971, 346
138 Ibid., 1967–8, 171; 1971, 348
139 Crawford, 2004e
140 A charter was issued in May 1471 relating to the marriage contract and acknowledging that in the event of James' death his widow could return to Denmark, and promising that if she did the 50,000 florins would be deducted from her 'terce' and the islands of Orkney returned to the kings of Norway (*APS*, ii, p.187)

It is a charter concerning the resignation of his lands, rents and possessions which he then held of the king in chief, and which the king promises that he will grant to the earl or his assignees by charter and seisin so that they would be held as freely as they were held before the resignation and 'without any dues having to be paid to the king' (*absque quibuscunque domino regi inde faciendo*).[141] From the terms of this charter it can be deduced that it was the lands which the earl already held in Orkney (and Shetland) which were being referred to, in particular those conquest lands which he had acquired recently, and which he did not already hold by charter or seisin because of the nature of odal tenure in the islands. This is a rather remarkable privilege in several respects. It shows that the earl was aware of the changes that were going to happen in landholding customs once Scottish tenurial arrangements were brought in to the islands, and that he was preparing for the implementation of those changes in the best way to preserve his own tenurial position.[142]

The short space of time between the marriage treaty and the 'excambion' arrangements of the following year suggests that the Scottish king and his advisers reacted rather quickly to the unexpected circumstances of the pledging of the islands. The Crown was acting in response to this development in order to ensure its acquisition of a permanent position in Orkney which the pledging of the lands did not assure them of. It can be assumed that the Crown was eager to buy out the right to the earldom which the earl is unlikely to have wished to surrender voluntarily. Despite the large number and wide range of the privileges given in exchange for the earldom, along with the magnificent royal castle of Ravenscraig, despite the build-up of a personal estate in the islands, and despite the reacquisition of the earldom of Caithness (which can probably be regarded as a transaction connected in some way with James II's original plans for the islands), Earl William and his family must have emerged from the events of the years 1468–70 with a pronounced loss of private income and with a very public loss of prestige.[143]

141 *RMS*, ii, no. 1001
142 Crawford, 1967–8, 173; 1971, 349
143 Crawford, 1971, 350

NINE

The Aftermath of the Old Earldoms

The final parliamentary act transferring Orkney and Shetland to the Scottish Crown was passed in February 1472, when the earldom of Orkney and the lordship of Shetland were annexed to the Crown permanently, 'nocht to be gevin away in tyme to cum to na persoune nor personis except anerly til ane the kingis sonnis of lachtfull [lawful] bed'.[1] This is the final piece of evidence for the Crown's determination to retain permanent rights and property in the islands, whatever the status of the pledged lands. There can never have been any intention that a prince of Scotland might be an earl of the kingdom of Denmark–Norway, which is what would have happened if the islands had been redeemed. All attempts to offer redemption money for the islands in the following century were ignored,[2] but the royal family acted directly against the terms of the 1472 annexation when the dignities of Orkney and Shetland were awarded to the illegitimate son of King James V.

9.1 THE REVIVAL OF SINCLAIR POWER AND INFLUENCE IN THE NORTH

It is also known – from a later document – that a letter was issued by King James under the privy seal to Earl William on 3 February 1472 (at the same date as the above parliamentary act) concerning the conquest lands within the bounds of the lordships of Orkney and Shetland, in which the king acknowledged 'he had na rycht thereto' and promised that the earl and his successor and factors 'suld be anserit of the samin without impediment'.[3] This is further indication of Earl William's concern about his legal rights over the conquest lands and shows that

1 *Shetland Docs.*, no. 27. This is the first time that the 'lordship of Shetland' is so named. It shows that it was a separate entity from the earldom of Orkney and almost certainly had not been reunited with the earldom in 1379 (see Chapter 8; Crawford, 1971, 366; 1983, 47)
2 Thomson, 2001, 240
3 Crawford, 1985, Appendix. This information is contained in a later petition of Henry, fifth Lord Sinclair, to the king in parliament concerning these lands, dated 18 November 1581, which indicates the problems which had been experienced in his family's continued possession of these conquest lands (see below)

he must have been seeking further assurance from King James that these rights would be recognised in the future.

9.1.1 *Lord Henry Sinclair, 'farmer' and 'leaseholder'*

These concerns were no doubt real, for the evidence shows that the family was allowed no role in the administration of the islands in the years after the acquisition of Orkney and Shetland, until the earl's grandson, Henry (son of the elder William), moved back north and managed to get powers granted to him under the bishop who had a lease of the lordship of Orkney, as the combination of royal and earldom lands and rights was then called.[4] Responsibility for administering the royal lands and rights in the islands (which now included all the earldom possessions) was given at first to Bishop William Tulloch who had been a trusted councillor of King Christian and involved in the marriage treaty negotiations, and who was given a lease for four years from 1474. This was quite an onerous but lucrative position to be in, and for the first time there are full details of the value of the lease and the commodities that had to be returned to Leith.[5] When Bishop William was translated to the diocese of Moray in 1478, the lease was given to his successor Andrew Painter, who held it until 1488, and during this prelate's period of control we find Henry Sinclair mentioned in connection with the Orkney accounts. Evidence suggests that his relationship with Bishop Andrew was embittered by disputes over the bishopric skats, which Henry considered he had a right to.[6]

Lord Henry was called *firmarius* ('farmer') of the lordships in 1484, and received in 1489 an official grant of the 'tack' (lease) for thirteen years, but he may have had some authority earlier than this.[7] The 1492 and 1500 Rentals of the lands of Orkney which he drew up show his remarkable business acumen in attempting to restore the family fortunes in Orkney.[8] In particular, the 1500 Rental was compiled with the purpose of distinguishing the conquest lands and keeping them separate, as Sinclair family estate. There was also a great need to sort out those skats which had been diverted to the bishop[9] and restore them to the Crown – or the tacksman. In 1490, the year following the grant of Lord

---

4 Peter Anderson (1982, Chapter 3, n.1) discusses the meaning of the term 'lordship'
5 Thomson, 2001, 221
6 Thomson, 2001, 225–6
7 Anderson, 1982, 20; Crawford, 1985, 242
8 Thomson, 1996, xx; 2001, 232. It seems likely that the whole Panmure Codex was written at the instance of Lord Henry Sinclair (see Section 2.5). If so, it shows that he had an especial interest in having a copy of the family 'Genealogy' which had been drawn up to provide proof of the validity of his grandfather's claim to the earldom
9 This may have been done as a reward for loyal service by King Christian (Thomson, 1996, xviii)

AFTERMATH OF THE OLD EARLDOMS 373

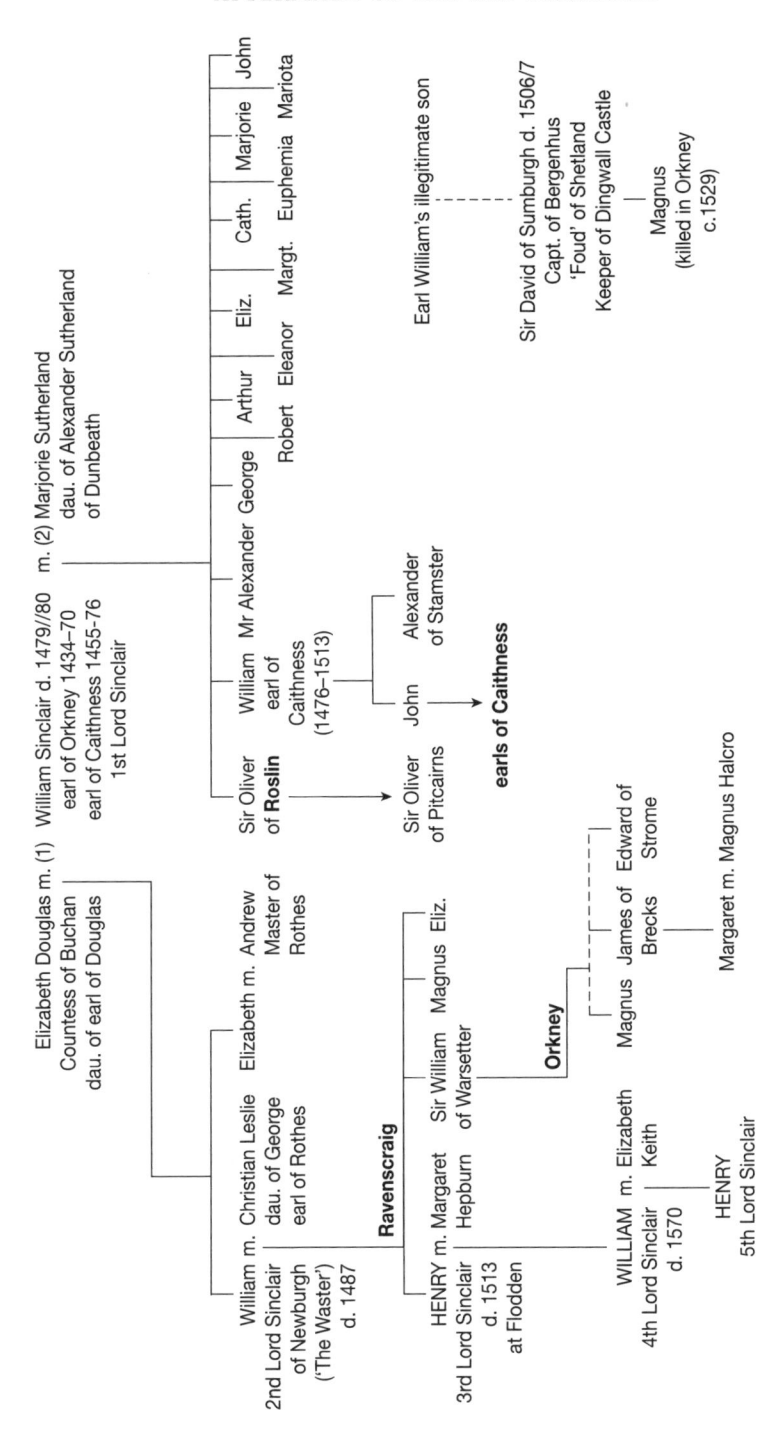

Figure 9.1 Family tree of Earl William's marriages and descendants. (Based on Crawford, 1985, Table 9)

The numbering of the title of Lord Sinclair follows that in SP *sub* 'Sinclair, Lord Sinclair'

Henry's lease, the bishopric was strengthened by the erection of its lands into a regality.[10] In 1501, Henry Sinclair's tack was renewed for a lease of nineteen years and the total tack payable was over £433, but Bishop Andrew also had confirmation of his rights in Orkney, and the Lords of Council warned Henry not to interfere with the bishopric skats and teinds. The rivalry of the two appointments continued and it was claimed that Lord Henry and his brother, William Sinclair of Warsetter, took forcible possession of some bishopric properties.[11]

Henry's efforts to establish his dominant position in Orkney were probably quite successful despite the problems of unravelling the complexities of the different lands,[12] and he retained the tack of the lordships until his death, after which it passed to his widow Margaret, (sister to the earl of Bothwell) with the judicial powers going to his brother, Sir William Sinclair of Warsetter. James III's attempts to make the bishops the principal royal representatives in the islands did not succeed, and it would appear that they were unable to resist the determination of the Sinclair family to restore their ancestral position.[13] After Lord Henry's death at Flodden in 1513, things eventually started to unravel as he left a minor, and royal officers were put into the islands who 'intromitted' with the conquest lands, as is said in the later document.[14]

Other members of the Sinclair family were powerful operators in the Northern Isles in the wake of the pledging of the islands to Scotland and the demise of the family earldom (see below for Sir David Sinclair). Lord Henry's brother, Sir William Sinclair of Warsetter, acted on his brother's behalf when Henry was busy in the south with the king's naval and military affairs. Sir William built up his power base on the island of Sanday in Orkney's north isles, based on his grandfather's conquest estates, along with other extensive Orkney estates, and he was exceedingly dominant in island history of the early sixteenth century, and an important continuator of Sinclair authority in the north.[15] After Sir William's death, conflict broke out between his sons and the young William, Lord Sinclair, leading to what the 1581 document describes as 'civil werres' through 'occasion and trubill'.[16] This internal power struggle, of

10 In 1489, identical grants to Lord Henry's (of the offices of Foud, Justice, Baillie and Custodian of Kirkwall Castle) were made to his brother-in-law, Patrick, earl of Bothwell, and Bothwell's uncle, Prior Hepburn of St Andrews, which 'may have been intended to provide an alternative power' to Lord Henry's position (Anderson, 1982, 20)
11 Thomson, 2001, 230. This counterbalance of lordly and episcopal power reflects the evidence of tension between earl and bishop in the fourteenth century (see Chapters 7 and 8)
12 See Thomson (2001, 222–8) for a discussion of the different lands and their management after Orkney was pledged to Scotland
13 Anderson, 1982, 21
14 Crawford, 1985, 252
15 Thomson, 2001, 23
16 Crawford, 1985, 243

vicious proportions, culminated in the pitched battle of Summerdale, fought in the hills of Stenness on the Orkney Mainland in 1529[17] (see below).

9.1.2 *Kirkwall's Burgh charter*

In the process of finding a workable solution for the governance of Orkney without an earl one very interesting royal charter was promulgated. On 31 March 1486, James III erected the town of Kirkwall into a Royal Burgh with a grant of lands and with special privileges.[18] This was the centre of the Scottish royal administration, and where the powerful community of burgesses lived and carried on their commercial enterprises. It sounds from the wording of the charter as if the situation which had developed in the islands in the vacuum left by the events of 1468 had been prejudicial to the commercial interests of the burgesses. It is said that their prosperity was being destroyed by 'foreigners, extraneous forestallers, and merchants that cometh from all parts not being burgesses of the said Burgh' and who were selling commodities as freely in the islands as any freeman or burgess. It may have been the case that the burgesses of Kirkwall had been unable to prevent other merchants from trading in the islands in the new situation which had developed since the pledging of 1468 and the change of political governance.

However, it seems clear from the phrasing of the charter that James was confirming privileges which Kirkwall had previously possessed, for the document continued to say that the burgh and city of Kirkwall had a long time since been erected into a Burgh Royal 'by our most noble predecessors'. These noble predecessors were of course the kings of Denmark and (prior to 1380) the kings of Norway. James continues to say that therefore he 'ratified and approved all privileges, liberties, immunities, and others whatsoever granted by any of our most noble predecessors in all heads, articles, conditions, and contents thereof', whether by charter, confirmation, donation, mortification, or any other way. But it does not sound as if any such still existed, and, if they did, they were not being cited as useful models for the new privileges being granted. There is no doubt that Kirkwall was a constituted burgh under the previous regime, for in 1460/1 a letter had been written to King Christian by Thomas of Kyrknes and John Mager who called themselves 'burgesses and bailies of your burgh of Kirkwall and of the community of the earldom of Orkney'.[19] There

---

17 Anderson (1982, 22) examines Storer Clouston's interpretations of the rights and wrongs of this internecine family warfare
18 *Kirkwall Chrs.*, 1–15. The original grant of James III is contained in the charter of Confirmation dating to 1536. A Scots translation is printed in Craven (1901, 123–28), probably the document referred to in 1658 (Mooney, 1947, 114)
19 *DN*, v, 599; *Orkney Recs.*, 52

are earlier fifteenth-century references to burgesses and baillies of Kirkwall.[20]

The charter continues by erecting the burgh and city into a 'full Burgh Royal' and gives a list of the area of lands surrounding the city which were included in its bounds, granting them to the 'said Provost, Baillies, Council and Inhabitants of our said Burgh and their successors'. Then comes a significant addition: 'as also, all and hail, the kirk called St Magnus Kirk, (*Totam et Integram ecclesiam illam nuncupatam Sancti Magni ecclesiam*)[21] and all other kirks, chapples and chapplandries, schools yards thereof, ... and all and sundry lands belonging to the said kirks, chapples, chaplaindries and schools ... and all and sundry prebendaries, tiends and others' including in particular the prebendary of St John, the income from which was to be used for the 'repairing and upholding' of St Magnus Kirk – as the cathedral is called in this charter.[22]

The significance of this transfer of the cathedral kirk to the ownership of the Burgh of Kirkwall has never been fully explained[23] (see Colour plate 39). It appears as if this was creating a new situation, and the reason must lie in the changed circumstances which had been created by the transfer of Orkney to the Scottish Crown. It seems likely that the cathedral had come into James' possession through William Sinclair's resignation of his 'right of the earldom' in 1470 rather than by the pledging of the islands in 1468.[24] If this is the correct explanation, it indicates that the cathedral had been the personal possession of the earls, who had of course founded and endowed it in the twelfth century (see Chapter 5). That foundation had created a very unusual situation – for a cathedral – although not an unusual situation, especially in Norway, where ordinary churches were concerned. It is not impossible that the earldom family had retained some proprietary rights over the building since its foundation,[25] although there is no other evidence to show us that this was the case. But if it was so, why was St Magnus Cathedral transferred to the Royal Burgh of Kirkwall in 1486 and why was it not given to the bishop of the day?[26]

Answers to this problem are not easy to find.[27] It may be that the intention was to strengthen the independence of the Burgh and to allow it to be free

20 Ibid., 47, 71
21 *Kirkwall Chrs.*, 5
22 Craven, 1901, 125
23 Local historian John Mooney grasped the extraordinary significance of this feature of the 1486 grant (1947, 5–8, and *passim*).
24 Mooney, 1947, 15
25 Anderson, 2003, 81
26 This was Bishop Andrew Painter (Pictoris) (1477–1505x1506) whom Craven (1901, 119) thought behaved magnanimously in permitting this grant of the Cathedral to be made to the Burgh. Brian Smith (1989) has studied Bishop Andrew's origins and his career
27 Crawford (2012a) discusses possible interpretations

of episcopal and also Sinclair control. As we have seen, there were tensions between the two stakeholders in the islands in this period, the bishop and the leaseholder, Lord Henry Sinclair, who first appears to have had a formal role in the administration in 1484 as 'farmer' of the lordships of Orkney and Shetland, and in 1485 when he rented them from Bishop Andrew (*sub reverendo patre Andrea episcopo eiusdem*).[28] The Burgh's privilege was granted shortly afterwards (1486) and may therefore reflect the royal response to the rivalry of these two, or to Lord Henry's ambitions to increase his powers of authority. Does it signify that Lord Henry had been making some attempt to restore family control over the cathedral, which James was forestalling by granting it to the Burgh? Or does it indicate that the bishop was conniving with King James to get the burden of financial responsibility which attended ownership of this building shifted away from episcopal resources?[29] Unfortunately, there is insufficient evidence for us to be certain about the reasons for James' unusual grant of the cathedral and other ecclesiastical possessions to his new Royal Burgh. What we can be certain of is that this was another constitutional plank in the process of building up Scottish royal power and authority in Orkney to delay and render the process of redeeming the islands difficult if not impossible.

9.1.3 *Earl William's family settlement*

Returning to the family settlement made by the old earl, William, we can note that there were problems and tensions already before his death between the sons of his two marriages, who were both called William. The elder William, known as 'the Waster', was the son of the first marriage with Elizabeth Douglas, and he was disadvantaged to some extent in the inheritance stakes, although not entirely disinherited (as has been said).[30] In 1476, the lands of the earldom of Caithness, along with the offices of justiciar, chamberlain and sheriff 'according to the bounds of the bishopric of Caithness' were granted to Earl William's son by his second marriage, also called William.[31] Roslin and the lands of Herbertshire with adjoining interests were resigned and made over to another son of

---

28 Anderson, 1982, 20
29 It is possible that episcopal resources had been over-extended in completion of the west front, which had probably taken place during the episcopate of Andrew Painter (Fawcett, 1988, 109)
30 The elder William held the Sinclair estates of Newburgh in Aberdeenshire and Carden in Stirlingshire
31 *RMS*, ii, 1267. This grant included the presentation to the hospital dedicated to St Magnus at Spittal (*unacum donatione hospitalis S. Magni in Cathania*), apparently the first reference to this earldom foundation, the site of which lies on the old road near the farm of Spittal Mains (see Section 2.7.1 and Colour plate 6)

the second marriage, Oliver, who also received the barony of Pentland.[32] Later evidence suggests that the Fife estates were likewise given to Oliver by his father, although he had eventually to cede them to his half-brother, the elder William.[33]

It is evident that the elder William was not treated as his father's prime heir, and the fact that the eldest son of the second marriage was also called William suggests that there was deliberate intention to treat the sons of the marriage with Marjory Sutherland as the old earl's main heirs. The reason probably lies in the mental weakness of the elder William which is indicated by a verdict of idiotry dating to 17 April 1482 when he was declared *incompos mentis et fatuus* ('of unsound and foolish mind'), and a 'waster of his lands and goods'.[34] This was two or three years after his father's death and no doubt had been procured by the half-brothers who were trying to resist the elder William's attempts to get possession of what he considered to be his rightful inheritance. It is very likely that Henry, the son of the elder William's marriage with Christian Lesley, was at this particular date himself becoming active in prosecuting what was thought to be his father's right to the Ravenscraig lands. This was the date also when Henry was beginning to be active in reviving the family affairs in Orkney, and in presenting himself as the heir to his grandfather, the old Earl William. He was clearly given the responsibility of bringing the conquest lands back under his family's control, either by his grandfather, or passed on to him by his own father. He was exceedingly successful, and ended up in 1489, after the death of his father, being recognised as Lord Sinclair 'chief of that blood': with the tack of Orkney and Shetland, the custody of Kirkwall castle and powers of 'justiciary, folderie and balliatus', which conferred authority to govern the islands and collect the rents.[35]

9.2 SIR DAVID SINCLAIR OF SUMBURGH

Henry was not the only member of the old earl's family to be successful in making good in the changed circumstances of the post-1468/9 era. The remarkable career of Earl William's only known illegitimate son, David Sinclair of Sumburgh, shows that he managed to survive, and flourish, as royal servant of both the Scottish and the Danish–Norwegian kings in this same period. This

32 *RMS*, ii, 1270; Hay, 1835 (2002), 82–90
33 Saint-Clair, 1898, 286
34 Crawford, 1985, 245. It might be thought that the earldom of Caithness should have passed to the earl's eldest son, however in the circumstances in which this earldom had been acquired during the lifetime of Earl William, it was not part of his inherited family estate. Therefore he could leave it to any of his sons
35 Thomson, 2001, 227 The 'folderie' was the office and jurisdiction of a 'foud', the Danish–Norwegian term used for a royal official or chamberlain in Shetland

Figure 9.2 Sketch of Sir David Sinclair (in the middle), King Hans of Norway–Denmark and King James IV of Scotland (from Crawford, 1978, fig. 1.1). Sir David is depicted wearing the golden chain which he says in his will (dated 1506) King Hans had given him (see Section 9.2.1). He was appointed Governor of Bergen Castle by King Hans, administrator in Shetland by King James, and was granted royal rights over the Church in Orkney by both James and Hans.

was a period when the relationship between the two countries was not always very easy, because of the circumstances of the pledging.

David was probably the son of an extramarital relationship in the Northern Isles, for he was closely associated with the north throughout his career, and particularly with Shetland, where his main seat was at Sumburgh in the south of Shetland (see Colour plate 40). There is no evidence of his relationship with his father, although it is probable that he was on the same footing as regards inheritance of the earl's lands in the north as were the legitimate children, for Norwegian law did not distinguish between the rights of legitimate and illegitimate offspring. In David's will, an illuminating document, on a par with the will of Alexander Sutherland, he left 'all the landis which I possessit eftir my Fader died in Zetland' to his nephew Lord Henry, which implies that he had inherited those lands. A charter dating from 1498 shows that his half-brothers and sisters granted him their shares of their paternal inheritance in Shetland (probably in return for payments or other favours).[36] This must have given him a good landed base in Shetland and David expanded possessions in Shetland (and Orkney) as is known from various documents and the Shetland Rental (called 'The Skat of Yetland') which is full of information about his land-purchasing activity.[37] The Shetland Rental also provides evidence for Lord Henry's land purchases alongside David's and other evidence shows that they had a good working partnership; when the former acquired the tacks of the lordships of Orkney and Shetland, his uncle (David) shared the administration with him by acting as 'foud' of Shetland (see note 35). It is probable that his rise to power in Shetland was a result of his connection with Lord Henry. They were both named 'Sheriffs in that part' in a royal letter of 1502 concerning Shetland.[38]

David's activities extended far beyond Shetland however, and spanned the North Sea in the traditional way. By 1496, he was so well regarded by King Hans (son of Christian I and uncle of James IV) that he had been appointed Governor of Bergen Castle and had authority over a large administrative district in western Norway. It is most likely that he was knighted by King Hans, for he is designated 'Sir David Sinclair, knight, our beloved man and servant' (*her David Sincklar, ridder wor elskelige man oc thienere*') by King Hans in 1491 in a grant for life of the rent and rights of the Crown over all the servants of the Church of Orkney.[39] There was uncertainty over royal appointments in the islands, as

36 *Shetland Docs.*, no. 34. This is a grant by Earl William of Caithness, and his twelve brothers and sisters (children of the second marriage) of their lands in 'Swinburgh' (Sumburgh) and all other lands in Shetland to their 'dearest brother' (David) 'for the fraternal love and affection' which they had for him. This indicates a close relationship between the legitimate children and their illegitimate half-brother
37 *Shetland Docs.*, Appendix 1; the rental itself may date from after his death (updated from reference to its compilation in Crawford, 1985, 248). Appendix 3 also provides a list of many purchases of land in the Northern Isles by Sir David
38 Crawford, 1977, 97
39 *OSR.*, no. 34. He is also called *høfdinghie i Hjaetland* ('chief man/official in Shetland') at the same time which may indicate that King Hans had been making a parallel appointment to the Scottish one (Crawford, 1977, 96–7; 1978, 4–5)

is seen from double grants of these ecclesiastical rights being made by the two kings.[40] This would appear to create a very difficult situation for an individual like Sir David who was pursuing a traditional lifestyle in Shetland and western Norway but in a changed political climate. The cross-currents of loyalties can be perceived from his involvement a few years later in the Norwegian rebel movement against King Hans, when he apparently joined the rebels against the king.[41] Whatever the motivation for this change of sides, we know that Sir David ended his career very much in favour with James IV, and a powerful royal servant of the Scottish king, who granted him offices and lands and military positions in north Scotland, as well as monetary gifts and pensions 'for service given'.[42]

9.2.1 *Sir David's will of 10 July 1506*

It is fortunate that Sir David's will has survived, drawn up at Tingwall in Shetland when he was ill, which gives a remarkable picture of his family and political relationships.[43] The strong Shetland/Norwegian/Scottish focus of his life is evident, and reveals a great deal about the wealth and social network of a northern member of the Sinclair family at a period when the old political structures were changing.

Tingwall in Shetland was the assembly site of the Shetland Lawthing, and the seat of the archdeadon of Shetland (see Colour plate 21). Sir David wished to be buried in St Magnus Church in Tingwall, and he left a velvet cloak to the church of Tingwall, as well as to St Magnus Cathedral and the Cross Kirk in Dunrossness; these would have been adapted for use as liturgical vestments. His most precious possessions included the golden chain which the king of Denmark had given him, and which he left to St George's altar in 'Rosskyill' (Roskilde?),[44] and his signet ring which he left to the provost of Bergen. Dr John Eke, a canon of Uppsala, who had been his chaplain and secretary was left twelve ells of black 'yper' (Ypres) cloth, two rose nobles, a saddle with attach-

---

40 Crawford, 1977, 93; 1978, 3. The impignoration documents of 1468–9 made no reference to the transfer of rights over church income or patronage
41 Discussion of the possible motives for Sir David's support of the rebel movement is in Crawford (1978, 5–8)
42 Crawford, 1978, 7
43 It has survived in a later Scots translation; see *Shetland Docs.*, no. 36. All the following references are taken from *Shetland Docs.* Previous discussion of the contents of Sir David's will is in Crawford, 1977, 1978
44 This golden chain 'which is callit a collar' is a symbol of the high esteem in which Sir David was held by King Hans, and may have been bestowed on him when he was knighted by the Danish king. Such collars signified 'a special relationship with a king or monarch' (Stevenson, 2004, 18)

ments, and a short black velvet coat.

The clothing Sir David possessed gives a vivid impression of the sumptuous manner of his dress when socialising with the Danish or Scottish nobility. It is worth listing them in detail: a doublet of cloth of gold, which along with a gray satin gown and three ostrich feathers were bequeathed to Sir William Sinclair (of Warsetter?); a black gown of damask with silver buttons, which was left to Allan Aiteson, along with his gray scarlet hose and a doublet of 'doune cramesse' (scarlet cloth?); his great silver belt and a piece of cloth of gold 'the length of a Flanders ell' which he left to Gertrude; a blue doublet with the bodice set with precious stones, and his hood set with precious stones and his golden chain 'the quihilk I weair dailly' which he left to Magnus Sinclair (probably his son); a black doublet of velvet and his red hose and short red cote of velvet without sleeves which he left to Peter Marshall; packs of green cloth and the best piece of a linen robe which he 'bought from the Flemings' and which were left to other individuals. These were mostly items of clothing for formal occasions, and the only reference to the local woollen cloth of Shetland, is the 'twa pak of wadmell' left to 'Sigrid in Rorik'.[45] There are a few references to objects of great value, prime among which are the 'silver stoups' (tankards or drinking cups) which had a series of smaller stoups which fitted inside; three sets of these were left to Lord Henry (Sir David's nephew and head of the family) and his wife Lady Sinclair, and their son and heir.

Sir David was a wealthy man, and his wealth probably came from diverse sources, political and commercial activities as well as landownership. We have seen that he inherited lands in Shetland from his father, the last earl, and he left these lands to his nephew, Lord Henry, thus ensuring that the inherited lands returned to the main line of the family. All his sisters' and brothers' portions of lands in Shetland, which he had acquired in 1498, along with his other 'conquest' lands were distributed among his friends, or perhaps servants. His own children, all of whom were apparently illegitimate, were given equal shares in his lands, the sons getting 100 marks of land each and the daughters 50 marks, or half that of a son, in accordance with odal practice.[46] These lands are not named (it was left to his executors to allocate them to his heirs), whereas the other territorial bequests are mostly named specifically along with the names of those inheriting them. The Flet brothers were given all his lands in Orkney, with the inns in Kirkwall, except for two named farms which were left to Alexander Borthwick. A James Sinclair (son?) who had succeeded him as captain in Dingwall was left all his 'geir' in Ross, of which there was a substantial

45 'wadmell' (ON *vaðmal*) – the coarse woollen cloth produced in the Atlantic islands
46 In addition, the 'geir' which was not disbursed in his will was to be divided between his sons and daughters

list. The two executors, Richard Leask and Thorvald of Brough, were left different parcels of land in different parts of Shetland, and the former also got 'my Inglis schipe with all geir'. This was not the only ship to be mentioned. There was an up-to-date ship called the *Carvell*,[47] which he left to Lord Henry; the little ship with all its gear which he left to the Flett brothers; and an item (illegible) which 'came hame to me with my schipe out of Norrowaye' was left to Thomas Boswell. Fifteen marks were to be paid to the Englishman 'that sauld me the schipe'. These incidental entries point to the maritime activity which occupied so much of his life spent crossing the North Sea between Shetland and Scandinavia and Scotland.

His political career in royal administration in Scotland is evident from mention of the pension of Shetland for that year, which he left to Lord Sinclair, and the links with Dingwall must have stemmed from his grant of the offices and lands of the chamberlain of the earldom of Ross and barony of Ardmannach. A strange entry says that the chalice of St Magnus in Tingwall was in Dingwall, which he commanded to be 'delivered'(perhaps back home to Tingwall). Perhaps it had been under repair at some silver workshop in Dingwall. The bequest of his inns in Edinburgh 'wyth the pertinents' to his brother, William, earl of Caithness, would have been welcome for the many meetings which the members of the old earl's family had when coming to agreements – or failing to come to agreements – over the division of the family lands in Lothian and Fife.

The lack of clarity over his own children must be a result of their illegitimacy. Nor is it clear who the important women in his life were (as we do know from Alexander Sutherland of Dunbeath's will). Who was Gertrude, who received the great silver belt? Or Sigrid in Rorik who received the two packs of wadmell and two cows? Or Ingarth in Cransetter who also received two cows? These are the only women named, except for Lady Sinclair, and none of them sound to have been of great significance, even if they may have been the mothers of his children. The only entries that sound a personal note are those referring to 'the puir folk that come out of Orknay with me', to whom he left their own land or else the equivalent in goods; and the bequest of the fruits of his lands of this year's crop (presumably in Shetland) to 'the puir folkis'. If these are the results of his piety and his attempt to bestow charity in preparation for the day of reckoning, it is all very undemonstrative, and with no apparent concession to deep religious scruples. The impression given is of a hard-headed careerist who was carefully disposing of his worldly wealth and goods with the minimum of fuss and with more concern for his powerful relatives and close companions than for his immediate offspring. This insight into Sir David's life and achieve-

---

47   See Crawford (1978, 9) for a discussion of the significance of such a ship

ments is of immense importance for our understanding of his wide-ranging contacts, but it reveals very little about him as a man, except that he had plenty of this life's goods and some exceptionally fine clothes.

Perhaps one item does reveal a little more about his concerns and priorities. The bequest of *The Buk of Gud Maneris* was made to Sir Magnus Haruode (Harwood/Herwood), along with two nobles (English currency). Sir Magnus was Sir David's secretary and chaplain, and was given a grant of the archdeaconry of Shetland by King Hans in 1502, although he was soon ousted by King James in favour of Henry Phantouch. This book was a translation of a French work by Jacques Legrand, *Le livre de bonnes moeurs*, written probably a century earlier but with an English translation published by Caxton at Westminster in 1487, and reprinted in the 1490s and 1500. The contents concern the state of princes and lords temporal and all chivalry, as well as the state of the common people, but also has a clerical component on the state of men of the Church and with a chapter on the seven deadly sins and the virtues.[48] The possession of this book suggests that Sir David was literate, which might be guessed from his association with Lord Henry, one of the most literate men of the time, and a most important patron of the arts.[49] It also hints at his interest in the nature of society, both clerical and lay, with perhaps a special interest in the political rule of kings and princes.

There is one puzzling thing about Sir David's lack of conformity to the accepted norms of the world he moved in. Despite his friendship with kings and clerics, he failed to learn that he needed to rectify the mistake of his birth if he was to maintain his landed wealth for his children. He never obtained letters of legitimation, nor indeed does he appear to have contracted a formal marriage so that his own children would be legitimate. Therefore his property escheated to the Scottish Crown, and his own children were not able to benefit from their father's bequests to them. Evidence for this development comes from the following decades when there were struggles among the family to obtain possession of the conquest lands of both Lord Henry and Sir David.[50] Indeed, the family's struggles to obtain possession of the wide estates of the last Earl William form a new and rather sordid chapter in the history of the northern Sinclairs.[51]

---

48 Acknowledgements to Elizabeth Henderson (Rare Books Librarian, Dept. of Special Collections, University Library, St Andrews) for this information
49 Addressed as 'fader of bukis, protector to sciens and lair' by Gavin Douglas who dedicated his translation of the Æneid to him (Chesnutt, 1985, 57 and references in n.10). See Section 2.5 above
50 Crawford, 1985, 248; Thomson, 2001, 236
51 These are not the concern of this book, for which see Anderson (1982, 22–8) and Thomson (2001, Chapter 17)

9.3 CHANGING WORLDS

Until the death of Lord Henry at Flodden in 1513 it can be said that the transition from the old earldom days to the new Scottish-dominated political rule 'had not proved bad for Orkney'.[52] The revival of the Sinclair governance of the islands saw the restoration of the old order with which the islanders were familiar, and the evidence of the Rentals tells us that Lord Henry's management of the economy – in difficult economic times – was maintained in a traditional paternalistic manner.[53]

The pledging of the islands did not affect the old order of social organisation either. The Norse Lawthings of Orkney and Shetland remained in full operation until 1541, when James V replaced the Lawthing and the office of lawman with a sheriff court and office of sheriff. That appears to have changed the social foundation of the traditional order of society.[54] But we still find that the court known as 'Hirdmanstein' (*hirdmanstevne*, 'the court of the hirdmen', or close followers of the earl) was in existence in 1561, even after the abolition of the Lawthing.[55] With the lack of an earl and the absence of the old paternalistic governance it is likely that the role of the native, wealthy families became even more significant as leaders of society. In general it seems that the odal ownership of land also remained unchanged until the mid-sixteenth century in the aftermath of the Reformation when the wholesale appropriation of episcopal estates created a new feudal aristocracy which held its lands by charter.[56] There is an earlier, and rather infamous, example of the feuing of lands, when in 1535 Sir James Sinclair of Brecks was given a feudal grant of the islands of Sanday and Stronsay, along with North Ronaldsay, Papa Stronsay and Auskerry for an annual payment of 200 marks.[57] This ignored the rights of landowners who had odal possession in these islands, and also gave James Sinclair the right to leave the feu grant to a single heir. Until this date the traditional way of holding lands according to odal custom, by which lands were divided equally among all children prevailed,[58] as is evident from Sir David Sinclair's acquisition of his brothers' and sisters' portions in 1498 (see Section 9.2).

The 'Scotticisation' of island culture did increase, and the upheaval of the Reformation compounded the deep changes in society. At the same time the

---

52 Thomson, 2001, 232
53 Ibid., 228
54 Imsen, 1994, 253, 260, 264
55 Thomson, 2001, 257; Imsen suggests that the Orkney hirdmen would be the king's hirdmen (2000, 175), but the 'hirdmanstein' of 1561 could not have been a court of royal Norwegian hirdmen
56 Thomson, 2001, 255; Jones, 2012, 394
57 Thomson, 2001, 241
58 Jones, 2012, 394

revival of the earldom of Orkney under the Stewart earls marked a new and problematical chapter in the history of the Northern Isles.[59]

9.3.1 Turbulence in Caithness

The situation in Caithness had long since changed from its role as the Scottish half of the dual earldom. The failure of the earldom line pre-1330 had meant the reversion of inheritance back to two heiresses and the division of earldom lands into two halves. We have seen how the earls of Ross were dominant in Caithness in the fourteenth century during the abeyance of the earldoms after Earl Malise's death, followed by the resignation of Caithness to the Crown by Alexander of Ard in 1375 (see Section 7.7). This was intended to prevent a repetition of the lawlessness which had pervaded the north in David II's reign, and royal possession of the turbulent northern earldom thus completed a process which had started many centuries before.

However, a prolonged process of feuding started in the northern Highlands between those families who had inherited Joanna's half of the earldom and the MacKays of Strathnaver, with the frequent participation of the earls of Sutherland. The turbulence was violent and continuous, and included battles between the families, murders and burnings from the 1370s and all through the fifteenth century.[60] The lack of an earl of Caithness, or of an earl who was resident in the locality, might be thought to be one cause of the problem, but nothing much seemed to change after William Sinclair received his grant of Caithness in 1455,[61] or after his son William was given all the earldom lands and judicial powers in the locality in 1476 and inherited the title on his father's death c.1480.[62] In 1503, there was said to be 'a great lack and fault of justice in the north parts', especially in the dioceses of Ross and Caithness,[63] which was thought to be because of the large size of the sheriffdom of Inverness. As a result the sheriff was empowered to appoint subordinate sheriffs, whose courts were to be at Wick and Dornoch, with appeal cases going to the justice ayre (circuit court) at Inverness. The contrast with the apparently well-ordered and judicious rule in Orkney at this time is rather striking.

The disaster of Flodden impacted heavily on the northern families, and both William, the earl of Caithness, and his nephew Henry Lord Sinclair lost their lives, as also did MacKay of Strathnaver. This merely left other powerful

---

59 Anderson, 1982, 2012
60 MacKay, 1914, Chapter VI, 'Conflict of the Clans'
61 A feud raged between the Keiths and Gunns in the later fifteenth century (ibid., 103–4)
62 In 1487 Mackays and MacLeods battled versus Ross of Balnagowan; in 1499 Sutherlands of Dirlot versus Dunbars (ibid., 104–6)
63 Ibid., 107

families to fill the vacuum, particularly the Gordons, who made a bond of friendship with the new earl of Caithness in 1516. Conflict continued to rage, and the family of the earl of Caithness was merely one of several families who were probably fairly equal in their power basis in terms of landed estates. That equality was so equal that one family never was able to dominate and to bring some semblance of order and peace to the area. The situation is rather different from most other northern parts of Scotland, and the circumstances may reflect the very different history and culture of Caithness.[64]

9.3.2 *The Pentland Firth – a barrier at last?*

The old links between the two earldoms across the Pentland Firth were broken. The lure of the rich arable lands in the islands constantly attracted the feudal lords of north Scotland, and the importance of having a powerful defender in the shape of an earl who ruled both earldoms is vividly recorded in the letter sent to King Christian of Denmark–Norway by the baillies of Kirkwall and the community of the earldom of Orkney when they were excusing Earl William from non-attendance in 1460.[65] They described the attacks against the islands which had been led by 'our old great enemy' John, Earl of Ross and Lord of the Isles, who had striven with all his power 'most savagely to destroy us from year to year and day to day burning our buildings, carrying away our goods, and destroying your loyal inhabitants to the uttermost'; and against whom they had 'no defender after God but your Highness' and 'our gracious and noble prince' the earl of Orkney and Caithness, who had laid himself out in the struggle 'to his no small suffering and loss, bearing the expense, labours and dangers of the war'. The importance of Caithness in this perilous situation is then stressed, for after the earl's deliberation with King James 'he has been wisely engaged in his earldom of Caithness and elsewhere in putting a stop to the malicious and savage attacks of these cruel enemies', adding significantly 'so that in this way praise be to the Highest, he has happily kept us safe, unharmed, and peaceful from these imminent dangers'. All this was written to convince King Christian of the good reasons why Earl William had not been to visit him, and promising that he would do so soon. If the dangers of the situation were stressed somewhat in order to convince King Christian of the validity of the excuse for the earl's absence, we nonetheless can believe – from what is known of the violent nature of north Scotland at this time – that the threats were real. The joint rule of one earl in both earldoms certainly appears to be helping to defend the inhabitants

---

64 These circumstances are worth much closer investigation, and the location and value of the lands held by the different families might throw light on the economic situation which underlay the violence and clan feuding
65 *Orkney Recs.*, no. XXII, already referred to in Section 1.4 above

of Orkney from the depredations of the earl of Ross, and doubtless other lawless chieftains in the north of Scotland.

Paradoxically it was when both Orkney and Caithness were part of the one kingdom, Scotland, that the links across the Pentland Firth and the anomalous situation of the joint earldoms came to an end. The Scottish Crown had relinquished the Caithness earldom which it gained in 1375 and granted it back to the earl of Orkney in 1455, who handed it over to his son William of his second marriage in 1476, and it remained a Sinclair earldom thereafter. King James made sure that he got the Orkney earldom after the impignoration and it was then granted out to the bastard son of the Stewart dynasty in 1565. The Sinclairs managed to hang on to Earl William's conquest lands (see Section 9.1), and these formed the basis of Sinclair family power in Orkney thereafter.[66] They also formed the basis of the great falling-out of the scions of the Sinclair clan, which resulted in the invasion of Orkney by Lord Sinclair and the earl of Caithness in 1529.[67] The invading army was met by a large force gathered under the leadership of James Sinclair of Brecks, the illegitimate son of Sir William Sinclair of Warsetter, and the two armed gangs met at Summerdale on Mainland Orkney. The battle was bloody and bitter and the invaders were routed. The legal rights of Lord Sinclair to his family lands were simply squashed, and the head of the family lost out to those cousins who were established in both Orkney and Shetland and who were determined not to relinquish their lands and rights easily or at all. The lack of an earl in the islands and the absence of any real governmental authority allowed this state of civil war to develop, and ensured the victory of those who held power in the land. It was the last time that an earl of Caithness tried to restore the territorial links with Orkney, but the Pentland Firth would appear by then to have become more of a barrier, even a frontier, than it had ever been in the past.

---

66 Crawford, 1985, 248–9
67 Thomson, 2001, 236

Retrospective Summary

We have traced the history of the earls, hereditary rulers of the Norwegian islands of Orkney, and the north Scottish mainland province of Caithness, over six centuries. This long period of time presents its own problems for the historian who is attempting to present the joint earldoms as the central feature of her study. The early Viking earls were a very different phenomenon from the Sinclair earls of the late fourteenth and fifteenth centuries, and the world of the wide-ranging ninth and tenth-century earls was long gone when the Stewart kings occupied the throne of Scotland, and Norway was ruled by the joint Danish–Norwegian monarchy. The authority of kings did not impact very heavily on the earlier earls, certainly not in their Caithness earldom, although the Orkney earls were subject to infrequent royal expeditions to their islands, as when Erik 'Blood-axe' used the islands as a base in the 950s for his raiding further south (see Section 3.4.3). For the rest of the tenth century and during the eleventh century the earls ruled their island world undisturbed by royal constraint – until the arrival of Magnus 'Barelegs' in 1098 gave them a jolt and woke them up to the reality of royal authority being extended from the home country out into their island domain (see Section 4.3).

The imposition of royal authority on the earls' independent command of their earldom resources is the main theme of Chapter 6 and the picture is mirrored in both earldoms. The growth of powerful kings striving to unify their kingdoms under their authority was happening in both Norway and Scotland, and the earl who suffered from the effects of this growth in royal power in both Orkney and Caithness was Harald Maddadson (see Sections 6.2–6.5). He is one of our most interesting earls and the one whose career is most fully recorded in Norwegian and Scottish sources, for there is a combination of saga, chronicle and documentary accounts to fill out the picture. He rampaged around the northern world in the spirit of his Viking ancestors, but his heart and soul were probably embedded in the north Scottish world from where he sprang (and from where he acquired one of his wives). Involvement in rebellions, or linking up with rebellious groups who were trying to overthrow the royal dynasties of Scotland and Norway was a dangerous game, but it seems as if Earl Harald thought these were activities earls were morally entitled to engage in and able effectively to prosecute. In the late twelfth century kings were indeed still vulnerable to a loss of support, and some did sit uneasily on their thrones. However, none of the risings Harald was engaged in, or implicated with, achieved anything except royal displeasure and royal retribution (see Sections 6.2 and 6.3).

This was all mistaken bravado and a misjudgement by Earl Harald about the kings' increasingly firm hold on power. Further misjudgements were made by Harald and his son John over the status of the bishop in Caithness and his sacrosanct position as a protégé of the Scottish king (see Sections 6.4 and 6.6). This was quite a different situation from that in Orkney where the bishop was firmly under the earl's wing and chosen by him. The ecclesiastical situation in Orkney had been created by the earls in the previous century; they had built both episcopal churches in Birsay and Kirkwall, and Harald was following in the footsteps of his predecessors in treating these churches as personal foundations and the incumbent as his own appointee. But in Caithness things were very different due to royalist policies regarding the Scottish Church. David I developed a modern church on the Norman model and endowed very generously the cathedrals whose bishops he chose and the monasteries which he founded. The Church was used as a vanguard for his policies of bringing the northern part of Scotland within a unified kingdom, and the creation of a Scottish diocese of Caithness meant the imposition of Scottish personnel and ecclesiastical constitutional arrangements, which may not have permitted the earl any participatory role at all. This did not suit Earl Harald and the resulting clash with Bishop John was perhaps inevitable (see Section 6.4). The attack on John's successor, Adam, was carried out by the Caithness *bondi*, but Earl John got the opprobrium for having failed to protect the bishop. Both occasions provided the kings with opportunities to lead expeditions north into Caithness for retribution against the earl, and in 1222 against the *bondi*.

The period of rule of Harald Maddadson and his sons (1158–1230) therefore marks the effective assertion of royal authority in both earldoms. But the problem was how to maintain that royal authority over succeeding decades by permanent administrative means rather than transient military action. Once more our clearest evidence for this process – and its limited success – comes from Earl Harald's period as sole earl. In Caithness King William attempted to replace him with a powerful appointee with earldom links through his mother, King Rognvald Gudrodson of Man and the Isles. Rognvald put in three stewards to run the earldom, but Earl Harald engineered the murder of one of them. In Orkney King Sverrir appointed a member of his new class of administrators (sysselmen) to manage the newly acquired royal estates and collect in half of the judicial dues to which the Crown now asserted a claim. But once King Sverre had died (in 1202), Earl Harald saw to it that the sysselman was murdered, and he reasserted his authority over the confiscated Shetland islands and all other powers of which he had been deprived. These two incidents reveal the earl's utter resistance to the installation of royal officials within his own domains and the difficulties facing the kings in attempting to impose a parallel royal administration in the earldoms. The traditional way to reduce an earl's power effectively was to give an alternative candidate with a good inherited claim a grant of half the earldom and thus create a situation of rival earls which might weaken or even lead to the death of the non-compliant one. However, in the case of Harald Maddadson the appointment of an alternative earl (Harald *ungi*) resulted in the death of the latter at the Battle of Wick, leaving the older Harald with a clear field and no further rival claimants for the rest of his life (see Section 6.5).

There were few earls with the ability and fearlessness and lack of respect for the long arm of royal authority that Harald Maddadson shows. His two sons David and John divided the earldoms between them, but John survived to become sole earl. Perhaps with a better sense of realism they visited Norway in 1210 and 1211 to repair relations with the new kings, while John also repaired relations with the Scottish king William and handed over his daughter as hostage for the maintenance of good relations (see Section 6.6.1). He similarly handed over his son to the Norwegian king. This was of course a classic method in all societies for ensuring a subject's good behaviour.[1] Earl John also lost authority over the southern province of Sutherland which was transferred into the keeping of loyal feudal vassals (see Section 6.6.2). Forfeiture of earldom territory at frontier zones (Shetland had been confiscated from Earl Harald in 1195) was another method of whittling away at the vassal's landed power base and reducing his source of wealth as well as his dynastic patrimony (see Figure 7.2).

Despite the repairing of relations with both sets of overlords, Earl John had a very troubled reign and never learned the necessity of maintaining good relations with the Scottish ecclesiastical authorities. So he allowed the Caithness *bondi* to attack and murder their bishop, with the dreadful consequences that resulted (see Section 6.7.1). The earl did not suffer the physical retribution which the *bondi* did, but he had to pay a large fine (as his father had had to do), and this was another means that the Scottish kings used to weaken their Caithness earls and impose their own authority. The Norwegian kings did likewise,

---

1 Harald had previously had to leave his son Thorfinn with the king of Scots who then caused him to be maimed

based on a long-established tributary relationship of the Orkney earls with their Norwegian overlords (see Section 2.3). Finally, Earl John was killed by the combination of a royal claimant to the earldom and the Norwegian sysselman, which meant the end of the old Norse line of earls.

The next phase of the earldoms' story is very different, dominated as it is by the Sottish dynasties of Angus (1231–1329) and Strathearn (1330–1350), who inherited the joint earldom situation, but about whom the sources tell us very little. As far as these sources reveal, this period did not have the violent incidents that were such a recurring feature of the preceding Norse epoch. It did however include the very difficult situation of warfare between the earl's two overlords when Hakon Hakonsson led his expedition west to assert his authority over the Hebrides and came to blows with King Alexander at Largs (see Section 7.3.2). The earl was faced with the dilemma of having to choose between them. The assessment of Earl Magnus III's difficult position indicates that fines may again have been imposed on him in Caithness. This was most likely the result of his reconciliation with King Magnus 'the Lawmender' along with the re-imposition of restrictive terms regarding his position in Orkney (see Section 7.4.1). There is no evidence for installation of permanent royal officials in Orkney in the period of these earls' rule, although there is in the periods of minority which occur in the fourteenth century and especially in the time of the earldom's abeyance after the death of Earl Malise in 1350 and during the Sinclair era (see Section 7.6.2).

When we come to the Sinclair earls of Orkney (1379–1470), we are in the late medieval world of overmighty subjects and kings of national states. The Sinclair lords of Roslin were important Scottish nobles who regarded their Orkney earldom as an adjunct to their Scottish landed position, although a very important family dignity which gave them their prestigious comital status (the Caithness earldom having been given up to the Crown in 1375; see Section 7.7.1). The three earls ruled their Norwegian earldom with scant regard for their vassal obligations to the Danish–Norwegian overlord, and exercising probably full control of earldom and royal rights of income. The realisation that the situation of dual allegiance could not last would have become increasingly clear. Fighting among earldom claimants, leading to the death of a cousin, and the killing of the bishop in the 1380s (see Sections 8.2.1 and 8.2.2) is reminiscent of an earlier age. But, of course, the fifteenth-century earldom(s) were a different world from the Viking earldoms. Royal authority was all-pervasive and independent action on the part of the earls was impossible, or only a temporary aberration. The two earldoms held by Earl William Sinclair from 1455 to 1470 were a very pale reflection of the former joint earldoms phenomenon. The remarkable fact is that he had restored it and these joint earldoms therefore survived in some shape or form for nearly 600 years. The history and vicissitudes of the joint earldom lordship make it a dramatic story of medieval power on the periphery. Students of medieval history can learn a very great deal from it about the survival of an institution, against the odds: a successful example of earldom power politics stemming from the Viking Age and lasting to the very end of the medieval period.

Bibliography

Abrams, L., 1998. 'History and Archaeology: the Conversion of Scandinavia', in Crawford, ed., 1998, 109–28
Adam of Bremen, *Gesta Hammaburgensis Ecclesiae pontificum*, ed. B. Schmeidler, Hanover and Leipzig, 1917.
Adam of Bremen, *History of the Archbishops of Hamburg-Bremen*, trans. F.J. Tschan, New York, 1959.
Aitchison, N., 1999. *MacBeth: Man and Myth*, Stroud
Almqvist, B., 1978–9. 'Scandinavian and Celtic Folklore Contacts in the Earldom of Orkney', *Saga-Book* lxx, 80–105
Almqvist, B., 2005. 'What's in a Word? Folklore Contacts between Norsemen and Gaels as reflected in *Orkneyinga Saga*', in Owen, ed., 2005, 25–38
Andersen, P.S., 1973. 'King Hakon the Old before the Bar of History', *Orkney Miscellany* 5 (King Håkon Commemorative Number), 27–36
Andersen, P.S., 1977. *Samlingen av Norge og Kristningen av Landet 800–1130*. Universitets forlaget Bergen-Oslo-Tromsø
Andersen, P.S., 1988. 'The Orkney Church of the Twelfth and Thirteenth Centuries: A Step-Daughter of the Norwegian Church?', in Crawford, ed., 1988, 56–68
Andersen, P.S., 1991. 'When was Regular, Annual Taxation Introduced into the Norse Islands of Britain? A Comparative Study of Assessment Systems in North-Western Europe', *Scandinavian Journal of History* 16, 73–83
Anderson, J., 1873 (and 1973 facsimile). *Introduction* to Hjaltalin and Goudie's translation of *The Orkneyinga Saga*, ix–cxiii, Edmonston and Douglas
Anderson, P. 1982. *Robert Stewart Earl of Orkney, Lord of Shetland 1533–1593*, Edinburgh
Anderson, P., 2003. 'Cathedral, Palace and Castle: the strongholds of Kirkwall', in Waugh, ed., 2003, 81–93
Anderson, P. 2012. *The Stewart Earls of Orkney*, Edinburgh
Andersson, T., 2006. 'Harray på Orkney', *Namn og Bygd* 94, 135–6
Andrew of Wyntoun, 1907. *The Original Chronicle of Andrew of Wyntoun*, vol. 5, ed. F.J. Amours (Scottish Text Society, vol. 56), Edinburgh, London
Bäcklund, J., 2001. 'War or Peace? The Relations between the Picts and the Norse in Orkney', *Northern Studies* 36, 33–48
Bagge, S., 1993. '*hirð*', in P. Pulsiano, ed., *Medieval Scandinavia: An Encyclopedia*, Garland Publishing, New York and London, 284

Bagge, S., 2010. *From Viking Stronghold to Christian Kingdom: State Formation in Norway, c.900–1350,* Copenhagen

Baldwin, J.R., ed., 1978. *Scandinavian Shetland: An Ongoing Tradition?* Scottish Society for Northern Studies, Edinburgh

Baldwin, J.R., ed., 1982. *Caithness: A Cultural Crossroads,* The Scottish Society for Northern Studies, Edinburgh

Baldwin, J.R., ed., 1986. *The Firthlands of Ross and Sutherland,* The Scottish Society for Northern Studies, Edinburgh

Baldwin, J.R., ed., 1994. *Peoples and Settlement in North-West Ross,* The Scottish Society of Northern Studies, Edinburgh

Baldwin, J.R., ed., 2000. *The Province of Strathnaver,* The Scottish Society for Northern Studies, Edinburgh

Balfour, D., 1859. *Oppressions of the Sixteenth Century in the Islands of Orkney and Zetland from original Documents,* Edinburgh

Balfour, D., 1860. *Odal Rights and Feudal Wrongs,* Edinburgh

Ballantyne, J. and Smith, B., 1994. *Shetland Documents 1580–1611,* Lerwick

Ballantyne, J. and Smith, B., 1999. *Shetland Documents 1195–1579,* Lerwick

Ballin Smith, B., 2007. 'Norwick: Shetland's first Viking Settlement?', in Ballin Smith *et al.,* eds, 2007, 87–97

Ballin Smith, B., Taylor, S. and Williams, G., eds, 2007. *West over Sea: Studies in Scandinavian Sea-Borne Expansion and Settlement Before 1300. A Festschrift in Honour of Dr. Barbara E. Crawford,* Leiden

Bandlien, B., ed., 2012. *Eufemia Oslos Middelalderdronning,* Oslo

Bangor-Jones, M., 1987. 'Ouncelands and Pennylands in Sutherland and Caithness', in MacGregor and Crawford, eds, 1987, 13–23

Barnes, M.P., 1991. 'Norwegian, Norn, Icelandic or West Norse? The Language of the Maeshowe Inscriptions', in J.O. Askedal *et al.,* eds, *Festskrift til Ottar Grønvik på 75-årsdagen den 21 oktober 1991,* Oslo, 70–87

Barnes, M.P., 1994. 'The Runic Inscriptions of Maeshowe, Orkney', Runrön 8 (Institutionen for nordiska Språk, Uppsala)

Barnes, M.P., 1998. *The Norn Language of Orkney and Shetland,* The Shetland Times Ltd, Lerwick

Barnes, M.P., 2003. 'Runic Tradition in Orkney: From Orphir to the Belsair Guest House', in Waugh, ed., 2003, 4–17

Barnes, M.P. and Page, R.I., 2006. 'The Scandinavian Runic Inscriptions of Britain', Runrön 19 (Institutionen for nordiska Språk, Uppsala)

Barrett, J., 2003. 'Culture Contact in Viking Age Scotland', in J. Barrett, ed., *Contact, Continuity, and Collapse: The Norse Colonization of the North Atlantic,* Studies in the Early Middle Ages 5 (University of York), Turnhout, 73–112

Barrett, J., 2004. 'Sweinn Asleifarson (d.?1171), pirate', in *Dictionary of National Biography (DNB)* Art. 49359

Barrett, J., 2007. 'The Pirate Fishermen: The Political Economy of a Medieval Maritime Society', in Ballin Smith *et al.,* 2007, 299–340

Barrett, J., 2008. 'The Norse in Scotland', in S. Brink, ed., *The Viking World*. London, 411–27

Barrett, J.H., 2012. *Being an Islander: Production and identity at Quoygrew, Orkney, AD 900–1600*, Cambridge

Barron, E.M., 1909. 'Robert the Bruce in Orkney, Caithness and Sutherland', *Old Lore Miscellany* 2, 90–4

Barrow. G.W.S., 1985. *David I of Scotland*, Reading

Barrow, G.W.S., 1997. '*De Domibus religiosis*: A Note on Dornoch', *Innes Review* xlviii, 83–4

Barrow, G.W.S., 1999. *The Charters of David I: the Written Acts of David 1 King of Scots 1124–1153 and of his Son Henry earl of Northumberland, 1139–52*, Woodbridge

Barrow, G.W.S., 2005. *Robert Bruce and the Community of the Realm of Scotland*, Edinburgh

Barrowman, R. 2011. *The Chapel and Burial Ground on St. Ninian's Isle, Shetland: Excavations Past and Present* The Society for Medieval Archaeology Monograph 32

Barry, G., 1805 (reprint 1975). *The History of the Orkney Islands*, Edinburgh

Batey, C.E., 1993. 'Viking and Late Norse Graves of Caithness and Sutherland', in Batey *et al.*, eds, 1993, 148–64

Batey, C.E., Jesch, J. and Morris, C.D., eds, 1993. *The Viking Age in Caithness, Orkney and the North Atlantic*, Proceedings of the Eleventh Viking Congress, Edinburgh

Beaton, D., 1908. *The Ecclesiastical History of Caithness*, Wick

Beuermann, I., 2009. 'Sveinn Asleifarson and the Irish Sea', in Woolf, ed., 2009, 131–68

Beuermann, I., 2011. '*Jarla Sǫgur Orkneyja*: Status and Power of the Earls of Orkney according to their sagas', in Steinsland *et al.*, 2011, 109–62

Bibire, P., 1988. 'The Poetry of Earl Rǫgnvald's Court', in Crawford, ed., 1988, 208–40

Bibire, P., 2002. 'The 1299 Shetland document, AM100, 3. Transcription and Translation', in Crawford, ed., 2002, 9–11

Bibire, P., 2004. 'Arnórr Earls' Poet', in DNB: www.oxforddnb.com/view/article/52276

Blindheim, M., 1988. 'St Magnus in Scandinavian Art', in Crawford, ed., 1988, 165–82

Blom, G.A., 1997. *Trondheims Historie, 997–1997: I, Hellig Olavs By. Middelalderen til 1537*, Universitetsforlaget

Boardman, S., 1996. *The Early Stewart Kings: Robert II and Robert III, 1371–1406*, East Linton

Bolton, T. 2009. *The Empire of Cnut the Great* (NW, vol. 40), Leiden

Bornholdt, K., 1999. 'Myth or Mint? The Evidence for a Viking-Age Coinage from the Isle of Man', in P. Davey, ed., *Recent Archaeological Research on the Isle of Man* (BAR British series 278), Oxford, 199–218

Bǫglunga Sögur II, ed. H. Magerøy, Norske Historisk Kjeldescrift-Institutt, Norrøne texter nr. 5, Oslo, 1988

Brady, K., 2002. 'Brei Holm. Papa Stour: in the Footsteps of the *papar*?', in Crawford, ed., 2002, 69–82

Bramman, J.I., 1972. 'The Vikings', in Omand, ed., 1972, 124–7

Brink, S., ed. (with N. Price) 2008. *The Viking World*, London

Brøgger, A.W., 1929. *Ancient Emigrants: A History of the Norse Settlements of Scotland*, Oxford

Brown, M., 1994. *The Stewart Dynasty in Scotland: James I*, Edinburgh

Brunsden, G.M., 2002. 'Earls and Saints: Early Christianity in Norse Orkney and the Legend of Magnus Erlendsson', in R.A. McDonald, ed., *History, Literature, and Music in Scotland, 700–1560*, Toronto, 60–92

Bull, E., 1912–13. 'The Cultus of Norwegian Saints in England and Scotland', *Saga-Book of the Viking Society* viii, 135–

Calder, J.T., 1861 (2nd edn 1887, reprinted 1971). *Sketch of the Civil and Traditional History of Caithness*, Wick

Caldwell, D. (with A. MacNiven), 2008. *Islay: The Land of the Lordship*, Edinburgh

Cant, R.G., 1972. 'The Church in Orkney and Shetland and its Relations with Norway and Scotland in the Middle Ages', *Northern Scotland* i, 1–18

Cant, R.G., 1984. 'Settlement, Society and Church Organisation in the Northern Isles', in Fenton and Palsson, eds, 1984, 169–79

Cant, R.G, 1988. 'Norwegian Influences in the Design of the Transitional and Gothic Cathedral', in Crawford, ed., 1988, 126–39

Carpenter, D., 2004. *The Struggle for Mastery: The Penguin History of Britain 1066–1284*, London

Carver, M., 2008. *Portmahomack: Monastery of the Picts*, Edinburgh

Chesnutt, M., 1968. 'An unsolved problem in Old Norse-Icelandic History', *Medieval Scandinavia* 1, 122–34

Chesnutt, M., 1981. '*Haralds saga Maddaðarsonar*', in U. Dronke *et al.*, eds, *Speculum Norroenum*, Odense, 33–55

Chesnutt, M., 1986. 'The Dalhousie Manuscript of the *Historia Norvegiae*', *Bibliotheca Arnamagnæana*, vol. xxxviii, opuscula viii (1985), 54–95

Chesnutt, M., 1993. 'Orkneyinga saga', in P. Pulsiano, ed., *Medieval Scandinavia: An Encyclopedia*, Garland Publishing, New York and London, 456–7

Chesnutt, M., 1997. 'Local Legendary in the Saga of the Orkney Islanders', *Copenhagen Folklore Notes* 1–2, 6–12

Chibnall, M., ed., 1956. *Historia Pontificalis of John of Salisbury*, Edinburgh

Ciklamini, M., 1978. *Snorri Sturlason*, Boston, MA

Clancy, T.O., ed., 1998. *The Triumph Tree: Scotland's Earliest Poetry AD 550–1350* (Canongate Classic), Edinburgh

Clancy, T. and Crawford, B.E., 2001. 'The Formation of the Scottish Kingdom', in R.A. Houston and W.W.J. Knox, eds, *The New Penguin History of Scotland*, Penguin Press, Harmondsworth, 28–95

Clarke, H.B., 1998. 'Proto-Towns and Towns in Ireland and Britain in the ninth and tenth centuries,', in H.B. Clarke, M. Ni Mhaonaigh, and R. O'Floinn, eds, *Ireland and Scandinavia in the Early Viking Age*, Dublin, 331–80

Clarke, H. and Ambrosiani, B., 1991. *Towns in the Viking Age*, Leicester

Close-Brooks, J., 1986. *Exploring Scotland's Heritage: The Highlands*, RCAHMS, Edinburgh

Clouston, J.S., ed., 1914. *Records of the Earldom of Orkney 1299–1614*, SHS, 2nd series, vol. 7, Edinburgh

Clouston, J.S., 1919. 'Two Features of the Orkney Earldom', *Scot. Hist. Rev.* xvi, 15–28
Clouston, J.S., 1923/4. 'The Orkney Lands', *POAS* ii, 61–9
Clouston, J.S., 1924–5. 'The "Goodmen" and "Hirdmen" of Orkney', *POAS* iii, 9–20
Clouston, J.S., 1925–6. 'The Old Prebends of Orkney', *POAS* iv, 31–36
Clouston, J.S., 1927. *The Orkney Parishes*, Kirkwall
Clouston, J.S., 1928–9. 'Three Norse Strongholds in Orkney', *POAS* vii, 57–74
Clouston, J.S., 1930–1. 'Some Saga Place-Names', *POAS* ix, 41–5 and 'The Orkney Arms', *POAS* ix, 57–9
Clouston, J.S., 1931–2. 'Our Ward Hills and Ensigns', *POAS* x, 33–41
Clouston, J.S., 1932. *A History of Orkney*, Kirkwall
Clouston, J.S., 1932–3. 'Something about Maeshowe', *POAS* xi, 9–18
Clover, H. and Gibson, M., eds and trans., 1979. *The Letters of Lanfranc*, Oxford
Cooper, R.L.D., ed., 2004. *The Voyages of the Venetian Brothers Nicolo & Antonio Zeno to the Northern Seas in the XIVth Century*. Masonic Publishing Co.
Cormack, M., 1994. *The Saints in Iceland: Their Veneration from the Conversion to 1400*, Société des Bollandistes, Bruxelles
Cowan, E., 1982. 'Caithness in the sagas', in Baldwin, ed., 1982, 25–44
Cowan, E. 1993. 'The Historical MacBeth', in Sellar, ed., 1993, 117–42
Cox, R., 1994. 'Descendants of *Bólstaðr*? A Re-examination of *bost* & Co.', in Baldwin ed., 1994, 43–67.
Craven, Rev. J.B., 1901. *History of the Church in Orkney: From the Introduction of Christianity to 1558*, Kirkwall
Craven, Rev. J.B., 1908. *A History of the Episcopal Church in the Diocese of Caithness*, Kirkwall
Crawford, B.E., 1967–8. 'The Earldom of Orkney and Lordship of Shetland: A Re-interpretation of their Pledging to Scotland in 1468–70', *Saga-Book* xvii, 156–76
Crawford, B.E., 1969. 'The Pawning of Orkney and Shetland: A Reconsideration of the Events of 1460–9', *Scot. Hist. Rev.* xlviii, 35–53
Crawford, B.E., 1971. 'The Earls of Orkney-Caithness and their Relations with Norway and Scotland 1158–1470', unpublished PhD thesis (University of St Andrews)
Crawford, B.E., 1973. 'Weland of Stiklaw: a Scottish Royal Servant at the Norwegian Court', *Historisk Tidsskrift (Norsk)* lii, 329–39
Crawford, B.E., 1974. 'Peter's Pence in Scotland', in G.W.S. Barrow, ed., *The Scottish Tradition. Essays in Honour of Ronald Gordon Cant*, Scottish Academic Press, Edinburgh, 14–22
Crawford, B.E. 1976. 'The Fifteenth-century "Genealogy of the Earls of Orkney" and its Reflection of the Contemporary Political and Cultural Situation in the Earldom', *Medieval Scandinavia* 10, 156–78
Crawford, B.E., 1976–7. 'The Earldom of Caithness and the Kingdom of Scotland, 1150–1266', *Northern Scotland* 2, 97–118. Also in K.J. Stringer, ed., 1985, *Essays on the Nobility of Medieval Scotland*, Edinburgh, 25–43
Crawford, B.E., 1977. 'Foreign Relations: Scandinavia', in J.M. Brown, ed., *Scottish Society in the Fifteenth Century*, London, 85–100

Crawford, B.E., 1978. 'Sir David Sinclair of Sumburgh: "Foud" of Shetland and Governor of Bergen Castle', in J. Baldwin, ed., *Scandinavian Shetland, An Ongoing Tradition?*, Scottish Society for Northern Studies, Edinburgh, 1–12

Crawford, B.E., 1978a. 'The Orkney Arms', *The Orcadian*, 13 July 1978

Crawford, B.E., 1979. 'The Shetland Lawthing seal', *The New Shetlander* 127, 22–4

Crawford, B.E., 1982. 'Scots and Scandinavians in Medieval Caithness; A Study of the Period 1266–1374', in J.R. Baldwin, ed., *Caithness. A Cultural Crossroads*, Scottish Society for Northern Studies, Edinburgh, 75–85

Crawford, B.E., 1983. 'Birsay and the Early Earls and Bishops of Orkney', *Orkney Heritage* 2, 97–118

Crawford, B.E., 1983a. 'The Pledging of the Islands in 1469: the Historical Background', in Withrington, ed., 1983, 32–48

Crawford, B.E., 1984. 'The Cult of St. Magnus in Shetland', in Crawford, ed., 1984, 65–81

Crawford, B.E., 1985. 'William Sinclair, Earl of Orkney, and his Family: A Study in the Politics of Survival', in K.J. Stringer, ed., *Essays on the Nobility of Medieval Scotland*, Edinburgh, 232–53

Crawford, B.E., 1986. 'The Making of a Frontier: The Firthlands from the 9th–12th Centuries', in J.R. Baldwin, ed., 1986, 33–46

Crawford, B. E., 1987. *Scandinavian Scotland: Scotland in the Early Middle Ages* 2, Leicester University Press

Crawford, B.E., 1990. *The History of Dunbeath in the Medieval Period*, Dunbeath Preservation Trust

Crawford, B.E., 1990a. 'North Sea Kingdoms, North Sea Bureaucrat: A Royal Official Who Transcended National Boundaries', *Scot. Hist. Rev.* lxix, 175–84

Crawford, B.E., 1991. 'Catanensis Eccl. (Caithness)', in Watt, D.E.R., ed., *Series Episcoporum Ecclesiae Catholicae Occidentalis*. Series VI Britannia, Scotia Et Hibernia, Scandinavia, Tomus 1 Ecclesiae Scoticanae, Stuttgart, 29–33

Crawford, B.E., 1992. 'Thorvald Thoresson, Duke Hakon and Shetland', in S. Supphellen, ed., *Kongsmenn og Krossmenn: Festskrift til Grethe Authén Blom* (Det Kongelige Norske Videnskabers Selskab, Skrifter 1), Trondheim, 69–90,

Crawford, B.E., 1993. 'Norse Earls and Scottish Bishops in Caithness: A Clash of Cultures', in C. Batey *et al.*, eds, *The Viking Age in Caithness, Orkney and the North Atlantic: Select Papers from the Proceedings of the Eleventh Viking Congress*, Edinburgh, 129–47

Crawford, B.E., 1993a. 'Birsay-Peel-Selja: Three Norse Bishops' Seats on Off-shore Islands: A Comparative Study', in *Kirkearkeologi og Kirkekunst: Studier tilegnet Sigrid og Håkon Christie*, Øvre Ervik, 21–36

Crawford, B.E., 1993b. 'Caithness', in P. Pulsiano, ed., *Medieval Scandinavia: An Encyclopedia* (Garland Encyclopedia of the Middle Ages, vol. 1), New York

Crawford, B.E., 1994. 'Earl William Sinclair and the Building of Roslin Collegiate Church', in J. Higgitt, ed., *Medieval Art and Architecture in the Diocese of St Andrews*, The British Archaeological Association Conference Transactions for the Year 1986, Leeds, 99–107

Crawford, B.E., 1995. *Earl and Mormaer. Norse-Pictish relationships in Northern Scotland*, Groam House Museum

Crawford, B.E., 1995a. 'An Unrecognised Statue of Earl Rognvald?', in Crawford, ed., 1995a, 29–46

Crawford, B.E., 1995b. 'Sigurd the Mighty', in *Artemis Lexikon des Mittelalters*, Munich

Crawford, B.E., 1996. 'Bishops of Orkney in the Eleventh and Twelfth Centuries: Bibliography and Biographical List', *Innes Review* xlvii, 1–13

Crawford, B.E., 1996a. 'Thorfinn', in *Artemis Lexikon des Mittelalters*, Munich and Zurich

Crawford, B.E., 1997. *Viking Graves, The Norse in Scotland, Royal Expeditions against the Earls in Orkney and Caithness,* in H. MacQueen and P. MacNeill, eds, *An Historical Atlas of Scotland*, 2nd edn, Edinburgh

Crawford, B.E., 1998. 'St Magnus and St Rognvald – the Two Orkney Saints', *Records of the Scottish Church History Society* xxviii, 23–38

Crawford, B.E., 1999. 'The Dedication to St Clement at Rodil, Harris', in B.E. Crawford, ed., *Church, Chronicle and Learning in Medieval and Early Renaissance Scotland* (essays presented to Donald Watt on the Occasion of the Completion of the Publication of Bower's *Scotichronicon*), Edinburgh, 109–22

Crawford, B.E., 2000. 'Medieval Strathnaver', in J.R. Baldwin, ed., *The Province of Strathnaver* (Scottish Society for Northern Studies), Edinburgh, 1–12

Crawford, B.E., 2001. 'Connections between Scotland and West Norway from the Viking Age to c.1500', in M. Synnove and H.R. Naley, eds, *Fiender og Forbundsfeller.*

Crawford, B.E., 2001a. 'Orkney and Caithness, Earldom of', in *The Oxford Companion to Scottish History*, ed. M. Lynch, Oxford University Press, Oxford, 467–70

Regional kontakt gjennom historien, Haugesund, Karmøyseminaret 1999, 81–96

Crawford, B.E., 2003. 'Orkney in the Middle Ages', in D. Omand, ed., *The Orkney Book*, Edinburgh, 64–80

Crawford, B.E., 2003a. 'The Bishopric of Orkney', in Imsen, ed., 2003, 143–58

Crawford, B.E., 2003b. 'The Vikings', in W. Davies, ed., *From the Vikings to the Normans* (The Short Oxford History of the British Isles), Oxford, 41–72

Crawford, B.E., 2004. 'Earldom Strategies in North Scotland and the Significance of Place-Names', in G. Williams and P. Bibire, eds, *Sagas, Saints and Settlements* (NW, vol. 11), Leiden, 105–24

Crawford, B.E., 2004a. 'Harald Maddadsson', in *DNB*: www.oxforddnb.com/view/article/49351

Crawford, B.E., 2004b. 'Einar', *DNB*: www.oxforddnb.com/view/article/49269

Crawford, B.E., 2004c. 'Sigurd II', *DNB*: www.oxforddnb.com/view/article/49270

Crawford, B.E., 2004d. 'Magnus Erlendsson', in *DNB*: www.oxforddnb.com/view/article/37728

Crawford, B.E., 2004e. 'Sinclair Family (*per.* 1280–*c.*1500)', *DNB*: www.oxforddnb.com/view/article/54321

Crawford, B.E., 2005. 'Thorfinn, Christianity and Birsay; What the Saga Tells us and Archaeology Reveals', in O. Owen, ed., *The World of Orkneyinga Saga,* Kirkwall, 88–110

Crawford, B.E., 2005a. 'The Sinclairs in the Late Middle Ages', in Oram and Stell, eds., 2005, 189–204

Crawford, B.E., 2006. 'Houseby, Harray and Knarston in the West Mainland of Orkney. Toponymic indicators of administrative authority?', in P. Gammeltoft and B. Jørgensen, eds, *Names Through the Looking-Glass, Festschrift in Honour of Gillian Fellows-Jensen*, Copenhagen, 21–44

Crawford, B.E., 2006a. 'Kongemakt og jarlemakt, stedsnavn some bevis? Betydningen av Houseby, Harray og *staðir*navn på Orkenøyenes West Mainland', *Viking*, 195–214

Crawford, B.E., 2006b. 'Ingebjorg' and 'Margaret', in E. Ewan *et al.*, eds, *A Biographical Dictionary of Scottish Women*, Edinburgh, 177–8, 250–1

Crawford, B.E., 2009. 'The Bishopric of Orkney within the Archdiocese of Trondheim, 1152/3–1472', *New Orkney Antiquarian Journal* 4, 47–68 (a reprint of the chapter in Imsen, ed., 2003, 143–58 with minor changes)

Crawford, B.E., 2010. 'The Joint Earldoms of Orkney and Caithness', in Imsen, ed., 2010, 75–98

Crawford, B.E., 2011. 'Tax and Tribute in the Joint Earldoms of Orkney and Caithness', in Imsen, ed., 2011, 33–56

Crawford, B.E., 2011a. 'Reply to "Random Thoughts on Sir Farquhar, Earl of Ross", in series 3, no. 15 (Oct. 2010)', *West Highland Notes and Queries*, 8–13

Crawford, B.E., 2012. 'Scapa Flow: The Nerve Centre and "Knarr" Centre of the Medieval Earldom': www.scapaflow.co/index.php/history_and_archaeology/the_norse/scapa_flow_the_nerve_centre_and_knarr_centre_of_the_medieval_earldom/

Crawford, B.E. 2012a. 'St. Magnus Cathedral: A Proprietorial Church of the Orkney Earls?', in S. Imsen, ed., *'Ecclesia Nidrosiensis' and 'Noregs veldi': The Role of the Church in the Making of Norwegian Domination in the Norse World,* Noregsveldet Occasional Papers No.3, Trondheim, 177–200

Crawford, B.E., forthcoming. 'The Kingdom of Man and the Earldom of Orkney – Some Comparisons', in J.V. Sigurdsson and T. Bolton, eds, *Celtic–Norse relationships in the Irish Sea in the Middle Ages, 800–1200* (NW), Leiden

Crawford, B.E., ed., 1984. *Essays in Shetland History, Heiðursrit to T.M.Y. Manson*, Lerwick

Crawford, B.E., ed., 1988. *St. Magnus Cathedral and Orkney's Twelfth-Century Renaissance,* Aberdeen

Crawford, B.E., ed., 1995. *Scandinavian Settlement in Northern Britain.* Leicester

Crawford, B.E., ed., 1995a. *Northern Isles Connections: Essays from Orkney and Shetland presented to Per Sveaas Andersen*, Kirkwall

Crawford, B.E., ed., 1998. *Conversion and Christianity in the North Sea World* (St. John's House Papers no. 8), Committee for Dark Age Studies, St Andrews

Crawford, B.E., ed., 1999. *Church, Chronicle and Learning in Medieval and Renaissance Scotland*, Edinburgh

Crawford, B.E., ed., 2002. *Papa Stour and 1299, Commemorating the 700th anniversary of Shetland's First Document,* Lerwick

Crawford, B.E., ed., 2002a. *The papar' in the North Atlantic. Environment and History,* (St. John's House Papers no. 10), Committee for Dark Age Studies, St Andrews

Crawford, B.E. and Ballin Smith, B., 1999. *The Biggings. Papa Stour, Shetland. The History and Excavation of a Royal Norwegian Farm* (Society of Antiquaries of Scotland Monograph no. 15: published jointly with The Norwegian Academy), Edinburgh

Crawford, B.E. and Taylor, S., 2003. 'The Southern Frontier of Norse Settlement in North Scotland. Place-Names and History', *Northern Scotland* 23, 1–76

Cronica Regum Manniae et Insularum. Chronicles of the Kings of Man and the Isles, transcr. and trans. George Broderick, Manx National Heritage, Douglas, Isle of Man, 1996

Crouch, D., 1986. *The Beaumont Twins: The Roots and Branches of Power in the Twelfth Century*, Cambridge

Cruden, S., 1961. 'Earl Thorfinn the Mighty and the Brough of Birsay', *Third Viking Congress*, Reykjavik, 156–62

Cruden, S., 1965. 'Excavations at Birsay, Orkney', in A. Small, ed., *The Fourth Viking Congress* (Aberdeen University Studies, no. 149), Edinburgh, 22–31

Cruden, S., 1988. 'The Founding and Building of the Twelfth-Century Cathedral of St. Magnus', in Crawford, ed., 1988, 78–87

Cuthbertson, B., 1996. 'Voyages to North America Before John Cabot: Separating Fact from Fiction', *Collections of the Royal Nova Scotia Historical Society* 44, 121–44

Dahlerup, T., 1990. 'Orkney Bishops as Suffragans in the Scandinavian-Baltic Area: An Aspect of the Late Medieval Church in the North', in Simpson, ed., 1990, 38–47

Davies, R.R., 2009. *Lords and Lordship in the British Isles in the Later Middle Ages,* ed. B. Smith, Oxford

De Geer, I., 1985. *Earl, Saint, Bishop, Skald – and Music. The Orkney Earldom of the Twelfth Century,* Uppsala

De Geer, I., 1988. 'Music and the Twelfth-century Orkney Earldom: a Cultural Crossroads in Musicological Perspective', in Crawford, ed., 1988, 241–63

Dockrill *et al.*, 2010. *Excavations at Old Scatness, Shetland* vol.1. *The Pictish Village and Viking Settlement*, Shetland Heritage Publications, Lerwick

Donaldson, G., 1984. 'Problems of Sovereignty and Law in Orkney and Shetland', *Stair Society Miscellany* ii,

Donaldson, G., 1988. 'The Contemporary Scene', in Crawford, ed., 1988, 1–10

Donaldson, G., 1990. *A Northern Commonwealth. Scotland and Norway*, The Saltire Society, Edinburgh

Donaldson, G., 1995. 'The Archdeaconry of Shetland', in Crawford, ed., 1995a, 77–89

Donaldson, G., 1999 (reprint of 1970), *Scottish Historical Documents*, Edinburgh

Downham, C., 2004. 'Eric Blood-Axe-axed? The Mystery of the last Viking King of York', *Medieval Scandinavia* 14, 51–77

Downham, C., 2005. 'The Battle of Clontarf in Irish History and Legend', *History Ireland* 13, 19–23

Downham, C., 2007. *Viking Kings of Britain and Ireland: The Dynasty of Ivarr to A.D.1014,* Edinburgh

Dumville, D., 2002. 'The North Atlantic Monastic Thalassocracy: Sailing to the Desert in Early Medieval Insular Spirituality', in Crawford, ed., 2002a, 121–32

Duncan, A.A.M., 1975. *Scotland. The Making of the Kingdom*. Edinburgh.

Duncan, A.A.M., 1999. 'Roger of Howden and Scotland, 1187–1201', in Crawford, ed., 1999, 135–60

Duncan, A.M.M., 1999a. 'John King of England and the Kings of Scots', in S.D. Church, ed., *King John: New Interpretations,* Woodbridge, 247–71

Duncan, A.A.M., 2002. *The Kingship of the Scots,* Edinburgh

Dunlop A. and MacLauchlan, D., eds, 1983. *Scottish Supplications to Rome* vol. 4, 1433–1447, University of Glasgow

Edmonston, A., 1809. *A View of the Ancient and Present State of the Zetland Islands,* 2 vols, Edinburgh

Ekrem, I. and Mortensen, L.B., eds, 2003. *Historia Norvegie,* Museum Tusculanum Press, University of Copenhagen, Copenhagen

Ekroll, Ø. 1997. *Med Kleber og Kalk. Norsk Steinbygging i mellomalderen 1050–1550,* Oslo

Ekroll, Ø. 2012. 'Erkebiskop Eystein, Oktogonen i Kristkyrkja og Kristi Gravkyrkje i Jerusalem', in K. Bjørlykke *et al.*, eds, *Eystein Erlendsson- Erkebiskop, politiker og kirkebygger,* Trondheim, 45–76

Erslev, K.1881–2. 'Tre Gavebreve af Dronning Margrethe fra Aaret 1411', *Kirkehistoriske Samlinger,* tredie række, tredie bind, 367–79

Etchingham, C., 2001. 'North Wales, Ireland and the Isles: the Insular Viking Zone', *Peritia* 15, 145–87

Eyrbyggja Saga, trans. Pálsson and Edwards, Penguin Books, 1989

Fagrskinna, A Catalogue of the Kings of Norway, a Translation with Introduction and Notes by A. Finlay (NW vol. 7), Leiden, 2004

Falk, H., and Torp, A., 1999 [1903–6], *Etymologisk Ordbog over det Norske og det Danske Sprog,* Oslo

Farmer, D.F., ed., 1978. *The Oxford Dictionary of Saints,* Oxford

Fawcett, R., 1985. *Scottish Medieval Churches,* Edinburgh

Fawcett, R., 1988. 'Kirkwall Cathedral: An Architectural Analysis', in Crawford ed., 1988, 78–87

Fawcett, R., 1996. 'The Excavation of the Church on the Brough by Sir Henry Dryden in 1866', in Morris, 1996, 210–15

Fawcett, R., 2011. *The Archaeology of the Scottish Medieval Church,* Newhaven, Conn.

Fenton, A., 1973. *The Various Names of Shetland,* Edinburgh

Fenton A. and Palsson H., eds, 1984. *The Northern and Western Isles in the Viking World: Survival, Continuity and Change,* Edinburgh

Fellows Jensen, G., 1990. 'Scandinavians in Southern Scotland', *Nomina* 13, 41–60

Fellows Jensen, G., 1996. 'Thingwall: the Significance of the Name', in D. Waugh, ed., *Shetland's Northern Links. Language and History,* Scottish Society for Northern Studies, Edinburgh,16–29

Fellows Jensen, G., 2000. 'Vikings in the British Isles: the Place-name Evidence', in S.S. Hansen and K. Randsborg, eds, *Vikings in the West,* Copenhagen; *Acta Archaeologia* 71, Supplementa 2, 135–46

Fernie, E., 1988. 'The Church of St. Magnus, Egilsay', in Crawford, ed., 1988, 140–61

Fisher, I. 1993. 'Orphir Church in its South Scandinavian Context', in Batey *et al.*, eds, 1993, 375–80
Flinn, D. 1988. *Travellers in a Bygone Shetland: An Anthology,* Edinburgh
Foote, P. 1988. 'Observations on *Orkneyinga Saga,'* in Crawford, ed., 1988, 192–207
Foote, P.G. and Wilson, D.M., 1970. *The Viking Achievement: The Society and Culture of Early Medieval Scandinavia,* London
Fordun, 1872. *Chronicle: John of Fordun's Chronicle of the Scottish Nation,* ed. W.F. Skene (Historians of Scotland, vol. iv), Edinburgh
Forte, A., Oram, R., and Pedersen, F., 2005. *Viking Empires,* Cambridge
Fraser, I., 1995. 'Norse Settlement on the North-west Seaboard', in Crawford, ed., 1995, 92–107
Fuglestvedt, I. and Hernaes, P., 1996. 'Rituell kommunikasjon i yngre jernalder', in J-F. Krøger and J.R. Naley, *Nordsjøen. Handel, Religion og Politikk,* Karmøyseminaret, 1994 and 1995, Stavanger, 140–61
Gammeltoft, P., 2001. *The Place-Name Element* bólstaðr *in the North Atlantic Area* (Navenstudier udgivet af Institut for Navneforskning Nr. 38), Copenhagen
Gammeltoft, P., Hough, C. and Waugh, D., eds, 2005. *Cultural Contact in the North Atlantic Region: The Evidence of Names,* Lerwick
Garipzanov, I., 2010. 'The Cult of St. Nicholas in the Early Christian North c.1000–1150', *Scand. J. Hist.* 35, 229–46
Gelting, M., 2004. 'Elusive Bishops: Remembering, Forgetting, and Remaking the History of the Early Danish Church', in S. Gilsdorf, ed., *The Bishop: Power and Piety at the First Millenium,* Neue Aspekte der Europäischen Mittelalterforschung 4, Munster, Hamburg and Berlin, 169–200
Gibbon, S-J., 2006.'The Origins and Early Development of the Parochial System in the Orkney Earldom', unpublished PhD thesis (University of the Highlands and Islands)
Gibbon, S-J., 2007. 'Medieval Parish Formation in Orkney', in Ballin Smith *et al.*, eds, 2007, 235–50
Goodare, J. 1999. *State and Society in Early Modern Scotland,* Oxford
Goudie, G., 1904. *The Celtic and Scandinavian Antiquities of Shetland,* Edinburgh
Gourlay, R., 1993. 'Castle of Old Wick', in Batey *et al.*, eds, 1993, 14–15
Graham-Campbell, J., 1995.*The Viking-Age Gold and Silver of Scotland (AD 850–1100),* National Museums of Scotland, Edinburgh
Graham-Campbell, G., 2006. 'Some Reflections on the Distribution and Significance of Norse Place-names in Northern Scotland', in P. Gammeltoft and B. Jørgensen, eds, *Names Through the Looking-Glass: Festschrift in Honour of Gillian Fellows-Jensen,* Copenhagen, 94–118
Graham-Campbell, J. and Batey, C., 1998. *Vikings in Scotland: An Archaeological Survey,* Edinburgh
Grant, A., 2000. 'The Province of Ross and the Kingdom of Alba', in E. Cowan and R.A. MacDonald, eds, *Alba: Celtic Scotland in the Medieval Era,* East Linton, 88–126
Gray, J., 1922. *Sutherland and Caithness in Saga-Time, or The Jarls and the Freskyns,* Edinburgh

Gray, J., 1923. 'Boundaries of Estates in Caithness Diocese Shortly after 1222', *Scot. Hist. Rev.* xx, 285–9

Grieve, S-J., 1999. 'Norse Castles in Orkney', unpublished MA thesis (University of Glasgow)

Grieve, S-J., 2005. 'Medieval Chapel Sites in Caithness: A Gazetteer', unpublished Orkney Collection, Orkney Library and Archive

Griffiths, D. and Harrison, J., 2011. 'Interpreting Power and Status in the Landscape of Viking Age Orkney', in Sigmundsson, ed., 2011, 132–46

Grönvald, K. *et al.*, 1995. 'Ash Layers from Iceland in the Greenland GRIP Ice Core Correlated with Oceanic and Land Sediments', *Earth and Planetary Science Letters* 135, 149–55

Gunnlaugs Saga Ormstunga / The Saga of Gunnlaug Serpent-Tongue, trans. R. Quirk and ed. P.G. Foote, London, Edinburgh, 1957

Guðrún Sveinbjarnardóttir, 2006. 'Reyholt, a Centre of Power: the Archaeological Evidence', in E. Mundal, ed., *Reykholt som Makt og Lærdomssenter i den Islandske og Nordiske Kontekst,* Reykholt, Snorrastofa, 25–42

Hacon's Saga = *The Saga of Hacon*, trans. G.W. Dasent. *The Icelandic Sagas* vol. IV, London, 1894

Haki Antonsson, 2005. 'The Kings of Norway and the Earls of Orkney: the Case of *Orkneyinga Saga,* Chapter 36', *Medieval Scandinavia* 15, 81–100

Haki Antonsson, 2005a. 'St. Magnús of Orkney: Aspects of his Cult from a European Perspective', in Owen, ed., 2005, 144–59

Haki Antonsson, 2007. *St Magnús of Orkney: A Scandinavian Martyr-Cult in Context*(NW, vol. 29), Leiden

Haki Antonsson, 2009. 'False Claims to Papal Canonisation of Saints: Scandinavia and Elsewhere', *Medieval Scandinavia* 19, 171–203

Haki Antonsson and Garipzanov, I., 2010. *Saints and their Lives on the Periphery: Veneration of Saints in Scandinavia and E. Europe (c.1000–1200)*, Brepols

Hamilton, J.R.C., 1953. *Jarlshof, Shetland,* HMSO, Edinburgh

Hansen, L.I., Holt, R. and Imsen, S., eds, 2011. *Nordens Plass i Middelalderens Ny Europa Samfunnsomdanning, Sentralmakt og Periferier* (Speculum Boreale nr. 16), University of Tromsø

Haug, E., 1996. *Provincia Nidrosiensis i dronning Margretes unions – og maktpolitikk* Historisk Institutt, NTNU-Trondheim (nr. 13 i Skriftserie fra Historisk Institutt)

Hay, R.A., 1835 (reprinted 2002). *Genealogie of the Sainteclaires of Rosslyn*, Edinburgh

Hedeager, L., 1990. *Danmarks Jernalder.Mellem Stamme og Stat.* Århus

Helle, K., 1964 (2nd edn 1974). *Norge Blir en Stat 1130–1319,* Universitetsforlaget

Helle, K., 1972. *Konge og Gode Menn i Norsk riksstyring ca.1150–1319,* Universitetsforlaget

Helle, K., 1973. 'Norwegian Consolidation and Expansion During the Reign of King Hakon Hakonsson', *Orkney Miscellany* 5: *King Håkon Håkonsson Commemorative Number,* Orkney County Library, Kirkwall, 7–16

Helle, K., 1992. 'Tidlig byutvikling i vestnorge', in I. Øye, ed., *Våre første byer*, Onsdagskvelder i Bryggens Museum – VII, 7–30

BIBLIOGRAPHY

Helle, K., 2007. Lecture on the earls of Orkney given at RSE Conference Sept. 2006 'The Vikings and Scotland' Published Report, 22 (Royal Society of Edinburgh)

Helle, K., ed., 2003. *The Cambridge History of Scandinavia.* vol.1, *Prehistory to 1520*, Cambridge

Hodnebø, F., ed., 1960. *Norske diplomer til og med år 1300*, Oslo

Hibbert, S., 1822. *A Description of the Shetland Islands, Comprising an Account of their Geology, Antiquities and Superstitions*, Edinburgh

Holman, K., 1996. *Scandinavian Runic Inscriptions in the British Isles: Their Historical Context.* Senter for Middelalderstudier (Skrifter 4), Trondheim

Hossack, B.H., 1900. *Kirkwall in the Orkneys*, Kirkwall

Hudson, B., 1992. 'Cnut and the Scottish Kings', *English Historical Review* 107, 351–8

Hudson, B., 1994. 'Knútr and Viking Dublin', *Scandinavian Studies* 66, 319–35

Hudson, B., 1998. 'The Scottish Chronicle', *Scot. Hist. Rev.* lxxvii, 129–61

Hudson, B., 2005. *Viking Pirates and Christian Princes*, Oxford

Huitfeldt, A., 1599. *Historiske Bescriffuelse om hvis sig haffuer tildraget under den Stormectigste Første oc herre/herr Christiern, den Første*, København

Hunter, J.R., 1986. *Rescue Excavations on the Brough of Birsay 1974–82* (Society of Antiquaries of Scotland Monograph Series 4), Edinburgh

Imsen, S., 1994. *Norsk Bondekommunalisme fra Magnus Lagabøte til Kristian Kvart.* Del 2 *Lydriketiden* (Universitet i Trondheim Historisk Institutt Skriftserie no. 7), Trondheim

Imsen, S., 1999. 'Public Life in Shetland and Orkney c1300–1500', *New Orkney Antiquarian Journal* 1, 53–65

Imsen, S., 2000. *Hirdloven til Norges Konge og hans Håndgangne Men,* Riksarkivet, Oslo

Imsen S., 2000a. 'Earldom and Kingdom: Orkney in the realm of Norway 1195–1379', *Historisk Tidsskrift* 79, 163–80

Imsen, S., 2002. 'Tingwall and Local Community Power in Shetland During the Reign of Håkon Magnusson, Duke and King', in Crawford, ed., 2002, 59–80

Imsen, S., 2003. 'Earldom and Kingdom. Orkney in the realm of Norway 1195–1379', (revised version of 2000a) in Waugh, ed., 2003, 65–80

Imsen, S., 2005. 'Grenseland i Vest – mellom Skottland og Norge', in Imsen, ed., 2005, 142–62

Imsen, S., 2007. 'landet Orknøy oc grefuescapet ther same stadhs', *Historisk Tidsskrift* 86

Imsen, S., 2009. 'The Scottish-Norwegian Border in the Middle Ages', 3rd Anderson Memorial Lecture, in Woolf, ed., 2009, 9–30

Imsen, S., 2010. 'Introduction', in Imsen, ed.,2010, 13–33

Imsen, S., 2011. 'From Tributes to Taxes', in Imsen, ed., 2011, 13–29

Imsen, S., 2011a. 'Norgesveldet som politisk System', in Hansen *et al.*, eds, 2011, 13–29

Imsen, S., 2012 'The Country of Orkney and the Complaints against David Menzies', *POAS,* 6, 9-33

Imsen, S., ed., 2003. *Ecclesia Nidrosiensis 1153–1537: Søkelys på Nidaroskirkens og Nidarosprovinsens historie*, Senter for Middelalderstudier, NTNU, Skrifter Nr.15 Tapir akademisk forlag

Imsen, S., ed., 2005. *Grenser og grannelag i Nordens historie*, Oslo

Imsen, S., ed., 2010. *The Norwegian Domination and the Norse World c.1100–c.1400*, 'Norgesveldet', Occasional Papers No. 1, Trondheim

Imsen, S., ed., 2011. *Taxes, Tributes and Tributary Lands in the Making of the Scandinavian Kingdoms in the Middle Ages,* 'Norgesveldet', Occasional Papers No. 2, Trondheim

Imsen, S. ed., 2012. *'Ecclesia Nidrosiensis" and 'Noregs veldi'.The role of the Church in the making of Norwegian domination in the Norse World,* 'Norgesveldet', Occasional Papers No.3, Trondheim

Inchaffray Chrs. = *Charter, Bulls and Other Document relating to the Abbey of Inchaffray*, 1908, SHS

Iversen, F., 2011. 'The Beauty of *Bona Regalia* and the Growth of Supra-regional Powers in Scandinavia', in S. Sigmundsson, ed., *Viking Settlements and Viking Society* (Papers from the Proceedings of the Sixteenth Viking Congress, Reykjavík, 2009), Reykjavík, 225–44

Jennings, A. and Kruse, A., 2009. 'One Coast-Three peoples: Names and Ethnicity in the Scottish West during the Early Viking Period', in Woolf, ed., 2009, 75–102

Jesch, J., 1993. 'England and *Orkneyinga Saga*', in Batey *et al.*, eds, 1993, 222–39

Jesch, J., 2005. 'Literature in medieval Orkney', in Owen, ed., 2005, 11–24

Jesch, J., 2006. *The Nine Skills of Earl Rögnvaldr of Orkney,* Inaugural Lecture delivered in the University of Nottingham, 1 March 2006

Jesch, J., 2010. *'Orkneyinga Saga:* A Work in Progress?', in J. Quinn and E. Lethbridge, eds, *Creating the Medieval Saga: Versions, Variability and Editorial Interpretations of Old Norse Literature,* University Press of Southern Denmark, Odense, 153–73

Jesch, J. and Molleson, T., 2005. 'The Death of Magnus Erlendsson and the Relics of St. Magnus', in Owen, ed., 2005, 127–43

Jexlev, T. 1988. 'The Cult of Saints in Early Medieval Scandinavia', in Crawford, ed., 1988, 183–91

Johnsen, O.A. and Jón Helgason, eds, 1941. *Den store saga om Olav den hellige*, vol. I, Oslo

Johnston, A.W. and A., eds, 1907–13. *Orkney and Shetland Records,* vol. 1 (Viking Society for Northern Research), London (cited as *OSR*)

Jón Viðar Sigurðsson, 2007. 'The Appearance and Personal Abilities of goðar, jarlar, and konungar: Iceland, Orkney and Norway', in Ballin Smith *et al.*, eds, 2007, 95–110

Jon Viðar Sigurðsson, 2008. *Det Norrøne Samfunnet. Vikingen, kongen, erkebiskopen og Bonden*, Oslo

Jón Vidar Sigurdsson, 2011. 'Kings, Earls and Chieftains. Rulers in Norway, Orkney and Iceland c.900–1300', in Steinsland *et al.*, eds, 2011, 69–108

Jones, M., 2012. 'Udal Law', in M. Mulhern, ed., *Scottish Life and Society. A Compendium of Scottish Ethnology, The Law*, Edinburgh, 389–417

Knirk, J., 1990. *Norges Innskifter med de yngre Ryner*, vol. VI

Knirk, J., 1993. *Konungasögur ("kings' sagas")* in P. Pulsiano, ed., *Medieval Scandinavia: An Encyclopedia*, Garland Publishing, New York and London, 362–6

Krag, K., 2003. 'The early Unification of Norway', in K. Helle, ed., 2003, 184–201

Kruse, A., 2005. 'Explorers, Raiders and Settlers: The Norse Impact upon Hebridean Place-Names', in P. Gammeltoft *et al.*, eds, 2005, 141–56

Kruse, S., 1988. 'Ingots and Weight Units in Viking Age Silver Hoards', *World Archaeology* 20(2), 285–301

Kruse S., 1993. 'Silver Storage and Circulation in Viking-Age Scotland: the Evidence of Silver Ingots', in Batey *et al.*, eds, 1993, 187–203

Lamb, R.G., 1972–4. 'The Cathedral of Christchurch and the Monastery of Birsay', *PSAS* 105, 200–5

Lamb, R.G., 1983. 'The Cathedral and the Monastery', in W.P.L. Thomson, ed., *Birsay: A Centre of Political and Ecclesiastical Power*, Orkney Heritage, 2, 36–45

Lamb, R.G., 1993. 'Kirkwall: Origins and Development' and 'Cubbie Roo's Castle', in Batey *et al.*, eds, 1993, 44–9, 57–8

Landnámabók: The Book of Settlements, trans. H. Pálsson and P. Edwards, University of Manitoba Press, Winnipeg, 1972

Lange, M.A., 2007. *The Norwegian Scots: An Anthropological Interpretation of Viking–Scottish Identity in the Orkney Islands*, Edwin Mellen Press, New York and Ontario

Larsen, A-C., ed., 2001. *The Vikings in Ireland*, The Viking Ship Museum, Roskilde

Larson, L.M., 1935. *The Earliest Norwegian Laws: being the Gulathing Law and the Frostathing Law*, translated from the Old Norwegian, New York

Lawrie, A.C., ed., 1905. *Early Scottish Charters Prior to 1153*, Glasgow

Lawrie, A.C., ed., 1910. *Annals of the Reigns of Malcolm and William, Kings of Scotland*, Glasgow

Laxdaela saga, trans. M. Magnusson and H. Pálsson, Penguin Classics, Harmondsworth, 1969

Liber Ecclesie de Scon, 1843. Bannatyne and Maitland Clubs, Edinburgh

Lidén, H-E, 1974. *Middelalderen Bygger i Stein*, Oslo–Bergen–Tromsø

Lidén, H-E. 1988. 'The Romanesque Cathedrals of Norway', in Crawford, ed., 1988, 72–7

Low, D.M., Batey, C.E. and Gourlay, R., 2000. 'A Viking Grave at Balnakeil, Sutherland', in Baldwin, ed., 2000, 24–34

Lowe, C., 2002. 'The *papar* and Papa Stronsay: 8th-century Reality or 12th-century Myth?', in Crawford, ed., 2002a, 83–96

Lowe C. *et al.*, 2000. 'St. Nicholas Chapel Papa Stronsay', *Discovery and Excavation in Scotland*, New Series 1, 67–8

Lustig, R., 1979. 'The Treaty of Perth; a Re-examination', *Scot. Hist. Rev.* lviii, 35–57

MacDonald, A., 2002. 'The *papar* and some problems', in Crawford, ed., 2002a, 13–30

McDonald, R.A., 1997. *The Kingdom of the Isles, Scotland's Western Seaboard, c.1100–c.1336*. Scottish Historical Review Monograph series no. 4, East Linton

McDonald, R.A., 2002. '"Soldiers Most Unfortunate": Gaelic and Scoto-Norse Opponents of the Canmore Dynasty, c.1100–c.1230', in R.A. McDonald, ed., *History, Literature, and Music in Scotland, 700–1560*, Toronto, 93–119

McDonald, R.A., 2003. *Outlaws of Medieval Scotland: Challenges to the Canmore Kings, 1058–1266*, East Linton

McDonald, R.A., 2007. *Manx Kingship in its Irish Sea Setting 1187–1229: King Rognvaldr and the Crovan Dynasty*, Dublin

McDougall, D. and I., 1998. Trans. and annotation of Theodoricus Monachus, *The Ancient History of the Norwegian Kings* (Viking Society for Northern Research, Text Series, vol. XI), University College, London

MacEwen, A., 1982. 'The Family Connections of Alexander Sutherland of Dunbeath', *The Genealogist* 3(2), 130–53

MacEwen, A., 2011. 'Random Thoughts on Sir Farquhar, Earl of Ross', *West Highland Notes and Queries*, Ser. 3, no. 16 (June 2011)

MacEwen, A., 2011a, 'Replies. Random Thoughts on Sir Farquhar, Earl of Ross', *West Highland Notes and Queries*, Ser. 3, no. 17 (Nov. 2011), 15–21

MacGibbon, D. and Ross, T., 1887 (reprinted 1971). *The Castellated and Domestic Architecture of Scotland from the Twelfth to the Eighteenth Century*, Edinburgh

McGladdery, C., 1990. *James II*, Edinburgh

MacGregor, L.J. and Crawford, B.E., eds, 1987. *Ouncelands and Pennylands*, St. John's House Papers, no. 3, University of St Andrews

MacIvor, I., 1962–3. 'The King's Chapel at Restalrig and St. Triduana's Aisle: A Hexagonal Two-storied Chapel of the Fifteenth Century', *Proc. Soc. Ant. Scot.* xcvi, 247–63

MacKay, A., 1906. *The Book of MacKay*, Edinburgh

MacKay, A., 1914. *The History of the Province of Cat*, Edinburgh

MacKenzie, G., 1750 (reprinted 1836). *The General Grievances and Oppressions of the Isles of Orkney and Shetland*, Edinburgh

MacKenzie, W. Mackay, 1936–7. 'The Dragonesque Figure in Maeshowe, Orkney', *Proc. Soc. Ant. Scot.* lxxi, 157–73

MacQuarrie, A., ed., 2012. *Legends of Scottish Saints: Readings, hymns and prayers for the commemoration of Scottish Saints in the Aberdeen Breviary*, Dublin

McMillan, A.R.G., 1923. 'The Admiral of Scotland', *Scot. Hist. Rev.* xx, 11–18

MacNeill, P. and MacQueen, H., 1996. *Atlas of Scottish History to 1707*, University of Edinburgh

Maggi, A., 2008. *Rosslyn Chapel An Icon through the Ages*, Edinburgh

Markús, G., 1998. 'Hymn of St. Magnus, earl of Orkney (late 13th century)', in Clancy, ed., 1998, 292

Markús, G., 2012. *The Place-Names of Bute*, Donington

Marwick H., 1927–8. 'Sir David Menzies of Weem', *POAS* vi, 13–16

Marwick, H., 1929. *The Orkney Norn*, Oxford

Marwick, H., 1932. *Orkney Farm-Names*, Kirkwall

Marwick, H., 1957. 'Two Orkney Letters of A.D.1329', *Orkney Miscellany* 4, 48–56

Matthew Paris, *Chronica Maiora*, ed. H.R. Luard (Rolls Series, 1872–83), London

Meulengracht Sørensen, P., 1993. 'The Sea, the Flame and the Wind: The Legendary Ancestors of the Earls of Orkney', in Batey *et al.*, eds, 1993, 212–21

Mooney, H., 1924–5a. 'Relics found in St. Magnus Cathedral', *POAS* iii, 73–8

Mooney, H., 1924–5b. 'Notes on Discoveries in St. Magnus Cathedral, Kirkwall', *Proc. Soc. Ant. Scot.* lix, 239–57

Mooney, H., 1935. *St. Magnus-Earl of Orkney,* Kirkwall
Mooney, J., 1947. *The Cathedral and Royal Burgh of Kirkwall*, Kirkwall
Morris, C.D., 1996. *The Birsay Bay Project: Sites in Birsay Village and on the Brough of Birsay, Orkney* (University of Durham, Dept. of Archaeology, monograph series no. 2), Durham
Mortensen, L.B. and Ekrem, I., eds, 2003. *Historia Norvegie* (Museum Tusculanum Press), Copenhagen
Munch, P.A., 1855. *Det Norske Folks Historie*, anden del, Christiania
Mundal, E., 1993. 'The Orkney Earl and Scald Torf-Einarr and his Poetry', in Batey *et al.*, eds, 1993, 248–59
Mundal, E., 2007. 'Orkneyinga saga: Its Literary Form, Content and Origin', Lecture given at the Conference organised by the Royal Society of Edinburgh (RSE) in September 2006 on 'The Vikings and Scotland – Impact and Influence' with summary in the Report of the Conference published by the RSE, 17–18
Mundal, E., in press. 'Rognvald Kali Kolsson: *Orkneyinga saga's* portrait of a good ruler'
Myatt, L.J., 1993. 'Congress Diary', in Batey *et al.*, eds, 1993, 2–10
Myrhe, B., 1992. 'Borre – et Merovingertids senter i Øst-Norge', *Universitetets Oldsaksamlings Skrifter*. Ny Rekke no. 13, Oslo.
Nicholls, K.W., 1983. 'Late medieval Irish annals: two fragments', *Peritia* 2, 87–102
Nicolaisen, W.F.H., 1969. 'Norse Settlement in the Northern and Western Isles: Some Place-name Evidence', *Scot. His. Rev.* xlviii, 6–17
Nicolaisen, W.F.H., 1976. *Scottish Place-Names, Their Study and Significance,* London
Nicolaisen, W.F.H., 1982. 'Scandinavians and Celts in Caithness; the Place-name Evidence', in Baldwin, J.R., ed., 1982, 75–85
Njáls Saga, trans. Carl F. Bayerschmidt and Lee M Hollander, Wordsworth Classics, London, 1998
Njåstad, M., 2003. *Grenser for Makt.Konflikter og konfliktløsning mellom lokalsamfunn og øvrighet ca.1300–1540* (Nr. 42 Skriftserie fra Institutt for historie og klassiske fag Akademisk avhandling NTNU), Trondheim
Øien, T., 2005. 'The Northern Isles – between two nations', *Northern Studies* 35, 80–104
Oleson, J., 2003. 'Inter-Scandinavian Relations', in K. Helle, ed., 2003, 710–70
Omand, D., 1972, 'From The Vikings to the "Forty-Five" ', in Omand, ed., 1972, 128–36
Omand, D., ed., 1972. *The Caithness Book*, Inverness
Omand, D., ed., 1989. *The New Caithness Book,* Edinburgh
Omand, D., 1993. 'The Landscape of Caithness and Orkney' in Batey *et al.*, eds, 102–10
Omand, D., ed. 2003. *The Orkney Book,* Edinburgh
Opedal, I., 1998. *De glemte skipsgravene, Makt og myter på Avaldsnes* (Arkeologisk museum i Stavanger) Stavanger
Oram, R., 1999. 'David I and the Scottish Conquest and Colonisation of Moray', *Northern Scotland* 19, 1–20
Oram, R., 2004. *David I: The King who made Scotland*, Stroud
Oram, R., 2011. *Domination and Lordship: Scotland 1070–1230* (The New Edinburgh History of Scotland, vol. 3), Edinburgh

Oram, R., 2011a. 'Ouncelands, Quarterlands and Pennylands in the Western Isles, Man and Galloway: Tribute payments and military Levies in the Norse West', in Imsen, ed., 2011, 57–75

Oram, R. and Stell, G., eds, 2005. *Lordship and Architecture in Medieval and Renaissance Scotland*, Edinburgh

Orning, H.J., 2008. *Unpredictability and Presence: Norwegian Kingship in the High Middle Ages* (NW, vol. 38), Leiden

Owen, O., 1999. *The Sea Road: A Viking Voyage Through Scotland*, Historic Scotland, Edinburgh

Owen. O., 2005. 'Scotland's Viking "Towns": a Contradiction in Terms?', in *Viking and Norse in the North Atlantic*, Proceedings of the 14th Viking Congress, Tórshavn, 297–306

Owen, O., 2005a. 'History, Archaeology and *Orkneyinga Saga*: The Case of Tuquoy, Westray', in Owen, ed., 2005, 193–212

Owen O., ed., 2005. *The World of Orkneyinga Saga: The Broad-Cloth Viking Trip*, Kirkwall

Paulsen, V.A., 2011. 'Fra Lendmann til baron-ridderkultur i Norge på 1200-tallet', in A. Ågotnes and Ingvild Øye, eds, *Fra kongssete til kulturminne. Håkonshallen og Bergenhus-området gjennom 750 år*, Bymuseet i Bergen

Penman, M., 2004. *David II, 1329–71*, Edinburgh

Perroy, E., 1933. *The Diplomatic Correspondence of Richard II* (Camden Society 3rd series, vol. xlviii),London

Peterkin, A., 1820. *Rentals of the Ancient Earldom and Bishoprick of Orkney: with Some Other Explanatory and Relative Documents*, Edinburgh

Platt, C., 2007. 'Revisionism in Castle Studies: A Caution', *Medieval Archaeology* 51, 83–102

Poole, R.G., 1991. *Viking Poems on War and Peace*, Toronto

Power, R., 1986. 'Magnus Barelegs' expeditions to the West', *Scot. Hist. Rev.* lxvi, 69–89

Power, R., 1990. 'Scotland in the Norse Sagas', in Simpson, ed., 1990, 13–24

Pulsiano, P., ed., 1993. *Medieval Scandinavia: An Encyclopedia* (Garland Encyclopedias of the Middle Ages, vol. 1), New York

Radford, Ralegh, C.A., 1959. *The Early Christian and Norse Settlements at Birsay, Orkney* (HMSO Guidebook), Edinburgh

Radford, Ralegh, C.A., 1962. 'Art and Architecture, Celtic and Norse', in Wainwright, ed., 1962, 163–87

Radford, Ralegh, C.A., 1983. 'Birsay and the Spread of Christianity to the North', *Orkney Heritage* ii, 13–35

Radford, Ralegh, C.A., 1988. 'St. Magnus Cathedal, Kirkwall, and the Development of the Cathedral in N-W Europe', in Crawford, ed., 1988, 14–24

Rae MacDonald, W., 1904. *Scottish Armorial Seals*, Edinburgh

RCAHMS, 1911. *Report with an Inventory of the Ancient Monuments of Caithness: The Inventory of Caithness*, Edinburgh

RCAHMS, 1946. *Twelfth Report with an Inventory of the Ancient Monuments of Orkney and Shetland* vol. II, *The Inventory of Orkney*, Edinburgh

Rendall, J., 2002. 'St. Boniface and the Mission to the Northern Isles: A view from Papa Westray', in Crawford, ed., 2002a, 31–8
Renfrew, C., 1979. *Investigations in Orkney*, London
Ritchie, A., 1985. *Exploring Scotland's Heritage: Orkney and Shetland*, RCAHMS, Edinburgh
Ritchie, A., 1993. *Viking Scotland*, London
Ritchie, A., Scott, I. and Gray, T., 2006. *People of Early Scotland from contemporary images*, Brechin
Robberstad, K., 1983. 'Udal Law', in Withrington, ed., 1983, 49–68
Ross, A., 2011. *The Kings of Alba*, Edinburgh
Rowe, E.A., 2005. *The Development of Flateyarbók: Iceland and the Norwegian Dynastic Crisis of 1389*, University of Southern Denmark Press, Odense
Saint-Clair, R., 1898. *The Saint-Clairs of the Isles*, Auckland
Sandnes, B., 2005. 'Fra norn til Skotsk. Det norrøne språkets sjebne på Vesterhavsøyene c.1300–1750', in Imsen, ed., 2005, 163–73
Sawyer, B., 1991. 'Women as Bridge-builders: the Role of Women in Viking-Age Scandinavia', in I. Wood and N. Lund, eds, *People and Places in Northern Europe, 500–1600*, Woodbridge, 211–24
Sawyer, P., 1988. 'Dioceses and Parishes in Twelfth-century Scandinavia', in Crawford, ed., 1988, 36–45
Sawyer, B. and P., 1993. *Medieval Scandinavia*, University of Minnesota Press, Minneapolis
Schei, L.Kjørsvik, 1998. 'Huseby- og Holland-Gårdene på Orknøyene', *Historisk Tidsskrift* 3, 336–44
Sellar, D., ed., 1993. *Moray: Province and People,* The Scottish Society for Northern Studies, Edinburgh
Sharples, N., 2009. 'Norse Settlement in the Western Isles', in Woolf, ed., 2009, 103–30
Sharples, N., 2012. *A Late Iron Age Farmstead in the Outer Hebrides: Excavations at Mound I. Bornais, S. Uist*, Oxbow Books, Oxford
Sigmundsson, S., ed., 2011. *Viking Settlements and Viking Society: Papers from the Proceedings of the Sixteenth Viking Congress.* Reykjavík
Simpson, G.G., ed., 1990. *Scotland and Scandinavia 800–1800* (The Mackie Monographs I, University of Aberdeen), Edinburgh
Sinclair, A., 1992. *The Sword and the Grail: Of the Grail and the Templars and a True Discovery of America,* New York
Skene, W.F., 1878/8. 'Notes on the earldom of Caithness', *Proc. Soc. Ant. Scot.* xii (1st series), 571–6. Also printed in *Celtic Scotland* iii (1880), 448–53
Skre D. and Stylegar, F-A., 2004. *Kaupang The Viking Town,* University of Oslo, University Museum of Cultural History, Oslo
Skre, D., ed., 2007. *Kaupang in Skiringssal* (Kaupang Excavation Project Publication Series 1, Norske Oldfunn 22), Aarhus University Press, Aarhus
Skre, D., ed. 2008. *Means of Exchange. Dealing with Silver in the Viking Age* (Kaupang Excavation Project), Aarhus University Press, Aarhus
Skre, D., ed. 2012. *Things from the Town: Artefacts and Inhabitants in Viking-Age Kaupang*

(Kaupang Excavation Project Publication Series 3, Norske Oldfunn 24), Aarhus University Press, Aarhus

Smith, Brendan, 2002. 'The Frontiers of Church Reform in the British Isles, 1170–1230', in D. Abulafia and N. Berend, eds, *Medieval Frontiers: Concepts and Practices*, Aldershot,, 239–53

Smith, Brian, 1988. 'Shetland in Saga-Time: re-reading the *Orkneyinga Saga*', *Northern Studies* 25, 21–41

Smith, Brian, 1990. 'Shetland, Scotland and Scandinavia, 1400–1700: the changing nature of contact', in Simpson, ed., 1990, 25–37

Smith, Brian, 1995. 'Scandinavian place-names in Shetland, with a study of the district of Whiteness', in Crawford, ed., 1995a, 26–41

Smith, Brian, 2000. *Toons and Tenants: Settlement and Society in Shetland, 1299–1899*, Lerwick

Smith, Brian, 2001. 'The Picts and the Martyrs or Did the Vikings kill the Native Population of Orkney and Shetland?' *Northern Studies* 36, 7–32

Smith, Brian, 2002. 'Earl Henry Sinclair's fictitious trip to America'. *New Orkney Antiquarian Journal* 2, 3–28

Smith, Brian, 2003. 'The Archdeaconry of Shetland', in Imsen, ed., 2003, 161–9

Smith, Brian, 2003a. 'Not welcome at all: Vikings and the native population in Orkney and Shetland', in Downes, J. and Ritchie, A., eds, *Sea Change: Orkney and Northern Europe in the later Iron Age AD300–800*, Balgavies, 145–50

Smith, Brian, 2009. 'On the nature of tings: Shetland's law courts from the middle ages until 1611', *New Shetlander* 250, 37–45

Smout, T.C., ed., 2003. *People and Woods in Scotland*, Edinburgh

Spurkland, T., 2005. *Norwegian Runes and Runic Inscriptions,* The Boydell Press, Woodbridge

Steinnes, A., 1959. 'The "Huseby" system in Orkney', *Scot. Hist. Rev.* xxxviii, 36–46

Steinsland, G., 2011. 'Introduction: Ideology and Power in the Viking and Middle Ages: Scandinavia, Iceland, Ireland, Orkney and the Faeroes', in Steinsland *et al.*, eds, 2011, 1–14

Steinsland, G., 2011a. 'Origin Myths and Rulership: From the Viking Age Ruler to the Ruler of Medieval Historiography: Continuity, Transformations and Innovations', in Steinsland *et al.*, eds, 2011, 15–67

Steinsland, G., Sigurðsson, J.V., Rekdal, J.E. and Beuermann, I., eds, 2011. *Ideology and Power in the Viking and Middle Ages: Scandinavia, Iceland, Ireland, Orkney and the Faeroes* (NW, vol. 52), Leiden

Stevenson, J., ed., 1870. *Documents Illustrative of the History of Scotland 1286–1306*, Edinburgh

Stevenson, K., 2004. 'The Unicorn, St Andrew and the Thistle: was there an Order of Chivalry in Late Medieval Scotland?', *Scot. Hist. Rev.* lxxxiii, 3–22

Stewart, W., 1858. *The Buik of the Croniclis of Scotland or A Metrical Version of the History of Hector Boece*, ed. W.B. Turnbull (Rerum Britannicarum Medii Aevi Scriptores, 3 vols), London

Stones, E.L.G. and Simpson, G.G., 1977–1978. *Edward I and the Throne of Scotland, 1290–1296*, Oxford University Press for the University of Glasgow, Oxford
Storm, G., 1880. *Monumenta Historica Norvegiae; latinske kildeskrifter til Norges histori i middelalderen*, Kristiania
Storm, G., 1888. *Islandske Annaler Indtill 1578*, Christiania
Sturlunga Saga, ed. O. Thorsson, 2 vols, Reykjavik, 1988.
Stylegar, F-A., 2004. '"Central Places" in Viking Age Orkney'. *Northern Studies* 38, 5–30
Sverres Saga. En Tale mot Biskopene, oversatt A. Holtsmark, Oslo, 1961
Sverrir's saga, ed. G.Indrebø, Oslo, 1920
Taranger, A. 1912–7. *Norges Historie*, 3 vols, Christiania
Taylor, A.B., 1930–1. 'Some Saga Place-Names', *POAS* ix, 41–5
Taylor, S., 1995. 'The Scandinavians in Fife and Kinross: the Onomastic Evidence', in Crawford, ed., 1995, 141–69
Taylor, S., 2004. 'Scandinavians in Central Scotland – *by*-place-names and their Context', in Williams and Bibire, eds, 2004, 125–46
Tennant, H., 1862. *The Norwegian Invasion of Scotland in 1263* (A translation from *Det Norske Folks Historie*, by P.A. Munch), Glasgow
Thomson, W.P.L., 1984. 'Fifteenth Century Depression: the evidence of Lord Henry Sinclair's Rentals', in Crawford, ed., 1984, 125–42
Thomson, W.P.L., 1987. 'Ouncelands and Pennylands in Orkney and Shetland', in MacGregor and Crawford, eds, 1987, 24–45
Thomson, W.P.L., 1996. *Lord Henry Sinclair's 1492 Rental of Orkney*, Kirkwall
Thomson, W.P.L., 2001, 2008. *The New History of Orkney,* Edinburgh
Thomson, W.P.L., 2002. 'Ouncelands and Pennylands in the West Highlands and Islands', *Northern Scotland* 22, 27–43
Thomson, W.P.L., 2003. 'St. Magnus: an exploration of his Sainthood', in Waugh, ed., 2003, 46–64
Thomson, W.P.L., 2008. *Orkney Land and People,* Kirkwall
Thomson, W.P.L., 2012. 'Ingibjorg *Jarlamoðir*', *Northern Studies* 43, 26–39
Thomson, W.P.L., 2012a. 'Who was Dufnjal? Did St. Magnus kill him?', *New Orkney Antiquarian J.* 6, 2–8
Thormodus Torfæus, 1697. *Orcades seu Rerum Orcadensium Historiæ Libri Tres*, trans. Revd. A. Pope, *Ancient History of Orkney, Caithness and the North* (1866), Wick
Thorsteinsson, A., 1968. 'The Viking Burial Place at Pierowall, Orkney', in B. Niclasen, ed., *The Fifth Viking Congress, Proceedings,* Torshavn
Topping, P., 1983. 'Harald Maddadson. Earl of Orkney and Caithness, 1139–1206', *Scot. Hist. Rev.* lxii, 105–20
Townend, M., 2005. 'Knútr and the Cult of St. Oláfr: poetry and patronage in eleventh-century Norway and England', *Viking and Medieval Scandinavia* i, 251–79
Tuck, A., 1972. 'Some evidence for Anglo-Scandinavian relations at the End of the Fourteenth Century', *Medieval Scandinavia* 5, 75–88
Tudor, J.R., 1883. *The Orkneys and Shetland: Their Past and Present State* (1987 facsimile reproduction with Foreword by G. Donaldson), Edinburgh

Turpie, T., 2013. 'The Many lives of St Duthac of Tain: Tracing the Origins of a Late Medieval Scottish Saint', *Northern Studies*, 44, 3–20

Vahtola, J., 2003. 'Population and Settlement', in Helle, K., ed., 2003, 559–80

Wade, T.C., ed., 1937. *Acta Curiae Admirallatus Scotiae, 1557–1562,* Stair Society

Wainwright, F.T., 1962. *Archaeology, Place-Names and History,* London

Wainwright, F.R., ed.1962. *The Northern Isles.* Edinburgh

Wallace, P., 2008. 'Archaeological evidence for the different expressions of Scandinavian Settlement in Ireland, 840–1100', in Brink S., ed., 2008, 434–8

Wallace-Murphy, T., 1993. *Rosslyn Chapel: An Illustrated Guidebook,* Friends of Rosslyn Chapel

Walsingham, 1865. *Annales Ricardi Secundi,* ed. H.T. Riley (Rolls series), London

Wamers, E., 1998. 'Insular Finds in Viking Age Scandinavia and the State Formation of Norway', in Clarke, H. *et al.*, eds, *Ireland and Scandinavia in the Early Viking Age,* Dublin, 37–72

Watson, W.J., 1904, 1996. *Place-Names of Ross and Cromarty,* Inverness

Watson, W.J., 1926. *The History of the Celtic Place-Names of Scotland,* Edinburgh

Watt, D.E.R., 1977. *A Biographical Dictionary of Scottish Graduates to A.D.1410,* Oxford

Watt, D.E.R., ed., 1963. 'List of Abbreviated Titles of the Printed Sources of Scottish History to 1560', Supplement to *SHR*, 42, i–xxxii

Watt, D.E.R.. ed., 1969. *Fasti Ecclesiae Scoticanae Medii Aevi ad Annum 1638* (Dept of Mediaeval History, St Salvator's College), St Andrews

Watt, D.E.R., gen. ed., 1987–1998. *Scotichronicon by Walter Bower in Latin and English,* 9 vols, Aberdeen/Edinburgh

Watt, D.E.R. and Murray, A.L., eds, 2003. *Fasti Ecclesiae Scoticanae Medii Aevi ad Annum 1638* (The Scottish Record Society, new series, vol. 25), Edinburgh; revised edition of Watt, 1969

Waugh, D.J., 1985. 'A Detailed Account of some Caithness Place-Names' *Scottish Language* 4, 37–90

Waugh, D.J., 1989. 'Place-Names', in D. Omand, ed., *The New Caithness Book*, Wick, 141–55

Waugh, D.J., 1993. 'Caithness. An Onomastic Frontier Zone', in Batey *et al.*, eds, 1993, 120–8

Waugh, D.J., 2009. 'Caithness: Another Dip in the Sweerag Well', in Woolf, ed., 2009, 31–48

Waugh, D.J., ed. 2003. *The Faces of Orkney: Stone, Skalds, and Saints,* Scottish Society for Northern Studies, Edinburgh

Wawn, A., 2011. Orkneyinga saga *in Victorian Britain: A Tale of Three Projects,* The Third Shetland Museum and Archives Memorial Lecture, Lerwick

Wegener, C.F., ed., 1856. *Diplomatarium Christierni Primi,* Copenhagen

Wærdahl, R.B, 2006. *'Norges konges rike og hans skattland' Kongemakt og statsutvikling i den norrøne verden i middelalderen.* Dr.art.-avhandling. NTNU, Trondheim

Wærdahl, R.B., 2010. 'The Norwegian Realm and the Norse World: a historiographic approach', in Imsen, ed., 2010, 35–57

Wærdahl, R.B., 2011. *The Incorporation and Integration of the King's Tributary Lands into the Norwegian Realm c.1195–1397* (NW, vol. 53), Leiden
Wærdahl, R.B., 2012. 'Dronning Isabella Bruce', in Bandlien, ed., 2012, 99–108
Westerdahl, C. and Stylegar, F-A., 2004. 'Husebyene i Norden', *Viking*, 101–38
Whaley, D., 1998. *The Poetry of Arnorr jarlaskáld: An Edition and Study*, Brepols
Williams, G., 1996. 'Land Assessment and Military Organisation in the Norse Settlements in Scotland, c.900–1266 AD', unpublished PhD thesis (University of St Andrews)
Williams, G., 2003. 'The *dabhach* Reconsidered: Pre-Norse or Post-Norse?' *Northern Studies* 37, 17–32
Williams, G., 2004. 'Land Assessments and the Silver Economy of Norse Scotland', in Williams and Bibire, eds, 2004, 65–104
Williams, G., 2007. '"These People were High-born and Thought Well of Themselves". The Family of Moddan of Dale', in Ballin Smith *et al.*, eds, 2007, 129–52
Williams, G. and Bibire, P., eds, 2004. *Sagas, Saints and Settlements* (NW, vol. 11), Leiden
Withrington, D.J., ed., 1983. *Shetland and the Outside World 1469–1969* (Aberdeen University Studies Series, no. 157), Oxford
Woolf, A., 2000. 'The "Moray Question" and the Kingship of Alba in the Tenth and Eleventh Centuries', *Scot. Hist. Rev.* lxxix, 145–64
Woolf, A., 2007. *From Pictland to Alba 789–1070* (The New Edinburgh History of Scotland, vol. 2), Edinburgh
Woolf, A., ed., 2009. *Scandinavian Scotland – Twenty Years After* (St John's House Papers no. 12), St Andrews
Yeoman, P., 1999. *Pilgrimage in Medieval Scotland*, Historic Scotland, Batsford

WEBSITES CONSULTED

Caithness Castles:
www.caithness.org/caithness/castles/lambaborg/
www.macdonald.cam.ac.uk/projects/Deerness/
www.paparproject.org.uk
Scapa Flow Landscape Partnership Scheme:
www.scapaflow.co/index.php/history_and_archaeology/the_norse/scapa_flow_the_nerve_centre_and_knarr_centre_of_the_medieval_earldom/
The THING Project (Thing sites International Networking Group) 2009–2012:
www.thingproject.eu/node/11

Index

Aalborg, Earl Thorfinn's visit to, 157
Aberdeen, revenues from, 225
Aberdeen Breviary, Scottish saints in, 225
abeyance of earldom, 37–8, 320–5
Adam, bishop of Caithness, 58
    burning of, 22, 149, 268–70, 390
Adam, chaplain of Orkney, 253, 259
Adam of Bremen, 146
Æthelred, Anglo-Saxon King, 126
Afreka, daughter of Earl Duncan of Fife, 246, 257
Agreement of 1312, 316
airigh, Gaelic term for shieling, 182
aith (portage), 191–2
Alba, kingdom of, 137
Alban, St, 230
Alexander II, king of Scots (1214–1249)
    and burning of bishop Adam, 271–3
    diplomatic approach to King Hakon, 294
    expedition against Ewen of Argyll, 294
    grants of Caithness, 281
    Sutherland policy, 264–5
Alexander III, king of Scots (1249–1286)
    Caithness policy, 296–7
    personal control of government, 294
    and the Treaty of Perth, 302
Alexander of Ard, 324–9
Alexander Borthwick, 382
Alexander of Klapam/Claphame, 345
Alexander Peterkin, Orkney sheriff, 29
Alexander Sutherland, 359
    family relationships of, *Fig.* 8.3
    will of, 359–60
Alladale, Ross, 154
altar frontals, 226

Anakol, fosterer of Erlend, 186
Anderson, Duncan, chief of the Clan Donnachie, 322
Anderson, Joseph, Scottish antiquary, 6, 26
Andrew, bishop of Caithness (1147/1151–1184), 185, 241, 251–2
Andrew Painter, bishop of Orkney (1477–1505x1506), 372, 374, 375n
Anglo-Saxon Chronicle, 45, 162
Angus, son of Moddan, 181
Angus dynasty, 392
Angus earls, inheritance of Orkney earldom, 277–9, *Fig.* 7.1, *Fig.* 7.4
Annals of Dunstable, 270–1
Annual, payment for the Isles, 360–1, 363, 365–6
architecture, and Orkney saints, 228
aristocracy, 104, 173–4
arm rings, as currency, 122
Arnamagnaean Collection of Icelandic manuscripts, Copenhagen, 65
Arnfinn, son of Earl Thorfinn 'Skull-Splitter', 47
    death of, 112
Arni Lorja, Norwegian sysselman in Orkney, 259
Arnkell, son of Earl Torf-Einar, 111
Arnor Thordarson *jarlaskáld*, poet, 49, 136–7, 139, 162
Arran, earl of, 365
art
    animal, 52
    Nordic, 52
    Ringerike style of, 52
Asbjorn, son of Grim of Swona, 176
Asgrimserg, place name, 182

ash woods, and shipbuilding, 118
Atholl, Earl Paul's captivity in, 183
Atholl family, alliance with Rognvald Kali Kolsson, 177
Aud the Deep-Minded, 94, 96n, 99n
Auskerry, feudal grant to Sir James Sinclair of Brecks, 385
Avaldsness, burial mounds at, 98
avenging head, Irish-Gaelic folk story motif, 93
Avondale, Lord, 365

Balfour, David, *Odal Rights and Feudal Wrongs* (1860), 29
Balliol, Edward, 319
Balliol, John, 309–10
Balnakeil Bay, boy's grave at, 103
Bangor monastery, Northern Ireland, Harald Maddadson's grant to, 258
Bannaskirk, Magnus dedication at, 224
banners, 116
    as emblems of war, 76
    Sigurd's raven banner, 127
Bannockburn, Battle of, 225
Barr, St, cult of, 185
Barry, George, minister of Shapinsay, 30
bathhouses, 72
    at Brough of Birsay, 72–3
beacon system, 151n
Beaumont family, allegiances of, 239
Bergen, 16
    Bergenhus at, *Col. pl.* 26
    Christchurch cathedral at, 245
    council meeting at (1223), 267–8
    diocese of, 221
    Hakon's Hall, *Col. pl.* 31
    maritime contact radius from, 13
Bernard Peff, Sir, 312
Bergen Castle, governor of, 380
Bergfinn Skatason, Shetland farmer, 202
Birgham, parliament at, 307–8
Birgisherað, Thorfinn's residence, 151
Birka, Sweden, as trading centre, 87
Birsay, *Col. pl.* 14
    bishopric at, 142
    church at, 145

earldom endowments of Orkney bishopric in, 218
    as episcopal estate, 74
    parish of, 151
    runestones from, *Col. pl.* 1
    Thorfinn's residence at, 141, 143, 147
Bjadmunja, daughter of king Myrkjartan of Connaught, 170
Bjarne Audunsson, 316
Bjarni Kolbeinsson, bishop of Orkney (1188–1223), 76, 214, 219–21, 227, 228–9, 244, 250, 255, 258, 263, 267, 305
Black Death, in Norway, 25
blood eagling, 105
boat building yard, at Easter Ross, *Pl.*3
boatslips, 73n
Böglunga sögur (Sagas of the Bagler), 259
bona regalia, royal estates belonging to the Norwegian Crown, 168n
bondi, farmers, 16, 131, 175, 272–3, 276, 287, 330, 390–91
Book of Miracles, 201–2
booty, 94
bordlands, 174, 191, 193, *Fig.* 4.6
Bornais, Viking settlement at, 86n
Borre, Vestfold, burial mounds at, 98
Bower, *Scotichronicon*, 34
Boyd family, and Scottish politics, 363
Brawl
    castle of, 325, 326n, *Col. pl.* 34
    estate of, 358
    Nicholas Breakspear, papal legate, 252
Breiðeyarsund (Broad-islands Sound), Shetland, Hakon's fleet at, 297
Brian Boru, king of Munster, 128
Broad-islands Sound, see *Breiðeyarsund*
Broch of Ness, Freswick, 176n, 196
Brough of Birsay, *Col. pl.* 7, *Col. pl.* 8
    church at, 68, 147, 228–31, *Pl.*5
    earldom power centre, 15, 143
    ecclesiastical complex at, 71–2, *Fig.* 2.3, *Col. pl.* 5
    geography of, 73
    geopolitics of, 142–3
    memorial stones at, 51
    monastic foundation at, 68

secular residences at, 70–2
Brown, Alexander, 315
Bruce, Isabella, queen of Norway, 347n
Bruce, Robert, king of Scots (d.1329), 309–10
Brusi Sigurdsson, earl (1014–1030x35), 42, 45, 130, 133
Bryggen, Bergen, runic finds at, 50n
Buchollie Castle, Caithness, 176n
Buk of Gud Maneris, 384
Burghead, Dark Age coastal stronghold at, 95n
burial mounds
    as power statement, 111
    purpose of, 98–9
burials, pagan, 98
Burray, 15
    silver hoard at, 159n
butter skats, 323
butter teind, 268

Cairston, castle at, 195
Caithness
    abeyance of earldom, 25, 320–5
    agriculture in, 16
    Alexander III's hostages from, 300, 301
    and Alexander of Ard, 325–9
    and Angus dynasty, 287–8
    Annual due from, 251
    battle in, 110
    bondi in, 391
    castles in, 196
    Christianity in, 231
    Crown authority in, 329
    deer hunting in, 188
    demesne estates in, 16
    detachment from Sutherland, 264–5
    ecclesiastical authority in, 268
    episcopal centres in, *Fig.* 4.1
    feudalism in, 175, 284, 329–31
    feuding in, 386–7
    Gaelic in, 12
    geography of, 11
    geology of, 16
    geopolitical significance of, 134–5, 188–97
    gödings in, 175
    granted to Erlend by King Malcolm, 186
    Hakon's fine from (1263), 298–9
    historical analyses, 27–9
    inheritance in, 59, 129–30
    as joint lordship, 6
    judicial arrangements in, 7, 273–4
    landholders in, 286
    links with Scone abbey, 260
    Magnus dedications in, 224
    marriages in, 108
    military routes in, 154–5
    mingling of belief (Celtic/Norse) in, 183
    Moddan family holdings in, 181
    Norse culture in, 181–2
    Norse settlement in, 96
    Norwegian links, 16
    Olaf Rolfsson's *yfirsókn* in, 175
    pagan burials in, 98
    parochial organisation, 232, 234
    as peripheral community, 21–2
    Peter's Pence in, 252, 258
    place names in, 12, 96, 99–101
    political history, 10, 18
    post-saga period, 26–7
    Ross family's control of, 25
    royal armies in, 22
    royal authority in, 17, 19, 23, 241, 287
    runic inscriptions from, 50
    skatlands in, 124
    social development of, 175
    stewards of, 251
    Thorfinn's troop raising in, 151
    tithes in, 268–9
    as tripartite maritime lordship, 15–16
    as war zone, 301
Carberry, 369
Carrick, earl of, 310
Carvell, ship owned Sir David Sinclair, 383
Castlehowe, Paplay, fortified structure at, 195
castles, 193–7
Cataibh, tribe of, 11
cathedrals, role of, 235
Céli Dé, monastic community, Dornoch, 185
Celtic language, erased in Orkney and

Shetland, 12
Celto-Norse society, in north Scotland, 181–2
Charles VII, king of France, 360n, 361, 366
cheese teind, 269
Christ Church, Birsay, 51
   Magnus Erlendsson's relics at, 205
Christ Church cathedral, Bergen, 245
Christ Church cathedral, Dublin, 147
Christian I, king of Denmark and Norway (1426–1481), 37, 360–3, 365–7
Christianity, 53, 126
Christopher of Bavaria, king of Denmark, Norway and Sweden (1418–1448), 353, 356
Chronicle of Melrose, 271
Church of the Holy Sepulchre, Jerusalem, 68
   as model for Round Church, Orphir, 212
Church
   in abeyance period, 324
   and appointment of Harald Maddadson as co-earl of Orkney, 184
   Gilbert de Moravia's ecclesiastical changes, 266
   and Harald Maddadson, 258, 259
   Norman, 56
   organisation of, 235
   role of bishops, 2
   and royal authority, 240–1, 251
   and state control, 73
churls, as class of men, 83
Clement, St, cult of, 2
Clement VII, pope, 341
Clontarf, Battle of (1014), 46, 125–6, 128
   Earl Sigurd *digri's* raven banner at, 76
Cnut the Great, 36, 133–4, 158
Cologne, archbishop of, and land assessment system of Orkney, 158
Cologne penny, 158–9
Comitis generosi militis gloriosi, sequence to St Magnus, 66
commaid, see conveth
Complaint of the People of Orkney against David Menzies of Weem (1425), 61–2, 349, 351, 352, *Col. pl.* 3

Comyn, John, 308
Conrad III, coronation of (1027), 158
conveth, Gaelic term for hospitality rent, 182
Copenhagen, William Sinclair in, 355–6
Cranstoun, David, 365
Crichton, George, Sir, 329, 358
Crookston writs, Hays's transcriptions of, 33
Cross Kirk, Dunrossness, 381
Cubbie Roo's Castle, Wyre, 194–5, 276, *Col. pl.* 17
currency, 122
Cyder Hall, farm-name, 98

Damsay island, castle at, 195
Danish-Norwegian monarchy, 340
Danish Royal Archives (Rigsarchiv), Copenhagen, 65
Darraðarlióð, Song of Dorrud, 128, 129
davach, Scottish territorial unit, 124, 330
David, earl, son of Harald Maddadson and Gormflaith, 20, 43, 240, 246, 259, 261 *Fig.* 6.2
David I, king of Scots (1124–1153)
   authority in Sutherland and Caithness, 23, 178
   authority in Orkney earldom, 185
   charter mandate to Earl Rognvald Kali Kolsson, 23, 184–5, 240–1
   establishment of Caithness diocese, 50
   involvement in appointment of Harald Maddadson as co-earl, 184
   and see of Orkney, 241
   support for Orkney earls, 183
   and Swein Asleifsson, 184, 186
David II, king of Scots (1329–1371), 322
David Menzies, governor of Orkney, 22, 61–2, 349, 350–3
David Stewart, earl of Caithness, 329
de Moravia family, 25, 286–7
   and Sutherland earldom, 265
Declaration of Arbroath (1320), 317
Deerness
   sea battle at, 136
   seal matrix from, 79
Denmark

burial mounds in, 98
Peter's Pence in, 252
wall paintings of St Magnus in, 226
devil possession, 201
Dibidale, Ross, 154
Dingwall, 155
derivation of place name, 155
Donald, son of Malcolm III, king of Scots, 44
Donald MacWilliam, 246
Dornoch
Céli Dé monastic community at, 185
sheriff court at, 386
Dornoch cathedral, 150, 266, *Col. pl.* 29
Foundation Charter of, 266–7
Dornoch Firth, 95
Dorrud, see *Darraðarlióð*,
Doune Castle, 366
Dubbo, 369
Dublin
as trading centre, 87
Christ Church Cathedral at, 147
Duffus, castle at, 286
Dufniall (Donald), chieftain, killed by Magnus and Hakon, 172
Dunbeath, Magnus dedication at, 224
Duncan, king of Scots, son of Malcolm Canmore, 'Long-Neck', 44, 159
Duncansby
derivation of name of, 108n
Olaf Rolfsson's *yfirsókn* at, 175
Swein Asleifsson's authority in, 176
Thorfinn's residence at, 141
Duncansby Head, battle of, 114
Dunfermline abbey, construction of, 211
Dungadr, Celtic chieftain, marriage to Groa, 96, 108
Dungalsnipa, see Duncansby Head
Dunstable, Annals of, 269
Durham cathedral, as model for St Magnus cathedral, Kirkwall, 211
Duthac of Tain, St, cult of, 69
dynastic marriages, 96
Dysart, Burgh of, 369

earl, title, meaning of, 83n
Earl Harald's Saga, 242

Earl's Bu, Orphir, longhalls at, *Col. pl.* 16, 19
earldom lordship, *Fig.* 1.2
earldom power centres, *Fig.* 3.13
earls
as class of men, 83
changing status of, 27–8
divided loyalty, 293–4
mythical origin, 80–5
Easter Ross, *Fig.* 4.2
boat building yard at, *Pl.* 3
Norse place names in, 117
Norse settlement of, 119
Echmarcach mac Ragnaill, Jemarc from the Rhinns, 134
Edgar, Scottish king, agreement with Magnus *berfættr* (Barelegs), 23
Edinburgh, Scottish royal power centre in, 22
Edward I, king of England
domination of Scotland, 309
letters of protection to Earl John, 310
tour of Scotland, 311
Edward II, king of England, son of King Edward I of England, 307–8, 316n
Egidia Douglas, 356
Egilsay
Bishop William the Old's residence at, 207n
earldom endowments of Orkney bishopric in, 218
Magnus Erlendsson killed at, 198–9
St Magnus church at, 228–31
Einar Rognvaldsson, 'Torf-Einar', earl (early 10th cent.)
contest with Halfdan Long-Leg, 105
and Harald Finehair, 106–7
nickname of, 104
progenitor of Orkney earls, 91, 105
Skaldic poetry of, 49
Einar Sigurdsson 'Wry-Mouth', son of Earl Sigurd II (1014–1020), 45, 131
Eithne, daughter of Kjarval, king of Ireland, 112
marriage to Earl Hlodver, 112
weaving the raven banner, 127
Eke, John, canon of Uppsala, 381

Ekkjalsbakki (banks of the River Oykel), 97
Elin, daughter of Erik Stay-Brails, 278
Elizabeth Douglas, 354, 356, 359
Ellisiv, queen of Harald Sigurdsson, 161
Elwick Bay, Shapinsay, Hakon's fleet at, 297
England
  king of, 239; *see also* Edward I, Edward II, John
  Magnus dedications in, 224–5
  Magnus Haraldsson's expedition to, 160
  Thorfinn's campaigns in, 139
Erik Haraldsson *blóðøx*, 'Blood-axe'
  forced out of Norway, 111
  and the Northern Isles, 104
  killed at Battle of Stainmore (954), 111
Erik Jedvardson, Swedish king, cult of, 200n
Erik Magnusson, king of Norway (1355–1380), 307, Pl. 7
  claim to Scottish kingdom, 309
Erik of Pomerania, king of Norway and Denmark (1382–1459)
  grant to David Menzies, 350–1
  grant to John Sinclair, 345
  grant to Thomas Tulloch, 350, 354
  and William Sinclair, 63, 354
Erik 'Stay-Brails', 248, 272
  daughters of, 278
Erlend Haraldsson, 185
Erlend Thorfinsson, earl (c.1060–1098), 45–6, 143, 162–3, 167, 186–7
Erling Erlendsson, son of Erlend, earl of Orkney, 44
Erngisl Suneson, earl of Orkney (1353–7), 319n, 320
Eskadale, Ross, 154
Eufemia of Strathearn, 323
Evie, church dedicated to St Nicholas at, 213n
Evreux, viscountcy of, 239
excambion, 369–70
Exchequer Rolls, 322
Eyiarskeggjar, Island-Beardies, 242
Eyiarskeggjar rebellion, Harald Maddadson's involvement in, 20, 57
Eynhallow
  ecclesiastical ruins at, 68n, 237

Eynhallow Sound, 143
Eyrbyggja Saga, 85, 114, 119, 125
Eystein Haraldsson, Norwegian king (1142–1157), 23, 186–7
  capture of Harald Maddadson, 23
  ransom of Harald Maddadson, 241
Eysteinsdalr (Ousedale), King William's camp at, 256

Faeroe Islands
  cult of St Magnus in, 225
  plague in, 320
Fagrskinna, 41
Falköping, Battle of, 343n
Ferchar Maccintsacairt, 266
Ferchard, bishop of Caithness (1304–1321x27), 315
feudalism, 174–5, 188, 239, 284, 329–31
Fife, Scandinavian place names in, 138n
Finlaggan, Islay, 152
Finnlaech, earl, ruler of Moray, 109
Finnleikr, earl, 114
  defeat by Sigurd II, 116
Firthlands (Moray, Cromarty and Dornoch Firths)
  geopolitical significance, 95
  Sigurd II's access to, 117
flame, as natural force, 81
Flateyarbók
  burning of Bishop Adam, 269
  composition of, 48
  text of, 41
Flet brothers, 382
Flodden, Battle of (1513), 374, 385–6
Floruvoe, Battle of (1193), 243
Fornjot, ruler of Finland and Kvenland, 81–2
Forse harbour, Earl John's grant to Reginald Cheyne II, 25
Frakokk, sister of Helga, 176–7
  attempted murder of Earl Paul, 179
  burning of, 181, 220
  and Clan Moddan, 179–83
  daughter of, 179, 181
France, kings of, 239
Freskin de Moravia, 25, 331
Freswick, Swein Asleifsson's estate in, 176

Fru Herdis Thorvaldsdatter, 342n, 343
fylker (Norwegian districts equivalent to a shire), 84

gæðingr, *see* göding
Gaelic language
   in Caithness, 12
   influence on Old Norse, 182
Gairsay, 176
Galloway, King William's authority in, 22
Gamla Uppsala, Sweden, burial mounds at, 98
Gaulverjabær, Iceland, hospital dedicated to Magnus Erlendsson, 226
genealogies, 32–5
Genealogy of the Earls
   Alexander of Ard, 326
   compilation of, 352–5
   in Corpus MS of Bower's *Scotichronicon*, 34–5, 37
   daughters of Earl Malise, 334
   description of, 63
   Gilbert II, 286
   Einar, 105
   eulogy for Rognvald Kali Kolsson, 227
   Henry I Sinclair, 346–7
   Henry II Sinclair, 348
   Isabella Sinclair, 344, 348
   Latin copy (part of Panmure Codex), 63
   Magnus III, 293
   Magnus V, 317
   Scots translation of, 62–3
   Sigurd II the Stout, 113
   Sutherland earldom, 265, 281–2
   Thorfinn the Mighty, 129n
Germany, Thorfinn's visit to, 157
Gesta Annalia, 242
Giants' Skerries, 162
Gilbert I, earl, successor of Magnus II, 282
Gilbert II, earl (1239–1256), 282
Gilbert, bishop of Hamar, 297
Gilbert of Moravia, archdeacon of Moray and bishop of Caithness (1222x23–1245), 265–6
Gilchrist, earl of Angus, 279
Gilla Odran, steward in Caithness, 187
   killing of by Swein Asleifsson, 188

Gilmakali, royal judge in Caithness, 273n
Gissur Thorvaldsson, Icelandic earl, 291n
Glen Harris, Isle of Rum, 151
Godfrey 'king of Man', defeat by Earl Sigurd II, 119
göding, upper strata of the landed aristocracy, 173–4
   Kugi, at Rapness, Westray, 174
göding-ship (*gæðingaskip*), loss of, 278
Godred, king of Denmark, 87
Godred, king of Man, 263
göfgra manna, nobleman, 174
Goi, descendent of king Fornjot, 81–2
Gor, descendent of king Fornjot, 81–2
Gormflaith (Hvarflöd), wife of Harald Maddadson, 57, 246–7, 257
graves, as evidence of pagan settlement, 99, 101
Great Cause, the, 309
Great Glen, 95
   as transport route, 119
Greenland, 18, 296
Gregory Kikr, sysselman from Shetland, 267
Grelaug, wife of Earl Thorfinn 'Skull-Splitter', 108
Grim of Swona, 176
Grimkell, Norwegian bishop, 148
Groa, daughter of Thorstein the Red, 96
   marriage to Dungadr, 108
Gulating lawcode of west Norway, 148
Gunnhild, daughter of Erlend, earl of Orkney, 44, 170, 201
Gunnhild, daughter of Harald Maddadson, 246
Gunnhild, wife of Erik 'Blood-axe', 112, 47
Gunni, farmer from Westray, 200
Gunnlaug, skald, 114
Guttorm Sigurdsson, 48, 104
Guttorm Sperra, 319n

hack silver, 120, 122
Hacon's Saga, 169, 268, 275–7, 294n, 297–9
Hafrsfjord, Battle of, 89
Hakon, son of Harald Maddadson, 246
Hakon the Good's Saga, 47
Hakon Hakonsson (IV), king of Norway

(1217–1263), 267, 292
  death of, 300
  grant of Orkney to Earl Magnus II, 282
  imposition of fines in Caithness, 242
  naval expedition (1263), 297–9, *Fig.* 7.3
Hakon Jonsson, 323, 325, 327
Hakon Ladejarl, 84
Hakon V Magnusson, king of Norway
    (1299–1319), 7, 292, *Pl.*8
  legal amendment of (1308), 84
  naval expedition of, 22, 295–7
Hakon VI Magnusson, king of Norway
    (1355–1380), 325, 340
Hakon Paulsson, earl (1104x5–c.1123)
  and bishop William the Old, 202
  and cult of St Nicholas, 213
  encounter with the soothsayer, 166
  killing of the royal official, 170–1
  and Magnus Erlendsson, 165
  and Norwegian kings, 165
  pilgrimage to Holy Land, 212
  political links, 171
  quarrel with Magnus Erlendsson, 198
  religious memorial of, 68
  in Sweden, 165–6
Hakon Sigurdsson, Norwegian jarl, 90
Hakon Sverrison's saga, 263n
Hakon's Hall, Bergen, 295
Háleygja-jarlar, earls of northern Norway, 84
Halfdan Hålegg 'Long-Leg', son of Harald
    Finehair, contest with Einar, 91, 105, 106
Halfdan the Old, 82
Halkirk, as place name, 149
Halkirk church, Caithness, 149, *Col. pl.* 30
  demoted by bishop Gilbert, 266
Hallad, son of Earl Rognvald of Møre, 48, 104
Hallvard Dufuson, 220
Halogaland, *Háleygja-jarlar* in, 84, 90
Ham, Caithness, 111
  prehistoric mound at, *Col. pl.* 12
Hamburg-Bremen, archbishop of, 56
Hanef *ungi*, steward of the king of Norway, 194, 264, 275–6
Hans, king of Denmark and Norway
    (1455–1513), 33, 380, *Fig.* 9.2
Harald 'Blue-tooth', king of Denmark
    (d.c.984), 114n
  memorial stone of, 52
Harald Eriksson, Harald *ungi* ('the Young'),
    earl (d.1198), 244, 248–50
  death of, 249
  as saint, 249, 250
  sisters of, 278
Harald Gilli, Norwegian king (1135–36)
  confirmation of Rognvald's claim to
    Orkney, 204
  grant of Orkney earldom to Rognvald
    Kali Kolsson, 177
  and St Olaf's church, Bergen, 209
Harald Godwinsson, king of England, 45, 161
Harald Halfdansson, *hárfagri* ('Finehair')
    (late 9th–early 10th cent.)
  burial of, 98
  creation of Orkney earldom, 91
  dynasty of, 91, 92
  Einar's reconciliation to, 106–7
  gift of Orkney and Shetland to
    Rognvald of Møre, 48, 63, 86
  in *Heimskringla*, 85
  unification of Norway, 86–7
Harald Hakonsson, *slettmali* ('Smooth-
    Tongue'), earl (c.1123–?1128)
  at Caithness, 176
  killed by poisoned shirt, 177, 179
Harald Maddadson, earl (1139–1206), 177, 389–90
  and Caithness, 19, 55, 261
  capture by King Eystein Haraldsson, 23
  career of, *Fig.* 6.1
  and the church, 258–9
  as co-earl of Orkney, 183
  death of, 50
  expedition into Moray, 247
  and the Eyiarskeggjar rising, 20
  grant to 'Benkoren' monastery
    (?Bangor), 258
  grant to Scone Abbey, 57, 257, 259
  Harald Maddadson's Saga, 98
  and King John of England, 253–4
  and King Sverrir, 242, 244–5

maiming of Bishop John, 251
marriage to Afreka, 246
marriage to Gormflaith, 246
murder of Arni Lorja, 259
murder of Hlifolf, steward of Caithness, 251
quarrel with bishop John of Caithness, 57–8
and royal authority, 240–6, 260
and Shetland, 16
submission to King William, 256–7
support of Donald MacWilliam, 246
Harald Sigurdsson *harðraði* ('hard-ruler'), king of Norway (1047–1066), 45, 133, 145, 156, 161–2
Harald Maddadson's Saga, 43, 98
Harray, parish of, 151
Harris, place name, 151
Haugar, Kormsund, Harald Finehair's burial at, 98–9
Havard the Fecund, son of Earl Thorfinn, 'Skull-splitter', 47
hay teind, 269
Hebrides
control of, 294
Earl Thorfinn's campaigns in, 138
Erik Blood-axe's raids in, 111
Honorius III's letter to, 269
lordship over, 36
Magnus Olafsson's war cruise to, 169
manpower from, 150
military organisation in, 150–2
place names in, 101
plague in, 320
and Treaty of Perth, 302
Heggen vane, 52
Heimskringla (Saga of the kings of Norway), 26
Orkney to Rognvald of Møre, 48
Harald Finehair in, 84–5
Olaf Haraldsson in, 133–4
as national history of the kings of Norway, 49
origin myth in, 81
relationship to *Orkneyinga Saga*, 41
as source for Genealogy of the Earls, 64
Thorstein the Red in, 96

Helena, daughter of Harald Maddadson, 246
Helga, daughter of Moddan, mother of Harald Hakonsson, 176–7, 179, 181
Helgi, farmer killed by Gilla Odran, 187
Helmsdale, Frakokk's court in, 183
Henry I, king of England, 165
Henry III, emperor, Thorfinn's visit to, 157
Henry, son of Harald Maddadson, 246, 259
Henry Phantouch, archdeacon of Shetland, 384
Henry Scott, 297
Henry Stiklawe, 310n, 313
hérað, district division, 151–2
heraldic emblems, of Orkney rulers, 76
Herbjorg, daughter of Earl Paul Thorfinnsson, 43
Herborga, daughter of Earl Harald Maddadson, 246
Herra district, Tingwall, Shetland, 151
Herries, district, Islay, 151–2
hersar (war-leaders), 84
hird (*hirð*), 5, 6, 20, 37, 73, 122, 142, 149, 156, 245, 276, 288–9, 305
hirðmenn, royal liegemen, 21, 50n, 142, 165, 167–8, 173, 192n, 231, 240, 245, 385
Hirdloven *see Hirðskrá*
Hirdmanstein, court of the hirdmen, 385
Hirðskrá, code of conduct for hird members, 288–91, 303, 305
Historia Norwegie (History of Norway), Latin text, 53–6, 63, 90–2, *Fig. 2.2*
Hlaðir, earls of Lade, 84
Hlifolf 'the Old', steward of Caithness, 251
Hlodver Thorfinnson (d.c. 980), 47, 67, 111–13
Hlodvir, baptismal name of Hvelp (or Hundi), Earl Sigurd II's son, 127
Hofn, Caithness, Earl Hlodver's burial at, 111
Holdbodi, companion of Magnus Erlendsson, 199
Hollandmaik, 'Earl's Cairn' at, 111n
Honorius III, pope, 269
Hordaland, 16, 156

Housebay, manorial farm, Stronsay, 189
Houseby, *Col. pl.* 15
Howes, burial mounds, 53
Hoy, island of, 15
Hroald, murder by Margad Grimsson, 176
Hrolf, hird-priest of Rognvald Kali Kolsson, 184
Hrolf, king, abduction of Goi, 81
Hrollaug, son of Rognvald of Møre, 91
Hugh, son of William de Moravia, 265
Huitfeldt, Arild, Danish chronicler, 363, 365
Humbleton campaign, 348
Hundi, son of Earl Sigurd II, 114, 127
Huseby, place name, 168n
Huseby farms
  in Norway, 168
  in Orkney, 168–9
huseby system, 169n
Hvarflöd, *see* Gormflaith
Hvelp, son of Earl Sigurd II, 127
Hymns, Magnus hymn, 223

Iceland
  cult of St Magnus in, 225
  governor of captured in Orkney, 360–61
  lordship over, 36
  Magnus dedications in, 226
  and Norwegian kingdom, 18, 60, 296
  self-government of, 175
Icelandic Annals, 132, 216, 221, 249, 268, 271, 281–2, 312, 320, 343
Icelandic Book of Settlements, see *Landnámabók*
Inga of Varteig, 267
Ingi Bardsson's saga, 263n
Ingi, king of Norway (1204–17), 20, 263–4
Ingibjorg, daughter of Erik Stay-Brails, 44–5, 138n, 159–62, 278
Ingigerd, daughter of King Harald Sigurdsson, 161
Ingirid, daughter of Earl Rognvald Kali Kolsson, 248
inheritance, 129, 130
  reversion of, 344
  single, 240
inheritance law, 347, 380

Innocent III, pope, 57, 252, 255
Inverness
  battle at, 247
  sheriffdom of, 386
investiture, procedure of, 288–9
Iona, abbot of, 268
Ireland
  Earl Thorfinn's raids in, 138
  Erik Blood-axe's raids in, 111
Irish Sea, Orkney as staging post for, 89, 90
Isabella, daughter of Earl Malise, heir to the earldom of Caithness, 319–20
Island-Beardies, see Eyiarskeggjar
Islay, silver hoard at, 158n
Isle of Man, *see* Man, isle of
Isle of May, plunder of monastery, 176
Ivar, son of Earl Rognvald of Møre, 86

Jacques Legrand, *Le livre de bonnes moeurs*, 384
James I, king of Scotland (d.1437), 354, 356
James II, king of Scotland (d.1460), 356, 360–2, 364
James III, king of Scotland (d.1488), 362–4, 371, 375–7, *Col. pl.* 38
James IV, king of Scotland (d.1513), 33, 381, *Fig.* 9.2
James V, king of Scotland (d.1542), 385
James of Cragy, 35n
James Kennedy, bishop, 360, 363
Janet Haliburton, wife of Earl Henry Sinclair (II), 346
jarl
  bestowal of title in Norway, 290
  meaning of Old Norse term, 83
  in Norwegian provincial laws, 84
  title of, 83–85
Jarla sǫgur, 39
Jarls' saga
  author of, 39
  Battle of Skitten, 114
  bondi in, 16, 175
  Book of Miracles, 201
  Caithness, 18–19
  classification of, 42
  conversion of Earl Sigurd II, 126
  creation of Orkney earldom, 85

death of Earl Magnus Erlendsson, 200
death of Earl Thorfinn, 162
evaluation of, 39–50
and Genealogy of the Earls, 64
grant of Orkney to Rognvald of Møre, 48
and historical analysis, 26, 42
Magnus Erlendsson's quarrel with Hakon Paulsson, 198–9
Olaf Haraldsson in, 133
Pentland Firth in, 23
reliability of, 42–8
rivalries of Earls Paul and Erlend's descendants, 172
and Earl Sigurd's raven banner, 76
Earl Sigurd II the Stout in, 114
Skaldic poetry in, 49
Earl Thorfinn the Mighty, 133, 145
Jarlshof, Shetland, longhouse at, 86n, *Col. pl.* 40
Jaroslav, prince, 133–4
Jarteinabók (Book of Miracles), 201–2
Jelling, Jutland, burial mounds at, 98
Jellinge stone, 52
Jemtland
  community seal of, 77
  as skattland, 21
Joanna, wife of Freskin de Moravia, 283–6
John, bishop of Caithness (1185/89–1202/1213), 250
  Harald Maddadson's attack on, 58, 151, 252, 254–5, 390
John, King of England (1189–1216), 253–4
John, earl of Ross, 387
John Drummond de Cargill, 345
John Haraldsson, earl (1206–30), 43, 240, 246, 259, 261
  authority in Sutherland 391
  and burning of Bishop Adam, 58, 268–72
  death of, 274–7, 392
  and Hakon Hakonsson, 267
John Magnusson, earl (1284–1303), 58, 307, 309
  betrothal to Isabella, 312
  charter issued by, *Col. pl.* 35
  and death of the Maid of Norway, 309–10
  land grant to Reginald Cheyne, 25, 58, 330–1
  and Robert Bruce, 311
  seal of, 76–7, *Col.pl.* 9a, b
John Pak, Roman bishop of Orkney, 342
Jon, bishop of Atholl, visit to Orkney, 184
Jon Hafthorsson, 342
Jon Hallkelsson, 243
Jón Hjaltalín, English translation of *Orkneyinga Saga* (1873), 26
Jón Jónsson, scholar, 41
Jon Langlifsson, 297
Jorsalafarar, Jerusalem farers, 51

Kalf Arneson, 125, 139, 156, 174
Kali Sæbjarnarson, 170
Kari, member of Earl Sigurd II's military following, 119
Karl, as personal name, 136n
Karl Hundison / MacBeth, king of Alba, 134–5, 137
Kateryn of Chaumer, 359
Katharine, countess, widow of Earl Magnus V, 59, 60, 317
Kaupang, Vestfold, Norway, as trading centre, 87
Ketil Flat-neb, 94
Kildonan church, Helmsdale, granted to canons of Scone, 260
King Olaf Tryggvesson's Saga, 126
Kings' Sagas, 41
kingship, role of, 23
kingslands, 289n
Kintradwell, Sutherland, place name, 254n
Kirkjubour, Faeroe Islands, 206n
Kirkwall, *Fig.* 5.1
  Bishop Reid's Tower at, *Col. pl.* 20
  Bishop's Palace at, *Col. pl.* 33
  Burgh charter of, 375–7
  castle at, 369, *Fig.* 2.4
  ecclesiastical, political and commercial centre, 191
  first reference to, 141
  Magnus Erlendsson's relics at, 205–6
  as place name, 141, 206n
  as proto-urban centre, 206–7

Rognvald Brusisson's church at, 141, 147
secular residences at, 70–5
strategic significance, 15
knarrs, transport ships, 191, 192
Knarston
mooring of ships at, 191–2
Earl Rognvald's farm at, 191
Knud, St, cult of, 200, 221
Kol, son of Kali Sæbjarnarson, 44, 170, 204, 206, 208–12, 217
Kolbein, brother of Hanef *ungi*, 275–6
Kolbein Heap ('Cubbie Roo'), 194
Kvitingsøy, peace of (1208), 263

Lade dynasty, 84
Lambaborg
as place name, 196
Swein Asleifsson besieged at, 176
Landlaw, law revision of Magnus *lagabætir*, 7, 24, 304
Landnámabók, 92, 96
Langlif, daughter of Harald Maddadson, 246, 261
Langwell, place name, 155n
Lapps, Nor's conquest of, 81
Largs, Battle of (1263), 299, *Col. pl.* 32
Latheron, south Caithness, 59
Latin documents, as historical sources, 53–9
Laurence, household priest of Harald Maddadson, 258–9
Lawthing assembly, Shetland, 16
lawthingmen, replica of letter written by, *Col. pl.* 2
Layyeld, royal due, 59, 330
leidang (*leiðangr*), national naval levy, 124n, 150, 295
leiðangr see *leidang*
lendman (feudal lord), 84
len, grant of Norwegian royal estate, 264n, 292
Leo IX, pope, Thorfinn's visit to, 158
leprosy, 201–2
Lerwick, Shetland, town hall at, *Col. pl.* 38
lið, chieftain's military following, 150–51
liegemen, royal, 21
'Life of St Magnus', in Latin, 226

Lifolf Skalli, 'Bald-pate', 248–9, 278
linguistic regions, of Scotland, 100
Linlithgow Palace, 366
Liot *níthing* ('renegade/villain'), Sutherland landowner, 181
littera regis Norwagie missa Cataniensibus, 242
Liturgical fragments, as historical sources, 65–7
Ljot, son of Earl Thorfinn 'Skull-splitter', 47, 108
Loch Glen Dubh, Kylestrome, 188
Longer Magnus Saga, 165, 171, 199, 226
longhalls, 73–4
Longhouses
at Brough of Birsay, 70–2
at Jarlshof, 86n
at Skaill, 86n
Lord of the Isles, 37
lordship, 35–8
comital, 38
definition of, 35
direct, 36
indirect, 36
royal, 38
Lumberd, papal culprit for the attack on Bishop John, 255–6, 258
Lund cathedral, Skåne, altar dedication to St Magnus, 226

MacBeth, earl, ruler of Moray, 109, 110, 134, 136, 158
MacEoth, Ivor, 330
MacHeth dynasty, 260–1
and insurrection in Moray, 266
Mackay clan, 331
MacWilliam clan, and insurrection in Moray, 247, 266
Maddad, earl of Atholl, 177-8
and death of Earl Paul, 183
madness, cures for, 201
Mael Coluim, *see* Malcolm, Scottish king
Mælbeath, *see* macBeth, ruler of Moray
Mælbrigte, earl of the Scots, 92, 97–8, 108
Mæra-jarlar (earls of Møre), 84
Maeshowe, chambered tomb, Orkney Mainland, runic inscriptions at, 50

Norse adaptation of 52–3
Maeshowe dragon, 52
Mager, John, 375
Magister Robert, 226
Magnus (II), earl (1235x6–1239), 279
    granted Caithness earldom, 281
    inheritance of the Orkney earldom, 291–2
    and the Treaty of York, 306
Magnus *berfættr* 'Barelegs', king of Norway (1093–1103), 23, 44, 134, 165–70, 238–9
Magnus the Blind and Harald Gille's Saga, 209
Magnus Eriksson, king of Norway and Sweden (1319/1332–1374), 319, 322
Magnus Eriksson, *mangi*, son of Erik Stay-Brails, 278
Magnus Erlendsson (earl and saint), *Col. pl.* 23
    at the Battle of the Menai Straits, 168
    churches dedicated to, 221, 223–4
    cult of, 30, 67, 199–212, 223
    death of, 69n, 198–9
    dedications to 224–6, *Fig.* 5.4
    as earl of Orkney, 171
    and Hakon Paulsson, 165
    and Henry I of England, 165
    martyrdom of, 2, 30
    political links of, 171
    quarrel with Hakon Paulsson, 198
    relics of, 68, 204–8, 211, *Pl.* 1
    sanctification of, 198
    skeletal remains of, 199
    statue of, 68, *Col. pl.* 24
Magnus (III) Gilbertsson, earl (1256–1273), 292–3, 295
    and Hakon's expedition (1263), 299, 300, 306
    reconciliation with King Magnus Hakonsson, 24–5, 288, 303–6
Magnus Hakonsson 'Lawmender', king of Norway (1263–1280), 7, 18, 23, 44, 134, 165–70, 238–9, 288, 303–5, *Pl.* 6
Landlaw, 18

Magnus Haraldsson, son of King Harald Sigurdsson, 160
Magnus Haruode, Sir, archdeacon of Shetland, 384
Magnus (V) Johnsson, earl (c. 1303–1320), 314–17
Magnus (IV) Magnusson, earl (1273–1284), 307, 317
Magnus Sigurdsson, 'the Blind', king of Norway (1130–1135), 209–10
Magnús saga lengri, see Longer Saga of Magnus
Magnusburgh, trading burgh at Inver, Dunbeath, 224
Maid of Norway, *see* Margaret, Maid of Norway
Mainland, Orkney, 15
Malcolm MacBrigte, ruler of Moray, 113, 136n
Malcolm MacHeth, earl of Ross, 246–7
Malcolm II MacKenneth, king of Alba, 46, 113
Malcolm III 'Long-neck' (*Ceann Mor/Canmore*), king of Scots (1047–1093), 44–5, 134, 178
    grant of Caithness to Erlend, 186
    marriage to Ingibjorg, 159–60
    settlement with King Magnus Olafsson 'Barelegs', 169
Malise, earl of Strathearn, 25, 61, 317–19, 323
    daughters of, *Fig.* 7.5
Malise (II) earl of Strathearn, 282
Malise (V), earl of Strathearn, 286
Malise Sperra, 334, 342–4
Man (Isle of Man)
    lordship over, 36
    manpower from, 150
    and royal authority, 263–4
    Earl Sigurd II's tribute from, 120
Mane prima sabbati, Easter sequence, 66
Mani Olafsson, steward of Caithness, 251
manorial farms, links with earls, 189
Margad Grimsson, 176
Margaret, daughter of King Alexander III of Scotland, 307
Margaret, daughter of King Christian of

Denmark–Norway, 365
Margaret, daughter of Earl Harald
    Maddadson, 246
Margaret, daughter of Helga, 177–8
    and death of Earl Paul, 179
Margaret, Maid of Norway, queen of
    Scotland (1286–90), 307–8
    death of, 308–9
Margaret, St, queen of Scotland, 45, 160
Margaret, sister of the earl of Bothwell, 374
Margaret, wife of James of Cragy, 35n
Margrete, queen, Danish and Norwegian
    regent (1387–1412), 340, 343–4,
    346
Maria, daughter of King Harald Sigur-
    dsson, 161
Marion/Mariota, daughter of Alexander
    Sutherland, 359
Mariota of the Isles, wife of Alexander
    Sutherland, 359
Marjorie Sutherland, second wife of Earl
    William Sinclair, 359
Marjory of Ross, 319
mark, unit of weight, 158
marriage
    earldom marriages, 112–13
    as indicator of external alliances, 112–13
Mary of Gueldres, wife of King James II,
    369
Mary de Moravia, 311n
Matilda, daughter of Earl Gilbert II, 282
Matilda, daughter of Earl Malise, 283–4,
    286, 320
Melkolf, earl, 114
Melrose Chronicle, 242
Melsnati, earl, 114
memorial stones
    Filippus/Philippus, Brough of Birsay, 51
    Jellinge stone, 52
    St Paul's Churchyard stone, 52
Menai Strait, Battle of, 44, 168
Methven, Battle of (1306), 311
Meulan, counts of, 239
miracles, 201, 202–4, 250
Moddan, Clan, 173, 179, 181
    and Frakokk, 179–83
    genealogical tree of, *Fig.* 4.5

monastic orders, 235
Moray, 19
    and authority over north mainland,
        109–10
    geography of, 108
    Earl Sigurd II's territories in, 117
Moray dynasty, 136n, 247
Moray Firth, 95
    as transport route, 119
Møre and Romsdal, Anglo-Saxon brooches
    and items of adornment from, 89
Møre dynasty, 89, 90–2
    in *Jarls' Saga*, 85
Møre jarls, mythic background of, 105
Morkinskinna, 41
Moster, Hordaland, proclamation of Olaf
    Haraldsson's laws at, 148
mounds, burial, 53
Muckle Flugga, Shetland, 162
Muddan, nephew of MacBeth / Karl
    Hundison, 136
    killing by Thorkel, 137
Munkaþverá monastery, Iceland, abbot
    of, 226
Murkle, Caithness, as earldom power
    centre, 112, 311
Music, polyphony, 65
Myrkvafjǫrðr, 188
myth
    in Orkney earldom, 182–3
    origin myth, 81–3
    and Viking earls, 80–3

Nereid, sister of Earl Sigurd II, 119
Ness, river, 119
Nicholas St, 212–13
Nicolaisen, W.F., mapping of Norse place-
    names in Scotland, 100
Nidaros
    archdiocese of, *Fig.* 5.8
    archbishopric of, 21, 53, 203, 221, 235,
        252
    church at, 147
Nithsdale, lordship of, 358
Njal's Saga
    Battle of Clontarf, 128
    Battle of Duncansby Head, 114

and raven banner of Sigurd, 76
Earl Sigurd II, 114, 117, 119, 125
Song of Dorrud, 128, 129
Nobilis humilis, St Magnus hymn, 65–6, Col. pl. 4
Nor, descendent of king Fornjot, 81–2
Normandy, duke of, 239
Norse culture
 in Caithness, 181–2
 in Sutherland, 181
Norse language, in Caithness, 12
North Mavine, grant of land to Alexander von Klapam, 345
North Ronaldsay, feudal grant to Sir James Sinclair of Brecks, 385
north way, sea route, 12
Norway, Fig. 1.1
 areas ruled by, 293–4
 burial mounds in, 98
 earls in, 20, 84
 feudal society in, 174–5
 governmental authority in, 339–40
 hereditary succession in, 18
 imprisonment of St Andrews merchants in, 314
 judicial arrangements in, 274
 kings of, 5, 139, 238, 240–2
 Møre-jarls control of Romsdal fjord, 90
 and Orkney earldom, 89, 288–93
 political situation in, 262
 provincial laws of, 84
 royal hird, 288
 royal lion of, 77
 and Scotland, 305, 310
 and Shetland, 16
 skattland communities, 21–2
 state development in, 295
 statues to St Magnus in, 226
 unification of, 86–7
Norwegian documents, as historical sources, 59–62
Norwick, Unst, Viking settlement at, 86n
Nothegane/Nottingham, Caithness, 25, 59, 330

odal estates, 176
odal law, 59n

odal rights, 106–7, 116
Odin, 81–3, 107, 189
Olaf, St, *see* Olaf Haraldsson
Olaf Haraldsson, king of Norway (1016–1030) (St Olaf)
 cult of, 141, 200, 221
 exile of, 133
 laws of, 148
 statue of, 68
 and Thorfinn the Mighty, 42, 131, 239–40
Olaf *jarlsmágr*, 243
Olaf Kyrre, king of Norway (1066–1093), 147
Olaf Rolfsson 'göding', 174
 burning of, 176
 as göding at Duncansby, Caithness, 174
 odal estate of, Gairsay, 176
 yfirsókn in Caithness, 175
Olaf Tryggvesson, king of Norway (995–1000), 46, 125–7
 see also King Olaf Tryggvesson's Saga
Olaf 'the White', king of Dublin, 94
Old Lore Miscellany, Viking Society publications, 29
Old Norse, Gaelic influences on, 182
Old Wick, castle at, Col. pl. 18
Oliver, son of Earl William Sinclair by second marriage, 378
Olvir Brawl, 176–7
Olvir *illteit* (Ill-Will), 275–6
oratam, Latin word for the ounceland, 330
Orc, tribe of, 11
Orkney
 agriculture in, 16, 110n
 Alexander of Ard's authority in, 326–7
 annexation to the Crown, 371
 annual (sum paid to Norway), 302–3
 bishopric of, 32, 145–50, 203
 Christianisation of, 53, 125–7, 145
 Christianity in, 231
 Church in, 56, 341
 churches dedicated to Magnus in, 223–4
 ecclesiastical situation in, 390
 economic significance of, 87–90
 Erik Blood-axe's launching pad, 47
 feudal hierarchy in, 175

Orkney *cont'd*
  geography of, 11
  geology, 16
  geopolitics of, 74, 111, 188–97
  Gunnlaug's visit to, 114
  historians of, 29–32
  inheritance in, 129–30
  and King James II, 360–2
  judicial provision in, 7
  land transfer in, 60n
  Landlaw (1274), 7, 24
  lawman of, 61–2, 362
  Lawthing of, 385
  lease to Henry 5th Lord Sinclair, 372, 374
  lease and grants to bishops, 350, 372
  lordship over, 36
  Margaret, Maid of Norway's death in, 308–9
  and marriage treaty of 1468, 365–8
  Møre dynasty in, 103
  Norse society in, 62
  as north European pilgrimage centre, 217
  and Norway, 24, 245–6
  Norwegian royal official in, 314–15
  Norwegian rule in, 325
  odal rights in, 106–7
  ouncelands in, 158
  pennylands in, 123, 158, 193
  as peripheral community, 21–22
  place name, 11
  plague in, 320
  political history of, 10
  as political power base, 15
  pre-Norse inhabitants of, 55
  as raiding base, 85, 89
  revenue collection in, 292
  royal authority in, 50, 246
  royal fleets in, 18
  royal hird in, 168
  runic inscriptions from, 50
  Scotticisation, 62
  as security for the marriage of King Erik Magnusson and Margaret, 307n
  settlement features of, 15
  skatlands in, 124
  -staðir names in, 100
  Storer Clouston's division of, 144
  as thalassocracy, 125
  Thorfinn's troop raising in, 150
  as trading centre, 87, 89
  and Treaty of Perth, 302
  tributary nature of, 55–6
  as tripartite maritime lordship, 15–16
  and twelfth century renaissance, 234–7
  Viking invasion of, 55
  as Viking strategic base, 13–15
  violence between Norwegians and Scots in, 314
  William Sinclair's land purchases in, 360
  see also Orkney community, Orkney earldom
Orkney community
  letters of, 77
  seal of, 77–8, *Fig.* 2.5
Orkney earldom
  creation of, 48, 85–92
  David I's authority over, 185
  defensive role of, 24
  dividing line of, 193
  episcopal centres in, *Fig.* 4.1
  governance of, 60
  heraldic emblem of, 76
  historical analysis of, 27
  inheritance of, 277, 305
  marriages in, 108
  music from, 66–7
  myths and motifs in, 182–3
  and Norwegian kings, 165–6
  and royal authority, 167–8, 390–1
  subjugation to kings of Norway, 106
  and Viking chieftaincies, 92
Orkney rentals (1492), Mackenzie's copy, 29
Orkneyinga Saga, 6, *Fig.* 2.1
  aristocracy in, 174
  derivation from *Jarls' Sagas*, 39–41
  and historical analysis, 26
  Hjaltalín & Goudie's English translation (1873), 26
  modern text of, 41
  Mooney's study of, 30
  narrator of, 178
  as national history, 49

and origin myth, 81
as source for Genealogy of the Earls, 63–4
Pálsson & Edwards' English translation, 27
Pope's English translation, 26
relationship with *Heimskringla*, 41
reliability as source, 43
Taylor's English translation, 27
Torfæus' Latin translation, 26
Orphir, 15, 192–3, *Col. pl.* 16
    Earl Paul's estate at, 191
    earls' centre of operations at, 189, 191
    round church at, 212–13
Osmundwall, Kirk Hope, 126, *Col. pl.* 13
Ottar, son of Moddan of Dale, 179, 181
Ottar the Black, poem on King Olaf, 131
Otterburn campaign, 346
ouncelands, 122–4, 144, 158–9, 162, 330, *Fig.* 3.10
Ousedale, Caithness, *Col. pl.* 28, and see *Eysteinsdalr*
Oykel, place name, 97
Oykel, river, 97, 99

paganism, 126
Panmure Codex, 63n, 283, 286, 372n
Papa Stour, 1, 60, 224n
Papa Stronsay
    church dedicated to St Nicholas at, 213, *Fig.* 5.7
    feudal grant to Sir James Sinclair of Brecks, 385
    Earl Thorfinn's attack on Rognvald Brusisson at, 141
papacy, 203, 255
papar project, 3
Paplay (Holm), church dedicated to St Nicholas at, 213
parishes, establishment of, 232, 234
parochial organisation, 232, 234
Patrick Mowat, Sir, 316
    imprisonment of, 314–15
Paul (II) Hakonsson, earl (c.1123–1126)
    banishment of Helga and Frakokk, 177
    blinding and maiming of, 183
    capture by Swein Asleifsson, 183
    death of, 179
    disappearance of, 183
    and division of Orkney earldom with Rognvald Kali Kolsson, 177
    kidnap of, 210
    poisoned shirt intended for, 179
Paul (I) Thorfinnsson, earl (early 1060s–1099), 43–6, 162–3, 165, 167
Peerie Sea, Orkney, 191
pennylands, 123–4, 144, 158–9, *Fig.* 3.10
Pentland Firth, 7, 11, *Fig.* 1.3
    as barrier, 387–8
    frontier, 23–5, 169
    political significance, 11, 15
    state border, 25–6
Perth
    Harald Maddadson at, 256
Perth, Treaty of (1266), 23–4, 292, 301–3, 305
    renewal in 1312, 314
    renewal in 1426 (at Bergen), 353
Peter's Pence, 251–2, 258
Philippa, queen, 351
Pierowall, Westray, as location for trading centre, 87–8
pilgrimage, 212–14
pine woods, and shipbuilding, 118
place names, *Fig.* 3.5, *Fig.* 3.6
    Asgrimserg place name
    -bó place names, 117
    -ból place names, 96, 117
    -bólstaðr place names, 96
    in Caithness, 12, 96, 99–101
    -dale place names, 117, 154
    evidence from, 3
    habitative elements in, 100
    hérað place names, 152n
    hross-völlr place names, 155
    Huseby place name, 168n
    Kintradwell place name, 254n
    and Norse settlement on Scottish Mainland, 100–3
    -setr place names, 96
    -staðr place names, 96, 100
    in Sutherland, 96
    þing-völlr place name, 155
    -völlr place names, 154

plague, 320
plógsland, land unit, 211–12
plunder, 94
   of graves, 53
polyphony, 65
pope
   of Avignon, 341
   Roman, 341
   see also Clement VII, Honorius III, Innocent III, Leo IX, Urban VI
Portmahomack, 9th century attack on, 95n
primogeniture, 20
provocation scenes, in Old Norse literature, 104

raðgjafi, counsellor, 173
raðuneyti, earls' counsellors, 173
Rafn the Lawman (*logmaðr*), steward of Caithness, 242, 251, 269–70, 273
Ragman Rolls, 311
Ragnhild, daughter of Erik Blood-axe, 47, 112, 278
Ragnhild Simunsdatter, 60
Ralph, nominee of Earl Paul Thorfinsson for Orkney bishopric, 56
Ralph Novell, bishop, 203
raven, the bird of Odin, 116
raven banner, 46
Ravenscraig Castle, Fife, granted to Earl William, 368–9, *Pl.*9
Reginald, bishop of Ross, 242, 252
Reginald Cheyne II, Lord of Inverugy, 58, 311n, 330–1
   Earl John's grant to, 25, 330–31
Rentals of Orkney (1492 and 1500), 29, 188, 364, 372
Ribe, Jutland, as trading centre, 87
Richard II, king of England, 346
Richard Leask, executor of Sir David Sinclair's will, 383
Rígsmál, Old Norse Eddaic poem, 83
Rígsþula see Rígsmál
ríki (ON, rule, realm), 36
ring money, 122, 124
Roberry Head, South Ronaldsay, sea battle at, 140, 156

Robert II, king of Scots (1371–1390), 325–6, 328
Rogaland, Norway, Anglo-Saxon jewellry at, 89
Roger, bishop of St Andrews, 256
Roger of Howden, English Chronicler, 242, 247
Rognvald, jarl of Møre, 48, 35, 63, 86
Rognvald, St, *see* Rognvald Kali Kolsson
Rognvald Brusisson, earl (1037x38–1046), 49, 140–1, 147
Rognvald Gudrodson, king of Man and the Isles, 250, 255, 263, 390
Rognvald Kali Kolsson, earl (1136–1158)
   acceptance of Harald Maddadson as co-earl, 183–4
   achievements of, 214–19
   alliances of, 177
   benefactor of St Magnus cathedral, 217–18
   claim of Orkney earldom, 177–8
   cult of, 219
   death of, 37, 219–20
   and division of Orkney earldom, 177
   expedition against Earl Paul, 204, 208
   at Knarston, 191–2
   and Maeshowe inscriptions, 51
   pilgrimage to Holy Land, 212, 216–17, *Fig.* 5.3
   relics of, 68
   sanctification of, 198
   and sanctification of Magnus Erlendsson, 208
   skaldic poetry of, 49
   statue of, 68, 218–19
   and Swein Asleifsson, 216
   support for Harald Gilli, 210
   and War of the Three Earls, 187
Rolf (Rodulfus/Rollo), son of Jarl Rognvald of Møre, 91
Rome, Thorfinn's visit to, 156–9
Romsdal, *Mæra-jarlar* in, 84
Rosemarkie Christian monastic site at, 95n
Roslin, Midlothian
   residence of Sinclairs, 332
   St Matthews church at, 67, 69, 332, 358
Roslin Castle, 33n, 332, *Fig.* 8.1

Ross, 152–6, 259–60
  as buffer zone, 152
  conquest by Thorfinn, 136
  earl of, 37
  Firthlands of, 95
  geography of, 152
  geopolitical significance, 117–19
  military routes in, 154–5
  Norse place names in, 154
  Sigurd II's territories in, 117
  social organisation of, 156
  as source of timber, 153–4, 156
Ross family, 25, 319, 323, 328
Rossall, place name, 155
Rousay, 15, 218
royal authority, 235, 238–42, 246, 263, 390–1, 393
rune carvers, 52
runic inscriptions, 50–53

Saemund Jonsson, 261
Saga of Gunnlaug Serpent-Tongue, 114
Saga of Harald the Stern, 161
Saga of Magnus Barefoot, 167
Sagas of the Bagler, 259
St Boniface kirk, Papa Westray, Rognvald's burial at, 141
St Duthac's chapel, Pickaquoy, and Thomas Tulloch's charter (1448), 69
St Lucy's Day, and death of Magnus Erlendsson, 205
St Magnus Bay, Shetland, 224n
St Magnus cathedral, Kirkjubour, Faeroe Islands, 206n, *Col. pl.* 22
St Magnus cathedral, Kirkwall, 66, *Fig.* 5.2, *Fig.* 5.5, *Col. pl.* 25, *Col. pl.* 39, *Pl.* 1, *Pl.* 4
  body of Earl Magnus at, 191
  building of, 207–12
  design of, 228
  masonry of, 194
  as monument to the earldom dynasty, 68
  tomb furniture, 67
  transfer to the Burgh of Kirkwall, 375–6
St Magnus church, Birsay, 74, 235
St Magnus church, Egilsay, 228–30, *Fig.* 5.6
St Magnus church, Tingwall, 381, 383, *Col. pl.* 21
St Magnus hospital, Spittal, Caithness, 224n
St Margaret's Hope, Hakon's fleet at, 297
St Matthew's collegiate church, Roslin, 69, 332, 358, *Col. pl.* 36
St Nicholas church, Papa Stronsay, 232, *Fig.* 5.7
St Nicholas church, Orphir, 68
St Olaf church, Kirkjubour, Faeroe Islands, 206n
St Olaf pre-cathedral church, Kirkwall, 141, 206
St Olaf's Saga, 85, 134
St Sunniva, Selja, Norway, 73n
St Tredwell's chapel, Papa Westray, 254n
saints
  as protectors, 209–10
  cults of, 69
  royal saints, 200
Salisbury, Treaty of, 308
Samuel Laing, translation of *Heimskringla* (1844), 26
sanctification, requirements for, 201
Sanday
  geography of, 15
  granted to Sir James Sinclair of Brecks, 385
  manorial farms in, 189
  William Sinclair of Warsetter's power base in, 374
Scandinavia, *Fig.* 3.2
Scapa Flow, 15, 189–93, *Fig.* 4.7
Scarmclath, Caithness, 328n
Scatness, Shetland, 86n
Scatwell, Easter Ross, place name, 156
Scone abbey, Harald Maddadson's grant to, 57, 257, 259–60
Scotland
  Admiral of, 336n
  Chancellor of, 356–60
  Cnut's authority in, 134
  land routes in, *Fig.* 3.9
  linguistic regions of, 100
  and Norway, 305, 310
  ouncelands in, *Fig.* 3.10

pennylands in, *Fig.* 3.10
political groupings in, 19
Earl Thorfinn's raids in, 137–8
Scots documents, as historical souces, 62–5
scotticisation, 385
Scrabster, Caithness
  bishops' castle at, 149
Scrabster Bay, Caithness, *Col. pl.* 27
sea, as a natural force, 81
sea routes, control of, 12, 189
seal matrix, from Durness, 79
seals, 75–9, *Col. pl.* 9, *Col. pl.* 10
  community of Orkney's, 61, *Fig.* 2.5
  community seals, 21–2
  Earl Henry I's, 76
  John's (earl of Caithness), 76–7, *Col. pl.* 9
Selja, island in western Norway, 230–1
  church at, 147
Serlo, chaplain of Adam, bishop of Caithness, 269
Shebster, Caithness, Magnus dedication at, 224
Shetland
  administrative relationship with Norway, 245
  annexation to the Crown, 371
  Christianity in, 231
  churches dedicated to Magnus in, 202, 223–4
  feudal hierarchy in, 175
  geography of, 15–16
  granted to Rognvald of Møre, 48
  inheritance in, 129–30
  Lawthing of, 381, 385
  lawthingmen of, 60
  leprosy in, 201n
  local historians of, 32
  lordship of, 36, 371
  and marriage treaty of 1468, 367–8
  and Northern Isles history, 32
  Norwegian control of, 16
  as part of the Orkney earldom, 16
  plague in, 320
  and royal authority, 245
  runic inscriptions from, 50
  Sinclair earls in 343–5

  and the Treaty of Perth, 302
  tripartite maritime lordship, 15–16
  as Viking strategic base, 13–14
Shetland Rental, 380
Shetlanders, and cult of St Magnus, 202
shieling system, 182
Shorter Magnus Saga, 199
Sidera, *see* Cyder Hall
Sigtrygg Silk-beard, Norse king of Dublin, 46, 147
Sigurd Eysteinsson, Earl Sigurd I ('the Mighty') (fl.870s x 890s)
  burial of, 67, 98–9, 108
  campaigns of, *Fig.* 3.3
  death of, 92–4, 97–8
  as first recorded earl of Orkney in *Jarls' Saga*, 48
  victory over Mælbrigte, earl of the Scots, 93–4, 96–7
Sigurd Hafthorsson, 342
Sigurd (II) Hlodversson, Earl Sigurd II (*digri* 'the Stout') (d.1014)
  administration of, 125
  banner of, 116
  at Battle of Clontarf, 119, 128
  at the Battle of Skitten Moor, 114, 127
  campaigns of, *Fig.* 3.8
  conquest of Ross, 95, 153–4
  conquests in Scottish mainland, 94
  conquests with Thorstein the Red, 94–6
  control of Caithness and Sutherland, 117
  conversion to Christianity by Olaf Tryggvesson, 125–7
  death of, 128–9
  descendants of, *Fig.* 3.11
  description of, 113
  fiscal organisation of, 120–4
  in Icelandic Sagas, 114
  marriage to the daughter of Malcolm, king of Scots, 45, 113
  and odal rights, 116
  raven banner of, 127
  taxation in Man, 125
  territory of, 114
  victory over Finnleik, 116
  victory over Godfrey 'king of Man', 119

Sigurd Magnusson, illegitimate son of King
    Magnus Erlingsson, 243–4
Sigurd Magnusson (*Jórsalafari*, 'Jerusalem-
    farer'), king of Norway (1103–
    30), 213
Sigurd *murtr* (Mite or Minnow), 249
Sigurd, son of King Magnus Olafsson
    ('Barelegs'), 167, 169–70
Sigurd's Hall, Brough of Birsay, 72–3
Sigurd's howe, *see* Cyder Hall
Sigurðarhaugr, *see* Cyder Hall
Sigvaldi Skjalgson, 276
silver
    silver hoards, 120, 122, 158n, *Pl.*2
    skat silver, 149
Simon, bishop of the Hebrides, 268
Sinclair
    Alexander, 323
    David, brother of Earl Henry I, 344–5
    David of Sumburgh, Sir, 33, 378–84,
        Fig. 9.2
    earls, 33–4
    Elizabeth, daughter of Henry Sinclair,
        345–6
    family of, 63, 336, Fig. 7.4
    Henry I, earl (1379–1400)
        appointment of, 334–41
        death of, 347
        defence of Orkney, 37
        in Genealogy of the Earls, 64n
        inheritance policy of, 345–6
        installation document of, 334, 336–8,
            340–2
        investiture at Marstrand, 328
        seal of, 76
    Henry II, earl (1400–1420), 332, 347–9
    Henry 3rd Lord Sinclair, 372, 375,
        rental compilation of, 30
    Henry 5th Lord Sinclair, 371n
    Isabella, mother of Earl Henry I, 336,
        344, 347–9, 358
    James, probable son of Sir David, 382
    James of Brecks, Sir, 385, 388
    John, son of Earl Henry I, 345, 349
    Lairds of Roslin, 332
    Magnus, probable son of Sir David, 382
    Robert, elected bishop 1383, 341

Thomas, 323, 336n, 351, 354
William, earl (1434–1470)
    and Caithness earldom, 34–5, 329,
        358–60
    burial at Roslin, 67n
    compilation of Genealogy of the
        Earls, 352–5
    and Danish overlord, 366–7
    earldom rights of, 349–51
    foundation of St Matthew's church,
        Roslin, 69
    installation of, 355–6
    land purchasing policy of, 364
    marriages of, 354, 359
    renunciation of right to Orkney
        earldom, 368–70
    seal of, 76
William 'the Waster', first son of Earl
    William Sinclair, 363, 377
William, earl of Caithness, second son
    of Earl William Sinclair, 377
William of Warsetter, Sir, 374, 382
Sinclair castle, Kirkwall, 74, 350, Fig. 2.4,
    Fig. 8.2
Skaill, Mainland of Orkney
    longhouse at, 86n
    silver hoard at, *Pl.*2
skaldic verse, 49, 217
Skalholt, Iceland, Magnus relic at, 225
Skaard, Iceland, embroidered altar frontal
    at, 226
skatlands, Orkney assessment system, 21,
    124
    historical research on, 6–7
skats, 120, 292–3, 323
    skat malt, 149
    skat silver, 149
Skattlands, Norwegian tributary lands, 18,
    21, 27, 124n, 267, 288, 291, 294,
    302
Skitten, Battle of, 108–9, 127
Skitten, 2nd Battle of, 108–9, 114
Skoldunga Saga, 81
Skuli, son of Earl Thorfinn 'Skull-Splitter',
    47, 109–10
Skuli Bårdsson, earl, 267–8
Snaekoll Gunnison, 275

Snorri Sturlason, 26
Sogn, Battle of, 279
Sogn and Fjordane, Anglo-Saxon brooches and items of adornment from, 89
Song of Dorrud, 128–9
South Ronaldsay, 15, 59–60
Spittal, Caithness
 church at, *Col. pl.* 6
 Magnus dedication at, 224
 pilgrims hospital at, 70
Stainmore, Battle at, 111
Stamford Bridge, Battle of (1066), 45, 162
standing stone of Asta, between Tingwall and Scalloway, 343n, *Col. pl.* 37
state development, Norwegian, 295
statues, of northern saints, 68
Stavanger
 cathedral at, 211n
 maritime contact radius from, 13
Stiklestad, Battle of, 133
Stirling, Scottish royal power-centre in, 22
Storhaugen, Norway, burial mounds at, 98
storm, as a natural force, 81
Strabrock, West Lothian, 286
Strath Halladale, 110n
Strathclyde, Erik Blood-axe's raids in, 111
Strathearn
 dynasty of, 392, *Fig.* 7.4
 earldom of, 328n
Strathnaver, 25, 181, 283–4
Stroma, island of, 176
Stronsay, 189, 385
Sturlunga Saga, 261
Sumarlidi Hrolfsson, 276
Sumburgh, David Sinclair's seat at, 379, *Col. pl.* 40
Summerdale, Battle at, 375, 388
Sunniva, St, 230
Sutherland, *Fig.* 4.2, *Col. pl.* 11
 comital lordship of, 287
 conquest by Thorfinn, 136
 detachment from Caithness, 264–5
 as earldom for de Moravia family, 265
 joint settlement in, 96
 military routes in, 154–5
 Moddan family holdings in, 181
 Norse culture in, 181

pagan burials in, 98
place names in, 96, 99, 101
Earl Sigurd II's control of, 117
Svein Forkbeard, king of Denmark, 126
Sveinn Estrithsson, king of Denmark, 157
Sveinbjornsson, Rafn, private seal of, 76
Sverre, king of Norway
 agreement with Earl Harald, 288
 conquest of Jemtland, 21
 death of, 259
 establishment of the office of sysselman, 245–6, 390–91
 Eyiarskeggjar rising against, 20
 and Harald Maddadson, 242–5
Svoldur, Battle of, 46
Sweden
 burial mounds in, 98
 Hakon Paulsson's visit to, 165–6
Swein Asleifsson
 and appointment of Harald Maddadson as co-earl of Orkney, 184
 authority in Duncansby, 172
 and Earl Paul, 179, 183
 death of, 227
 and death of Frakokk, 181
 feud with Clan Moddan, 173
 killing of Gilla Odran, 187–8
 at Knarston, 191–2
 Lambaborg castle of, 195
 as power broker, 184
 violent behaviour of, 172
 warships of, 173
Swein Breast-Rope, murder of, 192
Swelkie, whirlpool in Pentland Firth, 15
Swona, island of, 176
sysselman, office of, 170n, 245–6, 390–1
Syvardhoch, *see* Cyder Hall

Tankarness, sea battle at, 177
Tarbat, Christian monastic sites at, 95n
Tarbat Ness, Easter Ross, 104, 137
taxation, 120, 124, 159
 and construction of St Magnus cathedral, Kirkwall, 211–12
teinds (tithes), 232, 269
 butter teind, 268
 cheese teind, 269

hay teind, 269
thalassocracy, 125, 167, 296
Thomas, Archbishop of York, 56
   letter to Archbishop Lanfranc of Canterbury, 56
Thomas Boswell, 383
Thomas Kyrknes, 375
Thomas Tulloch, bishop of Orkney (1418–1461), 63, 350
Thora, mother of Magnus Erlendsson, 43, 200
Thorarin 'Bag-nose', 187, 220
Thorbjorn, outlaw, 37, 172
Thorbjorn Clerk, Earl Harald's counsellor, 187
   and death of Rognvald Kali Kolsson, 220
   feud with Swein Asleifsson, 220
Thord, tenant of Bergfinn Skatasson, 202
Thorfinn, son of Earl Harald Maddadson, 246
   blinding of, 253
Thorfinn Sigurdsson,'the Mighty', earl (1014–c.1060)
   area of influence, 162
   audience with the pope, 145–6
   authority in Scotland, 137–8
   and Caithness, 134–8
   conquest of Ross and Sutherland, 136
   conquests of, *Fig.* 3.12
   control of Ross, 153–4
   death of, 45, 159
   descendants of, *Fig.* 4.4
   dispute with Rognvald Brusisson, 140–1
   English campaigns of, 139
   governmental system of, 159
   Hebridean campaigns, 138–9
   inheritance of, 129–31
   as lawgiver, 148
   levy raised by, 150
   marriage to Ingibjorg, 160n, 161
   and Olaf Haraldsson, 131–4, 239–40
   and Orkney bishopric, 145–6
   reputation of, 137
   rivalries of, 138–41
   visit to Rome, 156–9, *Fig.* 4.3

Thorfinn's Hall, *Col. pl.* 8
Thorfinn's Palace, Brough of Birsay, 72, 73
Thorkel *fostri* ('Fosterer'), 133, 141, 187
Thorleif, daughter of Moddan, 181
Thorolfr, see Turolf
Thorstein the Red, 94–6
Thorvald of Brough, executor of Sir David Sinclair's will, 383
Thorvald Thoresson, 60
thralls, as class of men, 83
þursa skeriom (Giants' Skerries), 162
Thurso
   capture of Harald Maddadson at, 23
   castle at, 195
   Clan Moddan at, 181
   destruction of Earl Harald's castle at, 247
   killing of Karl Hundason's nephew at, 179n
   Muddan's forces at, 137
   murder of Earl John at, 275
Thurso Dale, Caithness, 179, 110n
Tigernach, Irish Chronicle, 161n
timber, 118
   for shipbuilding, 153–4, 156
Tingwall, 16
   archdeacon's church at, 223
tithes, *see* teinds
Tore, son of Jarl Rognvald of Møre, 91
Torfæus, Thormodus, Latin translation of *Orkneyinga Saga* (1697), 26
Torfness, 104
   battle at, 137, 153
trading centres, 87
treason, 289–90
Tredwell, St (ON Triduana,) 254n
Trøndelag, Anglo-Saxon brooches and items of adornment from, 89
Trondheim, 53, 90, 207
   Háleygja-jarlar in, 84
   as Jarl Hakon Sigurdsson power centre, 90
Tuquoy, Westray, runic inscription at, 51
Turolf, bishop, 146–7, 240

Ui-Meath, king of, 258
Uppsala, archbishopric of, 21

Urban VI, pope, 341
Urnes stave kirk, Norway, 52

Valkyries, in 'Song of Dorrud', 128
Valthiof, *göding*, Stronsay, 174
Van Bassan, 33
Vatican register, letter to bishops of Orkney and Ross (1198), 58
veizla, obligation of providing hospitality to the lord, 168n
Vestfold, Viken, Norway, Anglo-Saxon brooches and items of adornment from, 89
Viborg cathedral, Jutland, altar dedication to St Magnus, 226
Vigfússon, Guðbrandur, scholar, 41
Viking, definition of term, 3n
visionsdikt, Old Norse visionary poem, 128

Waleran, Beaumont twin, 239
Wales, Magnus' expedition to, 160
Walter of Buchan, canon of Orkney, 324n
War of the Three Earls, 187
Wars of Independence, 309–10
Waterford, battle at, 138
Weland de Stiklawe, churchman and royal administrator, 310n, 311–14
Welland de Ard, 320
Westminster Hall, 295
Westness, keep at, 195
Westray, 15, 189, 218
Wick
 battle at, 249
 sheriffs court at, 386
 stone tower at, 195
Wide Firth, Orkney, 191
William (IV), bishop of Orkney (c.1369–1382 or 1383), 323–4
William, earl of Ross, 61, 319–20
William, earl of Sutherland, 265

William of Buchan, archdeacon of Orkney, 324n
William de Crumbacy, valet of earl John, 309
William FitzDuncan, 251
William the Lion, king of Scots (1165–1214), 58, 253, 265
 capture of Harald Maddadson, 253
 destruction of Harald Maddadson's castle at Thurso, 247–8
 expedition to Caithness, 256
 Harald Maddadson's submission to, 256–7
 Earl John's dau. taken as hostage, 264
William the Noble, 44
William the Old, bishop (?1102–1168), 68, 184, 200
 and cult of St Magnus, 202–4, 207–8, 234
 and ecclesiastical organisation, 232
 miracles witnessed by, 203
 pilgrimage to Holy Land, 212
William Playfair, messenger of the earl of Orkney, 308
William Tulloch, bishop of Orkney (1461–1477), 362–3, 365, 372
Worcester, earls of, 239
worship, heathen, 189
Wyntoun, *Original Chronicle*, 272

Ynglingatal, skaldic poem, and origin myth of the Norwegian kings, 81
York
 archbishop of, and authority over Orkney bishopric, 203
 Treaty of (1237) 307
 Viking king of, 111–12

Zeno narrative, 343n
Zeno brothers, 343n
Zichmni, 343n